# Introduction to Business

# INTRODUCTION TO BUSINESS

## A SYSTEMS APPROACH

**Matt M. Starcevich**

*Phillips Petroleum Co.*

**James L. Wittenbach**

*University of Notre Dame*

**Charles E. Merrill Publishing Company**
*A Bell & Howell Company*
Columbus, Ohio

**to Judy and JoAnn**

Published by Charles E. Merrill Publishing Co.
*A Bell & Howell Company*/Columbus, Ohio 43216

International Standard Book Number/0-675-08755-4

Library of Congress Catalog Card Number/74-14497

Printed in the United States of America
1 2 3 4 5 6 7 8 / 79 78 77 76 75

# Preface

INTRODUCTION TO BUSINESS—A SYSTEMS APPROACH is written and organized to help the reader gain an appreciation for each of the basic processes which comprise the business system, the interrelationships of these processes, and the role of the environment within which every business must function. The six processes which comprise the business system—finance, production, distribution, manpower, management, and information—are covered in separate sections of the text. Although separate and distinct processes, each is dependent on and related to each of the others. Decisions made in one process area affect and are affected by the other processes which comprise the business system. The separate but related nature of each process is more easily understood by viewing every business as an ongoing system of interrelated activities. The text encourages the reader to constantly view the business, regardless of size or product, *not* as a collection of separate processes but as a *system* in which the processes of finance, production, distribution, and manpower are properly balanced, coordinated, and affected by the economic, political, and social environment of the United States.

The text is divided into eight sections. Section I concentrates on the economic, political, and social systems' impact on business decisions. Within this environmental context, the goals and central purpose of each business are discussed and the systems concept is presented as a model to help put into perspective decisions regarding the internal operation of every business institution.

Sections II through VII concentrate separately on each process of the system. To emphasize the interdependence of all processes, a flow diagram at the beginning of each section visually depicts the elements of the process being examined. It is followed by discussion of the relationship these elements have to the other processes and to the successful operation of a total business system.

Every business starts with and continues by defining the central purpose of that business. Concurrently the businessman must also reach certain financial decisions. The factors to be weighed in deciding on the forms of business ownership, the utilization of debt, and the impact of taxes on business operations will be discussed in Section II, "The Financial Process."

Section III centers on "The Production Process." It examines the factors the businessman must weigh in formulating that series of events which combine men and machines for the purposes of attaining and transforming raw materials into finished goods or services.

v

"The Distribution Process" is the subject of Section IV. Decisions must be made in the areas of pricing, wholesaling, retailing, advertising, selling, and transporting to assure that the consumer obtains the goods or services when he wants them, where he wants them, and at the prices he is willing to pay.

Section V concentrates on that series of events necessary to make sure the right number of people with the proper qualifications are available to the business when they are needed, and that they are willing to perform the tasks defined by the business. These events constitute what we have called "The Manpower Process."

The central role the manager plays in setting the environment in balance and integrating the various resources, processes, and objectives of the business system is discussed in Section VI, "The Management Process." After having discussed each of the five processes the reader can appreciate how the manager utilizes the information process to control the whole business system. Although each of these processes requires a certain amount of information to successfully make decisions concerning their operations, Section VII treats information as a separate process. The information will come from two sources: information outside of the business pertaining to its environments, such as market research and economic forecasting data, and information concerning the internal operation of the business system such as accounting, financial, and statistical data.

In Section VIII we bring together the parts of the business system into a meaningful whole and indicate future changes which will affect the operation of businesses in the United States.

Throughout the text, important terms or concepts which make up the language of business are printed in bold face to alert the reader to their significance. These terms are defined in a glossary at the end of the book. In addition to a summary and a set of review questions after each chapter, one or more incidents requiring the reader to apply the various principles and concepts as discussed are included at the ends of chapters 3 through 22. The incidents allow the reader to identify business problems and to find appropriate solutions to these problems.

A number of individuals deserve special recognition for the valuable assistance each provided. The encouragement and assistance provided by Dr. Ray Powell is sincerely appreciated. Critical comments by Dr. John Weber significantly improved chapter 24. The help given by John Bava, Dennis Pijor, and Michael Schumaker was instrumental in completing the book. We are indebted deeply to Sheryl Rossow for her patience and excellent work in typing the entire manuscript. In addition, we would like to thank Earl D. Purkhiser, Mount San Antonio College, and Chester R. Duckhorn, Fresno City College, for their helpful reviews of the manuscript.

*M.M.S.*
*J.L.W.*

# Contents

**I** **THE ENVIRONMENT OF THE BUSINESS SYSTEM**     **1**

**1**   **American Business and the Total Environment**     **3**

The Social System of the United States, 4
The Economic System of the United States, 4
Implications for Business and Businessmen in the United States, 5
The Governmental System of the United States, 7
The Total Environment and Business, 14
Questions, 15

**2**   **A Systems View of Business**     **16**

Goals of Business, 16
The Business System, 20
The Business System in Perspective, 23
Framework of the Book, 25
Questions, 26

**II**   **THE FINANCIAL PROCESS**     **27**

**3**   **Promoting a New Business Venture**     **29**

The Financial Process and the Systems Concept, 29
Promotion of a New Business, 31
Forms of Business Organization, 39
Summary, 44
Questions, 44
Incident, 45

**4**   **Sources of Long-Term Funds**     **46**

Equity Funds, 47
Nature of Long-Term Debt Funds, 53
Stocks Versus Bonds, 58

Leases, 60
Summary, 61
Questions, 61
Incident, 62

**5   Sources of Short-Term Funds**                                                   **63**

Nature of Short-Term Credit, 63
Computation of Interest Costs, 64
Cash Forecast, 65
Unsecured Credit, 67
Secured Credit, 74
Summary, 76
Questions, 77
Incident, 77

**6   Federal Income Taxes**                                                          **79**

Classes of Taxpayers, 80
Impact of Taxes on Selection of Business Organization, 86
The Small Business Corporation, 88
Accumulated Earnings Tax, 89
Impact of Taxes on Financial Arrangements, 90
Summary, 92
The Financial Process in Retrospect, 92
Questions, 94
Incidents, 95

**III            THE PRODUCTION PROCESS                             97**

**7   The Production Function**                                                       **99**

Production and the Business System, 99
Universality, 101
Input Procurement, 103
Summary, 111
Questions, 112
Incident, 113

**8   Manufacturing**                                                                 **115**

Types of Manufacturers, 116
Manufacturing Design, 118
Control of Manufacturing Operations, 121
Summary, 125
Manufacturing and the Production Process, 126
The Production Process in Retrospect, 128
Questions, 128
Incident, 129

# IV        THE DISTRIBUTION PROCESS     131

## 9   Distribution, the Marketplace, and the Consumer    133

The Distribution Process and the Business System, 134
The Market, 136
Who Are Consumers? 137
Summary, 147
Questions, 147
Incident, 148

## 10   The Distribution Process: Product, Price, and Availability    149

The Product, 149
The Product's Price, 153
Nonprice Competition, 156
Availability, 157
Summary, 161
Questions, 161
Incidents, 162

## 11   Promotion of the Product    165

Personal Selling, 165
Advertising, 171
Promoting a Product: Personal Selling and Advertising, 178
Summary, 181
Questions, 181
Incidents, 182

## 12   Physical Distribution    184

The Nature of Physical Distribution, 184
Modes of Transportation, 185
Should the Small Businessman Haul His Own Goods? 189
Transportation Rates and Special Services, 190
Determination of Inventory Locations, 193
Plant Location, 197
Retail Location, 198
Summary, 203
The Distribution Process in Retrospect, 203
Questions, 206
Incident, 206

# V        THE MANPOWER PROCESS     209

## 13   Manning the Business Systems    211

Manpower and the Business System, 211
Determination of Manpower Needs, 212

Developing Job Applicants, 215
Selection of Employees, 219
Legislation Protecting Employees from Employers, 221
Summary, 225
Questions, 226
Incidents, 226

**14  Employees as Individuals**                                         **229**

Characteristics of the Labor Force, 229
The Individual Employee, 233
Gaining Employee Cooperation, 237
Summary, 239
Questions, 240
Incidents, 241

**15  Employees in Groups**                                              **244**

The Informal Group, 245
Unions as a Formal Group, 248
Summary, 254
The Manpower Process in Retrospect, 255
Questions, 256
Incident, 256

**VI           THE MANAGEMENT PROCESS**                                  **259**

**16  The Manager's Job and Planning**                                   **261**

The Manager and the Business System, 261
The Management Process, 262
Planning, 263
Small Business Management, 271
Summary, 281
Questions, 282
Incidents, 282

**17  Organizing the Resources**                                        **284**

Importance and Nature of Organization, 284
Dividing the Work to be Done into Jobs, 285
Setting up Individual Jobs, 289
Organization Structure and Cooperative Endeavor, 290
Summary, 296
Questions, 297
Incidents, 297

**18  Directing and Controlling**                                       **300**

Directing via Communications, 300
Controlling the Business System, 306

The Basic Control Process, 307
Summary, 310
The Management Process in Retrospect, 310
Questions, 311
Incidents, 311


## VII    THE INFORMATION PROCESS    313


### 19   Internal Information Process—Financial Accounting    315

The Information Process and the Business System, 316
The Nature of Financial Accounting, 318
19X1 Transactions, 320
Users of Accounting Information, 329
Tools of Statement Analysis, 329
Summary, 334
Questions, 334
Incident, 335


### 20   Internal Information Process—
###        Managerial Accounting    338

Managerial Accounting Versus Financial Accounting, 338
Cost Determination, 339
Planning and Control, 344
Summary, 355
Questions, 356
Incidents, 357


### 21   Research: Generating Additional Information    358

Research and Business, 359
Systematic-Descriptive Business Research, 360
Competitive Adaptation and Business Research, 364
The Production Process and Business Research, 366
The Distribution Process and Business Research, 368
The Manpower Process and Business Research, 370
Summary, 373
Questions, 373
Incidents, 374


### 22   Tools to Aid in the Utilization of Information    376

The Computer, 376
Data Presentation, 383
Summary, 390
The Information Process in Retrospect, 390
Questions, 391

Incident, 392
    Appendix A—Volume-Profit Analysis, 394
    Incident, 399
    Appendix B—Inventory Planning and Cost Control, 400
    Incident, 404

## VIII   THE BUSINESS SYSTEM IN THE FUTURE AND IN RETROSPECT   405

### 23  Changes Affecting Business   407

Automation, 407
Social Responsibility, 411
Summary, 419
Questions, 419

### 24  International Business   421

International Trade, 421
The Multinational Firm, 431
To What Extent Should American Firms Engage in Business
   Abroad? 437
Summary, 438
Questions, 438

### 25  External Growth Through Business Acquisitions   440

Internal Versus External Growth, 440
Formal Plans for Combining Firms, 441
The Growth Pattern of a Firm, 442
Motives for Acquiring Another Firm, 444
Motives for Selling, 446
Antitrust Laws, 448
Summary, 450
Questions, 450

### 26  The Business System: A Restatement   452

Environmental Realities in the United States, 452
The Systems Approach, 454
Career Opportunities Open to Business Students, 458
Summary, 466
Questions, 466

Glossary, 469

Index, 475

# Introduction to Business

# THE ENVIRONMENT OF
# THE BUSINESS SYSTEM

Business is a fascinating and important subject. No other institution employs more people, utilizes more raw materials, or contributes more to the prosperity and power of the United States. The two chapters in Section I of this book set the stage for the study of business. Chapter 1, American Business and the Total Environment, analyzes how the total environment influences and is influenced by every business operation. Chapter 2, A Systems View of Business, serves as a basis for integrating and understanding the various functions of business. Chapter 2 also serves as a framework for the remaining chapters of the book.

# American Business and the Total Environment

People can either be independent or dependent upon others in seeking satisfaction of their wants and needs. However, very few people living in the advanced societies of the world are self-sufficient. In fact, most people are dependent upon others, those who are engaged in business activities and services, to satisfy the majority of their wants and needs. Business activities are all those events necessary for the provision and sale of goods and services for a profit.

Business activities range in size and shape from the one-man endeavor to the large corporate structure. Such diversity may be confusing, but common characteristics of all business activity can be identified. All business activity must take place in a framework provided by society. This framework is the sum of the social, economic, and governmental systems of that society. These three systems intertwine and form the total environment within which business must operate. There are considerable differences between various countries in the degree to which this environment shapes, and is shaped by, business. For now we are concerned with understanding the environmental setting of the United States.

---

A glossary will be found at the end of the text. Words defined in the glossary will be noted in boldface type when first mentioned within the text.

In our society *no* business operates in a vacuum or is immune to the environment surrounding it. For sake of discussion the three systems—social, economic, and governmental—will be discussed separately. However, it is important to remember that the three are in fact inseparable elements of one total environment.

## The Social System of the United States

The social system includes the values and beliefs held by the people of a society. The outward expressions of these cultural beliefs are found in the governmental and economic systems of that society. In the United States three overriding beliefs serve as the foundation for our society:

1. Equality of individuals.
2. Freedom of individual choice.
3. Freedom for individual effort.

These values guide in the formulations of our governmental and economic systems. By themselves they are almost meaningless. Their real meaning is evident when applied to the conditions under which people work and live.

## The Economic System of the United States

Every economic system of the world must solve two basic problems to continuity: (1) what goods and services are to be produced and in what quantity; (2) how will the productive capacity of the system be maintained and grow. The American economic system has many names. For our purposes the two titles **capitalism** and **free enterprise** will be used interchangeably. By definition either of these titles applies to a system where the production and distribution of goods and services is not organized and planned by some central authority. It is left instead to the private individual who engages in these activities for profit. Not *all* goods and services in the U. S. are supplied by private business. For example, we have a governmental postal system and a municipal water supply system. But the vast majority of the goods and services supplied to the public are produced by private enterprise.

The outstanding feature of the American system is the extent to which the belief in freedom of choice operates to solve the two basic economic problems. Each individual as a consumer is free to buy what he chooses, when and where he chooses. Problem number one, the determination of the quantity and quality of goods and services produced, is solved by the consumer exercising his freedom of choice. If consumers collectively do not want a good or service, or are unwilling to pay the price, no sale will be made. Production of this good or service will cease because it cannot pay for itself. However, if consumers want a good or service and are also willing to pay a price that is sufficiently high to provide a profit, someone will continue to produce and sell that good or service.

The second problem confronting every economic system, how the productive capacity of the country will be maintained and grow, is solved in the United States by relying on freedom of individual choice and freedom of individual effort. Each person in our society is free to establish his own business, to choose the type of business to engage in, and to produce the kind of product he thinks will sell. The motive for doing so, along with a feeling of independence, is the opportunity to make a profit. The productive capacity is maintained and the incentive for continual growth is provided by allowing individuals to retain the profits from their efforts.

### Implications for Business and Businessmen in the United States

Operating under a free enterprise system enables many businesses to prosper and grow. However, as the following examples illustrate, this is neither true for all business, nor automatic.

> In 1957 Ford Motor Company introduced into the American automobile market the Edsel. This was the culmination of twenty years of planning for a new medium-priced car. A six-volume report recommending the Edsel was based on the strong belief that there was a vast consumer yearning for a new medium-priced car. Yet, on November 19, 1959, Ford discontinued Edsel's production, having lost a total of $350 million and incalculable dealer and buyer confidence.[1]

> The *Saturday Evening Post,* founded by Benjamin Franklin, would have been 240 years old on October 2, 1969, but the last issue was printed February 8, 1969. This was in spite of a steady growth rate until 1952, when circulation was 4.2 million with advertising revenue of $75 million. A financially weak company in 1965, the *Post* went biweekly to cut its losses, but was eventually forced to circulate its last issue.[2]

> The Penn Central Railroad operated in sixteen states and serviced one-third of the nation's commuter and long-passenger customers. Over 300,000 commuters in the New York and Philadelphia area utilized the 903 passenger trains operated daily in the New York Area. In 1969 The Penn Central hit a new low in performance—on its Philadelphia lines, the road cancelled 117 train runs, and of the 296 that did run, 290 were late. The inability to meet expenses which included a $20 million payroll a week, for 94,000 employees, and a debt and rental charge on equipment in excess of $21 million and losses of $182 million forced the Penn Central to bankruptcy in 1969.[3]

There are many similar examples of business failures. Dunn and Bradstreet reports that of 2,490,000 firms in business in 1972, there were 9,566 failures.

---

1. *The New Yorker,* November 25, 1960, p. 57.
2. Michael M. Moody, "The Death of the *Post,*" *Atlantic Monthly,* November 1967, p. 70.
3. "The Biggest Bankruptcy Ever," *Time,* July 6, 1970, p. 58.

EXHIBIT 1–1

*Business Failures*

| Year | Total concerns in business | Number of failures |
|------|---------------------------|--------------------|
| 1960 | 2,708,000 | 15,445 |
| 1961 | 2,641,000 | 17,075 |
| 1962 | 2,589,000 | 15,782 |
| 1963 | 2,544,000 | 14,374 |
| 1964 | 2,524,000 | 13,501 |
| 1965 | 2,527,000 | 13,514 |
| 1966 | 2,520,000 | 13,061 |
| 1967 | 2,519,000 | 12,364 |
| 1968 | 2,481,000 | 9,636 |
| 1969 | 2,444,000 | 9,154 |
| 1970 | 2,442,000 | 10,748 |
| 1971 | 2,466,000 | 10,326 |
| 1972 | 2,490,000 | 9,566 |

Source: U.S. Bureau of the Census, *Statistical Abstract of the United States, 1973*, 94th ed. Washington, D.C.: 1974, p. 487.

The possibility of failure is ever-present; however, it is not inevitable. For every failure there are just as many long-lived business organizations and phenomenal success stories. The following examples illustrate that the free enterprise system is not so cruel in all cases.

James Cash Penney opened his first store in Kemmerer, Wyoming, in 1902, selling soft goods strictly on a cash basis. In 1957, Penney's was a dry goods chain selling mainly staples. It had 1,700 stores on the Main Streets of the country and was on the verge of becoming obsolete. A new direction was charted for Penney's in 1957, with the effect of a steady growth since 1960. During a period when Sears-Roebuck, the real giant in the business, posted a 60 percent gain in sales and earnings, Penney's earnings soared nearly 95 percent (to $107 million); it is increasing store space by 10 percent each year.[4]

In 1953 the first issue of *Playboy* was sold, with a circulation of 55,000 copies. Today *Playboy* sells over 3 million a month, will gross $28 million in 1965, with the total Playboy Corporation worth in excess of $70 million.[5]

International Business Machines (IBM) was chosen by the nation's top executives as the number one growth company in the United States. Sales have soared from one billion to seven billion in the last decade, with 69 percent of all computers shipped since 1964 carrying the IBM brand.[6]

These examples point up the two most important characteristics of our economic system, both of which revolve around the concepts of freedom of choice and individual effort. First, consumers, not business, collectively determine

4. "How They Minted the New Penny," *Fortune,* July 1967, p. 111.
5. "An Empire Built on Sex," *Life,* October 29, 1965, p. 68.
6. "The Power House Growth of IBM," *Dunn's Review,* December 1970, p. 26.

what and how much of a good or service is produced in our economy. Business only responds to consumer wants and needs. Secondly, the individual business-man or woman, along with the right to retain the profits of success, must also bear the risk of failure. In our economy business success is not guaranteed. Business failures more often than not are caused by the inability of that business management to determine properly what the consumer wants. It is indeed amazing how such a simple lesson is often forgotten.

Individual freedom of choice concerning what to consume and what to pro-duce is the basis for the U. S. economic system, with the profit incentive being the motivating force that keeps the economy running. But the profit incentive for producers is so great that controls must be put into effect to assure *all* in-dividuals their freedom of choice. This is one objective of the governmental system.

## The Governmental System of the United States

Absolute individual freedom is impossible: people can conflict in the pursuit of their freedoms, or can pursue their freedoms at the expense of the other's freedom. The following examples illustrate the dangers of a completely un-restrained economy.

> In the period between 1870 and 1882 *Standard Oil* of Ohio acquired nearly all the oil refineries in Cleveland and many others elsewhere and gained control of the oil pipelines from eastern oilfields to the refineries. Eventually the group dominated the industry, controlling some 90 per-cent of trade in refined products; it was able to set the price both of crude and of refined petroleum. Evidence was given that the combination, by obtaining heavy preferential rates and rebates from the railroads, had forced smaller competitors either to join it or go out of business.[7]

> There was never the least attention paid to what was cut up for sausage; there would come all the way back from Europe old sausage that had been rejected, and that was moldy and white—it would be dosed with borax and glycerine, and dumped into the hoppers, and made over again for home consumption. There would be meat that had tumbled out on the floor, in the dirt and sawdust, where the workers had tramped and spit uncounted billions of consumption germs. There would be meat stored in great piles in rooms; and the water from leaky roofs would drip over it, and thousands of rats would race about on it. It was too dark in these storage places to see well, but a man could run his hand over these piles of meat and sweep off handfuls of the dried dung of rats. These rats were nuisances, and the packers would put poisoned bread out for them, they would die, and then rats, bread, and meat would go into the hoppers to-gether. This is no fairy story and no joke; the meat would be shovelled into carts and the men who did the shoveling would not trouble to lift out

---

7. A. D. Neals, *The Antitrust Laws of the U.S.A. A Study of Competition Enforced by Law*, 2nd ed., NIESR Students' Edition. Cambridge, Eng.: University Printing House, 1970, p. 97098.

a rat even when he saw one—there were things that went into the sausage in comparison with which a poisoned rat was a tidbit.[8]

Wage data covering the payrolls of 21,922 textile workers in Lawrence for a period in 1911 is very revealing. The average rate of wages for this group was 16 cents an hour; of the total group, 23.3 percent received less than 12 cents an hour; and 20.4 percent earned 20 cents or more per hour. The work week was 56 hours. If they worked this full week, the average wage received by these 21,922 employees was $8.76 per week.[9]

An economic system based on total individual freedom will in fact result in an economy where few freedoms are preserved. This realization has been reached in the United States. In order to maintain the freedom necessary to make free enterprise function, the government has assumed the role of chief protector of the right of individual freedom of choice. President Franklin D. Roosevelt's New Deal legislation marked the start of active government intervention in altering the environment within which business firms operate for the benefit of *all* members of society. This intervention limits the degree of freedom business has in providing a good or service to meet consumers' demands.

The government has chosen to maintain the individual's freedom of choice by maintaining the ideals of free competition between businesses for the consumers' dollars. It has set certain minimum standards for employees, employers, and consumers in an attempt to protect their interests. To preserve these freedoms, the three branches of the federal government system—legislative, judicial and executive—and the state and local governments each play an active role.

## THE LEGISLATIVE BRANCH

Broadly speaking, government intervention can be classified into four categories of legislation:
1. Legislation protecting business from business,
2. Legislation protecting consumers from business,
3. Legislation promoting the general level of the economy,
4. Legislation protecting employees from employers.

The legislation is part of the environment within which business in the United States must operate and is the prime responsibility of this branch of our government. Each of these four categories of legislation carries with it certain implications for and limitations on the freedom of individual businesses. This chapter concentrates only on the legislation in the first two categories. Legislation falling into the third category impacts every business decision. Rather than discussing it in one place, it will be interspersed throughout the text. This legislation is the very heart of the American economic system and can best be understood as the various concepts of business are related. Legislation falling into the fourth cate-

---

8. Upton Sinclair, *The Jungle*. New York: New York American Library, Inc., 1905, p. 136
9. United States Congress, 62nd Congress, Senate, *Report on Strike of Textile Workers in Lawrence, Massachusetts in 1912*, Senate Document No. 870. Washington, D.C.: 1912, p. 72.

gory will be discussed in a later section of the text which deals specifically with the employees of the business firm.

## LEGISLATION PROTECTING BUSINESS FROM BUSINESS

Once in operation, most businesses would like to secure their positions. No one likes the thought of being forced out of business by a competitor. In the search for security, some managements have sought to decrease the amount of competition that their firms have to undergo. Competition, however, is a cornerstone of the United States' economic system. The Sherman Act, Federal Trade Commission Act, Clayton Act, and Robinson-Patman Act reflect the concern of the United States government with protecting the spirit and practice of competition among business firms.

*The Sherman Act* (1890) is a general declaration of intent to maintain a competitive economic environment in the United States. The act contains two main prohibitions:

> Section 1    Every contract, combination in the form of trust or otherwise, conspiracy, in restraint of trade or commerce is hereby declared to be illegal.

> Section 2    Every person who shall monopolize, or attempt to monopolize, or combine or conspire with any other person or persons to monopolize any part of the trade or commerce, . . . shall be deemed guilty of a misdemeanor.

This law does not stop businesses from expanding into large and efficient firms, but rather prohibits them from using their size and power to take unfair advantage of competitors or the public.

*The Federal Trade Commission Act* (1914) was designed to strengthen the Sherman Act by setting up a commission of specialists to investigate unfair business and industry practices and to enforce the law. The Federal Trade Commission (FTC), a part of the executive branch of the government, was charged with securing compliance with the general ban on "unfair methods of competition."

Since its establishment in 1914, the FTC has had its duties broadened. The Federal Trade Commission Act was amended by the Wheeler-Lea Act in 1938 to include not only unfair competition, but also unfair or deceptive acts and practices in commerce. It also gives the FTC jurisdiction over false advertising of foods, drugs, and cosmetics and the power to restrain false advertising through injunctions. Thus, the FTC is concerned with deceptive practices, as well as the promotion of free and fair competition.

In addition to creating the FTC, Congress attempted to strengthen the Sherman Act further by passing the Clayton Act. The Clayton Act (1914) makes the law more specific by singling out four practices in particular as illegal types of restrictive or monopolistic actions:

1. Price discrimination (section 2),
2. Contracts or agreements that require the buyer to purchase additional merchandise in order to secure the items desired (section 3),

3. Acquisition by a corporation of more than a limited amount of stock in a directly competing corporation (section 7),
4. Interlocking directorates in directly competing companies (section 8).

Each of these sections is qualified in that the practice concerned becomes unlawful *only* when its "effect may be to substantially lessen competition or tend to create a monopoly."

The enforcement of the antitrust laws does not depend exclusively on the Department of Justice and the FTC. The Sherman and Clayton Acts permit any private person who suffers damages as a result of violations to sue offenders.

*The Robinson-Patman Act* (1936), an amendment to the Clayton Act, is an anti-chain store act. Its intent is to prevent chain store monopolies from developing as a result of their power to induce their suppliers to grant them advertising allowances, price discounts, and price concessions not available to smaller retailers and wholesalers. It seeks to prevent the abuse of power, especially purchasing power, by large business to obtain unwarranted concessions that are not available to all on an equal basis.

Amending Section 2 of the Clayton Act, the Robinson-Patman Act states generally that:

1. To meet competition all purchasers must enjoy the same price unless costs vary in dealing with different competitors.
2. Advertising allowances and services must be made available to all customers on a proportionately equal basis.
3. It is unlawful to induce or receive knowingly a discrimination in price that is prohibited by law.

The intent of the act is to assure freedom of competitive opportunity. Large buyers still receive larger discounts than smaller buyers, but they do not receive price and other advantages because they are more important to the seller. Price differentials for large purchases are permitted only if they are based on actual differences in cost of manufacturing, selling, or delivering.

*State and Local Legislation.* There is an almost endless number of state and local laws which regulate intrastate commerce (within the state). Federal laws apply only to business involving *interstate* commerce (between the states). Virtually all states have their own statutory provisions against restraint of trade and against deceptive practices. By and large, however, most state and local legislation is in the field of protecting competition, perhaps reflecting the influence of small businesses on the state legislatures.

## LEGISLATION PROTECTING CONSUMERS FROM BUSINESS

Business' traditional attitude towards consumers is best described by the cliché "let the buyer beware." The federal government has stepped in and taken an active role in providing the consumer with some degree of protection; yet no agency, public or private, can completely cloak the consumer and prevent him from foolishly parting with his health, wealth, or energy. A series of executive agencies has evolved with the primary mission of offering the consumers some protection from business. It includes the Food and Drug Administration, the Federal Trade Commission, Post Office Department, Department of Agriculture, the Federal Communications Commission, and the Securities and Exchange Commission. These agencies are all involved in keeping business from taking advantage of the consuming public, although it is impossible to protect the consumer totally.

The *Food and Drug Administration* (FDA) is the oldest and most important government agency that protects the consumer. The FDA's mission is to insure that foods are safe, pure, and wholesome; that drugs are safe; that cosmetics are not harmful; that therapeutic devices are safe and effective; and that all these are honestly and informatively labeled and packaged. The FDA also inspects all imported foods, drugs, and cosmetics at the time of entry into this country. In the main, the FDA focuses its attention on areas which are most important to the public welfare. When a domestic violation is found, it is reported to the Justice Department with a recommendation for seizure, criminal prosecution, or injunction.

The "unfair methods of competition" of Section 5 of the Federal Trade Commission Act of 1914 has been interpreted to include deceptive practices. Where injury to a competitor through misrepresentation or false advertising could be shown, such practices could be attacked under this law. But the public did not receive specific protection from deception until the Wheeler-Lea Act (1938). This act gave the FTC clear power to regulate "unfair or deceptive acts or practices." No longer did injury to a competitor first have to be shown before the public interest could be protected. In addition, jurisdiction over the false advertising of foods, drugs, therapeutic devices, and cosmetics was given specifically to the FTC. Such advertisements are false when they mislead in a material respect, such as failing to reveal consequences of use. Other legislation administered by the FTC and designed to alleviate deception has been passed. These acts include the Federal Alcohol Administration Act (1935), the Securities Act (1933), the Federal Hazardous Substances Labeling Act (1960) and the Automobile Information Disclosure Act of 1958. Section 5 of the Federal Trade Commission Act, however, remains the principal regulatory effort with respect to goods in general.

In terms of consumer protection the *Post Office Department* is primarily interested in 'the prevention and suppression of fraud involving the use of the mails. No area is left uncovered; anyone using the mails to perpetrate a fraud or swindle may be fined up to $1,000 and imprisoned for up to five years or both.

The *Department of Agriculture* protects the consumer's food supply. Through its agricultural marketing service the supply of poultry and poultry products is protected by condemning, at processing plants or on farms, poultry that is unfit for human consumption. The agricultural research service of the department carries out the program of meat inspection and the supervision of the preparation of meat and meat products to assure their cleanliness and wholesomeness.

The *Federal Communications Commission (FCC)* was created by the Communication Act of 1934 for the purpose of regulating interstate and foreign commerce in communication by wire and radio. It aids the consumer by working with the Federal Trade Commission to eliminate false, misleading, or deceptive advertising over radio and television.

The *Securities and Exchange Commission (SEC)* administrates a series of laws designed to protect those people who choose to become investors. The truth in securities laws have two basic objectives:

1. To provide investors with information concerning securities offered for public sale;
2. To prohibit misrepresentation, deceit, and other fraudulent acts and practices in the sale of securities.

*State and Local Protection of Consumers.* Almost every agency of government protects the consumer either directly or indirectly. But it is impractical, and perhaps undesirable, that the federal government protect the consumer in all areas. A substantial amount of goods does not move in interstate commerce. State and local laws supplement federal regulation. Some states have better laws and enforce them more rigorously than others. Basically the states offer consumer services, food and drug laws, and laws affecting trading, labeling, gambling, advertising, frauds, and sanitary conditions.

This kind of legislation only prevents business from gross malpractices on consumers. In the U. S. the only complete consumer protection comes about when consumers take the responsibility to educate themselves. The consumer still must exercise good judgment in his choice of goods and services.

## THE JUDICIAL BRANCH

The legislation outlined above provides important laws needed to maintain the freedom which is so vital to the functioning of free enterprise. The responsibility for clarifying and interpreting those laws lies with the Judicial Branch of the government. The courts' protection of the business environment takes many forms. Of primary concern here is the protection the courts provide through the interpretation and enforcement of contracts between individuals and businesses.

Of all the legal devices in use today, probably the most important is the **contract.** Over the years, a legal structure has been developed whereby a guarantee is provided that contracts between individuals and businesses can be enforced. The contract makes it possible for people to make binding arrangements for the future; it enables business to expand beyond personal relationships. By stating what is and what is not a legal contract and providing the mechanism for enforcing contracts, the courts have set a positive framework that has enabled business to expand to its current level.

To simplify, clarify, and modernize the law governing commercial transactions as well as make uniform the laws among the various states and jurisdictions, the Uniform Commercial Code was adopted in 1962. Under this code, the basic principles of commercial law are expanded to provide a better understanding of the legal relationships of the parties in various commercial transactions. For the most part the code is designed to ascertain the intention of the parties to a contract; if a contract was intended, it upholds the agreement. To date, forty-five states, the District of Columbia, and the Virgin Islands have adopted the code.

## THE EXECUTIVE BRANCH

Actions taken by the president of the United States often have a significant impact upon the growth of business and industry and thus the growth of the economy of the United States. Every president is interested in increasing production of goods and services while maintaining high employment and stable prices. The president can affect levels of production, employment, and prices. For example, during periods of high unemployment, the president might recommend to Congress that federal income taxes be reduced so that consumers will have more money to spend on goods and services. Such increased spending would in turn create more jobs needed to satisfy the increased demand for goods and services, thereby reducing unemployment. Or the president could encourage Congress to allocate funds for public projects to provide additional jobs. Examples of such projects include the construction of roads, bridges, dams, and low-income housing.

In addition to jobs, the president is also concerned with controlling the level of inflation. An illustration of the president's authority to control and regulate the economy occurred on August 15, 1971, when President Nixon initiated what he called the most comprehensive new economic policy to be undertaken in this nation for four decades. President Nixon's new policy included a ninety-day freeze on wages, salaries, prices, and rents. The objective was to reduce the rate of inflation without slowing economic expansion. For the purpose of developing broad guidelines that would govern the economy after the ninety-day price and wage freeze, two panels were created. The Price Commission, consisting of seven members, developed guidelines for price and rent increases. Concurrently, the Pay Board, composed of fifteen members, watched over wages and salaries. The economic control measures designed by these two panels prevailed through most of 1972. Time will determine the long-range impact of this intervention for the economy and business activity. However, this move by the president is a historic change in government–business relationship. It may well be a prelude to an increased level of government intervention and the possible formation of an informal partnership between government and business for the welfare of our total economy.

Presidential power over business can be exercised in other ways including vigorously applying the antitrust laws against both labor and business monopolies, raising or lowering tariffs and other barriers, intervention into "key" wage negotiations of major industries, providing businessmen with tax credits as a means of stimulating investment in plant and equipment, and utilizing national television as a means of influencing public opinion. As in the past, the debate continues over the extent to which the government should intervene in the economic activity of the United States. Nevertheless, two facts remain: first, by all measures (unemployment, per capita income, and general standard of living) the United States must be considered a highly advanced economy. Secondly, government intervention is the result of the general population's reaction to business malpractices; it expresses our expectations about the general level of well-being for *all* the citizens of this country. Government intervention limits business in exercising freedom of choice for the purpose of retaining the society's freedom.

## The Total Environment
## And Business

Exhibit 1–2 illustrates how the environment, as discussed in this chapter, affects and limits the operation of every business in the United States. The

EXHIBIT 1–2

*The Business System in the United States*

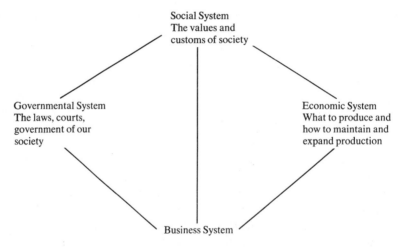

beliefs and values of our society are formalized and expressed through the choice of a governmental and economic system that will retain these values as well as satisfy the needs and wants of the population. Business activities are affected by these three systems and also have some impact on the nature of these systems. For example, business output and level of employment affect the operation of the economic system. The myriad of goods and services produced by business which make up our standard of living, affect our behavior and tastes as people, have some bearing on our attitudes and values or the make-up of our social system.

Finally, business as a whole has rights in the formulation of legislation that is favorable to its position. The relationship of business and the environment is too multifaceted for description. If you are sensitive to this interaction you can spot instances of it daily. Finally, to understand business operations, you must understand how these three systems in the environment affect and are affected by business operations.

## QUESTIONS

1. Illustrate, with specific examples of what you see happening around you, how changes in the social, economic, and governmental systems affect the operation of business in the United States.

2. Illustrate, again with specific examples of what you see happening around you, how changes in a given business operation can affect the social, the economic, and the governmental systems in the United States.

3. Freedom of choice is at the center of the economic system in the United States. Explain why.

4. How could you best summarize the role of government as it relates to business in the United States?

5. What illegal actions are specifically outlawed under the Clayton Act?

6. What is the function of the Federal Food and Drug Administration?

7. What impact does the Judicial Branch of our government have on business activity?

8. What role do you see the president and his advisors having in shaping and/or controlling business operations in the future?

# 2

# A Systems
# View of Business

The ultimate success of any business is based upon management's making correct decisions within the limits of the environment. These decisions are a means to the end of enabling a given business to reach its goals or objectives. Goals guide the businessman in making every decision that affects the organization's future. In this chapter the goals of business are discussed, and the systems concept is presented to help give the proper perspective on decisions regarding the internal operation of every business institution.

## Goals of Business

Every business is created and exists to accomplish some objective or goal. But what are the common ends toward which all businesses are striving? The economic environment of our society dictates that the end toward which *all* business, business activity, and each business decision is directed is *survival*. Survival is such a broad goal that it gives little direction to specific business activity and decision making. In order to survive, all business firms, regardless of size, must strive for the following secondary goals or objectives: (1) to produce a competitive good or service, (2) to make a profit, (3) to gain society's acceptance, and (4) to live up to the responsibility of the various "publics" the business deals with. Survival results when decisions are made with these four secondary goals in mind.

## TO PRODUCE A COMPETITIVE GOOD OR SERVICE

Every business must have a central purpose. This central purpose is to provide a good or service to consumers that has some distinct advantage over competing goods and services. The definition of this central purpose is the starting point for a new business endeavor, as well as an aid to insure a going concern of its continued survival. It is meaningless to discuss achieving the other goals of a business until the businessman is certain exactly what good or service he is going to provide the consumers. Identifying the central purpose is not easy, but the reward for successfully determining the consumer's needs is large. Every businessman must know what business he is in or wants to be in.

Too many times the businessman gets an idea for a good or service, produces it, and to his dismay discovers that no one will buy it. Unfortunately for this entrepreneur, people are not forced to buy his products. They buy only what satisfies their needs. Although the generation of new ideas is not to be discouraged, the potential businessman must analyze the needs of the consumer if his new ideas are to be turned into competitive goods or services. The accompanying diagram illustrates the process of defining which goods and services will be competitive, and thus fulfill the central purpose of the business.

### EXHIBIT 2–1

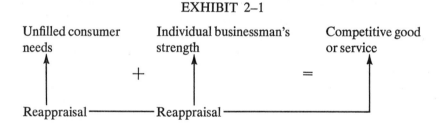

## DEFINING UNFILLED CONSUMER NEEDS

Information is the basis for defining the unfilled needs of a group of consumers. This information takes two forms: secondary information and primary information. Secondary information is already published by government or private agencies and is found by a thorough search of the libraries. To the astute observer, census data, current business trends, and newspaper articles dealing with local conditions present clues to the consumer's unfilled or changing needs. For example, indications that population is decreasing in one part of town may serve as an initial red light for construction of a new restaurant there.

Primary information is gathered to answer a specific question or problem. It is obtained by asking questions and watching the habits of particular consumers. Assume that a businessman wants to open a restaurant at a particular intersection of his town. The number of potential customers could be obtained by simply watching and counting the number of cars passing that intersection daily during the lunch and dinner hours. By further count of the number and type of competing restaurants in the immediate area, a reading could be attained on the degree of saturation of eating in that area. By asking all the household heads in a twenty-mile radius of that intersection to indicate (1) how often they eat lunch and/or dinner out, (2) the type of restaurant and meals they prefer when they are dining out, and (3) how far they are willing to travel to eat such a meal, he further defines the need for and type of restaurant needed in that area. All of these pieces of primary information are obtained to answer a specific question: what is the need for and potential success of a given type of restaurant at a given intersection.

Neither secondary nor primary information provides the potential business-man with all the answers to his questions. But if properly gathered and objectively analyzed, the information can increase the possibility of a correct answer to his questions, which is surely much better than producing a good or service and hoping a need exists. The study of information can save the businessman from making a costly error.

## BUSINESSMAN'S STRENGTHS

Having determined that a need exists, the next step is to analyze the business-man's strengths and weaknesses to determine if he can satisfy that need. Assume that all indications are positive for a family-type restaurant at the intersection in question. Will this business utilize the strengths of the individual business-man and bypass his limitations? This requires an indepth and objective ap-praisal by the individual of his ability, capabilities, and resources. For example, has he ever had any experience with managing a restaurant, does he know what is involved, can he raise the necessary funds to start and sustain this endeavor, and does he have contacts with food suppliers? Answers to these types of questions will determine if this is the right business. The right business is the one where the strengths of the businessman can be capitalized on to competi-tively satisfy an existing need. This is the formula for a competitive good or service, and one that initially insures the businessman's survival. But consumer needs are continually changing, as are the businessman's strengths and weak-nesses. The right business today may be the wrong business tomorrow. To remain competitive and thus survive he must reappraise both the needs of the consumer and how he is fulfilling those needs. This approach is applicable both to an individual who is contemplating starting a new business and to a going concern.

The businessman utilizing this approach can start with a search of the market for unfilled consumer needs or he may have a predetermined idea of what he wants to produce. If he starts with a predetermined idea, however, before he transfers it into an actual good or service he must see if a need exists and then modify or change his idea to match the need. To attempt production without checking consumer needs is definitely the formula for failure.

## TO MAKE A PROFIT

The level of profit made by a business is an indication of how competitive it is in providing a good or service. Profit means that business must operate over a period of time so that receipts exceed expenditures. A business can always be competitive by offering a good or service at the lowest price. But if this price does not cover production and operating costs, there is no profit and the business fails. On the other hand, a business could speculate that if the selling price of a good or service were three times the competitor's price, it would bring in additional profit. But if the competitor's goods and services were of equal quality and convenience, this speculation would be simply a dream. The two goals are related, but business must provide a competitive good or service at a competitive price *before* it can realize its profit goal. The order of realization of these two goals explains why the consumer, by exercising his dollar votes, has so much power in the United States economy. It also explains why the definition of the business' central purpose is so vital to long-term survival.

## TO GAIN SOCIAL ACCEPTANCE

Public opinion enables the consumer to exercise power over the formation of business objectives. Business must be concerned with the public's opinion of its product, service, and purpose. As an example, while many factors were responsible for the demise of General Motor's Corvair, Ralph Nader's book *Unsafe At Any Speed* and the resulting negative public opinion of the car had a definite impact. Business must be concerned and accept the responsibility for such matters as polluting of the environment, training and employment of minority group members, and selling safe and reliable goods and services, if they expect to remain a legitimate part of this society. Those who fail to accept this responsibility may find themselves on the negative end of public opinion, a proven detriment to survival. The term "social responsibility" has become a fashionable way to indicate business' general concern to be a giving member of the community rather than just a taking member.

## TO LIVE UP TO THE RESPONSIBILITY OF THE VARIOUS PUBLICS BUSINESS DEALS WITH

Business deals with various "publics" who expect a minimum respect for their specific demands. Such publics as consumers, employees, stockholders, and investors make demands on business which must be considered if the business is to survive. Legislation has set a minimum level of protection for these groups from unethical practices. In addition, the employees, stockholders, potential investors, and creditors expect more from business than the legal minimum provided by the government. Each group offers something necessary to the business; in return each expects certain considerations in the decisions that affect their interests. As with the consumer, the demands of employees, stockholders, and creditors must be satisfied if the business is to continue to operate.

Among other things, employees expect fair treatment, decent working conditions, and good wages. Stockholders expect, at a minimum, regular dividends, the right to a voice in the operation, and if not increasing value, at least a similar value for the stock they hold. Creditors expect a fair return on their investment in the form of interest on debt as well as repayment of the principal when the debt matures. Potential investors will evaluate at least the efficiency of management before investing or placing a value on the stock of the enterprise. If these publics are not satisfied, they, like the consumer, will take their business elsewhere. It would be impossible to meet all these responsibilities at the level each group expects, but some recognition must be given to each as a secondary goal for business. Without these publics the business would not be able to survive.

## DO THE GOALS CONFLICT?

Although at any time some of these secondary goals may conflict, looking at them in a broader perspective, emphasis on any of the secondary goals may cause conflict with the others. For example, high wages could lead to lower profits; high profits may be reduced by expenditures made for pollution control; high dividends to stockholders could result in low wages, low profits, and poor protection of the investor's money. High profits could result because no funds are being channeled into new product development, but this runs the risk of a poor competitive position. The combinations are endless. By seeing business' primary goal as survival, the relationship between the secondary goals is placed in its proper perspective. Businessmen make decisions that should result in a balanced achievement of all four secondary goals. At any one time one secondary goal may be more important than another. For example, the development of a competitive good or service may take precedence over the other three secondary goals in the short run; but the wise businessman realizes that for long-run survival, decisions must be made that result in all of the secondary goals being achieved to some degree.

Such decisions require the businessman to take many factors into consideration at once. To simplify his task and to indicate to him the consequences of his decision on each of his numerous secondary goals, he needs a framework within which to work. We suggest that the businessman think of his business, regardless of its size, or the good or service produced, as an ongoing system.

### The Business System

The basic idea of a **system** is that of a set of component parts related in the accomplishment of some purpose. An example of a system is the electrical wiring, terminal, sockets, bulbs, switches, etc., which must operate in the proper balance or combination to reach the objective of lighting a room. Each of these components is necessary and has a relationship to the other parts if the purpose is to be achieved. A larger system would be the country's military system. Each part (i.e., Army, Navy, Air Force, and Marines) has a function;

they are related or work in combination to accomplish the goal of the defense of our nation.

The value of the systems concept is that it forces those who make decisions about the operation of a business to analyze not only the objective of the business but also how the parts can best fit together to accomplish this purpose. Such an approach helps the businessman place the factors he must consider in making the decision in proper perspective. All business firms can be viewed as a system and depicted as in Exhibit 2–2.

EXHIBIT 2–2

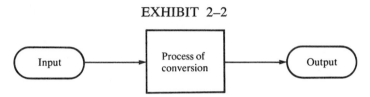

To endure or survive the business system must create value. Business creates value by receiving inputs from the society in forms of people, materials, and money; it transforms these into outputs of products, services, and rewards for organizational members sufficient to keep them participating in the system.

Such a general view is of little help in understanding the business system. More specifically, every business system must perform the following functions:

1. The business must *finance* its efforts.
2. Something of value must be *produced*.
3. The good or service must be *distributed* to the consumer.

These are basic to businesses' survival and have often been called primary functions of the business. To this list can be added the following three functions, which are also important to the survival of the business system:

4. Someone must *manage* the business system.
5. *Manpower,* in the form of workers and managers, must be employed.
6. *Information* must be obtained about the internal operations of the business system and about external changes in the environment to indicate how business will in the future adapt to these changes.

Each of these functions can be thought of as a separate series of interrelated events. For example, the production process requires that many events occur before a piece of steel can be turned into a car. Each of the six functions are "processes" occurring within the business system. A **process** may be defined as a series of actions or operations definitely conducive to an end. The end of each process is an efficient and effective business system. The simple diagram of the business system changing inputs into outputs can be expanded as in Exhibit 2–3 to include those processes that make up every business system.

Traditionally, major processes have been studied as separate and distinct activities. This emphasis on the efficiency of individual operating processes still holds in most businesses. Nevertheless, the growing tendency in business today is to examine each process as a part of the total system rather than in isolation. In other words, the company must be recognized not as a collection of separate processes but as a system in which the processes of finance, production, distribution, management, manpower, and information are properly balanced and coordinated.

In Exhibit 2–3, the systems approach is illustrated emphasizing the interrelationships between the various processes. It cannot be said that finance, for example, is more important than the other processes of the firm, any more than it can be said that the carburetor is a more important part of a gasoline engine than the ignition system. Businessmen who adopt the systems approach recognize that the operations and goals of the total firm rather than the activities of any one particular part or process, must be given primary consideration.

### EXHIBIT 2–3

*Major Processes of the Business System*

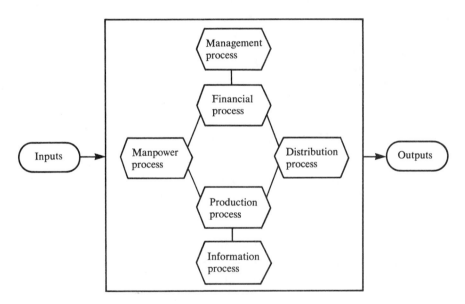

The business system can now be defined. A **business system** is a man-directed, multigoal, adaptive network of interaction processes. The points in this definition that need be stressed are:

1. *Someone must maintain the system; or, the business system is essentially man-directed.* It stands to reason that businesses do not run themselves. Human planning and direction of the business system is necessary. This is what we have called the *management process*. The manager/businessman must make decisions about the future of his business as well as how each of the other five processes will be run and interrelated. He gives this direction to the business system and determines its long-run success or failure.

2. *Business systems have many goals.* The four primary goals of all business systems were indicated earlier.

3. *The business system is adaptive.* In our economy the business system *must* be adaptive. Business systems in the United States are dependent upon and affected by the environment within which they operate. The social, economic, and governmental systems affect every aspect of the business system. Business systems are not only affected by consumers but also by competition, unions, government agencies, public opinion, and a host of other environmental factors.

The businessman must be constantly aware of this environment and any changes which signify his business should be headed in a new direction. This is part of the job of the *information process.*

4. *The processes within a business system are interacting.* Exhibit 2–3 indicates that each process overlaps the others. Each businessman must combine and integrate the four processes of distribution, production, finance, and manpower. He must perform certain managerial processes and have available information to guide his decisions. The decisions he makes on how to combine, integrate, and balance the four basic processes determines the success of the organization. Not one of these four processes should be allowed to dominate, for if it does, it does so at the expense of the other three processes and thus at the expense of the total business system. For example, if the production process operates as if it were the only part of the system, it will seek high output. High output is not in and of itself detrimental, but may have adverse effects on the total business system. Someone must sell the added output or warehouses will fill up with unsold inventory. This ties up funds in unsold merchandise, plus adds to selling and warehousing expenses. Carrying this example further, the required speed up in production effort may result in lowering the quality of the goods produced and increasing the amount of scrap produced. Furthermore, production costs will increase due to overtime wages. High output is now detrimental to the total system because the production process is out of balance with the other processes.

The essence of the systems concept requires that the subgoals of the individual processes be congruent with the goals of the total business. The six processes must be integrated for the best of the *whole* system. Each of the six processes are means to an end—the efficient operation of the business. The businessman must make the decisions that maintain that balance. This is the value of viewing the business as a system. Thus, when making a decision about production, or distribution, or personnel, the businessman must not only analyze the effect of his decision on that specific process but also on the operation of the total business system. Each decision must be put in this perspective, and it is in this perspective that we shall proceed in introducing the business system.

## The Business System in Perspective

Exhibit 2–4 summarizes what has been said in the first two chapters and indicates how this discussion relates to the study of business. Before each of the

# EXHIBIT 2–4

## The Business System in the United States

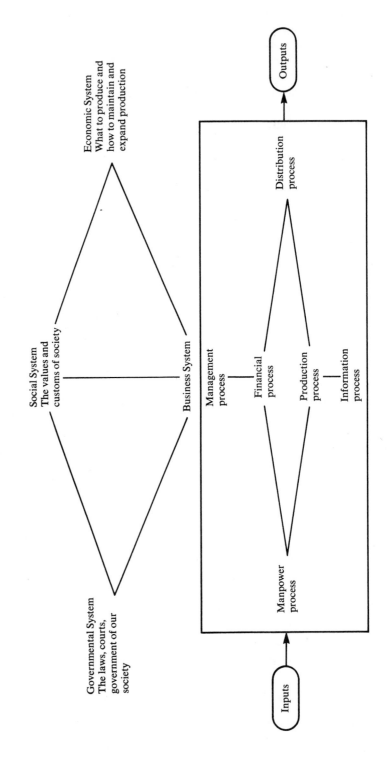

six processes of a business system is discussed as a separate entity, it is important to reemphasize the relationships of these processes and the relationship of the business system to its environment. In our society the business must create value in its *outputs*. To do this managers receive *inputs* from the environment in terms of raw materials, people, and money. These inputs are used or transformed into *outputs* and *distributed* to consumers through three processes: *production, finance,* and *manpower.* The businessman–manager uses an *information* system to detect changes in the environment affecting either inputs or outputs and to determine how each process is operating. This information is then used to make decisions of two general types: first, decisions about the effective operation of each process separately and secondly, decisions about relationships between the processes and the effect on the goals or objectives of the total business system. With this perspective in mind we can now turn to a discussion of each of the six processes separately, realizing that they never are totally separate and distinct, but are highly interrelated parts in the total business system.

### Framework of the Book

The next six sections of this book concentrate on the processes of the business system. Each section analyzes those factors that the businessman must take into consideration when making decisions concerning that process. Every business starts with and continues by defining its central purpose. Concurrently the businessman must also reach certain financial decisions. The factors to be weighed in deciding on the forms of business ownership, the utilization of debt, and the impact of taxes on business operations will be discussed in Section II, "The Financial Process."

Section III centers on the Production Process. It examines the factors the businessman must weigh in formulating that series of events which combine men and machines for the purposes of attaining and transforming raw materials into finished goods or services.

"The Distribution Process" is the subject of Section IV. Decisions must be made in the areas of pricing, wholesaling, retailing, advertising, selling, and transportation to make sure the consumer obtains the goods or services when he wants them, where he wants them, and at the prices he is willing to pay.

Section V concentrates on that series of events necessary to make sure the right number of people with the proper qualifications are available to the business when they are needed, and that they are willing to perform the tasks defined by the business. These events constitute what we have called "The Manpower Process."

The central role the manager plays in setting the environment in balance and integrating the various resources, processes, and objectives of the business system is discussed in Section VI, "The Management Process." After having understood each of the first five processes you should be able to appreciate how the manager utilizes the information process to control the whole business system. Although each of these processes requires a certain amount of information to make successful decisions concerning their operations, Section VII treats information as a separate process. Information comes from two sources: information outside of the business pertaining to its environments, such as market research, and economic forecasting data, and information concerning the internal operation of the business system such as accounting, financial, and statistical data.

In Section VIII we will bring together the parts of the business system into a meaningful whole and indicate some future changes which will affect the operation of businesses in the United States.

## QUESTIONS

1. How is it possible to reach all the goals a business system has? Do some of these goals not conflict?
2. What is a competitive good or service? Can this change over time?
3. Define the word *system*. How does the concept of a system apply to business and nonbusiness institutions?
4. Describe the basic processes found in every business system.
5. Illustrate how a decision concerning the financial process can have an effect on the performance of the manpower process.
6. Explain how changes in the social system can affect the performance of the management, production, and manpower processes within a given business system.
7. Explain how changes in the government system can affect the performance of the financial and distribution processes within a given business system.

# THE FINANCIAL PROCESS

The financial process is concerned with the following four events: (1) promoting and selecting the appropriate form of business organization; (2) raising the proper amount of funds on terms which will be favorable to the firm; (3) allocating these funds to fixed assets such as land, buildings, machinery, and equipment and to current assets such as merchandise inventory and supplies; (4) dealing with federal income taxes and their impact upon financial decisions.

The accompanying diagram illustrates the events which make up the financial process:

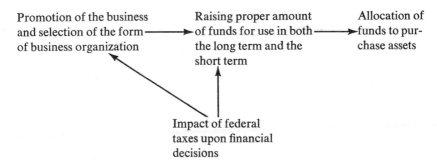

Financial problems first arise when the enterprise is being formed. At this point it is necessary for the business manager to provide information relating to the estimated revenues and expenses of operating the new business. This information is of utmost significance to those who are potential sources for funds. In Chapter 3 we discuss the stages in promoting a new business: conceiving a business opportunity; investigating the conceived venture; and assembling or putting together the various elements of the new business. In promoting an organization serious consideration must also be given to the alternative forms of business organization. The latter part of Chapter 3 is reserved for this subject.

In Chapters 4 and 5 some of the various sources of long-term and short-term financing are discussed. Chapter 6 contains a brief coverage of federal income taxes and their impact upon financial decisions.

# 3

# Promoting a
# New Business Venture

The choice of which good or service the business will offer is so critical that one approach to defining the central purpose of the business was presented in the last chapter. In summary, it was concluded that a businessman should first determine if consumer need exists. Having determined a need, he should then analyze his strengths and weaknesses to determine if he can satisfy that need. By matching his strengths and weaknesses with an unfilled customer need, the businessman will produce a competitive good or service. In this chapter, additional consideration is given to the importance of producing a competitive good or service by examining the three primary stages of promoting a business idea. During the process of promoting a new business venture, the businessman must also consider the form of business organization he will elect. Therefore, the advantages and disadvantages of the sole proprietorship, partnership, and corporation forms of organization are discussed.

## The Financial Process and the Systems Concept

Before discussing the promotion of a business, the role of finance in the business system should be examined. In noting the nature of the systems concept in Chapter 2 the importance of the interdependency of each of the processes within the business firm was emphasized. Such interdependency provides greater assurance that the goals of each process are contributing to overall business goals by achieving important parts of these overall goals.

Because production, distribution, and manpower require funds in order to carry out their assigned activities, the *financial process* is an interdependent part of the total structure of the firm. The *production process* requires funds for purchasing the necessary equipment and other facilities needed to convert raw materials or other inputs into finished products or services. The *distribution process* will need funds for acquiring delivery equipment and warehouse facilities in order to move the goods or services to the consumer. Funds must likewise be allocated to the *manpower process* so that a productive labor force will be maintained to carry out the other activities.

However, this is not a one-way street. By effectively utilizing the funds which have been provided, the production, distribution, and manpower processes in turn facilitate the financial process. Because funds are often limited, each process must attempt to minimize operating costs while at the same time maintaining product quality and good customer service. For example, by taking advantage of quantity discounts on the purchase of raw materials and utilizing efficient equipment, the production process will conserve funds. In similar fashion, the manpower process minimizes operating costs by providing finance, distribution, and production with competent and highly productive workers.

On the other hand, the creation of finished goods or services through the production process, combined with the movement of these goods or services to the consumer through the distribution process, provides the financial process with funds. A portion of these funds will be allocated to each of the processes of the business in order to maintain operating levels. The remaining portion will be retained by the financial process to pay for the future expansion and growth of the firm.

The information process provides data needed in the financial process for planning and control purposes. In order to determine the ability of the firm to meet its current obligations to creditors as they come due, the financial process requires daily reports on the amount of cash on hand and the amount of accounts receivable due from customers. Furthermore, it is vital that the firm have a reasonable estimate of its total needs for funds in the future. The information process must therefore provide data relating to expected sales three or perhaps five years into the future. In addition, information must be gathered on the estimated amount of plant facilities, personnel, and other resources which will be required in the future.

It is often said by those who have a special interest in finance that adequate funds will provide a means of correcting inefficiences in other processes. For example, if the distribution process is inefficient in performing certain functions, such deficiencies can eventually be eliminated if sufficient funds are provided. However, although funds are needed, they are not the sole solution for any and all problems. Strong and efficient production, distribution, and manpower processes are as vital to the survival of the firm as is the financial process. One process cannot be separated from the others. Each process, as indicated above, cannot fulfill its assigned function without support from the other processes. It is important to remember, as you read this book, that the financial process (like the production, distribution, manpower, and information process) is only one part of the firm's network.

## Promotion of a New Business

For the most part people tend to look at business firms as going concerns. When someone mentions the Ford Motor Company, he usually thinks in terms of a successful firm which manufactures beautiful cars, employs thousands of people, and operates at a substantial profit. When he looks at a manufacturing firm, a prosperous drugstore, or grocery store in his hometown, he admires the success of its owners and the respect given them by other members of the community. However, consideration is seldom given to the numerous problems, headaches, and uncertainties which were involved in creating the business. Although starting and operating a business may appear easy, there are many hurdles which every businessman must jump before the firm can become a competitive member of the business community. Many aspiring people who wish to become independent by going into business for themselves never achieve their goal. Of the 2,490,000 firms in business in 1972, there were 9,566 failures. Although success is never guaranteed to anyone who wishes to start his own business, it is possible to minimize the chances of failure by giving careful consideration to the problems involved in promoting a new venture.

Someone must be responsible for coming up with an idea such as a product or service and then combining the necessary human, physical, and monetary resources needed to exploit the idea. This process of developing and financing a new business or a new product is referred to as **promotion.** The promoter of large companies could very well be an outside specialist such as an investment banker or a management consultant. However, the great bulk of the small businesses today are promoted by the individuals who intend to manage them. Most retail stores, professional offices, and manufacturing concerns were established by the same people who now manage them. In many cases an individual who has gained experience and expertise by working for a company in a given industry will utilize this knowledge to build his own company. There are several phases in the promotion of a business, including (1) conceiving a business opportunity; (2) investigating the conceived venture; and (3) assembling or putting together the various elements of the new business. These phases will be examined briefly in this chapter.

## CONCEPTION

Conceiving a new business opportunity may happen in many ways. It may be spontaneous, as in the accidental discovery of oil or gold. Or the new idea may result from a well-defined and planned study in the research and development department of a large firm. Necessity may be the primary stimulus for seeking new products. Many of the tools presently used in agriculture were initially developed by enterprising farmers searching for better methods of tilling the soil. The need to control pollution, to improve the safety of automobiles, and to eradicate cancer are each taxing creative minds to develop new products.

However, a new business opportunity does not necessarily require the development of a new product. A new process or service may be developed. The success of the McDonald's and Holiday Inn franchises are good examples of providing a new service to satisfy wants and needs of new life styles. In addition, the need for more competition may spur people to start a new business. This kind of undertaking does not require a new product, service, or process, but rather the opportunity to satisfy the demands for established products resulting from population growth and increased purchasing power.

## INVESTIGATION

The second phase in promotion is investigation. Although it is understandable that the promoter of a business will often be optimistic and enthusiastic about his new venture, it is most important that he also recognize the inherent drawbacks. Once a thorough investigation of the pros and cons of the new venture has been conducted by the promoter, he should consult with experienced professionals such as lawyers, bankers, businessmen, and manufacturers about his idea and listen carefully to their reactions. Because of their experience and knowledge, they may be able to foresee some problem areas concerning the proposal and suggest methods or ways of avoiding them. Of course, the final decision to start the business rests with the promoter. He is the one who will be assuming the risk of losing all or gaining a great deal.

Once the decision to start a new business is made, the promoter must convince those who might provide financial assistance (backing) that the new venture will be profitable. He must explain why it is the right time to enter the market and what he expects his sales will be. He must convince others that the technology needed to manufacture the product or provide the service has been developed. In order to provide as much latitude as possible in price making, he must also show that the production process will produce the product at a low cost consistent with the quality desired. Other areas such as channels of distribution, supply of manpower, location of raw materials, and plant location must also be thoroughly investigated. In order to raise the necessary funds to finance the new business venture the promoter must present a convincing case.

In addition, he must be able to provide information relating to the estimated revenues and expenses of operating the new business. Consideration must be given to the amount of funds needed to finance the acquisition of permanent assets such as land, buildings, and equipment, as well as the amount of working capital required to acquire inventories and meet other recurring expenses such as payrolls and utility bills. By relating **net income** to initial investment the promoter can provide a measure of the rate of return on investment, which is of utmost importance to potential investors. For example, assume John Brown is interested in investing $80,000 in a shoe store. During the first year of operations, he expects sales will amount to $30,000 and that expenses will total $20,000. Mr. Brown's expected net income is therefore $10,000. This is computed by subtracting total expenses of $20,000 from total sales of $30,000. To compute Mr. Brown's return on investment, the following formula is used:

$$\frac{\text{Net income}}{\text{Investment}} = \frac{\$10,000}{\$80,000} = 12.5\%$$

On the other hand, if Mr. Brown estimates net income to be $4,000, his return on investment would be 5 percent ($4,000/$80,000). If the expected return on investment is only 5 percent, Mr. Brown may decide to invest his money in 5 percent municipal bonds. Interest on municipal bonds is nontaxable and the risk is minimal. However, if it appears that the proposed business venture will earn a 12.5 percent return on investment, Mr. Brown may feel that the higher return more than compensates for the risk involved.

Estimating future revenues, expenses, and initial investment is a difficult task which must be done with reasonable accuracy. Some of the more practical and popular methods are discussed below.

## REVENUE ESTIMATION

In order to arrive at the net income expected to be generated by the new venture, it is necessary to estimate total sales. The forecasting tools utilized for this purpose include survey of potential buyers, market tests, and others.

*Survey of Potential Buyers.* Regardless of the forecasting tool utilized, it is important that the benefits received be greater than the costs incurred in conducting the forecast. For example, the ideal technique would be to interview all potential customers personally to ascertain how much they will spend during the next year on a particular product. However, these interviews would entail a great deal of time and money. As a means of overcoming this limitation, a sample of potential customers could be chosen and those selected would, in turn, be interviewed. It is important that the sample selected have the same characteristics as the population, so that the accuracy or reliability of the data gathered may be measured. The survey does not necessarily require a personal interview approach. Two other types are the telephone interview and the mail survey. Regardless of the method used, the value of the data received depends upon the willingness and cooperation of those participating in the survey. In some instances potential buyers may either guess at what they might purchase or simply refuse to disclose the information.

*Market Test Method.* In those cases where surveys are not realistic measures of potential sales volume because of lack of data or unreliable data, a better technique may be a direct market test of the product. Under this method, the product is actually tried out in certain selected markets, giving information on characteristics of buyers as well as their attitudes and reactions to the new product. Such tests are often conducted by agencies specializing in marketing research.

*Other Sources.*    Because of the shortcomings of each forecast technique, no promoter should rely exclusively upon one approach. Although a businessman may rely primarily on one research method, other supplementary sources are usually considered. One valuable technique is to determine if a change in sales can be associated with a change in an economic indicator or other demographic data. For example, studies in various industries have shown that a given percentage increase in nationwide personal income will stimulate a certain percentage increase in sales. A person contemplating the manufacturing of diapers is interested in certain specific forecasts, such as the number of babies to be born in the coming year.

Another source is expert opinions from professional economists and specialists in particular industries. Information relating to future economic conditions in general or in specific industries can be purchased from private research firms. The government issues a wealth of data each year relating to such economic indicators as the unemployment rate, the index of industrial production, personal income, and business failures, to name a few.

## COST ESTIMATION

The task of estimating costs of operating a business is generally considered to be easier than that of estimating sales. However, if the promoter does a poor job of estimating sales, he will probably also do a less than admirable job of estimating costs. This is especially true in a manufacturing plant, because many costs vary with the level of production, which in turn is dependent upon the level of sales.

There are three broad categories of costs which must be considered in estimating the total costs of operating a manufacturing plant: product costs, selling and administrative expenses, and income taxes. There are three primary elements included in **product cost: direct materials, direct labor,** and **manufacturing overhead.**

Direct materials are materials which are incorporated into and become a part of the product being manufactured. Direct labor is the labor of employees who are working directly on the goods being manufactured. Both direct materials and direct labor are called variable costs because they vary in direct proportion to changes in production. For example, if sales increase 10 percent, then variable costs will increase 10 percent. Once production requirements are known, direct material and direct labor costs can be estimated quite accurately.

Manufacturing overhead includes all factory costs which are not classified as direct material and direct labor. Overhead usually includes such items as depreciation on plant and equipment, plant superintendent's salary, rent, insurance and repairs on factory equipment. Estimating manufacturing overhead represents a difficult problem because some of those costs are variable while others are fixed. A **fixed cost** is one which remains constant over various levels of production. Examples of fixed overhead include rent, insurance, depreciation, and property taxes. **Variable overhead** includes supplies and some repairs to equipment. It is therefore necessary to estimate both total fixed overhead and total variable overhead based upon the anticipated level of production. For example, depending upon the demand for the firm's products, the XYZ manufacturing company plans to produce either 10,000 or 15,000 units of output. The total overhead costs for each level of production are as follows:

|  | Units of output | |
|---|---|---|
|  | 10,000 | 15,000 |
| Variable overhead | $ 5,000 | $ 7,500 |
| Fixed overhead | 12,000 | 12,000 |
| Total overhead | $17,000 | $19,500 |

Notice that fixed costs remain the same under both levels of production. On the other hand, variable costs vary in direct proportion to changes in production. Consequently, by increasing output 5,000 units or by 50 percent, variable costs likewise increase by 50 percent, or $2,500.

Selling and administrative costs are not included in manufacturing overhead because they are not incurred as a part of the manufacturing activities. Selling expenses are commonly referred to as **distribution costs** and include those costs incurred in directing the flow of finished goods from the production department to the consumer or user. Selling expenses include advertising, delivery expense (including depreciation on delivery equipment), and salesmen's salaries and commissions. If salaries of salesmen are based upon sales made, the total cost will depend upon both the commission rate and the number of units sold. If the salesmen are paid a straight salary, then total costs will simply amount to the sum of the salaries. For a new company, estimating selling expenses may be difficult because the firm may be uncertain as to the exact number of salesmen needed. Of course, for some businesses there may be no need for salesmen. Advertising costs are usually based upon a given percentage of sales and therefore are not difficult to estimate. In many firms the amount spent on advertising is simply based upon excess funds which are not needed for production.

**Administrative expenses** include such items as office salaries, rent, insurance and property taxes on the office building, depreciation of the office building and office equipment, and expenses resulting from uncollectible accounts. However, bad debt expense is usually included as a part of selling expenses whenever the sales department regulates the credit policies of the firm. For an established firm administrative costs are usually based upon past experience adjusted for future increases in costs resulting from factors such as promotions, salary incentives, and business expansions. A new firm will not have the advantage of past experience and must therefore be more careful in making such estimates.

To compute net income, it is necessary for the businessman to recognize that income taxes, like selling and administrative costs, are expenses of operating a business. Taxes reduce the amount of income available for distribution to the owners of the business as well as the amount of money available for normal business operations and future expansion. If the firm does a good job of estimating net income before income taxes, the amount of estimated tax is simply a matter of multiplying the applicable tax rate times the taxable income.

EXHIBIT 3–1

*Total Costs of Operating
a Manufacturing Plant*

*Product Costs*

Direct materials
Direct labor
Manufacturing overhead
  Depreciation on plant and equipment
  Plant superintendent's salary
  Rent
  Insurance
  Supplies
  Repairs on factory equipment
  Factory wages
  Property taxes on factory facilities
  Other

*Selling Expenses*

Advertising
Transportation
Depreciation on delivery equipment
Insurance on salesmen's cars
Salesmen's salaries and commissions

*Administrative Expenses*

Office salaries
Rent on office building
Insurance on office building
Property taxes on office building
Depreciation of office building and office equipment
Clerical salaries

*Taxes*

Federal income taxes
State income taxes
City income taxes

## ESTIMATE OF INITIAL INVESTMENT

Once the promoter has estimated future revenues and operating expenses for the firm's first year of operation, he then must calculate the amount of investment required to start the new venture. It is not sufficient to show potential investors how much net income should be forthcoming from the business in its first year. More information is required. For example, assume the promoter predicts a net income of $10,000. If you are a potential investor, would this figure mean anything to you? The answer is no. The net income figure of $10,000 is pertinent only when it is examined in relation to the amount of investment required to generate that income.

If the initial investment is estimated to be $500,000, then the **rate of return on investment** would be 2 percent ($10,000 / $500,000). If the initial investment is approximated to be $50,000, then investors would earn a rate of return of 10 percent. In the first case, most investors would look to alternative forms of investment which would offer a much larger return than 2 percent. Simply depositing money in a savings account at the local bank, where the risk of losing it is minimal, earns a return of 5 or 6 percent. On the other hand, earning a potential return on investment of 10 percent would look quite attractive to most people and consequently they would give serious consideration to providing the necessary funds to start the business.

As the example illustrates, the initial investment required to get the business going is most important, and therefore the promoter must be careful to include all costs in his estimate. There are three primary needs which must be considered in estimating the amount of initial investment: (1) investment in property or fixed assets; (2) investment in working capital; and (3) organizational costs. Investment in property includes such items as land, buildings, machinery, and equipment. These are referred to as **fixed assets** because they are expected to be used in the business over a long period of time. When estimating the costs of buildings, machinery, or equipment, the promoter should consider such alternatives as buying versus leasing and purchasing new assets as opposed to used assets. Although every new business firm would like to start off with a beautiful new building and shining new machinery and equipment, other needs may require the promoter to consider used facilities which are still efficient and adequate.

The second need is for **working capital.** Many business ventures have failed simply because the promoters did not consider working capital in estimating initial investment. Working capital, which includes such assets as cash, accounts receivable (amounts due from customers), and merchandise inventory, is as essential to the operation of a business as fixed assets. If the new firm is in a retail business, cash will be needed to purchase **inventory** which will be later sold to customers. Inventory must be carefully planned so that a sufficient stock of each item handled will be available to meet the demands of future customers. Because a large percentage of sales will be on credit, it is important that the new firm has sufficient cash to meet current payrolls, utility bills, and other debts while awaiting payment from customers.

In addition the promoter must not overlook his own expenses as well as those of professional attorneys, accountants, and others which will be incurred in organizing the business.

## ASSEMBLY OF RESOURCES

The next task facing the promoter is to bring together the necessary human, physical, and monetary resources. The problems associated with monetary resources will be discussed here. Those associated with human and physical resources will be examined in later sections. The problems of raising the necessary funds are more severe for a new firm than for a firm which has been in operation for some time. The established firm which wants to expand or improve facilities can more easily acquire funds, because it has a financial record of past achievements. Bankers and investors can examine the past performance of the firm by analyzing such data as sales volume, operating expenses, net income from operations, and return on investment, in order to determine the desirability of providing additional funds. Because the new firm has no such record of past achievements, it is necessary to search harder and more diligently for funds. The promoter of a small business will often look to family and friends for financial assistance. In many cases the promoter will find that his only source of funds will be the personal savings which he has accumulated.

During the 1950s, special organizations designed to assist the small business-man were developed. Perhaps the most publicized is the federal Small Business Administration (SBA). When financing is not otherwise available on reasonable terms, the Small Business Administration makes loans with maturities of up to ten years. The SBA will not, however, loan funds to firms unless it is reasonably certain that the firm will have the ability to repay the loan in the future. The SBA and the assistance it offers the small businessman will also be discussed in a later chapter.

Once the business is operating, the small businessman may accumulate some capital by purchasing inventory on credit, purchasing equipment on install-ment plans, and borrowing small sums from banks and finance companies to meet seasonal conditions. Although financing a new business is difficult and trying, the promotor will find that the task of assembling funds will be made easier if he has done a thorough job of investigating future operating results.

## EXHIBIT 3–2

*Information to be Accumulated by the Promoter*

### *Estimation of Future Revenues*

Methods often used
  Survey of potential buyers
  Market tests
  Expert opinions
  Data accumulated by private research firms
  Data published by the government

### *Estimation of Future Costs*

Three broad categories of costs
  Product costs
  Selling and administrative expenses
  Income taxes

### *Estimation of Initial Investment*

Three primary needs to be considered
  Investment in property or fixed assets
  Investment in working capital
  Organizational costs

If the promoter does a thorough job of accumulating information on expected sales volume, operating expenses, and initial investment requirements, he will then increase the probability of acquiring funds from potential investors. Detailed discussions of both long-term and short-term sources of financing are provided in Chapters 4 and 5 respectively. However, before sources of funds are looked at, the various forms of business organization—the sole **proprietorship, partnership,** and **corporation**—should be examined; because the type of funds available to a business is, in many ways, affected by the form of organization which the promoter selects. For example, in order to acquire funds by issuing stocks or bonds, it is necessary that the corporate form of organization be selected.

## Forms of Business Organization

In the United States there are three common forms of legal organization: sole proprietorship, general partnership, and corporation. Data in Exhibit 3–3 indicate that sole proprietorships are still by far the most common form of organization in the U. S. today. However, since 1960, corporations have increased in number by approximately 45 percent. The amount of funds which

### EXHIBIT 3–3

*Proprietorships, Partnerships, and Corporations*

|  | *1960* | *1965* | *1968* | *1970* |
|---|---|---|---|---|
| Proprietorships | 9,090,000 | 9,078,000 | 9,212,000 | 9,400,000 |
| Partnerships | 941,000 | 914,000 | 918,000 | 936,000 |
| Corporations | 1,141,000 | 1,424,000 | 1,542,000 | 1,665,000 |
| Total | 11,172,000 | 11,416,000 | 11,672,000 | 12,001,000 |

Source: U.S. Department of the Treasury, Internal Revenue Service, *Statistics of Income, Business Income Tax Returns*, Washington, D.C.: various years.

an investor is willing to provide may depend to a large extent upon the form of organization elected by the promoter.

## THE SOLE PROPRIETORSHIP

A sole proprietorship is a business which is totally owned and controlled by one person. It is the simplest type of organization, in that almost anyone of legal age can form a proprietorship. Rather than concerning himself with complex articles of partnership or corporation charters, the sole proprietor must simply obey the local laws and pay those **franchise** or license fees which may be required. The sole proprietor has complete control of all phases of the business and therefore all gains or losses accrue to him. In many cases the sole owner of a business will delegate responsibilities for various activities to other personnel. Nevertheless, the final decisions concerning any and all matters rest with the sole proprietor. Although the majority of goods produced in the U. S. come from corporations, the sole proprietorship is still the most common form of organization and continues to play a significant role in the free enterprise system. Many of today's large and well-known corporations started as small single proprietorships.

The following list includes some of the advantages and disadvantages of a sole proprietorship:

*Advantages*
1. It is owned and controlled by one individual.
2. It is easy to organize.
3. Organization costs are minimal.
4. Whatever profits the business generates accrue to the proprietor as an individual.
5. Because of **unlimited liability,** it is usually easier for the sole proprietor of a small business to borrow money than for a corporation of comparable size. Unlimited liability means that creditors of a firm have a right to the personal assets of the owner where liabilities are greater than the assets of the company. Under the corporate form of organization, creditors are limited (should the corporation fail) to the assets of the corporation to satisfy their claims.
6. The owner does not report to several stockholders or to a board of directors. Consequently, he has total freedom to make decisions.
7. The sole proprietor is not subject to special regulations or taxation. Rather, the income from the sole proprietorship is included in the personal return of the owner.

*Disadvantages*
1. There is unlimited liability. Should the business fail, the creditors of the firm have a right to the personal assets of the owner, including his home, car, and personal savings.
2. It is extremely difficult to accumulate large sums of money for expansion because the business is totally owned by one person.
3. Continuity of life is subject to numerous influences. For example, the very survival of the business often depends upon the general good health and longevity of the sole proprietor. In contrast, the death of a General Motors stockholder will not dissolve or bring an end to G.M.

## THE PARTNERSHIP

The Uniform Partnership Act defines a partnership as "an association of two or more persons to carry on as co-owners of a business for profit." Most of the states today have adopted this act. Such an association is totally voluntary in that no one is forced to join a partnership against his will. The partnership form of organzation is usually found among the small enterprises in the United States in which competent individuals become partners by combining their talents and capital.

Because of statutes in many states forbidding certain professions to incorporate, the partnership form of organization is very popular among lawyers, medical doctors, and certified public accountants. The partnership comes into being by means of a contract, known as the articles of co-partnership, which represents the agreement made by the partners. Although such a contract is binding on each partner even if made orally, it is highly recommended that it be in writing. It should include provisions regarding the amount to be invested by each partner, the ratio in which income or losses will be distributed, and the amount of withdrawals allowed each partner.

## CHARACTERISTICS

*Limited Life.*  A life of a partnership is highly uncertain because events can cause the partnership to be dissolved or ended. These include death, retirement, bankruptcy, or insanity of one of the partners. A partnership may also be dissolved when the period for which the partnership was established expires or when the purpose of the partnership has been accomplished.

*Unlimited Liability.*  If a partnership becomes insolvent due to its inability to pay creditors, then those creditors have the right to the assets of the partnership to satisfy their claims. Should the assets of the partnership be insufficient, the creditors have a legal right to the personal assets of each partner until their claims are paid in full. Personal assets would include home, car, furniture, and savings of each partner. If one of the partners is unable to pay his share of the partnership debts, then the other partner or partners who are solvent are responsible for the unpaid debt.

*Participation in Income.*  Partners share income and losses of the partnership in accordance with the partnership agreement. If no provision is made for distribution of profits and losses, they will be shared equally.

*Mutual Agency.*  When a partner is conducting his duties which are within the ordinary scope of partnership activities, the partnership is bound to any agreement or contract entered into by him. For example, a partner in a clothing store may have the overall responsibility for managing the store. The partner can bind all other partners to any activity which would normally be included within the scope of managing a store. Because of this particular characteristic, it is vital that an individual electing the partnership form of organization choose competent and trustful partners.

*Withdrawal of Assets.*  The corporation is limited in the amount which may be withdrawn in the form of dividends to stockholders. However, no legal restrictions are placed upon the amount which may be withdrawn by partners.

The primary advantages and disadvantages of the partnership are as follows.

*Advantages*
1. Like the sole proprietorship, it is easy to organize.
2. It brings together individuals with varying talents, resources, and experience not possible under a sole proprietorship.

3. A partnership does not pay the taxes or file the numerous government reports of a corporation.
4. Whereas corporations may be required to pay license fees and special taxes to operate in foreign states (states other than the state of incorporation), no such provisions apply to partnerships.
5. It provides a means of bringing together professional skills of doctors, lawyers, and others.
6. Because partners are personally liable for partnership debts, a partnership has greater borrowing power than a corporation of similar size.

*Disadvantages*
1. There is unlimited liability for all partners.
2. **Mutual agency** may be abused.
3. The future life of the firm is uncertain.
4. There may be difficulty in achieving harmony among all the partners. If the partners are unable to work together effectively, the partnership will stand little chance of succeeding.

## THE CORPORATION

A corporation, as defined in 1819 by Chief Justice John Marshall, is "an artificial being, invisible, intangible, and existing only in the contemplation of the law." The essence of this definition is that a corporation is recognized by law as a separate legal person. A corporation, like you and me, can purchase and sell property, can sue or be sued, and is required to pay federal, state, and local taxes. Relative to sole proprietorships and partnerships, corporations are usually the larger firms. In order for a manufacturer to achieve mass production by means of assembly-line techniques, it is necessary to invest large sums in plant and equipment. Because the corporate form of organization provides the best means of accumulating large amounts of funds, it is often utilized by manufacturers. However, it is not necessary for a firm to be large before it can incorporate.

## CHARACTERISTICS

*Transferable Units of Ownership.* Ownership in a corporation is represented by shares of stock which are sold to investors. The owners of a corporation are called **stockholders.** Should a stockholder want to sell part or all of his ownership interest, it is usually simply a matter of endorsing the stock certificate and delivering it to the new stockholder. Millions of transactions involving such transfers between buyers and sellers occur daily on the New York and American Stock Exchanges.

*Lack of Stockholder Liability.* This **limited liability** means that the personal assets of the stockholders are not available to the creditors of the corporation. The stockholder can lose no more than he has invested in the corporation. This contrasts with the partnership or sole proprietorship forms of organization.

*Continuity of Life.*   Although the expected life of a partnership is highly un-predictable, the life of a corporation is determined by reference to the corporate charter. Because the charter may normally be renewed as a means of extending the original time period, the life of a corporation may be perpetual. Neverthe-less, a corporation may be dissolved by agreement of the stockholders, by ex-piration of the time stated in the charter, or by forfeiture of the charter to the state.

*Lack of Mutual Agency.*   While each partner is an agent for all of the other partners and therefore can commit them financially, this is not the case with corporate stockholders. No stockholder, when acting as a stockholder, can make an agreement which would bind the other stockholders.

*Restrictions on Withdrawal of Assets.*   Unlike a partnership or sole proprietor-ship, the corporation cannot withdraw or distribute its legal capital. Legal capital is usually the total amount of money invested by the corporation's stock-holders. This restriction is imposed upon corporations in order to protect cred-itors of the firm. Because of the limited liability of stockholders, creditors have access to corporate assets but not to the personal assets of each stockholder.

The advantages and disadvantages of the corporation are summarized below.

*Advantages*
1. It allows individuals to invest money in an enterprise without assuming the responsibilities of operating the business.
2. Continuity of life is reasonably certain in most states unless stockholders choose to dissolve the firm.
3. There is limited liability.
4. There is no mutual agency.
5. Ownership interests are easily transferred.
6. It facilitates the accumulation of capital necessary for expansion and growth.
7. A corporation is considered a separate legal person.
8. Because of the other advantages, the corporate form of organization is usually favored by investors.

*Disadvantages*
1. Corporations are required to complete and file numerous regulatory and governmental documents and reports.
2. It is authorized to engage only in those activities specified in the corporate charter.
3. Although limited liability is a definite advantage for medium- and large-size corporations, it may represent a disadvantage to the small corpora-tion.
4. Relative to other forms of organization, it is difficult and expensive to organize.

5. Stockholders have little to say in the actual operations of the firm.
6. It may incur problems in attempting to operate in states other than the state of incorporation.
7. Most professions are unable to use the corporate form of organization.
8. Firms in lower tax brackets may find the corporate tax rates higher than the individual rates applicable to income derived from partnerships or sole proprietorships.

## Summary

In promoting a new business, the promoter must first come up with an idea such as a product or service which will satisfy an unfilled customer need. Next he must convince potential lenders that the new venture will be profitable. He does so by accumulating data on expected revenues and expenses of operating the new business venture. He also provides information on the amount of initial investment which will be needed to acquire the necessary permanent assets and working capital. By relating new income to investment, the promoter can provide a measure of the rate of return on investment which is of utmost importance to potential investors.

Next, the promoter must determine which form of business ownership to select, which is significant because the number of potential investors or sources of funds available to a firm depends largely upon the form of organization that is utilized. For example, assume that an individual plans to open a local grocery store in a small city. Because of unlimited liability, it is generally easier for the sole proprietor of a small business to borrow money than it is for a corporation of comparable size. Therefore, in this case, the sole proprietorship form of organization would appear most favorable. On the other hand, assume that she is interested in constructing a new fifty-lane bowling alley in a large metropolitan area. In this case, the initial investment will most likely amount to one-half million dollars or more. Unless she is independently wealthy, the only way of accumulating the necessary funds will be through a partnership or corporate form of organization.

The tasks of promoting a business and selecting a form of business ownership are both related to the need to acquire sufficient funds with which to start the business. In the next chapter the different sources of long-term funds to which the businessman should give careful consideration are examined.

## QUESTIONS

1. Describe how the financial process relates to:
   (a) The manpower process.
   (b) The distribution process.
   (c) The production process.
   (d) The information process.

2. What is the purpose of the finance function?

3. Name the three phases of promotion.

4. What are the three categories into which costs are separated? Give a short definition of each category.

5. Distinguish between fixed and variable costs.

6. Name and explain the three primary elements in product costs.

7. Describe the sole proprietorship and give some of its advantages and disadvantages.

8. What are the distinguishing characteristics of a partnership?

9. What are the primary advantages and disadvantages of the partnership form of organization?

10. What are the distinguishing characteristics of a corporation?

11. List some of the advantages and disadvantages of the corporate form of organization.

12. Discuss the relationship between promoting a business and selecting a form of business organization.

## Incident 3–1

Ed Brown, Joe McQuire, and Anne Gould are interested in investing in a new business opportunity. The three have purchased the rights to a patent which will allow them to manufacture a new safety device for automobiles. The product is called the "Balloon" and is designed to reduce automobile accident fatalities. Upon impact at speeds over ten miles per hour, the balloon inflates in front of the driver, thereby protecting the driver from serious injury.

It is estimated that it will take approximately $300,000 to acquire the necessary production facilities and working capital. Therefore, each person will invest $100,000 in the business. Mr. Brown feels that the new business should be organized as a partnership. However, Mr. McQuire is of the opinion that the corporate form of organization would offer more advantages. Ms. Gould is undecided.

You have been called in as a consultant to advise the three. They have asked you to explain the advantages and disadvantages of the partnership versus the corporation form of organization. In your discussion, you should give consideration to the following three areas.

(a) Personal liability of each of the investors should the business fail.

(b) The ability of the business to borrow necessary funds.

(c) The way in which the business will be recognized for tax purposes and some of the major tax factors which should be carefully examined.

# 4

# Sources of Long-Term Funds

In this chapter some of the various sources of long-term funds which are available to the businessman will be examined. Long-term funds are of utmost importance to the businessman because it is these funds which are utilized to acquire land, buildings, equipment, and other fixed assets necessary to the formation of a business. Recognition will be given to both **debt** and **equity** securities. Debt funds are those which the business obtains from creditors, whereas equity funds are acquired from owners. The specific sources to be covered are the following:

Equity funds
    Common stock
    Preferred stock
    Retained earnings
Debt funds
    Secured bonds
        Mortgage bonds
        Collateral trust bonds
    Unsecured bonds
        Debentures

     Income bonds
     Long-term mortgage notes
     Purchase contracts
     Leasing
        Sale and leaseback

In some cases it will be advantageous for the firm to issue debt securities, whereas in other situations equity securities will be more favorable. For this reason, many businesses utilize both debt and equity in financing the acquisition of assets. The primary characteristics which differentiate the sources will be discussed. Each security or source will be analyzed in terms of the various arrangements by which it is possible to obtain long-term funds and the attractive features to both borrowers and lenders of each arrangement.

Before proceeding with the discussion, **long-term debt** should be differentiated from **short-term debt.** Long-term debt, which will be examined in this chapter, represents those liabilities of the firm which will not mature within the next twelve months. On the other hand, short-term debt, to be examined in Chapter 5, includes those obligations or liabilities of the firm which must be paid within the next twelve months.

## Equity Funds

For a sole proprietorship or partnership, equity funds represent the initial investment of the proprietor or partners in the business. As pointed out in Chapter 3, often the owners of unincorporated firms rely solely upon their personal savings in starting a new business venture. As the business prospers, the owners may acquire additional equity funds by retaining profits in the business as well as by investing additional capital.

Relative to the sole proprietorship or the partnership, it is easier to acquire greater sums of capital under the corporate form of organization, because ownership in a corporation is evidenced by shares of stock. These shares may be issued to hundreds or thousands of small investors. For a corporation, there are three primary sources of equity funds: **common stock, preferred stock,** and **retained earnings.** The discussion which follows examines corporate equity.

### SHARES OF STOCK

As a means of acquiring equity funds, corporations sell shares of stock to investors. These investors are called stockholders of the corporation. Each stockholder receives a stock certificate as proof of his ownership in the corporation. Although stockholders are the owners of the corporation, the responsibility for the general management of the business is delegated to the board of directors, who are elected by the stockholders.

The legal right of the corporation to issue shares of stock to potential investors is provided for in the corporate charter, which is granted by the state of incorporation. The number of shares which a corporation is permitted to issue is called **authorized shares.** When a corporation initially issues fewer shares than are authorized, the remainder is called **unissued shares.** These unissued shares may in turn be sold at a future date without further approval from the state of incorporation. Those shares which have been issued to stockholders are called **outstanding shares.**

## PAR VALUE OF STOCK

When each share of stock is arbitrarily assigned a value, such as $100.00, $5.00, or $.50, it is said to have **par value.** When no value is assigned to the stock it is referred to as **no-par stock.** Prior to 1912, each share of stock was required to have a par value assigned to each stock certificate. However, in 1912, the state of New York changed incorporation laws to allow shares of stock to be sold without a par value. Other states have since passed similar laws, although they are not uniform.

## STATED VALUE OF STOCK

Limited liability is one of the legal advantages of the corporate form of organization. Because of this characteristic, creditors are not allowed access to the personal assets of each stockholder in order to satisfy any unpaid claim. As a means of providing some protection to corporate creditors, the laws of the various states require a corporation to retain its stated capital in the corporation. Although definitions of *stated capital* vary in different states, generally the following definitions apply:

> When a corporation issues par value stock, the stated capital is defined as the total par value of the stock outstanding.
>
> When a corporation issues no-par stock, the board of directors of the company will assign a stated value to each share. Stated capital then represents the total stated value of each share outstanding.

For example, assume that a corporation issues 1,000 shares of no-par stock for $100 per share. The board of directors decides to assign a stated value to each share of stock of $100. The stated capital of the corporation is therefore $100,000 (1,000 shares × $100 per share). This means that the corporation cannot distribute or withdraw any portion of the $100,000 representing capital. It is to be retained by the corporation, thereby providing protection to the creditors who have loaned funds to help the corporation get started. This does not mean that creditors are completely protected by the retention of a corporation's stated capital. It is possible for a firm to lose all of its assets simply by operating at a loss year after year. Consequently, stated capital can be reduced as a result of losses but not because of distribution of corporate assets to shareholders.

## BASIC RIGHTS OF STOCKHOLDERS

There are certain basic rights which, unless restricted by the stock contract, each stockholder is entitled to exercise. These include the following: (1) to share in the dividends of the corporation; (2) to retain a proportionate ownership interest by participating in the purchase of additional shares offered by the corporation (this is referred to as the stockholder pre-emptive right); (3) upon liquidation of the corporation, to receive a share of the corporate assets which remain after all creditors have been satisfied; and (4) to vote at stockholder meetings, thereby exercising to some extent a voice in the affairs of the corporation.

## COMMON STOCK AND PREFERRED STOCK

When a corporation issues only one class of stock it is called common stock. Common stockholders, who have the rights outlined above, bear the heaviest risk as well as the greatest rewards. When two classes of stock have been issued, the second class usually receives certain preferential treatment and is called preferred stock. Generally speaking, preferred stockholders assume less risk than common stockholders. By offering two classes of stock, the corporation provides alternative investment opportunities for investors, thereby increasing potential sources for equity funds.

Two of the areas in which preferred stockholders receive preferential treatment are the right to first share of dividends before common stockholders and the prior right to assets upon liquidation. The amount of dividends to be paid preferred stockholders depends upon the characteristics or restrictions which have been attached to the stock.

### RIGHT TO DIVIDENDS

Although preferred stockholders have first right to a share of corporate earnings, no stockholder is entitled to any earnings until the board of directors elects to declare a dividend. The board of directors will not make a declaration until two prerequisites are satisfied: (1) there are corporate earnings from which to pay a dividend, and (2) the corporation has sufficient cash available with which to pay the dividends. It is important to recognize that even though a corporation may have an excellent earnings record, it may have invested its earnings in additional plant and equipment and consequently may have no cash available for dividends.

Once the board of directors decides to pay a dividend, the question becomes how much preferred and common stockholders will receive. The amount to be paid preferred stockholders depends upon the dividend rate as well as whether the stock is cumulative or noncumulative and participating or nonparticipating.

*The Dividend Rate.* If the preferred stock has a par value, the dividend rate is expressed as a percentage of par value. For example, if a corporation issues 1,000 shares of 6 percent preferred stock with a par value of $100 per share, the dividend rate per share would be $6.00 ($100 $\times$ 6%). If no par value is assigned to the stock, then it is necessary to express the dividend rate in terms of dollars and cents, such as $4.00 per share.

*Cumulative Versus Noncumulative.* Stockholders who own **cumulative** preferred stock are entitled to a dividend each year. Preferred dividends not paid go into arrears which means that such dividends must be paid before common stockholders are entitled to their share. The following example illustrates this feature of preferred stock. Assume that the M. Corporation was formed in January, 1972, with the following two classes of stock:

Common stock   $100 par value; 3,000 shares authorized and issued
Preferred stock   6 percent; cumulative $100 par value; 1,000 shares authorized and issued

The board of directors declares a dividend of $30,000 on December 31, 1975. The corporation had never paid a dividend prior to this time. The dividend will be distributed to the stockholders in the following manner:

|  | Preferred ($100,000 par) | Common (300,000 par) |
|---|---|---|
| Preferred dividends in arrears for 1972, 1973, and 1974 | $18,000 |  |
| Current dividends for 1975 | 6,000 |  |
| Remainder to common |  | $6,000 |
| Total | $24,000 | $6,000 |

Since the dividend rate is $6.00 per share (6% × $100 par value), the preferred stockholders are entitled to dividends of $6,000 ($6.00 × 1,000 shares) each year. Because the preferred stock in the example is cumulative, total dividends in arrears amount to $18,000 (3 years × $6,000). If the preferred stock were noncumulative, then there would be no dividends in arrears, and the preferred stockholders would receive the current dividends of $6,000 (whereas common would receive the remainder of $24,000). The difference between cumulative versus noncumulative in the example is therefore $18.00 per share. That is, cumulative preferred stock would earn $24.00 per share ($24,000/1,000 shares) whereas noncumulative preferred stock would earn $6.00 per share ($6,000/1,000 shares).

*Participating versus Nonparticipating.*   Although normally preferred stock is limited to a fixed percentage of dividends, there are preferred stocks in which the stockholders have a right to dividends in excess of a predetermined percentage. Such stock is said to be **participating.**

Continuing the example, assume that the preferred stock is also fully participating but that no dividends are in arrears on December 31, 1975. The dividend payment of $30,000 will be distributed between common and preferred in the following fashion:

|  | Preferred ($100,000 par) | Common ($300,000 par) |
|---|---|---|
| To preferred, 6% | $6,000 |  |
| To common, up to preferred rate, 6% |  | $18,000 |
| Remainder shared proportionally, 1.5% (Balance to be paid of $6,000 divided by total par value of all stock outstanding of $400,000 equals 1.5%) | 1,500 | 4,500 |
|  | $7,500 | $22,500 |

If the preferred stockholders were limited to the initial $6,000, the stock would be called nonparticipating. In this case, common stockholders would not participate with preferred but would receive all dividends paid in excess of $6,000, or $24,000 in the example.

## PRIOR RIGHT TO ASSETS UPON LIQUIDATION

When compared to common, preferred stockholders not only have greater assurance of receiving their dividends, they also assume less risk in losing their capital investments. Upon liquidation of the corporation, creditors have first claim on the corporate assets. Once the creditors have been paid in full, the remaining assets are used to satisfy first the claims of preferred stockholders and finally the demands of the common stockholders. The claims of the preferred shareholders will include the original capital paid into the corporation as well as any dividends in arrears, should the preferred stock be cumulative.

## STOCK SPLITS

You often hear on the radio or read in the newspaper that the stockholders of a particular corporation received a stock split. For example three new shares of common stock may be exchanged for one old share of common stock. The first reaction is that the shareholders have tripled the value of their securities. However, in reality, a stock split has no effect on the equity of the individual stockholders. To understand why this is so the purpose of a stock split must be explained.

Some corporations which have become highly successful find that the market value of their common stock on the stock exchange becomes very high. For example, assume a firm starting out sells 10,000 shares of stock for $30.00 per share, which is also the par value of the stock. As the firm grows and earns excellent returns on its investment, the market value of the stock grows because investors bid up the price of the stock. In the example, assume that the market value increases to $300 per share. Because of this high market value per share, the firm may have difficulty in trading its stock, because many people cannot afford to pay $300 for a share of stock. One means of reducing the market value is to initiate a stock split. For instance, the firm could call in its 10,000 shares of $30.00 par stock and in turn issue 30,000 new shares of common stock with a par value of $10.00 per share. By reducing the par value of the stock from $30.00 to $10.00 per share, the corporation is splitting the stock three for one. In other words, each shareholder receives three new shares of $10.00 par in exchange for one share of $30.00 par formerly held. The result is that the market value of the stock will decline from $300 per share to $100 per share, and consequently the firm's stock will be more marketable. Notice that in the example the total market value of the stock has not changed:

Total market value before split = 10,000 shares × $300 = $300,000
Total market value after split = 30,000 shares × $100 = $300,000

It is important to remember that a stock split is initiated for the good of the corporation. By reducing the price of the stock, more investors should find the stock more attractive and thus provide the corporation with additional funds.

## RETAINED EARNINGS

The net income of a firm is computed by deducting from total net sales the operating expenses and income taxes. The problem which next confronts the firm is how much of this income should be retained in the business and how much should be withdrawn. In the case of a sole proprietorship or a partnership, the owners make their own decisions. In a corporation, this decision is usually delegated by the owners (stockholders) to the firm's board of directors. The amount remaining after distribution of dividends to the stockholders is referred to as retained earnings. It is this portion of income which has been retained in the business that represents a significant source of funds needed to finance additional capital for the firm. Although this discussion focuses upon the corporation, it is equally applicable to the sole proprietorship or the partnership.

When a firm decides to retain funds in the corporation in order to acquire additional plant and equipment or to retire a bond issue or for some other purpose, it is keeping money from the stockholders by not withdrawing it in the form of dividends. The stockholders may feel that they deserve more dividends than they are presently receiving. The question may be raised as to whether or not retaining corporate income is advantageous to the stockholders. The answer is that it is advantageous to reinvest corporate earnings whenever the rate of return on new investments is greater than that which can be earned by the stockholders themselves. To illustrate, assume that the ABC Corporation has net earnings after taxes of $100 and its stockholders on the average are in the 40 percent tax bracket. The corporation has two alternatives: first, it may reinvest the $100 and earn a rate of return of 10 percent; or second, it may distribute the $100 in dividends to its shareholders. If the corporation elects to reinvest the $100 it will earn a return of $10 over the ensuing twelve months $(100 \times 10\%)$. However, should the corporation elect to pay the $100 in dividends, it will be included in the individual tax return of each shareholder, where it will be taxed at 40 percent. This means the shareholder will have $60 left to invest ($100 — $40 paid for taxes). However, in order for the shareholders to earn a return of $10, it will be necessary to invest in projects earning 16⅔ percent ($10/$60 = 16⅔%). Because it is difficult to find investments which will earn a return of 16⅔ percent, it would be advantageous for the shareholders to allow the corporation to reinvest the $100.

This illustration simply shows that stockholders can benefit from the corporation's decision to retain its earnings. This does not mean that no dividends should be paid. In fact, it is important to long-term financing to pay some dividends. There is evidence which indicates that investors are willing to pay a premium for stock in those corporations which have a record of paying stable and consistent dividends. However, the amount of dividends a corporation pays is often a matter of judgment. It depends to a large extent upon such factors as the needs of the corporation for funds to expand, whether or not the firm has alternative sources of funds, and the past dividend record of the firm.

There are several advantages to financing the growth of the firm internally. To summarize:

1. The use of retained earnings frees the firm from paying periodic interest payments and accumulating funds needed to pay bonds or notes as they mature.
2. Small firms are often restricted in their ability to raise needed equity funds or debt. Therefore, they have little choice other than to use retained earnings for additional capital. In fact, many small firms have expanded into giant corporations by relying almost exclusively upon retained earnings for their necessary capital. The Ford Motor Company is an excellent example.
3. The use of retained earnings does not result in reduction of stockholder control of the corporation. For example, assume that John Doe owns 10 percent, or 100 shares of the XYZ corporation's 1000 shares outstanding. Also, assume that the corporation elects to issue an additional 1000 shares and Mr. Doe chooses not to exercise his preemptive right. The result is that Mr. Doe's 10 percent ownership interest has now been reduced to 5 percent (100 shares/2000 shares outstanding). This could be avoided if the corporation has sufficient internal funds to expand.
4. In those firms in which there are only a few stockholders (closely held corporations) who are all in relatively high income tax brackets, the stockholders would most likely prefer that the corporation retain its earnings rather than pay dividends.

## Nature of Long-Term Debt Funds

In addition to using equity financing, a firm may also acquire funds by issuing long-term debt securities. Long-term debt represents those liabilities which do not mature within the ensuing year. The most common examples include bonds, notes, and purchase contracts.

The agreement between a borrower and a lender for long-term debt is usually quite formal because of the large sums of money involved and the length of time, which often covers several years. The agreement outlines in detail the obligations of the borrower (debtor) and the rights of the lender (creditor). The bylaws of a corporation may require the approval of the firm's board of directors and stockholders before long-term debt, such as bonds, may be incurred.

Debt differs from equity in that the use of debt requires the firm to pay interest throughout the life of the debt issue as well as the **principal** at maturity. Principal is the amount of money loaned by the lender whereas **interest** is a charge for the use of money. Should the firm default on its payments, the creditors could force the concern into bankruptcy. It is therefore to the advantage of a firm to search diligently for debt securities with favorable terms so as to minimize the cost of acquiring funds. A good example of this is the recent boom in sales of industrial revenue bonds. The industrial bonds are a close cousin of municipal bonds in that they are tax-exempt, which means that investors are not required to include interest from these bonds in their taxable income. As a result, borrowers are able to issue the bonds at a lower interest rate. However, in order to qualify for tax exemption, the bond revenue must be spent only for pollution control. The following excerpt from *Business Week* provides one example:

> Faced with a $25-million expenditure to cut pollution at its Philadelphia refinery, Gulf got the Philadelphia Authority for Industrial Development, a municipal agency, to issue $25-million worth of tax-exempt bonds. First Boston then sold the bonds to institutional investors at a net interest of 5.24 per cent. If Gulf had floated its own taxable bond, the interest would have been 7.36 per cent. The saving of Gulf: $9.9 million over seventeen years.[1]

## BONDS

The advantage of bonds to the corporation is that large sums of money needed for investment in fixed assets may be acquired from many individuals throughout the country. This is achieved by dividing the required funds into individual bonds with denominations of $100 or $1,000 thereby making them available to small investors. For example, if a small corporation needed to raise $500,000 for plant expansion, it might have a difficult time finding a single investor willing to provide the necessary capital. However, by breaking up the $500,000 into 500 bonds with denominations of $1,000 each, the corporation will be able to reach the small investor.

In most instances, the corporation will not issue the bonds itself, but rather will utilize the services of a professional investment banker. Investment bankers are essentially middlemen who channel funds from investors to borrowers. The investment banker may elect to underwrite the bond issue by guaranteeing the corporation a certain sum of money. He then assumes the risk of selling the bonds to the public for whatever price he can get. As an alternative, the investment banker may choose to sell the bonds on a commission basis, deducting a certain amount from each bond sold.

When a corporation decides to sell bonds, an agreement is drawn up which outlines restrictions and other terms to which the corporation must adhere. This agreement, called an **indenture,** is a contract between the bondholders and the corporation. Some of the usual provisions are:

1. The life of the bond issue;
2. Rate of interest;
3. Due date for payment of interest and principal;
4. A list and detailed description of each property used as security;
5. Amount of additional debt which the corporation can issue;
6. All deposits required to cover bond interest as well as deposits to the sinking fund;
7. Any restrictions placed upon the amount of dividends the corporation can pay.

To make sure the corporation abides by the provisions in the indenture, a trustee is named to represent the bondholders. It is the trustee's duty to inform

---

1. July 29, 1972, p. 50.

the bondholders of any major act by the corporation which does not comply with the terms specified in the indenture.

## SPECIFIC BONDS

Investors and borrowers are each interested in acquiring the best terms possible before buying or selling a bond. Those terms which are attractive to an investor may be unattractive to a borrower and vice versa. Consequently both sides will bargain until a satisfactory agreement is reached. The result is that there are so many varieties of bonds traded in the marketplace that it is impossible to describe each type. The discussion below includes some of the more popular varieties.

## SECURED BONDS

### MORTGAGE BONDS

The businessman is in a better position to offer bonds to the public if he is willing to pledge property as security for funds provided by the investors. The security is created by means of a **mortgage.** A mortgage is a transfer of title on property from the borrower to the lender. In reality there is no physical transfer of title to the property, but rather the mortgage provides a lien or claim on the property. If the claim is a first mortgage, the bonds are referred to as *first mortgage bonds.* When the debt is paid in full, the borrower regains complete control of the title. However, should the corporation default on its payment and be unable to pay the principal or the interest on the loan, the lender has a lien on the pledged assets, which gives him first claim on them. This means that the lender can instruct the trustee to sell those assets to satisfy the lender's claim.

The mortgage may be any specified property or it may cover all of the firm's fixed assets, in which case it is called a *blanket mortgage.* An important provision under a blanket mortgage is the after-acquired clause, under which any additional property acquired by the borrower will also be pledged as security for the original issue. Usually an after-acquired clause will contain an open-end provision which allows the borrower to issue additional bonds using the existing mortgage as security for the loan. This is advantageous to the borrower because the same bond indenture is used for all issues.

### COLLATERAL TRUST BONDS

The use of mortgage bonds requires the pledge of tangible assets as security for a loan. Eventually, however, the firm may reach the point where all of its tangible assets are mortgaged. In order to prevent the issuance of second mortgage bonds, which usually carry a high rate of interest because of the higher risk assumed by the investors, the firm might consider collateral trust bonds. If the firm has investments in stocks and bonds of other firms it may transfer these to a trustee to serve as security for the issuance of the bonds. Although popular with the railroads at one time, collateral trust bonds are not frequently used today.

## UNSECURED BONDS

### DEBENTURES

**Debentures** are unsecured bonds in that no property is pledged as security. The bondholders have no liens on any assets which could be sold in the event the borrower defaults on his agreement. The bondholders rely solely on the earning potential of the firm and its general financial condition. Because no security is set aside, the indenture agreement will usually stipulate certain restrictions to which the borrower must adhere in order to maintain the firm's current financial status. These restrictions might include the amount of dividends the firm could pay out in the future or the level of working capital which must be maintained. This type of financing is often resorted to by firms in times of emergency where no other alternatives exist.

### INCOME BONDS

Income bonds are unsecured and require the firm to pay interest only when it has sufficient earnings. They are used frequently during periods of reorganization when the earning power of the firm is uncertain. They are similar to preferred stock in that they may be cumulative or noncumulative. If cumulative, the bondholders have a claim on future income for any interest not paid in a particular year. Dividends paid on preferred stock are nondeductible, whereas interest paid on the income bond would be deductible for tax purposes. Because income bonds are debt securities, investors in these bonds are entitled to the full amount of any interest due them before preferred stockholders are entitled to a dividend.

## BONDS WITH SPECIAL FEATURES

Because of the financial condition of the corporation or, perhaps, because of general economic conditions, a corporation may find it rather difficult to issue bonds at a reasonable price. In order to provide added incentive to the investor, a corporation might add certain accessories to the bonds to make them more attractive. Two examples are convertible debt and debt with stock purchase warrants.

### CONVERTIBLE BONDS

Convertible bonds contain a provision which allows the investor the opportunity to exchange his bonds for common stock of the issuer. The exchange is usually restricted to a predetermined time limit and a specific price. For example, on January 1, 1976, a corporation issues 250 bonds with a par value of $1,000 per bond. Each bond may be converted into ten shares of the corporation's common stock at any time prior to January 1, 1983. Assuming Jane Brown purchases ten $1,000 bonds, she then has the opportunity of acquiring at her option 100 shares of the corporation's common stock. The conversion ratio is ten to one, or ten shares of common stock for each bond. The conversion price is computed by dividing ten shares into $1,000; it is $100 per share.

Convertible bonds are advantageous to both investor and issuer. Because the bonds are convertible, the issuer can usually sell them at a lower rate of interest than nonconvertible bonds. On the other hand, the investor has the opportunity of becoming a stockholder and, perhaps, receiving an attractive profit in the process. In the example, should the market value of each share of common stock rise to $110 per share, Ms. Brown could elect to acquire 100 shares at a cost of $100 per share.

## DEBT WITH STOCK PURCHASE WARRANTS

A corporation may sell bonds with attached warrants. The warrants may be used by the investor to purchase shares of common stock at a specified price. The warrants are usually detachable, which means that the bondholder can sell or surrender the bonds without selling the warrants. In other words, the bonds and the warrants are actually treated as separate securities.

As with convertible bonds, the use of stock warrants allows the issuer to issue bonds at a lower cash interest cost. In some instances, the use of warrants may change unsaleable bonds into marketable securities. The investor benefits in that the exercise price (the cost to the investor) of each share may be lower than the market value of the security at the time of purchase. For example, the holder of the warrants may use them to purchase common stock at a cost of $50.00 per share when the common stock is selling on the stock exchange for $52.00 per share.

## LONG-TERM MORTGAGE NOTES

Although corporations frequently utilize mortgage bonds to accumulate large sums of money, sole proprietorships and partnerships often use the mortgage note. The terms of the loan between the borrower and the lender are outlined in a promissory note and the mortgage provides the necessary security. A mortgage note is usually used with smaller sums than a mortgage bond, because the lender is usually one or two persons rather than many. This may be a disadvantage of the mortgage note in that it is difficult for the borrower to find a few lenders with sufficient funds to loan.

## PURCHASE CONTRACTS

Rather than issuing bonds or stocks to acquire funds for investment in fixed assets, the firm may purchase equipment and other assets under a purchase contract. For example, a businessman might purchase several trucks from the Ford Motor Company to be paid off over a period of ten years. The financing arrangements would be completely handled by Ford, which would retain title to the trucks until the purchase price is paid. The businessman would have full use of the trucks during the period of the purchase contract.

## Stocks Versus Bonds

There is no simple answer to the question of whether a firm should use stocks or bonds to finance long-term investments. However, a discussion of the pros and cons of each security will help to provide a framework for analysis.

### COMMON STOCK

1. No dividends are paid until the firm earns a profit.
2. Unlike bonds, there is no fixed interest charge which must be paid periodically, nor is there a fixed maturity date.
3. Because the issuance of common stock increases the amount of assets which can be mortgaged, the firm's ability to secure long-term debt financing through the issuance of bonds is strengthened.
4. Although common shareholders assume the greatest risk, it may be easier to sell because of the greater rewards.

### PREFERRED STOCK

1. The advantages of preferred stock include the first three advantages of common stock.
2. The preference attached to preferred stock may make it easier to sell than common.
3. Because preferred stock may be convertible or callable, it is a more flexible form of financing than common stock.
4. The firm's existing stockholders may retain their control of the corporation by issuing preferred stock in which voting rights are restricted.
5. If the preferred stock is not fully participating, common shareholders will not be required to share all profits proportionately with preferred shareholders.

### BONDS

1. The issuance of bonds does not reduce the control of the present shareholders. Issuing additional common stock would spread the control of the firm over more shares.
2. Interest payments are tax deductible. Dividends paid common or preferred shareholders are not deductible in arriving at taxable income.
3. If the rate of return on the assets employed is greater than the interest rate, it is to the advantage of the firm's shareholders to issue bonds.
4. Because bondholders have preference to the firm's assets in the case of liquidation, the interest rate in bonds is usually less than the dividend rate on preferred or common stock.

The data in Exhibit 4–1 provide information relating to new issues of corporate securities from 1940 to 1972. The information in this table indicates that bonds and notes are used much more frequently than stocks as a source for additional funds. There would appear to be three reasons for this trend:

## EXHIBIT 4–1

### New Issues of Corporate Securities
### 1940 to 1972

| Year | All types | Bonds and notes | Stocks |
|------|-----------|-----------------|--------|
| 1940 | $ 2,751,000,000 | $ 2,472,000,000 | $ 279,000,000 |
| 1950 | 6,692,000,000 | 4,804,000,000 | 1,888,000,000 |
| 1960 | 10,797,000,000 | 8,072,000,000 | 2,725,000,000 |
| 1971 | 46,687,000,000 | 31,917,000,000 | 14,769,000,000 |
| 1972 | 42,306,000,000 | 27,065,000,000 | 15,242,000,000 |

Source: U.S. Bureau of the Census, *Statistical Abstract of the United States, 1973*, 94th ed. (Washington, D.C.: 1973), p. 461.

(1) the issuance of bonds does not reduce the control of present shareholders; (2) interest payments are tax deductible; and (3) bonds allow trading on equity.

## TRADING ON EQUITY

The directors are the representatives of the stockholders and are elected to manage the corporation. As representatives of the stockholders, they are interested in earning the highest possible return on the equity invested in the corporation by the stockholders. One method by which the directors may increase the rate of return on stockholders' equity is by issuing bonds to acquire additional funds rather than selling more stock. It is necessary, however, that the borrowing rate on the bonds be smaller than the rate of return to be earned on the funds obtained from the bond issue. Suppose that stockholders have invested $100,000 in common stock of the New Corporation, which has no outstanding liabilities. The $100,000 paid in by the stockholders represents the total equity of the corporation, which earned $10,000 during its first year of operations. The rate of return on stockholders' equity is therefore 10 percent ($10,000/$100,000). The board of directors would like to expand operations by acquiring an additional $100,000. They could either issue another $100,000 in common stock or they could issue $100,000 in bonds. If the board elects to issue additional common stock, the corporation would then earn $20,000 per year and again the return on the stockholders' investment would be 10 percent ($20,000/$200,000). However, should the board of directors elect to issue $100,000 in 7 percent bonds, the rate of return on stockholders' equity will increase as follows:

| | |
|---|---|
| Earnings before interest expense | $20,000 |
| Interest expense | 7,000 |
| Net income available to stockholders | $13,000 |
| [2]Rate of return on stockholder equity (13,000/$100,000) | 13% |

2. Taxes are not considered in these computations.

By issuing bonds rather than common stock, the stockholders have increased their rate of return from 10 percent to 13 percent on the $100,000 in stockholders' equity. The firm's return on the money obtained from the bond issue (when invested in operations) was greater than the cost of borrowing. This technique is referred to as **trading on equity** or financial leverage.

## Leases

A lease is a contractual agreement whereby the lessor (the owner) provides a right to use personal or real property to the lessee for a specified period of time and at a specified rental charge. It represents an alternative form of financing the acquisition of plant and equipment. Many small firms lack the necessary financial credit to issue bonds, and consequently leasing represents an excellent means of debt financing. Whereas the purchase of equipment on an installment contract might require an initial down payment of 20 or 30 percent, leasing agreements require no down payment except for perhaps a small deposit. In addition, the terms of a lease agreement are generally less restrictive than those included in an indenture or a note.

When a firm issues bonds to secure funds it must show a liability on its balance sheet representing the future amount due bondholders. On the other hand, leasing is not recognized as a liability and therefore is not included in the firm's balance sheet. However, the lessee is still committed to periodic lease payments to the lessor, even though a liability does not appear on the firm's financial statements.

In summary, the following are primary reasons for leasing:
1. The risk of ownership is transferred to the lessor.
2. It provides a means of acquiring assets when alternative forms of financing may not be available.
3. The lease payments are completely tax-deductible.
4. The lessor often assumes additional costs such as taxes, insurance, and maintenance.
5. It provides 100 percent financing not available under purchase contracts because a purchase usually requires a down payment.
6. Leasing provides the lessee an opportunity to utilize up-to-date and modern equipment.

## SALES AND LEASEBACK

Even though leasing does provide a means of acquiring additional property, it does not provide added money as bonds and notes do. One form of financing which results in returning cash to the firm that was originally spent on constructing a fixed asset is called sale and leaseback. For example, a firm may construct a building, sell the building at its fair market value to an investor, and then lease it back. The unique feature of this method of financing is that the firm does not tie up money in fixed assets, which may be needed for working capital purposes. Of course, the firm becomes a lessee and is required to make periodic payments to the lessor according to the terms of the lease. The primary advantage to the businessman lessee is that he acquires cash equal to the fair market value of the building. If he had used the building as collateral for a loan, he would have received cash equivalent to about 70 percent of the fair market value of the building.

## Summary

Long-term capital is generally used to acquire land, buildings, equipment, and other fixed assets. Equity funds in a sole proprietorship or a partnership consist of the investments of the owners in the business and any profits not withdrawn. For a corporation, equity funds come from three primary sources: preferred stock, common stock, and retained earnings.

There are certain basic rights which each stockholder is entitled to exercise unless restricted by the stock contract. These include the rights to share in dividends, to retain a proportionate ownership interest, to share in assets upon liquidation, and to vote at stockholder meetings. When a corporation issues only one class of stock, it is common stock. Common stockholders bear the heaviest risk. When two classes of stock have been issued, the second class is called preferred stock. Preferred stockholders are entitled to certain preferential treatment, including first preference as to dividends and a prior right to assets upon liquidation. Preferred stock may be cumulative or noncumulative; it may be participating or nonparticipating.

In addition to using equity financing, a firm may also acquire funds by issuing long-term debt securities. Long-term debt is debt which will not mature within the ensuing year. Debt differs from equity in that if the firm defaults on its debt obligations, the creditors could force the concern into bankruptcy. Examples of debt financing include secured bonds, such as mortgage bonds and collateral trust bonds; unsecured bonds, such as debentures and income bonds; long-term mortgage notes; purchase contracts; and leasing. The agreement between a borrower and a lender under long-term debt is usually quite formal.

Because both stock and bonds have a number of advantages, most business firms issue both types of securities. In some instances, issuing additional debt instruments will result in increasing the stockholder's rate of return. This is called trading on equity.

## QUESTIONS

1. Distinguish between debt and equity financing.
2. Define the following terms: par value stock, no-par value stock, and stated value of stock.
3. List the basic rights that each stockholder is entitled to exercise as the owner of stock in a corporation.

4. (a) What is preferred stock?
   (b) In what areas do preferred stockholders receive preferential treatment?
   (c) Distinguish between the different types of preferred stock: cumulative versus noncumulative and participating versus nonparticipating.
   (d) Under what conditions will the board of directors declare a dividend?
   (e) What does it mean to say that preferred dividends are in arrears?

5. Why do corporations have stock splits?

6. Explain retained earnings.

7. When is it advantageous to reinvest corporate earnings rather than distribute them in the form of dividends? Give some advantages to financing the growth of a firm through reinvestment of retained earnings.

8. (a) Define long-term debt and give examples.
   (b) How do debt and equity financing differ?

9. What are some of the considerations that should be looked at in the determination of which type of security that a firm should issue?

10. (a) What is meant by trading on equity?
    (b) Why are leases used as a means for debt financing?
    (c) What is meant by a sales and leaseback arrangement?

## Incident 4–1

Assume that the Monte Carlo corporation was formed on January 1, 1973, and had the following two classes of stock:

Common stock    $50 par value 1,000 shares authorized and issued.

Preferred stock    5%; $10 par value, 3,000 shares authorized and issued.

The board of directors decided to declare its first dividend of $20,000 on December 31, 1975. What would be the amount of dividends paid to the preferred and common stockholders under the following circumstances?
(a) The preferred stock is noncumulative and nonparticipating.
(b) The preferred stock is cumulative and nonparticipating.
(c) The preferred stock is noncumulative and participating.
(d) The preferred stock is cumulative and participating.
(e) Assume that the market value of the common stock is currently $200 per share. What will be the effect of a four for one stock split on the number of shares outstanding and the market value of the stock?

# 5

# Sources of Short-Term Funds

## Nature of Short-Term Credit

In Chapter 4 equity and long-term credit were examined. Long-term is defined as those liabilities which will not mature during the ensuing twelve months. In fact, the life of long-term debt may extend over a period of twenty-five years or more. Because the funds acquired through long-term financing are primarily used to purchase the more permanent capital of a firm such as land, buildings, and equipment, there are generally large sums of money involved. For this reason arrangements between lenders and borrowers are very formal with such documents as bonds, indentures, or contracts outlining in detail the obligations and rights of both sides.

In contrast, short-term debts have a maturity of less than one year. Examples of short-term debt include trade credit, short-term bank loans, and commercial papers. The funds acquired from these sources are usually invested in current assets such as inventory and accounts receivable. Rather than being formal, the agreements between lenders and borrowers are frequently informal. This is particularly true with trade credit.

In this chapter some alternative sources of short-term debt and the special characteristics of each type will be discussed. However, before discussing the various sources available to business enterprises, we will examine two factors which are very much a part of debt financing: the computation of interest and cash forecasting.

## Computation of Interest Costs

All credit or debt arrangements have two things in common: an amount of money (called *principal*) is loaned for which the lender receives a fee (called *interest*). The amount of interest paid by the borrower is equal to the difference between the amount of money initially borrowed and the amount of money actually paid when the loan comes due. Three factors are considered in the computation of interest: the principal amount of the loan, the interest rate on the loan, and the time period for which the loan is borrowed. The formula used to compute the total interest charges is as follows:

Principal $\times$ rate $\times$ time = Interest

To illustrate, assume that Ed Beck borrows $1,000 on June 1 for sixty days from the Greenville City Bank. The bank charges interest at the rate of 6 percent. The total interest charges would amount to $10.00 which would be computed as follows:

$$\text{Principal} \quad \text{Rate} \quad \text{Time} \quad \text{Interest}$$

$$\$1,000 \times \frac{6}{100} \times \frac{60}{360} = \$10.00$$

A common business practice is to use 360 days rather than 365 days as the denominator in the fraction for time. The use of 360 days makes the interest computation easier, although 365 days would be more accurate.

One method often used by businessmen as a shortcut to computing interest is the "6 percent, 60-day method." The interest computation for a 6 percent, 60-day loan is computed simply by moving the decimal point in the principal two places to the left. In the example above, the principal of the loan is $1,000.00. When the decimal point is moved two places to the left, the interest comes out to $10.00. The decimal point is moved two places to the left because the terms 6 percent, 60 days are equivalent to an annual interest rate of 1 percent. Since 60 days represents one-sixth of a year $(60/360 = 1/6)$, then one-sixth of 6 percent equals 1 percent $(1/6 \times 6\% = 1\%)$. One percent of any figure is always computed by moving the decimal point two places to the left.

The 6 percent, 60-days method can be used to compute interest charges on loans even though the interest rate or the time period differs from 6 percent or 60 days. For example, the interest on a 6 percent, 90-day, $1,000 loan would be computed as follows:

| | |
|---|---:|
| Interest for 60 days (decimal moved 2 places to the left) | $10.00 |
| Interest for 30 days ($\frac{1}{2} \times \$10$) | 5.00 |
| | $15.00 |

The interest on a 3 percent, 60-day, $1,000 loan would be computed by first calculating interest at 6 percent and then making an adjustment:

| | |
|---|---:|
| Interest for 60 days at 6% (decimal moved 2 places to the left) | $10.00 |
| Interest for 60 days at 3% (½ of $10) | $ 5.00 |

## Cash Forecast

A **cash forecast** is a schedule which summarizes the amount of cash receipts expected to be realized in the future, the estimated expenditures which will be incurred, and the resulting cash balance. It is used to find out how much money the firm should borrow during the ensuing period. This estimate is usually determined for the coming year of operations. However, for those firms in which the future outlook is highly unpredictable, one year may be too long. In such circumstances, the firm should make estimates over a shorter period, such as one-half year. For most business situations one year is a suitable time.

In order to provide better planning and control of cash, the estimates should be broken into months. If the forecast is made so that careful consideration is given to all possible inflows and outflows of cash, the monthly schedules will disclose signficant information which the businessman can use. An example of a cash forecast in which the cash receipts and expenditures are allocated to specific months is presented in Exhibit 5–1.

The cash forecast helps the businessman to plan his needs for additional funds. Its primary purpose is to show the variations in inflows and outflows of cash during the months of the year. Therefore, the forecast should be constructed to emphasize these extremes. For example, data in Exhibit 5–1 disclose that cash expenditures are expected to exceed cash receipts for the months of January, February, March, and April. The total deficiency for these four months amounts to $61,000 (10 + 10 + 37 + 4). By recognizing this potential cash deficit early, the businessman is in a position to consider alternative sources of borrowing short-term debt, thereby increasing the firm's chances for acquiring the right amount at the least cost. Not only does the businessman know the probable amount of his deficiency, he also knows how long the shortage will last. Such a forecast is also important to lenders. For example, a banker is in a position to examine first hand the firm's future cash position and can consequently determine its debt-paying abilities. Again, in Exhibit 5–1 receipts exceed expenditures for the months of May through December. The excess funds received in these months can be used to pay back short-term funds borrowed in the first four months of the year.

For a firm which has been in business for some time, much of the data in Exhibit 5–1 can be accumulated from accounting records. Of course, for an enterprise just beginning operations, there are no prior accounting records to help project future cash inflows and outflows. As a result, the cash forecast may not be as accurate as it might otherwise be.

## EXHIBIT 5-1

### Cash Budget for the Witt Corporation for 1975
*(thousands of dollars)*

| | Jan | Feb | Mar | Apr | May | June | July | Aug | Sept | Oct | Nov | Dec |
|---|---|---|---|---|---|---|---|---|---|---|---|---|
| Beginning cash balance | 10 | (10) | (10) | (37) | (4) | 30 | 47 | 115 | 195 | 253 | 124 | 88 |
| **Cash receipts** | | | | | | | | | | | | |
| Cash sales | 50 | 50 | 45 | 45 | 70 | 80 | 90 | 100 | 90 | 80 | 70 | 60 |
| Collection of accounts rec. | 50 | 50 | 40 | 40 | 40 | 60 | 70 | 80 | 80 | 75 | 70 | 60 |
| Sales of plant assets | | | | | | | | | | | 100 | |
| Total | 110 | 90 | 75 | 48 | 106 | 170 | 207 | 295 | 365 | 408 | 364 | 208 |
| **Cash expenditures** | | | | | | | | | | | | |
| Purchase of merchandise | 40 | 40 | 32 | 32 | 56 | 64 | 72 | 80 | 72 | 65 | 56 | 48 |
| Wage and salary | 10 | 10 | 10 | 10 | 10 | 10 | 10 | 10 | 10 | 10 | 10 | 10 |
| Rent | 2 | 2 | 2 | 2 | 2 | 2 | 2 | 2 | 2 | 2 | 2 | 2 |
| Administrative expense | 5 | 5 | 5 | 5 | 5 | 5 | 5 | 5 | 5 | 5 | 5 | 5 |
| Interest expense | | | | | | 4 | | | | | | |
| Insurance premiums | 1 | 1 | 1 | 1 | 1 | 1 | 1 | 1 | 1 | 1 | 1 | 1 |
| Payroll taxes | 2 | 2 | 2 | 2 | 2 | 2 | 2 | 2 | 2 | 2 | 2 | 2 |
| Federal income taxes | 20 | | 20 | | | 20 | | | 20 | | | |
| Loan installments | 40 | 40 | 40 | | | 15 | | | | | | |
| Replacement for plant assets | | | | | | | | | | 200 | 200 | 200 |
| Total | 120 | 100 | 112 | 52 | 76 | 123 | 92 | 100 | 112 | 284 | 276 | 172 |
| Ending cash balance | (10) | (10) | (37) | (4) | 30 | 47 | 115 | 195 | 253 | 124 | 88 | 36 |

In addition to the accounting records, it is necessary for the businessman to consider future plans which will affect inflows or outflows of cash. Examples of such plans are future acquisitions of plant and equipment, cash dividends or withdrawal, sale of properties not used in operations, and sale of stocks or additional investments by owners.

Having pinpointed when and how much short-term money he needs, the businessman can now attempt to borrow these funds. There are two distinct types of short-term credit: unsecured and secured. The businessman can increase his chances of getting the funds needed if he has done some preplanning in the form of estimating his specific cash forecast. If he does not know exactly what his needs for short-term funds are, chances are that these needs will go unsatisfied or oversatisfied, in that he borrows too much, perhaps from the wrong source.

## Unsecured Credit

### TRADE CREDIT

Once a firm has acquired the various fixed assets necessary to conduct business, it must consider the alternative ways of acquiring inventory and the other working capital items needed to begin operations. For a small firm just starting out, it may be difficult acquiring loans from banks and other financial institutions because of the lack of **collateral** for the repayment of a loan. Collateral is security such as property which is given as a pledge. Therefore, a very common form of financing for the acquisition of inventory is trade credit. Suppliers of merchandise are generally more liberal in their credit arrangements than are banks.

The most common form of trade credit is called *open account*. Under this arrangement the buyer telephones or mails a purchase order to a supplier, requesting certain merchandise. The supplier will in turn check the credit standing of the purchaser to determine the acceptability of his financial status. If acceptable, the supplier will ship the goods to the buyer along with an invoice which indicates the quanity of goods shipped, the price per unit and in total, and the credit terms of the arrangement. The creditor (seller) will enter on his books an account called *accounts receivable,* and the debtor (buyer) will set up an account called *accounts payable* on his books. The unique feature about an open account arrangement is that no formal agreements are signed by the parties involved. The seller simply relies upon the general financial well-being of the buyer. Trade credit is similar to buying gasoline with a credit card. The gasoline company has an account receivable with the customer's name on it. At the end of thirty days they bill him for the total amount shown on his account.

It may seem difficult to understand why trade credit is a source of funds in that no money has been provided for the firm. However, in reality, funds have been provided because the buyer has acquired merchandise without paying the seller. For the time period which begins with the receipt of the goods by the buyer and ends when payment is due, the supplier is extending credit to the buyer. In other words, the buyer is not required to pay the seller immediately upon receipt of the goods; but rather, he is allowed to defer his payment for a short period, usually thirty days. The buyer can use his cash for other items during the credit period. For example, if a businessman purchases some material worth $100, he can either pay cash for it or buy it on thirty-day credit. If he buys it on credit, he has the use of the $100 during the credit period. The seller has in effect extended the buyer's spending capacity by giving him thirty days to pay for the material.

The larger the amount of goods purchased and the longer the period allowed before payment is due, the greater the amount of credit provided by the creditor or supplier. Even for firms which have been in existence for some time, trade credit is an important means of financing seasonal and temporary fluctuations in business conditions. For example, during the months of spring, summer, and fall a ski lodge will generate little or no inflow of funds. Nevertheless, during this time period considerable expenditures may be incurred for maintenance and improvement of buildings and equipment. Because the inflow of funds will not materialize until the winter, the firm may rely upon trade credit as a means of financing some of its operating costs during the off season.

### TRADE DISCOUNTS

Wholesalers and retailers are often allowed deductions from the suggested retail list price called *trade discounts*. For example, a manufacturer of lawnmowers might offer a wholesaler a trade discount of 40 percent and 10 percent from the retail list price. Because two discounts are provided, this is often called a *chain discount*. Assuming the retail price of the lawnmowers was $100, the wholesaler would pay the manufacturer the following amount for each lawnmower.

| | |
|---|---:|
| Retail list price | $100 |
| First discount—40% × $100 | 40 |
| Remainder | 60 |
| Second discount—10% × $60 | 6 |
| Sale price to wholesaler | $ 54 |

It is important to note that a trade discount of 40 percent and 10 percent does not mean 50 percent off the retail price; it means 46 percent; because the first discount of 40 percent is based upon the retail list price of $100 and amounts to $40 ($100 × 40%), while the second discount of 10 percent is based not upon the retail list price of $100, but rather upon $100 minus the first discount of $40, or $60. Consequently, the second discount amounts to $6 ($60 × 10%). The two discounts added together amount to $46 ($40 + $6), which represents 46 percent ($46/$100) off the original retail list price. Similarly, trade discounts of 50 percent and 50 percent would not result in a 100 percent price reduction, but rather 75 percent. In the lawnmower example, the manufacturer may require the wholesaler to pass the first discount of 40 percent on to the retailer. As a result, the wholesaler would pay the manufacturer $54 for each lawnmower and the retailer would pay the wholesaler $60 for each lawnmower. The purpose for trade discounts is to enable each retailer and wholesaler to cover his selling and administrative expenses and earn a profit.

## CASH DISCOUNTS

A cash discount, ranging from 1 to 3 percent, is used to encourage the buyer to pay his debt promptly. Assume that a customer purchases a lawnmower from a retailer on January 1 at a cost of $100, with terms of 2/10, n/30. This means that the customer will receive a 2 percent discount if he pays his invoice within ten days from the date of sale. If he does not pay within ten days, then the full amount will be due in thirty days. If the invoice is paid on January 8 the amount due the retailer would be:

| | |
|---|---|
| Invoice price of lawnmower | $100.00 |
| Discount offered by seller (2%) | 2.00 |
| Net amount due | $ 98.00 |

Another cash discount which is often provided is 2/E.O.M., n/60. This allows the buyer a 2 percent discount from the selling price if the obligation is paid by the end of the month (EOM). No discount is allowed after the end of the month, and the debt must be paid within sixty days of the date of the invoice.

In addition to encouraging a buyer to pay his debt promptly, cash discounts are offered by sellers in order to meet competition. That is, if one seller in a certain region offers cash discounts to its customers, other sellers do so in order to be competitive.

## COMMERCIAL BANKS AS A SOURCE FOR SHORT-TERM FUNDS

Commercial banks are strategically located in every city and town and most villages throughout the United States. Although large and established firms rely heavily upon commercial banks for funds, these same firms also have access to alternative sources of funds. On the other hand, small firms often find the local banker to be their only source of funds. For this reason it is important that the businessman develop a good relationship with the bank with which he chooses to do business. Once the businessman develops the confidence and trust of his banker, he must be careful not to loose it.

If the bank requests important summaries of the firm's accounting and financial records, the businessman must make certain that these records are not only provided but also that they are accurate. Furthermore, the businessman should clearly explain to the banker why the loan is needed and how it will be spent. In other words, if the bank provides funds with the understanding that the businessman will purchase additional inventory, then the funds should be spent for that purpose. Certainly, spending these funds on a new car for the family would be one way of destroying relations with the bank.

The businessman must also adequately plan his cash forecast to make certain he will have sufficient funds to repay the loan. If the loan provisions require that monthly installments are to be paid, then these payments should be made when due and no later.

## SHORT-TERM NOTES

When a firm borrows money from commercial banks for less than a year, a promissory note is used as the instrument for the loan. An example of a promissory note is presented in Exhibit 5–2. In this note Joe Brown is the maker of the note and First Security Bank is the payee. The note is dated June 1, 1976, bears interest at the rate of 7 percent, and is payable in ninety days, or on August 30, 1976. There are six characteristics to a promissory note.

### EXHIBIT 5–2

*A Promissory Note*

| | |
|---|---|
| $ 1,500.00 | Belding, Michigan      June 1, 1976 |

_____Ninety days_____ after date ___I___ promise to pay to the

order of _____First Security Bank_____

****One Thousand Five hundred and 00/100**** _____ dollars

Payable at _____First Security Bank_____

Value received with interest at _____7%_____

No. ___86___          Due ___August 30,___ 1976          *Joe Brown*

1. It must be an unconditional promise made by one person called the maker to another called the payee.
2. It must be in writing.
3. It must be signed by the maker.
4. It must be payable on demand or at a fixed or determinable future date.
5. It must be for a certain sum in money.
6. It must be made payable to order or to bearer.

Generally speaking, if the loan is for less than $1,000, no collateral will be required. If the loan exceeds $1,000, the bank will either require collateral or ask for financial statements which provide evidence of the firm's debt-paying ability.

When a firm is approved for a loan, the bank has two options regarding interest. First, it can require the firm to pay the interest at the maturity date of the loan; second, it can deduct the interest from the initial loan. The second option causes the effective interest rate to be higher. For instance, assume that the Johnson Shoe Store borrows $10,000 from the local bank for one year, signing an 8 percent promissory note. At the expiration of one year, the shoe store will pay the bank principal plus interest, or $10,800. The effective rate of interest is computed as follows:

$$\frac{\text{Interest cost}}{\text{Money provided by bank}} \quad \frac{\$\ \ 800}{\$10,000} = 8\%$$

Now assume the same example, but that the bank elects to deduct the interest from the initial loan so that the Johnson Shoe Store does not have the use of $10,000 but only $9,200 ($10,000 — $800 = $9,200). At the end of twelve months, the amount due the bank would be $10,000. Under this approach, the effective rate of interest is not 8 percent but rather 8.7 percent, computed as follows:

$$\frac{\text{Interest cost}}{\text{Money provided by bank}} \quad \frac{\$\ 800}{\$9,200} = 8.7\%$$

It is obviously to the businessman's advantage to pay the interest at maturity rather than initially.

Some bank rates on short-term loans are included in Exhibit 5–3. These rates are broken down by size of loan and by geographical center. Some interesting variations are apparent in this table. For example, interest rates in February, 1973, averaged 7.6 percent on loans in the $1,000 to $9,999 range; they averaged 8.1 percent in February of 1971. This indicates that the cost of borrowing money fluctuates drastically during a period of twenty-four months. The

EXHIBIT 5–3

*Bank Rates on Short-Term Business Loans*

| | 1971 | | | 1973 | |
|---|---|---|---|---|---|
| *Center* | *Feb.* | *May* | *Nov.* | *Feb.* | *May* |
| Average, 35 centers | 6.6 | 6.0 | 6.2 | 6.5 | 7.4 |
| New York City | 6.3 | 5.7 | 5.9 | 6.2 | 7.0 |
| 7 other Northeast | 6.8 | 6.3 | 6.4 | 6.9 | 7.7 |
| 8 North Central | 6.7 | 6.0 | 6.1 | 6.5 | 7.5 |
| 7 Southeast | 6.9 | 6.4 | 6.5 | 6.8 | 7.4 |
| 8 Southwest | 6.6 | 6.2 | 6.4 | 6.6. | 7.3 |
| 4 West Coast | 6.6 | 6.1 | 6.2 | 6.5 | 7.3 |
| Size of loan, 35 centers | | | | | |
| $1,000–$9,999 | 8.1 | 7.5 | 7.5 | 7.6 | 8.1 |
| $10,000–$99,999 | 7.5 | 6.9 | 7.1 | 7.3 | 7.9 |
| $100,000–$499,999 | 6.9 | 6.4 | 6.5 | 6.8 | 7.6 |
| $500,000–$999,999 | 6.6 | 6.0 | 6.3 | 6.5 | 7.3 |
| $1,000,000 and over | 6.4 | 5.8 | 5.9 | 6.3 | 7.2 |

Source: U.S. Bureau of the Census, *Statistical Abstract of the United States, 1973*, 94th ed. Washington, D.C.: 1973, p. 457.

businessman should consider these fluctuations and try to secure a loan when the rates are most favorable. Interest rates also decline as the amount of the loan increases. For example, interest rates in May, 1973, averaged 8.1 percent on loans in the $1,000 to $9,999 range and 7.9 percent on loans in the $10,000 to $99,999 range. This would mean the businessman could save interest costs by borrowing in larger amounts a few times during the year rather than smaller amounts more frequently. For example, rather than borrowing $6,000 every three months, the businessman could reduce his interest costs by borrowing $12,000 once at the beginning of the year and $12,000 around the middle of the year.

One of the primary advantages of the commercial bank is its flexibility. That is, loans can be arranged to meet the seasonal needs of different businesses. For example, some businessmen, such as farmers, incur most of their costs at certain months of the year such as the planting season. However, income may not be available to pay the interest and principal portions of the note until the crops are harvested. Factors such as these are taken into consideration by commercial bankers in order to provide businessmen with terms tailored to meet the firm's needs.

Other features have been added by many commercial banks in order to provide greater flexibility in serving their clients. One in particular is called **line of credit.**

*Line of Credit.*   Because many firms establish a regular pattern of borrowing funds from commercial banks, it is customary for bankers to establish lines of credit. A line of credit is established for a firm by allowing it the opportunity to borrow funds up to a certain figure simply by requesting the amount desired. For example, a firm may estimate on January 1 that it will need to borrow $40,000 over the next twelve months. Rather than making separate applications for each loan, the bank could establish a line of credit of $40,000. This allows the manager to borrow any amount he desires to at any time, provided it does not exceed the line of credit, $40,000 in this case. As an illustration, this firm could borrow $10,000 on four different dates during the year without having to make a separate application for each loan.

A bank will not establish a line of credit until it carefully examines the credit worthiness of the applicant. The bank will give consideration to the firm's financial records, other outstanding loans, and the amount of property pledged as security for each loan before determining the size of the line of credit, if any, to be granted to a firm.

## ENDORSEMENTS

In those instances in which a lender will not loan money to a borrower on a short-term basis unless assets are pledged as collateral, the lender may accept a guarantee by an outside third party. The person who guarantees payment is called the *guarantor.* Evidence of such a guarantee is given when the third party cosigns the borrower's promissory note. Should the borrower fail in his promise to repay the lender, the guarantor will be responsible for any unpaid balance. The bank or any other lender will not accept such a guarantee until it is satisfied with the guarantor's financial position. For example, a major stockholder in a small closely held corporation may guarantee the corporation's promissory note. A closely held corporation is one in which the outstanding stock is owned by a few shareholders. The most common type is the family-owned corporation.

## COMMERCIAL PAPER

Another form of short-term loan is commercial paper. Commercial paper is an unsecured short-term promissory note which has a maturity date that varies from a few days to approximately nine months. Commercial paper differs from short-term bank credit in that the interest rate is usually lower. The data in Exhibit 5–4 indicate that commercial paper rates have been lower than short-term bank loans as far back as 1950. In 1950 interest rates on bank loans amounted to an annual average percent of 2.69, compared to interest rates of 1.45 percent for commercial paper (the difference amounting to 1.24 percent). However, the latest figures available (March, 1973) indicate that interest rates in commercial paper are slightly higher than short-term bank loan rates.

### EXHIBIT 5–4

*Money Market Rates: 1950 to 1973*

| Type | 1950 | 1960 | 1970 | 1971 | Mar. 1973 |
|---|---|---|---|---|---|
| Prime commercial paper | 1.45 | 3.85 | 7.72 | 5.11 | 6.85 |
| Short-term bank loans to business | 2.69 | 5.16 | 8.48 | 6.32 | 6.52 |

Source: U.S. Bureau of the Census, *Statistical Abstract of the United States, 1973,* 94th ed. Washington, D.C.: 1973, p. 457.

There are two ways for a businessman to sell commercial paper. One way is to sell these promissory notes directly to investors. This method, referred to as the *direct placement market,* accounts for approximately two-thirds of all commercial paper sales in the United States. Investors in commercial paper generally include universities, insurance companies, governmental units, and even other business firms which have excess funds available for a short period of time. The second way of selling commercial paper is through commercial paper dealers who in turn sell to investors. This method is referred to as the *dealer market.*

Investors find commercial paper a good investment because the rate of return on these notes is reasonable, the risk involved is minimal, and it provides a temporary outlet for excess funds. However, the availability of commercial paper as a source of funds is often contingent upon economic conditions. For example, in periods of tight money there may be few investors willing to part with their funds. As a result, it is recommended that businessmen not rely solely on commercial paper but rather recognize it simply as an alternative source of securing short-term funds.

Because commercial paper is sold by well-established firms which have a good credit standing, it would be difficult for a small firm just getting started to consider commercial paper as a source of funds.

## Secured Credit

Some firms are unable to acquire funds without providing some form of security for the lender's protection. These firms may be just starting in business and therefore have no past earnings record, or they may simply be carrying too much debt relative to their total assets. In order to compensate for such weaknesses, the lender may require the borrower to pledge certain assets. Therefore an examination of some types of secured credit—assignment and factoring of accounting receivables; public and field warehousing; chattel mortgages; and trust receipt loans—is included below.

## ASSIGNMENT

One method of securing additional cash which is becoming more and more popular with businessmen is assignment of accounts receivable. With this technique the firm simply assigns its accounts receivable to a finance company in exchange for cash. The finance company will loan the firm cash which will be equivalent to a certain percentage of the accounts receivable assigned. This percentage varies from 70 percent to 95 percent, depending upon the quality and size of each account receivable involved.

Assume that A & B Partnership needs $7,000 for working capital. The partners assign $10,000 of the firm's accounts receivable to a finance company which in turn loans the partnership $7,000. The purpose of the assignment is to provide the lender with security for the loan. By assigning accounts receivable in excess of the loan, the finance company is protected in the event some of the receivables prove to be uncollectible.

Two important terms which are often included in the contract assignment agreement are "with recourse" and "nonnotification." *With recourse* means that the borrower must make good those receivables which are uncollectible by replacing them with additional receivables of equal value. *Nonnotification* means that the borrower will not notify the debtors of the assignment of their debts to a finance company. Therefore, the debtors will simply continue to make payment to the borrowing company, which will in turn forward the payments to the finance company. Once the loan is paid in full, any remaining accounts receivable assigned to the lending agency are turned over to the borrowing company.

## FACTORING OF ACCOUNTS RECEIVABLE

Factoring differs from assignment in that a factor actually purchases accounts receivable from the selling firm. A factor is any person or finance company which is in business to purchase accounts receivable from other firms. With this arrangement, the firm selling the receivables notifies the debtors of the sale and instructs them to make payment to the factor. In addition, a factor may agree to purchase future accounts receivable which will result from future credit sales. In regards to future sales, it is necessary for the selling firm to first obtain approval from the factor before extending credit to a potential customer. Once approval is granted, the goods are shipped and the invoice is mailed to the factor. The factor, after deducting certain commission fees for his services, will forward cash to the selling firm. The commission fee usually varies from 1 percent to 3 percent of the net receivables sold, depending upon the quality and size of the receivables purchased. The primary advantage of this method is that the factor extends credit to the selling firm's customers and also assumes the risk of collection. The selling firm is able to convert receivables into cash immediately and is generally not responsible for any uncollectible accounts. For a new firm or a small business which cannot afford to tie up cash in the form of accounts receivable for thirty or sixty days, factoring represents a uniquely advantageous arrangement.

## PUBLIC WAREHOUSE RECEIPTS

Warehouse receipts represent one means of acquiring cash from funds which are tied up in merchandise inventory. This is particularly significant to those firms which spend a large portion of the year manufacturing products which are not sold immediately but rather are stockpiled because of seasonal demands. Examples include manufacturers of lawn fertilizer and snowmobiles.

The businessman is first required to store inventory in a public warehouse. The warehouseman, acting as a third party, provides the businessman with a warehouse receipt. The receipt is evidence that collateral in the form of merchandise inventory is being held in a public warehouse. By turning these receipts over to a banker or other lender, the businessman is able to borrow money. Once the merchandise has been sold and the loan paid off, the lender will turn the receipts over to the buyer so that the merchandise can be withdrawn from the warehouse.

This form of financing is particularly important to small businessmen who may have no alternative source for necessary funds. The use of warehouse receipts as collateral for loans was greatly enhanced by the Uniform Warehouse Receipt Act of 1907. This act, which defines the rights and liabilities of public warehousemen, has been accepted by all fifty states.

## FIELD WAREHOUSING

In using public warehousing, the businessman must physically transfer his inventory to facilities provided by the public warehouseman. However, in order to avoid such transfers, some businessmen utilize the services of field warehousing. Field warehousing is a storage technique whereby the public warehouseman goes to the premises of the businessman where the inventory is already located. The public warehouseman takes possession by segregating the applicable inventory. This may be done by constructing a fence around the inventory used as security for the loan or simply by placing the inventory in a separate part of the warehouse. The public warehouseman will then issue a warehouse receipt to the businessman. As in public warehousing these receipts may then be used as collateral for a loan.

## CHATTEL MORTGAGES

Funds may be acquired by means of a chattel mortgage. A chattel is an article of movable property such as inventory. The lender obtains a lien on certain specified property such as merchandise inventory which the borrower owns or is acquiring. Title in the inventory remains with the borrower but he cannot sell it without the permission of the lender. It is necessary that the inventory be specifically identified. One means of identification, among others, would be serial numbers. Because of the rigorous identification requirements, inventory items which are small in size, represent a low unit value, and have a high turnover are not recommended as collateral. Items commonly used include movable property other than merchandise inventory such as machinery and equipment.

## TRUST RECEIPT LOANS

The use of the trust receipt technique, also called floor plan financing, is most popular in the durable goods industry. The financial institution involved will actually purchase the inventory from the manufacturer or the wholesaler and order it delivered to the borrower or retailer. The borrower will in turn issue a trust receipt to the lender. For example, the borrower may be a retailer of televisions and appliances. When a television set is sold for cash, the retailer must turn the proceeds over to the lender in payment of the loan. If the television is sold on an installment basis, the installment contract may be substituted for the trust receipt held by the lender. In order that the lender may be assured the borrower is not selling television sets or appliances without remitting the proceeds to him, the lender takes periodic inventory checks to compare the outstanding trust receipts with the merchandise in stock. Despite these necessary checks, this method is one of the most popular means for businessmen to finance their inventories.

### Summary

Short-term debt has a maturity of less than one year. The funds acquired from these sources are usually invested in current assets such as inventory and accounts receivable. The agreements between lenders and borrowers are frequently informal.

In order to determine how much to borrow on a short-term basis, the businessmen should prepare a monthly cash forecast schedule. The monthly schedules will disclose significant information which the businessman can use. The primary purpose of this schedule is to show the variations in inflows and outflows of cash during different months of the year. By recognizing potential cash deficits early, the businessman is in a position to consider alternative sources of borrowing short-term funds, thereby increasing the firm's chances for acquiring the right amount at the least cost.

Examples of short-term fund sources include unsecured credit such as trade credit, commercial paper, commercial bank loans, and special endorsements by third parties; and secured credit, such as assignment of accounts receivable, factoring of accounts receivable, public warehousing, field warehousing, chattel mortgages, and trust receipts.

## QUESTIONS

1. What is the nature of short-term debt that distinguishes it from long-term debt? Give some examples of short-term funds.

2. (a) What is the purpose of a cash forecast?
   (b) What information is needed in the preparation of a cash forecast?

3. (a) What is meant by *trade credit?*
   (b) Explain the nature of a trade discount.
   (c) Why do sellers of merchandise offer a cash discount to the buyer?

4. (a) Define *commercial paper.*
   (b) What does the availability of commercial paper depend on? Why?

5. What advantages does a commercial bank offer to the businessman who wishes to acquire a short-term loan?

6. What are the two options that are available to a bank in relation to the interest on short-term loans?

7. What is a guarantor and what is his purpose in short-term financing?

8. What does a firm do when it assigns its accounts receivables? What is the purpose of this arrangement?

9. How does the factoring of accounts receivable differ from assigning them? Explain.

10. (a) What is the purpose of warehouse receipts in short-term financing?
    (b) How does field warehousing differ from public warehousing?

## Incident 5–1

Scott Johnson and Myra Weeks are both residents of Cannonsburg, Michigan, a small village located in the southern part of Michigan. Although the population is only 500 people, it is located just fifteen miles north of Grand Rapids, where the population approximates 500,000 people.

In 1968 a ski resort was developed in Cannonsburg. The resort accommodates thousands of skiers daily during the winter months. Although ski equipment can be rented at the lodge, there was no facility in Cannonsburg where skiers could purchase ski equipment or clothing. As a result, in July 1975, Mr. Johnson and Miss Weeks each contributed $20,000 of their personal savings in order to start a ski equipment and clothing center. The partnership, which is called the J & W Sports Center, is located near the entrance to the ski lodge. In addition to their savings, each one borrowed $20,000, using their homes as security for the loan. Of the $80,000 in cash which was invested, they used $8,000 to acquire the land, $25,000 to construct a building, and $30,000 to purchase such inventory as skis, poles, boots, and clothing. This left $17,000 in cash to meet their expenses such as wages (four sales clerks were hired), utility bills, and office supplies.

The partnership opened for business on December 1, 1975. During the month of December, the firm sold $25,600 of merchandise on credit and $3,000 of merchandise for cash. Both Mr. Johnson and Miss Weeks decided not to accept any credit cards but rather to establish their own credit terms which were 10 percent down with remainder to be paid in sixty days. Before a buyer was allowed credit, he was required to fill out a personal data sheet. Both Mr. Johnson and Miss Weeks were particularly interested in three pieces of information: age, income, and place of employment. If the buyer was twenty-one or over, earned a minimum of $9,000 per year, and was employed within a radius of fifty miles of the lodge, he was automatically allowed credit.

In order to replace the merchandise sold during the month of December, the partners purchased an additional $18,000 of merchandise on December 31, 1975. Both partners felt that it was important that they pay the vendor (seller) immediately for all items purchased. Therefore, although the credit terms provided by all suppliers they did business with were 2/15, n/30, Miss Weeks wrote a check for the entire purchase on December 31. After the discount of 2 percent, the check amounted to $17,640. Other cash outlays (expenses) of operating the store amounted to $3,420 during December.

As a result of the above transactions, the cash balance for the J & W Sports Center on December 31, 1975, amounted to only $1,500, computed as follows:

| | | |
|---|---:|---:|
| Cash inflow | | |
|    Original amount invested | $80,000 | |
|    Deposit on credit sales ($25,600 × 10%) | 2,560 | |
|    Cash sales | 3,000 | |
|      Total inflow | | 85,560 |
| Cash outflow | | |
|    Land | $ 8,000 | |
|    Building | 25,000 | |
|    Merchandise inventory (30,000 + 17,640) | 47,640 | |
|    Other expenses | 3,420 | |
|      Total outflow | | 84,060 |
|    Balance | | $ 1,500 |

Both partners expect cash to begin flowing into the firm during the second half of January from the December credit sales. However, during the first two weeks of January, both expect cash outflow to exceed cash inflow by approximately $10,500. Therefore, they need to borrow $10,500 for two weeks. Both partners agree that once customers who purchased merchandise on credit begin to make their payments, the partnership will never again experience a cash shortage.

(1)  In your opinion, could the partners have avoided having to borrow $10,500 for two weeks? Substantiate your answer by pointing out specific details.

(2)  What sources of short-term credit are available to the partners?

(3)  Do you share the partner's contention that once credit customers begin to pay, their cash shortage problems will be over? Explain.

(4)  Looking ahead, do you feel that the ski shop will be a success or a failure? Why?

# 6

# Federal Income Taxes

Income taxes are of such importance that special attention must be given to their implications. Because income taxes do represent a cost of doing business, it is vital that the promoter consider tax factors before choosing a form of business organization and form of financing. This chapter does not provide in-depth coverage of federal income taxes, but rather it examines briefly the basic computations involved in individual and corporate taxes. Consideration is then given to the effect that taxes may have upon the selection of form of organization and type of financing.

Taxes play a dominant role in most financial decisions. The primary source of revenues for financing the operations of the federal government has been the income tax. The right to levy a tax on income was provided in the sixteenth amendment to the Constitution in 1913. The rules and regulations governing the income tax are incorporated into the Internal Revenue Code. The Internal Revenue Service, a division of the Treasury Department, is responsible for both the enforcement of these laws and the collection of the tax. Today there are four major taxes which together account for most of the revenues received by governments: income tax, sales tax, property tax and excise taxes. Our discussion will be limited to the federal income tax because it has the biggest impact on business operations.

## Classes of Taxpayers

The income tax law provides for four classes of taxpayers: individuals, corporations, estates, and trusts. Each of these classes must file a return to pay the appropriate tax, if any, to the federal government. The sole proprietorship and partnership are not treated as separate taxable entities or units and therefore pay no tax. Rather, the income from a sole proprietorship is included in the individual tax return of the proprietor. Similarly the income from a partnership is included in the individual tax return of each partner whether or not it is withdrawn from the business. The individual tax return, called Form 1040, includes all income and tax deductions in arriving at taxable income. Although a partnership does not pay an income tax, it must file an information return. This return, form 1065, shows the computations of partnership income, along with each partner's portion of that income.

The corporation is treated in the eyes of the tax law as a separate taxable unit and therefore must pay an income tax on its taxable income. Furthermore, dividends distributed by the corporation must be included as part of gross income in the individual tax return of each stockholder. The tax on corporate income plus the tax on dividends distributed to stockholders results in double taxation of corporate earnings. For example, assume that the XYZ Corporation has $50,000 in taxable income for its latest year of operations. Furthermore, the board of directors declared and paid $30,000 in dividends to the firm's fifteen shareholders. Under the provisions of the Internal Revenue Code, the corporation will be taxed on its $5,000 of taxable income. In addition, each of the fifteen shareholders will be taxed on $2,000 of dividends ($30,000/15 = $2,000; this ignores dividend exclusion). Consequently, corporate earnings end up being taxed twice—once to the corporation in the form of a corporate tax and once to the shareholder in the form of an individual income tax.

## THE INDIVIDUAL INCOME TAX

The formula used in arriving at taxable income for individuals is outlined in Exhibit 6–1. This formula follows the basic content of the U.S. Individual Income Tax Return (Form 1040).

### GROSS INCOME

For federal income tax purposes, gross income is defined as all income not specifically excluded by law. Four examples of income excluded by law are (1) interest on state and municipal bonds; (2) the first $100 of dividends ($200 if filing a joint return); (3) social security income, and (4) life insurance proceeds. The income from a sole proprietorship is included in gross income on the individual tax return of the proprietor. Likewise, the income from a partnership is included in gross income on the individual tax return of each partner.

## EXHIBIT 6–1

*From Gross Income to Income Taxes Payable—Simplified*

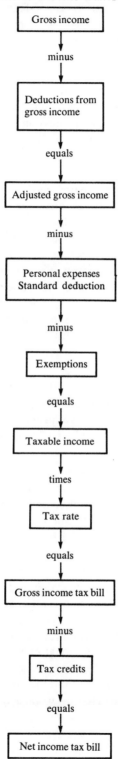

Gross income

minus

Deductions from gross income

equals

Adjusted gross income

minus

Personal expenses
Standard deduction

minus

Exemptions

equals

Taxable income

times

Tax rate

equals

Gross income tax bill

minus

Tax credits

equals

Net income tax bill

## DEDUCTIONS TOWARD ADJUSTED GROSS INCOME

The law provides for certain deductions from gross income to arrive at taxable income. Two relevant categories of deductions are business expenses and employees' business expenses.

*Business Expenses.*   The Internal Revenue Code authorizes a deduction of all the ordinary and necessary expenses incurred during the taxable year in carrying on any trade, business, or profession. Examples include advertising, bad debts, depreciation, repairs, rent, salaries, insurance, supplies, and selling commissions.

*Employee Expenses.*   Only five major classifications of employee expenses are deductible in arriving at adjusted gross income. They are: (1) costs incurred by a traveling salesman in soliciting sales for his employer (referred to as *outside salesman's expenses*); (2) transportation expenses including local bus, taxi, and so on, other than costs of commuting to and from work; (3) moving expenses resulting from accepting a new job in a different community; (4) expenses incurred for meals and room while away from home overnight; and (5) reimbursed expenses (these expenses are deducted *only if* the reimbursement is *included* in the employee's gross income).

This brings the taxpayer to an intermediary point referred to as *adjusted gross income.*

## DEDUCTIONS FROM ADJUSTED GROSS INCOME

Gross income minus the applicable deductions allowed by law results in adjusted gross income. Deductions from adjusted gross income may be classified into two areas: (1) personal exemptions (2) personal deductions.

*Personal Exemptions.*   Each taxpayer is allowed a deduction of $750 for each exemption in computing his taxable income. The taxpayer is allowed one exemption each for himself, his spouse, and each individual who meets the test as a dependent of the taxpayer. One exemption each is also allowed for the conditions of old age (65 and over) and blindness.

*Personal Deductions.*   The taxpayer has an option regarding deductions of a personal nature in that he may take the standard deduction or choose to itemize his deductions. The standard deduction for 1973 and thereafter is 15 percent of adjusted gross income, limited to a maximum of $2,000. If the taxpayer elects to itemize his deductions he will not be limited to any particular amount. Itemized deductions include such personal expenses as:

(1) Charitable contributions to certain precise classes of organizations such as the Red Cross, Boy Scouts, and the American Cancer Society.
(2) Child-care expenses incurred by women or widowers who must work outside of the home to earn a living.

(3) Medical and dental expenses not compensated for by insurance.

(4) Personal taxes such as state and local property taxes, income taxes, general sales taxes, and gasoline taxes.

(5) Personal interest expense such as interest on a mortgage on one's home.

It should be noted carefully that some of the deductions listed are subject to well-defined limitations outlined in the Code. For example, only medical expenses in excess of 3 percent adjusted gross income may be deducted. Those taxpayers who do not maintain adequate records which properly support their itemized deduction are encouraged to take the standard deduction. The taxpayer should select that option which will be to his best interest.

The figures in Exhibit 6–2 reflect the average deductions taken by people who itemize. The figures are for 1970, the latest year available.

### EXHIBIT 6–2

*Average Itemized Deductions*

| Adjusted gross income classes | Average deductions for contributions | Average deductions for interest | Average deductions for taxes | Average medical and dental deductions | Total deductions as % of AGI |
|---|---|---|---|---|---|
| $ 5,000–$ 6,000 | $ 228 | $ 382 | $ 423 | $ 373 | 25% |
| 6,000– 7,000 | 218 | 438 | 470 | 405 | 23% |
| 7,000– 8,000 | 241 | 544 | 536 | 406 | 23% |
| 8,000– 9,000 | 260 | 600 | 598 | 348 | 21% |
| 9,000– 10,000 | 275 | 666 | 671 | 318 | 21% |
| 10,000– 15,000 | 313 | 783 | 858 | 325 | 19% |
| 15,000– 20,000 | 415 | 966 | 1,177 | 325 | 17% |
| 20,000– 25,000 | 557 | 1,181 | 1,548 | 358 | 17% |
| 25,000– 30,000 | 694 | 1,436 | 1,944 | 432 | 17% |
| 30,000– 50,000 | 1,007 | 1,900 | 2,615 | 490 | 16% |
| 50,000– 100,000 | 2,186 | 3,376 | 4,581 | 681 | 17% |
| 100,000 or more | 13,553 | 11,832 | 13,068 | 1,146 | 22% |

Source: Reproduced by permission from 1974 U.S. MASTER TAX GUIDE, published and copyrighted in 1973 by Commerce Clearing House, Inc., Chicago, Ill. 60646.

## INDIVIDUAL TAXABLE INCOME

The taxpayer is now ready to compute his taxable income, the taxpayer's gross income minus deductions from gross income, minus either the standard deduction or the itemized deduction, minus the personal exemptions. The taxpayer then applies to his taxable income the applicable rate as outlined in the tax tables. The tax rates vary depending upon whether the taxpayer is single, single but qualifying as head of a household, married filing a joint return, or married filing separate returns. Although the Internal Revenue Service provides four separate tax rate tables, only the table for married individuals filing joint returns is reproduced here. The federal income tax is progressive; that is, taxpayers earning higher incomes pay at a higher rate. Exhibit 6–3 shows that a married taxpayer in the lowest income bracket pays a tax of 14 percent, whereas those in the top bracket pay the progressively higher rate of 70 percent.

EXHIBIT 6–3

*Income Tax Rates for Married Individuals Filing Joint Returns*
*Effective for 1971 and following years*

| Taxable income | Tax on column 1 | Percentage on excess |
|---|---|---|
| $  — | $  — | 14 |
| 1,000 | 140 | 15 |
| 2,000 | 290 | 16 |
| 3,000 | 450 | 17 |
| 4,000 | 620 | 19 |
| 8,000 | 1,380 | 22 |
| 12,000 | 2,260 | 25 |
| 16,000 | 3,260 | 28 |
| 20,000 | 4,380 | 32 |
| 24,000 | 5,660 | 36 |
| 28,000 | 7,100 | 39 |
| 32,000 | 8,660 | 42 |
| 36,000 | 10,340 | 45 |
| 40,000 | 12,140 | 48 |
| 44,000 | 14,060 | 50 |
| 52,000 | 18,060 | 53 |
| 64,000 | 24,420 | 55 |
| 76,000 | 31,020 | 58 |
| 88,000 | 37,980 | 60 |
| 100,000 | 45,180 | 62 |
| 120,000 | 57,580 | 64 |
| 140,000 | 70,380 | 66 |
| 160,000 | 83,580 | 68 |
| 180,000 | 97,180 | 69 |
| 200,000 | 110,980 | 70 |
| 300,000 | 180,980 | 70 |
| 400,000 | 250,980 | 70 |

To calculate an individual's income tax, assume the following. The taxable income of Mr. Ed Brown and his wife amounts to $13,200 in 1973. Their tax is computed as follows, using the rates in the table above:

| | |
|---|---|
| Tax on $12,000 | $2,260 |
| 25% of $1,200 excess over | |
| $12,000 | 300 |
| Total | $2,560 |

## CORPORATION TAXABLE INCOME

Corporations, unlike sole proprietorships and partnerships, are separate taxable units. Therefore, like individuals, they are required to pay an income tax on their annual taxable income. However, the tax formula (see Exhibit 6–4) followed in arriving at taxable income is slightly different for a corporation in that there is no such concept as adjusted gross income, because a corporation is not allowed deductions for exemptions or personal expenses. Deductions from gross income include the ordinary expenses of operating a business, such as salaries and wages, depreciation of plant facilities and equipment, uncollectible accounts (bad debts), rent, interest, utility bills, repairs

### EXHIBIT 6–4

*Corporation Income Tax Return—Simplified*

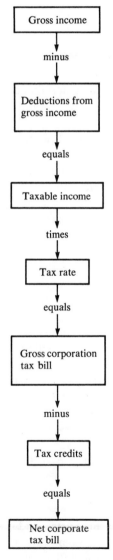

Gross income

minus

Deductions from gross income

equals

Taxable income

times

Tax rate

equals

Gross corporation tax bill

minus

Tax credits

equals

Net corporate tax bill

to business property, insurance, advertising, supplies, and contributions to charity.

Another major difference between individuals and corporations is the tax rate. The corporate tax rate is not progressive. It consists of two separate elements: a normal tax of 22 percent on all taxable income and a surtax of 26 percent on taxable income in excess of $25,000, resulting in a total rate of 48 percent on all income above $25,000. Assuming a corporation has a taxable income of $100,000, its tax liability would be computed as follows:

| | |
|---|---|
| Normal tax of 22% on first $25,000 | $ 5,500 |
| 48% on all taxable income in excess of $25,000 | 36,000 |
| Total | $41,500 |

## Impact of Taxes on Selection of Business Organization

There is no simple formula for determining which form of organization to elect. However, the following factors should be considered when making a decision of this nature.

1. Individual tax rates vary from 14 percent to 70 percent.
2. Corporate tax rates are 22 percent on the corporation's first $25,000 of taxable income and 48 percent on taxable income in excess of $25,000.
3. Income from a sole proprietorship or partnership is included in an individual tax return whether or not withdrawn.
4. Dividends paid by a corporation are included in the individual tax returns of each shareholder but are not deductible from the corporation's gross income.
5. Reasonable salaries or wages paid stockholders for services rendered are deductible from the corporation's gross income. Such salaries are included in the individual tax return of the stockholder.

Recognizing these basic tax factors, a businessman must select either corporate or noncorporate form of organization. Assume that Robert Dean, a married man with two children, is interested in starting a men's clothing store. Mr. Dean has had years of experience as a salesman of men's clothes and has acquired considerable knowledge about the clothing industry. He expects that his gross income from the store will be approximately $80,000 the first year. His original income as a salesman was $20,000, and therefore he plans to withdraw this amount from the business as his salary. He expects his business expenses (not including the salary) to amount to $25,000; his itemized deductions are estimated at $2,500. Exhibits 6–5 and 6–6 illustrate the amount of tax which Mr. Dean would be required to pay under the corporate and sole proprietorship forms of business.

Notice that when the corporate form of organization is used, Mr. Dean's salary of $20,000 is treated as an expense and is subtracted from gross income in arriving at taxable income. The salary is then included in his personal return as income. On the other hand, using the sole proprietorship form of organiza-

## EXHIBIT 6–5

### *Corporate Form of Organization*

| | | |
|---|---:|---:|
| Gross income | | $80,000 |
| Less: Business expenses | | |
| (not including salary) | $25,000 | |
| Mr. Dean's salary | 20,000 | 45,000 |
| Taxable income | | 35,000 |
| Computation of corporate tax | | |
| 22% on first $25,000 | $ 5,500 | |
| 48% on excess $10,000 | 4,800 | 10,300 — |
| Net Income | | $24,700 |
| Total corporate and individual taxes due | | |
| the federal government: | | |
| Corporate tax on $35,000 income | | $10,300 |
| Individual tax | | |
| Mr. Dean's salary | | $20,000 |
| Less: Personal exemptions (4 × $750) | $ 3,000 | |
| Itemized deductions | 2,500 | 5,500 |
| Taxable income | | $14,500 |
| Computation of individual tax | | |
| Tax on $12,000 | $ 2,260 | |
| 25% on excess of $2,500 | 625 | 2,885 |
| Combined corporate and individual tax | | $13,185 |

## EXHIBIT 6–6

### *Sole Proprietorship Form of Organization*

| | | |
|---|---:|---:|
| Gross income | | $80,000 |
| Less: Business expenses | | 25,000 |
| Adjusted gross income | | 55,000 |
| Less: Personal exemptions (4 × $750) | $ 3,000 | |
| Itemized deductions | 2,500 | 5,500 |
| Taxable income | | $49,500 |
| Computation of individual tax | | |
| Tax on $44,000 | $14,060 | |
| 50% on excess of $5,500 | 2,750 | $16,810 |

tion means that Mr. Dean cannot treat his salary as an expense. Rather, it is considered to be simply a distribution of profit.

The figures illustrate that Mr. Dean will save $3,625 in the first year by electing the corporate form of organization. This is computed as follows:

| | | |
|---|---:|---:|
| Taxes resulting from electing the sole proprietorship | | |
| (Exhibit 6–6) | | $16,810 |
| Taxes resulting from electing the corporate form of | | |
| organization (Exhibit 6–5) | $10,300 | |
| Plus Mr. Dean's individual tax (Exhibit 6–5) | 2,885 | 13,185 |
| Tax savings by incorporating | | $ 3,625 |

However, the example should be carried one step further. Mr. Dean elected to retain the net income of $24,700 (see Exhibit 6–5) in the corporation rather than paying a dividend. If he later elects to pay this amount in dividends, it will be included in his individual tax return as a part of gross income. As long as he continues to retain the net income of the corporation in the corporation it will not be taxed. What would the result be if he chose to pay the net income in dividends to himself? His taxable income on his individual return would increase from $14,500 to $39,000. This is computed in the following manner:

| | |
|---|---:|
| Taxable income before dividends (see Exhibit 6–5) | $14,500 |
| Plus: Dividends paid to Mr. Dean | 24,700 |
| Minus: $200 dividend exclusion permitted by the Internal Revenue Code | (200) |
| Taxable income after dividends are paid | $39,000 |

Mr. Dean's individual tax on $39,000 amounts to $11,690. Combining $11,690 with the corporation tax of $10,300 results in a total tax of $21,990.

The picture has now changed. Whereas the data in the first illustration indicated that the corporate form of organization would minimize total taxes, data in the second illustration, which assumes that net income is paid out in dividends, suggests that the sole proprietorship form of organization is preferable.

It is often difficult to determine which form of organization will help the businessman minimize his tax burden. However, generally speaking, the corporate form is preferred when the following conditions are fulfilled:

1. The owner is in a high income tax bracket.
2. The owner retains most of the earnings in the business.

Consequently, the sole proprietorship is preferred when:

1. The owner is in a low tax bracket.
2. The owner withdraws most of the firm's profits.

## The Small Business Corporation

In 1958 a provision was added to the Internal Revenue Code which allows some corporations to elect to have their income treated as though it were the income of the shareholders. That is, the corporation could elect to be taxed like a partnership. This means that the shareholders are taxed on the income of the corporation in much the same fashion as partners are taxed on the income of a partnership. In other words, the corporation pays no tax and thereby avoids the burden of double taxation on dividends while at the same time enjoying such legal benefits of a corporation as limited liability. The titles given to this type of organization can be "Subchapter S corporations," "Tax-option corporations," or "Small business corporations."

In order for a corporation to make this election, the following requirements must be satisfied:

1. It must not have more than ten shareholders.
2. All shareholders must be individuals or estates.

3. No shareholder can be a nonresident alien.
4. There cannot be more than one class of stock.
5. The corporation cannot be a member of an affiliated group.
6. It must be a domestic corporation.

These requirements are such that a large number of small corporations in the United States could easily qualify. In fact, a recent estimate indicates that there are approximately 200,000 enterprises in the United States today electing to be taxed as "Subchapter S Corporations.[1] Furthermore, the Internal Revenue Code also allows sole proprietorships and partnerships to incorporate and subsequently elect Subchapter S.

## WHY ELECT SUBCHAPTER S

The primary reason for electing the Subchapter S corporation treatment is that the owners of an unincorporated firm (such as a partnership) want to have the legal and business benefits of a corporation without the burden of double taxation on corporate earnings paid out as dividends. In order to acquire these privileges, it is necessary that the unincorporated business first incorporate and then elect to be taxed as a Subchapter S corporation. Likewise, owners of existing corporations can elect the Subchapter S corporation treatment to avoid double taxation of dividends. For example, the owners of a business may wish to withdraw all of its earnings each year. If the owners elect the regular corporate form of organization, the corporation will be subject to a minimum tax of 22 percent on the first $25,000 of taxable income. In addition, the dividends paid to the shareholders will be included in the individual tax return of each shareholder, where they will be subject to a minimum tax of 14 percent. On the other hand, by electing the Subchapter S corporation treatment, it is possible that the same earnings might be subject to a minimum tax of only 14 percent, because the income from the corporation is included in the individual returns of the shareholders in the same way that income from a partnership is included in each of the partners' individual returns. Consequently, the corporation escapes the corporate tax. A word of caution—if owners have reasonably high incomes it would probably be to their advantage to elect the regular form of corporation treatment in order to substitute lower corporation tax rates of 22 percent and 48 percent for high individual tax rates of as much as 70 percent.

### Accumulated Earnings Tax

One way for a regular corporation to avoid the double taxation problem is simply to retain its net earnings in the company by not paying any dividends. Although this appears to be safe, there is one major problem. The Internal

---

1. William L. Raby, The Income Tax and Business Decisions, 2nd ed. Englewood Cliffs, N. J.: Prentice-Hall, Inc., 1972, p. 71.

Revenue Code contains a provision whereby a penalty tax is provided for every corporation which allows its earnings to build up for the purpose of avoiding double taxation. The penalty tax is a rate of 27½ percent on the first $100,000 of accumulated earnings considered unreasonable. Consequently, a regular corporation could find itself in the unenviable position of paying a minimum 22 percent on earnings plus an additional 27½ percent in penalty taxes. Again, by electing the Subchapter S Corporation treatment, this pitfall could be avoided. However, if a corporation can justify its retention of earnings there is no penalty tax for unreasonable accumulations. An accumulation of earnings is considered reasonable when the purpose of such accumulation is plant expansion, debt retirement, plant replacement, etc. Accumulations of $100,000 or less are not questioned by the Internal Revenue and therefore will not be classified as unreasonable.

### Impact of Taxes on Financial Arrangements

A corporation can acquire funds to finance expansion through the issuance of common stock, preferred stock, and/or bonds. Deciding which security to issue is not easy. In making a comparison of the advantages and disadvantages of each type of security, consideration is given to a number of factors such as the amount of debt the firm already has and the stability of its earnings, that is, whether earnings are about the same from year to year or fluctuate (high in some years and low in other years). Another factor which affects the form of financial arrangements selected by the firm is taxes.

Taxes are important because interest on corporate bonds is deductible for tax purposes. On the other hand, dividends on common stock and preferred stock are not deductible. Instead, they are considered to be a distribution of corporate earnings. In order to see the effect taxes have upon differing financial arrangements, assume the following situation: the G. Bird Corporation, which presently has 1,000 shares of common stock outstanding, needs to raise

EXHIBIT 6–7

*Financial Arrangements: Stocks Versus Bonds*

|  |  | Preferred Stock |  | Bonds |
|---|---|---|---|---|
| Earnings before interest and taxes |  | $100,000 |  | $100,000 |
| Minus: Interest on bonds ($50,000 × 8%) |  | —0— |  | 4,000 |
| Taxable income |  | $100,000 |  | $ 96,000 |
| Taxes |  |  |  |  |
| 22% on first $25,000 | $ 5,500 |  | $ 5,500 |  |
| 48% on excess over $25,000 | 36,000 | 41,500 | 34,080 | 39,580 |
| Earnings after taxes (net income) |  | 58,500 |  | 56,420 |
| Dividends on preferred stock ($50,000 × 8%) |  | 4,000 |  | —0— |
| Earnings retained by the firm |  | $ 54,500 |  | $ 56,420 |
| Income per share of common stock |  | $   54.50 |  | $   56.42 |

$50,000 in order to purchase equipment to produce a new product the firm is introducing to the market. Two alternatives which are being considered are: (1) issue 1,000 shares of $50 par value, 8% preferred stock, or (2) issue 1,000 shares of $50 par value, 8% bonds. Exhibit 6–7 shows the impact which taxes would have on this decision.

The figures in the exhibit indicate that by issuing bonds rather than preferred stock, the corporation will end up with an extra $1,920. The extra amount results from the fact that interest, unlike dividends, is tax deductible. As a result, the corporation saves $1,920 ($41,500 — 39,580) in taxes by issuing bonds rather than preferred stock. Furthermore, earnings of common stock amount to $56.42 per share by issuing bonds versus $54.50 per share by issuing preferred stock. The formula for computing earnings per share (EPS) of common stock is as follows:

$$EPS = \frac{\text{Net income} - \text{Preferred dividends}}{\text{Common shares outstanding}}$$

If the G. Bird Corporation elects to issue preferred stock, the earnings per share of common stock would be computed as follows:

$$EPS = \frac{\$58,500 - \$4,000}{1000} = \$54.50$$

The dividend of $4,000 is subtracted because this money belongs to the preferred stockholders.

If the G. Bird Corporation elects to issue bonds rather than preferred stock, the earnings per share of common stockholders would be computed as follows:

$$EPS = \frac{\$56,420}{1,000} = \$56.42$$

The increase in earnings per share of $1.92 is again due to the savings in taxes of $1,920 resulting from the issuance of bonds. The earnings per share figure simply expresses in dollars and cents the relationship between the total earnings of common stockholders and the number of shares of common stock outstanding. Investors attach a great deal of significance to EPS. Generally, the higher the EPS figure, the higher the market value of the corporation's common stock. Market value is the amount of money a shareholder can receive by selling his stock to another buyer.

In this example, the businessman should also consider the fact that interest is a fixed expense in that it must be paid regardless of the firm's earnings. On the other hand, dividends are not payable until declared by the firm's board of directors. Therefore, the firm assumes more risk by issuing bonds. However, this risk appears to be overshadowed by the deductibility of interest in computing taxable income. In fact, of the total dollar value of new issues of corporate securities in 1972, 64 percent were bonds and notes. The other 36 percent were stock. Debt securities are obviously a popular means of acquiring additional funds.

Although this discussion compared preferred stock with bonds, the same type of analysis can be used in comparing common stock with bonds. Furthermore, it is not necessary that the firm be a corporation. The tax advantages of debt funding are also available to the owners of sole proprietorships and partnerships.

## Summary

Because income taxes represent a cost of doing business, it is vital that the promoter consider tax factors before choosing a form of business organization. The income tax law provides for four classes of taxpayers: individuals, corporations, estates, and trusts. Members of each of these classes must file a return. The sole proprietorship and partnership are not treated as separate taxable entries or units and therefore pay no tax. Rather, the income from a sole proprietorship or a partnership is included in the individual return of the owners. The corporation is treated as a separate taxable unit and must pay a tax on its taxable income. Corporate income is subject to "double taxation" in that dividends paid to stockholders are included in the stockholder's individual returns.

The taxable income of an individual is computed as follows: gross income minus deductions from gross income equals adjusted gross income minus personal expenses or standard deduction and minus exemptions equals taxable income. The taxable income of a corporation is simply gross income minus deductions from gross income.

Generally speaking, if the owner of a business is in a high tax bracket and retains most of the earnings in the firm, the firm should be organized as a corporation. On the other hand, the owner in a low tax bracket who withdraws most of the business profits should elect the sole proprietorship form of organization.

In order that a corporation might avoid double taxation on dividends without losing the legal benefits of a corporation, it may elect to be taxed as a Subchapter S Corporation. However, a corporation must meet certain requirements before it will be allowed to make this election.

Taxes are important in considering different types of financial arrangements. Although dividends are not deductible for tax purposes, interest on corporate bonds is deductible in arriving at taxable income.

## The Financial Process in Retrospect

The financial process is concerned with four major events. The first is promotion and selection of the appropriate form of business organization. The financial process plays a critical role in not only getting the business started but also keeping it going after it begins operations. Once the decision is made to start a new business venture, the promoter must convince those who might provide financial assistance that the new venture will be profitable. In order to do so, he must be able to provide information relating to the estimated revenues and expenses of operating the new business. Consideration must be given to the amount of funds needed to finance the acquisition of permanent assets such as land, buildings, and equipment. Likewise, careful attention must be given to the amount of working capital required to acquire inventories and meet other recurring expenses such as payables and utility bills. Once the amount of funds required is determined, the next task facing the promoter is to bring together the necessary monetary resources needed to conduct business activities.

The amount of funds forthcoming is often dependent upon the form of organization selected. If a businessman, for example, is interested in acquiring equity funds by issuing stock or debt funds through the sale of bonds, it will be necessary to incorporate. Consequently, the promoter must decide whether the new business will operate as a sole proprietorship, partnership, or corporation. The tasks of promoting a new business venture and selecting a form of business ownership are both related to the need to acquire sufficient funds with which to start the business.

This leads to the second and third events of the financial process; raising the proper amount of funds on terms which will be favorable to the firm and allocating these funds to fixed assets and to current assets. The financial process is concerned with acquiring both long-term funds and short-term funds. Long-term funds are utilized to acquire land, buildings, equipment, and other fixed assets. The sources of long-term equity funds and debt funds available to the business firm often depend upon the form of organization. For a sole proprietorship or partnership, equity funds represent the initial investment of the proprietor or partners in the business. As the business prospers, the owners may acquire additional equity funds by retaining profits in the business as well as by investing additional capital. For a corporation there are three primary sources of equity funds: common stock, preferred stock, and retained earnings.

In addition to equity financing, a firm may also acquire funds by issuing long-term debt securities. Corporations often issue bonds whereas a sole proprietorship and partnership frequently use the mortgage note. The advantage of bonds to the corporation is that large sums of money needed for investment in fixed assets may be acquired from numerous individuals. On the other hand, it is difficult for a sole proprietorship or a partnership to borrow large sums of money because the number of lenders is usually limited to one or two persons rather than many.

Short-term funds are used to acquire current assets such as inventory and accounts receivable. In many instances the businessman will be able to acquire funds without putting up collateral as security. Common examples of unsecured credit include trade credit, small loans from commercial banks, accommodation endorsements, and commercial paper. Some firms, because of certain weaknesses, are unable to acquire funds without providing some form of security for the lender's protection. In order to compensate for such weaknesses, the lender may require the borrower to pledge certain assets. Some of the more popular forms of secured credit include assignment and factoring of accounts receivable, public and field warehousing, chattel mortgages, and trust receipt loans.

The fourth event which makes up the financial process is evaluating the impact which taxes have upon financial decisions. When analyzing which form of organization to select and which type of funds to acquire, the businessman closely examines the impact of taxes upon these decisions because he can minimize taxes through electing the proper form of organization or the proper source of funds. The sole proprietorship and partnership are not treated as separate taxable entities and therefore pay no tax. Rather, the income from noncorporate firms is included in the individual tax returns of the owner or owners. On the other hand, the corporation is a taxable unit. The tax on corporate income plus the tax on dividends distributed to stockholders results in double taxation of corporate earnings. The corporate form will usually minimize taxes if the owner is in a high income tax bracket and most of the earnings are to be retained in the business. The unincorporated form is generally preferred if the owner is in a low tax bracket and most of the firm's profits are withdrawn. Before making a final decision in this regard, those firms which have ten or fewer owners should give serious consideration to the opportunities provided by electing to be treated as a Subchapter S corporation.

The impact of taxes upon the type of funding to select is important because interest on corporate bonds is deductible in arriving at taxable income. Dividends on common stock and preferred stock are not deductible. The savings in taxes resulting from the interest deduction makes the issuance of debt securities a very attractive alternative to equity securities.

## QUESTIONS

1. What are the four classes into which taxpayers can be divided? What classification would a partnership fall under?

2. Explain the implications of double taxation as it relates to the corporate form of organization.

3. Assume that Mr. Smith asks you to help him fill out his tax return for 1975. You find that his gross income totals $20,000; he has business expenses of $2,500, and employee expenses of $4,000.
   (a) Define and give two examples of business and employee expenses.
   (b) What is Mr. Smith's adjusted gross income for the year 1975?

4. What are the differences between the determination of taxes for the corporation and the sole proprietorship and partnership?

5. Assume that the X Corporation has a *taxable income* of $77,000 for 1975. What would be the tax rate used in the determination of the taxes owed and how much would the X Corporation have to pay in taxes in 1975?

6. What factors should be considered in the selection of a particular form of business organization?

7. Why is the Subchapter S corporation sometimes elected?

8. What requirements must be met in the formation of the Subchapter S corporation?

## Incident 6-1

Assume that for the year ending December 31, 1975, Mr. Anderson has gross income of $90,000 from an office building which he leases to business and professional clients. He plans to deduct $6,500 in business expenses that were incurred by him for the purpose of repairs on the building, depreciation, and property taxes. Further assume that Mr. Anderson incurs $10,000 expense associated with the entertainment of clients during 1975. He is married and has one child living at home, along with Mrs. Anderson's mother, who will turn 71 at the end of next year. Mr. Anderson is planning to take the standard deduction for 1975.

(1) What is Mr. Anderson's adjusted gross income for 1975?
(2) What is a personal exemption and what would Mr. Anderson show on his tax return as exemptions?
(3) Distinguish between the standard deduction and the itemized deductions; show what Mr. Anderson would show as his standard deduction.
(4) What is Mr. Anderson's taxable income for 1975?
(5) How much would Mr. Anderson pay in taxes in 1975?

## Incident 6-2

Assume that Mr. Wilson, a married man with three children, is interested in starting his own real estate offices. He plans to deduct $30,000 a year as a salary and he expects his business expenses (not including his salary) to be $16,000. Mr. Wilson plans to take the standard deduction.

(1) What would Mr. Wilson's tax bill for 1975 be under the corporate form of organization and under the sole proprietorship form of organization, given the fact that the gross income from the real estate firm for 1975 is $150,000?
(2) Which form of organization should he choose? Why?

## Incident 6-3

In this chapter there is an example involving Robert Dean, who is interested in starting a men's clothing store. The assumptions are:

(a) Robert Dean is a married man with two children.
(b) Gross income from the store will be approximately $80,000.
(c) Mr. Dean's salary will be $20,000.
(d) Business expenses (not including salary) will amount to $25,000.
(e) Itemized deductions are estimated at $2,500.

The illustrations in the chapter show that if he decides to pay no dividends, the corporate form of organization would minimize total taxes. On the other hand, should he decide to pay out all of the firm's net income in dividends, the sole proprietorship form of organization would minimize taxes.

Discuss the feasibility of Mr. Dean electing to have his business taxed as a Subchapter S corporation. Should he do so?

# THE PRODUCTION PROCESS

The **production process** is that series of events which creates value in the form of finished goods or services. It is one of the major functions of all business ventures. Unless something of value can be created there is no business.

Countries and citizens of the world marvel at the degree to which business-men in the United States have developed the production process. In no other country or economic system can the application of ingenuity and technology for production purposes be witnessed to such as extent as it can in the United States. Many of our companies conduct daily tours displaying and explaining their production process.

In general, the sequence of events and activities included in the production process can be diagrammed as follows:

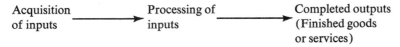

Acquisition of inputs ⟶ Processing of inputs ⟶ Completed outputs (Finished goods or services)

These events are discussed in the next two chapters, Chapter 7, The Production Function, and Chapter 8, Manufacturing.

III

INTERDISCIPLINARY PROCESS

# 7

# The Production Function

Evidence of production activity is so much a part of our lives that we take it for granted or associate it only with the factory situation. We often think of the production of such goods as steel, automobiles, and chemicals, but all business systems must create a competitive good or service and thus be involved in production activities. Something of value must be produced by every business. In this chapter those activities which start the production process and keep it going will be discussed. To begin, the nature, some relationships, and universality of the production function will be examined.

## Production and the Business System

The discussion of the business system has thus far revolved around two concurrent decision areas. The first centers on defining the central purpose of the business system in terms of that combination of goods and services which could best satisfy the unfilled wants and needs of consumers. The second decision area is involved with obtaining the funds necessary to start and maintain the business system.

At this point the businessman has only an idea and a commitment for funds to finance his idea. Through the production process, ideas are converted into tangible goods and services, and funds are spent to generate profits for the business system. Through the production process, men, machines and materials are combined in an orderly fashion to produce a tangible good or service. Furthermore, funds are used to purchase raw materials and equipment and to pay employees' salaries. Through the production process the ideas and financial support generated by the businessman are in a sense put to work—put to work to create that tangible good or service which should be sold for a profit.

The production process is also related to the other processes of the business system. A good or service is created which in turn must be priced, promoted, and sold through the distribution process. The good or service needs to be available in the right quality and quantity to meet and satisfy consumers' demands. Production and distribution efforts are not carried on independent of one another. Consumer wants and needs are communicated to the businessman through the distribution process. In this way he learns what his product must be to be competitive with similar products. In turn, raw materials are transformed into products via the production process to meet these consumer needs. Production efforts affect the style, cost, quality, and quantity of the good or service made available for distribution. Thus production is affecting the price, promotional efforts, and in sum the total distribution process of a business. Production and distribution within a business system are interdependent; each affects the other.

The production efforts of a business create jobs that are filled through the manpower process. The type of good created and the production process used affect the number and type of employees needed by a given business system. For example, in one situation welders may be needed; in another, bakers; in another, chemists; and in yet another, engineers. The production process defines the skills a large proportion of any business' labor force will need. Therefore, manpower cannot be sought until these skill needs have been defined by setting in motion a production process.

The manager performing these activities directs the production efforts of a business and coordinates it with the other processes. He decides what quantity, quality, and type of products to produce. These decisions are made in light of what those in the distribution area have told him about changing consumer demands and what those in the financial and manpower areas have told him about the availability of capital and employees, respectively. These areas are important considerations for the manager. For example, an impending strike or a projected shortage of credit and funds or a new lower-priced competitor's product all affect his decisions in the production area.

Finally, in addition to directing the production efforts of a business and coordinating these efforts with the other processes carried on within the business, the manager needs to control the various elements of the production process, including the amount of inventory on hand, production costs, quality levels, the amount scrap or waste, and production schedules. To aid in control various information is needed. The control needs within the production process determine what information should be gathered. The information process is vital to efficient performance of the production process.

In reality no production decision can be made without considering its impact on the performance of the financial, manpower, and distribution processes. And in turn, many of the decisions made within the manpower, financial, and distribution processes either are made to facilitate production efforts or are affected by decisions made in performing the production process.

## Universality

Those events which transform inputs into outputs of goods and services have been called the production process. This definition emphasizes that creating value is the primary purpose of production and points up its universal nature. Viewed in this perspective, every business system has a production process since every business system does something of value. Every businessman must make decisions relating to the production process. Railroads, restaurants, dry cleaners, grocery stores, chemical processors, steel manufacturers, and even such public institutions as hospitals and universities all create something of value. These institutions create value by transforming inputs into outputs and thus are involved in production activities. Even the businessman who deals only in a service is involved in making production decisions.

The value created through production activities can conceptually be illustrated as:

$$\text{Output value} - \text{Input value} = \frac{\text{Value created through production}}{\text{activities}}$$

In creating value, every business obtains inputs and in some way alters their value. If they did not, the two values in the formula would be the same, resulting in no profits. No businessman buys an input and then sells it for the same price. All businesses in some way alter the inputs they receive. Whatever the nature of this alteration, it has been broadly defined as production. The word *production* has, however, commonly been associated with factory operations. In the factory it is easy to see raw materials being actually formed, altered, and shaped into finished goods. But the serving of food in a restaurant, transporting of goods, selling of food in a store, and healing of people are all production processes. The input in each case has been altered. The grocery store owner takes a side of beef and cuts it into steaks, roasts, and so on. The hospital takes in a sick patient, applies medicine and medical techniques, and releases a healthy person. Regardless of what is being produced, transforming inputs into outputs involves certain common types of decisions and actions, so that the resultant output conforms to predetermined standards, meets certain specifications, is in the quantity and quality desired, is within the agreed upon time schedule, and does not exceed a stated cost. These decisions and actions are involved in increasing the effectiveness of the production process. These decisions must be made and taken regardless of what value the particular business is creating.

Three types of businesses illustrate the concept that value is added or created through production by all businesses, manufacturers, wholesalers, and retailers. The manufacturer converts raw materials and assembles component parts into saleable goods: automobiles, televisions, chemicals, steel. The production process employed by manufacturers is both complex and highly refined. Chapter 8 is devoted to discussing **manufacturing. Wholesalers** supply other businesses with the inputs used in their production processes: meat to restaurants, tires to automobile manufacturers, drugs to pharmacies, and so on. The wholesaler's production process involves channeling goods to the appropriate retailer of these goods. Production for wholesalers deals with such functions as bulk storage, distribution, marking, and grading. These activities are how the wholesaler alters the input or adds value to them. They add value to the input and are properly classified as production activities. **Retailers** can be typified by the drugstore, supermarket, discount chain store, gas station, dry cleaner, or barber shop. Their purpose is to sell goods or services to consumers. The inputs are usually either finished goods received from manufacturers or wholesalers, or manpower which is used to generate newly created services. Production occurs when manpower creates the service: cleaning clothing, cutting hair, or altering the form in which the finished goods are received—marking, shelving, merchandising, filling prescriptions, or pumping gasoline. For the one-man retail operation, the production process is relatively simple. However, it can quickly become complicated as operations expand. Sears and Safeway, with their extensive production processes, illustrate this point.

This emphasizes that the production process is universal among businesses. It can range from the very simple to the very complex—contrast the production process of a shoe repairman to that of the manufacturer of shoes. The shoe repairman's production process involves a very few events and is simple to visualize. He takes dilapidated shoes in and resoles, reheels, resews, or reglues them. The manufacturer, on the other hand, must balance many complex variables to convert leather and synthetic material into shoes of various sizes and styles. Both, however, make the same type of production decisions. Each is involved in meeting cost, time, and quantity specifications as well as maintaining the final product's quality. The only things that vary between the shoe repairman and the shoe manufacturer are the magnitude and complexity of these decisions.

Every businessman procures and transforms inputs. The inputs may be raw materials, finished goods, paperwork, customers, or patients. Regardless of type or form, a series of production activities, usually in a preplanned sequence, is performed on these inputs. The production process is the sum total of those operations necessary to procure and transform inputs. It can be characterized as a mechanical, chemical, assembly, or personal contact process, depending on the nature of the input. The resulting output can be in the form of parts, products, substances, or services. Regardless of this output, the method by which it is achieved revolves around production decisions and actions, decisions that someone in every business system must make. The production process, and so the discussion of it, starts with the first decision area—input procurement.

## Input Procurement

The production process starts with the procurement of inputs. Four inputs are employed in achieving the business' goals: labor, equipment, materials, and supplies. Labor is the only commodity that is not the concern of procurement activities. The manpower process is designed to provide the business system with the needed type and number of employees. The complexity of the activities involved in obtaining the right type and kind of manpower warrants discussing them as a separate process, in Section V.

**Procurement** is defined as obtaining the proper materials, equipment, supplies, and other inputs used within the business. The ability of the businessman to procure these in the right quantities, qualities, prices, and at the right time affects the success of his business activities. When combined, these commodities or inputs represent the largest expenditures made by most business firms. In addition, the procurements or purchases made in these areas determine, to a large extent, the quality of the finished goods or services which are produced. Materials of poor quality or defective equipment adversly affect the quality of the finished product. Thus, the negative impact on business profitability is definitely noticeable when procurement is inefficiently performed.

### PROCUREMENT AND THE PRODUCTION PROCESS

Uninterrupted production demands that materials, supplies, and equipment be available when needed. The quantity and quality of the goods or services produced starts and guides procurement activity. For example, the number and type of pizzas a local pizzeria expects to sell on certain days of the week dictates the type and amount of flour, sausage, cheese, and other ingredients that will need to be purchased. The volume of business also affects the equipment purchased, including the size of the oven, number of tables, and number of platters.

In addition, procurement activities have some impact upon the production process. Those responsible for procurement are usually the first to hear of new materials, supplies, and equipment available to facilitate and improve production activities. These ideas are the basis for changes and alterations in the production process. This two-way relationship makes procurement an inseparable part of the production process. Procurement is more than just making materials, supplies, and equipment available when needed by production. It plays an integral part in design of and later changes in, the entire production process.

The important role procurement activities play in the design of the production process can be seen when the first production decision every business must make is evaluated. This decision is which inputs the business should make and which should be bought from others. In reality the businessman could make most of the inputs used in the production of a finished good or service. However, this is impractical in most instances, and therefore he should use procurement and production information to help resolve his make–buy problem.

## MAKE OR BUY DECISIONS

The businessman can be totally self-sufficient, making every item used in production or elsewhere in the business. Of course, the futility and cost involved in making everything from paper clips to heavy-duty equipment is readily recognized. However, where to draw the line between what to make and what to buy from other suppliers demands continual analysis. Production and procurement circumstances which indicate that buying a certain input is the best decision today may change tomorrow. Procurement cannot begin until the businessman identifies exactly which materials, supplies, and equipment to buy.

### WHEN TO MAKE

*When Quality and/or Performance Cannot be Met by Suppliers.*   The available suppliers of a material, supply, or piece of equipment may offer only a selection, limited in quality or ranges of performance. When the businessman's demand is higher or lower than these levels or ranges, he may consider making the items to meet his exact demands. The quality and performance of available materials, supplies, or equipment can be either too high or too low for the specific situation faced by the businessman. If the quality and performance is higher than needed by the business, the make decision is based solely on economic terms. Why, for example, should the businessman pay the added cost for a motor designed to last ten years when the one that only lasts two years is needed? On the other hand, when the available materials, supplies, or equipment are of a lower quality or performance than needed, the decision to make may be based on other considerations. These other considerations may include such factors as the finished goods' safety, durability, or performance. For example, the engines manufactured for street automobiles cannot meet the high performance requirements of race car drivers. Thus, many racing teams build their own engines to meet their strict performance requirements. When the level of quality or performance cannot be compromised, regardless of cost, it may be the only factor to consider in determining whether to make or buy. An excellent example of this is the recent manned-space flights. Safety and performance were the main criteria, not the costs of making or buying the various component parts. Therefore, many of the parts were custommade to meet the high quality and performance standards set by NASA. Many times, suppliers will modify an item's quality and performance to meet a specific business demand. This is especially true if the business represents a large proportion of the supplier's annual sales.

*When the Business Can Produce the Merchandise at a Substantially Lower Cost.*   The businessman may think that the merchandise can be produced at a cost lower than the supplier's selling price. However, he needs to evaluate carefully future as well as present costs so that a fair decision can be made. For example, what are the "costs" of not being able to make sufficient quantities of the materials needed for production of the business's main good or service? In this case the "costs" might include lost sales or poor relationships with customers. In addition to determining costs, the businessman should be certain that he wants to produce the material forever if his decision forces present suppliers out of business. These "costs" and decisions are difficult to foresee and calculate but should serve to illustrate that the make decision should be based on more than just today's facts, figures, and prices.

*When the Business' Manufacturing Experiences and Equipment Are Well Suited to Manufacture the Material.* Some businesses find that certain employees and equipment are idle during the day. In other words, the main production effort is of insufficient volume to keep all employees and equipment working for the full eight hours. The equipment and manpower may be adaptable to the production of secondary products without too much difficulty. Secondary products are those used in the production of the main product or service. The opportunity to utilize men and equipment fully may make the decision to produce rather than buy these secondary items an economical one, in the sense that the present employees and equipment will be fully utilized. After all, the employee receives the same pay and the equipment costs the same whether they are idle or working. If production of secondary items takes the place of some of this idle time, the businessman can realize a savings.

These are several good reasons why a business might decide to make rather than buy materials, supplies, or equipment. However, there are also some compelling reasons for purchasing materials, supplies, or equipment.

## WHEN TO BUY

*When the Costs of the Equipment Needed to Make an Item Are so Large that the Business Is not in a Position to Make the Investment.*    The lack of funds could quickly discourage a businessman from sinking huge amounts of money into the extensive equipment necessary to produce some relatively simple products. For instance, the cost of a press to punch out metal tops for containers will run into thousands of dollars. The funds available to the business must first be applied to the production of primary products. Only when excess funds are available can the businessman think about investing them in the equipment necessary to manufacture secondary materials.

*When the Quantities Required Are Small.*    When there is a limited demand for some materials, supplies, or equipment the businessman cannot in many cases justify the high costs of producing them. The high cost of the machinery to produce many materials, supplies, or equipment cannot be justified when only a few items are needed. The machinery used in production probably presents the best example of this limitation. The purchase of one drill press, lift truck, or hoist every twenty-five years hardly justifies the time and expense of attempting to make these items. Although they may be expensive to buy, chances are that the costs of making them would be prohibitive.

*When Other Companies Hold Patents or "Trade Secrets" on a Required Material.* Under these conditions it is legally impossible for the business to consider making a patented item. Many products and processes are protected by law, and the businessman has no choice but to buy these goods from those suppliers who hold the patent.

These reasons for buying versus making materials, supplies, and equipment present the businessman with difficult decisions, which must be resolved before procurement activities can continue. Having identified which materials, supplies, and equipment to buy, the business' procurement efforts can be started.

## PROCUREMENT OBJECTIVES

The objectives of procurement are purchasing the proper quality and quantities of various materials, supplies, and equipment from the proper suppliers at the proper time and at a proper price. What is "proper" in reaching each of these objectives depends upon the individual business.

The proper quality is that quality which is necessary for accomplishing the purpose for which the item is intended. Quality has no meaning in and of itself. For example, metal of a thickness, composition, and design to withstand all abuse for twenty years is of too high quality for an automobile body, too low quality for a space ship, and in the right quality range for an ocean liner. Quality is relative, and often means that quality which the business' customers want and are willing to pay for.

The proper quantity refers to that volume necessary to keep the production efforts on schedule or to take care of continuing sales. The businessman seeks a balance between undersupply and oversupply of material, both of which are costly. Undersupply causes interruptions in production, while oversupply increases the costs of such factors as storage and interest on the money tied up in material investments.

The proper supplier is the one whom the businessman can depend on for the various factors agreed upon in the purchase contract. The supplier is contractually responsible for delivering the quantity and quality ordered, at the proper place and time, and at the agreed upon-price. The integrity of the supplier in many instances, however, determines if he will live up to these contractual responsibilities. This integrity should be weighed more heavily than the contractual obligations created by the purchase agreement.

The proper time is when the materials, supplies, or equipment are needed. Planning when these items are needed is important so that orders can be placed far enough in advance of this date to guarantee their receipt.

The proper price is the one which bears a fair relationship to the quality and service required by the businessman.

## PROCUREMENT ACTIVITIES

Procurement activities are the same for such diverse products as paper clips, iron ore, desk calculators, heavy duty equipment, and bulk chemicals. These activities can either be among the many responsibilities of the small businessman or the responsibilities of a separate purchasing department. Regardless of the business' size or who is responsible for procurement, the following steps are taken for any materials, supplies, or pieces of equipment purchased:

1. Recognizing and describing the need.
2. Negotiating for possible sources of supply.
3. Selecting the supplier.
4. Following up, receiving, and inspecting goods.

### RECOGNIZING AND DESCRIBING THE NEED

Procurement activities originate with a need that can be satisfied by new purchases. The need must be stated so that the person or department responsible for procurement can determine exactly what it is. Information is gathered on what exactly is wanted, how much is wanted, and when it is wanted.

For securing some needs—paper clips, typewriter ribbons, and so on—the businessman can anticipate from past usage the advance need. The supplier can be granted the freedom of automatically shipping a gross of paper clips, or five reams of typing paper, every month unless told otherwise. For materials utilized in the production process, future plans for the number of units to be produced indicate when and how much of a particular type of material will be needed. For example, if the local Dairy Queen operator knows that during the month of August, fifty gallons of ice cream needs to be produced she can place her order in advance for the required amount of milk. For equipment and other sporadic purchases, the need is usually indicated by one individual within the business, such as a foreman, worker, or secretary who knows when equipment needs to be replaced. The procurement activity is not started until this need is indicated.

For all these purchases a detailed description must either be on record (for recurring purchases), or developed (for those sporadic purhases). Incomplete descriptions are costly in terms of lost time taken to determine what exactly is wanted, lost production time due to improper materials on hand, and delivery and return of wrong materials and supplies. To decrease such problems the businessman should utilize a standard requisition form similar to that shown in Exhibit 7–1. A requisition form forces the user to describe specifically what, how much, and when the good is needed. A completed requisition can be filed and used for items where repeat purchases are necessary. As a record-keeping device, these requisitions serve as the basis for information necessary to anticipate the future need for recurring purchases. The person or department in charge of purchasing the product receives the requisition or goes to the files, makes sure that the description is in sufficient detail, and then processes it through the remaining steps.

EXHIBIT 7–1

*Purchasing Requisition*

| | | Requisition | | |
|---|---|---|---|---|
| Quantity | Unit | No. or Size | Description | Price |
| | | | | |
| | | | | |
| | | | | |
| | | | | |

Confirmation _____     Suggested vendor _____     Wanted _____

Requisitioner _____     Approved _____     Date approved _____

Buyer _____

## NEGOTIATION FOR POSSIBLE SOURCES OF SUPPLY

Sources of supply are developed to fill the need as indicated on the purchase requisition. There may be only one source of supply for the material needed, but usually the businessman has many alternative suppliers available. The nature of the negotiation between the suppliers and the businessman depends on the nature of the material sought.

For recurring purchases, a group of approved reliable soures can generally be developed because of the common nature of the supplies needed. Price may be the same for these suppliers, and the only decision needed is whether to spread the purchases around to many suppliers or to concentrate the orders with one supplier. Generally, the service a purchaser can expect from a supplier will be better when orders are concentrated with one or a few suppliers. When supplier services are an important element of a purchasing agreement it is probably advisable to place the purchases with only a few suppliers. The supplier will then feel it is worth his time and effort to insure the level and type of service the particular business expects. The supplier who, on the other hand, is only getting a small part of the order economically cannot justify spending a lot of time servicing that particular business or account.

For items which are bought infrequently or completely new purchases, the procedure is a little different. The sources of supply can be developed by analysis of the various vendor's categories, talking with salesmen who invariably call, or contacting manufacturers of items similar to the one in question. The list of tentative suppliers can be narrowed by investigating the suppliers' abilities and capacities to provide the items and by interviewing the representatives of these suppliers. After going through this process, the businessman will select two or more suppliers which he feels can meet his demands. He is now ready to enter into negotiations with each. Price is usually at the center of these negotiations and can be obtained using two methods. The first is through the supplier-published price lists. Published price lists leave little or no room for negotiation. The second is to have the suppliers quote a price based upon the specifications. A typical quotation request is reproduced in Exhibit 7–2. This form allows various suppliers to bid competitively for the specific items. Note that the businessman is already confident that each of the suppliers can meet

EXHIBIT 7–2

*Request For Quotation*

| XYZ Company<br><br>Inquiry<br>This is not an order | Date _____<br>Page _____ of _____<br><br>Bid closing date<br><br>Our inquiry no. | Request for quotation |  |
|---|---|---|---|
| | | Submit cost breakdown if quotation exceeds<br>$ _____ | |
| | | Vendor complete below this line ↓ | |
| | | Total price | Pym't terms |
| | | | Shipping wt. |
| | | | F.O.B. |
| | | | Comments |
| | | | Schedule<br>Can be met<br>Yes _____<br>No _____ |
| Retain duplicate for your files.<br>Fill out and return one copy to bid room,<br>Procurement Dept.<br><br>Buyer: _____ | | Vendor | |
| | | Per | |
| | | Title | |
| | | Date | |

his demands. What he is questioning is the difference in price. Once this price information has been returned, he can select the one or group of suppliers with whom he will place the order.

## SELECTION OF THE SUPPLIER

The selection of a specific supplier involves two events: analysis of the supplier and placement of the actual order.

Analyzing the various suppliers has as its objective the selection of the right suppliers. This is the most difficult of the procurement activities because so many intangible factors must be weighed. Price is certainly a basic factor, but it may not be the most important. Such factors as the plant facilities, technical know-how, financial soundness, location, attitude, honesty, fairness, and services provided should also enter into the decision. In some cases the businessman might choose the supplier with the highest price if he feels assured these other factors are worth the additional cost. All these factors determine which supplier is the right one. In many cases the final decision is based upon personal judgment of the situation. The evaluation of a supplier's honesty and integrity is a good example of the type of judgment required.

For legal and internal records the placing of an order should always involve the use of a purchase order. A standard **purchase order** is presented in Exhibit

## EXHIBIT 7–3

*Purchase Order*

| XYZ Company | | | | | Purchase Order |
|---|---|---|---|---|---|
| To: | | | | | NO. (This number must appear on all papers, packages and invoices) |
| | | | | | Account no. |
| | | | | | Requisitioned by |
| | | | | | Contract no. |
| | | | | | Deliver material to |
| Item | Quantity | Description | | Part no. | Net unit price |
| | | | | | |
| Delivery at destination | | | "X" indicates confirming order | | Total |
| Item | Qty. rec'd | Date rec'd | Balance due | Chk by | Gross wt. | Rec'd via | Trans chg. |
| | | | | | | | |
| | | | | | | | |
| | | | | | | | |
| | | | | | | | |
| | | | | | | | |
| | | | | | | | |

7–3. The purchase order, once accepted by the supplier, is a legally binding contract and contains the conditions of the sale plus any other internal record-keeping information the businessman feels should be included. Such information is illustrated at the bottom of the purchase order in the exhibit. Care should be taken in filling in the purchase order because it may be the only way of identifying exactly what the supplier's employees need to know. Procurement activities do not end when the order is placed. The order has to be followed up until the supplies are received.

## FOLLOW UP, RECEIPT, AND INSPECTION OF GOODS

The procurement responsibilities of the businessman do not end with the completion of the purchase order. It needs to be followed up on. Following up on an order consists of holding a supplier to his promises of delivery. The businessman should keep in contact with the supplier until there is an explicit notice of acceptance of the purchase order and a commitment made on the stated delivery date. Follow-up procedures may not need to be initiated for all items purchased, but just for those where delayed deliveries or nondeliveries could be critical to the business. Most businesses will not be harmed by the late delivery of office supplies but, running out of production raw materials is another question. For these items follow-up procedures should be initiated.

A supplier's invoice usually precedes the delivery of the items purchased. An invoice is a notification of exactly what the businessman should receive and the amount of money owed the supplier. The procurement activities are not completed until the invoice has been checked against a receiving report which shows the quantity received and the condition of the material. A receiving report is prepared by the businessman. An example of a standard receiving report is found in Exhibit 7–4.

Careful checking of the purchase is important. Goods received must be checked against the invoice with any deviations noted. The quantity stated on the invoice is no guarantee that this is the number shipped from the supplier. The quality of the goods should also be inspected. Except for hidden defects, once the goods are accepted, the supplier's liability for poor quality ends. Therefore, any defects need to be spotted at this point and adjusted for by the supplier. Only now are procurement activities completed. The quantities purchased are ready to be used or go into storage for future use.

## Summary

Every business creates value or produces something of worth, making the production process universal to all businesses. Production occurs when inputs are modified to form outputs. The first step in the production process is the procurement of inputs in the form of the materials, supplies, and equipment necessary to create outputs of value. Procurement activities include recognition and description of need; negotiation for possible sources of supply; selection of suppliers; and follow up, reception, and inspection of goods. Procurement feeds the production process with a constant flow of materials, supplies, and

## EXHIBIT 7–4

### *Receiving Report*

| | Your Business<br>3000 Shadeland Avenue<br>South Bend, Indiana | | |
|---|---|---|---|
| Receiving report | | | |
| From:  South Bend Supply Company<br>6690 South Commerce Street<br>South Bend, Indiana | | Date: May 15, 19....<br><br>Carrier:  Carter<br>Trucking Co. | |

| Quantity | Description | Remarks |
|---|---|---|
| | | |
| | | |

Signed _____

Title _____

equipment. Inefficiency and waste in performing procurement activities decreases the efficiency of the whole production process. Manufacturing operations best exemplify how these inputs are changed into outputs and are
discussed in the following chapter.

## QUESTIONS

1. How does the production process relate to:
   (a) The financial process?
   (b) The manpower process?
   (c) The management process?
   (d) The information process?
   (e) The total business system?

2. Give an example of production activities for each of the following:
   (a) Restaurants.
   (b) Drugstores.
   (c) City governments.
   (d) County jail.

3. What factors affect the businessman's decisions to make or buy a given material, supply or piece of equipment?

4. The Smith Company has prior manufacturing experience in producing widgets
but no experience in producing gadgets. How would the factors in a make-or-
buy decision differ between widgets and gadgets?

5. What extra costs could be incurred by a business when the descriptions of the good to be purchased are incomplete?

6. For what types of purchases is price a negotiable factor?

7. What factors would the businessman weigh in selecting a supplier?

8. Discuss in detail each of the steps in the procurement process as they relate to the procurement of high grade carbon steel.

9. What are the objectives of procurement? Explain what these objectives mean.

10. Do procurement activities end when the purchase order is mailed to the supplier?

## Incident 7–1

The Walk-Away Company, Los Angeles, manufactures a complete line of men's and women's shoes. Each year it purchases about 2,000,000 shoe boxes. The shoe style and size are printed on the end of each box by Walk-Away.

The purchasing agent had always maintained at least two sources of shoe-box suppliers in order to protect Walk-Away from the inability of a supplier to meet a contract. It was custom to renegotiate the contracts with suppliers in November of each year. In November the Top Box Company, located in New York, submitted a bid of $4.25 per thousand boxes; the Blue Bird Company, located in Dallas, $4.12 per thousand; the Jet Box Company, Chicago, $4.10 per thousand; and Pandora Box Company, Omaha, $4.09 per thousand. Freight costs from each of the plants' home locations would be paid by Walk-Away.

Satisfactory purchases have been made in the past from all of these companies. Within the last two years all of Walk-Away's requirements have been supplied by Blue Bird and Pandora Box Companies.

Shortly after receiving these bids the president of Walk-Away received a call from the mayor of Los Angeles. The mayor indicated that a new box company, the Silver Lining Company, had just been started by a group of black entrepreneurs in the Los Angeles Watts area. Since the mayor was 100 percent in favor of black enterprise, he was wondering if Walk-Away would accept a bid from the Silver Lining Box Company. Walk-Away's president informed the purchasing agent to get in touch with the people at Silver Lining.

The purchasing agent furnished the people at Silver Lining with detailed specifications of the work desired and was told that Silver Lining was anxious to submit a bid. Two days later Silver Lining's sales manager stated that his company would furnish the boxes exactly as specified at a price of $4.00, delivered at Walk-Away. This bid was only good if an order of not less than 1,500,000 boxes was placed. The sales manager produced many samples of excellent quality work. He also told the purchasing agent that the $4.00 quotation would return no profit to Silver Lining but keep the present work force employed until other accounts could be obtained. The purchasing agent visited Silver Lining's facilities and found them to be small but adequately equipped.

(1) What facts should the purchasing agent use in evaluating Silver Lining's bid in relation to other bids he has received?

(2) Should Walk-Away purchase from a firm whose future is suspect?

(3) Should Walk-Away continue its policy of purchasing from two suppliers? If so, how should the orders be divided?
(4) Do you think that as time passes any factors in this case will change? What effect will these future events have on the decision?
(5) Considering costs, convenience, public relations, reliability, and other relevant factors, what should the purchasing agent of Walk-Away do?

# 8

# Manufacturing

The central purpose of the business system is achieved through the production process. A competitive good or service of value is created. The production process entails *all* those events necessary to procure and transform inputs into competitive goods or services. While all business systems have a production process, not all businesses are involved in **manufacturing.** Manufacturing concentrates on that series and sequence of operations which transforms raw materials into finished goods. Manufacturing is peculiar to a factory situation and only represents one phase of a manufacturer's production process. It is one approach, the most efficient and refined method of converting inputs into outputs available, to processing or converting inputs into outputs. Yet not all businesses are manufacturing concerns. Therefore, not all business' production processes ential manufacturing activities. In this chapter the concepts that make manufacturing so efficient shall be discussed. The manufacturer can apply those concepts to increase the efficiency of his production process. Then, the application of these manufacturing concepts to situations other businessmen face shall be examined in order to improve the efficiency of nonmanufacturing production processes.

## Types of Manufacturers

All manufacturing efforts differ somewhat. However, a general manufacturing model can be developed. Such a model is presented in Exhibit 8–1. After

EXHIBIT 8–1

*General Manufacturing Model*

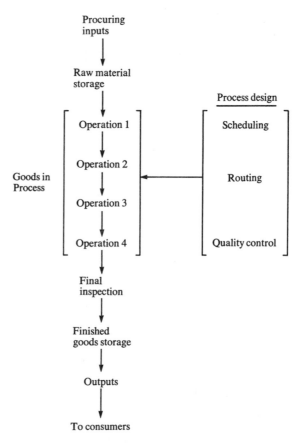

inputs are acquired, the manufacturer stores them until they are needed. Then, several preplanned operations occur. In Exhibit 8-1 these operations are shown as numbers 1, 2, 3, and 4. Through these operations the inputs are converted into outputs. As inputs move through this conversion process or through the preplanned operations they can be called "goods in process." Inputs are going through the process of becoming finished goods. Decisions must be made concerning the design of this process, or the type and number of operations which shall be involved. Plans then must be laid for the scheduling and routing of the inputs through these processes or operations. At various points in the transformation, quality is checked and controlled. After the finishing operations, a final inspection is made in order to separate any goods which are defective.

Finished goods which pass inspection are then held in storage until they are shipped to the customer. Regardless of the size or type of the manufacturing operation, this general model presents a fair picture of how it operates.

Beyond this general model two types of manufacturing operations can be identified: **intermittent manufacturing** and **continuous manufacturing** operations.

### INTERMITTENT AND CONTINUOUS MANUFACTURING

As the name implies, *intermittent manufacturing* has an intermittent, interrupted, or uneven flow of inputs, goods in process, and outputs. Intermittent manufacturing is represented by the custom or job order type of shop. Examples of intermittent manufacturers would include cabinet shops, machine shops, batch type chemical operations, tailors, general contractors, and so on. No single sequential pattern of operations is appropriate. In other words, in these operations there are no such things as Exhibit 8–1's operations 1, 2, 3, and 4. For custom or job order manufacturers, everything, including the sequence of operations, must be flexible to adapt to changing jobs and orders.

*Continuous manufacturers,* on the other hand, have a continuous, even, uninterrupted flow of inputs, goods in process, and outputs. Continuous manufacturing is represented by petroleum refineries, food processors, and mass production industries such as automobile and home appliance companies. These manufacturers can adapt a standard set and sequence of processes, as in the diagram. In other words, they can preplan and set out a definite sequence of operations. For example, in the processing of soft drinks, work is required in four operations or departments: mixing, blending, bottling, and packing. As work is completed in one department, it is transferred to the next department in the order listed.

In general the intensity and predictability of consumer demand as well as the type of raw material processed has a considerable influence on the type of manufacturing operation. For example, fine teak wood used for ornamental carving is not as adaptable to continuous manufacturing as is crude petroleum oil. On the other hand, even though home construction is conducive to continuous manufacturing, the variability and fluctuation of consumer demand precludes the stringent preplanning, scheduling, and standardizing necessary for a continuous manufacturing operation. For the businessman to operate a continuous manufacturing operation, product demand must be stable and predictable. He must be able to plan his manufacturing efforts around a fairly stable number and type of units of output. In addition, the raw materials used in manufacturing the finished product must be conducive to machine processing. Intermittent manufacturing is best when these conditions in *total* cannot be met. It is best when product demand is not stable from year to year and when the transformation of the raw materials into finished goods involves a great deal of hand labor. Under these conditions the instability of product demand keeps the businessman from being able to preplan his operations and output. If his manufacturing efforts were continuous, he would run the risk of over-producing during certain times of the year. If the raw material is not conducive to machine processing, much of the economy the planned, automated production lines offer the continuous manufacturer is eliminated. To cover the high costs of continuous manufacturing machinery, output usually must be at a high level. Any time human labor is required the output level decreases. Thus, the more human labor required, the less economical it becomes to invest in continuous manufacturing machinery.

Whether or not the manufacturing operations are continuous or intermittent, basic manufacturing decisions need to be made. First, a plan or design for the manufacturing operations must be established; and second, a system to control the manufacturing operations needs to be designed and implemented.

## Manufacturing Design

The first area with which either the continuous or intermittent manufacturer must be concerned is manufacturing design. He must be concerned with design from two standpoints. The first is the actual design of the product. What the end product must do and look like affects the way the manufacturer deals with the second design area—the actual manufacturing operations and methods. The manufacturer cannot determine the types of machinery needed until he knows what the end product's design should be.

### PRODUCT DESIGN

The purpose of product design is to transform what the businessman feels are unsatisfied consumer demands into a physical product. Product design is the first step in manufacturing a competitive product; it centers around the functional design and style design of the product.

### FUNCTIONAL DESIGN

Funtional design is that phase of product design which focuses on the purpose the product is to achieve. In other words, what function should the product perform? A ballpoint pen manufacturer, for example, is concerned with designing a product that writes without skipping or smudging ink on the paper, is light and fits the hand, can be carried in pocket or purse, will write on material other than paper, and is durable. A ballpoint pen which has these characteristics fulfills the purpose for which it is intended and is "functional." If the pen were not functional, sales would suffer because it would be an inferior product—inferior because it does not perform the same functions that competing ballpoint pens do. But being functional does not insure the manufacturer that his product will be competitive.

### STYLE DESIGN

To be competitive the manufacturer must also conern himself with style design. *Style design* is that phase of product design which focuses on the fashion, distinction, elegance, attractiveness, and aesthetic value of the product. Functional design concentrates on how the product works, while style design concentrates on how the product looks. Both are important aspects in determining a product's competitiveness. For example, the ballpoint pen manufacturer (once he has designed a functional pen) must also design it so that it is distinctive and connotes either elegance and wealth or practicality, masculinity or femininity, boldness or delicacy. The style together with the functional aspects determine the product's competitiveness.

For some manufacturers the objectives of style design are incorporated into *package design*. Package design deals with the container which holds the product. The package for such products as breakfast food, cigarettes, and aspirin, to name a few examples, is the only place where distinctiveness and aesthetic value can be added to the product.

Functional and style design are equally important aspects of product design. Both help assure the manufacturer that his product will competitively satisfy consumers' demands. Certain types of raw material may be needed so that the finished good can both perform its intended functions and yet be stylish. The raw material which will meet these requirements could have a huge impact on actual manufacturing operations. For example, metal and plastic cases for the ballpoint pen would present two completely different sets of manufacturing problems. Both functional and style design decisions greatly affect manufacturing operations and methods.

## MANUFACTURING OPERATIONS AND METHODS DESIGN

The manufacturer who knows what the product must do and look like next turns his attention to designing those operations and methods that will transform inputs into the desired product design. Manufacturing operations and methods are designed to bring together the men, materials, and machinery necessary to manufacture the product. The most important and complex aspect of manufacturing operations and methods design is plant layout. In laying out the plant, the manufacturer plans for the proper position and utilization of men, equipment, and materials. The primary objective here is to arrange the machines, men, and materials so that maximum value is created through manufacturing operations. A controlling factor in plant layout is whether the manufacturing operations are intermittent or continuous. This affects both the layout of the plant and the types of machinery to be used in the manufacturing efforts.

The intermittent manufacturing operations of custom or job order shops, utilize general-purpose machinery. For example, in a machine shop, general purpose lathes and drill presses are used because of their wide adaptability to a variety of situations. The varying types of jobs performed by intermittent manufacturers demand flexibility both in equipment and plant layout. The flexibility in plant layout is attained by employing a *functional,* or *process plant layout.* The men, materials, and machines are grouped on the basis of the functions or processes being performed. All equipment of the same functional type is grouped together. For example, all drill presses are grouped together. A process layout for a machine shop is illustrated in Exhibit 8–2. Note that a particular or single product does not control or dictate the layout of the plant and the position of the equipment. Products are not mentioned at all in this type of plant layout because the manufacturer must produce a great variety of products from raw materials. The different processes (grinding, milling, and

EXHIBIT 8–2

*Process Layout*

| Forges | Millers | Lathes | |
|--------|---------|--------|-------------------------------|
| | | | Finished product storage |
| Saws | Grinders | Drill presses | |
| Raw material storage | | | |

so forth) form the basic divisions of the plant. Raw materials will take various paths through the plant, depending on the nature of the finished product. One order, for example, may require raw materials to move from the sawing to lathes and to finished goods storage. Another might require a completely different pattern of movement. In this example of product movement, flexibility is guaranteed. This flexibility is the chief advantage of the process plant layout. The utilization of general-purpose machinery and the process layout enables the machine shop manufacturer to retain the flexibility which intermittent manufacturing operations usually demand.

Continuous manufacturing operations of mass production industries utilize a number of special-purpose machines. The auto industry uses many examples of special-purpose machinery, such as five-headed air wrenches that tighten the lug nuts on car wheels. The high volume and standardized products justify the special-purpose machines. The *product plant layout* is best suited for continuous manufacturing operations. The men, machines, and materials are arranged according to the sequence of operations required to produce a specific product. Since only one or a limited kind of products are manufactured, they dictate the way in which the plant is layed out. A product layout is schematically illustrated in Exhibit 8–3.

The sequence of operations required to produce product A determines the layout of the plant. Unlike the process layout where the products manufactured can take various paths through the plant, in the product layout plant, product A takes only one path. The machinery is placed at the proper points along this path. Unlike the process plant layout where all the same type of equipment is grouped together, in the product plant layout the same type of equipment

EXHIBIT 8–3

*Product Layout*

| Raw material storage | Stamping process | Welders | Assemblers | Painters | Finish sanders | Finished product storage |
|---|---|---|---|---|---|---|
| | Ⓐ | | | | | ▶ |

may be placed at many points along the path the raw materials take. The flexibility needed by the intermittent manufacturer is replaced by the continuous manufacturer's demands for high volume production of a specific, single, standardized product. This high volume is necessary to justify the large investment in special-purpose equipment.

It is not uncommon to find a combination of process and product layouts in a given plant. In mass production industries such as automobiles, the assembly function often uses a product layout while such functions as maintenance and repair are arranged according to a process layout. The nature of the product manufactured is the controlling factor. If there are a number of different products, a plant layout which provides for a high degree of flexibility is desirable; such flexibility is realized through the utilization of a process plant layout. However, if the product is standardized, flexibility in plant layout is unimportant. Speed in manufacturing is the important factor. The product plant layout design allows for special-purpose machinery to be set up in a fixed pattern, thus increasing the speed of production. Speed is probably the single most important factor for the continuous manufacturer.

### Control of Manufacturing Operations

Designing manufacturing operations and methods is only part of the manufacturer's job. The other part involves setting in motion a system of control to assure that those manufacturing operations are performing at the level and way they were intended. The manufacturer's control system centers around two areas: manufacturing planning and control and quality control.

### MANUFACTURING PLANNING AND CONTROL

Manufacturing planning and control represents the nerve system of the manufacturer's operations. The purpose of these activities is to insure that the goods are manufactured on time and in accordance with a set standard. Depending on the type of manufacturing operations, one of two types of control systems can be used—**order control** and **flow control.** *Order control* is the most common type of manufacturing control and is used in businesses with intermittent manufacturing operations. Intermittent manufacturing is characterized by a job shop employing general-purpose machinery and process plant layout.

Because orders come into the shop for different quantities of different products, manufacturing planning must be based on the individual order, thus the title **order control.** When an order is received the businessman determines (1) the quantity and quality of the raw materials and parts which will be necessary to fill the order and (2) the series of operations which will be required to complete the manufacturing of that order. For the intermittent manufacturer these two factors can be different for each order. Once these two factors have been determined, a schedule can be developed.

Developing a schedule for each order entails determining the time requirements for completing the order. It sets forth when particular manufacturing operations should be performed. In developing a schedule, the manufacturer works backwards in time from the date the finished product must be delivered. The manufacturer seeks answers to these questions: how long will the manufacture–assembly process take? What is the manufacturing capacity of particular machines and departments which will be responsible for completing the order? How far ahead are these departments, machines, and their operators booked up? How long does it take to procure the necessary raw materials and purchased parts? How long does it take to buy any additional tooling? How many raw materials and parts are already in inventory and therefore do not need to be made or purchased? What is the priority of the order under consideration?

Answers to these and similar questions allow the manufacturer to schedule the dates on which orders should be placed for purchased parts, raw materials, and tools, when parts manufacturing should commence, and when final assembly should be started. These are all elements of a well thought-out schedule. If the order is kept on this schedule, every aspect of the manufacturing operation will be on time and the final delivery date will be met. The final step is to put these plans and time schedules into operation by issuing *work orders.* Work orders instruct employees what to do and when to do it. If the work orders are followed, the schedule will be met and thus the order completed on time. When a work order or a scheduled event is not completed on time, the manufacturer will have to make adjustments in the schedule. Such adjustments will balance the unforeseen slowdowns and allow the order to be completed either close to or on time. The schedule is the key under an order control system. Poorly thought out schedules, or unrealistic schedules which cannot be met, give the intermittent manufacturer little control over his operations. In addition, as guaranteed order dates go unfilled due to poor scheduling, consumer satisfaction and the number of new orders the manufacturer receives are likely to decrease.

**Flow control** is used by businesses with continuous manufacturing operations. The manufacturing planning and control procedures used by the intermittent manufacturer are not necessary for continuous manufacturing operations. For the continuous manufacturer scheduling is not a problem. Unlike the intermittent manufacturer, each order involves the same raw materials and sequence of operation. The raw materials, parts, and sequence of operations are predetermined and standardized. An order control system therefore is not applicable.

Even issuing work orders to employees is not necessary; because they do not do a variety of jobs, but do the same specialized tasks every day. The continuous manufacturer does not control each order; instead he controls the entire flow of raw materials through the various manufacturing operations, thus, the title *flow control*. It is similar to controlling the flow of water from a faucet. Once it is turned on, the water flows in only one direction. Therefore control is mainly concerned with regulating the speed at which the water will flow. How fast the water is allowed to flow is dependent upon how much is needed during a given time. So it is with the control exercised by the continuous manufacturer. The speed of the manufacturing flow is determined by the number of finished products needed during a time period. The main control problem the continuous manufacturer must solve is determining how many units of the standardized product to produce to put into inventory for future orders. This number determines the speed at which the manufacturing efforts should flow. Once this determination is made, manufacturing planning and control centers around two activities. First, enough raw materials and supplies need to be on hand to keep the manufacturing efforts going at the speed required to produce the predetermined number of units. Second, the rate at which the product is manufactured needs to be set so that the required number of products will be produced. This second activity involves keeping the manufacturing operation running efficiently.

Even though continuous manufacturing operations require simpler manufacturing and control than intermittent manufacturing operations, the importance of this function is not diminished. The extensive amount of preplanning and control necessary should be evident when you consider that many continuous manufacturers operate around the clock, seven days a week, never stopping except for periodic equipment overhauls. This level of operation requires detailed manufacturing planning and control.

## QUALITY CONTROL

Manufacturing planning and control concentrates on synchronizing those activities which convert raw materials into finished goods. In **quality control,** the emphasis is on seeing that the finished goods will meet a desired specification or quality level. While manufacturing planning and control involve keeping raw materials moving through the manufacturing operations, quality control concentrates on keeping the quality of the finished product up to a desired level.

Quality levels are met by inspection. Through periodic checking and measuring before, during, and after various manufacturing operations, the quality level set for the product can be achieved. Before a quality inspection program can be initiated two questions must be resolved: first, when should inspection occur, and second, what needs to be inspected.

The first question, when should inspection occur, concentrates on defining at which points during the manufacturing operations product quality should be evaluated or inspected. At a minimum two inspection points should be built into most manufacturing operations. First, raw materials should be inspected to see that they meet the necessary quality and quantity requirements. This inspection point was discussed in chapter 7 as the last step in the procurement activities. The second inspection should occur at the end of the manufacturing operations before the products are shipped to consumers. These are the minimum inspection points. Building in inspection points during the actual manufacturing operations is also wise. These inspection points should allow quality problems to be spotted and corrected before the product is finished. But how many inspection points during the manufacturing operations are necessary? To inspect at all possible points in the manufacturing operations would be too costly. Employing quality inspectors and slowing down manufacturing operations for inspection both cost money, which can be justified only if product quality is improved because of its expenditure. Each manufacturer should analyze his own manufacturing operations. If during an operation any of the following three events occur, it would be wise to inspect *before* this event:

(1) If the product enters into a costly operation. Inspection at this point insures that the product is free from fault before the heavy expense of the process is added.

(1) If an irreversible operation occurs. Usually this goes hand in hand with expense. Expensive operations are usually irreversible. For example, there would be no reason to go ahead and gold plate a piece of jewelry if the basic design had a flaw in it. This operation is expensive and irreversible. *Before* it is performed, the design should be inspected.

(3) If a manufacturing operation could cover previous manufacturing defects. The assembly of parts may hide certain internal parts. In these cases it is easier to check those internal parts before they are covered from view. For instance, it is easier to inspect the pistons of an engine before they are put into the engine than after, when they cannot be seen, let alone inspected.

Inspection points before any of these three events can save the manufacturer money and headaches. Poor quality spotted before any one of these three events occurs makes it easier and cheaper to rectify. An adjustment at this point is minor when compared to what would be required to correct faulty quality once any of these three events had taken place.

The second question, how much to inspect, deals with the quantity of products inspected at each inspection point. After the decision has been made concerning the points at which inspection should occur, this second problem can be solved.

The quantity inspected can either be 100 percent or only a sample of the total items passing the inspection station. Complete 100 percent inspection is expensive and only occurs when there is a chance for large variation in quality or where the risks of poor quality are great. Manual labor (as compared to machine labor) allows for human error in output, and thus large quality variations. An extreme example illustrates this point. A craftsman will not do the same job twice in exactly the same way. The quality of the final product will vary each time he does the job. Those operations which require manual labor are likely candidates for extensive inspection. Total inspection would also occur when the risk of unacceptable quality is high. The aerospace industry is a good example of high risk attached to product quality. A malfunction in an airplane or missile would cause a disaster. The cost of inspection in this example is outweighed by the costs of a malfunction.

Due to the high cost of 100 percent inspection, most manufacturers inspect only a sample of the total items at each inspection station. Sample inspection is most widely applied when machines are incorporated into the manufacturing procedures. Samples can be relied upon because machines keep human errors and quality variations to a minimum. The products are highly uniform in terms of quality. It is therefore safe to assume that if one unit out of every 100 units passing an inspection point meets the quality specifications, the other 99 are of the same quality. The assumption is usually safe, considering the reliability of today's machinery. Were it not a safe assumption, inspection would have to revert to the costly 100 percent method. Sample inspection techniques are also used when a large quantity of bulk items are to be inspected. For bulk items, 100 percent inspection is impossible. In this situation samples are accurate indicators of the total product's overall quality. Examples of bulk items include vats of beer, carloads of grain, and tankloads of liquid products. Sampling is really the only feasible method of inspecting these bulk items.

Product quality is maintained through inspection. The manufacturer must be selective in determining the number of inspection points and the quantity of items to inspect at each point. There is no general answer; for each situation, the manufacturer needs to weigh the cost of inspection against the loss of business and company good name defective goods could create. Quality inspection in these terms is an investment made to maintain consumers' satisfaction with the product's performance.

## Summary

The manufacturer is concerned with one type of production—the transformation of raw materials into finished goods. Depending on the intensity of demand and nature of the raw materials, manufacturing efforts can either be intermittent or continuous. However, regardless of the type, there are two general problems the manufacturer faces in reaching his objectives. The first problem centers around the manufacturing operations themselves and deals with the areas of product design and operation design. The second problem focuses on the planning and control necessary to insure that the goods are manufactured within a specified time and meet a predetermined quality standard. Exhibit 8–4 summarizes the problems and possible solutions facing all manufacturers. Every manufacturer is concerned with designing a competitive product. Therefore all manufacturers need to evaluate what the consumers want and what their competitors are doing in the areas of product design. From this evaluation a product can be designed which will be both functional and stylish. The manufacturing operations and control procedures set in motion to produce this product will differ depending on the type of manufacturer. As indicated in Exhibit 8–4, the

EXHIBIT 8–4

*Problems and Possible Solutions*
*Facing the Manufacturer*

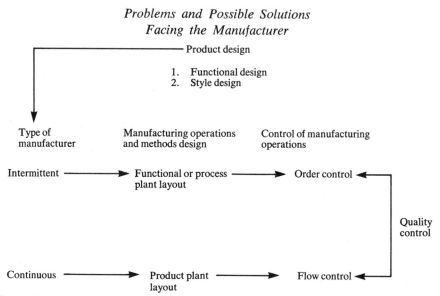

intermittent manufacturer would probably find that the process plant layout and order control systems fit his situation best. The continuous manufacturer would most likely find that the product plant layout and flow control systems best fit his particular situation. Thus, depending on the type of manufacturing operation, certain alternative solutions to the problems facing all manufacturers appear better than others. These alternatives are presented in the diagram, along with the area of quality control. Quality control is an area all manufacturers, regardless of type, need to be concerned about. The focus now will be redirected to applying manufacturing ideas and concepts to increasing the efficiency of the total production process.

## Manufacturing and the Production Process

The manufacturer creates value by transforming raw materials into finished goods. These finished goods are either sold to consumers or utilized in the manufacture of other goods. Businesses other than manufacturing also create value and are thus involved in some sort of production. The concepts used by manufacturers can be applied to all businesses, especially those creating a service. Nonmanufacturing businesses can thus improve their production efficiency by utilizing some of the concepts manufacturers have so highly refined. The production process was illustrated in the following diagram:

Acquisition of inputs ─────► Processing of inputs ─────► Completed outputs

This diagram applies to all businesses: services, wholesalers, retailers, and manufacturers. The manufacturer processes inputs. He concerns himself with the layout of facilities, the flow of inputs through the plant, and the control over manufacturing operations to achieve the maximum utilization of men, equipment, and materials. All those engaged in providing goods and services be concerned with similar events.

As an extreme example, consider a hospital. The output of the hospital's production process is a service, medical care to those in need. The inputs are patients requiring the medical care. These inputs are processed or transformed through a series of steps. Each of these steps is different for different illnesses. To accomplish a given series of steps, a number of other inputs must be procurred and utilized. Examples of these inputs would be medical personnel, specialized equipment, rooms, lights, nurses, and other support personnel. Like the manufacturer, the hospital administrator must determine how to design his product to be competitive with other hospitals. Such factors as building appearance, general reputation, and so on would be included in the hospitals product design. Additionally he needs a proper layolt of facilities: obstetrics on one floor, X-ray on another floor, a certain number of nurses per floor, etc. The flow of inputs (patients) through receiving, general examination rooms, intensive care, and a control system for the entire process with time schedules, equipment checks, instructions, and so on must be developed. The production process of the hospital can utilize many of the manufacturing concepts discussed in this chapter. In fact, using the discussion of manufacturing operations, hospitals can be classified as intermittent manufacturing operations. Thus a process plant layout and a control system similar to an order control system and scheduling could increase efficiency in creating the output—medical care. Since all businesses have a production process the manufacturing concepts of product and operation design and scheduling and quality control can and should be applied to increase their effectiveness in transforming inputs into outputs. The elements of the production process can be expanded into the following general production diagram.

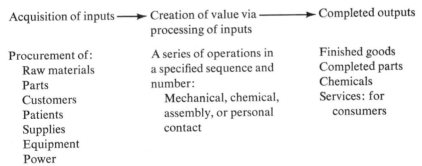

| Acquisition of inputs | → Creation of value via → processing of inputs | Completed outputs |
|---|---|---|
| Procurement of: <br> Raw materials <br> Parts <br> Customers <br> Patients <br> Supplies <br> Equipment <br> Power | A series of operations in a specified sequence and number: <br> Mechanical, chemical, assembly, or personal contact | Finished goods <br> Completed parts <br> Chemicals <br> Services: for <br> consumers |

The inputs may be raw materials, paper work, people, or anything the particular business needs to create value. The creation of value occurs once these inputs have been assembled. Inputs flow through a specified sequence and number of operations. The result is the completion of outputs, or finished products and services. Although the production process varies with different industries and businesses, every business has a production process. The concepts developed by manufacturers can be applied to increase the efficiency with which the production process is performed. Manufacturers have refined their production process to such an extent that it approaches a science. What is proposed here is that other businesses can apply manufacturing techniques to increase their efficiency in transforming inputs into outputs.

## The Production Process in Retrospect

All business systems perform the basic function of production. Value is created in the form of a competitive good or service. To create this good or service every businessman is concerned with that series of events entitled the production process: the procurement and transformation of inputs into competitive outputs, goods, or services.

The production process transforms what the businessman feels to be a competitive idea into a tangible good or service. In doing so the funds generated by the financial process are spent on equipment, materials, supplies, and inventories in the hopes of generating the income necessary to maintain the system.

The production process results in finished goods and services which must be promoted, sold, and distributed. This process is vital for all businesses and links the financial and distribution processes together. The distribution process picks up where the production process ends and is the subject matter of the next section.

## QUESTIONS

1. What is the relationship between the production process and manufacturing?
2. How does the intermittent manufacturer differ from the continuous manufacturer?
3. For each of the following products, indicate whether the intermittent or the continuous manufacturing concepts would be utilized:
   (a) Chemicals
   (b) Cigarettes
   (c) Motion pictures
   (d) Automobiles
   (e) Homes
   (f) Dairy products
   (g) Airplanes
   (h) Car repairs
   (i) Pizzas
   (j) Preparation of tax returns by a public accountant
4. All manufacturing efforts are similar. Explain how.
5. What is the difference between the following pairs?
   (a) Functional and style product design
   (b) Process and product layout
   (c) Order control and flow control
   (d) 100 percent quality inspection and sampling quality inspection
6. Determining when to inspect products as they are processed through the various operations is often a judgment which the manufacturer must make. However,

certain events are signals to the manufacturer that inspection should take place prior to these events. List three such events. Explain why inspection may be beneficial before each of them.

7. Using the concepts of manufacturing, evaluate and offer suggestions for improving any one of the following production processes.
   (a) The student union on campus
   (b) A local bank
   (c) The business curriculum and scheduling at your school

## Incident 8–1

### THE PIT

A midwestern university with an enrollment of about 10,000 students has in operation a sandwich–snack bar called The Pit. Customers range from students who do not like the offering at the school's cafeteria or just want a snack, to secretaries, professors, and other university personnel who buy their breakfast, lunch, dinner, or snacks at The Pit.

The Pit's layout is illustrated in Exhibit 8–5. Customers find an open space at the counter and place their order with one of twelve female employees. The employee then fills the entire order, whether it be for candy, ice cream, hamburger, coke, hot dog, or potato chips. She collects the money, makes change, and then waits on another customer. During lunch hours it is not uncommon to find customers three and four rows deep all along the counter. Getting waited on during these times becomes a matter of strategy.

The manager, Mr. Cotter, has noted that sales have remained constant over the years, even though student enrollment and the number of university personnel has increased. In addition, the level of sales is below what comparable-size universities with similar operations are experiencing.

Mr. Cotter feels that The Pit should be rearranged to get the best possible flow of customers and workers. Since all the equipment is fixed in place, he really does not know how to accomplish a rearrangement without incurring a large expense.

(1) What are the advantages and disadvantages of the present facility layout?
(2) What types of new layouts would you recommend and why? What are each of the advantages and disadvantages?
(3) If only $1,000 can be spent on the rearrangement, what recommendation would you make?

EXHIBIT 8–5
*The Pit's Layout*

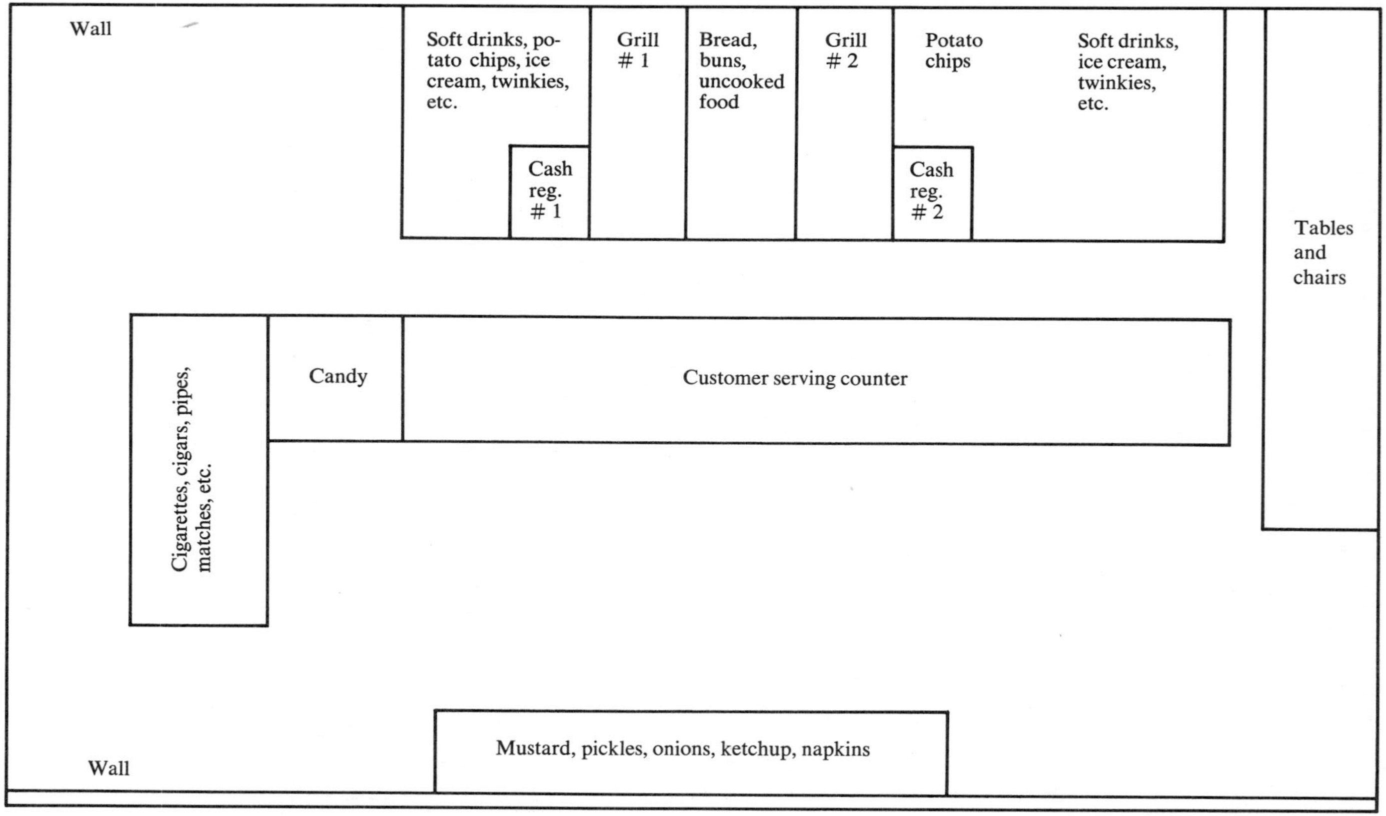

| | | | | | |
|---|---|---|---|---|---|
| Soft drinks, potato chips, ice cream, twinkies, etc. | Grill #1 | Bread, buns, uncooked food | Grill #2 | Potato chips | Soft drinks, ice cream, twinkies, etc. |

Cash reg. #1

Cash reg. #2

Tables and chairs

Customer serving counter

Candy

Cigarettes, cigars, pipes, matches, etc.

Mustard, pickles, onions, ketchup, napkins

Wall

Wall

# IV

# THE DISTRIBUTION PROCESS

The creation of value, or the production of goods and services, is only the beginning. Unless these goods or services are bought they really have no value to the business. For the goods or services created by the business to be bought they must be distributed. In this section the distribution process—that series of events or activities necessary to move goods or services from the point of production to the consumer—will be discussed.

Goods or services are distributed or moved from producer to consumer in two ways. First, the businessman physically moves or transports the goods or services *to* the consumer; and second, the consumer can create a movement *from* the producer by continually demanding goods or services. The businessman needs to concern himself with both types of movements. The physical movement or transportation of the goods or services is totally controllable by the businessman and makes the goods or services available to the consumer. Once available, however, the goods or services must be moved by or bought by the consumer. This movement can only be partially influenced by the businessman. He can exert some influence through the decisions he makes about the nature of the product itself, the price of the product, and the promotional efforts behind the product. The activities involved in moving goods or services from producers to consumers and the relationship of the distribution process to the business can be diagrammed as follows:

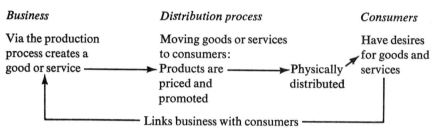

*Business*                          *Distribution process*                        *Consumers*

Via the production          Moving goods or services          Have desires
process creates a            to consumers:                            for goods and
good or service ──────► Products are ──────►Physically  services
                                     priced and                          distributed
                                     promoted

                                     ── Links business with consumers ──

   The distribution process links the business with the consumer and is central to the business' survival. Through the distribution process the businessman is attempting to influence the consumer to buy, in sufficient quantity, his output. Before the consumer can be influenced he must be understood. The presentation of the distribution process thus starts with the consumer and then discusses the activities involved in moving the good or service from producer to consumer. The distribution process will be discussed in the following four chapters: Chapter 9, Distribution, the Marketplace, and the Consumer; Chapter 10, The Distribution Process: Product, Price, and Availability; Chapter 11, Promotion of the Product, and Chapter 12, Physical Distribution.

# 9

# Distribution, the Marketplace, and the Consumer

The efficient movement of goods and services from producers to consumers is so much a part of our lives that we take it for granted. The thought of pulling into a gas station and being told that they are temporarily out of gas never used to cross most people's minds. And yet the gas stations which are out of gas have become a part of life. Another expectation is going to a food store and finding exactly what you want on the shelf in the size and price range you are looking for. Whenever we need something, the solution is simply to go to one type of store or service establishment and buy it. Our attitude is that if consumers want something, and have a sufficient amount of money, they should be able to buy it, whether it is a car, loaf of bread, pair of shoes, or dinner. To meet this seemingly simple demand of consumers requires that businesses are involved in a very complex process for the distribution of their goods or services. The complexity of moving goods and services from producers to consumers increases when business is conducted throughout the U.S. on a national level. A moment's thought on the problems a business like Sears and Roebuck faces in just making sure particular goods are always available in the right quantity, quality, and variety in all of its stores throughout the country will point out the complexity of the distribution process.

The distribution process—in fact the whole business system—centers around an important point developed in chapter 1: successful businesses respond to consumer wants and needs. In this chapter the consumer will be discussed to better understand what these wants and needs are. In our economy the consumer is at center stage. That is, his wants and needs are of prime importance to the businessman. The importance of the consumer is seen in the relationship of the distribution process to the total business system.

## The Distribution Process and the Business System

If there were no sales, there would be no business. Because the distribution process ends with the sale of goods or services to consumers, it therefore can be seen as the most important process of the business system. There are those people who present such an argument. However, just as valid an argument could be made for *any* of the other processes of the business system. For example, if the business could not be financed or the goods could not be produced, the business would not exist. Therefore, the financial, or maybe the production process is the most important one to the business system, depending on your point of view. Such arguments are of course futile. All the processes are important to the business' continued existence. Every one must be performed efficiently for the business to reach its objectives.

What then is the perspective, importance, or role of the distribution process in the business system? How does the distribution process relate and interrelate with the other processes of the business system? Distribution is one of the three primary processes (finance and production are the other two) performed by all business. Diagrammatically, the relationships of these three primary processes are shown in Exhibit 9–1.

Every potential businessman starts with an idea of what he can do in terms of fulfilling unfilled consumer needs. A business is then established and financed to accomplish this central purpose or realize this idea. Raw materials, equipment, and other inputs are purchased and a production process is set in motion to transform the ideas and raw materials into finished goods or services. These finished goods or services are next distributed to consumers, who hopefully will buy the good or service. If they do, the sales dollars can be used to finance future production and equipment expenditures. A level of sales tells the businessman his idea or central purpose is in line with present consumer needs, for customers only buy those products which will fulfill their specific need. Sales also indicate to the businessman that his distribution process (price, promotion, and physical movement of goods) has been accepted by the consumer.

A business meeting consumer needs through effectively performing the financial, production, and distribution processes, as outlined in Exhibit 9–1, is likely to be successful. But consumer needs are constantly changing. The clothing you bought four years ago, for example, is not likely to satisfy your needs today. As the diagram indicates, consumer needs must be taken into account both *before* and *after* the three primary processes are initiated. Thus, as consumer

## EXHIBIT 9–1

### *Three Primary Functions of the Business*

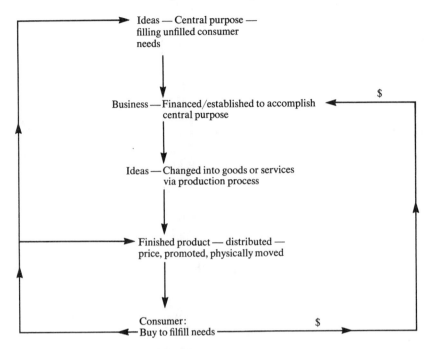

needs change so too must the financial, production, and distribution processes change to take account of the new and different consumer needs.

The relationships between these three primary functions are so close that it is hard to separate them. The businessman does not just make financial decisions, or production decisions, or distribution decisions. He makes business decisions realizing that financial considerations will affect the performance of the production process (e.g., how much capital to spend on equipment) and the distribution process (what price will allow a desired level of profits). Distribution considerations will also affect the performance of the financial process (how much to pay salesmen) and the production process (how much inventory will be required). The same can be said for the production process as it relates to the financial and distribution processes. Decisions made in one process will have an effect on the performance of the other primary processes. The decisions made in the area of distribution will have an impact on the performance of the financial and production processes. Keep this in mind as you read this section on the distribution process. It is important to remember that the three processes are so related that a poor job done in one of the three affects the other two. No single process can compensate for a poor job done in another. Distribution cannot, for example, make up for a poor job done in production, any more than a well-financed business can make up for poor product quality.

In Sections II and III the ways the financial and production processes can be performed effectively have been discussed. If a businessman has a good idea (an unfilled consumer want), the financial problem can be overcome. Similarly, due to our level of technology, a production process can be designed to make just about anything. However, a problem that is not so automatically solved is distributing the good or service that is produced. Many a product or service which would fulfill a need fails to sell because of a poor distribution process. The good can be the best around; but if it is sitting in a warehouse with consumers unaware that it exists, it is worthless.

Having discussed the first problem faced by a businessman—how to finance a business—as well as the second problem—how to produce a good or service —we now turn to the third problem area—how to distribute this good or service. The third problem is just as important as the first or second. Before the businessman can set in motion a process for distributing his goods or services, he first must understand the type of situation he will face in "the market."

## The Market

The concept of the **market** is a carryover from before the Industrial Revolution. The market was wherever people gathered—a town square, a fair, a street. It was customary for the businessman to take his pushcart full of goods to the market. The consumer also went to the market to buy certain goods or services. Although the picture of a group of sellers and buyers haggling over prices is far removed from the ultramodern shopping centers of today, the term *market* is still applied to both. The same two groups are necessary to make up a market—businessmen with goods and services to sell and consumers with money to spend on the goods and services they want.

But today, rather than talking about all consumers or all businesses, specific markets can be defined, such as the automobile market, the food market, or the clothing market. Within each of these markets is a relatively set number of consumers and businesses. Every consumer in the market has at least one thing in common: they all want the same type of product. Every business in this market also has one thing in common: they are all competing for the specific consumer's dollars. They compete by offering consumers variations on the same product. For example, there are countless variations of automobiles and shoes. A simplified version of a given market can be visualized as in Exhibit 9–2. In this figure eight businesses are trying to influence the consumer to buy their specific product. This situation could apply to products from hats to steak dinners to gasoline. For sake of illustration, assume the product is beer.

If all beer drinkers are represented by the consumers in the middle of Exhibit 9–2, each of the eight businesses producing beer may ( 1 ) reason that one-eighth of the consumers will buy their product, or ( 2 ) try to develop a competitive edge over the other seven and sell beer to *more* than one-eighth of the beer consumers. If alternative ( 2 ) is achieved, then naturally the success of one occurs either at the expense of lost sales to one or all seven of the other beer producers or through encouraging *more* people to drink beer than formerly did. In fact, most businesses are trying to achieve alternative ( 2 ).

## EXHIBIT 9–2

### *The Market*

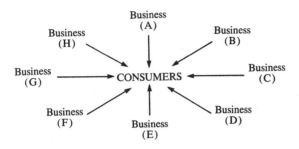

But, since the products are basically the same, that is, beer is beer, how can one producer or business gain a competitive edge over the other seven? Businesses compete on the basis of product, price, promotion, and availability of the product. These elements are, in fact, the distribution process. Businesses compete or gain a competitive edge over others in a market, then, through their distribution process. Every business in the U.S. offers consumers some combination of products, prices, promotional efforts, and availability. The combinations are too numerous to mention but the end results are always the same —either you are competitive in the market or you are not. If you are not, then as a business, you have to alter one or all of the elements in the distribution process to get competitive or go out of business.

In the example, business A may offer consumers a high quality beer at a lower price and in more places than any of the other seven competitors. Or, business B might promote more than any of the other seven. Sales indicate how well they have competed in the market, the success of their total distribution efforts.

To be competitive, the businessman can alter the parts of the distribution process–product, price, promotion efforts, and product availability. How these four elements are combined and accepted by the consumer determines how successful the distribution efforts have been. The consumer will dictate to the businessman how these four elements of the distribution process can be combined for optimum success. Thus, the first question the businessman must ask is what is the market, or who are the consumers?

### Who Are Consumers?

A **consumer** is an individual having a specific definable desire with the economic ability and motivation to satisfy this desire. In other words, a consumer is someone willing to spend his money on the things that he wants. Thus, everyone at one time or another is or will be a consumer for certain goods or services. Everyone will sometime have the desire, money, and motivation to buy, for example, a hamburger, pair of shoes, or car. However, not everyone will be a consumer for all goods or services. Everyone may have the desire for a Rolls

Royce but few people will have the money or motivation to spend this much money for one automobile.

Thus, rather than talking about all consumers, the businessman needs to know who are his *potential consumers*. In other words, who are the people who possess the three key elements that define them as consumers of *his* good or service: the desire for the specific good or service, the money, and the motivation to spend this money on the specific product. If any of the three are lacking, the individual may be a consumer but not a potential consumer as far as the particular businessman is concerned. For example, a vegetarian is a potential consumer for many goods and services. But if the businessman owns a restaurant which serves only steaks, the vegetarian is not a potential consumer.

Probably one of the most important jobs the businessman faces is defining who exactly his potential consumers are. His whole distribution process is geared toward satisfying these potential consumers. If he does not know who they are, what they want, and what characteristics they have, his attempts at designing a competitive distribution process will at best be weak.

A businessman's specific market is the sum of all his potential consumers, where the businessman competes with others for a share of the consumers' purchase dollars. Each business competes in this market by developing what is felt to be a competitive distribution process. Return to the beer producers illustration. How each of the eight beer producers goes about defining who their potential consumers are and what they want will directly affect their distribution process and thus how competitive each will be. Let's concentrate on only two of the eight beer producers, producers A and B.

Beer producer A defines his market as anyone over age eighteen. In this definition he has assumed all potential beer consumers' desires are the same. He distributes his beer in six packs to all liquor stores in the U. S., wth a suggested price of $2.00. His promotional efforts consist of salesmen calling on and stocking liquor stores and advertisements on the radio. His market or potential consumer definition has not been very precise and thus neither is his distribution process. He has blanketed the total market with one product which he hopes will fulfill everyone's desires. How competitive he will be, of course, can only be estimated. However, let us contrast him with beer producer B.

Beer producer B initially defines his market as anyone over age eighteen. But he feels that within this large number a definable number of potential consumer groups can be identified, each group having needs peculiar to that group. He defines three groups within this market: (1) beer consumers in bars, taverns, and restaurants; (2) beer consumers between the ages of 18 and 30; (3) beer consumers with incomes exceeding $20,000 per year. Each of these three is a market within the total market of beer consumers. The point is that consumers in each market may have specific desires around which a specific distribution process must be developed. The tavern market may require beer to be in bottles, cans, and barrels for tap service and may need special advertising display material. The 18 to 30 age market may have different tastes, wanting a malt liquor along with conventional beer; whereas those consumers whose income exceeds $20,000 may prefer a higher priced premium quality beer. Each of the three markets would require a special product and promotional efforts designed solely for the consumers in that market. These are but a few of the effects on producer B's distribution process and competitive position this further definition of the market would have. The two producers are contrasted in Exhibit 9–3.

### EXHIBIT 9–3

*A Comparison of Distribution Processes*

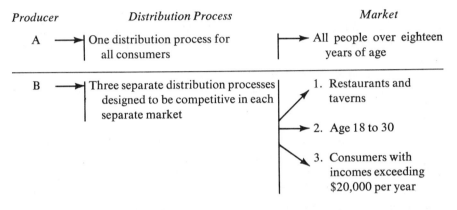

Since producer B has defined each market he can tailor the distribution process to each specific market. He will be in a better competitive position in each market as well as the total beer market than producer A is because he is meeting specific consumer demands.

Businessmen must be very careful in defining who exactly their consumers are. These consumers will be able to be grouped in specific categories. Each category will have specific needs and desires which the businessman must cater to via his distribution process. Some general classifications of consumers can be developed. Two such classifications are industrial consumers and ultimate consumers, each of which has its own peculiar needs.

### INDUSTRIAL CONSUMERS

Industrial consumers buy goods or services for use either in their operations or for reprocessing into other products. The industrial market includes other businesses and institutions such as banks, hotels, restaurants, governmental agencies, schools, hospitals, and prisons. As consumers of finished products we tend to forget the industrial market or minimize its importance to our economy. But approximately 53 percent of all wholesale sales is in industrial goods.[1]

Industrial consumers buy three types of goods: (1) capital goods, such as physical plant and equipment to be used in the production of other goods, which do not become a part of the goods produced. Such items as factories,

---

1. Ralph S. Alexander, James S. Cross, and Ross M. Cunningham, *Industrial Marketing.* Homewood, Ill.: Richard D. Irwin, Inc., 1956.

production machinery, furniture, and fixtures would be included in this category; (2) components and materials which become part of the final product produced. Such items as tires, batteries, and spark plugs are components purchased by the auto industry, while lumber is a material purchased by furniture manufacturers; (3) supplies which include goods bought to help in the production process. They usually do not become part of the finished good, but are used up in production. Such items as lubricating oil for equipment and office stationery would be included in this group of industrial goods.

The businessman whose market is wholly made up of or includes some industrial consumers needs to be aware of certain distinctive characteristics of this market, characteristics which will ultimately affect the business distribution process. The following characteristics are particular to industrial consumers:

(1)  A high concentration of buyers,

(2)  A high average value of sales,

(3)  Technical-service requirements of buyers.

*High Concentration of Buyers.*    The industrial consumer market is highly concentrated from two standpoints. First, the number of industrial consumers is much smaller than ultimate consumers. Whereas all ultimate consumers buy clothing, only a few textile manufacturers buy yarn and textile machinery. Second, industrial consumers are concentrated geographically, around the larger cities in the U. S.; while ultimate consumers are dispersed throughout the country.

*High Value of Sales.*    Industrial goods are usually purchased in large quantities, for example, a trainload of corn or tons of iron ore. They may have a high unit value, such as $500,000 for a steel press or $400,000 for a computer. Thus one sale may frequently amount to several thousand dollars or much more.

*Technical-Service Requirements of Buyers.*    The computer is an excellent example of the technical complexity of industrial goods. Many industrial consumers also have highly technical demands. For example, a manufacturer might require a machine custom-built specifically for his purposes. The businessman must then be involved in the technical design of a one of a kind piece of equipment. Or an industrial consumer may need technical advice on which grade of lubricant would be best for his specific conditions. These are all examples of the complexity, both in form and application, of industrial goods.

In addition to the technical nature of the products, service is a critical demand of industrial consumers. If something goes wrong with a piece of equipment the industrial consumer wants the producing company to fix it immediately. If a computer is not working the way it should, the industrial consumer wants it to be either fixed or instructed on how it should be used. The relationship with the industrial consumer does not end with the sale of the product. Many industrial sales are made, in fact, because of the excellent reputation a business has for after-sale advice, assistance, and service.

## THE DISTRIBUTION PROCESS FOR INDUSTRIAL CONSUMERS

The three unique characteristics of industrial consumers dictate that in order for a company to be competitive in the market, the distribution process must be very direct and personal. Many industrial products are custom-made to the specifications of the buyer. Even when the industrial product is standardized (e.g., lubricating oil), the buyer must be educated in the application of the product. The businessman himself or his sales representative will personally contact industrial consumers to find out their specific needs. Since these consumers are highly concentrated geographically and in number, it is less difficult to contact the consumer personally. The need for after-sale service and advice also increases the need to develop a personal relationship between buyer and seller. The businessman can justify the cost of his or a salesman's time spent with each industrial consumer because of the large sums of money involved in each transaction.

These factors frequently mean that products, prices, promotional effort, and physical distribution are custom-made and personally determined for each industrial consumer. In the industrial market, personal selling and personal contact between seller and buyer is the central concept behind the distribution process.

## ULTIMATE CONSUMERS

Ultimate consumers buy goods or services for personal or household use. The ultimate and industrial consumer are different in many ways. First, as a group, the industrial consumers are relatively small in number whereas ultimate consumers can be anyone in the population. Although certain sections of the country have higher concentrations of population than others, the ultimate consumer is not geographically concentrated as the industrial consumer is. Second, the need for goods and services is a personal matter for the ultimate consumer. He alone determines how much meat, furniture, haircuts, clothing, and vacation he needs this year. The industrial consumer does not have this freedom. His production efforts dictate what kinds of goods and services he will buy. The ultimate consumer, then, has total freedom in deciding what he needs and which goods and services will satisfy those needs. This freedom of choice, coupled with a degree of individuality each person possesses, limits the generalizations that can be made about *all* consumers. However, there are two choices every ultimate consumer must make.

## THE CHOICES ULTIMATE CONSUMERS MUST MAKE

In the American economy, the ultimate consumer is free to buy anything he wants. However, as most people painfully know, the money available to buy goods and services is not unlimited. At any one time each consumer has a fixed amount of disposable income (income after taxes have been deducted). The first choice every consumer must make is how much of this disposable income to spend on goods and services, and how much to save. Most people want the security "money in the bank" or "saving for a rainy day" gives them. The proportion of disposable income consumers elect to spend is important for two reasons. First, the amount of current income spent along with access to credit determines the quantity of goods and services they will purchase. Second, the amount of money saved will affect the amount of future purchases that will be made.

The first thing to note is that consumers differ in the way they make this first choice of how much of their disposable income to spend on goods and services and how much to save. One factor affecting this choice is the consumer's age. As a generalization, younger consumers spend more of their income and save less. With increasing age comes the need to save and invest for future security. Businesses selling to younger consumers can be sure then that more of the income these consumers have will be spent on goods and services. Those businesses selling to older consumers, however, must compete not only with other businesses but with the consumer himself who spends less of his disposable income. An increase in savings has the same effect as decreasing the amount of disposable income consumers have. Both adversely affect the two criteria used to define consumers: available income and the motivation to spend it. Increases in savings decrease the amount of income available to spend on goods and services in the present. Although these savings may be used for future purchases, businesses must compete in the present for a smaller number of consumer dollars. Increases in savings also affect the consumer's motivation to spend money for certain goods or services. If savings increase or disposable income decreases for whatever reason, less money would be spent on luxury goods and services in general. Decreasing the consumer's available disposable income or motivation to spend this income will have a detrimental effect on a given business' distribution process.

In the U. S., increasing amounts of income will be available for the purchase of goods and services. Affluence is rapidly spreading over the country. By 1980 one-third of the households will reach or exceed an annual income of $15,000 (the current level of affluence).[2] Ultimate consumers will have more and more available disposable income to spend. But will they spend it? In the U. S., the public appears to be saving from 6 to 8 percent of disposable income. Since the rate of consumer savings appears to be constant, the increase in income will result in more disposable income being spent by consumers. This trend spells a bright future for U.S. businesses. The ultimate consumer is making and will continue to make his first choice to the benefit of the businessman. Consumers will increasingly have both the *ability* and the motivation to buy more goods and services.

Each consumer with a given amount of disposable income now faces a second choice: how do I spend this income? From a business standpoint this second choice must be analyzed from two directions. First, how do consumers allocate their income *across* certain categories of goods and services? Exhibit 9–4 indicates how the total populations in 1950 and 1970 made this allotment.

---

2. "Affluence Spreading over the U. S.—Findings of a New Study," *U. S. News and World Report,* Dec. 6, 1971, pp. 28–29.

The way consumers are making these decisions indicates whether certain markets are increasing, decreasing, or staying the same. For example, the percentage of income spent by the population on "recreation" was 5.8 percent in 1950 and 6.3 percent in 1970. If businessmen are attempting to discover and satisfy

EXHIBIT 9–4

*Personal Consumption Expenditures by Product*

|  | 1950 | 1970 |
| --- | --- | --- |
| Food, beverages, tobacco | 30.4% | 23.2% |
| Clothing, accessories, jewelry | 12.4 | 10.1 |
| Personal care | 1.3 | 1.6 |
| Housing | 11.1 | 14.8 |
| Household operations | 15.4 | 13.9 |
| Medical care | 4.6 | 7.7 |
| Personal business | 3.6 | 5.8 |
| Transportation | 12.9 | 12.6 |
| Recreation | 5.8 | 6.3 |
| Other | 2.4 | 3.9 |

Source: U.S. Department of Commerce, *Statistical Abstract of the United States, 1972,* 93rd ed. Washington, D.C.; U.S. Government Printing Office, 1972, p. 315.

consumer needs, they can study the expenditures across the categories of goods and services to understand which needs are growing, stagnating, changing, or decreasing in importance.

The second choice consumers must make needs to be analyzed from a second perspective: why do consumers spend their income the way they do *within* a given category? The businessman who is attempting to sell within the "clothing, accessories, and jewelry" category needs to know what styles and fashions consumers will be spending 10.1 percent of their incomes on. For the businessman who is competing in a *given market,* the factors that influence consumer spending within a given market are the important ones. He must ask what factors influence his ultimate consumers to act the way they do. Answers to this question will affect every element of the distribution process. The product, price, promotion, and availability of the product will be designed around the answer, to get the most favorable reaction from consumers in this market: sales for a given business.

Each consumer is an individual, thus making it difficult to generalize about all consumers' behavior within a given market. However, some of the factors which influence consumer choices *within* a given market can be identified.

## FACTORS INFLUENCING ULTIMATE CONSUMERS' CHOICES

No one factor can be identified as influencing the consumers' choice. Instead, many factors must be taken into consideration in trying to explain why one consumer buys a good or service, and another does not. Consumers themselves cannot, many times, explain all the factors that caused them to buy a particular good or service. The three types of influences which, when taken together, explain most reasons consumers behave the way they do are economic, environmental, and attitudinal.

*Economic Factors.* The amount of income and access to credit an individual has will affect his buying choices. Given the economic ability to consume certain goods and services, other economic factors will influence consumers in a given market. The price of a good and of competing goods is an economic consideration that may influence his decision. The price of a good or service is so important that part of Chapter 10 will be spent discussing it in detail.

In addition to price, other economic factors such as product durability, reliability, dependability, and expense of operation and repair may be important in influencing the consumer's choice. However, important as they are, economic factors are not the sole determinant of consumer behavior. The classic example in the U. S. is the automobile. If economic factors were the only influence in this decision, producers and consumers would be selling and buying vastly different types of automobiles than are on the road today. In fact, the Cadillac and Lincoln car owners probably do not give much consideration to economic factors. As with other products, economy of price and operation are only part of the reason people buy the goods or services that they do. Environmental and attitudinal factors also affect ultimate consumer choices.

*Environmental Factors.* In this category are those elements, personal and otherwise, that make up the environment in which the consumer lives. Included are such factors as the consumers' age, sex, marital status, and family size.

People of different age groups buy different products in varying quantities. The teenager spends a tremendous amount of money on records and certain types of clothing, but very little on houses, household furniture, and cars. Older, retired people, on the other hand, who may not even own a car, already have a house and furnishings, and demand very little in the way of clothing. The age of the consumer has a tremendous influence on the type of goods and services bought.

The demand for certain products is directly determined by the consumer's sex. Distributing goods or services to men is an almost completely different undertaking from distributing to women. For instance, men do not tend to buy in the same stores that women buy in.

The creation of a new spending unit through marriage usually necessitates many new purchases: household goods, furniture, homes, etc. Marital status also affects future purchases. For example, prime candidates for such items as campers, life insurance, and station wagons are married couples. The effect of the factor of marriage is hard to separate from the factor of family size. Larger families' purchases are different from those of smaller families. The economy and family size packages are illustrative of one of these differences. Many of our products today are made and packaged for big families. However, the steadily declining birth rate may spell a change in this variable, which may partially explain the growth in popularity of apartments and condominiums at the expense of the once popular larger home.

These environmental factors are important in influencing a consumer's buying behavior. They all change with time and thus keep businessmen from being able to say the consumer will behave in the same way always. For example, many college students may shun the idea of buying a station wagon, but they may see the day when they will seek out such a product.

*Additudinal Factors.* In this category are included the range of attitudes and opinions held by ultimate consumers toward various goods and services. Everyone has a set of attitudes and opinions. The effect of these on buying behavior can be understood by discussing the three primary sources of attitudes: society, individual, and reference group.

The *society* imposes certain attitudes on people. For example, an engagement to be married is usually accompanied by an engagement ring; a person wears a suit and tie when making a business call. Such attitudes have a very positive effect on the diamond jewelry and men's suit businesses. The effect of culture on what is bought is everpresent. A consumer's attitudes and opinions as to what is right, acceptable, or correct cannot be divorced from the specific culture of that person.

Everyone lives in a society and is affected by it. Yet everyone is still an *individual*. Individuals form their own attitudes and opinions about products. These attitudes are based upon what they as individuals want to be and what they want to be seen as. If, for example, someone strives to be a leader or a pacesetter, then his opinion of new and fashionable products is positive.

Individual attitudes and opinions towards products are also influenced by the reference group of which the person is a member. A *reference group* is a number of people with whom the individual socializes and to whom he looks for social acceptance. Examples are a group of students, workers, or neighbors. Within this group certain common attitudes and opinions develop. Certain ways of behaving are acceptable, while others are not. The clearest example of the effect of the group on individual attitudes toward products is in clothing. In fact, the phrase "in fashion" implies a positive attitude by a group of people towards a type of clothing. Suspenders for men are definitely out, whereas levis and army surplus clothing are another story. How a group of people feel, or their attitudes toward a product, will determine its success or failure. If the consumer wants to be "in," or a part of the group, he must hold attitudes and opinions towards products similar to the group's.

Attitudes and opinions are formed by individuals. An individual's attitude is affected by his own goals and ambitions, the people or group he associates with, and his society. These three elements affect the attitudes a consumer has towards a good or service. In many cases it is not necessary that a businessman understand *why* consumers hold certain attitudes and opinions toward specific products. He must, however, know *what* these attitudes are and how the distribution process can be adjusted to them.

Three factors—economic, environmental, and attitudinal—alone or together influence consumers to buy certain goods or services instead of competing goods or services. The businessman is attempting to influence consumers to buy his specific good or service. To do so he must take account of the three factors influencing ultimate consumers as he develops his distribution process.

## THE DISTRIBUTION PROCESS FOR ULTIMATE CONSUMERS

The ultimate consumer has many characteristics—age, attitudes, family size, amount of income, and so on. These many characteristics make it impossible to describe a distribution process for all the ultimate consumers of a given good or service. The businessman must classify his ultimate consumers into groups by the dimensions discussed and ask if there is any difference in what these groups want in the way of product, price, promotion, and availability of goods. If there is, he must have more than one distribution process for *each* classification or group of his specific ultimate consumers.

For a product as basic as toothpaste, the businessman needs to know, for example, if the female college student is different in her attitudes and desires from the middle-aged housewife with three children. Does each group want the same product? Or does the mother's concern for cavity prevention versus the college student's concern for whiter teeth indicate the need for two types of toothpaste? What about size and price? Do different size and priced tubes of toothpaste need to be offered to the college student and the mother? How about promotion efforts for each class of consumer? Do the advertisements aimed at the mother need to be different in content and message than those for the college students? Most people would answer yes. And finally, how about the availability of the good? Should certain size and priced toothpaste tubes be placed in drugstores and foodstores, while other sizes and priced tubes are placed in bookstores? These and similar questions should be answered before a competitive distribution process can be developed for each category of consumer. Where the groups have different desires, the distribution process should be different. This approach of first categorizing the consumer into groups and then designing a distribution process for each group can be applied to any product from soap to automobiles to restaurants to clothing stores.

The same approach can be applied when the business is trying to sell a service. This can be illustrated by the banking business. The bank serves many categories of consumers—young, old, businessmen, newlyweds, investors, etc. Each category of consumers wants a different service from the bank. One may want low interest, long-term loans; another, safety deposit services; and another, advice on wills and trusts. The banking businessman, if alert, does not offer just one service but determines what each category of his consumers wants and designs a distribution process specifically for that group. This approach applies to any service, including such diverse services as television repair, dry cleaning, automobile repair, and advertising agencies.

Any business, regardless of its product or service, must define exactly what each specific group of consumer wants to be competitive. The factors that influence the consumer to buy certain products or services are useful in categorizing consumers into groups with similar desires. Each group is, however, different from the other groups in its needs. Separate distribution processes must be designed for each group of consumers. An important point is that businesses do not have one distribution process for all consumers. Businesses have many distribution processes, each designed to satisfy the needs of a specific consumer group.

The ultimate consumer market is more diverse than the industrial consumer. For this reason, the discussion of price, promotion and product availability will be pointed toward the ultimate consumer only. In the following chapters the various alternatives the businessman has in price, promotional effort, and product availability will be discussed. In designing a distribution process for each consumer group, the businessman needs to be aware of what his alternatives are in these areas. Then, and only then, can a competitive distribution process be designed to fill the needs of each consumer group.

## Summary

In this chapter some important concepts relating to the distribution process have been discussed. Without a doubt, the movement of goods or services from producer to consumers is vital for any business success. In our economy consumers carry a tremendous veto power. If they do not like a good or service, its price, promotional efforts behind it, or its availability, they will not buy it. Businesses must compete in this market. Thus, consumers' demands must be considered before anything is done in the areas of production or distribution.

Two categories of consumers, industrial and ultimate, have been discussed. The businessman must identify the unique characteristics that influence the buying behavior of groups of consumers within these two categories. These characteristics must be understood, because it is around these that the businessman designs his distribution process. In the next three chapters, specific elements of this distribution process will be discussed, based upon the concepts developed in this chapter. Before continuing, you should have a firm grasp on the ideas presented here.

## QUESTIONS

1. How does the distribution process relate to each of the following:
   (a) The financial process
   (b) The production process
   (c) The business system
2. Define a consumer. Why is it important for a businessman to determine who his potential consumers are?
3. What role does the consumer play in shaping the distribution process for a given business? Illustrate this with a product you are familiar with.

4. What three characteristics are peculiar to industrial consumers? How do these characteristics affect the distribution process of the businessman?

5. What is the difference between industrial and ultimate consumers?

6. What elements affect ultimate consumers' buying choices?

7. Define the various groups of consumers for Chevrolet automobiles. How does each group differ? How would the total distribution efforts for each group be different?

8. Name some specific goods or services which you have purchased recently. Identify one or more factors which influenced your decision to buy those particular goods or services.

## Incident 9–1

The Fresh Air Company manufactures a wide line of industrial air conditioning systems. Fresh Air serves as the standard of quality for industrial air conditioning. Fresh Air's forty-five man sales force concentrates their efforts on the architect-designers of new plant or office facilities. These efforts have proven successful in the past, and Fresh Air feels its industrial market is secure.

In 1971 Fresh Air's top management decided to capitalize on the growing trend toward developmental housing. All projections seemed to indicate that the residential housing industry would remain a big business and that the materials going into these houses would increase in demand. In 1972 Fresh Air introduced a complete line of quality residential central air conditioning units. This market already had some established competitors, such as Fedders, General Electric, and Westinghouse. But Fresh Air's management felt that the quality image which had been developed in the industrial field would carry over into the residential home market.

With the rising construction costs, the materials going into residential homes are chosen because they meet the minimum standards and allow the builder a large profit per house. Price of materials is becoming more and more a factor. As one builder stated, "When you're building homes in the $20,000 to $30,000 range, price is the big factor." Fresh Air's prices range from 10 to 20 percent higher on their central air units than competitors' models. As another builder aptly put it, "I know Fresh Air offers reliable, high quality units but I can't afford them. Besides I don't feel people who buy a home today are that discriminating. All they care about is whether or not the home has central air, not whether it has a Fresh Air or Westinghouse unit."

(1) How should Fresh Air's distribution efforts be different for the industrial and residential air conditioner user?

(2) Can residential home buyers be made so conscious of air conditioners that they will insist on a given brand being used in their homes?

(3) Are all home buyers the same or are there definable groups of home buyers with similar interests? If there are definable groups, what specific factors would you use to define these groups?

(4) Should Fresh Air produce a lower-priced line of air conditioners, even though this would result in lower quality? Should Fresh Air use the same name on this air conditioning unit in the event the company decides to go ahead with it?

# 10

# The Distribution Process:
# Product, Price, and Availability

In designing a distribution process the businessman must think of all elements of that process—the product, its price, availability, the promotional efforts, and physical movement of the product. A decision made in one area of this process will have some effect on the other areas. For example, a decision on the product's design will affect its cost and thus price. For sake of discussion, however, each area of the distribution process can be treated separately. This chapter concentrates on three areas of the total distribution process: the product, its prices, and its availability. Keep in mind that the businessman develops a total distribution process, not just one area or element. In addition, the discussion will center around only one category of consumers, the ultimate consumer. Ultimate consumers are very difficult for the businessman to understand because of the wide variety of their demands. In the design of a competitive distribution process this wide variety creates many unique problems.

## The Product

Businesses survive in the United States when they can satisfy consumers wants or needs, or consumer demands. Products are developed and distributed to satisfy consumer demands. Thus a **product** could be defined as whatever satisfies consumers demand. It can be either a good or service. Television repair service is just as much a product as are cigarettes. Including services expands the definition of products to include intangible as well as tangible items.

Consumers gain satisfaction from both functional aspects of the product and from other elements of the product, including design, color, and style. The actual product's design was discussed in the section on the production process. The focus here is on how a business can go about developing new products to satisfy consumer demands.

Consumer demands are constantly changing. The resultant effect is that the product, like people, has a life cycle. That is, products are introduced (born), gain popularity (live), and eventually are taken off the market (die). The life cycle of a product can be divided into four periods: introduction, growth, maturity, and decline. The sales of the product and profits generated vary in each of these periods. This relationship is shown in Exhibit 10–1.

EXHIBIT 10–1

*Product's Life Cycle*

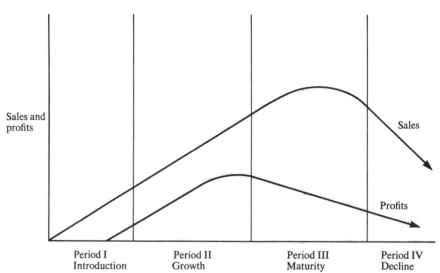

PRODUCT'S LIFE CYCLE

## INTRODUCTION

New products are being introduced into the market daily. During this introductory stage the business is spending a considerable amount of money to inform consumers that the product is available. Money has also been invested in the production of the product in hopes of future sales. These costs exceed the few sales during this period of the product's life, as indicated in the graph.

## GROWTH

Some products fail to reach this second stage, resulting in a huge loss to the business. Products that do reach this second stage are accepted and bought by consumers. Sales and profits increase. But competitors see the success of this product and attempt to offer the consumers a better variation of the same type of product. During this stage the market is flooded with a variety of the same type of products. Profits are at their peak for the original producer of the product.

## MATURITY

In the third stage competition is intense. Competitors may cut prices or increase promotional efforts to attract consumers. These costs have an adverse effect on profits. Although sales are increasing, the individual business' profits are declining. Each competitor is making a lower level of profits on each unit of product sold, because each business' product is basically the same. To attract consumers, prices are being cut while promotional costs are increasing. The net result is depicted in Exhibit 10–1—increasing sales but decreasing profits. Automobiles and household appliances are good examples of products in the maturity period. Intense price and promotional competition between automobile and appliance dealers is evident. When these costs are subtracted from the sales revenue, a level of profits lower than that during the growth period is the result.

## DECLINE

The maturity period continues until a new product type is developed. A steam-powered automobile or a microwave oven would be examples of new products. These new products replace the old. Businesses continue to manufacture the old products until, as depicted in the exhibit, sales and profits are so low that they cannot afford to continue production. The new replacement product will now go through these same four periods.

The life of a product, or the time it takes to go through these four periods, depends on consumers' demand and the amount of competition. For some products it is as short as a year; for others, as in the case of automobiles, 100 years. During different periods of a product's life cycle, different distribution alternatives (price, promotion, and product availability) may have to be developed to keep the product competitive.

The life of a product depends upon consumer demands and the amount of competition. Since consumer demand is constantly changing and the economy's trademark is competition, the businessman needs to be concerned about the development of new products to replace those that will decline.

## NEW PRODUCT DEVELOPMENT

The development of new products is very risky business. Of course not all new products succeed; in fact, very few do. Some writers indicate that only 5 percent of the new products introduced succeed. The businessman is then faced with a dilemma. If he does not develop new products, the sales and profits from the business' old stand-bys will probably dwindle away as the product reaches maturity. However, there is a high chance of failure and cost involved in developing new products. If he wants to stay in business and be competitive, at some time or other he will have to give some thought to new product development.

One way of minimizing the chance that the new product will fail and increasing the chance of new product sales is to establish a systematic procedure for new product development. One such procedure involves four steps: ( 1 ) exploration, ( 2 ) development, ( 3 ) test, and ( 4 ) commercialization and reevaluation.

## EXPLORATION

This first step is the search for and analysis of new product ideas and opportunities. The concepts developed in Chapter 9 are particularly important here. The businessman is attempting to find an unfilled demand of a particular consumer group. Basic studies of consumers' desires and changing demands may point up new opportunities. For example, the recent emphasis on environmental issues has resulted in a new demand for ten-speed bicycles, a demand so big that current manufacturers can not immediately fill it. The key is to always be sensitive to consumers and their changing attitudes and values. The idea of considering what the consumer wants both before and after the business is started is important to remember here.

Once the idea is developed, it must next be analyzed for its economic possibilities. Although many times this involves the judgment of the businessman involved, two sets of data should be developed. The first is the demand for the product in number of units. The second is whether the product can be produced feasibly in the light of the business' resources. The time and effort spent to obtain these estimates is well worth spending. From this point forward the idea starts costing money. A decision based upon the businessman's best judgment is required to determine if the idea is a good or bad one.

## DEVELOPMENT

If the idea is a good one it is now ready to be turned into a tangible product. A production process, on a small scale, is initiated to produce a limited number of the new products. During this time the businessman gets a view of the production problems he may run into. The idea is now reevaluated with this new information. The product may be either dropped at this point or continued.

## TEST

The products produced are now tested to check if, in fact, consumers will accept them. Failure to test an idea ignores a central fact: the consumers determine if the product will be a success, not the businessman. Details on product testing are beyond the scope of this text. It is no simple matter; misleading results can come from faulty testing procedures.

## COMMERCIALIZATION AND REEVALUATION

Once the businessman is satisfied that he has satisfactorily tested his idea for a new product, then the decision to go ahead with full scale commercial production and sale must be made. When the product is out in the market, it should be reevaluated. Many judgments were made in deciding to go ahead and produce this product. Reevaluation checks are now necessary to see if these judgments were made correctly. Such questions as the following are asked: Does the product satisfy consumer demands? Should it be changed or altered? Are sales up to the expected level? What is competition doing? These questions help the businessman monitor the product's movement through its life cycle, indicating when he should start to develop a new product again. The commercialization (full scale production and sales) of a product requires the development of a complete distribution process. One important element that needs to be determined is the product's price.

## The Product's Price

Pricing is one of the major elements in the distribution of a product. Although not the only factor, it is a very critical factor in the consumer's buying decision. From a business standpoint, price affects both the volume or number of products sold and the amount of profits earned by a business. This relationship can be depicted as follows:

$$\text{Revenues} = \text{Product Price} \times \text{Volume}$$

$$\text{Profits} = \text{Revenues} - \text{Costs}$$

The following example will illustrate the relationship between price, volume, and profits. Business A prices its product at one dollar per unit. At this price, 50,000 units are sold. It costs $30,000 to produce this many units. Therefore:

$$\text{Revenues} = \$1.00 \times 50,000 \text{ units} = \$50,000$$

$$\text{Profits} = \$50,000 - \$30,000 = \$20,000$$

Let us further assume that business A lowers its price to $0.80 per unit. At this price 70,000 units are sold, because more people are willing to buy the product at its new, lower price. The increase in production increases costs to $35,000. Therefore:

$$\text{Revenues} = \$ \ .80 \times 70,000 \text{ units} = \$56,000$$

$$\text{Profits} = \$56,000 - \$35,000 = \$21,000$$

In this example, decreasing the price by $0.20 increased profits by $1,000. Price affects both volume and revenue. In determining the product's price, then, two elements must be considered. First, what price will generate at least enough revenue to cover the costs of producing the product; and second, which price will enable the business to sell the desired volume of the product.

### COSTS AND PRICE

The revenue generated beyond costs determines the amount of profit a business will make in a given time period. The businessman at least would like to cover his costs. A simple approach to pricing the products would be a **cost-plus approach.** In the example, the total cost of producing 50,000 units was $30,000, or $0.60 per unit. The lowest price the businessman could offer the products for would be $0.60. Any price lower than that would lose money. The cost-plus approach to pricing would be to add a "reasonable markup" to the cost per unit. Assume, as the businessman in this example did, that $0.40 per unit is a reasonable markup. Thus, the selling price on a cost-plus approach becomes $1.00 per unit. The businessman makes $0.40 profit on each unit of the product sold.

The cost-plus approach, although simple, fails to take account of two factors. The first is the effect increases in production have on unit costs. In the second part of the example, the total cost of producing 70,000 units was $35,000, or $0.50 per unit. Although increasing production from 50,000 units to 70,000 units increased total costs by $5,000, the cost to produce each unit declined from $0.60 ($30,000/50,000 units) to $0.50 ($35,000/70,000 units). This decrease in cost per unit could be attributed to a savings from a fuller utilization of plant and equipment. A machine which costs $10,000 and only is needed for one-half day's production will add less to the unit cost of the product if it can be used a full day's production, because the cost of the machine is spread over a greater number of units. Increased sales volume would also result in this type of savings.

The second area that the cost-plus approach fails to take into consideration is the relationship of price to volume. Assume the businessman feels the same reasonable markup of $0.40 should apply to the $0.50 unit cost figure calculated above. The cost-plus price would then be $0.90 per unit. What effect will this price have on the demand for this good or service?

## DEMAND AND PRICE

In the example, selling 70,000 units required that the product be priced at $0.80 per unit, not $0.90, as the cost-plus method might indicate. In fact, in this example, it could be guessed that the following relationship between volume demanded and price exists:

| Unit price | Volume in units |
|:---:|:---:|
| $ .80 | 70,000 |
| .90 | 60,000 |
| 1.00 | 50,000 |

This is a typical relationship between price and demand: as price decreases more people demand, or are willing to buy, the product. Conversely, as price increases fewer people demand, or are willing to buy, the product. In the example it was assumed that when the businessman produced 70,000 units of output, he was operating at full capacity. Consequently, the supply of the product is fixed (only 70,000 units will be produced *this* year.) Therefore, demand is in fact what determines the product's price. If people demand more than 70,000 units, the price will rise. If they demand fewer, the price will fall. Compare this to football tickets. If only 60,000 seats are available and more than 60,000 people want to see the game, they will pay a higher price than what the cost-plus markup indicates the price should be. If less than 60,000 want to see the game, the opposite is true. The cost-plus method of pricing, by ignoring the effect of demand on price, fails to realize a very important point. Selling price is only partially determined by what it costs to make the product. The product's price is strongly influenced and determined in the market by demand conditions. The market determines how much the consumer is willing to pay for the product. It is the market, not production costs, that sets the price. Costs determine only the price below which the firm is unwilling to go. The market determines how high the price can go.

Thus, the businessman does not have complete freedom in establishing whatever prices he desires. He faces many restrictions, one of which is competition. The amount of competition and level of product demand affects the freedom the businessman has in setting his prices. And the amounts of competition and demand vary throughout a product's life cycle.

## PRICING AND PRODUCT LIFE CYCLE

### INTRODUCTION AND GROWTH PERIOD

The businessman who has developed a new, unique product has two choices in pricing the product during the introductory stage:

1. *Skim pricing* would set a high price to maximize profits on the new product. When a product is new or different, some consumers will buy it regardless of the price. The businessman is attempting to top or "skim the cream" off the market.

2. *Penetration pricing* is just the opposite of skim pricing. A low enough price is set that the new product penetrates the market. That is, a lot of people buy the new product because of its newness and reasonable price.

However, during the growth stage competition increases. Similar or better versions of the same products compete. The price set in the introductory stage could affect the rate at which competitors decide to produce the new product. A skim price could tell competitors that there is a lot of money over costs to be made, thus hastening their entry into a good market. A penetration price, on the other hand, could discourage competitors. The business might sell to such a large proportion of the market that other businesses may feel they cannot compete with the loyal following.

### MATURATION PERIOD

Eventually, as the product increases in popularity, competition is going to emerge. During the maturity stage many similar products will be competing for the increased level of sales. One way of competing is via the product's price. The original businessman must lower his price if it was set at a high skim level. He has three choices in setting his prices during this stage:

*Market Price.*   In highly competitive products businesses must meet competition—the market price. A prime example here is gasoline. No gasoline station owner would think of increasing or decreasing his price per gallon of gas by himself. Gas wars were an indication of what happened when a station reduced its price per gallon. Many familar products follow this pricing approach. The producers would like to charge higher prices, but competition does not allow it. If they cannot meet their costs and make a profit at the market price, they cannot raise their price, and will probably be forced out of the market.

*Above the Market Price.*   Few products which reach the maturity stage can be priced above the market price. The only way the product can be consistently priced above the market is if consumers think it is better than those it must compete with. Some products carry a quality image and thus consumers are willing to pay more for these products than for their competitors. One way of achieving this distinction is by using another element of the distribution process which will be discussed in the next chapter—promotional activities.

*Under the Market Price.*   Discount stores offer products below the prices of conventional stores. The objective of this pricing approach is to appeal to the economy-minded consumer. The economy-minded consumer feels all products of a given type are alike in quality and buys on the basis of price alone.

DECLINE PERIOD
   New products bring about the decline of old products. Those businesses that continue to produce the product during this stage continually must lower prices in the attempt to attract consumers. The demand for the product is decreasing. Consumers are attracted by the new products. A few producers will stay in the market with the old products until the bitter end. At this time prices will be close to the costs of production. Eventually producers remaining will stop production of the product.
   Throughout the life of a product the businessman must decide on what price to charge. This decision is based upon the demand for the product and what his competition is doing or likely to do. These two factors may be different at different stages of the product's life cycle. Thus it is quite possible for the price also to be different to take account of these changing conditions. In the price decision the costs of production are taken into consideration only as a limit on the amount of profits that will be made and as a factor in the decision to stop production of the product because the market will no longer pay a price that covers these production costs.

## Nonprice Competition

   One factor on which most products must compete is price. However, there are other factors with which businesses can compete. These other factors are called nonprice competition. In a highly competitive market product prices tend to be uniform, but some producers sell more of their product than do others. Winston cigarettes is one example; Texaco gasoline is another.

When price is a constant, businesses must compete on other factors, including product design, promotional efforts, availability, and physical distribution.

The objective of a businessman engaged in nonprice competition is to distinguish his product in the mind of the consumer from other competing products. Any or all of the elements (except price) of the distribution process can be used to achieve this objective. Through product design a fashionable or stylish product can be used to create various images in the mind of consumers. Such images as quality and sex appeal will distinguish one product from another. The availability of a product may make it easier for a consumer to find, thus setting it off from all other products. Most products must enter into some form of nonprice competition. How products and product design can be used as competitive elements has already been discussed. The next element to be discussed is the product's availability.

## Availability

For businessmen to sell their products or consumers to buy these products, they must be available to consumers at the time they want them and at the right place. Making products available to consumers involves two actions: initiating a physical transportation and storage system for moving products from producers to consumers and deciding which institutions are necessary to help sell the products to consumers. Physical distribution is discussed in Chapter 12. The concern here is analyzing the alternative institutions which help businesses sell their products.

## CHANNELS OF DISTRIBUTION

Channels of distribution are the institutions a product passes through in going from producer to consumer. These institutions help the producer sell his product. Exhibit 10-2 depicts the various institutions or channels of distribution a business can use in selling his product to consumers.

The businessman has three alternatives in selling his products:

(1) Selling products directly to consumers;
(2) Using retailers to sell the product;
(3) Using wholesalers and retailers to sell the product.

The first alternative involves no other outside institutions. The other two alternatives involve the two basic types of distribution institutions—wholesalers and retailers. There are many different kinds of wholesalers and retailers, thus giving the businessman more than just two or three choices.

## RETAILERS

Retailers are institutions which sell products to the ultimate consumer. The producer, as indicated in Exhibit 10–2, can sell his own product directly to consumers, and thus be a retailer. Direct selling can be accomplished by three basic methods.

(1) Door-to-door selling,
(2) Producer's retail stores,
(3) Direct mail.

EXHIBIT 10–2

*Channels of Distribution*

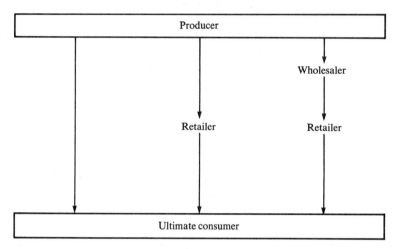

Producer

Wholesaler

Retailer          Retailer

Ultimate consumer

*Door-to-door selling* has been used with success by Avon, a leader in the cosmetic industry, and encyclopedia producers. This alternative is attractive when the producer feels that he can sell more products this way than when by displaying his goods in retail stores.

*Producer's retail stores* are operated to sell only the producer's products. Such companies as Singer, Firestone, Goodyear, Thom McAnn, and many small jewelry producers own their own retail stores. This alternative is attractive when the producer feels that his product must be aggressively sold by highly trained salesmen. The producer of tires rightly feels that if all brands were sold in the same store, the salesman could not aggressively push one brand of tire over another. Therefore it is probably wise to have his own store selling exclusively his tires.

Producers can also use *direct mail* in selling their products. Catalogs and mail order promotions are quite popular methods of retailing products. This method is attractive only when a good mailing list that contains the names of good prospects for the products can be obtained.

In addition to the direct approach, where the producer becomes a retailer, the producer may decide to use a specialized retailing institution to sell his products. Retail institutions are by far the most popular means of selling goods and services to ultimate consumers. Retailing institutions offer the prime advantage for making the products available to a lot of consumers at a lot of places. The following types of retail institutions or stores are available to help the businessman sell his products:

(1) Department stores,
(2) Specialty stores,
(3) Discount stores,
(4) Supermarkets,
(5) Vending machines.

*Department stores* have a wide range of products for sale, and in fact are often nothing more than a combination of many small retail stores. *Specialty stores,* on the other hand, sell a limited number of products, for example shoes, jewelry, or sporting goods, all of the same basic nature. *Discount houses* handle many types of products. They sell products at low prices and offer little or no services to the consumers. Examples of discount houses are Korvetts, K-Mart and T.G.&Y. *Supermarkets* are basically large grocery stores. But, unlike grocery stores, many nonfood items are sold in supermarkets. *Vending machines* are growing in popularity to help sell such items as cigarettes, candy, milk, ice, beer, and hot and cold foods. In the future the consumer will be seeing more and more items sold through vending machines.

## WHOLESALERS

Wholesalers are true middlemen. They take the product from producers and sell it to retailers. Although they are important parts of the channel of distribution for consumer products, they never deal directly with the ultimate consumer. In addition to helping the producer sell his products, wholesalers also perform two important services: they store inventory for producers and they deliver goods to retailers. Although no two wholesalers operate exactly the same way, there are two major types of wholesalers:

(1) Merchant wholesalers,
(2) Merchandising agents and brokers.

Of the two types, merchant wholesalers are the most numerous and do the most business. They buy and take title to the products, thus getting their sales money to the producer immediately. The wholesaler's salesmen call on retail stores and fill their orders. Many of these wholesalers carry thousands of products, making it impossible for their salesmen to give special attention to any one product. Although this is a disadvantage, the increased availability of the product to retail outlets many times outweighs it. The merchant wholesaler extends an individual producer's capacity to sell his product. Not all producers can afford a sales force. The merchant wholesaler not only provides a sales force but also delivers the goods to retail outlets, all at a cost way below what it would take the businessman to provide these services.

Merchandising *agents* and *brokers* do not buy or take title to the products. The main service they perform is to negotiate a sale between producers and retailers. They help the producer in the performance of his selling function. The producer using an agent or broker does not have to undergo the expense of developing his own sales force because agents and brokers bring buyers and sellers together. For this service they receive a fee or commission.

## CHOOSING A CHANNEL OF DISTRIBUTION

The channel the businessman chooses depends upon three factors: the nature of the product, the consumers of the product, and the business itself. Certain products—perishables and services, for example—do not lend themselves to lengthy channels of distribution. The businessman who is selling to a few customers does not need to distribute his product through a national discount house. Putting aside the third factor, the business itself, the effect the product and consumer of the product have on channels of distribution can be discussed.

## EFFECT OF THE PRODUCTS AND CONSUMERS

When discussing channels of distribution all products cannot be equated. However, categories of consumer products which are similar in nature and in what consumers want in product availability can be developed. The following are four such categories of consumer products.

1. *Convenience goods* are purchased by consumers with a minimum amount of effort; the purchase must be convenient to them. If you run out of cigarettes, candy, razor blades, or deodorant, for example, you seek the most convenient place to buy them. It is highly unlikely that the consumer will spend a lot of time going from store to store comparing prices before he selects a convenience good.

The businessman producing convenience goods seeks an intensive distribution of these goods. That is, he wants his product in as many different types of stores and outlets as possible. For this reason many middlemen of distribution institutions are used, especially merchant wholesalers and retailers. In this way the producer's product can be available almost anywhere the consumer goes. It is thus truly convenient for the consumer to buy that producer's product.

2. *Shopping goods* are those products for which the consumer shops (compares prices, quality, and style of more than one assortment of goods) before making a purchase. When you buy a new suit or dress, you compare not only many suits or dresses but also the suits and dresses in different stores. The higher the price of the product, the more likely it is to be a shopping good. Consumers shopping to get exactly what they want are willing to spend the time and effort this shopping and comparing takes. Because the consumer is willing to take more effort in obtaining a shopping good, the businessman can be selective in the distribution of his product. He selects a few retail outlets in his market rather than many. The producer can in many cases get along without wholesalers. He deals directly with a small number of retailers.

3. *Specialty goods* are those which the consumer knows that he wants. He is willing to exert considerable effort to get the exact specialty good he wants. If the consumer wants a Maytag washer or Uniroyal tires he will go to all extremes to satisfy this need.

The producer of a specialty good can use a very exclusive distribution system. The consumer will in effect seek out the store that carries these items. Therefore a very few retail outlets can be used, or the product can be sold door to door, through the producer's own retail outlet, or by mail order.

4. *Service goods* are by their nature intangible. They include services, car washes, haircuts, television repairs. They can only be distributed directly from producer to consumer. Often these services are "distributed" in the producer's office or place of business. Services cannot be distributed through middlemen. How, for example, could dental work be performed through a wholesaler and retailer?

## THE BUSINESS AND CHANNELS OF DISTRIBUTION

In addition to the product and consumer of the product the business itself limits the type of distribution channels which can be used. Two factors, business size and financial strength, affect the choices which can be made.

A small company usually does not have the financial position or product diversity to own retail outlets and large warehouses and employ a full sales force. For this reason many small producers must use the services of merchant wholesalers and retailers. They may have no other choice.

On the other hand, a larger company usually has the financial strength and diversity of products to justify employing their own sales force and owning retail outlets, and large warehouses. However, even though they can afford to use a direct channel of distribution, wholesalers and retailers may be the most economical choice, based upon their product and consumers.

### Summary

This chapter concentrates on three elements of the total distribution process: the product, the product's price, and the product's availability. Each is discussed to determine how it can aid in increasing the business' competitive position.

The concept of a product's life cycle shows how new product eventually become old products. Thus all businesses should involve themselves with new product development. New product development is centered around continually satisfying consumers' wants and needs.

The product's price is an important factor affecting the consumer's buying choice. The impact of producer's costs, demand, and competition on prices are discussed. As demand and competition change, so too must the price of the product. Thus at various stages in a product's life, various prices might apply. Nonprice competition has been introduced. One element of nonprice competition is product availability. Products are made available by using various channels of distribution, which vary depending on the nature of the consumer, the product, and the business itself.

An important factor in nonprice competition is the promotional efforts behind a product. This element of the distribution process is discussed in Chapter 11.

### QUESTIONS

1. Explain the differences in sales, profits, and competition level during each of the four stages of a product's life cycle.
2. What is the relationship between a product's price, costs, and volume of sales?

3. The Clean Corporation manufactures 10,000 mudguards per year at a total cost of $20,000. The selling price of the mudguards to the wholesaler is $3.00. A new merchant wholesaler has offered to purchase an additional 10,000 units provided the price per unit is decreased 30 percent. Doubling production would increase total cost of production by 75 percent. The president, in rejecting the proposal, made the following statement: "Any time you increase costs by 75 percent and decrease selling price by 30 percent you cannot possibly make a profit." Do you agree with the president? Are there any errors in his logic? If the Clean Corporation accepted the offer to produce an additional 10,000 units, what would the firm's profit amount to?

4. The price of a product is determined by its demand, not its cost. Explain.

5. Differentiate between skim pricing and market price.

6. What is the objective of a business engaged in nonprice competition? What forms of nonprice competition might the producer of the following products or services utilize?

   (a) Cigarettes            (d) Toothpaste
   (b) Automobiles        (e) Beer
   (c) Banks               (f) Nursing homes

7. What factors determine which channel of distribution is best for a given business system?

8. What is the difference between a convenience good and a specialty good?

## Incident 10–1

### WHITE FENCE FARMS

John Daniels owns and farms 200 acres on the outskirts of Little Rock, Arkansas. In the past the majority of the acreage has been put into crops. As a hobby, John raises turkeys, ducks, and chickens. These fowl were either consumed by John's family or given to close friends as holiday gifts. Increasingly people have been asking John to sell them his birds. Over a five-year period these sales have increased and added handsomely to John's income.

In 1974 John decided to spend the majority of his time raising these birds. A local store in Little Rock agreed to sell John display space in its freezers, and a large restaurant has a standing order for ducks and chickens. In the Little Rock area White Fence Birds enjoy a very favorable image, and demand has exceeded John's wildest predictions. John would like to turn his entire 200 acres into a bird ranch, but to support such an effort sales would have to be less seasonal and the product distributed in a larger area than just Little Rock.

The demand for chickens is fairly constant throughout the year, but the turkey and duck demand is highly seasonal. Almost the entire turkey and duck crop has to be pointed to Thanksgiving Day and Christmas Day business. The birds are hatched at times which will allow them to be brought to maturity primarily for these two periods. To even out demand, John has developed a line of canned turkey and duck products. This line includes canned thinly sliced white and dark meat, canned concentrated soup, canned smoked and canned barbecued turkey and duck. These products, he hopes, will minimize wastage and even out demand. They would also be an addition to the whole turkeys, ducks, and chickens currently being sold. John has found that he can have his various products canned on a custom basis in a Little Rock cannery, thus avoiding the expense of canning equipment.

The product's distribution presents another problem that must be resolved before converting White Fence Farms totally over to bird ranching. John cannot afford to hire salesmen, and he cannot leave the farm and preparation of his canned products to do the selling himself. His attempts at selling to chain food stores have to date been met with little success. The chainstore buyers admit that White Fence Farm products are of exceptional flavor and quality, but they doubt consumer acceptance and need bigger quantities of the products than John has planned to offer at the start.

John has since contacted a food broker who represents a group of noncompeting goods producers on a commission basis. This particular food broker maintains a sales force of twenty salesmen who call on wholesalers or retailers. White Fence Farms would have to make their own arrangements for shipping the merchandise to regional warehouses.

John knows his standard of living could be quite comfortable if he just continued his local activities; but he feels that if his new products were accepted and his total line of products distributed nationally, success is only a year or two away. Just how these two goals could be achieved still puzzled him.

(1) Evaluate John's present method of new product development.
(2) What steps would you propose John follow in evaluating his new product line?
(3) Should he go ahead with his distribution plans before he has evaluated his new products idea?
(4) What channels of distribution are available to John? What are the strengths and weaknesses of each?
(5) What factors should be weigh in choosing the right channel of distribution for his situation?
(6) Can new product development and channel of distribution selection be carried on at the same time?

## Incident 10–2

Geno Palmeri was the head cook for a leading Italian restaurant in the Chicago area for ten years. During this time he saved his money with one thought in mind, to own his own restaurant. Finally he accumulated enough money to fulfill his wish.

Geno purchased a small building in Arlington Heights, Illinois, a growing northwestern suburb. The building was renovated into three major rooms: a family dining room, a cocktail lounge with wall booths, and a kitchen. The menu was to be standard Italian fare: pizza, spaghetti, veal parmesan, lasagna, etc. Lunch, dinner, carryout, and delivery services were to be provided. Geno's cooking reputation was well known, and he hoped some of his boss' former customers would frequent his restaurant. The cost would be held to a minimum with Geno doing the cooking, his wife serving and bartending, and one additional waitress.

Geno felt his location, right across the street from a major shopping center, was excellent. Competition would be rigorous, but he felt his overall quality and family style restaurant would offset the advantages of the chain pizza houses. His biggest concern was his prices. Since he had never been involved in figuring out costs and prices, this was a totally new area.

(1) What specific type of information does Geno need to determine his pricing policy?

(2) What method of pricing would you recommend for a restaurant of this type?

(3) Should different prices be installed for the lunch, dinner, and carry-out menus?

(4) What effect will Geno's prices have on his volume, profits, and revenue?

(5) What forms of nonprice competition would you suggest that Geno should engage in?

# 11

# Promotion
# Of the Product

Having developed a product, priced it, and established a channel of distribution, the businessman has one remaining job to complete the distribution process. He must promote the product. Sales do not just happen. Consumers have to be told about the product and shown why they should buy it. Promotion completes the distribution process in that it makes sales occur.

The objective of promotional activities is to influence or encourage potential consumers to buy the product. Promotional activities are nothing more than communicating to consumers. The businessman has two methods of communicating to consumers: personal selling and advertising. These two communication or promotional techniques will be discussed in this chapter. Each businessman will combine various types of each to help distribute his product. Before how much of each is required can be discussed, personal selling and advertising must be covered.

## Personal Selling

Personal selling is face-to-face communication between a seller and potential consumer. Personal selling is used at every point in the channel of distribution. Businessmen or their representatives communicate with wholesalers, retailers, and of course consumers. Each is a potential consumer; and thus businessmen are always involved in some form of personal selling, even if they do not come into face-to-face contact with ultimate consumers.

The concern here is not with the techniques of salesmanship. However, to better understand the rest of the discussion, some mention must be made of what a personal salesman does. Regardless of what is being sold, personal salesmen: (1) locate and meet potential customers; (2) discover what customers' needs and attitudes are; (3) develop a sales presentation aimed at informing the customer of their product attributes and persuading him to buy; (4) close the sale; and (5) follow up to be sure the consumer is satisfied. If you are interested in the actual techniques of personal salesmanship, you can consult the many excellent textbooks in this area.

With this brief exposure into the salesman's job, attention can be turned to the main concern. Potential businessmen must understand *when* to use personal selling versus advertising, *what* to expect from personal selling, and what factors to consider in putting together an efficient sales force. The discussion of personal selling will center around these three points.

## WHEN TO USE PERSONAL SELLING

Each individual businessman must make the decision on how much personal selling and advertising will be used in promoting his product. There are, however, certain factors which make personal face-to-face selling a more attractive method of communicating with potential consumers than advertising. These factors are:

### A SMALL NUMBER OF POTENTIAL CONSUMERS

A business often does not need to communicate with the number of people who read *Newsweek* magazine. Thus advertising in *Newsweek* would be an overkill when the number of potential consumers the business needs to communicate with is small. The fewer the number of potential consumers, the more likely personal selling can be used. This is one of the basic reasons why personal selling is used more in communication with industrial consumers than with ultimate consumers. Personally selling shampoo or personally contacting every man, woman, and child who uses shampoo is almost impossible. The number alone makes it impossible for each to be personally contacted.

### CONCENTRATION OF POTENTIAL CONSUMERS

The geographic concentration of consumers makes personal communication easier. Although the number of potential consumers may be large, salesmen do not have to travel great distances to sell these consumers. Chicago and New York are excellent examples of places where certain potential consumers are highly concentrated. In these cities sellers find a great concentration of buyers at such central locations as the Merchandise Mart and the Grain Market.

## SIZE OF AVERAGE SALE

The average dollar value of each sale is an important consideration in covering the costs of personal selling. The costs per individual salesman can easily exceed $50.00 per day when meals, transportation, room, and salary are taken into consideration. Thus a salesman who sells ten units of a $5.00 product only covers his costs. But the salesman whose average sale is $500 would probably exceed his costs per day. Based upon costs alone, those businesses whose average sale is small will use less personal selling than those whose average sale is large.

## NEED FOR DEMONSTRATION

Personal selling is almost mandatory when products must be demonstrated to convince consumers of their merits. Included in this category are most mechanical products: vacuum cleaners, automobiles, televisions, stereos, etc. If consumers will believe in the product's merits without a demonstration, advertising may be used as a method of communication.

## UNRECOGNIZED CONSUMER NEEDS

Most families don't recognize that they "need" encyclopedias or life insurance. This is probably the most important reason for using personal selling. Personal selling can be used to prove this need to consumers. On the other hand, most people recognize that they need toothpaste. In this case advertising might be all that is needed to get consumers to buy one specific type of toothpaste.

Although not exhaustive, these factors appear to be some of the more important considerations in deciding when to use personal selling. Personal selling does not answer all the promotional needs of a business. The businessman needs to know realistically what he can expect from personal selling.

## WHAT TO EXPECT FROM PERSONAL SELLING

In evaluating personal selling versus advertising, the businessman should realize that each has certain strong points and weaknesses. Personal selling offers the businessman the following advantages.

## SALESMEN KNOW EXACTLY WHO
## POTENTIAL CONSUMERS ARE

The salesman can seek out and define potential prospects. Advertising, however, does not discriminate between potential and nonconsumers. An advertisement communicates to everyone. Personal salesmen communicate only to potential consumers. From an economic standpoint, promotional dollars may be more efficiently spent because there is less wasted effort and time in personal selling.

## SALESMEN CAN MEET SPECIFIC OBJECTIONS

Advertising is really one-way communication—telling which is aimed at many consumers. Personal selling involves two way communication—telling and listening to one consumer. The salesman can custom-make his sales presentation to fit the needs and objections of the specific consumer he is talking to. Personal selling is far more effective in convincing a consumer of the product's good points, because the sale is directed toward what a specific consumer wants, needs, and objects to. Custom-made promotional efforts are more likely to result in sales.

## SALESMEN HELP CLOSE THE SALE

Unless promotion creates action in terms of actually buying the product being promoted on the part of consumers, it has failed. Many people hear or see an advertisement and fully agree with it, but never buy the product. In advertising there is no one there to move the consumer into action. This is not true for personal selling. The salesman is there and in a position to push for an order and close the sale. Possibly the biggest advantage in personal selling is that salesmen can keep consumers from delaying their purchases. All consumers face a moment of indecision—maybe I should wait or think it over. Salesmen personally help the consumer at this time and are thus the most effective method of closing a sale.

## SALESMEN PROVIDE INFORMATION TO PRODUCERS

Because selling is two-way communication, the salesman receives valuable information, such as consumer suggestions and attitudes, from consumers. This information is invaluable to the producer of a product who wants to remain competitive. It helps the producer align his distribution process—product design, price, availability, promotional efforts, and physical distribution—with changing consumer needs and attitudes. The salesman, unlike the advertisement, can tell the producer what the consumer really thinks about his product and the whole distribution process.

## DISADVANTAGES TO PERSONAL SELLING

Not all businesses, however, rely heavily on personal selling. Personal selling has some limitations that the businessman should be aware of before he formulates his promotional activities. These disadvantages include:

## SALESMEN COST MONEY

Like everything else, the cost of maintaining a salesman in the field is rising. A few years ago $18.00 per day per salesman might have been within reason, but today that is probably the cheapest a motel room alone would cost. The average salesman's salary is also increasing, from $5,000 a year during the 1960s to between $10,000 and $20,000 per year at a minimum. Businesses can reduce these costs by increasing the efficiency of their sales forces. Such proposals as increasing the number of successful sales calls, substituting telephone calls for some of the personal calls, minimizing the distance traveled between potential consumers, and using central showrooms to encourage consumers to come to the salesmen are steps in reducing these high costs.

## SALESMEN CANNOT BE EVERYWHERE

The salesmen should be with the potential consumer when the buying decision is being made. This, however, is physically impossible. Thus the absence of the salesman at the crucial moment might result in a decision detrimental to a given business. These lost sales can be prevented if the salesman can build enough good will with a consumer that he will be called when a decision is going to be made. Or, the business can use advertising in hopes of being on the consumer's mind when the buying decision occurs.

## GOOD SALESMEN ARE HARD TO FIND

Selling as a profession historically has not been an attractive career. The best students do not, as a generalization, see the life of a salesman as attractive. This view may be hard to understand in light of the freedom, responsibility, challenge, and pay a selling career offers. Be that as it may, this negative attitude can cause problems for some businessmen who feel that personal selling is the best approach for promoting their products. The problem these businessmen face is finding competent people to perform the tasks of personal selling. In attempting to solve this problem, the businessman has two alternatives. The first is to rely less on personal selling and more on advertising: the second is to develop his own sales force. If the indication is that more personal selling should be used than advertising, the first alternative is a waste of the company's promotional efforts.

## DEVELOPING AN EFFICIENT SALES FORCE

The shortage of capable people willing to make selling a career has forced many businesses to develop their own sales forces. A sales force is part of the manpower of a business. The process for recruiting and hiring good salesmen is the same as that for blue collar employees, managers, secretaries, etc. This process will be discussed in detail in the next section, The Manpower Process. As you read that section you can apply it to the problems of developing an efficient sales force. For regardless of the type of employee, the procedure for increasing the utilization of human resources is the same. There are two important considerations in developing a sales force to be discussed here: training salesmen and compensating salesmen.

## TRAINING SALESMEN

The importance of sales training can be illustrated by stating a generally accepted truth—good salesmen are not born; they are trained. A poorly trained sales force is worse than no sales force at all. All new salesmen must undergo some type of formal or informal training. The time the business spends on training new and retraining old salesmen will be returned in increased sales and salesman job satisfaction.

The sales training program should cover three areas: (1) familiarity with the company, (2) familiarity with the product, and (3) selling techniques.

*Familiarity with the Company.*   The salesman is a representative of the company. Many times he is the only company representative the consumer ever sees. He should be able to answer the consumers' questions about the company, such as size, number of employees, and growth potential. Often he must sell the company before he can sell the product. Inability to discuss the company may indicate to the consumer that the salesman really doesn't know that much about the product he is selling.

*Familiarity with the Product.*   The salesman should have enough information about the product and the way it is produced to satisfy consumers. If the product and the product's applications are highly complex and the consumer is very sophisticated, the salesman will need a good deal of in-depth product knowledge. Computer salesmen, automobile salesmen, shoe salesmen, and magazine salesmen need different amounts of information about individual products. Many computer salesmen are graduate electrical engineers. Their depth of product knowledge and training is more extensive than that of an automobile salesman, because the person who buys a computer requires more answers to detailed questions than does the typical automobile buyer. The important point is that the salesman needs to be able to answer the consumers' questions or find these answers. Consumers are bound to lose confidence in the salesman who cannot answer their questions. How then can they be expected to believe the salesman who tells them the product is best for them?

*Selling Techniques.*   Note that this is the last of three training areas. All the selling techniques in the world cannot help the salesman who does not know his company and product. Today's consumers are too sophisticated to have the wool pulled over their eyes. However, selling techniques are important. They can be taught in two ways: first, by discussing how to make sales calls, presentations, close sales, and answer consumer objections; second, by practicing and observing salesmen in action. Most businesses assign new salesmen to older successful salesmen for this second reason. The technique (how to make sales calls, presentations, close sales, and answer consumer objections) can thus be seen and analyzed in action. Most good training involves both classroom and field experience.

How long good salesmen stay on the job and the effort they put into the job affects the efficiency of the total sales force. One element that has some impact on salesmen staying on the job and putting forth more than minimal effort is the way they are compensated while doing their jobs.

## COMPENSATING SALESMEN

The type of compensation a salesman receives has an important influence on the effectiveness of the sales force. If salesmen are unhappy with their pay, they will either quit or work less. Some will do both. Salesmen can be paid either (1) a straight salary, (2) a straight commission, or (3) a combination of salary and commission. The nature of the product and the consumer determines which of the three plans would be best for the sales force.

A *straight salary* gives the salesman a maximum amount of security. If the sales vary from month-to-month, salesmen may want the security of knowing exactly how much they will make. Straight salary also gives the business control over the salesmen. The business can be sure, for example, that routine selling activities such as consumer service and repair or stocking shelves get done. Thus the greater the routine selling activities or the larger the fluctuation in sales volume, the more likely the straight salary method of compensation. For these reasons department stores usually pay their salesmen a straight salary.

The *straight commission* gives the salesman a maximum amount of incentive. He receives a certain commission on each item sold. For example, a salesman selling ten cars in January would receive $1,000 for that month if he received a $100 commission on each car sold. This method can be used where routine selling activities are of minor importance, as in life insurance, encyclopedia, and magazine sales. These are hard selling jobs and require a lot of incentive. However, if routine selling activities are important, straight commission is not attractive from a business standpoint. The salesman is not paid for routine selling activities, and therefore he often will ignore them.

Because most people want some security and some incentive, a combination plan of *salary plus commission* is most widely used. The various combinations are too numerous to list. Under most, the salesman receives a set salary (say, $200 per month) and so much ($10.00) on each item sold. For salesmen selling products that require a lot of routine selling duties and fluctuate in sales, the salary represents a larger proportion of their income. On the other hand, the salesmen whose products require a lot of selling work receive little salary and must rely on large commissions. The commission provides the salesmen the incentive to engage in the hard selling these products require.

## Advertising

**Advertising** is a form of indirect communication between a seller and many potential consumers. It is indirect because the seller communicates to potential consumers through media other than personal face-to-face contact.

The personal salesman is limited in the number of consumers he can contact and the time he has to spend with each. Advertising does not have these limits. A huge variety of products that are distributed across the United States require an advertising promotional effort. Advertising is mass promotion, reaching millions of people at a time. Many products—not just those of large businesses—require this mass communications effort.

Businessmen need to know how to use this promotional tool effectively. There are four basic questions to be asked before an advertising campaign is launched. (1) When should advertising be used instead of personal selling? (2) What can a businessman expect from advertising? (3) What factors should be considered in constructing an effective message? (4) What **medium** should be used?

# WHEN TO USE ADVERTISING

In answering this question the businessman is attempting to determine the extent to which his product can be advertised. Under certain conditions, some products can be advertised more easily than others. The following conditions should be evaluated.

## AVAILABLE MONEY

This is not the money consumers have, but the money the business has to spend on promotional efforts. While selling is expensive, advertising is even more expensive. A commercial minute on one of the major television networks during prime time runs between $45,000 and $55,000. A one-page ad in a major newspaper such as the *Chicago Tribune* or *Los Angeles Times* runs around $5,000. A one-page ad in a widely read magazine such as *McCalls Magazine, Reader's Digest,* and *Better Homes & Gardens* can exceed $50,000. These are only the costs of buying the space or time. Expenses are also incurred in creating the ad and hiring the talent to produce and act in the advertisement. In addition, one of the principles behind effective advertising is repetition. Multiply these costs by ten or twenty times per year, and you can readily see why advertising is so expensive.

Of course, not all businesses need national advertising. Local businesses will find local television and newspapers' rates considerably less than those cited above. For example, the *Oklahoma City Journal* (circulation 60,000) charges the advertiser $0.39 per line. *The Miami Beach Sun Reporter* (circulation 50,000) charges advertisers a flat rate of $0.30 per line. Even though it is cheaper for local businessmen to advertise locally, they still usually have much less money to spend on advertising than do national businesses. Once the businessman realizes the high costs involved in advertising, he must consider other factors to determine if advertising is a wise investment for *his* product.

## HIDDEN QUALITIES

One function of advertising is to inform consumers of a product's qualities. If these qualities are apparent to the consumer, advertising is of less importance in the final sale of the product. However, if these qualities are hidden, unable to be seen upon inspection by the consumer, then advertising has a very important role to play. To illustrate, consider the classic example, gasoline. The consumer has no way of telling a gasoline's quality. It is completely hidden; two jars of gasoline look exactly alike. Advertising can inform the consumer of hidden qualities such as special additives, filtering processes, and blending processes. Consumers do develop preferences for the kind of gasoline they use. These preferences are built up by advertising the hidden qualities of the particular brand. Many other products have hidden qualities. The important question for the producer to ask is this: if a consumer were to look at two products side by side, one mine, one my competitor's, would there be any apparent differences? If not, advertising can be used to inform the consumer of my product's hidden qualities.

## HIGH CONSUMER INTEREST

Advertising, whether it be on television, radio, newspaper, magazine, or billboard, must compete for the consumers' attention. Of course if it cannot gain this attention, the advertisement will not inform the consumer of a product's qualities.

What factors, besides the ad itself, which will be discussed later, cause consumers to give an advertisement their attention? One is whether the consumer is really interested in buying the products. Analyze yourself on this point. Of all the ads you see and hear, which do you look for and pay attention to? The answer is the ads of the products you are thinking about buying. Consumers will ignore what they are not interested in.

This principle can be generalized; when a product is growing in demand, many people will be interested in buying it; and thus advertising will be effective. However, when a product's demand is declining, few people will be interested in buying it; and thus advertising will go unnoticed or be ineffective.

## CONSUMERS' BUYING MOTIVES

The nature of consumers' buying motives affects the *type* of advertising more than decision whether or not to use it. If a product is bought for *rational* reasons—price, quality, durability, and reliability—then advertising can only be informative. Such advertising is designed to inform consumers of these rational qualities of the product.

However, if the product is bought for emotional reasons—status, fear, sex appeal, security—the type of advertising changes radically. Advertising can stimulate these emotions. For example, Lincoln Continental advertisements do not stress price and reliability. They do stress the status and prestige associated with the car. Tobacco companies advertise from a purely emotional basis, conjuring up images of virility, sex appeal, or femininity in their ads. Mouthwash and toothpaste are two other examples of products with ads based upon emotional buying behavior. When strong emotions are involved, advertising can do a great deal to stimulate buying.

These factors determine the product's ability to be effectively advertised. If more than one is negative—that is if the businessman has a small amount of money to spend on promotional efforts, if the product does not have any hidden qualities, if consumer interest is low, if consumers' buying motives are purely rational—the business should look to other promotional tools. This does not mean that the product cannot be advertised, only that the funds allocated to promotion can be more efficiently used in other types of efforts.

## WHAT TO EXPECT FROM ADVERTISING

Advertising is limited in what it can accomplish, as is personal selling. The businessman should not expect too much; he should realize what advertising is likely to accomplish. There are several realistic expectations for advertising campaigns.

## BRAND RECOGNITION

A producer's product is distinguished from competing products by the brand name the firm attaches to it. Examples of brand names would include Texaco, Winston, Larry's Service Station, and the Hideaway Steak House.

Through advertising consumers will get to know and recognize the firm's brand name. One of the main objectives of advertising is to build up a *brand preference* among consumers. In other words, they seek, ask for, and prefer a particular brand over all other brands of the same product—for example, Coke rather than just cola, Winstons rather than just cigarettes, Bayer rather than just aspirin, and McDonald's rather than just hamburgers. A start to building this brand preference among consumers is gaining widespread recognition of the firm's brand of products.

## TRIAL BUY

If a firm's advertisements can create enough interest, new consumers may try the products just once instead of buying their regular brand. The businessman hopes that once they try it, the product will sell itself, and a loyal consumer will be the result. A loyal consumer is one who repeatedly purchases the same brand of product. If the original claims made in the advertisements are true, this is not too far-flung an expectation. However, it holds true only until another producer convinces the consumer to *try* his brand instead of yours.

## REACH MANY CONSUMERS

The circulation of periodicals and the number of television viewers in the United States are indicative of the many consumers advertising can reach. Advertising can also reach consumers inaccessible to salesmen. For instance, breakfast food ads reach many children, none of whom would be accessible to door-to-door salesmen.

## AID IN PERSONAL SELLING

The detailed ways advertising and personal selling work hand-in-hand will be covered later in this chapter. Advertising can open the door for salesmen and make their job easier and more effective. If potential consumers do not recognize the product's brand name, the salesman has a more difficult time.

## CONSTRUCTING AN ADVERTISING MESSAGE

What the businessman expects from his advertising campaign will have a great effect on the type of advertising done. For example, if he wants consumers to trial buy his product, a refundable coupon may be included in a printed ad. The coupon can save the consumer money and thus is likely to entice the consumer into a trial buy. What the businessman wants his advertising to do should be clear in his mind. When he knows his goals, he can develop an advertising message and place it in the proper media to get the proper results.

In constructing an advertisement to communicate to a *group* of potential consumers, their attitudes, desires, and outlooks must be kept first in the businessman's mind. Each product may be bought by a number of different groups of consumers. Each group is likely to have different attitudes, desires and needs. The businessman is trying to talk to each group of consumers. Unless he knows what each group wants to hear, and what their thinking and attitudes are, they might not listen to him. This is the first step in creating a message. Businessmen need to know not only what different consumer groups are going to be listening to the message, but what each group's attitudes, beliefs, and feelings are. Thus the message "buy my product" might be the same for all the groups of potential consumers; but how, when, and where it is stated could definitely be different for each group.

Next the businessman should determine what exactly should be contained in the message. As a general statement he will be trying to communicate (1) the features that are unique to his product and (2) his product's strengths. These two are communicated around a third point, how consumers evaluate the alternative products. An example can best illustrate how these three points came together in forming a message. Purina Company found that dog owners wanted a pet food that was palatable, nutritious, economical, and convenient to store. The dry Purina Chow was developed and in taste tests on dogs found to be preferred six to one. Similar to other dog food companies, Purina initially used advertising messages which stressed the product's high nutritional value (the product's uniqueness and strength). Further evaluation of how consumers evaluated the alternative dog foods revealed that nutritional value was irrelevant. The consumers' main concern was whether or not the dog would really eat the given dog food. Consequently, a new advertising message was created, saying "new Purina Dog Chow makes dogs eager eaters." With this message, Purina has been able to sell more dog food than any other company.[1]

This story shows that simply telling the product's uniqueness and strengths does not necessarily result in an effective advertisement. The message must be centered around the consumer's attitudes and beliefs about what a given product should do or should be.

The third step is the actual construction of the advertisement. Whole books have been written on advertising design, color, and makeup. You can consult these books for an in-depth discussion of advertising construction. This is an important part of advertising communications, but the subject is too involved for the discussion here. A properly constructed advertisement can attract and hold consumers' attention as well as get them to read or hear the message. The best message unnoticed is the same as no message at all. Advertising construction is no place for amateurs; the businessman should seek specialized help from advertising agencies or his own advertising department.

---

1. Noel Digby, "Purina Dog Chow: All You Add Is Love," Central Region Convention, American Association of Advertising Agencies, Oct. 14, 1966.

## EVALUATING ALTERNATIVE MEDIA

The nature of the medium chosen by the businessman has a great impact on the message. Each medium has its own distinct strength and weaknesses the businessman should be aware of.

An advertising medium is the vehicle which carries a message to a chosen group of potential consumers. Each medium has its own characteristics, limitations, and strengths. In certain situations one medium will be superior to another. The times each medium can be most effective must be understood for selection of the right media to fit the situation faced by the businessman. If the medium is not chosen properly, the message either is ignored by the potential consumer or misinterpreted, both of which mean that the advertisement is un-effective. This discussion will be limited to the four media most commonly used in business advertising: newspapers, magazines, television, and radio.

### NEWSPAPERS

This is the vehicle most used in delivering a message to potential consumers. It offers the advertisers, especially the small business, numerous advantages. Newspapers have extensive coverage; in fact, in excess of 80 percent of the adults in the U.S. read a newspaper on a weekday. In addition to contacting many people, newspapers are confined to local markets. Most cities and towns have a local newspaper. The local businessman can thus contact only those people who will likely buy his product. Finally, the businessman can advertise his product within a few hours notice since most newspapers are printed either daily or weekly.

However, newspaper advertising does have its disadvantages. Probably the severest disadvantage is the short life of a newspaper. Newspapers are not read and reread; they are skimmed through once. If the ad is not seen in the first reading, it never will be. A second disadvantage is the large amount of compe-tition within newspapers for the reader's attention. One ad may become lost or buried among all the ads in a paper. Try to recall the advertisements you *noticed* (not read) in yesterday's paper. Our guess would be that most readers cannot recall more than two advertisements.

The newspaper as a vehicle is best used to tell consumers about a product which already has a demand. If the product is new, newspapers are not the best vehicle available. In newspaper advertising, size and newsworthiness of the ad are of major importance. Full-page ads seldom get lost in the shuffle, nor do newsworthy ads. Newsworthy ads tell the consumer something he did not know, such as the sale price of a product.

### MAGAZINES

*Magazines* are a specialized vehicle of communication. Most people read a newspaper; however, only people with special interests read such magazines as *Popular Mechanics, Better Homes & Gardens, Modern Photography, Adver-tising Age,* or *Dog World.* This is the prime advantage of magazine advertising, extensive readership among a certain interest group. Regardless of the product there are probably several national magazines read by only those people who would be interested in it. The advertiser thus can be very selective about who will be given the opportunity to see his ad. Advertising in newspapers does not offer this selectivity. Another advantage magazines have over newspapers is in their longer life. Magazines are kept, read, and reread. Thus the chances for a consumer noticing and reading a particular advertisement are enhanced.

The biggest disadvantage of magazines is that unless the product has national demand and distribution, the advertiser is paying for a lot of wasted circulation. An advertisement by a local restaurant would not be suitable for a magazine. Many magazines have minimized this disadvantage by publishing regional editions for advertisers whose products are not nationally distributed. *Better Homes & Gardens* for example, has ten different regional editions of each issue.

Magazines would seem to be best for products having national or at least regional distribution and for products whose consumers are classified as a special interest group: skiers, home owners, photographers, dog owners, etc.

## TELEVISION

*Television* is a central part of most Americans' entertainment. It has been estimated that 95 percent of all homes have a television set and that more than one-fourth of the population's leisure time is spent watching television. No other medium commands so much of our time or reaches as many people as does television. This mass audience is probably the biggest advantage to television advertisers. In addition, from an advertising standpoint, things can be done on television that cannot be done with any of the other media. Products can be demonstrated and shown in use. This combination of sight and sound comes very close to personal selling to literally thousands of people at a time.

The advertiser has the same selectivity offered by magazines. By picking time slots and shows, some control is gained over who will see the advertisement. Such shows as *Days of Our Lives, The Wide World of Sports,* and the *Bugs Bunny Show* are not all seen by the same type of consumer. Thus advertising on television, as in magazines, can be directed to special interest groups. Like magazines, television offers various combinations of local and regional advertising.

Unfortunately television has two very prohibitive disadvantages. The first is cost. Cost of television time and production efforts are tremendous. One ad, shown one time during prime time, may exceed $100,000 in time costs alone. The second disadvantage of television is that its messages are instantaneous. They have no life span. Consumers cannot go back to an ad on television and study it or ask questions. If the message does not register or is not seen the first time, it is lost until next time, if there is a next time.

## RADIO

*Radio* is like television in that it gives a sound dimension to advertising. However, it lacks the sight appeal of television, newspapers, and magazine advertising. Radio does offer the advertiser a mass audience. Almost 99 percent of the homes in the United States have at least one radio. Like television and magazines, radio is a selective media. Stations specializing in classical, soul, jazz, or rock music or in commentary or sports programming have listeners with specialized interests. The radio advertiser knows the type of audience each type of programming attracts. The radio and television are also alike in one disadvantage, the life of the message. Once the message is given, it may be gone forever.

Unlike television, however, radio is entirely a local and relatively inexpensive media. Local businessmen appealing to certain types of consumers will find the radio a valuable medium. For it to be effective, however, the advertisements needs to be aired quite often, with a great deal of repetition.

## Promoting a Product:
## Personal Selling and Advertising

Promotional efforts are not made up of either personal selling or advertising; instead the business' promotional efforts should be a combination of both, if for no other reason than that a personal salesman is almost always needed to complete or close a sale. There are, however, other reasons for combining personal selling and advertising. The most important is that the two elements complement one another. Thus to get the most for a certain amount of promotional dollars, they should be combined into one promotional effort. This does not mean that they will get equal emphasis. In one situation more emphasis might be given to personal selling than advertising. The factors which determine how much each will be emphasized are the potential consumer, the product's life cycle, and the nature of the product.

The *potential consumer* has been classified as either industrial or ultimate. The industrial consumer, by his nature and product demands, requires more personal attention. In addition geographic concentration and high average sale makes it possible for those businesses distributing products to industrial consumers to emphasize personal selling over advertising. The ultimate consumer, unless very localized, usually represents a large number of geographically dispersed people. When this is so, those businesses selling to a large group of ultimate consumers must rely more on mass promotion (advertising) than personal selling.

As Exhibit 11–1 indicates, whether the consumer is industrial or ultimate, advertising does some preselling of the product, company, and salesman because of its ability to reach consumers. The other two factors play an important role in deciding when personal selling or advertising should be emphasized.

The four stages in the product's life cycle—introduction, growth, maturity, and decline—each require a different emphasis on personal selling and advertising.

## EXHIBIT 11-1

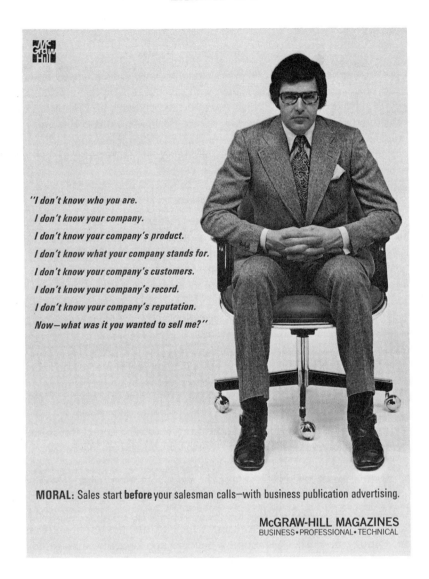

"*I don't know who you are.*
*I don't know your company.*
*I don't know your company's product.*
*I don't know what your company stands for.*
*I don't know your company's customers.*
*I don't know your company's record.*
*I don't know your company's reputation.*
*Now—what was it you wanted to sell me?*"

**MORAL:** Sales start **before** your salesman calls—with business publication advertising.

**McGRAW-HILL MAGAZINES**
BUSINESS·PROFESSIONAL·TECHNICAL

Source: *Business Week*, Jan. 8, 1973, p. 33.

During the introduction stage few people know of the product, its advantages or uses. Personal selling is especially important during this stage. New products need the special push that only personal selling can supply. Because the product is new, questions and objections will have to be answered, demonstrations given, and sales closed. These are functions which are best performed by a personal salesman. Advertising is limited to letting consumers know a new product is available and to arousing the consumers' curiosity so that they will either inquire about or come to look at the new product. When they do, personal salesmen must finish the job of promoting and selling the product.

As the product goes into its growth stage, competition forces the producer to try and differentiate his product from competitors' offerings, because the product has been accepted by a larger number of consumers. During this stage advertising is emphasized over personal selling. Advertising should now persuade consumers to buy and stay with one brand of the product. This strategy is carried through the third stage of the product's life, maturity. Mass selling (advertising) is particularly aggressive during this stage. You can prove this point to yourself by counting the number of ads on television, radio, newspapers, and magazines done by the automobile companies or pharmaceutical companies.

As the product reaches the decline stage, all promotional efforts are decreased in an attempt to cut costs. Personal selling receives the emphasis necessary to keep the few remaining customers satisfied. Thus at each stage in a product's life cycle the amount of advertising and personal selling used by a business changes. The nature of the product will have some impact on how personal selling and advertising are combined into a total promotional effort.

*The nature of the product* has an impact on all decisions which affect the distribution process. The concern here is with the impact on promotional efforts. Four types of products have been identified: convenience goods, specialty goods, shopping goods, and services.

Convenience goods require more mass selling and less personal selling than the other three types. The primary influence on consumers who buy one brand of razor blades or cigarettes, for example, is the advertising efforts of their producers. No personal selling is involved; razor blades are on a display rack and cigarettes in a machine or behind a counter. The consumer has already made up his mind which brand to buy before he enters the store. The brand of convenience good purchased is usually bought on habit, which was started and is maintained through advertising.

The comparisons consumers make between products when looking for shopping goods make it necessary for more emphasis to be placed on personal selling than advertising. Advertising is used to point up the different characteristics of a product. But, once the consumer is in a store, the salesman is important in pointing up certain differences between the products and getting the consumer to buy one product over another. For example, the salesman points up many different features between competing brands of televisions.

The consumer is willing to seek out a specialty good. Advertising which reminds consumers where they can find a certain specialty good is emphasized over personal selling. Additionally, advertising efforts must continue to keep the product a specialty good. Personal selling plays only a minor role in promoting these goods because the consumer already has his mind made up that he is going to buy one product. The only question is when and which size or price range. Salesmen can help solve these problems.

Service products require advertising to let the consumer know the service is available and personal selling almost in equal proportions, except when the service is of a professional nature, as for doctors, lawyers, dentists, etc. In these cases advertising is prohibited. For other services, since they are intangible, consumers buy and rebuy the service on personal impressions of the ability and reliability of person performing the services. This person must be involved in selling both himself and the service. While in the presence of a consumer he is always selling himself. Advertising fulfills the role of telling a consumer where he can find the particular service and in many cases portraying an image that the person performing the service is to be trusted.

These three elements—the potential consumer, the product's stage in its life cycle, and the nature of the product—separately and in total determine the emphasis personal selling and advertising will receive in a given situation. Knowing how these elements affect the consumer's buying decision, the business-man can determine the right mix of promotional alternatives for his product and situation.

## Summary

The promotion of a product is an important part of any businesses distri-bution process. Few products, especially new ones, sell themselves. The busi-nessman who doesn't promote his product is taking a big chance. With all the products competing for a limited number of consumers' dollars the consumer is not likely to buy a new product purely by accident.

Businesses promote their products by communication with consumers. This communication or promotional effort can take two forms, personal selling and advertising. Each is different in its strengths and weaknesses. When using either, certain precautions should be taken to insure the businessman that the strengths will be maximized and the weaknesses minimized. What is done with each and the amount of each used by a business depends upon the par-ticular consumer, the nature of the product being promoted, and the stage in the product's life cycle.

## QUESTIONS

1. What factors determine when personal selling is better than advertising?
2. What can the businessman expect from the personal selling effort?
3. What is involved in training effective salesmen?
4. When should the business system emphasize advertising over personal selling as a method of communicating with consumers?
5. What can the businessman expect from a sound advertising campaign?
6. What does every advertising message try to communicate to consumers?
7. When should the business system rely on:
   (a) Newspapers,
   (b) Magazines,
   (c) Television,
   (d) Radio?

8. What mix of advertising and personal selling do most convenience goods require, and why?

## Incident 11-1

The First National Bank operates in a midwestern town of approximately 150,000 people. The main bank is located in the downtown business area, and six branch banks are located throughout the city. Although each bank carries First National's name, they are evaluated separately. Thus, there are some branches that have more depositors, make more loans, and in general are operated more efficiently than others. First National's growth and branch success have in the past been taken for granted and could be very easily attributed to convenience of location. No promotional efforts have been instituted. Scott Prentise, First National's president, wonders if in fact the more successful branches are just more convenient than competitor's branches.

Until recently the competition has not been severe among the banks. But two years ago Security National Bank added a Vice-President of Business Development to its staff. This new vice-president has put in motion a continuing promotional campaign. As a result, Security's depositors and loans have increased at the expense of First National. Prentise is considering a full-fledged promotional campaign, but wonders just what exactly can and should be done.

(1) What personal selling and advertising efforts could Prentise utilize?

(2) What type of information does he need to emphasize in this promotional effort?

(3) What media would you advise Prentise to rely on and why?

(4) How should the promotional efforts of First National be evaluated?

(5) Construct an example of a promotional message for Prentise's evaluation.

## Incident 11-2

Interiors of Chicago, a partnership formed in 1970, manufactures custom wood interior decorating dividers and panels. Sales and distribution are carried on in the Chicago office, which consists of a showroom and sales office. Manufacturing and production facilities are located in a plant on the near-north side of town. One partner runs the manufacturing end of the business. He purchases the necessary material and supervises six workers who build to meet customer orders. This partner installs the order on the customers' premises with the help of one installer.

A second partner is responsible for sales. She spends her time at the office and contacts interior designers and architects. Once an order is obtained, she carefully measures the job and designates the material, color, and dimensions of each order. Because of the custom nature of the product, an error in measurement results in a high-cost scrap item.

The Interiors line is priced on a cost-plus basis. After the customer's requirements are carefully analyzed, the final cost is production costs plus a mark-up of 75 percent. Interiors has been very successful for the following reasons:

(a) They have a substantial reputation for originality and dependability of design

and manufacturing. For example, Interiors is the only firm in the Chicago area to still work with bamboo inlays.
(b) A succession of satisfied customers have recommended the line to others.
(c) They have developed a good rapport with many interior designers in the area.
(d) Two of Chicago's main department stores will only have Interiors do the custom display windows.
(e) There are many apartment-dwellers in the Chicago area wanting custom interiors.

Both partners agree that in view of the profitable nature of the business, efforts should be concentrated on increasing sales volume. Area surveys indicate that a substantial potential market exists in the suburbs. But sales representatives employed in the past have proven unreliable, and an ad in the Chicago classified telephone directory has resulted in only a moderate sales volume.
(1) How should personal selling efforts be increased?
(2) What recommendations would you have for training and compensating this sales force?
(3) How should advertising efforts be increased?
(4) What recommendations would you have for construction of this advertising? What media would you use?
(5) How much reliance should Interiors place on personal selling and advertising in their total promotional efforts?
(6) How can these personal selling and advertising efforts be coordinated into a united promotional effort?
(7) Would it be feasible to employ two non-firm members, one to take charge of manufacturing, the other to take charge of the sales office, and have the two partners serve as outside sales representatives?

# 12

# Physical Distribution

## The Nature of Physical Distribution

Up to this point, primary consideration has been given to three parts of the distribution process: product, price, and promotion. The fourth part, product availability, was introduced in Chapter 10 with a discussion on channels of distribution. The other aspect of product availability—physical distribution—is analyzed in this chapter. In order to provide good service to the firm's customers, it is necessary that the right amount of goods be transported to the right place at the right time in the right condition. As a matter of fact, the customer's intention to buy in the first place could very well depend upon the time needed to expedite the shipment of merchandise.

Professional people who provide a service must also be concerned with physical distribution. For example, a barber must not keep his customers waiting too long or they will leave. An accountant or an attorney preparing a client's federal tax return must not file the return with the IRS later than April 15. If he does, the client will likely look to others to provide the service.

In this chapter, physical distribution will be examined in a much broader perspective. Physical distribution is much more than the delivery of merchandise to the firm's customers. In fact, for a manufacturing firm there are, at a minimum, four functions to be performed in the area of physical distribution:

(1) Selecting the mode of transportation to be used in shipping raw materials that are used in the production process to the plant site.

(2) Selecting the mode of transportation to be used in shipping finished goods to the firm's customers.

(3) Determining the appropriate number and location of the firm's warehouses.

(4) Selecting the right plant location.

Except for the shipment of raw materials, these functions also apply to retailers and wholesalers.

Throughout this text the importance of the systems approach to operating a business has been emphasized. Nowhere is this approach needed more than in the area of physical distribution. Each decision the business manager makes concerning one facet of physical distribution will in turn affect the other parts. For example, the decision to construct a manufacturing plant close to the source of raw material will mean that transportation costs on finished goods will be higher than if the plant was built close to the market where the goods are to be sold. Likewise, decisions concerning the location and number of warehouses will affect the amount of transportation and storage costs. Although decisions of this nature are difficult, the business manager must coordinate the four functions rather than looking at each as if it was a separate segment independent of all others. As a guide to decision making, the business manager must try to minimize total costs to the firm while at the same time providing good service to the customers. One such cost area to be considered is physical distribution.

In the remainder of this chapter, consideration will be given to modes of transportation, warehousing, and plant location. All of these elements are involved in the physical distribution of a good or service. A section on basic principles of locating a retail store is also included.

## Modes of Transportation

In the United States there are five modes of transportation which the retailer, wholesaler, or manufacturer may use to move goods: (1) railroads, (2) motor vehicles, (3) ships, (4) pipelines, and (5) airplanes. Each of these is discussed in detail below. Exhibit 12–1 indicates the changing pattern of use of each of these five modes of transportation. As the advantages and disadvantages of each of these transportation modes for the businessman are discussed, the exhibit will be referred to.

### RAILROADS

Although the railroads at one time represented the primary means of transporting goods in America, they no longer hold this distinction. As shown in the graph, railroads accounted for 63 percent of the total volume of domestic intercity freight traffic in 1940. However, this percentage has been steadily declining. The preliminary indication for 1971 was that railroads would account for 39 percent of the total intercity freight traffic. This represents a decline between 1940 and 1970 of approximately 38 percent.

EXHIBIT 12–1

*Percent Distribution of Ton-Miles of Domestic Intercity*
*Freight Traffic, by Type of Transportation*[1]

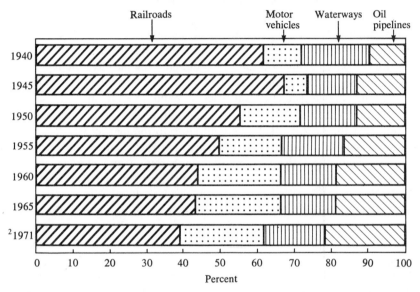

Source: U.S. Bureau of the Census, *Statistical Abstract of the United States: 1973*, 94th ed. Washington, D.C.: 1973, p. 537.

This drastic decline in rail traffic is due to the increased competition provided by trucks and pipelines. Trucks, because of their speed and flexibility, have become increasingly popular as a means of transporting high value, low bulk items over short distances. Because of the higher rates charged on these items, the railroads have been losing an important source of their earnings to the trucking industry.

The reduction in the amount of traffic handled by the railroads has resulted in rather drastic actions on the part of railroad management in order to reduce costs or improve service. For instance, the Penn Central, a giant railroad in financial difficulty in late 1972, set as some of its goals to reduce its 20,000 miles of track by 5,000 miles; to eliminate one brakeman from each freight train crew, thereby eliminating 5,700 jobs; and to encourage truckers to use piggyback service by taking trailers off the highways and on to the railways.

1. Airways not shown separately; less than 1 percent.
2. Preliminary data.

This third goal was necessary in order to encourage new business which would add to tonnage and revenue.[3]

The railroads are noted for their ability to carry large volumes of heavy, bulky low-value commodities long distances at a low cost. For this reason, the products of the forest, mines, and agriculture are often shipped by rail. Because of the highly interconnected railroad system which covers the entire country, it is possible for some railroads, upon notice from a shipper, to divert a shipment to a different destination with little or no increase in freight charges to the shipper. This service, referred to as "diversion in transit," will be discussed in more detail later in this chapter.

## MOTOR VEHICLES

Where the railroads are the most efficient and economical carriers of low-value items such as iron, coal, and wheat traveling long distances, motor vehicles provide the most economical and efficient service on medium- to high-value items traveling a short distance. Trucks can travel on almost any road at relatively high speeds and are not limited, as are ships and trains, to predetermined canals and roadbeds. Due to this flexibility, merchandise can be loaded on to a truck at the point of origin and unloaded at the point of destination. As a result, a shipper will incur less cost over short distances with a truck than a train, because the latter requires the use of a truck for pick-up and delivery. Furthermore, merchandise shipped via a motor vehicle sustains less wear and tear because of reduced handling and less shock during movement. This in turn means lower packaging costs for the shipper.

Because of the flexibility and speed provided by trucks over short distances, they have become increasingly popular as a mode of transportation. Although motor vehicles accounted for only 10 percent of domestic intercity freight traffic in 1940, they accounted for 22 percent in 1971. This represents an increase of 120 percent. The slogan used by the trucking industry—"if you bought it, it came by truck"—is not far from the truth.

## SHIPS

Like the railroads, water carriers have the capacity to handle large tonnages of bulky commodities such as iron, ore, coal, petroleum, and grain. Although the cost of shipping via rivers, canals, the Great Lakes, or the ocean is the lowest of all the modes of transportation, it is also the slowest. In many parts of the United States freezing conditions prevent shipments during the winter months. Consequently, manufacturers and others who depend upon raw materials transported by water order larger quantities during the summer and fall than are actually needed for production. The excess is stored and then used during the winter months.

In 1940, inland waterways accounted for 18 percent of domestic intercity freight traffic. This percentage has declined slightly over the past thirty years,

---

3. *Business Week,* January 13, 1973, p. 44–45.

and the preliminary figure for 1971 is 16 percent. In reality, these figures understate the total significance of water carriers because ocean transportation to and from United States ports is not included in the statistics.

As a new source of traffic, ships have been designed to handle truck trailers. This type of service is often referred to as "fishyback." Another service which water carriers are emphasizing to shippers is the use of ships as "floating warehouses." Because of the low speed which is characteristic of water carriers, commodities in transit can be stored for several days. Those companies which lack sufficient storage facilities find this to be a very attractive alternative.

## PIPELINES

Pipelines, like motor carriers, have played a significant role in capturing traffic from the railroads. The railroads at one time shipped much of the crude oil and other petroleum products from production fields to the consuming markets. With the construction of pipelines, which are owned for the most part by major oil and gas companies, the railroads have lost much of this traffic. In fact, the crude oil shipped via rail today is limited to those areas in which pipelines have not yet been constructed or the production of oil is so small that the construction of pipelines is not warranted.

The characteristics of pipelines are such that they are limited to the transporting of liquid products such as oil and gasoline. The use of pipelines by oil companies has had a significant impact upon the location of refineries throughout the United States. Because of the low cost incurred in transporting crude oil via pipelines, it is no longer necessary for refineries to be located near the production fields. On the contrary, today many oil companies utilize pipelines to transport the crude oil to the refineries which are located near markets where the refined products will be sold to consumers.

The rapid increase in the use of pipelines is evident from the data in Exhibit 12–1. Whereas in 1940 oil pipelines accounted for only 9 percent of intercity freight traffic, in 1971 they were expected to account for 23 percent of this traffic. To make matters more difficult for the railroads as well as other modes of transportation, experiments are being conducted today whereby it may be possible in the near future to ship solid products in capsules via pipelines.

## AIR TRANSPORT

The characteristics of air freight are almost in direct contrast to those of water freight. As previously indicated, shipment by water is both the slowest and least expensive of any mode of transportation. Air freight is both the fastest and the most expensive of all modes of transportation. For this reason, freight shipped via the airways is restricted to high-value items such as electronic components and perishable goods. In many businesses today, time is of the essence. Having materials available when they are needed may keep the firm from stopping production. The following example illustrates the vital role played by air transport in the automobile industry.

Jet Way Inc., a tiny air-charter firm in Ypsilanti, Mich., is busy day and night making "last-resort" flights of parts to one or another of the Big Three's assembly lines to prevent them from grinding to a halt, says Jack Mars, vice-president and chief pilot. Jet Way charges up to ten times the normal air-freight cost and rarely flies more than a few hundred pounds of parts at a time, but its 550-m.p.h. Lear jets can reach 39 percent of the industry's forty-four U.S. car plants in ninety-five minutes or less. To auto makers faced with a plant closedown, that's worth every dime.[4]

Although air transportation is expensive, total distribution costs may be reduced through savings in other areas. For example, a buyer in a large metropolitan area can expect to receive merchandise that was shipped by air within a few hours or, at the most, one day after it is ordered. This may mean considerable savings in inventory costs if warehouse facilities which are no longer necessary can be eliminated. Furthermore, goods shipped by air freight suffer less spoilage and have lower packaging requirements.

The percentage of total intercity freight hauled by air transport is increasing each year. However, today it still represents less than 1 percent of the total. The percentage is so small that the graph does not include air transport. This does not mean that air transport will be insignificant in the future. Significant changes are being implemented to accommodate additional sources of traffic. With the development of supersonic transport, increased cargo capacity, improved pick-up and delivery service, and more efficient terminal operations, air shipment will become more popular.

### Should the Businessman Haul his own Goods?

Transportation carriers are grouped into three classifications: common carriers, contract carriers, and private carriers. Common carriers receive a franchise from a government regulatory agency such as the Interstate Commerce Commission. They are required to maintain regular services and to carry freight for any shipper who requests it. Examples of common carriers include the major truck lines such as Ryder Truck and Lee Way Motor Freight. Contract carriers enter into contracts with specific shippers to transport specific goods over a specific period of time. Contract carriers are subject to less government regulation than common carriers.

Private carriers are owned and operated by firms for the purpose of hauling their own goods. In other words, rather than hiring someone else to transport goods, the businessman may elect to operate his own transportation equipment. Private trucking has always been, and still is, an important means of shipping goods short distances. For example, retail stores use trucks to make local deliveries to their customers, farmers use trucks to haul produce to the local market place, and gasoline stations use trucks to make service calls. However, today, with the advent of major expressways and turnpikes, private truck-

---

4. The *Wall Street Journal,* Tuesday, May 29, 1973, p. 1.

ing is utilized for long haul shipments as well. Many of the trucks on the highways today bear the names of the companies whose products they haul. Many companies own a fleet of trucks which carry their products to every corner of the country. Although the truck is the most popular mode of private transportation, the other modes (rail, ship, airplane, and pipeline) are also utilized as private carriers.

In many instances private transportation results in speedier delivery to the firm's customers. Rather than waiting to ship merchandise via common carriers, the firm which uses private carriers can ship merchandise the moment it is ready. The private carrier is also advantageous in those situations where specialized equipment is needed. For example, the major oil and gas companies own and operate the pipelines used to transport oil from the fields to the refineries. These companies likewise own fleets of tank trucks which are used to transport their products to the service stations.

Although private transportation provides an alternative to paying for the sevices of common or contract carriers, it is not economically feasible for all businessmen to elect this approach for long haul shipments. Unless the businessman ships large quantities on a regular and frequent basis, he will most likely find the common carrier a less expensive means of transporting the firm's goods. In any event, before making a decision on this question, the businessman should carefully compare the cost and services provided by for-hire carriers with the cost and service to be realized through private transportation.

The transportation rates and special services provided primarily by railroads will be discussed next. Using the railroads may appear questionable since they have recently experienced significant losses in traffic. However, centering attention on the railroad is appropriate because the rate structure and a number of services provided by other modes of transportation are patterned after rates and services developed by the railroads.

## Transportation Rates and Special Services

### CLASS RATES

Through the use of a freight classification device, railroads are able to divide thousands of products into a limited number of groups or classes. This process of classifying products into specific classes is *rating*. The present freight classification contains a rating on approximately 10,000 products. This technique eliminates the need to publish separate rates for each product. The class into which a particular commodity or product is placed depends mostly upon the characteristics of the product and the distance it will travel. For example, products with one or more of the following characteristics would pay a high rate:

(1) Products which require special equipment for loading or transporting (i.e., fruits and vegetables require refrigerator cars).

(2) Products which take up lots of space but weigh little (i.e., bicycles).

(3) Products which could cause damage to other goods while in transit (i.e., acids and paints).

## COMMODITY RATES

Unlike a class rate, which is determined by rating goods into specific classifications, a commodity rate is one which is usually negotiated between the shipper and the railroad. A commodity rate is the one established for bulky, low-value products such as iron ore, lumber, and agricultural products. However, other products which are regularly shipped in large quantities may also be subject to negotiation between shipper and carrier. Most of the goods shipped via the railroad receive a commodity rate. The commodity rates supersede the class rates on the same commodity. In many instances, a class rate may be just high enough to prevent a shipper from competing in a particular market. For example, assume that it costs the Wolverine Co. $2.00 to produce and harvest a bushel of peaches at point A which it wants to sell at point B for $3.00 per bushel, which is the going market price. However, the class rate from point A to point B (200 miles) is $1.00 per bushel, which

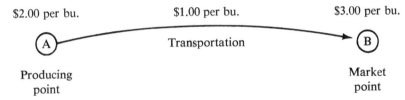

means that the Wolverine Co. will realize no profit for its efforts. This is computed as follows:

| | | |
|---|---|---|
| Selling price per bushel of peaches | | $3.00 |
| Cost to produce one bushel | $2.00 | |
| Cost to transport one bushel | 1.00 | 3.00 |
| Profit | | $ –0– |

The only opportunity the Wolverine Co. has of competing in the market at point B is to negotiate a commodity rate with a carrier which is less than $1.00 per bushel. If it is assumed that the Wolverine Co. is successful and negotiates a commodity rate of less than $1.00, say $0.50, then the company will be able to earn a profit of $0.50 on each bushel of peaches sold at point B ($3.00 — $2.50 = $0.50).

This example illustrates the fact that freight rates are not fixed. Lower rates may be available through effective negotiation on the part of the business manager who wants shipment and the carrier who is interested in providing additional traffic.

As a means of developing new business to increase revenues, the railroads have developed special services. Three examples discussed below are transit privileges, diversion in transit, and incentive rates.

## TRANSIT PRIVILEGE

A transit privilege is often granted by railroads (and in some cases by trucks) to shippers who find it necessary to stop the goods in transit before they reach their final destination. The purpose in stopping the shipment may be to have the goods stored for a period of time or perhaps to have the goods processed into a different form.

For example, a wholesaler buys New York grown apples in Albany to be sold in California. However, before reaching California, the fruit is to be shipped to Michigan, where it will be stored in a cold storage for two weeks. The transit privilege allows the shipper to pay the through rate from New York to California even though the apples are stored for two weeks in Michigan. For a small transit charge, the freight bill for the services rendered by the railroad will be based upon a through rate from point of origin to point of destination, providing the same general direction is maintained. The through rate will be smaller than if the railroad based its freight bill on two separate shipments, from point of origin to point of storage and from point of storage to point of destination.

The carrier is not obligated to provide this attractive service to the shipper. Rather it is up to the businessman to negotiate with the carrier a transit privilege which will be beneficial to both parties.

## DIVERSION IN TRANSIT

Diversion of the goods in transit often occurs when perishable or hard-to-store goods are being sold. For example, the wholesaler in the previous illustration could ship a carload of New York apples directly to California, anticipating a buyer for his fruit. While searching for a buyer, he finds that the California market is saturated; and consequently he diverts the shipment to Washington state, where market conditions are better.

Although the goods have been diverted, the shipper will receive the privilege of paying the through rate from New York to Washington plus a small transit charge. This rate is much less than the rate from New York to California plus the freight charge from California to the next destination, Washington.

## INCENTIVE RATES

In a retail establishment such as the local tobacco store, there are usually cigars which sell for ten cents apiece or three for a quarter. By purchasing three cigars the buyer saves five cents. This is a simple, but basic example of a quantity discount. By selling in large quantities, the cigar store owner is able to reduce his operating costs on a per unit basis, spreading the costs over more units (cigars). Some of these savings are therefore passed on to the buyer in the form of smaller prices for larger quantities purchased.

This same concept is used by various modes of transportation to encourage shippers to ship in large quantities. Rates are, therefore, published in terms of LCL (less than carload), CL (carload), LTL (less than truckload), and TL (truckload). For example, a motor transport carrier may quote a price of $0.50 per 100 for shipments of 5,000 pounds, which we will assume is less than a truckload. To provide incentive to the shipper to ship in large quantities the same trucker will charge $0.40 per 100 for truckload shipments of 10,000 pounds. Consequently, by shipping in truckload quantities throughout the year, it is possible for retailers, wholesalers, and manufacturers to realize considerable savings.

## IMPORTANCE OF UNDERSTANDING RATES

The cost of transporting goods from seller to buyer is a significant part of the total cost of running a business. Approximately 50 percent of total distribution costs are spent on physical distribution. In order to minimize these costs, the business manager must constantly be on the outlook for possible savings. Although a higher class rate may be published in the tariff on a particular product, the business manager may be able to negotiate a lower commodity rate with the carrier. Lowering the transportation rate may enable the business manager to turn an unprofitable market into one which is lucrative.

Further savings can be achieved through making application with the appropriate carriers for such additional services as storage in transit, processing in transit, and diversion in transit. Utilizing incentive rates by means of truckload, carload, or planeload shipments will likewise reduce costs.

The rate structure in the transportation industry is extremely complex. Only the surface in terms of the rates and services available to the business manager has been touched here. Suffice it to say at this point that the business manager must always be on guard for possible savings.

## Determination of Inventory Locations

### STORAGE FACILITIES

Because the production of goods does not necessarily coincide with the immediate demand of customers for the goods, it is necessary for most business firms to have storage facilities. Through the use of proper storage, the business manager can adequately protect his goods and make them available to customers throughout the year. For example, in certain industries production is seasonal, whereas consumption is more or less continuous. Wheat is harvested in the summer but its consumption in the form of bread and other goods is continuous. Conversely, in some industries production takes place year-round while consumption is seasonal. Snow tires are in high demand by customers during the winter, but yet they are produced year-round.

Storage facilities also enable buyers to achieve lower purchasing costs. In many instances business firms will purchase larger quantities of raw materials than are actually needed for current production. This allows the firm to take advantage of quantity discounts offered by sellers as well as lower transportation costs resulting from carload shipments. Similarly, in order to realize the low cost of water transport, manufacturers will ship large quantities of raw materials during the summer months. Those materials not required for current production are placed in storage and used during the winter months when the ships are inoperative. A portion or perhaps all of these savings can be passed on to the consumer in the form of lower selling prices.

So that the firm can provide good service to its customers as well as lower the total cost of distributing its product, the business manager must determine the type of warehouse facility to use.

## TYPES OF WAREHOUSE FACILITIES

Generally speaking, the business manager has two alternative ways of providing for storage. He may utilize private warehouse facilities or he may elect to use the services of a public warehouse. A private warehouse is one which is owned and operated by the business firm for its own purposes. The use of a private warehouse usually requires a sizable outlay of capital by the firm in order to construct and equip it efficiently. Additionally, the costs of operating the warehouse in terms of insurance, property taxes, utility bills, and employee salaries are constant from month to month whether or not the warehouse is being used. For these reasons, a private warehouse is most appropriate for those firms which have a continual flow of goods both into and out of storage.

### LOCATION OF PRIVATE WAREHOUSES

Determining the number and location of warehouse facilities to be used is not easy. The decision the business manager makes should be one which lowers the firm's total distribution costs while at the same time providing good service to its customers. For example, if a manufacturer constructs a single warehouse at the factory site, he will be able to reduce the total inventory needed at any one time and increase the control necessary to reduce loss from pilferage and vandalism. However, using one warehouse will increase total transportation costs and may mean that potential customers will be lost due to the length of time needed to transport the goods. On the other hand, a firm can overdo it by building warehouses in every town and city it serves. Although this would provide shipment to all customers within a matter of hours after each order is received, the cost of maintaining the warehouses and keeping them well-stocked could be staggering.

Many businessmen have now concluded that by strategically locating a few warehouses in the market area the firm serves, it is possible to reduce significantly warehouse and transportation costs while maintaining good customer service. As an example, many businessmen who market their products throughout the entire country are able to provide delivery the day after an order is received to 90 percent of their customers by using fewer than twenty-five warehouses.[5] For a firm which serves only one region, such as the Northeast or the

---

5. James A. Constantin, *Principles of Logistics Management*. New York: Appleton-Century-Crofts, 1966, p. 366.

Midwest, it is obvious that the number of warehouses would be much less than twenty-five. Savings in transportation costs are often realized through long haul carload shipments to each of the warehouses. As customer orders are received, trucks are used for smaller short haul shipments directly to the buyer.

## PUBLIC WAREHOUSING

For some firms the service provided by a public warehouse is adequate. A public warehouse is one operated for the purpose of providing storage and other services to the public. The firm pays only for the actual time during which the storage space is used. Because the public warehouseman is a custodian of the goods placed in his facility, he is expected to take reasonable care in protecting the stored goods. Those firms which require storage facilities only part of the year or have need for year-round storage but in a relatively small quantity often find the service of a public warehouse very attractive. In both situations, the costs of maintaining private storage would probably exceed the charge for services performed by a public warehouse.

The popularity of public warehousing is evident in the data in Exhibit 12–2. In 1963 there were 8,838 public warehouse facilities in the United States occupying a floor space of 355,450,000 square feet. By 1967 these figures had increased to 9,433 facilities with a floor space of 392,865,000 square feet.

EXHIBIT 12–2

*Public Warehousing Facilities—Summary,*
*By Region: 1963 and 1967*

| | | *Occupiable public storage space Dec. 31* | | |
|---|---|---|---|---|
| *Region and type of facility* | *Estab-lish-ments* | *Floor space (1,000 sq. ft.)* | *Refrigerated space (1,000 cu. ft.)* | *Bulk liquid storage (1,000 gal.)* |
| 1963, United States | 8,838 | 355,450 | 474,199 | 467,480 |
| Northeast | 1,589 | 78,012 | 111,547 | 341,456 |
| North Central | 2,661 | 70,696 | 147,000 | 35,781 |
| South | 3,026 | 166,022 | 93,228 | 52,803 |
| West | 1,562 | 40,720 | 122,422 | 37,440 |
| 1967, United States | 9,433 | 392,865 | 533,960 | 519,601 |
| Northeast | 1,688 | 84,311 | 118,846 | 421,992 |
| North Central | 2,689 | 87,735 | 158,042 | 12,448 |
| South | 3,271 | 165,493 | 123,321 | 28,071 |
| West | 1,785 | 55,326 | 133,751 | 57,090 |

Source: U.S. Bureau of the Census, *Statistical Abstract of the United States: 1973*, 94th ed. Washington, D.C.: 1973, p. 758.

*Services Provided by Public Warehouses.* The primary service provided by the public warehouse is storage. Different types of public warehouses have been developed to provide storage for the public. A general merchandise warehouse will store items of almost any nature. In contrast a special warehouse is designed to store specific types of commodities such as cotton, wheat, and fruit. Products of this nature require special services which specialty warehouses are specifically designed to handle. Other services a public warehouse provides are examined below.

*Breaking Bulk.* As noted earlier in the chapter, considerable savings in transportation costs can be achieved by shipping in TL or CL shipments. Therefore, if a retailer, wholesaler, or manufacturer has a number of small shipments to make to separate buyers, it would be advantageous to consolidate these shipments into one or more carloads and ship directly to a public warehouseman in the area. The warehouseman would then break the consolidated shipments into separate lots and deliver them to the appropriate places.

Without this particular service rendered by the public warehouseman, it would be necessary for the seller to ship his goods at LTL or LCL rates directly to the individual buyers.

*Warehouse Receipt as a Source of Credit.* Many small firms which might not otherwise have access to credit often find the public warehouse an attractive service. When goods are placed in storage a warehouse receipt is issued, giving evidence that goods are stored under his control. The receipt may in turn be used by the firm as collateral for a bank loan. Once the goods are sold and the loan is paid in full, the receipt is turned over to the new owner and the goods are then released from the warehouse. For further discussion on the use of warehouse receipts as a source of short-term credit, refer to Chapter 5.

*Other Services.* When a firm elects to use its own facilities for storage, it is necessary that a portion of management's time be directed to the operations of the warehouse. However, in many cases the demand placed upon management's time for other activities is so great that insufficient attention is given to warehouse operations. Unless the firm is large enough that a full-time managerial position may be developed to handle this assignment, the firm may find it advantageous to use a public warehouseman. Because public warehouses utilize management personnel and other workers whose expertise is in this area, the public receives the benefits of the newest methods in the storing and handling of goods.

Furthermore, public warehouses are plentiful in that they are located in all parts of the country. Often a firm which is considering the feasibility of selling its products in a new area is uncertain of the success it will achieve. Rather than investing considerable capital in constructing a warehouse in the area, the firm can utilize a public warehouse during the initial stages of entering the market. If the new venture proves successful, the business manager is then in a better position to evaluate the advantages of continuing with a public warehouse or using private facilities.

## Plant Location

### FACTORS TO CONSIDER IN SELECTING A PLANT SITE

Three factors which affect the decision a business manager will make in selecting a plant site are (1) transportation costs, (2) production costs, and (3) personal considerations. Each of these is examined below.

### TRANSPORTATION COSTS

Transportation expenses are incurred on two types of shipments: first, transporting raw materials from their source to plant site, and second, transporting the finished goods from the plant site to the market where they will be sold. The impact which transportation costs have upon the plant location decision depends upon how important these costs are relative to other production costs. If transportation costs account for a large percentage of the total expenses in running the business, then they should have a significant impact on where the plant is to be located. On the other hand, if transportation costs are but a small or insignificant portion of the total costs incurred then selection of a plant location will be based on other factors.

As previously mentioned, the businessman can select from five different modes of transportation: railroad, truck, ship, airplane, and (in some instances) pipelines. In making his decision as to the modes of transportation to utilize, he is interested in lowering or minimizing his transportation costs while at the same time maintaining good service to his customers. For example, sending by ship is the least expensive means of shipment but also the slowest. If the firm's customers do not need the goods immediately, then shipping will allow the firm to minimize its costs and provide good service to its customers. On the other hand, if the firm's customers need the merchandise the day after it is ordered or sooner, then sending by truck or perhaps plane will be necessary.

Another means of minimizing transportation costs is selecting the appropriate plant location. Depending upon the nature of the industry, the businessman will usually find it advantageous to locate his plant either at the source of the raw material or at the market where the goods will be sold to customers.

*Plant Located Near Raw Material.* In some industries the business manager has no choice other than locating near the source of the raw material. For example, if a person is interested in starting up a farming operation to cultivate and grow vegetables, he must locate his business on rich and fertile soil that is conducive to growing vegetables. However, in most industries the manager does have a choice regarding the location of his plant. As an illustration, suppose you are interested in building a plant to manufacture paper. You have two plant sites in mind. One is located in the forest area of the Northwest where the supply of pulpwood is abundant, and the second site is located in the Southwest where you expect to market your paper products. In making a decision of this nature one of the most important factors to consider is the weight loss which results from processing the raw material into the finished product. If the weight loss is significant, considerable savings in transportation expenses will be achieved by locating the plant near the source of the raw material.

In this illustration, assume that transportation rates are the same on both raw materials and finished goods. Under this assumption, the cost of transporting logs from the Northwest to a plant site in the Southwest would be much greater than the cost of transporting paper products from the Northwest to markets in the South. This is due to the significant weight loss which results when pulpwood is processed into paper.

*Plant Located Near the Market.* In certain industries, the opposite occurs. That is, weight is added during the processing of raw materials into finished goods. In the beverage industry, the water which is added to the concentrate (raw material) in the production process substantially increases the weight of the finished goods. Lower transportation costs are therefore realized by locating the plant site near the markets where the beverage will be sold.

For those industries in which the weight of the raw material is the same as the weight of the finished goods, it is generally more favorable to locate the plant close to the market. This is because the value of raw materials is usually less than the value of the finished product. Consequently, the transportation rates are lower on raw materials simply because lower-value commodities cannot be charged the high rates which are often levied on high-value products.

## Retail Location

Where to locate the facilities of a business is a universal problem. This discussion has been limited to the plant location problems facing the manufacturer. However, retailers must also resolve the location problem. Unlike the manufacturer, transportation costs are not one of the most important considerations for the retailer who must select a particular business location. Although the retailer will purchase from many manufacturers and wholesalers, he would never give serious consideration to locating his store close to these suppliers simply to save transportation costs. The retailer must be where the consumers are. Thus, the market place, not transportation costs, is the greatest influence over the retailer's store location decision. Consequently, retail store location and transportation costs are unrelated. However, the retailer's decision is still part of the physical distribution system for his goods.

A retail store is a place where ultimate consumers purchase goods or services. In this book the typical definition of a retail store has been expanded to include services. Thus, with this definition a retail store includes such businesses as grocery stores, pharmacies, gasoline stations, barber shops, bakeries, theaters, taverns, clothing stores, jewelry stores, car wash facilities, and restaurants. As pointed out in Chapter 1, every business is not a success. This is especially true in retailing. In fact, the failure rate for retail stores is higher than in any other industry. Statistics show that out of every ten business failures, seven are in the field of retailing.[6] A prevalent reason for this high rate of failure is poor store location. The controlling theme underlying the proper selection of a location for a retail store is customer convenience. Since customers must visit the retailer in order to purchase a good or service, it is important that the retailer locate his facility where it will be convenient and easy for the customer to visit.

## THE TRADING AREA

The trading area is that area from which the retailer draws his customers. Every business, regardless of size, has its own trading area. The size of a store's trading area is largely dependent upon three factors. The first factor is the nature of the community. For example, the trading area of a pharmacy in a small country town would include the town itself as well as the surrounding rural areas. On the other hand, a neighborhood pharmacy in a large city might simply include the residents living within a few blocks of the store. Second, the size of the trading area is generally dependent upon the nature of the product sold by the retailer. Since consumers are willing to shop carefully and to take extra time in purchasing a specialty good or a shopping good, the boundaries of the trading area will be larger than they would be for a convenience good. That is, goods or services which are expensive and which the consumer buys infrequently would generate a larger trading area than those goods and services which cost little and are purchased frequently. As a consumer, you would probably visit a number of dealers before purchasing a new automobile, but you would go to the nearest retail store for a tube of toothpaste. Third, the larger the store, usually the larger the trading area. This is because larger stores generally offer a wider selection of goods and services, and therefore consumers are willing to travel large distances to visit these establishments. For example, the trading area of a large department store such as Neiman-Marcus in Dallas would be larger than the trading area of a Thom McAn shoe store located in a Dallas suburb.

The size of the trading area, along with the number of existing retail stores in the area, determines to a large extent if a new store can exist in this area. Only a few of the factors which should be considered in determining the general size of the trading area have been mentioned. Actually measuring the boundaries of a trading area is not easy. In fact, an individual interested in starting a new retail outlet should seek the advice of experts in measuring the extremities of the area from which the store can expect to draw customers.

Once the businessman has determined the trade area he is interested in serving, the next problem is to determine whether the area is adequate to support the new retail establishment.

---

6. Robert D. Entenberg, *Effective Retail and Market Distribution.* Cleveland: World Publishing Company, 1966, p. 166.

## TRADE AREA ADEQUACY

The retailer should ask himself the following question: Does the trade area have the necessary population, buying income, and retail sales to support the proposed retail venture when present competition is considered? The potential retailer should give careful thought to these factors because an over-stored condition (number of retail outlets exceeds the buying desires of consumers) may spell disaster for the business.

There are a number of indices or guidelines available to the retailer which can aid him in determining the adequacy of a given trade area. Two of these— rate of return on investment and degree of saturation—will be discussed.

*Rate of Return on Investment.* The rate of return on investment is computed by dividing net income by total assets. Assume that Henry Tinkner, who is presently a salesman for the Wicks Furniture Company, is interested in starting a furniture store in Gratton, Michigan. The city has a population of 35,000 and is presently served by four furniture stores. According to figures published by the trade association representing furniture stores throughout the country, the average rate of return on home furniture stores is 12 percent. Because of his experience as a salesman of home furniture to retailers in the Gratton area, Mr. Tinkner has estimated that the average rate of return on investment for the other four furniture stores in Gratton is approximately 24 percent. Since this return is double the national average, there appears to be strong evidence that there may be room available for another retail furniture outlet in Gratton.

*Degree of Saturation.* Another index for determining the adequacy of a given trade area is the degree of saturation for a given trading area. Whenever the trading area has more stores than it can adequately support, it is called "over-saturated." One way of measuring saturation is to use the following formula:

$$\frac{\text{Population of area}}{\substack{\text{Number of individuals} \\ \text{needed to support the} \\ \text{store}}} = \substack{\text{Maximum number of} \\ \text{stores that can} \\ \text{be supported in a} \\ \text{trading area}}$$

To illustrate how the degree of saturation is computed, actual U.S. Census of Business data will be used.

Data in Exhibit 12–3 indicate that the average population needed to support an average home furniture store with sales of $197,283 was 5,934 people. Using this figure as the denominator and the population of Gratton as the numerator, the maximum number of furniture stores which the city of Gratton could support would be computed as follows:

$$\frac{35,000}{5,934} = 5.89 \text{ or } 6$$

Since there are presently four furniture stores in Gratton, it would appear that this particular trading area is not oversaturated. This figure, together with the high rate of return on investment the four stores are experiencing, is a good in-

## EXHIBIT 12–3

*Selected Data on Furniture Stores in the United States, 1967*

| Number of establishments | Sales | Average population per store[7] | Average sales per store[8] |
|---|---|---|---|
| 33,274 | $6,564,388,000 | 5,934 | $197,283 |

Source: Information on number of establishments and sales taken from U.S. Department of Commerce, Bureau of the Census, *Census of Business, 1967*. Washington, D. C.: 1967, Vol. II, *Retail Trade—Area Statistics*, pp. 1–4.

dication that Mr. Tinkner should give serious consideration to opening a new furniture store.

Once the retailer is convinced that the trading area is capable of supporting another retail store, the next step is to determine the proper site within the trading area.

## SITE SELECTION

The businessman should select that site which will provide the greatest customer convenience. Three important aspects of site selection are covered here: site traffic, compatibility of neighboring stores, and parking.

### SITE TRAFFIC

The retailer should analyze the traffic passing by the particular site on which he would like to place his store. If the site is such that the store will be dependent upon automobile traffic for potential customers, a count should be made of the number of cars passing by during the course of a day. If the site will draw pedestrian traffic, a count of people walking by would be appropriate. Obviously the greater the traffic, the more customers the site will draw. For example, in many shopping centers there are two competing department stores at each end of the center. The purpose is to increase the amount of traffic between the two sites. In other words, in order for shoppers to compare products in the two department stores, it is necessary to walk past the other stores in the center.

### COMPATIBILITY OF NEIGHBORING STORES

The retailer should carefully examine the type of stores which will be located close to each other. He should obviously avoid unfriendly competition. For example, if a pharmacist were interested in establishing a retail drugstore he would not find it to his advantage to locate the store adjacent to a discount center specializing in the filling of prescriptions. On the contrary, the business-

---

7. Computed by dividing the total 1967 resident population of 197,457,000 by the number of establishments.

8. Computed by dividing the total sales of furniture stores by the number of establishments.

man should look for neighboring stores which have a high degree of retail compatibility. For example, locating a Singer sewing machine outlet next to a retail store specializing in yarns and fabrics would generate increased business for both stores.

PARKING

The availability of parking facilities is important for the businessman to attract and retain customers. The significance of sufficient parking facilities is reflected by the exodus of many retail stores from downtown business districts to shopping centers in outlying areas. Equally important is the ease with which customers may enter or leave the parking area. Customers are interested in getting off the highway and into the parking area quickly. Upon completion of their visit they want to return to the road without having to deal with traffic congestion. This principle is so basic and simple that there may appear to be little need to mention it. However, one expert has estimated that four out of five existing shopping centers have an entirely unnecessary traffic congestion problem at the entrances and exits.[9]

In retail location the selection of a site within a trading area is as important as selecting the trading area itself. Insufficient site traffic, incompatibility of neighboring stores, or poor parking facilities can be just as disastrous as selecting an oversaturated trading area. Thus, the two problems of picking a trading area and the site location within a trading area are deserving of the retailer's time and energy. These two represent the problems facing the retailer in facility location. The importance of location for retailers and manufacturers cannot be overstated.

## Summary

Four functions to be performed in the area of physical distribution are:
(1) Selecting the mode of transportation to be used in shipping raw materials to the plant site.
(2) Selecting the mode of transportation to be used in shipping finished goods to the firm's customers.
(3) Determining the appropriate number, location, and type of warehouses.
(4) Selecting the right location for the business' facilities.

In the United States there are five modes of transportation used to move goods: (1) railroads, (2) motor vehicles, (3) ships, (4) pipelines, and (5) airplanes. The railroads are noted for their ability to carry large volumes of heavy, bulky, low-value commodities long distances at a low cost. Trucks, because of their speed and flexibility, have become increasingly popular as a means of transporting high-value, low-bulk items over short distances. Like the railroads, water carriers have the capacity to handle large tonnages of bulky commodities such as iron ore, coal, petroleum, and grain. The characteristics

9. Richard L. Nelson, "The Selection of Retail Locations," *F. W. Dodge Corporation*

of pipelines are such that they are limited to the transporting of liquid products such as oil and gasoline. Freight shipped via the airways is restricted to high-value items such as electronic components and perishable goods. Air freight is both the fastest and the most expensive of all modes of transportation.

The cost of transporting goods from seller to buyer is a significant part of the total cost of running a business. Approximately 50 percent of total marketing costs are spent on physical distribution. In order to minimize these costs the businessman must constantly be on the outlook for possible savings. Savings can be achieved through applying with the appropriate carriers for such additional services as storage in transit, processing in transit, and diversion in transit. Utilizing incentive rates by means of truckload, carload, or planeload shipments will likewise reduce costs.

The business manager has two alternative ways of providing for storage. He may utilize private warehouse facilities, or he may elect to use a private warehouse. A private warehouse is most appropriate for those firms which have a continual flow of goods both into and out of storage. In determining the number and location of warehouse facilities, the businessman should strive to find that combination which lowers the firm's total distribution costs while at the same time providing good service to its customers. Those firms which require storage facilities only part of the year or have need for year-round storage but in relatively small amounts often find the services of a public warehouse very attractive. Other services provided by a public warehouse include breaking bulk and utilizing warehouse receipts as a source of credit.

Transportation costs affect the decision a manager will make in selecting a plant site. Transportation expenses are incurred on two types of shipments: transporting raw materials from their source to the plant site and transporting the finished goods from the plant site to the market where they will be sold. In making a decision regarding the location of a manufacturing plant, the businessman should give careful consideration to the weight loss which results from processing raw material into finished goods. If the weight loss is significant, considerable savings will be achieved by locating the plant near the source of the raw material. On the other hand, if weight is added during the processing of raw materials into finished goods, transportation costs will be lower by locating the plant site near the markets where the goods will be sold.

When selecting an area in which to locate a retail store, the businessman should first determine the ability of the area to support another store. The particular site selected should be one which will be convenient and easy for the customer to visit.

## The Distribution Process in Retrospect

The distribution process is that series of events or activities necessary to move goods or services from the point of production to the consumer. Through the activities of new product development, pricing, promotion, and physical movement, the businessman makes available the goods or services which consumers desire. However, in order to perform these activities effectively, the businessman must first define exactly his potential consumers. This is very important because the whole distribution process (product, price, promotion and physical movement) is aimed toward satisfying these consumers.

Industrial consumers and ultimate consumers are two general classifications of consumers. The following are characteristics of industrial consumers: a high concentration of buyers, a high value of sales, and a need for technical service and advice. Therefore the businessman must utilize a distribution process which is both direct and personal. In contrast to the industrial consumer, who must purchase those goods and services required for the production process, the ultimate consumer has total freedom in deciding what he needs and which goods or services will satisfy these needs. This freedom of making decisions plus the unique individuality each person possesses tends to restrict the generalization relating to ultimate consumers as a whole. Nevertheless, certain factors which influence the ultimate consumer's decision to choose one product or service over another can be identified. These factors include those classified economic, environmental, and attitudinal. In developing his distribution process, the businessman must take into consideration all of these factors in order to influence ultimate consumers to purchase his particular good or service. However, because of the variety of consumer characteristics, it is impossible to develop one particular distribution process which will satisfy the needs of ultimate consumers. He varies in his economic status, age, sex, marital status, family size, attitudes, opinions, and so on. Therefore it is vital that the businessman identify certain groups of consumers which have similar characteristics and needs. Once he has done so he must then tailor the distribution process to each specific market he is interested in serving. Each part of the distribution process must be developed with the intention of satisfying the needs of each potential group of consumers.

The word *product* includes goods and services. For example, the automobile dealer who sells cars (goods) and the service station mechanic who performs motor tune-ups (services) are both selling products. The life of a product consists of four phases: introduction, growth, maturity, and decline. This life varies depending upon the demand for the good or service and the extent of competition. Because every product eventually reaches the period of decline, the businessman must concern himself with new product development in order to remain competitive. Although developing a new product can be very risky, the businessman can minimize these risks by following four steps: exploration of new product ideas and opportunities; development of the idea; test of the products to determine consumer acceptance; and full-scale commercial production and subsequent reevaluation.

Commercialization of a new product requires the businessman to give careful attention to the elements or areas of the distribution process: price, promotion, and product availability. Although consumers generally give a number of reasons why they chose one particular product over another, one factor almost always cited is price. As a result, the price of a good affects the volume sold. The price a businessman places on his product depends upon the cost of doing business, the demand for his product, and the level of competition he faces.

These three factors do not remain stable; rather they change as the product goes through its life cycle. Consequently, the businessman generally sets a relatively high price during the introduction and growth period and then lowers his original price as the products pass through the maturity and decline stages.

For many products intense competition forces prices to be similar. Therefore businessmen emphasize other parts of the distribution process in order to gain a competitive edge. By emphasizing product availability and/or product design and/or promotion efforts, the businessman is trying to influence potential consumers into believing that his product can better satisfy their needs than competitors' products.

Product availability involves getting the product to the right place at the right time in the right condition to satisfy a consumer need. In order to do this effectively, the businessman must first utilize a physical transportation and storage system to transport products from producers to consumers. Second he must select a channel of distribution which will help the firm sell its products to the ultimate consumer. Three alternative channels of distribution are available to the businessman: use no outside institution, use a retailer only, or use both a wholesaler and a retailer. The channel the businessman elects will vary depending upon the nature of the product, the consumer, and the firm itself.

In addition to developing a product, competitively pricing it, and establishing the channels of distribution, the businessman must also promote the product. Through promotional activities he is communicating to potential consumers. He can communicate either by personal selling or advertising. Although he may elect to use both techniques, personal face-to-face selling is generally more effective when the following factors are present: the number of potential consumers is relatively small; potential consumers are concentrated; the average sale is relatively large; products are of such a nature that demonstration is required; and the potential consumer is not aware a need exists.

On the other hand, advertising is an indirect means of communicating with potential consumers. Certain conditions also exist which signal to the businessman that advertising will most likely be more effective in communicating to the consumer than personal selling. The presence of more than one of the following conditions would indicate that the product can be advertised: the product is one which has hidden qualities; the product is one consumers purchase because of emotional reasons; the product is growing in demand and therefore consumer interest is high; the company has a lot of money to spend on promotional efforts.

Both personal selling and advertising have strengths and weaknesses. The businessman should be aware of the characteristics of each type in order to better select the proper combination of media for communicating his message effectively to potential customers. In addition, he must give careful attention to both the nature of the product and stage in its life cycle it is presently passing through. Both affect the combination of personal selling and advertising the businessman should utilize.

Although physical distribution is commonly thought of as the transportation of goods from the seller to the buyer, it can be looked at it in a much broader perspective. Two other areas are very much a part of physical distribution: determining the appropriate number and location of the firm's warehouses and selecting the right location. The businessman's guide to decision making in each of these areas is to minimize costs of the firm while maintaining good service to the firm's customers. This emphasis upon minimizing costs is critical because figures indicate that the amount of money spent on physical distribution accounts for approximately 50 percent of total distribution costs.

Putting together each of these four areas (product, price promotion, and physical movement) of the distribution process in such a way that the firm maximizes its sales is not an easy task. However, the businessman who does an effective job in tailoring his distribution process to meet the needs of the market he is serving will in turn acquire a competitive edge in that market.

## QUESTIONS

1. What are the four functions that must be performed to facilitate physical distribution?

2. Name the five modes of transportation that are used to transport goods and give a short description of each in terms of the materials that commonly are shipped by each means.

3. What is meant by *rating* as used by railroad companies?

4. What is a commodity rate?

5. Name and explain three special services that have been developed by the railroads to increase revenues.

6. Why is it important that the businessman have a thorough knowledge of rate structures when carrying out various business operations?

7. What are the implications of the determination of whether to use storage facilities?

8. What are the distinguishing characteristics of private and public warehousing?

9. What are the three factors that must be considered in the selection of a plant site? What part do transportation costs play in carrying out business operations?

10. What factors should a retailer take into consideration when searching for a location to conduct business?

## Incident 12–1

Paul Soby has been the sales manager for the Ravel Household Appliance Store for the past twelve years. He has been solely responsible for sales and service. Under his direction sales at the Ravel Appliance Store have increased each year. The store is owned by Walter Ravel, president, who has two children, Arthur and Diane, who hold positions as purchasing agent and treasurer, respectively. Realizing that the store will eventually be taken over by the two children, Paul is seriously considering going into business for himself by starting his own household appliance store.

The Ravel Store is located in Greenville, Michigan. There are presently two household appliance stores in Greenville, and both are doing very well. In fact, Mr. Soby is aware that the return on Mr. Ravel's investment in the appliance business is above average. Greenville is a growing community which presently has a population of approximately 32,000 people, including the outlying rural areas. The city does not rely upon one industry for its prosperity. On the contrary, there are six different industries in Greenville in addition to the fertile farmlands and orchards which surround the city. It is also the home of a new community college. Many of Greenville's young people attend the college and plan to stay in the city to pursue their careers.

A new shopping center is under construction across from the community college. The shopping center is located one mile from the downtown business district. In addition to a department store (which will not handle appliances initially), one theater, and a restaurant, fifteen other stores to be included in the center will handle a large variety of shopping, specialty, and convenience goods. Paul is of the opinion that the shopping center would be an ideal location for a new household appliance store. He has been notified by Frigidaire executives that, should he decide to go ahead with his plans, he would be given the exclusive right to sell the Frigidaire products in the Greenville area.

In analyzing the capability of the Greenville area to support another appliance store, Paul Soby has accumulated the following data from the U.S. Census of Business.

*Data on Household Appliance*
*Stores in the United States*
*1967*

| Number of establishments | Sales | Average population per store | Average sales per store |
|---|---|---|---|
| 20,806 | $3,013,817,000 | 9,490 | $144,853 |

(1) In your opinion, what strengths and weaknesses does Paul Soby possess in relation to starting a new household appliance store?

(2) List some of the characteristics of the Greenville trading area which you feel are positive indications that Paul should start a new store. Are there any negative factors?

(3) Measure the degree of saturation as it relates to appliance stores in Greenville. According to this measure, do you feel Paul should go into business for himself?

(4) List three factors which he should consider in selecting a site.

(5) Given the factors you mentioned in question (4), do you feel the shopping center would be an appropriate site?

(6) List two examples of stores which would provide retail compatibility for the planned appliance store. List two examples of stores which would represent unfriendly competition.

# V

# THE MANPOWER PROCESS

People are a central resource for almost every operation performed within a business. No business could continue without employees, but there is more to it than just having people employed. How well people perform their assigned jobs is an important consideration.

The businessman has many decisions to make concerning the labor force, including how many and what type of employees will be needed, how can the "right" employees be hired, what are the legal rights of employees, what do they want from their jobs, and how should management act with the employees' representatives. In total these decisions are concerned with the manpower employed by the particular business. In this section, the manpower process is examined to aid the businessman in resolving these and similar questions.

The **manpower process** is that series of events which concentrates on the attainment and maintenance of a productive labor force. This diagram illustrates those activities involved in attaining and maintaining a productive labor force.

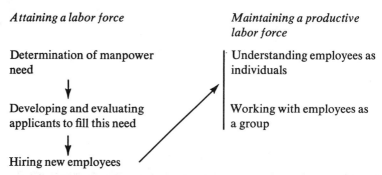

These activities will be examined in three chapters: Chapter 13, Manning the Business System, Chapter 14, Employees as Individuals, and Chapter 15, Employees in Groups.

# 13

# Manning the Business System

The discussion of the basic processes of the business system up to this point has assumed that employees are available to perform the various jobs created by the production and distribution processes. Meeting this assumption requires that employees in the right quantity and quality are available when needed. The activities necessary to obtain this labor force are discussed in this chapter. In the discussion the terms *labor force* and *manpower* are meant to include all employees of the business firm: laborers, managers, secretaries, salesmen— everyone.

## Manpower and the Business System

The manpower process is directly related to the survival of the business system. Only through the efforts of people can goods and services be produced and distributed. Even the most advanced, automated factory requires employees. The number of employees required may be less than for the nonautomated factory, but without employees neither could operate. No business system can accomplish its objectives without people.

There are strong relationships between the manpower process and the other processes of the business system. The production and distribution processes set the stage for the manpower process. To create chemicals, shoes, or clean clothes in any given quantity requires a certain number of people to perform the various production jobs. The number and type of goods or services produced create jobs. The same is true for the distribution of these goods or services—jobs are created. Those jobs created directly by the production and distribution processes and the additional support and managerial jobs such as foremen, secretaries, and maintenance men, must be filled, before anything can happen. Without manpower it would be impossible to produce or distribute goods or services; and thus impossible for the business to exist or achieve its objectives.

Labor is a resource bought by the business through the payment of wages. The wages paid employees represent an expense that the businessman involved with the financial process must weigh and consider. Profits (income minus expenses) are affected by the total amount of wages paid to employees. Wages are one of the larger expenses of all businesses, and thus directly affect a business' continued profit level, growth, and existence.

In addition, people are not just placed on the job and then forgotten. As is well known, once on the job the employee can perform at a minimum, average, or superior level. Employees do more than just work and fill job slots. They also think and have feelings. These thoughts and feelings affect their level of performance. Through the management process, the businessman utilizes what is known about individual employees and groups of employees to increase the performance level of each employee.

Like any other resource utilized by the business, certain manpower information needs to be obtained and analyzed. The information process needs to generate a certain amount of manpower data. Such manpower data as the level of absenteeism, accident rates, and payroll are useful in making decisions on the utilization of the labor force. Manpower needs to be managed and controlled for the business system to receive value for its wage expenditures. Through the information process the businessman can control this vital resource.

Manpower is a necessary and supportive process. It supports the production and distribution processes. The huge sums of money spent for wages are one indication, however, that it is not a secondary process, but a process of vital concern for any successful business system.

### Determination of Manpower Needs

Every businessman is searching for the right employee, the one who has the proper qualifications to fulfill the needs of the business. Right is relative to what the business needs. For example, an individual with a masters degree in aeronautical engineering would be right for a job in the engineering department of an aerospace organization, but the same individual would be the wrong person to operate a lathe in the factory. This person could learn to operate the lathe, but he is the wrong person if for no other reason than the probable personal dissatisfaction this job would cause him. The job to be filled determines what qualifications the right person will have. For different types of jobs, different people will prove to be right.

The duties, scope, and level of individual jobs in the business are dependent upon the nature of the business. For example, the number and type of jobs would differ greatly between restaurants, machine shops, bookstores, and florists. However, even though the jobs to be done are different for different types of businesses, the activities involved to insure that the right employee is found to fill a job are the same, regardless of the level, type, or number of employees sought. These activities are the subject matter of this chapter.

Before a job can be filled, the businessman needs to know what is involved in doing the job. The starting point, then, is to analyze each job within the business. The businessman needs a current picture of each job that is necessary to achieve his objective. For each job in the organization there should be on record a one- or two-page job summary. A **job summary** is a statement of the basic tasks performed on that job. This is a basic document around which much of the manpower process revolves. Care should be taken to assure that the job summary for each job is accurate and up to date.

Exhibit 13–1 illustrates the job summary for a secretary's job in the customer complaints department of a fictitious business. As the businessman reads the job summary he should be able to answer three questions:

(1) What must this employee who fills this job do?

(2) How does the employee do it?

(3) Why does the employee do it?

These same three questions also provide the guidance necessary to prepare a job summary for each job within the business. If anyone read the job summary and could accurately answer these three questions, the businessman has done a complete evaluation and write-up of a job.

The next step to insure that the right employee fills this job is to state the minimum qualification necessary to fill this job. For example, are there any educational requirements necessary to do this job? If so, what is the minimum? Exhibit 13–2 illustrates the qualifications an employee should have to perform the secretarial job summarized in Exhibit 13–1.

In combination these two documents provide the businessman with the necessary information to fill the various jobs within a business. Now he can go about systematically finding people who can fill the jobs when they are needed.

Employees are needed to fill the current jobs in an organization. But as the current employees and organization change, so too does the need for employees. Information concerning these changes must be analyzed to prepare for the future employee needs. The businessman needs to plan for his future manpower needs, because often a long lead time is needed to find the right person. For instance, if a businessman wants to hire an employee to do some typing for the first time, he would need time to ask around or locate a number of possible people to do the typing and to evaluate the applicants based upon what he is willing to pay, the people's reputations, and their availability to do

EXHIBIT 13–1

*Job Summary*

Job title:    Secretary
Department:    Customer complaints
Date:    April 17, 1975

*Statement of the Job*

The secretary performs such clerical tasks as taking dictation and typing and assuming minor duties which relieve organization officials from certain responsibilities.

*Duties of the Job*

Schedules appointments, gives information to callers, takes dictation, and otherwise relieves officials of clerical work and minor administrative and business detail. Reads and routes incoming mail. Locates and attaches appropriate file to correspondence to be answered by employer. Takes dictation in shorthand or on Stenotype machine and transcribes notes on typewriter, or transcribes from voice recordings. Composes and types routine correspondence. Files correspondence and other records. Answers telephone and gives information to callers or routes call to appropriate official. Places outgoing calls. Schedules appointments for employer. Greets visitors, ascertains nature of business, and conducts visitors to employer or appropriate person. May arrange travel schedule and reservations. May compile and type statistical reports.

EXHIBIT 13–2

*Job Qualifications*

Job title:    Secretary
Department:    Customer complaints
Date:    April 17, 1975

*Job Qualifications*

| | |
|---|---|
| Education: | A broad education in office procedures including the ability to type 50 wpm, take dictation, and operate a ditto/mimeo machine. |
| Experience: | Practical experience in handling people's complaints and phrasing business correspondence. |
| Contacts: | Frequent public contact by phone and in person. Courtesy and tact required. |
| Job conditions: | Average office conditions. |

his typing. This time may not total more than one hour, but it could take two weeks to find and employ a full-time salesman. Exhibit 13–3 illustrates the information the businessman should analyze to help plan for new or different types of employees.

## EXHIBIT 13–3

### *Manpower Information Needs*

| Changes in the present + labor force | Changes in the future = business plans | Number and type of employees needed |
|---|---|---|
| Retirement | For example, plant | ? |
| Transfers | expansion, product | |
| Promotion | line deletion, or | |
| Discharges | new product efforts | |
| Resignations | | |
| Deaths | | |

First, to accomplish its current objectives, every business requires a labor force of a given quantity and quality. If nothing else changes, these employees will. Some will retire, some will resign, some will be discharged, and some will be promoted or transferred to new and different jobs. With each one of these changes new employees must be hired to fill the vacated jobs. Thus, time creates a certain need for new employees. The businessman himself also creates a need for new employees. As he changes the objectives or direction in which his business is headed, he also alters the job to be done, and thus types of employees needed. Something as basic as a planned expansion either through increased sales, or a venture into the production and distribution of different goods or services, triggers the need for new or different employees. In addition to expansion, the possibility of stopping the production of products also changes the number of employees needed.

The necessary information is presented in Exhibit 13–3 in formula form. Changes in the present labor force, plus the number of employees to man the jobs future business change will create, equals the number and type of employees needed at some date in the future. The businessman probably should anticipate at least once a year how future changes will affect number of employees. One year gives him lead time to find suitable employees to fill his projected needs.

The businessman now knows the number and type of employees he needs. The jobs he wants these employees to fill have been summarized, along with the qualification necessary to fulfill these jobs stated. Now he can intelligently develop a number of job applicants to fill his specific needs.

### Developing Job Applicants

The people who will apply for any given job can be classified into two groups: those already employed by the business and those in the external labor market. Present employees should *automatically* be considered for promotion or transfer to a vacated or newly created job. Generally speaking, if an employee is qualified to fill the new job, there is a positive effect on his attitude if he is promoted or transferred to the position. However, none of the present employees may be qualified to fill the vacant jobs in a business, or the business-man may feel that a new employee will bring in fresh ideas. He then faces the problem of getting a number of qualified people from the external labor market to apply for the job.

At one time or other, every business will seek new employees from the external labor market. The businessman has a number of ways to find people to apply for a job. Among these sources are unsolicited and recommended applicants, advertising, employment agencies, and recruiting. The choice or combination of choices the businessman decides to use depends a great deal on the type of employee sought.

## UNSOLICITED AND RECOMMENDED APPLICANTS

Many of you have probably tried to find summer or part-time jobs by going to the businesses in your community and asking if a job were available. If so, you were an unsolicited applicant. From a businessman's standpoint, this is a highly unreliable method of filling a job. If a job needs to be filled, it usually needs to be filled right now. The businessman cannot afford the luxury of waiting until someone walks in the door and applies. Even if he could, the chances of the applicant's qualifications exactly matching those needed for the job, except for low skill jobs, are extremely small.

The businessman can seek the recommendations of present employees. The number of applicants obtained by this method, however, is restricted to the number of people a given employee knows. As a result the number is usually small. Recommendations also can come from other companies. Occasionally, other employers will try to find a job for those employees they have to let go. In these situations the reason the employee is being let go usually is that his skills are no longer needed, rather than that he was a poor employee. For the employer to attempt to find the employee another job is a good indication that the employee is an excellent worker and should be considered as a potential new employee.

Because of the small number of applicants received and the unpredictability of the number that will apply, this method is the least frequently relied upon by businesses.

## ADVERTISING FOR APPLICANTS

The large number of help-wanted ads in the newspaper is an indication of the wide usage of advertising to attract job applicants. Like any advertising done by a business, help-wanted advertising is intended to be informative. The possibility exists of informing many people of the need for employees. How effective it will be in informing people depends upon two factors: the nature of the advertisement itself and its placement. Both of these factors point out that if an advertisement goes unread, or gives the reader the wrong information and impression, it is useless.

The advertisement should be worded so that it attracts attention, is clear, and is informative. Vagueness in a help-wanted ad will either cause people to not apply for the job, or it will lead the wrong person with the wrong qualifications to apply. At a minimum the job title, a brief statement of what the job involves if the job title is not self-explanatory, the requirements the applicant must possess, salary or hourly rate to be paid, the business' name, and where the applicant may apply should be clearly stated. All of this information is readily available to the businessman if he has done a thorough job in preparing the job summary and job qualification forms.

A well-written ad, however, is only one-half of the solution. The business-man must also determine the best way of getting this job information before the group of people who are qualified to fill the job. The choice of which medium (television, radio, newspaper, etc.) to place the help-wanted ad in is usually limited to one. The selection of which exact newspaper or magazine to place the advertisement in depends upon the type of person sought for the job. People have different reading interests. Placing an ad for carpenters in the *Wall Street Journal* is probably useless. The same ad, however, will probably be read and lead to action if placed either in the local newspaper or in bulletin form on the pegboard of the carpenters' union building.

Even if the advertisement is properly worded and placed in the correct medium, there is no assurance that people will apply for the job. This method is better than relying on unsolicited applicants, but still carries no guarantee that people will inquire about the job. The next two sources at least assure the businessman that he will have a number of people to evaluate for the job in question.

## EMPLOYMENT AGENCIES

There are two general types of employment agencies: public and private. Both perform the service of bringing employers and employees seeking jobs together. For this service, a direct or indirect fee is charged either to the em-ployee or the employer.

### PUBLIC EMPLOYMENT AGENCIES

Public employment agencies are directed by the federal government's U.S. Employment Service. Each state has a number of public employment agencies. A national employment service has developed to find employment for those who are willing and able to work. The need for such a service was brought to the public's attention by the employment problems created by the World Wars and the Great Depression. The growth of the system has been furthered by legal requirements that *all* unemployed persons must register with their state agency before they are eligible for unemployment or welfare payments. There are a staggering number of unemployed people in our nation. A conservative esti-mate of the number of unemployed people would be 3 percent of the total pop-ulation, although it varies up to as much as 7 percent with economic conditions. The coordination of such large numbers of unemployed people almost requires that the government be a leader in solving some of the unemployment problems.

The state public employment agencies are clearinghouses for jobs and job information. The businessman submits requests for employees with certain qualifications. Those people who are unemployed or seeking new employment can learn what jobs are available and be referred to the business seeking employees. The agency does not send just anyone to the business but evaluates the people in an attempt to refer only those suitable for the job.

Every businessman pays for this service. The Social Security Act authorizes the government to collect a payroll tax which amounts to 3.1 percent of the total payroll up to a maximum of $3,000 per employee. The bulk of these funds cover unemployment welfare payments, but a small part of the funds is applied to the expenses of administering the public unemployment agencies. Thus an indirect fee is charged to every businessman, whether he uses the service or not.

## PRIVATE EMPLOYMENT AGENCIES

While the public agency handles all types of employees, most private agencies specialize by type of employee. For example, there are private agencies who only deal with secretaries, or accountants, or salesmen, or executives. This specialization presumably allows them to be more efficient in bringing employers and employees together. Concentrating on only one type of employee puts them in a better position to match the needs of the particular employer with the qualifications of those seeking employment. The private agency provides many of the same services the public agency does in bringing employers and employees together. The big difference is that the fees charged by the private agency are direct and paid either by the employer or employee only for services rendered. As a generalization, the employer pays the fees for employees with high skills—engineers, accountants, and executives, for example. Lower-skilled employees (secretaries, laborers) pay the fee themselves. The fee is based upon a fixed percentage of the employee's first, weekly, biweekly or month's pay. The percentage and method of computation varies between agencies.

Employment agencies provide the businessman an economical source of job applicants. The fee charged is minor when the amount of work they save the businessman is considered. Of all the sources available, the employment agency should be the first the businessman considers. In fact, the majority of a business' employee needs can be filled by employment agencies.

## RECRUITMENT SOURCES

If the other three sources fail to produce job applicants, the businessman can initiate his own recruiting system. Such a move is costly and time consuming. Recruiting is usually used when a particular type of employee is in scarce supply. The businessman must go directly to where the employee can be found and try to interest him in applying for the job. The yearly recruiting efforts on college and technical school campuses is a good example of this process.

Very few small businesses can afford the time and expense involved in recruiting, and therefore they must rely on other sources for job applicants. Regardless of the source or combination of sources chosen, the businessman must carefully analyze which will give him the best applicants to choose from.

Advertising in the local newspaper, for example, would hardly provide a blue-ribbon list of candidates for a vice-presidential position. The quality of employees hired depends on the quality available to choose from. One way of increasing the quality to choose from is to pick the right source of supply for generating job applicants.

## Selection of Employees

Generally speaking, if the right source has been used, the businessman will not have much trouble obtaining a number of applicants for a specific job. All the applicants at least have something approaching the qualifications necessary for the job. If they do not, the businessman has done a poor job of getting people to apply for the job. Now, a decision must be made: to which *one* shall the job be offered? The businessman must select the right applicant for the job in question.

To help in this decision he can set in motion a screening procedure. Screening is similar to a series of hurdles each applicant must successfully jump. Failure to clear any hurdle removes him from further consideration for the job. At each hurdle certain information that is weighed in making the decision is sought from the applicant.

### CRITERIA USED IN SELECTION

The criteria or standards the businessman uses in evaluating the information supplied by the applicant are specific. In other words, the criteria are different for each job. The requirements of the job determine the standards against which applicants are evaluated. For example, a welder's job might require that an applicant be able to weld aluminum, cast iron, and steel; while for an office manager's job, this may be an irrelevant criterion. Based upon this one standard, the same person might be acceptable for the office manager's job but unacceptable for the welder's job. For each job a group of criteria can be involved. These criteria come from the job statement. The businessman should have these criteria in mind as he evaluates the information supplied by the applicant.

### THE SCREENING PROCEDURE

Applicants are screened by comparing the requirements of the job against information supplied by the applicant himself. This information is obtained by three methods: the application blank, employment tests, and the interview. These three methods represent the screening procedures most persons applying for a job must go through.

### THE APPLICATION BLANK

The application blank is the most common source of applicant information. Although the forms vary, the following information is usually sought:
  (1) Identifying information such as name, address, telephone number, social security number, height, weight, health;
  (2) Personal information such as marital status and number of dependents;

(3) Education, including degrees held, and institutions attended;

(4) Work experience, usually in detail through the last three or four employers;

(5) References, often restricted to former employers.

The applicant provides information on an application blank concerning his past. Based upon the job opening, information supplied by the applicants will eliminate some of them from further consideration. The two prime bits of information, education and work experience, will immediately eliminate some of the applicants. Those who remain in consideration have supplied the businessman with a potential source of additional information, the references.

References as a source of information are only useful if checked. The best approach for checking references is to discuss the applicant with his former employer. The businessman is seeking an evaluation of the applicant as a person and as an employee. He should state specifically the duties and responsibilities of the job and then ask the past employer for an evaluation of how well the applicant can meet these duties and responsibilities. Past employers have seen the applicant in an actual work situation and are a valuable source of information, one that should not be ignored by the businessman.

## EMPLOYMENT TESTS

Employment tests provide the businessman with very specific information. Depending on the job, two types of employment tests can be given the applicant: ability or skill tests and personality tests.

Ability or skill tests are usually given to applicants for clerical and manual jobs. Although too numerous to identify specifically, tests for dexterity, mechanical ability, mathematical ability, verbal ability, and clerical skills can be administered.

Personality tests are usually given to the applicants for managerial and professional jobs. Tests that indicate sociability, tolerance, emotional stability, and cooperativeness are available.

Either type of test is contructed for very specific information—in one case a mastery of specific skill, in the other a personality factor. The weight placed upon a test score in the employment decision depends upon the importance of the tested factor on job performance. For example, if typing is only 10 percent of a secretary's job, then a test to determine typing speed would not be the only factor weighed in making the employment decision. An applicant who has mediocre typing ability would probably not be dropped from further consideration for the job.

Tests are not infallible. The businessman needs to be very careful in choosing and interpreting test results and is best advised to seek expert assistance in this area.

## THE INTERVIEW

Those applicants still being considered for the job move into the last phase of the selection procedure, the interview. The interview is a more personal evaluation of the applicant that the application blank or employment test. Information is sought from the applicant in a face-to-face meeting with the employer. The employer formulates an opinion of the applicant in this meeting. Most businessmen trust their own opinions and thus put a lot of weight on the interview in making the employment decision.

The interview is more than just a conversation. The purpose is to evaluate the applicant. A false evaluation of the applicant needs to be guarded against. False evaluation can be avoided if the businessman receives enough specific information to form an opinion. Thus the success of the interview depends on the amount of preparation the businessman has done *before* he meets the applicant. He must determine the information he wants to receive from the applicant and the information he wants to give the applicant. He will want to receive any information important for the performance of the job which cannot be obtained from the application blank or employment test. If, for example, the job requires a person who can think on his feet, the businessman may want to pose a problem or situation to the applicant and watch his reaction. Such a problem or situation might be: "You have just found one of the employees using drugs on the job. What would you do and why?" The specific information sought can only be determined for a specific job, so it must be thought through and planned before the interview.

The interview is not all one-sided. The applicant is also evaluating the job. He must be given information that will help him decide whether or not to accept the job if it is offered to him. The businessman should truthfully explain what the job entails and answer any of the applicant's questions.

The businessman who started with a large number of applicants is now faced with a smaller number of applicants from which he must offer one job. He needs to weigh the three types of information received from the applicants: past education, experience, and job performance, present indications of ability (employment tests), and his opinions of the applicant. Each source of information is important because it tells something different about the applicant. Thus no one source of information should receive more weight than another in making the final employment decision.

It is advisable for the businessman to list the applicants' names in order of preference from first choice to last and then write out the reasons for this order. This forces the businessman to formalize his reasons and helps clarify his choices. Once the decision has been made, the businessman makes the job offer. If the applicant accepts, he becomes an employee. If he rejects the offer, then a new job offer can be made to the second choice on the list. If the second choice would not be the right employee, then the process must be started again with a *new* group of applicants. This will continue until he is happy that the applicant offered the job is right for the business.

## Legislation Protecting Employees from Employers

Historically, the business has been viewed as the domain of the businessman. He had the right to make any decision affecting his property or domain. One such group of decisions were those affecting the employees of the business. The assumption was that if a person seeks to enter the domain of the businessman, he forfeits certain "rights" to the businessman. For efficiency of operation, the businessman could decide who to hire and fire, and what working conditions and wages were offered to employees. If the employee thought the decision was not in his best interest, his only recourse was to quit. The employee had no rights.

Numerous cases indicate that the employee's best interests were of minor importance in the decision-making process. The following example illustrates this point:

> Wage data covering the payrolls of 21,922 textile workers in Lawrence for a period in 1911 is very revealing. The average rate of wages for this group was $0.16 an hour; of the total group, 23.3 percent received less than $0.12 an hour; and 20.4 percent earned $0.20 or more per hour. The work week was fifty-six hours. If they worked this full week, the average wage received by these 21,922 employees was $8.76 per week.[1]

Without protection, the labor force was exploited by the business community. Legislation slowly evolved to protect employees (whether they be potential or actual employees) from employers. Businessmen now face the problem of obtaining and maintaining a labor force. Legislation affecting their decisions in these areas must be understood. Two types of legislation protecting individual rights are discussed in this chapter: legislation protecting employees against discrimination and legislation protecting the economic position of employees. A third type of legislation protects the employees' rights to form a **union,** a formal employee group. Unions and the legislation protecting them shall be discussed in Chapter 14, Employees in Groups.

## LEGISLATION PROTECTING EMPLOYEES AGAINST DISCRIMINATION

Groups of people in our society have been and are being discriminated against because of their race, religion, age, sex, or handicaps. Discrimination of various kinds has resulted in the Civil Rights Act of 1964 and the Age Discrimination in Employment Act of 1967.[2] These bills have a tremendous impact on the manpower process.

### THE CIVIL RIGHTS ACT OF 1964

The Civil Rights Act of 1964 is aimed at eliminating discrimination in employment related to race, color, religion, sex, or national origin. Key organiza-

---

1. United States Congress, Senate, *Report On Strike of Textile Workers In Lawrence, Mass., in 1912,* 62nd. Congress, Senate Document No. 870. Washington, D.C.: 1912, p. 72.

2. As this book goes to press, thirty-three of the required thirty-eight states have ratified the Equal Rights Amendment to the Constitution. All indications are that the necessary five states needed for the amendment to become law will ratify shortly. The amendment outlaws discrimination between the sexes in the application of the laws of the United States.

tions concerned are (1) employers, an employer being defined as "a person engaged in an industry affecting commerce who has twenty-five or more employees for each working day in each of twenty or more calendar weeks in the current or preceding calendar year," (2) employment agencies, and (3) labor organizations. The most significant aspects of the law read as follows:

Sec. 703.
  a. It shall be unlawful employment practice for an employer—
    (1) To fail or refuse to hire or to discharge any individual or otherwise to discriminate against any individual with respect to his compensation, terms, conditions, or privileges of employment, because of such individual's race, color, religion, sex, or national origin.
    (2) To limit, segregate, or classify his employees in any way which would deprive or tend to deprive any individual of employment opportunities or otherwise adversely affect his status as an employee, because of such individual's race, color, religion, sex, or national origin.
  b. It shall be an unlawful employment practice for an employment agency to fail or refuse to refer for employment, or otherwise to discriminate against, any individual because of his race, color, religion, sex, or national origin, or to classify or refer for employment any individual on the basis of his race, color, religion, sex, or national origin.
  c. It shall be an unlawful employment practice for a labor organization—
    (1) To exclude or to expel from its membership, or otherwise to discriminate against, any individual because of his race, color, religion, sex, or national origin.
    (2) To limit, segregate, or classify its membership, or to classify or fail or refuse to refer for employment any individual in any way which would deprive or tend to deprive any individual of employment opportunities, or would limit such employment opportunities, or otherwise adversely affect his status as an employee or as an applicant for employment, because of such individual's race, color, religion, sex, or national origin; or
    (3) To cause or attempt to cause an employer to discriminate against an individual in violation of this section.
  d. It shall be an unlawful employment practice for any employer labor organization, or joint labor-management committee controlling apprenticeship or other training or retraining including on-the-job training programs to discriminate against any individual because of his race, color, religion, sex, or national origin in admission to, or employment in any program established to provide apprenticeship or other training. . . .

Sec. 704. . . .
  b. It shall be an unlawful employment practice for an employer labor organization or employment agency to print or publish or cause to be printed or published any notice of advertisement relating to employment by such an employer or membership in or any classification or

referral for employment by such a labor organization, or relating to any classification or referral for employment by such an employment agency, indicating any preference, limitation, specification, or discrimination, based on race, color, religion, sex, or national origin.

An Equal Employment Opportunity Commission composed of five members was created by the act to hear and investigate charges and attempt to resolve problems. Penalties for violations of the act vary. They include the court's enjoining the accused from engaging in the unlawful practice, reinstatement or hiring of employees with or without back pay, and the payment of reasonable attorney's fees. In cases occurring in states and cities having laws on fair employment practices, appropriate agencies are given a period of time in which to process charges before the Commission acts further.

## THE AGE DISCRIMINATION IN EMPLOYMENT ACT OF 1967

The Age Discrimination in Employment Act of 1967 was designed to protect workers against arbitrary age discrimination in hiring, pay, and other conditions of employment. The act is specifically designed to protect individuals at least forty years of age but younger than sixty-five. However, organizations may discriminate against those younger than forty and against those sixty-five and older; in short, employers may give the forty to sixty-five group preference in employment. The act applies to the same organizations as the Civil Rights Act of 1964.

## LEGISLATION PROTECTING THE ECONOMIC POSITION OF EMPLOYEES

### FAIR LABOR STANDARDS ACT

To keep employers from exploiting employees, a federal minimum wage law has been enacted. Under the Fair Labor Standards Act of 1938, as amended in 1974, employees engaged in commerce or in the production of goods for commerce must now be paid wages of at least $2.00 per hour, effective May 1, 1974. The Equal Pay Act of 1963 amends the Fair Labor Standards Act and prohibits discrimination in wage payments on the basis of sex. According to this law, "No employer . . . shall discriminate between employees on the basis of sex by paying wages . . . at a rate less than the rate at which he pays wages to employees of the opposite sex . . . for equal work on jobs the performance of which require equal skill, effort, and responsibility, and which are performed under similar working conditions."[3]

In addition to protecting the base pay of employees, the social system seeks to give employees a degree of economic security, in the sense that if an individual is unable to work his income will not totally stop. Legislation has been passed to provide a degree of protection against the three major reasons for economic insecurity: accidents, old age, and unemployment.

---

3. U. S. Department of Labor, "Equal Pay for Equal Work Under the Fair Labor Standards Act," *Interpractices Bulletin,* Title 29, Part 800, Washington, D.C.: 1967.

## INDUSTRIAL COMPENSATION LAWS

All states have industrial compensation laws establishing mandatory insurance funds. The fund is used to pay employees for financial losses incurred due to on-the-job accidents. The funds for such pay come from the employers. The charges and methods of computation vary from state to state; a businessman should see the specific law of the state in which his business operates.

## SOCIAL SECURITY ACT

The Social Security Act of 1935 provides for old-age and survivor benefits. These benefits are financed through taxes shared equally by the employer and the employee or paid entirely by the self-employed. The Social Security tax was expanded in 1965 to include a tax for hospital insurance for the aged, "Medicare." The Social Security tax and the Medicare tax now account for a combined rate of 5.65 percent on the first $12,000 of wages paid during the calendar year. The combined rate for self-employed individuals is 7.65 percent on the first $12,000 of income. The employer collects the taxes and pays the sum to the Internal Revenue Service. The payment is credited to the account of each employee. The account is identified by a social security number.

Retirement benefits are payable to the wage earner and his family upon retirement at age 65 for standard benefits, or 62 for lower benefits. Survivor benefits are payable to the insured's family, no matter what the age at death is. Disability benefits accrue to the worker if the insured becomes totally disabled before the age of 65.

The unemployment title of the Social Security Act gives the federal government authority to administer an unemployment insurance plan in cooperation with the states. The Federal Unemployment Tax Act authorizes the collection of a payroll tax for this purpose which amounts to 3.1 percent of the payroll up to $3,000 per employee.

With these funds the states have provided for varying benefits. The benefits vary according to amount, length of time paid, and individual employee records. The maximum payable for a week of unemployment (excluding allowances for dependents, provided by eleven states) ranges from $30.00 to $60.00. The maximum weeks of benefit range from twenty-two to thirty-nine. And the qualification of individuals for benefits depends (1) upon how long he worked in covered employment before becoming unemployed and (2) upon his registration with the state employment office for suitable work, should it become available.

## Summary

The manpower process deals with attaining and maintaining a productive labor force. This chapter has concentrated on the procedures for obtaining a labor force.

The businessman must be aware not only of how to obtain the needed employees, but also the legal rights potential employees (applicants) and actual employees have. The legislation discussed in this chapter affects the total man-power process and is particularly important in restricting the businessman's freedom to obtain a labor force.

Once a labor force has been obtained the businessman must direct his atten-tion to how a productive labor force can be maintained. He must understand the employee. The next chapter concentrates on understanding employees as individuals.

## QUESTIONS

1. How does the manpower process relate to or affect the following:
   (a) The business system,
   (b) The financial process,
   (c) The distribution process.

2. What is involved in developing a job summary for each job in the business?

3. What specific information does the businessman need when determining the future number of employees needed by his business?

4. What are the various sources of job applicants available to the business?

5. For which type or kind of employees are the various sources you identified in question (4) best suited?

6. In evaluating applicants, what types of information can the employer obtain from:
   (a) The application blank,
   (b) Employment tests,
   (c) The interview.

7. Who is covered and what businesses are affected by the Civil Rights Act of 1964?

8. Name two types of payroll taxes a businessman is responsible for today. List some benefits which are available to an employee as a result of these taxes. What qualifications must an employee meet in order to collect these benefits?

## Incident 13–1

### THE POTENTIAL EMPLOYEE

Golden Products Company employs 200 people to manufacturer plumbing fittings of various shapes and sizes. Richard Furman has been the foreman and general plant manager for the last fifteen years. With the help of a secretary, he keeps the plant running. The president, Daniel Taylor, is concerned about who will replace Richard when he retires. Richard will be sixty-three next month.

Mr. Taylor has always handled manpower matters in the past. He would be the first to admit that his approach has been very informal. After evaluating the present group of employees, many of whom have not completed high school, he feels that someone from the outside should be brought in and trained to take over when Richard retires. This new employee would at this time fill the newly created position of assistant foreman. Mr. Taylor has discussed this matter with Richard, and both men agree that this is what needs to be done. Although neither man has discussed what exactly is involved in this new job, both feel that Mr. Taylor should begin his search for job applicants immediately.

Mr. Taylor spent one afternoon discussing his problem with the local college placement director. After looking through the June graduates' personal resumés, he decides to contact Kenneth Lee for an interview. Kenneth agrees to spend a day discussing the possibilities of working for Golden Products Company. Exhibit 13–4 is a copy of Kenneth Lee's resumé.

---

*Exhibit 13–4*

Resume of Kenneth Lee          Single
402 Niles Avenue               Excellent health
Mishawaka, Indiana 46653       6'2"
219-283-1711                   Age 21

Job objective: To have managerial responsibilities for market or production in a small to medium-sized organization.

Education: Indiana University at South Bend
          Class: 1974
          Degree: B.S.
          Major: Industrial Management
          Minor: Chemistry

Honors: Beta Gamma Sigma National Honor Society in Business Administration, and Dean's list.

Activities: Member Society For the Advancement of Management, Phi Sigma Epsilon Social Fraternity, Active in Student Senate, and intramural athletics.

Experience: Summer and part time: Various and sundry jobs to finance college education including laborer, mechanic, and guitar instructor.

Personal background and interests: Attended public elementary and high school in Chicago, Illinois; active in clubs; honor society; and student government. Interests: golf, tennis, music, and fishing.

References: Reference available upon request at Indiana University, South Bend Placement Center, South Bend, Indiana 46656.

---

Upon returning to the plant, Mr. Taylor gives Richard a copy of Kenneth's resumé. Both men agree that Richard should plan on spending about two hours interviewing Kenneth. The remainder of the time will be spent talking to Mr. Taylor and touring the plant facilities. At the end of the day Richard and Mr. Taylor will discuss the possibility of extending Kenneth a job offer.

(1) Evaluate Mr. Taylor's approach to determining the manpower needs of Golden Products Company.
(2) Evaluate Mr. Taylor's approach to developing applicants to fill the present job.
(3) What criteria will Mr. Taylor and Mr. Furman use to evaluate Kenneth Lee?
(4) What screening procedure would you recommend that Mr. Taylor consider?
(5) Select two students from the class and role play the interview between Kenneth Lee and Richard Furman. Before the interview think through what infor-

mation each party would like to give and receive. After the interview critically
evaluate what happened during the interview and make suggestions on how it
could have been improved.

(6) If neither man likes Kenneth Lee, what would you suggest they do next?
(7) Comment on what you feel to be the strengths and weaknesses of Kenneth
Lee's resumé.

## Incident 13–2

### EMPLOYEE DISCRIMINATION

Two black married sisters, Susan Standish and Judy Jones, lived in the same
community, Riveredge, Arkansas. Their children were all attending school, and
they both felt that it was time for them to find work and supplement their families'
incomes. Riveredge contained some light manufacturing operations. The largest
employer in the community was Hotstuff, Inc., a dry soup manufacturer.

Hotstuff, Inc., employed 500 persons in the plant, 400 white and 100 black. All
100 black employees were males.

On two different days Susan and Judy made application for employment at Hotstuff. They filled out the application forms and provided all the information required by the company. They were each interviewed by the personnel manager.
Neither Susan nor Judy had ever worked in a food processing plant before (in fact,
Susan had never held a job before), and none of their relatives or close friends
worked at the plant.

Both ladies were informed that no present vacancies were available. Susan further
reported that the personal manager told her that Hotstuff did not employ black
females.

Six months later a vacancy occurred at the Hotstuff plant for which Judy was
qualified. She was not contacted, and an inexperienced white female was given
the job. Judy and Susan have since filed charges with the Equal Employment Opportunity Commission. The commission reported that it found reasonable cause
to believe that Judy and Susan were not considered for employment at the Hotstuff plant because of their race. The commission felt that Hotstuff's policy of
giving priorities in hiring former employees and close friends of existing employees
discriminated against black females. The commission also felt that Susan and Judy
should each be offered a job and back pay for the time they could have worked if
the company had not discriminated against them.

Hotstuff's public stance was that in two obvious places on the application blank
were printed the following words, "Applications for employment must be renewed
every two months to remain active." The company's public relations director further stated that the lack of black female employees was a result of their previous
lack of interest in becoming employees at Hotstuff, Inc.

(1) What are Susan and Judy's legal rights? Are they different for each woman?
(2) What are Hotstuff's legal rights?
(3) What other information would you need to know about Hotstuff before a decision could be made?
(4) Would you advise Judy and Susan to take legal action? Why?
(5) What, if anything, would be your future advice for Hotstuff's personnel manager?

# 14

# Employees as Individuals

In the last chapter the first phase of the manpower process, obtaining a labor force, was examined. Once a labor force has been obtained, the businessman must next determine how he can maintain it. Maintaining a labor force involves solving two problems: first, how to keep the good people as employees; and second, how to obtain a desired level or amount of work from each employee. These two problems are related. Their solution centers around understanding what employees want. To oversimplify, if the good employees are given what they want, they are likely to remain employees of the business. And if a desired level of output is a condition of getting what they want, their production will be at a satisfactory level. Thus, the key to maintaining a productive labor force is to understand the employee. This understanding involves two levels: understanding the employee as an individual and understanding the individual as a member of an employee group. This chapter concentrates on the employee as an individual. Chapter 15 looks at the employee as a group member.

## Characteristics of the Labor Force

Since who and what employees are has an effect on what they want, a good starting point in understanding the employees as individuals is to evaluate the qualities or traits of a "typical employee." The labor force is continually growing and changing. Predictions are that the labor force will increase by more than 20 million workers between 1970 and 1985. By that time the total number of workers will exceed 107 million.[1] What statements could be made about a "typical employee" when there are 107 million workers? To help provide answers to the question of who the typical employees of a business are and what characteristics they possess, four factors will be evaluated. These four factors are the sex, age, education, and racial make-up of the labor force. These four factors are changing enough to indicate that the typical employee of the future will be different from the typical employee of today.

## SEX

A substantial proportion of the additional 20 million workers to be added to the labor force between 1970 and 1985 will be women. By 1985, two out of five American workers will be women. These women will be seeking more than secretarial and clerical jobs. They will be looking for jobs at every level of the business organization from factory work to managerial positions. Those jobs that were once held exclusively by men are rapidly disappearing. Women are now, for example, working in the construction trades and mining industries. Women will increasingly qualify for more and more of the jobs being performed in business and industry today.

This influx of women may present unique problems for the businessman or businesswoman, including such problems as how to get men and women to work together cooperatively; whether women should supervise men or vice-versa; what happens to the job when the woman must leave because of pregnancy; and whether baby-sitting service will have to be provided by employers. These are but a few of the problems that the businessman of the future will have to resolve. Women are and will increasingly become an important part of the labor force. Ways must be devised to handle some of the unique problems this trend will present.

## AGE

By 1985 the labor force will be younger than it currently is. Exhibit 14–1 illustrates the projected age and sex profile of the total labor force by 1985. There will be an overwhelming number of workers within the age range of twenty-five to thirty-four. In this age group there will be one woman seeking employment for every two men who also will be seeking work. For the businessman, the married, older worker represents a more stable employee than the younger, single worker. The older worker has often already decided where he wants to go and what he wants to accomplish. In addition, he is more likely to stay on the job for a longer period of time than the younger employee.

The whole shift towards a younger labor force, when considered along with some of the other characteristics, has widespread implications for the businessman. One such characteristic is the level of education of the work force.

---

1. Sophia Travis, "The U.S. Labor Force: Projections to 1985," *Monthly Labor Review, 93,* May 1970, pp. 3–12.

EXHIBIT 14–1

*Age and Sex Profile of the Total Labor Force by 1985*

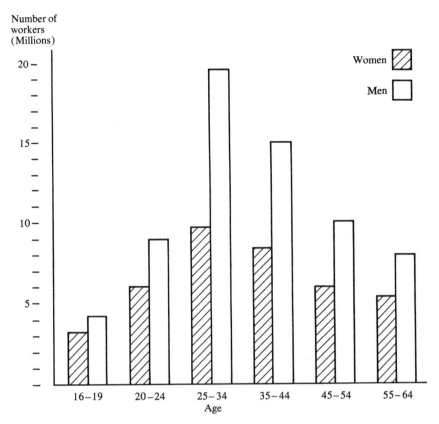

Source: Sophia Travis, "The U.S. Labor Force: Projections to 1985," *Monthly Labor Review, 93*, May 1970, p. 3.

## EDUCATION LEVEL

In every country of the world except the United States, education beyond the early teenage years is a privilege for the wealthy few. In the United States the number of high school and college graduates are continually increasing. Exhibit 14–2 illustrates how the number of people in college has been and will continue to increase. By 1980, nearly one-half of all college-age people in the United States will be enrolled in post-secondary education.

The trend is set. Those people seeking jobs in the future will have a higher level of formal education than employees of the past. At first glance this may appear to be a beneficial trend for business. In fact, the economic achievements of this country can be directly related to the population's level of education. However, it is a double-edged sword. An increasing level of education may present the businessman with some problems.

The more educated a person, the higher are his expectations. With the rising level of education, the population may come to view some jobs (e.g., janitors,

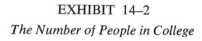

EXHIBIT 14–2

*The Number of People in College*

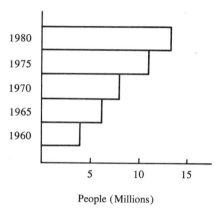

People (Millions)

Adapted from S. E. Harris and A. Levensohn (eds.), *Education and Public Policy.* Berkeley, Calif.: McCutchan Publishing Corporation, 1965, p. 226.

laborers, factory jobs, clerical jobs, and maintenance jobs) demeaning or below them. The problem a higher level education could create for the businessman is finding good people to do some of these necessary jobs. As more people go to college, a smaller number will be available for apprenticeship in the skilled trades (e.g., tool and die makers, machinists, carpenters, etc.). There is a projected shortage of these skilled employees. Most businesses need at a minimum a few highly skilled employees. Without these skilled employees they will be in real trouble. As it looks now, certain skilled jobs will in the future go unfilled.

On the positive side, the businessman of the future can count on a more educated worker which presumably, because of his level of education, will make a better employee. However, in the face of a general rise in the level of education, some people will be *overeducated* for the unskilled jobs they will have to accept if they want to be employed. And some people will be *miseducated.* They will have the wrong type of education for some of the skilled jobs that then will remain unfilled. It is not hard to see the time when college graduates will be unemployed while businesses search for qualified tool and die makers to employ.

An underlying theme of U.S. culture has been to raise the general level of education of the population. It is quite possible that this goal may need to be revised. Although a population with high education is beneficial, some of the educational effort may need to be redirected. The new theme may be to educate some of the population in the skills that are needed by the economy. Some government-funded training and retraining has already been started to alleviate some of the problems miseducated groups will cause.

RACE

For discussion purposes, the labor force can be thought of as two groups, white and nonwhite. The nonwhite group is made up primarily of Chicanos, Indians,

Orientals, and Black Americans. The Blacks are by far the largest subgroup of the nonwhite group. The composition of the labor force in terms of race is slowly changing. By 1985, the labor force will be made up of 87 percent white and 13 percent nonwhite members. In understanding what employees want from their jobs, the distinction of race is really not a meaningful one. The businessman must deal with each employee as an individual person, not as a member of one race or another.

However, the businessman is feeling and will continue to feel the impact of an increasing percentage of nonwhite workers. In the U.S. a moral and legal commitment has been made to provide equal employment opportunities to the members of the nonwhite groups. The antidiscrimination legislation discussed in Chapter 13 is just a prelude to this commitment. Increasingly business will feel the pressure to hire, promote, and train *more* nonwhite employees. Businesses are being asked to share the burden of rectifying a historical trend that has placed nonwhites at a disadvantage in obtaining employment and competing for advancement. The impact of this request on business is too wide for discussion in this text. You must try to imagine the time, effort, and expense necessary to undo years of racial discrimination and to reach the time when a section on race in a book such as this need not even be mentioned.

## THE "TYPICAL EMPLOYEE" OF THE FUTURE

On the whole the labor force of the future will only slightly differ from the labor force of today. The majority will still be middle-aged white males with a high school education. However, for part of the total labor force this generalization is inaccurate, and this part will become larger as time passes. There will be an increasing influx of women, younger workers, higher educated workers, and minority group employees into the labor force. The businessman will have to bring together people of different sex, age, education, and racial backgrounds in a common work setting. How effective he is in bringing these people together will determine how effective his labor force will be.

To talk about or attempt to classify within the labor force a "typical" or "average" employee will mean less and less. The labor force of the future will be mixed. Within the labor force members of any one group—men, women, young, old, black, etc.—may have certain things in common. But the important point is that regardless of which group an employee may fall into, as an individual each employee is and will continue to be different. To maintain a productive labor force, the businessman needs to understand how each employee is different as an individual.

### The Individual Employee

The changing nature of the labor force does carry with it certain implications for the businessman. However, to discuss employees only from this viewpoint is too general. The businessman still needs to solve the two problems stated at the beginning of this chapter: keeping good employees and getting a desired level and amount of work from them.

The answer to each problem depends upon the individual employee. For each individual, it is quite possible that the solutions for these two problems could be different. For example, one employee may want clean working conditions whereas for another employee that is of no concern. Or a monetary incentive may make one employee very productive and have no effect on the output of another employee.

Solving the two problems requires that the businessman understand what it is that an employee wants from his job. If this can be understood, then giving the good employee what he wants helps keep him as an employee and thus solves the first problem. The second problem can be solved by exchanging what the employee wants for a certain amount of work. The employee is rewarded for good work and penalized for poor work by giving or taking away what he wants most from the job. This is, of course, an oversimplification of a very complex situation. To illustrate how this concept might be put into action by the businessman, assume that an employee only wants money from a job. Therefore, to keep him, the businessman must be sure that his wages are at least equal to what he could be making at other jobs he is qualified to do. Secondly, to insure that this employee will continue to be productive, part or all of his wages should be tied to his level of output, through some form of incentive system.

To help explain employees and thus solve these two problems, two views of what employees want from work can be contrasted. The first is the view of the employee as a totally rational-economic person.

## THE RATIONAL-ECONOMIC EMPLOYEE

Traditionally most businessmen have assumed that their employees were economic and rational in nature; that is, that the "rational-economic" employee wants money from the job. Two important characteristics of the rational-economic employee can be identified:

(1) The employee constantly seeks economic gain and will do whatever gets him the greatest economic gain.

(2) The employee rationally weighs the effort required on the job against the resulting economic gain from doing the job.

If the businessman follows these beliefs, the employee can be thought of as a commodity to be bought like any other commodity. The two problems are easily solved. If you want to retain the good employees, pay them more money; because if the employee can make more money working for someone else, he will leave. The type of work is really not important. What is important is that, as an employee, if a man can make more money collecting garbage than he can teaching school, he will collect garbage. Thus the solution to the first problem is simple: pay good employees more money than they could make anywhere else.

If the businessman believes in the second idea, then the other problem he faces is also very easily solved. If you want people to work harder, pay them more money, because employees weigh the effort on the job against the economic gain from the job. And if the employee does not work as hard as you think he should be working, decrease his pay.

What an easy job the businessman would have in maintaining a productive labor force if the solutions to his problems were so simple. Money is a very important consideration in taking a job, staying on a job, and performing on a job, but it is only a part. It is not the money, but what the money will buy that is important. Money allows people to satisfy their basic needs—food, clothing, and shelter. It allows them to survive. But most individuals want more than just survival out of life and out of a job. Employees want more than just a paycheck.

Your own desires, or wants, can serve to illustrate this point. If, on completion of this course, you were offered ten jobs in line with your present level of ability, you would immediately recognize two things. First, most likely the pay you would be offered would not vary more than $25.00 per month among the ten jobs. And second, some of the ten jobs would be more pleasing and more attractive to you than others. Why are some jobs more attractive than others? And why will you accept one job versus another? The pay you will receive may have little to do with which job you select. The "something else" you see in that job, the chance for something other than pay, is the important factor. It might be the chance to be your own boss, the chance for responsibility, the opportunity to work with other people, or any number of things. The "other things" will motivate you to accepting one job and performing on that job. If you find, once on the job, that these "other things" are missing, the money you receive will not be a strong enough force to keep you on that job. Not even an increase in salary will do.

So it is with all people and all employees. Money is a very important *first* consideration. However, once the money is there, "other things" become more important. To understand what these other things are requires moving away from the simple view of the employee as a rational-economic employee.

## THE TOTAL EMPLOYEE

The economic desire is one need of the employee. However, each employee is very complex. This does not mean that the employee is nonrational and noneconomic. He is rational as well as emotional, and economic as well as noneconomic. Businessmen need to understand what the "total employee" wants from the job. What the total employee wants from the job can be expressed as a combination of the following three factors:

(1) Economic factors (E),

(2) Social factors (S),

(3) Personal factors (P).

For each individual employee, the combination of these three factors will vary. The degree to which money will satisfy one employee will be different from that for the next person. The same holds true for the social and personal factors. However, the order of importance of these factors can be illustrated as follows:

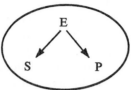

Economic considerations are first and foremost in the minds of employees. Given that an individual is employed and receiving adequate pay, the social and personal aspect of the job become important. They determine whether an employee stays on a given job and how he performs on a given job—the two problems the businessman faces in maintaining a labor force. Thus once the economic factors of a job have been dealt with, understanding the social and personal factors is the key to maintaining a productive labor force.

Man is social; he needs contact with other people. Employees like to associate with other people on the job. One of the severest forms of punishment is solitary confinement. The same can be said for work which keeps people from coming into contact with one another. Employees seek social contacts on the job. Through these social contacts, groups are formed. Their full effect will be discussed in the following chapter, where the employee as a member of a group is considered.

At the same time the employee seeks a certain feeling of personal worth from the job. He wants a sense of achievement, recognition for a job well-done, a feeling of importance, and a sense of responsibility. These are of maximum importance once the economic need of the employee has been satisfied.

Each employee as an individual places differing values on these three factors, just as certain students require more social activity than others. The same can be said for the other two factors. The desires will vary from person to person. The difficult part of the businessman's job is to understand what each individual employee wants from the job in terms of these three categories of factors.

## THE TOTAL MAN AND JOB SATISFACTION

When a job can provide an individual with what he wants, he is generally satisfied with it. To be satisfied with a job usually means that the person stays on the job and is productive on that job. People look for other jobs when they are dissatisfied. They also perform poorly on a job that they are dissatisfied with.

To maintain a productive labor force means to attempt to satisfy individual employees. The total man is satisfied when his job provides him with sufficient economic, social, and personal rewards. In seeking to understand the employee, it is of utmost importance that the businessman keep in mind the following concepts:

(1) *There is no average man.* People are not all alike. Each is a unique individual.

(2) *The individual wants to have a degree of economic security.* Everyone strives for an equitable payment for his efforts in order to make a living. This is first and foremost in most employees' minds.

(3) *The individual wants to work in a social environment.* Man is largely social. Although at times he may want to be alone, most of his time he wants to spend with other people.

(4) *The individual wants to use his full capabilities.* The individual seeks a degree of personal satisfaction from work. He resents the lack of opportunity to apply his knowledge and skills and to be held responsible for specific results.

(5) *The employee can be persuaded to cooperate in achieving the business' objective.* Employees can be persuaded to cooperate through many means, which must be selected to meet the individual's nature.

## Gaining Employee Cooperation

A cooperative employee willingly and enthusiastically carries out the work assigned him. The businessman tries to gain the cooperation of his employees, because cooperative employees do more than the minimum amount of work expected from them. The businessman can increase employee cooperation by considering the nature of individual employees.

People have many different reasons for working which can be classified as economic, social, and personal. These function as incentives to work. In addition to making people want to work, they also affect the *way* an employee performs his job. People are enthusiastic about work that satisfies their economic, social, and personal desires. Since the businessman can control these incentives, he can also control the degree of cooperation he receives from his employees. He is faced with a matching problem, matching the job to be done with the individual employee's job desires. If properly matched, the result will be a cooperative employee. Before such a match can be successful, the two elements involved—the individual and the job—need to be analyzed.

Because each employee is an individual, the economic, social, and personal desires of each will differ. The kind and amount of the three incentives each requires from work will have to be determined for each employee of the business.

Next, an analysis of each job should be performed. This analysis should determine the kind and amount of economic, social, and personal satisfaction an employee would receive by performing each job in the business.

Each employee can now be matched to that job which will provide him with the kind and amount of the three incentives he desires. For example, an employee who wants a lot of social contact on the job would probably be better suited for a salesman's job than for a bookkeeper's job. Or an employee who desires a lot of recognition and feelings of achievement would probably be suited for a job which offers him the freedom to make his own decisions. It may be impossible to have a perfect match between all employees and their jobs, but to come as close as possible should be one goal of the businessman. Non-cooperative employees are usually on a job which fails to provide the kind or amount of at least one of the three incentives they want. To keep an employee cooperative or gain the cooperation of an uncooperative employee, the job needs to be such that it provides him with what he wants. This does not mean that if each employee receives a $2,000 raise every year he will be cooperative. Cooperation cannot be bought. Cooperation is given to employers in return for jobs which offer a suitable amount of *all* three of the important job incentives.

People are basically cooperative. Whether they remain so as employees depends largely on the jobs they are given to do. If the job satisfies their desires they will be cooperative. If not, they will be uncooperative, doing only the minimal amount of work required, or they will quit. Both of these alternatives are undesirable for the business if the person is a potentially good employee.

In summary, to maintain a labor force or to keep good people as employees, and to obtain the desired level or amount of work from these employees, requires three things: (1) to understand what each employee wants from work; (2) to understand what each job would give to the person performing it in terms of economic, social, and personal returns; and (3) to match the right employee with the right job. In this way the businessman and the employee will both benefit from a job well done.

## COOPERATION AND THE IMPACT OF A CHANGING LABOR FORCE

In the first part of this chapter the changing composition of the labor force was discussed. As the labor force becomes more and more mixed, two problems will present themselves as the businessman seeks to gain the cooperation of employees. First, the businessman will not be able to generalize about what all his workers want. The different backgrounds, races, educations, and sexes of employees will result in a wider variation in what each employee wants from the job. Thus in the future it will even be more important to understand each employee as an individual. Second, the worker of the future will increasingly demand work that satisfies his personal and social desires. Money may still be the important factor for the people supplementing their families' incomes or for the culturally deprived employees. But for the career woman, the young workers, or the more educated workers, the jobs will have to offer more than just a paycheck. If cooperation is to be maintained, the nature of work will have to take account of these demands. Increasingly the once-popular production line with its routine jobs will be questioned. Although the production line concept will always be a part of industry, there may need to be certain modifications to add a more personal touch. In the future these routine jobs will most probably be redefined to emphasize the personal and social satisfaction they offer employees.

## DISCIPLINE

Up to this point, only the positive rewards of a job have been discussed. Cooperation, employees willingly and enthusiastically performing their jobs, also means that employees adopt certain kinds of behavior while at work. For any business to function properly, certain kinds of behavior are necessary. For example, a business may require certain behavior in showing up for work, maintaining acceptable output, being careful, observing no-smoking and no-drinking rules, or accepting official orders. Persistent failure of employees to behave properly requires disciplinary action.

Disciplining is an inescapable part of the businessman's job. How he disciplines an employee can have a lasting effect on the cooperation he will receive from his employees in the future. Disciplining will be most beneficial in terms of employee cooperation if the businessman observes the following guides. All discipline should be:

## PROMPT

The best time to correct an error is soon after it occurs. If an employee is caught smoking in a no-smoking area, bringing it to his attention two days later will have very little effect on him.

## WITH FOREWARNING

Employees should know in advance what they are expected to do and what not to do. If the employee is unaware that the area where he is smoking is, in fact, a no-smoking area, then disciplinary action would be unfair. The job of communicating to employees what is and is not expected of them is the businessman's responsibility. No disciplinary action should be taken unless the employee has received this forewarning.

## FAIR AND CONSISTENT

The discipline should be proportional to the severity of the behavior. For example, firing an employee for hitting a supervisor may be fair, but it would be unfair for the violation of a no-smoking rule. The discipline should also be applied consistently to all employees. For example, if two employees hit a supervisor, firing one and verbally reprimanding the other is inconsistent. The result is likely to be a charge of favoritism by other employees; it would be disruptive of future relationships.

The purpose of disciplinary action is solely to improve the *future* behavior of the employee being disciplined and other employees. Discipline should not be detrimental to maintaining or gaining employee cooperation. This does not mean that the businessman should ignore those situations requiring disciplinary action. Even though disciplining employees is a distasteful aspect of the businessman's job, failure to do so will lead to a failure in achieving employee cooperation. Employees know when they are out of line and expect to be disciplined. Failure to discipline, or discipline which is late in coming, unexpected, or excessive will have an adverse effect on future employee–employer cooperation.

## Summary

To maintain a productive labor force the businessman must understand his employees, which requires an understanding of how the labor force of the future will differ from the labor force of today. In general, it will be made up of a greater variety of people. There will be a larger influx of females, racial minority group members, and younger and better educated workers. Each of these workers will vary in what he wants or expects from a job. Each will expect and want a varying amount of economic, social, and personal satisfaction from work. To gain the cooperation of employees the businessman needs to understand what each employee as an individual wants in each of these areas. To maintain this cooperation, the businessman will on occasion have to discipline some employees. If the discipline is prompt, with forewarning, fair, and consistent the end effect will be to increase cooperation.

The employee seeks social contact with other employees. In Chapter 15, some of the effects of this desire are discussed. It is just as important that the businessman understand the employee as a member of a group as it is to understand him as an individual.

## QUESTIONS

1. What is involved in maintaining a productive labor force?

2. What impact will more women in the labor force have on maintaining a labor force?

3. What are the pros and cons of a labor force whose educational level is constantly increasing?

4. What two important beliefs about the rational-economic employee were identified?

5. If the businessman pays his employees high wages, he will not have to worry about his workers willingly and enthusiastically carrying out their work assignments. Is this statement correct or incorrect? Give your reasons.

6. What other factors besides money does the employee want from his job? Give some examples of what is involved in each of these factors.

7. Listed below are five basic satisfactions which employees desire from their jobs. As a future college graduate, you will probably have an opportunity to select from a number of job offers. Which of these basic satisfactions will be most important to you in choosing your new job? List them in order of decreasing importance.
   (a) Doing something which is interesting and varied,
   (b) Receiving recognition for job performance,
   (c) Wages which allow for a decent living,
   (d) A position which affords job security,
   (e) A working environment which is conducive to trust, support from your fellow workers, and little pressure.

8. How can the businessman gain the cooperation of employees?

9. When and how can disciplinary action increase cooperation between employees and an employer?

## Incident 14–1

### THE ENGINEER DEPARTMENT

Jim Hastings, age forty, was a design engineer for Sleep-Not mobile homes. Sleep-Not was a leader in innovative design in the industry. Many of Jim's ideas had helped give Sleep-Not this leadership. The only reason Jim had not been promoted to head of the design department was his apparent dislike for managerial duties. He was quite happy to continue doing the design work and leave the managerial tasks to Bob Vanner, his supervisor for the last eleven years. Bob respected Jim's ability and education, a masters degree in design. As a result Jim was given a great deal of freedom on his job.

Jim roamed through the plant, talking with supervisors and employees as well as observing operations. Through the years Jim had developed some close personal relations with some people in the plant. As Jim stated, "a mutual respect has developed—they don't try to snow me and I don't try to snow them." He also talked to suppliers and attended conventions where new ideas were on display. Through these channels, he generated new ideas which he incorporated into designs, once back in the office. On occasion a competitor of Sleep-Not had tried to hire Jim at a substantial salary increase. To date all such attempts have failed. Sleep-Not's top management felt very fortunate to have a man of Jim's loyalty and ability and have publicly stated this on numerous occasions.

On the day after Christmas Jim received some very upsetting news. Bob Vanner had suffered a severe heart attack while shoveling snow out of his driveway. Although the heart attack was not fatal, Bob would be out of work for at least six months. The president asked Jim if, under the present circumstances, he would manage the design department until Bob's return. Jim reluctantly agreed.

As a manager, Jim had very little time to do any actual design work himself. He planned the work for the other designers and made sure they were on schedule. It seemed to Jim that 90 percent of his day was taken up with administrative work, such as top management meetings, reports, budgets, and personal conferences. The other 10 percent was planning for future events. He very rarely left his new office. On more than one occasion he commented to his wife that he didn't feel that as an administrator he was making the kinds of contributions he was trained for. After six months the president informed Jim that Bob's condition had not improved. He further asked if Jim would take the manager's job on a permanent basis. Jim said he didn't really feel suited for the manager's job but the president insisted.

Two months later Jim handed in his letter of resignation. He was immediately hired by a competitor of Sleep-Not as a design engineer.

(1) What did the president fail to recognize about what Jim wanted from a job?
(2) What does Jim want from his job? When will Jim be satisfied with a job? What will make Jim the most satisfied?
(3) What does this case illustrate about matching the man with the job?
(4) Is Jim peculiar in what he wants from work? Would these needs be different for a laborer, secretary, or teacher?
(5) Could the same things that made Jim satisfied as a designer make him satisfied as a manager? If so, how would you change the manager's job to give him these things?
(6) What recommendations would you have for Jim's new boss?

**Incident 14–2**

## THE SECRETARY POOL—PART A

Kevin Ryan had been the supervisor of a secretary pool in a large insurance company. All of the employees were women whose age averaged about twenty-one years. They received typing to do from various managers in the company. The work came in two forms, either on a dictaphone tape or through written reports. Kevin's goal was to get the work back to the managers in completed form one day from receipt. Therefore, each morning the work for the day was divided among the women. Any typing that came in during the day was either assigned to the women or held for the next day's assignment. This schedule had allowed Kevin to reach his one-day turnaround goal.

Kevin permitted the women to have a maximum amount of freedom as long as they did their work. He was not strict in enforcing the time limits for the coffee and lunch breaks. The atmosphere was very relaxed and to an outsider might appear to be too casual, but the women appreciated this freedom and tried to do their share of the work to make up for it. Nancy Wagner's comments best summed up the feeling of the other secretaries when she said, "Where else can I have the freedom to take some extra time at lunch when I need it without having a boss always checking on me? Kevin trusts that you have a good reason for taking the extra time, and as long as you do your share of work that's good enough for him."

The morale and output of Kevin's department were high. He was promoted to a new position and replaced by Sharon O'Malley, who had a somewhat different philosophy. Sharon was a recent college graduate, and this was her first management job. She believed that as long as there were rules they should be enforced, particularly those relating to coffee breaks and lunch periods. During her first week on the job Sharon called a meeting of the secretaries and announced that in the future they would be expected to observe the time limits established for coffee breaks and lunch periods. Although most of the women complied with her request, Sharon couldn't achieve the one-day turnaround on typing work Kevin had achieved. A few employees also continued to take a longer lunch period than was permitted. When Sharon discovered one of the women returning from lunch one-half hour late, she warned her that she or anyone else would be sent home and not be paid for the remainder of the work period if they overstayed their lunch period in the future. The woman was noticeably upset because the reason for her lateness was a teacher–parent conference, which could not be attended either before or after work.

Two weeks later all the secretaries went out to lunch to celebrate the birthday of one of them. Many had too much to drink. The entire group came back from this lunch an hour late. Faced with the alternative of backing down or enforcing the rule and sending the entire group home, Sharon chose to enforce the rule. The next day Sharon's boss came to investigate the mass suspension; a short time later he requested that Sharon be transferred to another department.

(1) Under existing circumstances, was Kevin's or Sharon's approach to gaining employee cooperation better? Why do you feel this way?

(2) Was Sharon wrong in enforcing the rules?

(3) Evaluate Sharon's approach to the employees and her disciplinary action.

(4) If Sharon could not be transferred but instead had to stay on this job, what as Sharon's boss would you advise her to do?

(5) Do you think the fact that Sharon was a woman caused her to act differently than a new male supervisor might have? If so, how? Do you think it caused the secretaries to act differently?

(6) If you were the new supervisor who was assigned Sharon's job, what would you do, and why?

# 15

# Employees in Groups

Every business, except for the one-man operation, requires the efforts of many people with specialized skills. These people are brought together to perform the work of the particular business. One of the trademarks of modern society is men and women working together. Today, throughout business and industry, people are working as members of **groups** in an attempt to solve a wide variety of problems. The work to be done requires a certain number of formal groups, including committees, departments, task forces, and teams, which are required within any business. In addition, because man is social, certain groups are formed other than those required to perform the work of the business.

People have found that the attempt at self-sufficiency—producing your own food, clothing, shelter, and all other goods—at best leads to a meager standard of living. But when people join together, combine their efforts, and exchange the results of their labor, they can maintain a higher standard of living. In addition, they can better protect what they have if they join together. People naturally form groups to better gain and protect that which is important to them. This is true in the business situation. Employees will group together to gain and protect what is important to them. When these groups are formalized, they are called *unions*.

People, and employees, will form groups for reasons other than protection. One of the three factors identified in the last chapter as being important to all employees is the social factor. People need and seek social contact in every aspect of life, including the job. Employees will form informal groups on the job. These groups are not needed to do the job but occur solely to satisfy the individuals' social desires. A tour through any plant during lunch hour will readily illustrate this concept. Card and checker groups abound, some of which may have had the same members for many years. Informal groups also form during working hours. Within a secretarial pool, the causal observer can ofen witness a number of different informal groups. Informal groups spring up naturally whenever people work together.

With this background the concept of a *group* can be defined as any number of people who (1) interact with one another, (2) identify themselves as a group, and (3) have a purpose. All three of these elements are important for a group to exist. A crowd watching a football game is not a group. They may be aware of one another, but they do not interact nor do they identify themselves as a group. They are a mere aggregate of people. *All* the people in a given business are only an aggregate of people. Within this aggregate of people there are two types of groups: formal and informal.

Formal groups are created in order to perform specific jobs with the business. A committee to investigate a certain problem, a number of maintenance employees, and a crew of carpenters are examples of formal groups. The union is a type of formal group with a purpose other than performing specific jobs within the business. The purpose of a union is to protect the interests of its members. The informal group is created by the employees and for the employees, for social contact, not for any specific business function.

In this chapter the discussion will be limited to one formal group—the union—and the informal group. The impacts of these two groups on the activities of a business are very widespread. If understanding employees is the key to maintaining a productive labor force, the businessman needs to understand how to operate with these two types of employee groups. In many cases he has no choice.

## The Informal Group

The only way the businessman can keep an informal group from forming is to keep employees physically separated from one another. The nature of the work to be done usually makes this an impossible alternative. The practical solution is for the businessman to learn how to work with informal groups. The starting point is to understand why informal groups form. Informal groups are formed because they offer employees several benefits.

### A SOURCE OF FRIENDSHIP AND SOCIABILITY
Usually at least eight hours of the business day are spent at work. The rest of an individual's time is spent in many cases with the family. The only contact

some people have with other people occurs on the job. On-the-job friendships are quick to grow. These friendships are particularly important during time on the job when a person does not work (coffee breaks, lunch hours, etc.). The importance of these friendships is illustrated in the common practice of factory workers who come to work an hour early just to sit and talk or play cards.

## A SOURCE OF IDENTITY

This is particularly important in larger organizations where the individual may feel that he is an insignificant member. A small group of friends gives him something to belong to and identify with.

## A SOURCE OF PROTECTION AND SECURITY

The idea that there is strength in numbers is important for individual workers. By banding together, the group can protect members through a united stand against unreasonable pressures from the boss or business organization.

These three are all compelling reasons for workers to form informal groups. Businessmen need to be concerned about them because they may have an adverse effect on the activities carried on in a business.

## INFORMAL GROUPS AND BUSINESS ACTIVITIES

In exchange for membership in the group, the individual gives up a degree of his freedom. The informal group holds some power over the individual because it can literally withhold one or all three of the benefits mentioned above. With this power certain influences can be exerted over the attitudes, beliefs, and behavior of individual group members. This influence can have at least two negative effects on the employee.

## PRESSURE TO CONFORM TO GROUP STANDARDS

Conformity is common in every aspect of life. Children tease playmates if their clothing is too fancy or not in the accepted style. The length and style of a person's hair is an example of standards imposed upon individuals. Even the nonconformist conforms to standards set by the group of nonconformists he identifies with. Of course, the particular matters on which to conform vary from group to group.

On the job, as in school, the prime standard seems to be an accepted level of output. In school, no one likes a "curve breaker." In fact, the student who scores continually higher than the rest of the class will feel some social pressure. The same can be said about employees on the job. The group informally determines the acceptable level of work output. The employee who goes beyond the accepted standard will be subject to social pressure, occasionally severe. Members of the group may no longer associate with him, treating him as an outcast. Each individual's craving for the respect and acceptance of fellow employees makes such pressure very unpleasant. The result is that the majority of the members of the informal group will conform to the standard of output as set by the group. The businessman may find that his efforts to stimulate higher output will have little effect in the face of a group-imposed standard level of output.

## PROVISION OF BELIEFS AND VALUES TO THE EMPLOYEES

Feelings are passed on to individuals by the group. The informal group can influence an individual's feelings about many matters on the job. For example, the employee may accept the group's belief that the boss is "unfair" without any personal observation to confirm it. The group may feel that it is all right to steal small tools and material from the business, or that expense accounts should be padded. Once these values and beliefs are formed, even though they might be wrong, the individuals view them as "right." Stealing small tools and material from the business for example, is not viewed as a crime, but as an acceptable practice. This feeling could be costly to the business. Many group feelings and values do not really affect the business' operation and thus should not concern the businessman. But when the standards, feelings, and values of the informal group interfere with the operation of a business something needs to be done.

### WORKING WITH THE INFORMAL GROUP

If the businessman feels an idea held by an informal group is not in the best interests of the business, he must take action. Many times a standard, value, or belief results from misinformation. For example, a rumor could start that one-half the employees will be laid off by Christmas or that there will be no raises this year. These situations are easily remedied by getting the correct information to the employees. But often just telling employees that they should not behave or feel a certain way is not sufficient. They may simply not believe the businessman. Then what?

At this point the businessman must try to understand why these employees feel as they do. He needs to secure a full understanding of their feelings and problems. This will only happen if and when employees as a group and individually are ready to confide in him. If employees feel that whatever information they pass on to the businessman will be held against them, or that the manager will only hear what he wants to hear and ignore what is really important to the employee, very little information will come to him.

The whole process of changing an informal group's standards is one of influence. Before the businessman can influence employees, two things must happen. First, he must fully understand the feelings of these employees; and second, he must be willing to have them influence him. There is a possibility that the employees are right, and in fact, he needs to change, not the informal group.

Working with an informal group requires a degree of openness in both the businessman and the group, a willingness to explain why a value is the way it is. Only then can some agreement be reached on what is the best value for the system. This agreement may require a change by both the businessman and the informal group. Once the standard is accepted by the group, the power the group has over individuals can work for the benefit of the businessman. If, for example, an employee does not produce up to the agreed-upon standard, social pressure will be brought to bear on him. Thus, the informal group can also be a positive force within the business.

## Unions as a Formal Group

The natural tendency for men to band together to protect and maintain what is important to them has already been mentioned. A natural outflow of this informal banding together is the whole social system. The same can be said about unions. Workers informally banding together naturally resulted in a more formal structure or group, the union.

### GROWTH OF UNIONS

The growth of unions in the United States can be directly attributed to the individual's desire for protection, in this case protection from the power businessmen could exercise over employees. It is generally accepted that, given the chance, businessmen would exploit employees, as was illustrated by the conditions in the factories prior to the development of the unions.

> We were not aware until within a few days, of the modus operandi of the factory powers in this village, of forcing poor girls from their quiet homes, to become their tools, and like the southern slaves, to give up her life and liberty to the heartless tyrants and taskmasters. Observing a singular looking "long, low, black" wagon passing along the street, we made inquiries respecting it, and were informed that it was what we term a "slaver." She makes regular trips to the north of the state, cruising around in Vermont and New Hampshire, with a "commander" whose heart must be as black as his craft, who is paid a dollar a head, for all he brings to the market, and more in proportion to the distance—if they bring them from such a distance that they cannot easily get back. This is done by "hoisting false colors," and representing to the girls that they tend more machinery than is possible, and that the work is so very neat, and the wages such, that they can dress in silks and spend half their time in reading.[1]

> We went through many of the mills, talked particularly to a large number of the operatives, and ate at their boarding-houses, on purposes to ascertain by personal inspection the facts of the case. We assure our readers that very little information is possessed, and no correct judgments formed, by the public at large, of our factory system, which is the first germ of the Industrial or Commercial Feudalism, that is to spread over our land . . . in Lowell live between seven and eight thousand young

---

1. From *A Documentary of American Industrial Society*, Vol. 12, p. 141, as quoted in Raymond S. Iman and Thomas W. Koch, *Labor in American Society*. Chicago: Scott, Foresman and Company, 1965, p. 437.

women, who are generally daughters of farmers of the different States of New England; some of them are members of families that were rich the generation before . . . the operatives work thirteen hours a day in the summer time, and from daylight to dark in the winter. At half past four in the morning the factory bell rings, and at five the girls must be in the mills. A clerk, placed as watch, observes those who are a few minutes behind the time, and effective means are taken to stimulate to punctuality. This is the morning commencement of the industrial discipline (should we not rather say industrial tyranny?) which is established in these Associations of this moral and Christian community. At seven the girls are allowed thirty minutes for breakfast, and at noon thirty minutes more for dinner, except during the first quarter of the year, when the time is extended to forty-five minutes. But within this time they must hurry to their boarding-houses and return to the factory, and that through the hot sun, or the rain and cold. A meal eaten under such circumstances must be quite unfavorable to digestion and health, as any medical man will inform us. At seven o'clock in the evening the factory bell sounds the close of the day's work.

Thus thirteen hours per day of close attention and monotonous labor are exacted from the young women in these factories . . . So fatigued—we should say, exhausted and worn out, but we wish to speak of the system in the simplest language—are numbers of the girls, that they go to bed soon after their evening meal, and endeavor by a comparatively long sleep to resuscitate their weakened frames for the toils of the coming days. The young women sleep upon an average six in a room; three beds to a room. There is no privacy, no retirement here; it is almost impossible to read or write alone, as the parlor is full and so many sleep in the same chamber. A young woman remarked to us that if she had a letter to write, she did it on the head of a band-box, sitting on a trunk, as there was not space for a table. So live and toil the young women of our country in the boarding-houses and manufactories, which the rich . . . have built for them.[2]

Under these conditions it was inevitable that groups of wage earners would arise to protect themselves against some of these abuses and to improve their lot in life. Labor unions spread from factory to factory.

Today, in excess of 25 percent of the total nonagricultural labor force belongs to a union.[3] Indications are that this percentage will remain about the same in the future, due to a projected standstill in union growth. Thus, it is safe to say that one out of four workers is today, and will be in the future, a union member.

The American labor movement consists essentially of blue-collar workers. This is shown in the six largest labor unions in the country:

(1) The International Brotherhood of Teamsters, Chauffers, Warehouse-men, and Helpers of America,

(2) The United Auto Workers,

---

2. From *A Documentary History of American Industrial Society,* Vol. 7, pp. 132–35, as quoted in Iman and Koch, *op. cit.,* pp. 37–39.

3. U. S. Department of Labor, Bureau of Labor Statistics, *Handbook of Labor Statistics, 1972,* Bulletin #1735. Washington, D. C.: 1972, Table 153, p. 333.

(3) The United Steelworkers of America,

(4) The International Brotherhood of Electrical Workers,

(5) The International Association of Machinists,

(6) The United Brotherhood of Carpenters and Joiners of America.

In spite of the historical predominance of blue-collar unions, in 1956 white-collar workers outnumbered blue-collar workers for the first time.[4] All indications are that the trend toward a higher and higher proportion of white-collar workers appears likely to continue for the foreseeable future. These shifts in proportions mean that unions will gradually lose their membership strength unless they are able to organize more white-collar workers. Those groups where unions will find their most success in organizing appear to be among clerical and governmental employees. The promise of organizing the large number of employees in these two groups alone assures the continued existence of unions in the U.S. In short, unions are here to stay. They are an additional group that the businessman must work with, because of the legal rights of employees.

## LEGAL RIGHTS OF EMPLOYEES

Initially, labor unions were declared by the courts to be illegal. Slowly, public opinion towards unions has changed. Today's legal definition of a union is vastly different from its once illegal position because of numerous pieces of state and federal legislation dealing with labor–management relations. Probably the single most important piece of federal legislation with the greatest impact on businessmen is the Taft-Hartley Act, which was enacted in 1947.

The Taft-Hartley Act recognizes that the inequality of bargaining power between one employee and a large organization necessitated the establishment of employee organizations (unions). The increasing size of businesses had given them a greater degree of power over employees. To balance out this power required an organization of equally large size. The union was seen as a check on the power big business could wield over individual employees and viewed as restoring equality of bargaining power between employers and employees. The employees were guaranteed certain legal rights, as follows:

(1) The right to form, join, or assist labor organizations,

(2) The right to bargain collectively through representatives of their own choosing,

(3) The right to engage in other concerted activities (strikes and picketing) for the purposes of collective bargaining,

(4) The right to refrain from any or all of such activities.

The employee cannot be forced to join a union. Union membership is a right which is legally guaranteed, but exercised at the will of each individual employee. However, it is generally accepted that without employees' legal protection, businessmen would not recognize the existence of a union. Labor history is full of violent examples illustrating this point. Unions complicate the

---

4. Carol A. Barry, "White Collar Employment, Trends and Structure," *Monthly Labor Review, 84,* January 1961, p. 17.

life of a businessman. Before employees were legally protected, businessmen would, and *did,* go to extremes to keep unions out of their businesses.

## UNFAIR LABOR PRACTICES

Any practice that is intended to deny the rights of employees to form, join, or assist labor unions is an unfair labor practice. More specifically the Taft-Hartley Act made it an unfair labor practice for an *employer:*

(1) To interfere with, restrain, or coerce employees in the exercise of their rights to organize a union and bargain collectively or to refrain from union activity. This prohibits such activities as direct or implied threats to employees of what might happen if they joined a union and prohibits promises of rewards for refraining from joining a union.

(2) To discriminate against any employee for union activity. This applies to such matters as initial hiring, conditions of employment, or discharge.

(3) To refuse to bargain collectively with the representatives of his employees.

As labor unions grew in number, size, and power it became evident that their officials were capable of limiting the employees' rights, and occasionally did so. Consequently unfair labor practices were extended to include practices of *labor organizations* or their *officials:*

(1) To restrain or coerce employees in their rights to refrain from union activity or to ask an employer to discriminate against an employee for the purpose of forcing him to join a union.

(2) To stick against an employer to compel the employer to recognize or bargain with that union when another union has already been certified as representative of the employees.

(3) To refuse to bargain collectively with an employer.

(4) To require employees to pay excessive or discriminatory membership fees.

## PROTECTING EMPLOYEE RIGHTS

The Taft-Hartley Act empowered the National Labor Relations Board (NLRB) to administer the unfair-labor provisions of the act. The NLRB cannot initiate an unfair-labor practice charge on its own; action must originate from an individual. When an unfair labor practice has been committed by either an employer or a union, the other group can file an unfair-labor practice charge with the NLRB. The charge is investigated, and the NLRB issues a ruling on the case. The NLRB may require persons to "cease and desist" from the unfair labor practice or to reinstate employees, and it may petition federal courts to enforce its orders. The NLRB's orders are subject to review by the courts and may be appealed ultimately to the Supreme Court.

The NLRB is also empowered to determine the employees' choice of a particular union, by conducting a certification election. Typically, if a union is attempting to organize a group of employees, they must show to the NLRB that a substantial interest for the union exists among the employees. Usually, the union can present evidence of sufficient interest if 30 percent or more of the employees sign a petition stating this interest. An election will then be held and the employees given the opportunity to choose among, (1) the particular union in question, (2) any other union that shows an interest in representing the employees, and (3) no union. A majority vote by the employees is necessary for the NLRB to certify the union as the bargaining agent for these employees. The employer then is legally required to bargain with this union.

The process can also be reversed to decertify a union. If 30 percent of the employees petition to decertify their bargaining agent, such an election will be held. Employers may not petition for decertification of a union, only employees. This procedure is a means whereby workers who are dissatisfied with their union can revoke their representative rights.

## LABOR RELATIONS

Once a union has been certified, the businessman legally must enter into the area of labor relations. Before the union the businessman can make all employment decisions by himself. With the union, he must consult and bargain for the way certain decisions will be made. He must negotiate with the employees' representatives.

### COLLECTIVE BARGAINING

The businessman and the union are required by law to bargain collectively with each other over matters pertaining to the wages, hours, and working conditions of employment. The purpose of such bargaining is to reach agreement on a contract both parties are willing to sign and live by for a period of time. This contract becomes the basic law governing the working lives of the employees, and thus its contents are of extreme interest to employers.

**Collective bargaining** is like the bargaining that goes on between a car salesman and a customer. Both parties are trying to achieve the best deal. In the end they settle on an agreement that is satisfactory to both. In actuality, collective bargaining is more than this because it takes place between two parties wielding a vast amount of power. The union can strike until an agreement is reached, or the businessman can lock out employees (refuse to let them work).

Actual collective bargaining consists of three stages:
(1) The formulation of demands for changing the terms and conditions of employment, on the part of both the union and the business.
(2) The actual negotiation process, where agreement is reached.
(3) The administration of the labor contract which involves the implementation of the agreement.

The key to collective bargaining is planning before the actual bargaining begins. It is similar to preparing a case for debate. The businessman must know as much as he can about both sides of the problem. He needs to know what he wants, what the union wants, and how much each will cost. He then collects data and prepares his arguments, so that the final agreement is in his best interest. The worst position to be in during collective bargaining is to be unprepared for a union demand. If he does his homework on the issues and plans his strategy *before* the actual bargaining takes place, he will be in a good position. However, it is possible that no agreement between the two parties can be reached. They are then faced with an impasse.

## COLLECTIVE BARGAINING IMPASSE

When the two parties cannot reach an agreement, they may seek outside help. The Federal Mediation and Conciliation Service was created by the Taft-Hartley Act. The major responsibility of the service is to help unions and businesses in reaching agreements by providing people to do one of two things: **mediation** or **arbitration.** A mediator helps the two parties reach an agreement through friendly intervention. The mediator can only advise each party on the action he thinks they should take. The parties may accept or reject his advice. An arbitrator, on the other hand, hands down a decision that both parties must follow. The arbitrator decides how the impasse will be solved, while the mediator only advises the parties. Both arbitration and mediation are provided to the parties as a service. They cannot be forced on unwilling parties. But once the parties mutually agree to use an arbitrator, his decision must be followed and is binding.

When an agreement cannot be reached an additional alternative is available —stop work. In essence one party (either the union or the businessman) says to the other "We will stop work unless you see things our way."

The businessman can stop work by literally locking employees out. The lockout is legal but exceedingly rare these days. The union can stop work, and does, by calling a strike. The strike brings economic pressure on the businessman by workers withholding their services. Since a strike seriously interrupts the business operations, the threat of a strike and the strike itself are effective in forcing an agreement to be reached. Strikes are also costly to the union in that some financial support must be given to the workers during the period of the strike. As a result, the impasse will have to be a major one from the union's standpoint before they will strike. What is a "major point" varies from time to time. For example, a two-week paid vacation at one time was a strikeable issue. In other words, the union was willing to take a strike rather than compromise on this demand. Today, such a demand is probably not a major strikeable issue; others, such as paid dental care and guaranteed annual wages, have taken its place.

## ADMINISTRATION OF THE LABOR CONTRACT

The actual negotiation and strike, if it occurs, are only a minor portion of the area of labor relations. The largest part of labor relations falls in the day-to-day working with employees under a labor contract. Once the contract is signed, it becomes law for its duration. The really important job ahead of the businessman is to interpret and apply—or administer—the agreement throughout its duration.

The contract is interpreted and applied through the *grievance procedure*. The grievance procedure involves a systematic deliberation of a complaint between the representative and the businessman. The central purpose of the grievance procedure is to seek an interpretation of the contract with a degree of fairness for both parties. If the employee has a complaint arising because of interpretation of the agreement, he may file a grievance. In practice most businesses allow employees to file a grievance any time they have a complaint.

The procedure is the number of steps an employee's complaint must follow. Most grievance procedures include several steps. Normally, the first step permits the aggrieved worker to present his grievance with union representation (usually his steward) to his immediate supervisor. The supervisor then makes a decision, based upon what he feels to be the intent of the contract. If the worker is dissatisfied with the decision, he many appeal it by taking it to the next step in the procedure. This next step usually involves the next higher level in the organization. The number of steps in the grievance process varies from business to business. Most contracts, however, provide that the last step in the grievance procedure be arbitration. In other words, a third party makes a binding decision and settles this grievance forever.

To illustrate, assume that as a student you have union representation, a contract, and a grievance procedure in your college. Further assume that your teacher takes a disciplinary action you feel uncalled for under the existing contract. The teacher expels you from class for one week, during which time you miss an examination which the teacher will not allow you to make up. You file a grievance and with your representative present it to the teacher. The teacher reviews the facts of the case and your story and decides the disciplinary action was justified. You appeal to the next higher step in the grievance procedure, the dean, who agrees with you. But the teacher is unhappy with the decision and decides to take it to the next level, the president's office. The president listens to your case and the teacher's, and decides in favor of the teacher. You still feel you were right and submit your case to the last step, arbitration, which in this case is a committee of neutral students and teachers. Their decision—you were right, the teacher will formally apologize in front of class, readmit you to class, and give you a make-up examination of similar difficulty to the one you missed. This decision is binding on the parties and must be followed. By changing the words *student* to *worker* and *teacher, dean,* and *president* to various administrative titles such as *foreman, personnel director,* and *plant supervisor,* you can see how the grievance procedure works in a business setting.

The grievance procedure is an effective way of solving workers' complaints and solving the day-to-day problems under a labor agreement. Each decision will set a precedent for future decisions. As such, they should be studied very carefully. In addition, each grievance represents possible changes that will have to be made in future labor contracts.

## Summary

Man has found that he can best obtain satisfaction for his social desires and protect what is important to him by banding together into groups. In the business situation this conclusion results in two types of groups, the informal work group and the union. The informal group satisfies social desires, while the union is a method of protecting what is important in a job. Either group could have a positive or negative effect on business activities. If the businessman understands why these groups exist and attempts to work *with* them, not against them, the results will most likely be positive. A businessman who feels he only is working with individuals, in other words, who ignores the existence of groups, is in for trouble. Groups are a trademark of our society. Building effective relationships with the group is the key to working with the various informal and formal groups the businessman must deal with, and an important element in maintaining a productive labor force.

## The Manpower Process in Retrospect

The manpower process specializes in the utilization of one resource—the human resource. Every business requires employees with certain qualities and qualifications. Obtaining the right number and type of people is the first step in the manpower process.

To obtain the right number and type of people, the businessman needs to know beforehand the number and type of employees his business needs to employ to reach its objectives. He then can develop applicants for the jobs which need to be filled. The applicants can be screened, and the best one, based upon the demands of the job, offered the job. Obtaining employees can be visualized as a flow of people into the business system, just as raw materials flow through a business. Raw materials are purchased and altered in a fixed fashion until at the end they have been changed into finished products. So too people flow into the organization. They are hired and trained until they are able to perform the jobs for which they were hired.

But obtaining a labor force is only part of the manpower process. An effective labor force must be maintained by keeping good people as employees and keeping their output up to a desired level. To do this the businessman needs to understand his employees. He must understand what each individual wants in the way of economic, personal, and social rewards from his job, and understand how to work with and through the various formal and informal groups formed by individual employees.

In summary, the manpower process can be successfully performed when the businessman knows and understands the jobs that must be done by the business. From this he can determine the number and qualifications of employees by way of economic, social, and personal factors. The businessman also needs to know and understand his employees as individuals and members of groups. He can then determine what each wants from work and attempt to match these wants with the jobs that need to be performed. This knowledge can also aid in working with employee groups.

The human resource is important to any businesses success. Yet its effective utilization is usually not given the attention the other resources in the business system are given. We feel this to be an error, and throughout the last three chapters have tried to indicate how the human resources can be better utilized by any business system. These comments do not apply to any one group of employees, but rather to all employees—executives, salesmen, factory workers, secretaries. Every employee is a resource, and therefore the businessman should be concerned with its effective utilization.

## QUESTIONS

1. Why is the formation of groups in business and society a natural phenomena?
2. What benefits does an informal group offer its members?
3. Specifically, how can the informal group be both positive and negative in its effects on the operation of the business system?
4. What are the legal rights of employees in regards to unions? Be specific in your answer.
5. What are unfair labor practices? What is considered an employer unfair labor practice? What is considered a labor organization unfair labor practice?
6. What specifically is involved in collective bargaining?
7. Differentiate between mediation and arbitration.
8. What is a grievance procedure? Illustrate how in your school such a procedure could be set in motion. What advantages and disadvantages do you see of such a procedure?

## Incident 15–1

### THE SECRETARY POOL—PART B

All of the women of the secretary pool went to lunch to celebrate one of the women's 21st birthday. The celebration lunch extended one hour beyond the normal lunch period and caused a confrontation with the newly appointed manager, Sharon O'Malley, who was cracking down on extended lunch periods. This crackdown was a position totally opposite to Sharon's predecessor, who ran a very loose department. Sharon sent all the women home without pay for the remainder of the day. Her boss, after an investigation, felt that the situation necessitated her transfer. For a more detailed description of events, see The Secretary Pool—Part A, Incident 14–2.

After being informed by Sharon that they were being suspended, the secretaries were agitated. Nancy Wagner, one of the older and more vocal secretaries, suggested that they all return to Nickey's Lounge (the scene of the original lunch) and "talk about it." After a lot of heated discussion at Nickey's, Nancy suggested that "If we don't look out for ourselves, no one else will. We're all pretty fed up with the way Mrs. O'Malley has been treating us. I wouldn't put it past top management to have told Mrs. O'Malley to crack down on our department. I just don't trust them any more." Mary Willard agreed, and stated that she felt they should all stick together until "we can go back to the way things used to be." The rest of the women agreed with Mary and suggested that they purposely slow down on their typing and increase the number of errors until they got their way. Nancy also felt that every Friday after work they should meet at Nickey's and figure out what they should do next week to "get our way." With that, the meeting adjourned.

Rod Jerstad, a middle-aged manager, was assigned to be the new manager of the secretarial pool. He had heard rumors of the trouble and was a little nervous about stepping into that hornet's nest. Before doing so he felt, that he'd better hear Sharon's side of the story. Sharon told Rod that she felt that she and the women never really hit it off, and that most of the secretaries had been conscientious about their jobs at the start. If they would have just abided by the rules, everything would have been fine. The only warning that she could give Rod was to be very careful with Nancy Wagner and Mary Willard because the other women respected them.

Rod knew that on Monday he would have to walk into the secretarial pool office and do something, and that if he did the wrong thing top management would view it as a failure, which would probably spell the end of any future promotions for him with this company.

(1) How would you describe the informal groups before and after the suspension occurred?

(2) What does the informal group offer each secretary that is missing in her job?

(3) Is the informal group as it exists now detrimental to the business? If so, how?

(4) How could this situation have been avoided? Is allowing the women to continue breaking the rules on extended lunch hours the only alternative?

(5) What are Rod Jerstad's alternatives? What consequences would you predict for each alternative, and which alternative would you advise him to take?

## Incident 15–2

West Bend Toy employs 400 people, 300 of whom work in the factory at jobs requiring very little skill. The company has grown from a handful of employees to its present size. The founder of the company, Thomas Murphy Sr., always believed in "taking care of his employees." Wages, hours, and working conditions have always been better than other local manufacturing operations in the area.

Thomas Murphy Jr. has followed in his father's footsteps. Even though inflation and competition have caused some efficiency moves, the employees are still treated fairly. Of course, the relationships between Tom and the employees are more formal than they were in Tom Sr.'s days, because of the increased number of employees.

The present labor force is about evenly divided in age. Half are older and have been with the company for a long time. The other half of the employees are under twenty-five years of age. Although the younger employees "complain" more than the older employees, Tom Jr. generally feels the employees like the way things are run around West Bend Toy.

The other day Tom was walking through the plant when one of the older workers asked if he could talk to him privately. During the conversation, Tom learned that some of the younger employees were discussing the possibility of a union. Much to Tom's surprise, this employee felt the idea was being received favorably by both the younger and older workers.

Tom had seen a competitor close its doors after it became unionized. He was very upset and decided to contact his father for his advice. Tom Sr.'s advice was pure and simple—find out who the trouble-makers are and fire them. For the rest of the employees, declare a 5 percent wage increase and pass the word informally that management would look unfavorably on any employee who in the future started "this union business" again. West Bend is a fair employer but will not tolerate a union or employees who want a union.

(1) Why might these employees want a union? Do you think the 5 percent increase in wages will keep the union out?

(2) What are the legal rights of the employees on this matter? What are the legal rights of the management of West Bend?

(3) What alternative actions might you suggest to Tom Jr., other than to follow the advice of Tom Sr.?

(4) What is the procedure Tom should follow if, in fact, other employees want to unionize?

(5) If a union should come into West Bend Toy, what advice would you give Tom on the content of the contract and procedures he should follow during the first collective bargaining session?

## Incident 15–3

### DISOBEYING THE SUPERVISOR

Mark Fry worked in the machine shop for Flexo-Matic manufacturers. As a machinist he could do and often did a variety of jobs. At 10:00 on a Monday, Mark's foreman told him to stop what he was doing and handle an "emergency job." Mark told his foreman that he would handle the "emergency job" after he finished what he was working on. The foreman returned about an hour later and saw Mark still working on the same job. The foreman dismissed Mark for the rest of the day. The union contract prohibited "any employee from refusing to perform assigned work and from refusing to obey a reasonable order." Violation carried with it the penalty of lay-off.

Mark felt that his punishment was unjust and filed a grievance. The union argued that the contract stated "any lay-off required twenty-four hours advance notice." Since Mark was not given this notice, he should be reinstated with pay.

(1) Who is right?

(2) What additional facts would you like to have before making a decision?

(3) Is a disciplinary lay-off different from a regular lay-off?

# VI

# THE MANAGEMENT PROCESS

In the introductory section the point was made that the ultimate success of a business is based upon decisions made within certain environmental limits or constraints: legislation, consumer attitudes, competition, and so on. Four broad areas where such decisions are made—the financial, production, distribution, and manpower processes—have been discussed. With each of these areas covered separately we now can turn to the area of managing the total business system.

The terms *businessman* and *manager* are synonomous. The word *businessman* has been used in describing those areas of concern within the four processes of the business system. Now it is necessary to look at how the businessman, either by himself or with the help of other managers, manages the business system.

Every business has at least one manager and probably more. As the name implies, these people manage the business. The **management process,** or what these managers do, will be discussed in this section. This process involves a very complex flow of events. In general, the management process consists of the following sequence of events or activities: (1) planning the direction the business will take in the future, (2) organizing the resources of the business,

(3) directing the efforts of the business, and (4) setting in motion a system to control the business. The management process can be shown as in the diagram:

The Management Process

Planning ⟶ Organizing ⟶ Directing ⟶ Controlling

These activities are discussed in three chapters: Chapter 16, The Manager's Job and Planning; Chapter 17, Organizing the Resources; and Chapter 18, Directing and Controlling.

# 16

# The Manager's Job and Planning

On a very basic level every individual must manage himself. That is, he must determine where he wants to go or what he wants to do, organize his time and energy to get there, and periodically check to see if he is progressing at a satisfactory rate. Everybody is a manager of at least himself or herself.

On a broader level, whenever people join together to accomplish something, someone must manage their efforts. *Someone* must make decisions that affect the whole group. Hopefully, because of these decisions, organized effort results. This someone, the manager, makes the group effort effective. The need for managers exists wherever people are working together to accomplish something. Managers are needed in colleges, hospitals, football teams, business firms. Such terms as *teacher, coach,* and *captain* could be used interchangeably with the term *manager*. But this book is concerned only with groups of people engaged in business activities and therefore concentrates only on the business-manager. The importance of the manager's role can be illustrated by discussing the relationship between the manager and the business system.

## The Manager and the Business System

The business system is man-directed and controlled. Nothing happens until man brings other men together with materials, money, and machinery. The business system is neither self-starting nor self-perpetuating. Someone, or a group of people, must oversee and control its operation. These are the managers. They are the men in charge and responsible for the results attained by the system.

The manager may have any one of many different titles: president, chief executive, vice-president, division manager, foreman, or supervisor. If the business is small, one individual can make all the financial, production, distribution, and manpower decisions. But as a business grows, the work to be done and decisions to be made outrun the ability and time of one manager. Other managers are added and their work and decisions are indicated by such titles as financial manager, production manager, personnel manager, marketing manager, and office manager. Although their positions, titles, and work vary, all of them have in common the responsibility of management, the responsibility for the efficient operation of the total business system and its separate processes.

Managers give life to the business system. They start, construct, promote, and keep it going. Managers decide where the business system will go, what the processes of the system should be, and how the process will be brought together; coordinates the activities within the system; and inspires the people associated with the business system to work together. In short, if there were no managers there would be no business system. The manager is a catalyst whose influence is felt throughout the business system.

There are those who might argue that the management process should have been the first area of discussion. We chose, however, to first discuss the processes the manager must bring together to form the total business system. Now that you have been exposed to the financial, production, distribution, and manpower aspects of every business, we can explore how these merge into a total, ongoing business system. These processes are merged through the management process.

## The Management Process

Management is a complex process. It is a process because it is made up of a series of actions that lead to the accomplishment of a goal. These actions can conveniently be identified as: planning, organizing, directing, and controlling. All four actions are present in the managing of every kind of enterprise—small and large, manufacturing and services, corporations and sole proprietorships, hospitals and governments. Each action is vital to the continued success of the enterprise.

It is equally important to understand that the management process is a continuous one. The business system always needs to be managed. The manager does not just plan, organize, direct, and control once. He replans, reorganizes, redirects, and recontrols as conditions change or new problems present themselves. Thus, continual attention should be given to those actions constituting the management process.

In this chapter the first action of the management process—planning the future direction of the business system—is discussed. Chapters 17 and 18 in this section discuss the other three activities of the management process—organizing, directing and controlling.

## Planning

A *plan* can be defined as any detailed method formulated beforehand, for doing or making something. Implicit in this definition are the following points:
(1) Planning involves thought and decision making: *thought* on what as a business, department, or person, one wants to do; *decision making,* in that a course of action must be chosen among alternative courses of action.
(2) Planning is concerned with the future. Managers must decide in advance what they want to do and how they are going to do it.

For the business system, planning is of the utmost importance. No individual within the business can operate unless he knows where he is going. For a manager, planning is more important than the other activities he performs. In fact, planning sets the tone for the other activities which constitute the management process. A manager organizes, directs, and controls to assure that the plan will be accomplished.

Planning involves selecting business objectives, translating business objectives into operating objectives, and developing programs, policies, procedures, and rules for achieving these objectives.

### SELECTING BUSINESS OBJECTIVES

Objectives are expected results or goals. Business objectives are the results the manager expects the business system to achieve. In the second chapter the following goals or objectives of a business system were identified:
(1) To produce a competitive service or good,
(2) To make a profit,
(3) To gain society's acceptance,
(4) To live up to the responsibilities of the various "publics" business deals with.

The business system can be visualized as moving through time (days, months, years). Managers usually plan for time periods of five years in length. At the end of each time period the manager can review the progress to determine if his original objectives were achieved and then state what objectives he will plan for in the future. The objectives he will strive for are the four objectives as listed above. However, the nature of each objective will be different because the conditions facing the business will differ from time period to time period. Consumers' wants, competition, government regulations, investors expectations, may all change. Thus for each planning time period the manager will go through a thought process, as outlined in Exhibit 16–1.

EXHIBIT 16–1

*Planning Thought Process*

| *Today* | | *In the future* |
|---|---|---|
| The business system is: → | | → The business system should be: |
| 1. Producing a competitive good or service | | 1. Producing the same or a different good or service |
| 2. Making a level of profits | Changing Environment | 2. Making the same or a different level of profits |
| 3. Maintaining a certain public image | | 3. Maintaining a certain public image |
| 4. Living up to the public's expectations | | 4. Meeting the same or different publics' expectations |

The four general objectives of the business system have not changed. However, what is involved in each is constantly changing, because the environment the business system lives in and competes in is changing. Business objectives should not be based on the conditions of today, but on the conditions the manager thinks will exist in the future. The past and present may serve as a guide for the future, but there is no assurance that conditions will remain the same. In fact, a safer bet would be that conditions will change and be different in the future.

Before the goals or objectives the manager is going to plan for can be stated, he needs to have some estimation of how the environment will change in the future. Businesses and managers are increasingly involving themselves in "futurology," guessing and predicting what the future will be like so that objectives and plans can be made to meet the future demands of consumers, government, and the businesses "publics."

In our rapidly changing world the poorest prediction or guess the managers could make is that at some point in the future things will be the same as they are today. A moment's thought on these questions will indicate why this is a poor prediction: in five years, what will the social and political environment be? What new technical developments, competition, tax rates will emerge? Even the manager of a local business will be affected by changes in these areas. In short, the one thing that is sure is that the future will *not* be the same as today.

Planning helps the businessman go from where he is to the objectives he wants to achieve in the future. Before his planning can be successful, the future objectives need to be clearly stated in the four areas outlined above. This can only happen after the manager predicts how the environment will look in the future.

The end result of the first phase of planning is a set of realistic business objectives in four areas: the good or service to be produced, the level of profits, the business' image, and the business' public responsibility. These objectives represent the business' attempt to adapt to a changing environment. These are targets towards which the whole business system will strive during the coming planning period. Plans can now be made to achieve these four objectives. The next step is to translate these business objectives into specific operating objectives.

## TRANSLATING BUSINESS OBJECTIVES INTO OPERATING OBJECTIVES

The statements that the business objective five years from now is to phase out the production of a toy line in favor of a low-priced wrist watch or to have an increased social conscience, or to dry clean clothing better each provides direction for the business system. Each serves as a target toward which all the resources of the business system are to be directed. The problem with business objectives is that the manager who states them knows exactly what they mean for operations in the years to come, but they are vague and hard for others in the system to identify with, let alone work toward achieving. What do general business objectives mean for the people and departments within the business system? What do managers expect them to do or what part do managers expect them to play in reaching the business objectives? It is certainly implied that they will be involved in some sort of activity. Unfortunately, this activity may only be understood by the top manager, not by the people who must do the work.

What is needed is for the manager to define and redefine what results (or objectives) are going to be expected from each of the departments and individual employees during the planning period. For example, a restaurant manager might want her business objectives to be to increase the level of customer satisfaction during the coming year. What she needs to do is translate this into operating objectives for the employees. She might tell the waitresses that their objectives are to be pleasant to customers and have them seated and waited on within five minutes after they enter the restaurant. She might additionally tell the cook that his objective will be to do the cooking in the order in which the waitresses give him their orders. These are operating objectives. They are objectives on which people can go to work. Note that if the cook and waitresses reach their operating objectives, the manager has reached her business objective of increasing customer service.

By redefining the business objectives into personal operating objectives, the manager gives people something they can work on. People and departments cannot plan around a vague set of general business objectives. The business objectives must be defined for each unit and person in the business system. This point is so important that the following hypothetical situation is presented to illustrate how it might be done for the total business system.

## AN EXAMPLE

Assume that the manager feels the business should change its direction and product line. That is, he feels that by 1977 the business should be producing sewing machines rather than the product they are currently producing, whatever it is. This is a general business objective and states *what* the business system is going to do. This business objective must first be translated into operating objectives for the operating units in the business system. In line with the previous discussion, assume that the following are the four departments within this business system: finance, production, distribution, and manpower. The manager must define the role each of the four departments will play in achieving the general business objective. Each department's role represents the operating objectives for a given time period. Each of these four department's operating objectives might be:

| | |
|---|---|
| Finance department: | To obtain $500,000 for new equipment only from private investors |
| Production department: | To design a production line capable of producing 100 sewing machines a day |
| Distribution Department: | To establish a distribution system which will realize sales of 20,000 sewing machines in the first year. |
| Manpower department: | To have three full crews of men ready to man the production line by August of this year. |

The operating objectives give meaning to the general business objective. If each department were to achieve its objective, the business system would achieve its general business objective. But these operating objectives need to be further defined or broken down until specific individual objectives are established. Each of the four department managers needs to define the part each person in his department will play in reaching the departmental operating objective. To illustrate, concentrate on only one department, the distribution department. The distribution department's operating objective is to establish a distribution system which will produce sales of 20,000 sewing machines in the first year. Toward this end these four objectives might be defined:

(1) Study the sewing machine consumer's buying motives and determine what type of outlet (store, catalogue, door-to-door salesmen, etc.) is the most effective.

(2) Develop an advertising campaign for the new product.

(3) By August have four regional salesmen ready to go.

(4) Establish the necessary warehouse and transportation routes.

These represent specific objectives for employees within the distribution department to work on. These objectives give specific direction to each distribution employee's efforts. They now can plan their time and resources to achieve one specific objective.

Through this process a vague business objective has been translated into specific areas in which people can work. Plans and courses of action can now be developed to accomplish the major business objective. For example, establishing outlets for the sewing machines might require detailed plans to buy or lease land, get contractors to build stores, get employees for the new store, and so on. The important point is that when each of these smaller plans has been completed and the objective gained, the sum of these accomplishments is the department's and thus the business system is achieving the stated general business objective.

## THE VALUE OF OBJECTIVES

The process of defining general business objectives and then translating these into specific operating objectives unifies the planning effort in a business system. This process can be illustrated with an inverted triangle as in Exhibit 16–2.

EXHIBIT 16–2

*The Objective Structure for any Business System*

General business objectives become narrower through a process of redefinition until every person has a job to do or a specific set of objectives to achieve. Thus the effort and plans people make to achieve these objectives are unified. In the final analysis, each employee and department plans lead to the achievement of a common set of general business objectives.

Two points need to be reemphasized. First, as new circumstances arise, general business objectives need to be reevaluated in light of these changing conditions. The business system adapts to changing conditions by reformulating where it wants to go or its general business objectives. Thus the process of determining business objectives, operating objectives, and plans to achieve them is continual. Second, the process of establishing general business objectives, operating objectives, and plans to achieve these objectives is important for all business systems regardless of size or product. The manager of a small service business must direct and guide it. Unless he knows where he is going or what he wants to accomplish (general business objectives), he cannot guide or direct the business system. In short, he is not managing the business system, it is managing him. Without objectives and plans, the manager can only respond haphazardly to things that happen in the life of his business. Passively responding is a far cry from guiding and directing the business system. On the other hand, the manager can take the initiative only when he knows what his objectives and plans are for the future.

In making plans to achieve a general business or operating objective, certain problems will arise which stand in the way of achieving a given objective. Planning must be done to surmount two types of problems the manager of a business system runs into: recurring problems and one-time problems.

## PLANS FOR RECURRING PROBLEMS

Every institution faces certain problems that occur over and over again. In school, for example, such problems include the sequence and course types can a student take, the action taken if a student receives below a *C* average, the effect of attendance on students' grade. A business is no different; it has problems such as the amount of vacation an employee should receive, the way to handle customer complaints, determination of operating hours, and grounds for dismissal.

A manager develops plans which will provide guidelines for solving these recurring problems. Three such types of plans are policies, procedures, and rules. Each of these is formulated only after the recurring situation has been studied and alternative ways of handling the problem evaluated. The manager then states a **policy, procedure,** or **rule,** depending on the situation. Each represents his intent on how the problem should be solved everytime it reoccurs. The three types of plans are suited for different situations.

## POLICIES

A policy is a formal statement of the manager's belief in a given area. It is intended to guide the action and thought of people within the business as they approach a recurring problem. For example, a business's policy might be to "promote from within, whenever qualified employees are available." Thus, when the problem of filling a new or vacated job develops, the policy guides the thinking of the person who faces this problem. If a present employee is qualified to fill the job he should be promoted. If not, a new employee should be brought in from the outside.

The larger the business, the more important policy statements become. In a large business one manager cannot make all the decisions. Lower-level managers must make some of the decisions. However, the top manager would like to make sure that these decisions are consistent with his beliefs. Policy statements help him give direction to those people who must make the decisions: they guarantee him that the final decision will be in line with his philosophy. When a lower-level manager faces a problem where there is a policy, he simply reads the policy statement and handles the problem accordingly. The top manager can be sure that his feelings will be known by all lower managers faced with a problem through a policy statement which guides their thinking.

The typical business system has hundreds of policy statements. What subjects these policies should cover and what they should say about these subjects depends entirely on what will be helpful in solving these recurring problems. The policy on employee vacations would be quite different from the policy on determining if a customer is a good credit risk, for instance.

## PROCEDURES

Unlike a policy, which guides a person's thinking, a procedure details the sequences of steps one or several individuals *must* take to achieve a specific purpose. For example, there are standard procedures for filling out income tax forms, filing complaints, applying for jobs, billing customers, ordering materials, etc.

Procedures are essential for the smooth operation of a business. Reflect on the confusion a lack of procedure for student registration, or for handling a customer's complaints, or for filing invoices, or for employing people, would cause. Most procedures apply to the flow of paper work—bills, orders, reports, requests, applications. Excessive procedures—called "red tape"—receive their fair share of criticism. However, they do bring order to many a potentially confusing and chaotic situation.

## RULES

Rules are statements of required or mandatory behavior. Examples would be: no smoking, all food handlers must wear clean white smocks, no one is admitted to the plant unless they show the guard a proper form of identification, safety glasses must be worn at all times. A rule requires that a specific and definite action be taken or not taken. Thus it is a specific management decision.

Policies, procedures, and rules can be distinguished by the amount of discretion or freedom offered in their application. A policy offers the widest discretion or freedom, and a rule offers no discretion. If conditions warrant, policy and procedures can be modified slightly; but a rule cannot be broken.

## THE VALUE OF PLANNING FOR RECURRING PROBLEMS

Planning for recurring problems by issuing policies, procedures, or rules results in several distinct advantages to the business system.

## SAVE TIME

Problems can often be quickly and easily solved if a policy, procedure, or rule has been established to cover the situation. For example, if an employee is smoking in a no smoking area, the manager does not have to take the time to decide what should be done. The employee has broken a rule which is evidently justified by conditions. Therefore, a warning to the employee that he is breaking a rule or another specified punishment must be carried out.

## SAVE EFFORT

For recurring activities the manager only studies the problem *once*. He then issues a policy statement, determines a procedure or makes a rule to cover the situation. Each time the problem recurs, the manager does not have to restudy the problem but simply must apply the policy, procedure, or rule. For example, if a set procedure exists for handling customer complaints, every time a new customer complaint occurs, the manager simply follows the pre-established procedure.

## PROMOTE EFFICIENCY

Policies, procedures, and rules save time and effort, thus promoting efficiency. Efficiency is promoted because they represent what the manager feels to be the *best* way to handle the problem. Without a set policy, procedure, or rule, every time a problem occurs some inefficient methods for resolving it could result.

## BUILD CONFIDENCE

When a policy, procedure, or rule has been established, the people a business system deals with know that they will be treated consistently. They are confident that no favoritism will be shown. For example, no smoking areas apply to everyone. Or a policy of awarding a contract on the basis of the lowest bid means those competing for the contract will be treated equally every time.

Policies, procedures, and rules help give order to the business system by providing guides for solving recurring problems. However, not all problems a manager deals with are recurring. Some in fact, only occur once.

## PLANNING FOR ONE-TIME PROBLEMS

Problems stand in the way of achieving objectives. Solving these problems requires a well thought-out course of action. When the problems recur, the course of action (policy, procedure, or rules) can be applied over and over again. However, some problems are not routine; they occur only once. For example, the development of an advertising campaign, the financing of a new acquisition, hiring a new president, training plant supervisors, introducing a new product, or increasing the morale of employees are not routine problems. Handling these nonroutine problems takes up a great deal of a manager's time. For these problems, a plan or course of action must be devised. Once the problem has been solved the plan is no longer needed, because the problem is not likely to occur again—it has been solved.

The plan for one-time, nonroutine problems is called a *program*. A program sets forth the specific steps for solving a problem, the personnel who should take these steps, and the approximate time each step should occur. Thus a manager involved in establishing a program must do three things:

1. Divide into steps the activities necessary to solve the problem. If a businessman wants to move his offices to a new location, or train a new employee, what steps are involved? Thinking through these steps helps in planning because each step can be concentrated on by itself.

2. Decide who is to be responsible for doing each step. Having decided what needs to be done, the manager must next assign specific steps to people

in the system. If he alone is to perform all the steps in the program, it is not an important consideration. But if he is going to rely on other people, serious consideration should be given to the ability and capability of others in the business system. Matching the people who can do the various steps is an important determinant of how well the steps get done.

3. Decide on the time for each step. A program designs a course of action from beginning to end. Each step needs to be coordinated in time with the next. Each step then has two time estimates: (1) the date on which those performing the step can begin their work, and (2) the time required to complete a step once work on it has started. The more complex the program, the more important the element of time becomes. Introducing a new product and erecting a new building are complex programs with many steps. Each step must be coordinated with the next, which means that the two time estimates are needed. Coordination is impossible without reliable time estimates.

Programs are not used solely for solving complex problems. For example, the complexity of a program designed to merge two companies would exceed the complexity of a program designed to train a new secretary. Since many nonroutine problems stand in the way of achieving objectives, skill in programming is a major plus for managers.

## Small Business Management

Often business writers fall into the easy trap of referring to only large businesses such as General Motors, Western Electric, or United Airlines. This is particularly true when discussing the management aspect of business. It is easy to illustrate one's point by using only examples of large businesses. Unfortunately most people get the impression that large businesses are the only ones who have or need managers. This impression could be no farther from the truth. In fact, managers of the small business probably play a more important role than managers in a larger business. A wrong decision on their part almost always means business failure, while for a large business it usually means a less profitable year. Managerial expertise and excellence is of utmost importance to the small business.

Most people would agree that the corner drugstore, local garage, and local bank are "small businesses," and that Miles Laboratory, General Motors, and Chase Manhattan Bank of New York are "big business." But, when does the small business become a big business? The answer would depend on your own personal experience and the yardstick you used to measure size: sales, number of people employed, size of the physical plant, geographic dispersion of operations, etc. For some people a business employing 200 people with sales of $2,000,000 per year would be considered big, but another would classify it as small.

The federal government makes certain financial assistance available to small businesses only. To make our discussion more specific, we can use their definition of a small business. According to the Small Business Administration Act of 1953, a small business is "one which is independently owned and operated and not dominant in its field of operations." In addition to this the act states that a manufacturing firm is considered small if it has 250 or fewer employees and large if it has more than 1,000 employees. Thus a manufacturing firm which employs between 250 and 1,000 employees is neither a small nor big business. In wholesaling, a small business is one whose net sales do not exceed $5,000,000 per year. The top net sales figure for most retail and service establishment to be considered small is $1,000,000. However, as far as the government is concerned, small is not absolute, but relative to the industry under consideration.

The Committee for Economic Development provides a more definitive way of defining a small business. This organization would define *any* business displaying at least two of the following characteristics as small:

(1) Management is independent and usually the managers are the owners.
(2) Capital is supplied and ownership is held by an individual or small group.
(3) The area of operation is mainly local. While the product need not be sold only in a local market, workers and owners live in one home community.
(4) Relative size within the industry—the business is small when compared to the biggest units in the field. Because the size of the biggest units vary so greatly, large in one field would be definitely small in another.[1]

By definition, a small business which meets these criteria is limited in its ability to compete in *all* business ventures. For example, producing steel, or operating a transatlantic airline are pretty much precluded by the first three criteria. This does not mean that small businesses are always inferior to large business. In fact, as will be shown, small businesses are superior and better able to compete than large businesses in many situations. The small business manager needs to recognize the realities of his situation, realities which affect the planning efforts of this manager, by placing some limits on feasible small business objectives.

## SMALL BUSINESS OBJECTIVES

The small business, like the large business has survival as its primary objective. The evidence of big business surrounds the American public to such an extent that some people assume the economy is dominated by giant corporations. Some authors have even professed the doom of small businesses in the U.S. Statistical projections fail to draw the same conclusion. In Exhibit 16–3, projections indicate that in 1976 in excess of five million small business firms will be in operation in the U.S.

---

1. Committee for Economic Development, *Meeting the Special Problems of Small Business.* New York: 1947, p. 14.

## EXHIBIT 16–3

### *The Outlook for Small Business*

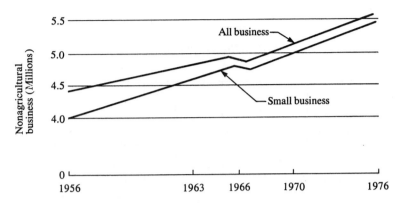

Source: *Business Week*, July 31, 1965, p. 35.

This is hardly a bleak picture, but indicates that as long as the economy grows, the number of both small and large businesses will continue to increase. But the opportunities for small businesses are not the same in every industry. As Exhibit 16–4 indicates, in the manufacturing industries the big companies are getting bigger. Indications are that there will continue to be less and less

## EXHIBIT 16–4

### *Manufacturing Opportunities for the Small Company*

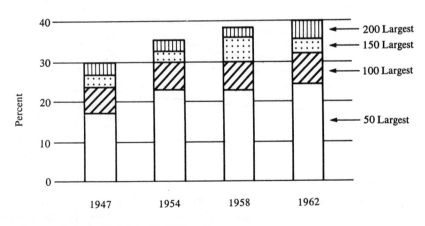

Source: *Business Week*, July 31, 1965, p. 35.

room for small businesses within the manufacturing world. Information in Exhibit 16–5 indicates that in the retailing industry, chain stores are continuing to grow. An analysis of the stores in any shopping center should tell you that this trend is sure to continue. Chain store retailers are apparently making it difficult for the small businessman to compete in certain types of retail operations.

EXHIBIT 16–5

*Retailing and Small Stores*

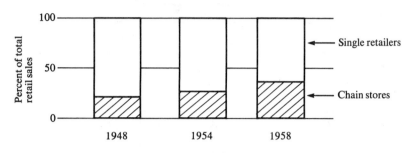

Source: *Business Week,* July 31, 1965, p. 35.

Where can the small business compete? What is a realistic central purpose (good or service) for the small business? Exhibit 16–6 indicates that small businesses are best suited for the fastest growing sectors of our economy: spe-

EXHIBIT 16–6

*Services and Other Sectors of the Economy*

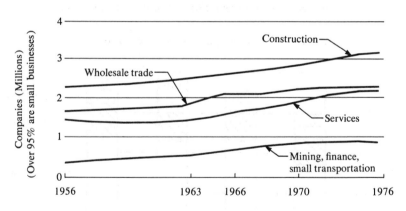

Source: *Business Week,* July 31, 1965, p. 35.

cialty retailing (jewelry, auto supplies, clothing, etc.), services (dry cleaning, repairs, etc.), finance, transportation, and construction. Why are these areas more attractive for small business than others? In Chapter 2 the following illustration of how any business system defines which goods and services will be competitive and thus which it should produce was offered:

Unfilled Consumer Needs + Business Strengths = Competitive Good or Service

The reason certain areas are more attractive for small businesses is that their specific strengths are capitalized on in these situations. Or, to put it another way, the reason that manufacturing and retailing are being dominated by big businesses is because their strengths are capitalized in these areas. In planning for a small business' survival, the manager should understand what these strengths are, thus giving him some assurance that the direction he is leading the small business system towards is the right one.

## SMALL BUSINESS STRENGTHS

Specialty retailing, services, finance, transportation, and construction have been singled out as areas where small businesses are likely to be competitive. The following are strengths of being small and thus why these areas are favorable for small businesses:

### ECONOMICAL DISTRIBUTION POINTS

Small businesses provide big businesses an excellent source of help in distributing their products. It might be too costly for a producer of one product such as auto supplies, aspirin, shoes, cameras, or clothing to operate stores that sell only his product. Small businessmen, however, can establish speciality retail stores to sell many different brands of auto supplies, aspirin and other pharmaceuticals, shoes for all ages and both sexes, cameras and other photographic supplies, and various forms of clothing. Even though the producers of these items are big businesses, they need small businesses to serve as distribution points between them and the consumer. The more big businesses specialize their products, the more important small businessmen will become in distribution.

### PRODUCING CUSTOM-MADE PRODUCTS

Small businesses flourish where the product is custom-made or the production facilities are not suited to mass production. The technology required to produce the goods or service can be a determining factor in the size of the business. For example, painting, plumbing, repair work, upholstering, and carpentry are not conducive to large-scale operations, nor are they conducive for mass production.

### WHEN THE MARKET IS SMALL

The size of business that can be supported is directly related to the size of the market. A business operating locally in a town of 50,000 is limited in its growth potential. Or a firm producing "exact replicas of Indian water pipes" is not going to become a large operation. Markets where there is limited demand and local markets are best served by small businesses.

### SEASONAL PRODUCTS

The sales volume of seasonal products fluctuates throughout the year. Good examples of seasonal products are swimming pools, christmas trees, income tax services, ice cream, and root beer. Most large businesses require a regular level of sales for growth. Erratic and seasonal sales prohibit the chance for business growth. Businessmen which want their companies to remain small find seasonal products well-suited.

## THE SERVICE INDUSTRY AND SMALL BUSINESS

As a mark of the United States' rising affluence, the economy in the early 1970s moved beyond its industrial base and become the world's first full service economy, to the extent that in excess of 60 percent of the private work force was engaged in supplying services.[2]

The service industry offers "products" which are intangible, which cannot be counted or inventoried. This results in production and consumption occurring simultaneously. Hair cuts, auto repairs, lawn mowing, are produced and in a sense consumed at the same time. When compared to a business which produces a tangible product, the service industry's biggest cost is not machinery, equipment, or raw materials, but labor. The owner of a service establishment spends his time providing a highly specialized service to the consuming public. For example, there are now companies which specialize in the following services: balance your budget; baby sit for your child or pet; wake you up in the morning; drive you to work, find you a new home, job, car, wife, clairvoyant, cat feeder, gypsy, or hippies to decorate your next cocktail party. The service industry indeed encompasses a bewildering jumble of businesses. But the intangible nature of the product coupled with the high labor costs makes the service industry particularly attractive to the small businessman.

The broad diversity of services offered the consumer makes classification difficult, However, most service concerns can be fitted into the following categories:

## BUSINESS SERVICES

Business concerns of this type render service to other business organizations. These firms include accounting firms, advertising agencies, public relations counselors, collection services, private employment agencies, blueprint services, tax consultants, management consultants, and addressing services.

## PERSONAL SERVICES

In the personal service group are found such concerns as barber and beauty shops, shoeshine stands, cleaning-pressing shops, laundries, funeral homes, photographic studios, travel agencies, and business colleges. Other examples include baby-sitting services, piano teachers and tuners, and public stenographers.

---

2. "Services Grow While the Quality Shrinks," *Business Week,* Oct. 30, 1971, pp. 50–57.

## AUTOMOBILE AND REPAIR SERVICES

The repair services include automobile repair, shoe repair, jewelry repair, upholstery and furniture repair, electrical repair, and blacksmith shops. In addition, automobile parking garages, parking lots, automobile and truck rental services, and car-wash establishments may be classified in this group.

## ENTERTAINMENT AND RECREATION SERVICES

These include not only sports promoters and owners of professional athletic organizations, but also bowling alleys, swimming pools, racetracks, motion picture theaters, theatrical presentations, amusement parks, dance bands, orchestras, and the like.

## HOTELS AND MOTELS

The operation of hotels, motels, tourist courts, automobile trailer camps, and mobile home parks is still another type of service provided by many small business establishments.

Perhaps the outstanding characteristic of the service trade industries is their small size. It is the one point at which small entrepreneurs can often get the better of larger competitors. In a business that is exclusively service, an impressive advantage rests with the small operators.

It is probably safe to say that as the American consumer becomes more affluent, more people will be willing to part with some of their incomes for services which in the past were considered luxuries. Thus, the future for the service industry and small service business appears bright. However, operating a small business operation is not without its limitations. These limitations need to be realized and planned for by the manager.

## SMALL BUSINESS LIMITATIONS

The small business faces two severe limitations which prohibit it from competing in all areas of our economy. The first is the inability to raise huge sums of money. It is a vicious circle—lenders will not lend large sums to small businesses; thus small businesses stay small. In those areas and markets requiring huge capital investments, the small businessman in general is out of luck.

The second limitation centers around the concept of specialization. The small business-manager-owner must often be a "jack of all trades and master of none." The large organization can afford to hire specialists in production, finance, distribution, and manpower, but the small businessman must be the true "general manager," making the decisions in all of these areas without, in many instances, the expert knowledge required to make these decisions. No one person can be expected to be an expert in all of these areas. Thus, the small businessmen are at a distinct disadvantage—they lack *managerial depth*. How can the husband who is manager and worker with occasional aid from his wife and children or a few hired employees compete with a large organization which has specialists thinking and planning eight hours a day on topics the small businessman *might* be able to devote five minutes to.

Two different approaches have been developed to overcome these two major limitations: franchising and using the Small Business Administration.

FRANCHISING

In 1954, a manufacturer's representative in California named Ray Kroc sold milkshake machines to a chain of seven drive-in restaurants operated by two brothers named McDonald. Gradually as time passed, and he sold more milkshake machines, he realized that the McDonald's venture offered a gold mine of opportunity: why shouldn't its 15-cent hamburgers, french fries, and milkshakes be sold across the country? The vision was dazzling. After all, hamburgers and milkshakes were the common diet of nearly all Americans, regardless of their class, color, and creed.

Accordingly, he and two associates, June Martino and Harry J. Sonneborn, bought the **franchise** rights to the McDonald's name and operation and rapidly started selling franchises.

The rest is history. Of all the fast food drive-in chains that grew up during this era (and there were literally thousands), McDonald's is still the biggest and most successful. Right now McDonald's ranks as the largest of all food service operations in the country. Its franchises number 2,500 (145 of which are outside the U.S.). In 1965 it really hit the big time by going public. The 1973 sales were $1.03 billion, passing the U.S. Army as the nation's biggest dispenser of meals. If you've never stopped at a McDonald's, its quite probable you just don't get around.[3]

Such going concerns as Kentucky Fried Chicken, Midas Mufflers, the various automobile dealers, Walgreen Drugstores, Hertz Rentals, Dairy Queens, Schwinn bicycles, Dunkin' Donuts, Howard Johnsons, Coca-Cola bottlers, and Western Auto Supply companies are all franchise operations. A comprehensive and accurate definition of modern day franchising is as follows:

> Franchising is a system for the selective distribution of goods and/or services under a brand name through outlets *owned* by independent businessmen, called "franchisees." Although the "franchisor" supplies the franchisee with know-how and brand identification on a continual basis, the franchisees enjoy the right to profit and runs the risk of loss. The franchisor controls the distribution of his goods and/or service through a contract which regulates the activities of the franchise, in order to achieve standardization.[4]

There has been a rapid growth in the franchise system because franchising is a means of combining the advantages of both big and small business, or of keeping the limitation faced by small businesses to a minimum. Franchising has had such a phenomenal growth because it offers advantages to both parties: franchisor and franchisee.

---

3. "The Burger That Conquered the Country," *Time,* Sept. 17, 1973, p. 84.
4. Robert Rosenberg with Madelon Bedel, *Profits from Franchising.* (New York: McGraw-Hill Book Company, 1969), p. 41.

*Advantages for Franchisors*   The big business which has exclusive rights to a product, process, or service finds the franchising arrangement particularly advantageous. It is one of the most effective solutions to two persistent contemporary problems of big business: how to secure top flight management personnel for local distribution outlets and how to achieve rapid growth with a limited amount of capital.

Each party in a franchising agreement takes a financial risk. Each invests a fixed sum of capital, which both lose if the franchise fails. The local franchise is likely to put in a concerted effort in insuring the success of the franchise. The franchisor additionally can open more outlets under this plan than would be possible if attempting to finance each outlet himself. In addition to allowing for rapid growth in outlets on a limited amount of capital, the franchise agreement provides the local distributor a high degree of personal incentive. To the local franchisee this arrangement is similar to private ownership. He alone enjoys the profits and suffers the losses of his efforts. This incentive acts as insurance for the parent company that the local franchisee will put more effort into making the venture a success than he would if it were just a job.

If the parent company is selective in choosing local franchisees, it will reduce the risks inherent in operating a business. It is possible, of course, if the product, process, or service is bad, for the franchise to fail. But the franchise agreement offers the parent company highly motivated local managers running a large number of distribution outlets all on a limited amount of capital investment.

*Advantages for Individual Franchisees*   The desire to be able to make a decent living and at the same time to be your own boss are the chief incentives the franchisee offers the individual. Many people dream of owning their own business, but the fear of failure and economic loss as well as the inability of most people to accumulate the large sums of money needed to finance their own businesses keeps these dreams from ever being realized. The franchising system helps to solve these two problems and more.

A person with limited capital can enter into a franchising arrangement. For this investment, he is given certain concrete things: the right to use the name of the franchising company and to sell or manufacture its goods or services and certain initial equipment fixtures and/or supplies. Note that he is "set up" as a private businessman with a small initial investment. Just as important, he owns a company which has already established itself or been proven as offering a successful good or service. He is the selective distributor in his area for an already proven good or service. This advantage is tremendous when one analyzes the number of *new* products or services that fail.

In addition to the security that goes with a proven good or service, the individual has the flexibility of being his own boss without the disadvantages that go with being a small businessman: lack of management depth. In return for his investment in the franchise, the franchisor is obligated to supply a mix of services and aids such as training, consultation, management know-how, promotional support, and accounting or bookkeeping aids. This is why the franchise offers the advantages of the big and small business without some of its disadvantages. The local franchisee provides the flexibility and adaptability to local conditions; while the parent company provides the local franchise the expert advice, or management depth, so often lacking in the small business.

The incentive is great for the successful local franchisee. For example, the profits of the Coca-Cola Bottling Corporation of Los Angeles are in excess of $2,300,000, and Robert Demery and his brother Gerald are reported to be quite happy with their modest gross of $2,000,000 from ten Dunkin' Donuts shops in Connecticut.[5] These successes were not automatic. A great deal of the success in franchising, as in any business, depends upon the value the consumer places on the good or service being offered him. No matter what the advantages of franchising may be, without a superior good or service, its future is suspect.

*Disadvantages of Franchising.*   A franchise is no guarantee of success. Daily franchises are going out of business. The same pitfalls which can trap any businessman can also affect an individual franchise. The franchisee as a businessman-manger should thus view the problems discussed in this text as also facing him. He needs to develop an effective business system.

Franchising is not the best form of ownership for everyone. While offering a high degree of independence, some restrictions are still placed on franchisees by the parent company. These restrictions and in some cases the high costs of obtaining a franchise are the two disadvantages peculiar to franchising. These restrictions are too varied for inclusion in this discussion. The individual should realize that there will be some restrictions over his freedom as a businessman. The potential franchisee is advised to study the franchise arrangement carefully. If he can live with the restrictions and the costs of obtaining the franchise, they will not represent disadvantages for him. If not, he may be wise to seek another form of business ownership.

## THE SBA

In 1953 the Small Business Administration (SBA) was established. Its purpose is to help small businesses and thus maintain the freedom of competition in the United States. The government's attitude toward small businesses is best expressed in the Small Business Act:

> It is the declared policy of the Congress that the Government should aid, counsel, assist, and protect insofar as is possible the interests of small-business concerns in order to preserve free competition enterprise.[6]

More specifically the SBA has the following three responsibilities:
(1)  To assist small concerns in the procurement of credit. The SBA works

---

5. *Ibid.,* p. 7.
6. Small Business Administration, *Small Business Administration—What It is, What It Does.* Washington, D. C.: 1954, p. 1.

closely with local banks in its business lending program to aid small business in the form of loans to finance construction; purchase equipment, supplies, and inventory; and finance other useful business purposes. This minimizes one limitation small businessmen face, the inability to raise money.

(2) To help small business get a fair share of government contracts. The SBA issues certificates of competency certifying the financial and productive capacity of small firms to fulfill government contracts. In addition the SBA supplies information to small firms on government buying practices and assists small firms in obtaining subcontracts from prime contractors. This helps small business compete with larger businesses for government contracts.

(3) To provide management and technical assistance to managers of small businesses. The SBA publishes information directly related to the management of a small business. Staff personnel both in Washington and in field offices are available to counsel managers of small business on various management problems. Finally, the SBA helps colleges to organize extension courses covering small business management. These aids help overcome the lack of management depth of most small business managers.

## MANAGEMENT AND THE SMALL BUSINESS

In small as well as large businesses, managers make decisions which give the business system direction. The size of a business does not change the demand for good management. The small business must be managed just as well as the large business. Size affects those strengths a particular business system has in producing a competitive good or service. There are areas where the small business has advantages over the large business and vice versa. These are realities that each manager must take into consideration in performing the management process. This means that the manager of a small business must plan, organize, direct, and control his business system in the same fashion as the big business executive. The only thing that differs are the details of the situation each manager faces, the number and type of conditions which affect the plans, organization, directions, and control procedures. This is all that differs. It is important to remember that a businessman manages the business system regardless of its size.

## Summary

All managers plan, organize, direct, and control the business system. This chapter centers on the first of these duties: planning. Planning involves selecting business objectives, translating business objectives into operating objectives, and developing programs, policies, procedures, and rules for achieving these objectives.

Size places some limits over the feasible objectives for the small business. The small business manager must realize this in his planning efforts. He must additionally learn to cope with the two primary limitations of small businesses:

the inability to raise large sums of capital and a general lack of management depth. The Small Business Administration and the franchise form of ownership help minimize these two limitations.

The manager, regardless of the size of the business system, who has set forth a plan of action must now further direct his thinking. His next area of consideration is how the resources available to him can be organized to best achieve his plans. This area is the topic of Chapter 17.

## QUESTIONS

1. What activities are involved in the management process? How does it relate to the successful operation of the:
   (a) Financial process,
   (b) Production process,
   (c) Distribution process,
   (d) Manpower process,
   (e) Total business system?

2. Define the concept of business planning.

3. What is the difference between general business objectives, operation objectives, and personal employee objectives?

4. Define and give an example of each of the different types of plans used for recurring activities. What are the values of plans which deal with recurring activities?

5. What is a small business? What two limitations do all small businesses face?

6. Identify the areas where small businesses can compete effectively and explain why.

7. What are the advantages and disadvantages of the franchise system of ownership?

8. What services does the Small Business Administration provide the small businessman-manager?

## Incident 16–1

For the last fifteen years Roy Kaiser has been a highly successful independent salesman representing a prominent tool manufacturer. He seems to have a knack for talking to people, and many of his clients thought of him as a close personal friend. But all of this has come to an end. The company Roy used to represent has been acquired by a larger firm which manufactures and sells a complete line of tools and tooling products. The new company already has a full salesforce, and there was no room to add Roy to the present sales staff. But the president, having heard of Roy's past success as a tool salesman, has offered him the job of sales manager of the midwestern division. Roy's first reaction, because he had been a salesman all of his life, was to look for another selling job. But the president convinced him that if he could be a successful salesman, he could be a successful manager.

In his new job Roy spent his time in hiring and firing salesmen, in setting up sales programs for his division, in reviewing the daily records of his thirty salesmen, and in supervising the activities of his office staff. After his first year on the new job, sales in the midwestern division had increased by 10 percent, an improvement none of the other divisions of the company could match.

One evening Roy was talking to his friend Bud Warden about his new job. "Bud, two things bother me. First, it seems like I'm putting in longer hours and falling further behind. It always seems like I'm fighting fires or solving other people's problems. Sometimes I wonder if the other salesmen really know what they're supposed to do, or where they're going in the future. If I were sick I think the office would stop running. The second thing that bothers me, Bud, is that I wish I were back selling again where I can do some real work. I feel like all I'm doing in the office is shuffling papers."

(1) Does a good salesman automatically make a good manager? What, if anything, is the difference?

(2) What would lead you to believe that Roy is a good or bad manager?

(3) Where and how might Roy specifically improve as a manager?

(4) If you were to explain to Roy how a manager manages, what would you say?

(5) How would you explain to Roy the functions he should be performing as a manager?

## Incident 16–2

The Open Road Company was one of the oldest and most respected names in the motorcycle industry. During the company's seventy-year history every effort has been made to produce the highest quality road motorcycle. Road motorcycles are built for long distance travel and durability. It is not uncommon to find many ten to fifteen year-old Open Roads on the major crosscountry interstates today.

Two groups of customers buy Open Road motorcycles. The first is the true motorcycle enthusiasts, who are enthusiastic enough to pay between $2,000 and $3,500 for a high quality road motorcycle. This person is usually middle-aged and uses the motorcycle as his primary means of transportation. The second group of consumers are city and state governments. Open Road motorcycles are ridden by 95 percent of the motorcycle police forces in this country.

Recently Mr. Clark, Open Road's president, has become very worried as sales have fallen to only a small fraction of previous levels. Other companies, both foreign and domestic, have diversified into numerous types and sizes of mini-bikes, trail bikes, and motorcycles, as well as associated equipment. Mr. Clark has stood firm in his commitment to produce only the finest quality road motorcycle.

(1) Evaluate the planning Mr. Clark has done for his company.

(2) What type of information does Mr. Clark need to formulate future plans for Open Road Company?

(3) List four specific objectives you feel Open Road should have for the upcoming business year.

(4) Draw up a list of the types of plans Open Road should have, if in fact no formal plans are in existence. Explain and illustrate with an example each of the type of plans on your list.

# 17

# Organizing the Resources

Knowingly or not, everyone determines how much time and effort will be required to accomplish a particular task. For example, most readers will estimate how long it will take then to read this chapter. Then, given all the things they want to accomplish today, this week, or this month, a problem must be solved: when can and should I read this chapter? To solve this problem requires organization of all the things there are to do. In other words, every person organizes his resources of time and effort to achieve the many things he desires. This is true even though some people are better organized and thus do more than others. In this section how the manager organizes the resources of the business system is examined.

## Importance and Nature of Organization

The plans developed by a manager are just ideas on the direction he would like to see the business system take. These ideas only become reality when people do the work necessary to fulfill the plans. Achieving plans requires the manager to organize or bring together the resources of the business system. Good plans are meaningless until an organization is devised to implement them.

If the business system is a one-man operation, the manager faces the same organization problem everyone does: how can I best organize my time and effort to achieve my plans? But, usually, many people are employed by the business system. This addition of other people complicates the organization problems faced by the manager. He does not just organize himself, but must organize others as well. A formal business organization is required as soon as two or more people combine their efforts to achieve a common purpose.

A business organization could be defined as a group of people, each with special jobs, who must work together in order to achieve a goal or plan. This definition applies to small business organizations (of more than one person) as well as to large business organizations. When the manager organizes, he creates such a business organization. The definition states the two basic activities the manager performs in creating a business organization: (1) dividing the work to be done into jobs for people to do, and (2) making sure that the people performing these jobs work together.

### Dividing the Work to be Done Into Jobs

This phase of organization is a logical extension of those planning activities discussed in the previous chapter. The manager who knows what his plans and objectives are must now answer the following questions:

(1) What activities are necessary to accomplish these plans and objectives?
(2) How should these activities be grouped into jobs?
(3) Who will be responsible for performing these jobs?

These questions are not pertinent for the one-man business. They only become pertinent when the work to be done must be divided among other employees. To show why the manager must organize and give an approach he is likely to take, the growth of a ficticious business producing lounging chairs will be discussed. At various stages in the business' growth, the work to be done needs to be divided or organized in different ways.

### STAGE 1—THE OWNER-MANAGER STAGE

This stage starts with the formation of the business. Its name comes from the fact that one man, the owner-manager, totally operates the business. His plans are to sell and produce lounge chairs. To do so he has accumulated a small sum of money and has a production process of sorts set up in his basement. During this stage the owner-manager does everything. He sells his chairs door-to-door on Monday through Wednesday. On Thursday through Saturday he manufactures the chairs in his basement to fill the sales orders received during the first part of the week. The bookkeeping, purchasing of materials, and delivering of the finished product are sandwiched in during the week. There is no need for a formal business organization because there is no division of work. The owner-manager does everything. He must only organize his own time to best accomplish the work to be done.

## STAGE 2—GROWTH AND SPECULATION

Assume that the chairs are extremely popular with the people the owner-manager has sold them to, and that they in turn tell their friends, some of whom contact the owner for an appointment to discuss the purchase of a chair. Further assume that the owner has convinced a local furniture store to carry his chairs. The local furniture store contracts with the owner for 500 chairs the first year.

This increased growth creates an organizational problem for the owner-manager. No matter how well he organizes his own time, there is not enough time to do everything. He must specialize or concentrate on a few activities only and hire one or a group of employees to do the other activities that must be done. Before he hires someone, however, he must answer the three organizational questions mentioned above: What activities are involved in accomplishing his business objectives? How should these activities be grouped into jobs? Who should be responsible for performing these jobs? Answers to these questions help determine what the new employee will do or specialize in.

You should already be able to answer the first question of what activities are involved in accomplishing his business objectives. Three broad groups of activities have been defined as common to all business systems. They must be performed if a business' objectives are to be achieved. Certain financial, production, and distribution activities are essential to all business systems. Specialization usually occurs along these three activity areas. One or all three of these activities are usually the first jobs to be established formally in a business organization.

The activities the owner-manager chooses to keep performing and those he groups together to form jobs in the organization can and do vary. In this case, the owner-manager is willing to let someone else perform the production activities. By specializing in this way, he can concentrate his time on the financial and distribution activities necessary to achieve the business' objectives. This specialization allows each person to perform his job better, because each now has more time to spend on fewer activities. The owner-manager now only has two activities to concentrate on instead of three. The new employee can devote all his time and effort to only one activity area—production. Note this specialization has occurred only because the owner-manager can afford it. The increased growth and sales have made it economically possible to add a new employee.

There are now two people in this organization, each performing specific activities. The organization may look something like this:

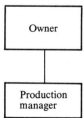

Depending on the situation, the production manager might perform all or only some of the production activities. At first he is likely to be both manager and worker. But if the business continues to grow, a time will come when he is no longer able to both manage and work in this area. A new employee will be hired and specialization in this organization will occur again. The owner and production manager must decide which activities the new employee should perform. Assume that two new employees are hired. One specializes in building the frames for the chairs and the other worker stuffs and upholsters the chairs. The production manager no longer is a worker but now performs such activities as scheduling production, keeping the two employees working, and devising new methods to increase production efficiency.

The work to be done has been divided into four jobs. This new organization, along with a brief statement of each employee's responsibilities, could be diagrammed as in Exhibit 17–1.

### EXHIBIT 17–1

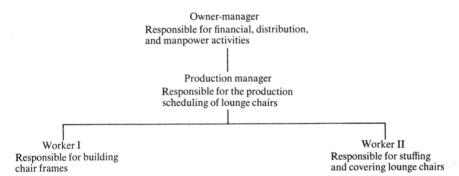

Further growth of this business will not only dictate but make economically possible increased specialization. The owner-manager may feel that there is a potential for increasing sales and that what is keeping his business from growing is not the inability to produce lounge chairs, but rather his own inability to perform the financial and distribution activities adequately. To grow, the owner-manager must specialize further, thus allowing a new manager to concentrate his efforts on these activities. Assume that he hires a distribution manager and a financial manager. The new organization, with a brief description of the new people's responsibilities, would look something like Exhibit 17–2.

### EXHIBIT 17–2

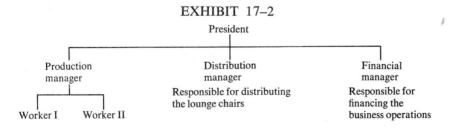

In this case the owner-manager now carries the title of president. He is no longer directly responsible for any of the three activity areas defined as crucial to the business' success. A specialized manager is now responsible for the work in each of these activity areas. The president coordinates the work of these three managers. He is responsible for the direction each manager takes, as well as for the direction of the total business system.

It is important to remember that specialization and growth go hand-in-hand. Growth leads to specialization, not vice versa. Specialization can only facilitate growth. A level of sales must be reached before a business can afford the degree of specialization this particular business has undergone. It is also important to note that the pattern discussed here is the way businesses often initially specialize and organize their resources. The three primary processes of any business—production, finance, and distribution—are the areas where specialization comes first.

The formal business organization depicted above can allow for a great deal of continued growth and specialization. Specialization can continue to occur *within* the three primary processes without any new units or departments added to the business. For example, the distribution manager might add one employee to specialize in sales, another in advertising, another in transportation, and so on. New employees can be hired and additional specialization can occur in the production and financial areas as the growth of this business demands. This type of organization can accommodate continued growth and specialization for quite some time. It is suitable for most small and medium-sized business sytsems. A businessman employing upwards of 200 people would still find this type of organization well suited for his needs.

## STAGE 3—THE ADDITION OF SERVICE UNITS

In the growth of most businesses there comes a time when certain administrative burdens interfere with the attention and time each manager can give to his primary responsibilities. In this example *each* of the three managers—production, distribution, and finance—must perform such administrative tasks as keeping employee records, finding employees to replace those that leave the business, gathering and analyzing data, and compiling various reports. When the business is small these tasks can be performed by each manager in a short period of time. But as the business increases in size, the time to perform these administrative tasks becomes burdensome, to the point where they are commanding a major part of the manager's day. This does not allow each manager to concentrate on his designated area of specialization. When these administrative tasks become burdensome, the owner-manager may want to add a service unit or department. The service unit's sole responsibility would be to take some of these administrative burdens off the managers within the business. The service unit would perform a service for the business by doing some of the administrative tasks for all the managers, thus freeing their time to concentrate only on their area of specialization. The service unit, which is sometimes referred to as a **staff** unit, specializes in a certain type of work: it takes from the other managers those administrative burdens which are outside their area of specialization.

The service unit or department added at this stage in a business' growth is often headed by an individual with the title of office manager. The office manager is responsible for most of the clerical work, record keeping, and report preparation that each individual manager in the past had to worry about. The organization with the addition of this service unit might look like Exhibit 17–3.

EXHIBIT 17–3

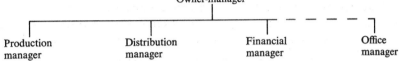

Owner-manager

| Production manager | Distribution manager | Financial manager | Office manager |

The chief advantage of creating a service unit is that it allows each manager to concentrate his time on that specialized area for which he is responsible. In the example, the production, distribution, and financial managers now have more time to spend on their respective areas of responsibility. This has been accomplished by taking some of the clerical duties, which each were responsible for, and making these the responsibility of one manager—the office manager. Regardless of the type of service unit used in a business, the aim of all service units remains the same: to help a manager manage by minimizing the time he spends on administrative work incidental to his specialization.

This example shows in general how a manager can (1) define the activities necessary to accomplish a business' plans or objectives, (2) group these activities into jobs, and (3) decide who will be responsible for performing these jobs. In addition to grouping activities into jobs the manager should be aware of a number of specific factors in setting up each individual job within the business organization.

## Setting up Individual Jobs

When dividing the work of the business into jobs, the manager should make sure that certain conditions are fulfilled.

(1) The duties to be done for each job should be clearly defined and understood by all those concerned. Each employee must be perfectly clear on the *activities* he will be expected to perform. Each job should be described so that it can be distinguished from other jobs within the organization. In this way an employee keeps from performing some activities others in the business should perform or doing less than is expected of him.

(2) The results expected should be clearly stated. This is different from the activities and duties set out in point (1). Every employee must also understand the level of accomplishments expected of him. In the example of the chair

manufacturer, one production employee performs all the activities necessary to make the chair frames. This is his job; these are his duties. But in addition to these duties, a part of his job is to achieve a level of production or to achieve certain accomplishments. For example, he may be held responsible for producing five chair frames a day. This represents the results which are expected from him. Every job must be thought of both in terms of activities to be performed and results that should be achieved. Activities only indicate what is to be done, while stated results tell the employee the minimum acceptable level of output on a specific job.

(3) The overlap in duties must be kept to a minimum. To increase efficiency, work should not be duplicated. The manager therefore must not only set up each job but see to it that no two jobs are involved in performing some of the same duties. This does not mean that if three secretaries are needed each must perform different activities. What it does mean is that no other employee's job should include activities that the three secretaries are performing.

(4) Accompanying every job should be a corresponding amount of authority. If an individual is assigned duties to perform and a stated level of results is expected, he should have the authority to carry out these duties and achieve these results. The production worker who makes chair frames must have the authority to order or obtain from inventory the material necessary to perform his job. Without this authority he cannot efficiently perform his job.

(5) Individual jobs should be so ordered that the individual performing the job knows who his supervisor is. Each individual in the business should know who his boss is. This boss or supervisor is the person to whom the employee must turn for help, advice, orders, or directions. The supervisor is the person who will evaluate how well the employee has performed his job. No individual job holder should be placed in the confusing state of having to report to two or more supervisors. It should be made clear to the employee which one individual will be his supervisor.

(6) Adaptability should be built into the job. The duties, results, authority, and reporting relationships of all jobs should be flexible enough to adapt to changing conditions. Changes in the business' plans, the people doing a job, and types of technology used to produce a good or service will all affect specific jobs within a business. Jobs are not just set up once and then forgotten. They need to be reevaluated to determine if they are still necessary to achieve the plans of a business system.

Once the content of each job has been determined, the jobs and activities must be grouped into an overall organization structure which will increase the likelihood that employees will work cooperatively together.

## Organization Structure and Cooperative Endeavor

The first area of organizational concern, dividing up the work to be done into jobs, utilizes the concept of specialization. The concept of specialization includes the belief that efficiency is increased when employees concentrate their thinking and efforts on only a few activities at a time. Thus the total work to be done is divided into specific jobs.

Every business, except the one-man operation, employs the concept of specialization. Therefore, in the vast majority of cases it is not a question of whether to specialize or not, but to what degree. The best illustration of extreme specialization is the modern mass production line. Some jobs are so speciailzed and repetitive that they can be and are done by machines.

Regardless of the degree of specialization, it presents the manager with a second organizational problem: coordinating the work of many specialists. The efforts of employees who are doing only a specialized part of the total work to be done need to be synchronized. The higher the degree of specialization, the greater is the need for coordination. The need for coordination when two craftsmen built one car is vastly different from that of today's mass automobile production plants. The organization structure is one method of coordinating the work of the many specialists within the business system. In fact, one of the reasons for organizing is to guard against uncoordinated effort.

The formal organization structure represents the grouping of certain jobs and activities into departments. Departments are distinct areas of the business over which a manager has authority for the performance of specific activities. Examples of departments within a business might include the production department the personnel department, and the sales department. Each department is made up of at least one manager and a number of employees performing different aspects of the same departmental activity. In a small business there may be no departments if all activities fall under the direction of one manager, the owner. However, as a business grows beyond what this one manager can manage, departmentalization occurs. That is, a specialized group of activities are defined and a manager made responsible for the performance of these activities. There are certain guidelines the manager can use in developing the departments within his business organization.

## GUIDELINES TO DEPARTMENTALIZATION

Each department is set up to increase the likelihood of cooperation among people in the business system. The manager has a number of departmentalization patterns or designs to choose from. Among these patterns the three most widely used, functional, product, and geographic, will be discussed. Each of these is a logical and appropriate pattern for particular situations.

### FUNCTIONAL

The functional pattern of departmentalization has been used in the examples in this chapter. All the activities related to a single function, or technical area of knowledge, are placed under one manager. If this pattern is chosen, such departments or functions as manufacturing, sales, finance, legal, public relations, accounting, and marketing would be found within the organization structure. A functional pattern of departmentalization is illustrated in Exhibit 17–4. One

EXHIBIT 17–4

*Functional Organization Pattern*

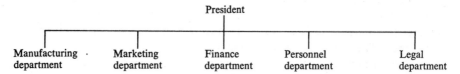

manager is responsible for all the activities of a function or department. Of course, the number of employees and the jobs under each function depend on the type and size of business in question. This pattern is found in small to medium-sized businesses which produce a single or few products. The chief advantage of the functional organization is that it increases specialization and thus the effectiveness with which a function is performed. As the size of the business or number of products increase, other patterns of organization are better suited to coordinate the efforts of people in the business.

## PRODUCT

The product pattern groups all the functions necessary to produce and distribute one product in the same department. Product patterns are used by businesses which produce multiple products. An illustration of this pattern is presented in Exhibit 17–5. Each product group in the exhibit represents a

EXHIBIT 17–5

*Product Organization Pattern*

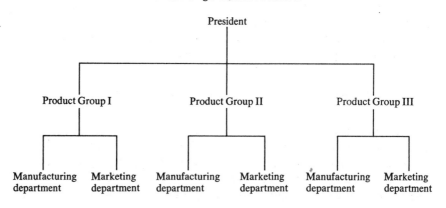

department. The functions necessary to produce and distribute each product group are grouped under that department. In Exhibit 17–5 each product group has its own respective manufacturing and marketing departments. The classical example of this form of organization is General Motors Corporation. In Exhibit 17–5, Chevrolet, Buick, and Cadillac could be substituted for the titles Product Group I, II, and III. Smaller companies may find this form of organization useful when different products are manufactured. The chief advantage of this form of organization is that one manager can coordinate the production and distribution efforts for his product. He is assured that his product will receive the special attention that is needed. He can also use production and distribution techniques different from those used by other product group managers. Thus a second advantage for this type of organization structure is the flexibility it provides each product group manager. He has the flexibility to adapt to the special demands of the consumers of his product group.

## GEOGRAPHIC

With a geographic pattern of departmentalization each department is responsible for the business in the designated geographic location. This pattern is beneficial for businesses operating in many locations, especially when each geographic market has differing demands. An illustration of this geographic pattern is presented in Exhibit 17–6. This illustration could be representative

### EXHIBIT 17–6
*Geographic Organization Pattern*

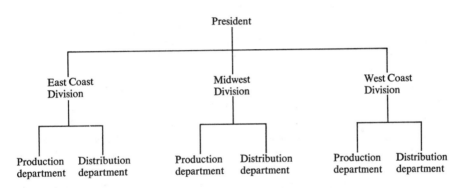

of a national food store operation where local food stores are stocked with items out of a regional department.

Different patterns of departmentalization aid in coordinating the activities of a business. The most desirable pattern depends upon the relationships among people and functions necessary to accomplish the business' objective. Those activities which need close coordination should be grouped together in one department, thus allowing one manager to coordinate them. For example, sales and advertising activities need close coordination, whereas production scheduling and bookkeeping activities are fairly distinct. In one case sales and advertising might logically be grouped under one manager in the same department, whereas production scheduling and bookkeeping need not be grouped together. As a business grows, when new products are added or new markets are explored, functional organization becomes increasingly difficult to coordinate. The product and geographic patterns in effect establish small organizations within a larger one. Both of these patterns allow a manager to coordinate all those activities necessary.

No one single pattern is best; it depends on the size of the business and the nature of products and market served. Each manager must analyze his specific situation to determine which pattern will allow for the greatest coordination of effort.

## THE ORGANIZATIONAL PYRAMID

The organizational structure indicates the formal relationships that should exist between the jobs in an organization. Just as important in gaining cooperation are the relationships between the people who perform these jobs. Departmentalization creates an organizational pyramid or series of superior–subordinate relationships. These personal relationships can be used as an additional way of gaining cooperation.

The organizational pyramid and resulting superior–subordinate relationships hold the organization together. Every business has a top manager, or president, responsible for running the entire business. As mentioned, except in the very small business, this individual does not have the time to do all the work himself. He defines activity areas over which other people manage. These activity areas have been defined as departments.

The top manager sets up a series of departments, and department managers coordinate the work of employees within their respective departments. These departmental employees no longer report to the president but to their department manager. The president has added a layer of management between himself and the employees. In turn, these department managers frequently find they do not have enough time to perform all the managerial duties of their departments. Some of the work must be done by subordinate managers within the departments. Thus a second layer of management between the president and employees can be added. In this situation every clerk, secretary, salesman, or employee in general has his boss, who in turn has his boss, and so on up to the president. Every member of the organization has a connection to the president. The employee's position determines the number of managerial layers between him and the president.

The definition of departments and redefinition of the administrative work within each department until each specific manager has the time and ability to perform it well can be illustrated with the familiar pyramid structure, as in Exhibit 17–7.

In most business organizations of any size three layers of **management** can be conveniently defined: **top** management, **middle** management, and **first-level** management.

Top management as a group includes the president and department heads, or vice presidents. This group is very small in number, even in large organizations. Together they plan the direction the business will take and make decisions which affect large parts of the organization. For example, this group might consider which products to produce, the amount of money to spend on capital equipment, how to distribute the products, or what profits should be.

The small number of managers at this level helps in coordinating the efforts of all people in the organization. The president does not have to work with 100

EXHIBIT 17–7

*The Organizational Pyramid*

production workers or thirty salesmen. He only coordinates and works with two people: the production department manager and the sales department manager. At this level the efforts of hundreds of people are tied together. As top management formulates total organization plans, each department manager realizes his role in achieving these plans. In addition to this, the between-department cooperation necessary to achieve the plans is clearly established. For example, top management might want to increase sales by 10 percent during the next year. To do this requires at least three things: (1) the available quantity of products for sale is increased by 10 percent, (2) distribution efforts are increased to sell an additional 10 percent volume, and (3) production and distribution efforts are coordinated. Points (1) and (2) are clearly the separate responsibility of the production and distribution department managers. However, point (3) requires the cooperation of both the production and the distribution departments. Salesmen cannot promise goods that do not exist to consumers, nor can goods be produced and placed in inventory for long periods of time. Each department manager has to coordinate his plans with the next. Without this coordination and cooperation, departmentalization would work to the disadvantage of the business system. Each department would function as a totally independent unit, when in fact it is only a part of the total business system. In general, coordinated effort occurs through the members of top management working as a team where each member (department manager) can be counted on to fulfill his responsibility and work with the other members for the best results of the total business system, not just his department.

Middle managers are subordinate managers within a department. They report to the head of their particular department. Within each department, a number of middle managers develop operational plans to implement the plans and ideas of top management. They are involved solely in helping the department manager live up to his responsibilities. In the previous example, for the production department to increase output by 10 percent certain middle managers, such as the purchasing manager, production planning manager, and plant manager, must alter their plans. Middle managers' jobs and responsibilities result from plans made by top management. Each middle manager is responsible for a piece of the total department's responsibility. The department manager coordinates the various middle managers to insure that the department's plans are achieved efficiently.

First-level managers supervise the work of operating employees. As a group they are the lowest level of management, only one step above operating employees. In some situations first-level managers are called *foreman* or *supervisors*. They are the only group whose subordinates are not managers. Top managers supervise a group of middle managers, while one middle manager supervises a group of first-level managers. One first-level manager in turn supervises a group of operating employees. The first-level manager's main responsibility is to get employees to efficiently perform that part of the department's job the middle manager has given him to do.

At each level in the organizational pyramid, managers are concerned with coordinating the work of those under them. If top management as a team has spent the time to coordinate the plans across the department, middle and first-level managers' coordination job is easier. The middle manager works within the boundaries set by top management. These boundaries help assure interdepartmental coordination. In turn the first-level manager lives with the boundaries set by middle management. This pyramid helps to maintain coordinated effort as the work of a business is continually divided up. The relationship between the managers of a business and between a manager and his subordinates is the mechanism for achieving cooperative action. A manager, regardless of his level, whose job is not related to other administrative and operative jobs is not a member of the total management team. The organization pyramid as a series of manager-employee relationships helps to keep the manager and employees working in a coordinated effort.

## Summary

Creating a sound organization is an essential part of effective management. The manager achieves the plans he has for the business by organizing the efforts of people within that business. Two organizational decisions must be made by the manager.

First, he must decide how the work to be done shall be divided into jobs. This problem involves the question of how much specialization is needed to accomplish the objectives of the particular business. This problem, once solved, results in specific jobs within the business. Every employee performing one of these jobs must be clear as to exactly what duties, results, and authority are involved in that job.

Once the content of each job has been determined, it is necessary to group jobs and activities together to increase cooperation between the people performing these activities. This second organizational problem is one of departmentalization. Activities can be grouped into one of the following patterns of departments: functional, product, or geographic. Each is a logical and appropriate pattern for particular situations. Whichever pattern is chosen, an organizational pyramid with at least three levels of management results. The relationships between these managers play an important role in coordinating the various activities performed within any business system.

## QUESTIONS

1. What does the manager do when he establishes a formal organization structure?
2. How would the organization structure of a small business differ from the organization structure of a large business?
3. What function does a service or staff unit within an organization perform?
4. In establishing an individual's job, what factors must the manager be sure are clearly defined?
5. When should the manager use a functional, product, or geographic pattern in establishing organizational departments? What disadvantages do you see for each of these patterns?
6. In general define the duties of top managers, middle managers, and first-level managers.
7. How does the organization structure aid the manager in coordinating the efforts of departments and employees?
8. Study the organization chart of your university. What pattern of departmentalization is employed? What functions do the various service units perform? Indicate who you would classify as top, middle, and first-level managers within this structure.

## Incident 17–1

A. M. Jackson & Sons manufactures and distributes men's and women's industrial shoes. The home office and manufacturing operations are in Cicero, Illinois. The plant operates on two shifts, with the total number of employees fluctuating between 200 and 225. Exhibit 17–8 illustrates the present organization chart.

T. J. Jackson is responsible for purchasing the equipment and raw materials needed for production, planning the production schedules for the two shift foremen who report to him, and determining the wages for the factory employees.

R. Ross handles the sales and financial end of the business. From her projections of sales she evaluates the need for new and additional financing. The sales force is broken down into two groups of five salesmen each. Each group is managed by a sales manager. One group concentrates on men's industrial safety shoes, and the other group on women's industrial–professional shoes such as those for nurses, waitresses, and female janitors. Each salesman sells directly from a completely equipped van which he drives from site to site. For example, a salesman would park his van on the hospital or industrial plant premises and take orders for shoes as the

EXHIBIT 17–8

*A. M. Jackson & Sons—Organization Chart*

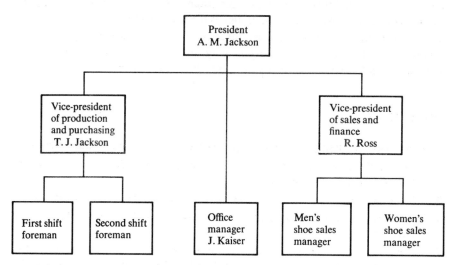

workers passed by. Sales were limited to the states of Illinois, Indiana, and Ohio due to the high concentration of industry in these states.

The office manager, J. Kaiser, and his staff were responsible for typing the orders received from the salesmen, forwarding these to T. J. Jackson for production, shipping the orders to the customer, handling customer complaints, and handling the necessary paper work.

Every Monday morning the four managers (A. M. Jackson, T. J. Jackson, Ross, and Kaiser held a planning and review meeting. During this meeting the past week's performance was evaluated and plans for the present week were made. Each felt these meetings were necessary to coordinate their individual efforts. It was at one of these meetings that A. M. Jackson made the following announcement:

"As you well know our company has experienced rather consistent profits even in the face of inflation. I have been thinking about our future and feel that we should expand our efforts into men and women's dress shoes. A leading shoe company has agreed to buy dress shoes from us and sell them under their name brand. I think our present organization is well-suited for this addition to our present product line. I feel it could be accomplished with three changes. First, combine the second and first shift into one and with the necessary plant expansion have this shift keep producing our industrial shoe line. A new second shift could be added which would now produce the new proposed dress shoes. Second, put a third group of salesmen called "dress shoe salesmen" under your control, Ross. These salesmen would sell to and act as a communication link between A. J. Jackson & Sons and the dress shoe company. And finally, add an assistant office manager to help Kaiser handle the additional work load this move would create. These changes can all be made rather quickly and with very little difficulty. I definitely feel the time is right for A. J. Jackson & Sons to broaden our base of operation. I want you three to think about these proposals and their implementation so that we can discuss them at our next meeting."

(1) What are the advantages and disadvantages of A. M. Jackson & Sons' present organization structure?

(2) What organization changes would you recommend to eliminate or minimize these disadvantages?
(3) What are the strengths and weaknesses of the three proposed organization changes sugggested by A. M. Jackson?
(4) What organization changes would you recommend to eliminate or minimize the disadvantages this new line of dress shoes might cause?
(5) Do you see any need for new service departments with A. M. Jackson & Sons, either before or after the addition of the dress shoe line?
(6) How do you think each of the three managers will react to these specific proposals which will alter their jobs?

## Incident 17–2

### THE NEW ASSISTANT

Peter Knapp has been the owner-manager of six motel-resort areas in Wisconsin for the last four years. He has built his business around his initial motel-resort area, Chain-O-Lakes Lodge. Each of the other five resort areas is run as a separate complex with a superintendent residing at each one. These superintendents report directly to Peter, who sets out guidelines for the resort area's operation. Each superintendent has the freedom to make decisions within these guidelines Peter has set.

Peter has just submitted his bid to buy two additional resort areas, which would bring his total holdings to eight areas. Peter feels that if these bids are accepted, his job will become too big for him to handle. With this in mind he has already hired a recent graduate of the University of Wisconsin's hotel management program to be his new assistant. Since this is to be a new job Peter wants to provide the employee with a statement of exactly what his job will involve. After some thought, Peter decides to show the following statement to the new employee during his first day on the job:

> The assistant manager of Chain-O-Lakes Lodges Inc. shall be directly responsible to the manager, Peter Knapp. He will act as a relief valve for the manager. Any work which the manager is too busy for automatically becomes the assistant manager's responsibility. Once a month he will visit each of the other motel-resort areas and evaluate their operations. He will also evaluate with the manager any new lodges that may be of interest to Chain-O-Lakes, Inc.

(1) What are the strengths and weaknesses of Chain-O-Lakes' present organization structure?
(2) What are the strong and weak points of the job statement Peter has written up for the new assistant manager?
(3) How would you change this job statement to minimize these weaknesses?
(4) From what you know write a new job statement for the assistant manager's job.

# 18

# Directing and Controlling

A manager cannot assume that jobs within the organization will automatically get done or that plans will be realized. In short, his responsibilities do not end once plans, organizations, and jobs have been outlined. He must direct the work of employees who perform at these jobs and review the progress departments, people, and the organization are making toward achieving the desired plans. In this chapter the focus is on the last two functions every manager performs: directing and controlling the business and the work of people in the organization.

## Directing via Communications

Managers direct employees and subordinates through **communications.** There is no other way to direct the work of individual employees or work groups. Just think of the impossibility of laying out the work to be done, instructing subordinates, or coordinating efforts without being able to communicate. Communication is a must when people have to work together. Communication is how managers go about transforming ideas and ideals into action.

Effective management and good communication skills go hand in hand, yet most people take for granted the ability to communicate with others. After learning how to talk and write, most people feel they have mastered the skill of communications. And yet every day they are indirectly told that they have not mastered this skill. For example, how many times has someone misunderstood what you said? Or have you ever said to a teacher who graded you low on an essay question, "I didn't state the answer exactly like you put it, but that's what I meant." These examples illustrate that good communication does not automatically happen. As a matter of fact, poor communication, with misunderstanding, is more often the rule than good communication. Good communication is difficult; it is one of the most important skills an individual or manager needs to work on and devote time to.

## ELEMENTS OF COMMUNICATIONS

Communications can be defined as passing information and understanding from one person to another or from one person to a group of people. An important point is part of this definition. Communication involves *both* information and understanding. Most people would agree that if they stand in a room alone and speak or shout they are not communicating. Information has been passed out but it has not been understood, because no one heard it. The same thing can happen when talking or writing to other people. In class, the teacher passes out a lot of information but many times communicates very little. Students who don't listen can't understand. On the job a manager may talk to an employee who does not listen or fails to understand what was said. In either case no communication has occurred. Information has only been passed between the parties. Words or messages are not communication; they are only information. They only become communications when someone hears and understands them.

The manager is responsible for gaining employees' cooperation, in achieving predetermined plans. He is also responsible for getting the jobs done within an organization structure. He can not fulfill these responsibilities unless action is created in people or the departments of the organization. The action must be directed towards plans and performance on a given job. These actions are created and his responsibilities met through good communications.

The manager could be viewed as a communication center receiving information, understanding it, and passing it out to other points and people in the business. This information and understanding gets jobs done and plans accomplished. The purpose of the first part of this chapter is to provide guides for increasing the communication skills of a manager. Doing so requires an understanding of the role each element in communications plays. Any communication could be broken down in diagram form into the five elements depicted in Exhibit 18–1.

The *sender* and *receiver* could be any two people. In this context we will talk about employees and managers, either of which could be a sender or a receiver. When the employee complains or offers an idea to the superior in

EXHIBIT 18–1

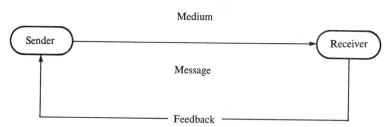

charge, he is a sender and the superior is the receiver. Conversely, when a manager talks to one or a group of employees, the manager is the sender. These two parties and the remaining three elements are necessary for communication to occur. There is a *message* the sender wants to get across to the receiver. This could be information, an order, a complaint, reassurance, or friendly conversation. The message is presented to the receiver through some **medium.** The basic concern here is with the written or oral media used in business situations. Finally, the sender must seek *feedback* from the receiver. By seeking feedback, the sender is asking, in a sense, "Did you understand my message the way I intended it?" Or, "Did we communicate?" Without feedback, the process of checking for understanding, the sender might just be sending only information and not communicating. Viewing communications this way points up a fact often forgotten: in the final analysis the receiver, not the sender, determines if communications have occurred. If he does not understand, the sender has only sent information and thus has not communicated.

Each of the five elements (sender, receiver, medium, message, and feedback) can be a cause for communications failure. The sender has some control or influence over all five of these elements. He can understand what he wants to say, know with whom he is communicating, plan his message, choose the appropriate medium, and foster feedback. All of this means that communications should be planned with the receiver in mind. If the receiver does not understand the message, fails to read or hear it, or feels embarrassed to admit he has not understood it, the communication has failed. The idea of planning communications with the receiver in mind cannot be overemphasized. It is the key to successful communications.

The manager is involved in two main types of communication: formal written communication and oral communication. For both types he can increase his communication effectiveness by planning communication with the listener or receiver in mind.

## FORMAL WRITTEN COMMUNICATION

Many messages in a business are communicated in written form. Memorandums, contracts, designs, advertisements, policies, procedures, rules, manuals, legal documents, purchase agreements, and various reports are just a few examples of the mountains of paper used in written business communications. Probably the biggest advantage to using written communication is that it can be kept on record. The permanence is a definite legal advantage where contracts are concerned. A written communication also allows the receiver to refer to it to refresh his memory on what exactly was said.

The prime disadvantage of written communications is that they are often poorly written. The sender cannot personally correct any misunderstanding but must rely totally on his written word. Therefore, poorly written communications increase the chance of misunderstanding and misinterpretation. A second disadvantage is that the intended receiver may never see the written communication. A report might very easily bypass the intended receiver or never get to him. Written communication is often initiated to save a manager's time. If he were to personally see to it that his written communication was received by all those for whom it was intended, he might as well have just communicated to them orally.

To minimize the chances that the intended receiver will not see the communication, the manager can initiate a formal communication network. Formal communication networks are made up of the numerous channels through which messages flow from person to person in a business. A purchase order might be started by a foreman, who sends it to his boss to approve, who in turn sends it to the purchasing department, who sends it to accounting for approval, then back to the purchasing department for order, then back to the accounting department for their records. This is a very short communication network. It does make sure that those departments or people who should see the purchase order do. Formal communication channels or networks are no small matter. Visualize the number of hands a customer's complaint or financial report would have to pass through, and what would happen if the right people never saw the communiqué.

To assure that only the right people receive a message at the right time, the manager must decide what formal route or channels his various communications will take. The example of the purchase order is an example of a formal communication route or channel. Many formal reports contain multiple copies, each of which goes to a separate person. Well-designed forms can alleviate many of these problems. For more general information, such as bulletins, policy handbooks, and manuals, copies are usually distributed to all persons affected.

Once these communications have been received by all the right departments or people the written message becomes important. It must be written so all those who receive it understand it. If a receiver does not understand it, he might as well have never received it. If the receiver misinterprets it, the results may be worse than if he never received it. Planning for effective written communications, those that are understood, involves being aware of why communications fail. Both oral and written communications fail for the same reasons, which will be presented after the discussion of the general area of oral communications.

## ORAL COMMUNICATION

Written words and numbers fit standard situations, but they do not convey feelings to the receiver. Oral, face-to-face communications include both *facts* and *feelings,* feelings because the receiver can see and hear the sender. He can see his facial and body expressions and hear his emphasis and tone of voice. Although feelings are usually not stated, they "color" the message. They make it personal.

The biggest advantage oral, face-to-face communication offers the manager is the opportunity for speedy and complete communication. Communication can be complete because each party can question the other until the meaning is clear. Added explanation is readily available; all the parties have to do is ask for it. Thus, there is no reason why face-to-face communication should be ineffective or fail. But often it is ineffective and does fail. Misunderstanding is just as likely to occur in personal face-to-face communications as in formal written communications.

## REASONS COMMUNICATIONS FAIL

### SENDER FAILS TO TAKE RECEIVER INTO CONSIDERATION

People's viewpoints and opinions differ. These viewpoints and opinions are the basis for evaluating and interpreting the messages others send them. For example, everyone attaches different meanings to such words as *black power, unions, drugs,* and *lay-off.* Similarly, messages are and can be interpreted differently by different people. For example, a manager (teacher) might pass an employee (student) in the morning and say "I'd like to see you this afternoon." The meaning is or should be very clear. But if the employee (student) is insecure, or knows he has done something wrong, a different meaning may be attached to this seemingly simple statement.

The meaning attached to a message depends upon the receiver's background and situation. The receiver always attaches a meaning to the message. Failure to think about the receiver's background, viewpoint, or situation means that the sender assumes that the meaning the receiver attaches to the message will be the same the sender attached to it. However, this may not be so; and thus, communications do not occur. The familiar song "Walk a Mile in my Shoes" best explains the solution to this problem. The sender needs to put himself in the receiver's situation to look at communications the way he thinks the receiver will and try to anticipate problems before they occur.

### SEMANTICS

Semantics is the science that deals with the meaning of words. Very simple words have many different meanings. For example, the word "face" can mean:

> the front part of the head
> the amount expressed on a note
> the surface of anything
> the end of a wall or tunnel
> the upper printing surface of a type
> to oppose
> to turn a card upwards
> to confess . . .

Most words have several different meanings. Thus if the sender either uses specific words which the receiver does not know, uses words which have many meanings and assumes they are interpreted the way they are meant, talks over the head of the receiver, or makes a message complicated and long, he has run into a problem with semantics. Many times senders try to impress receivers with their command of the language. They might say *mendacity* instead of *lie,* or *aphelion* instead of *distance,* or *want of symmentry* instead of *ugliness,* or *arborescence* instead of *roughness.* These attempts at impressing receivers usually backfire and create a negative impression and negative results.

Some of the best teachers, paid communicators, and managers are able to put their messages in words their receivers understand. This does not mean that either their written or oral communications are made up entirely of words of one syllable. It simply means that they know which words their receivers are most likely to understand, and that they go to great lengths to be sure the receiver attaches the same meaning to the words that the sender intended.

## THE SENDER DOES NOT LISTEN

A sender who fails to listen cannot get feedback to see if his message is understood. In the purest sense, listening only occurs with the ears. However, the sender can also "listen" with his eyes. Facial expressions such as a wrinkled eyebrow or a questioning look should be signals that the sender and receiver are not on the same wave length. They are not communicating. When these signals are being sent to the sender by the receiver, it is best to stop and clear up the situation before continuing. Many people, however, are not sensitive to these signals. As a consequence, the messages are not communicated effectively.

Listening 100 percent of the time requires work, as any student can attest to. You can listen faster than people can talk, which leaves time for your mind to wander. Senders may be so intent on getting their point across that as people question them, they only pretend to be listening. In reality they are thinking about their response or where to start once the questioner finishes. The result is that they really have not received any feedback from the receiver.

Just as dangerous is another practice many managers have. They do not allow questions or discourage them by abruptly answering them when they arise. The feeling is that the superior knows best so the receiver should just listen. But if the receiver has a question, he is not listening; he is thinking about his question. Supervisor's may also fail to recognize how uncomfortable a subordinate may be in asking questions or offering an opinion. Some people feel that asking questions or asking for clarification is a sign of ignorance. They would rather ask other workers (classmates) to clarify the message than show the supervisor (teacher) how ignorant they are. For a manager this is a delicate situation. The situation where employees are afraid to give feedback is very unhealthy. The manager needs to try continually to set an environment of belief among employees that feedback is honored, not looked on as a sign of weaknesses or ignorance.

Good communications do not occur by accident. They require continual planning and analysis—analysis of the receiver's beliefs, attitudes, and situation. Through analysis, the manager can anticipate where communication problems might occur and then plan his approach to avoid them. All of these reasons for communication failure could be summed up under one phrase—a lack of communication planning. Before every communication, written or oral, the manager should answer these questions:

(1) What is the message or idea I want to communicate?

(2) How can this best be accomplished? In a speech, memorandum, talk to a group, or individual conference?

(3) When is the best time for the receiver to listen to this message? When will he be most receptive and willing to listen?

(4) Why is this message necessary? If I don't know, how do I expect the receiver to know its importance?

Managing and directing the work of other people requires good communications. An unplanned communication is likely to be a poor one. Similarly a manager who takes communications for granted will likely be a poor communicator. We cannot overemphasize the importance of communication to the manager and how through communication planning this important technique can be made more effective.

## Controlling the Business System

The last function performed by every manager is control. Once plans have been put into operation, control is necessary to review progress, uncover deviations from plans, and take corrective action. Very simply, the manager controls to make sure that what is done is what was intended.

The manager controls the business system by controlling the many parts and elements of the business system. He must control such diverse factors as product quality, cash, employee wages, inventory levels, purchases, and employee morale. However, the control process is essentially the same for anything, money, products, or employees.

Before the managerial function of control is discussed, an important point must be made. Control and control techniques cannot be considered until plans, organization structure, and direction are clear, complete, and integrated. If a manager is unsure of what he wants the business to accomplish or what he wants an employee to do, it is difficult to control their activities. It is also difficult to control the business system when the jobs to be done are not clearly defined. There is a definite reason why the control function is covered last. It cannot be effective if the manager has been ineffective in performing his planning, organizing, and directing functions. Control cannot make up for a poor job done by the manager in planning, organizing, and directing. It will only point up when a poor job has been done in these other management functions. For the control function to be performed effectively, the manager will have to have done a good job in planning, organizing, and directing the resources of the business system.

## The Basic Control Process

Regardless of what is being controlled, the basic control process involves three elements: 1) establishing standards that represent desired performance, 2) measuring actual performance, and 3) correcting any deviations from these standards. The essential ingredient of control is information of what departments, employees, and processes are accomplishing. Without information on what is happening, the manager must assume that events are meeting standards. The ingredient of information is so important that the following section, The Information Process, is devoted to it. This chapter looks at the control function in total and indicates what types of information the manager needs to have to control the business system. The actual generation and use of this information will be discussed in the next section.

### ESTABLISHING STANDARDS

Performance standards represent an expression of planning objectives. The manager must answer the following question: How will I know when my plans have been achieved? If there is more than one manager, each must answer this question for his department or for that part of the total business objective he is responsible for. The production manager, distribution manager, president, and foreman must each set their own standards, based upon the objectives for their part of the business.

One approach to answering the question is to consider output and expenses, both of which affect whether a planning objective is achieved.

### OUTPUT

The manager must know what services, outputs, or functions he or the people in his department must perform. For example, a production manager knows that so many units of product must be produced in a given time period to meet his department's objectives. This is easy to measure; it is more difficult for, say, an advertising manager. What is his output? One function the advertising manager might be trying to fulfill is to affect the attitude of those buying the product in a certain way. For a foreman one function or output that affects his plans is the number of products rejected for quality defects. The manager, regardless of his responsibilities, should define a number of outputs of which he can say, "If I achieve these I have met my plans." Each of these outputs, when possible, should be defined in terms of quantity, quality, and time. However, it is not enough to say as a foreman, "I will decrease the number of products rejected." A further determination must be made of the exact number of rejections he is trying to achieve and within what time limits. This defines the performance standard, gives it meaning, and gives him something to judge his efforts against.

EXPENSES

Having thought about the type and level of output a manager should achieve, he must give some thought to expense. How much should I spend to achieve this output or accomplish this function? Given unlimited funds, almost any output can be realized. But each manager does not have this freedom; he needs to allocate the money available over the many outputs he is responsible for. The foreman who wants to decrease his rejection rate could do so by hiring more inspectors and having his men work slower. But he may not have the freedom to incur the added expenses this decision would involve. He has to accomplish his plans within economic restrictions.

These two conditions (outputs and expenses) can be used to establish the standards against which a manager will control the factors under his control. If a manager wants to control the activities of a secretary he only needs to state the standard in terms of the number and quality of letters typed (outputs) and salary paid (expense). However, if the manager wanted to control the sales efforts of a department store he would have to set standards for such outputs as level of sales for each item and customer services. In addition he must be concerned that expenses do not exceed a set limit for such items as advertising, salaries, shop lifting, merchandise displays, and equipment.

Standards in terms of specific levels of outputs and expenses translate plans into specific goals or targets against which results can be measured and controlled. A manager cannot control something unless he has stated what exactly should be accomplished. Establishing standards gives the manager a level of achievement or accomplishment against which he can measure actual results or performance.

## MEASURING ACTUAL PERFORMANCE

In this phase the manager is monitoring the performance of those people and activities under his control. The nature of the activity determines to a large extent the type of measurement used. Some activities lend themselves to easy quantification: man-hours worked, wages paid, units produced, expenses paid, level of sales, number of customers, and so on. The actual measurement of the activities involves the gathering of numbers and figures, data against which the manager can easily determine how well an employee or department is doing in meeting the standard of performance. This hard data is the central theme of the following section. Such numbers as accounting figures, cost data, and research information can be obtained by the manager.

For many other activities, the measurement of performance is extremely difficult. For example, it is difficult to measure the performance of an engineer, waitress, florist, receptionist, cook, computer programmer, or even student. As an activity moves away from being quantifiable, measurement and control become complex and often more important. In fact if the types of work performed in any business were analyzed, a large number of jobs for which quantifiable measures of performance cannot be obtained would come up. A manager cannot just forget controlling these activities or assume that if an activity or department is not too costly it must be doing something. For those activities where no quantifiable data can be generated, the manager should at least do two things:

(1) Personally observe what is happening, not every minute, but periodically to give him a feel for how the activity, department, or person is doing. During these observations and discussions with employees he should also note symptoms as a possible indication of what is happening. For example, the attitude of employees is hard to measure directly. But such symptoms as the number of absences and tardiness might be observed to indicate whether the employee attitude is favorable or negative.

(2) Require periodically that employees state, in writing, what they feel their performance is and why it is at the present level. Reading these reports can help give the manager insight into actual performance and ideas for improving it. The value of these reports depends on the honesty of those reporting. Some employees may pad the reports to look good for the boss.

Although these two suggestions do not solve the problem of measuring seemingly nonquantifiable activities, they do help in giving the manager a reading on what is going on. Any information must be evaluated as to its worth, even numerical data. These two suggestions do, however, provide the manager with some different information to use in evaluating performance, more than he would have if he just relied on some vague feeling about performance.

## CORRECTING DEVIATIONS

The information generated by measurement, whether it be quantifiable or not, only indicates what has happened. If performance is below the standard, the trouble needs to be corrected. Before this can happen, the manager must investigate the difficulties creating this trouble. Corrective action starts with identifying the reasons performance is deviating from a standard.

At this point the other managerial functions come into the picture. He must investigate all those activities performed in planning, organizing, and directing to see how they can be changed to increase performance. If sales, for example, are not up to expectation, the manager might investigate such questions as whether his product, consumer, or competition warrants such a sales goal (planning), whether he has enough salesmen (organizing), whether they work as hard as they should (directing), or whether the drop in sales is a result of forces in the economy beyond his control. Questioning each of the functions he has performed is valuable regardless of the scope of the control problem. Even the smallest control problem occurs because actions are not living up to plans. The reasons could be faulty plans, organization, or poor direction of people in the organization. Unless corrections are made in all or one of these areas, the problem will continue. Control is not an end in itself, but indicates where corrective action is needed. The control function forces the manager to reevaluate how well he has performed his other functions, as well as the abilities and capabilities of people within the business to meet his plans and perform the jobs as outlined.

## Summary

The manager, in performing the direction function, gives life to plans and the organization structure. He directs subordinates in performing jobs and achieving the business' plans. An important skill in directing the efforts of others is communications. Good communications are not automatic but rather require work and effort on the part of the manager. Probably the two keys to improving communications skills are analysis and planning—analysis of who the manager will be communicating with, their situation, attitudes, and beliefs and planning his communications in terms of what needs to be communicated, how, and when. Managers should analyze and plan to increase the chance of a communication being listened to, understood, and properly responded to.

The last function performed by a manager is that of control. This function encompasses the review and regulation of every activity carried on within the business system. The prime purpose of control is to make sure that these activities are conforming to those plans as outlined by the manager; and, if they are not, to find where corrective action needs to be taken. The business system cannot be controlled without information, both of quantitative and qualitative.

## The Management Process in Retrospect

The business system is not self-perpetuating. It is man-directed and controlled. One individual or a group of people make decisions which direct and control the total business system and its various elements. This person is called a manager; and in this section of the book we have tried to analyze what every manager does. Two immediate conclusions could be drawn from the discussion. First, a manager of a small business is involved in the same types of activities as a manager of a large business. Second, where many managers are found in a business, they all perform the same basic functions. This is true for the foreman in the plant and the president. Thus, all managers, regardless of the size of business or the level within the organization, perform the same basic functions. All managers plan, organize, direct, and control the efforts of those under them.

Planning involves determining a course of action for the business as well as for each department in the business. Objectives are determined; employee behavior is regulated through policies, procedures, and rules. In organizing, the manager determines the nature and content of the jobs to be done within the business and he then sets up a formal organization structure which will coordinate the jobs with one another. Employees are provided direction via communications. The manager cannot direct the work of others to comply with plans and jobs to be done without being able to communicate effectively. Finally, a control procedure must be initiated whereby the manager can review and evaluate the progress people, departments, and the total business system are making towards accomplishing the firm's predefined objectives. This last function gives unity to the manager's job and indicates its continuous nature. For if performance is not up to par, corrective action must be taken. This corrective action will be felt in altered plans, jobs and organization of work, and directional efforts.

You should appreciate by now the central role the manager plays in the success of the business system. He plans, makes decisions, organizes, directs, and controls all the activities or processes discussed so far. He or his associate managers make each process go. Without managers there would be no business system.

## QUESTIONS

1. Define the concept of communications. What role does communications play in performing the managerial functions of planning and organization?
2. Does face-to-face communications have any advantages over written communications? Describe why you answered as you did.
3. How can the manager increase his effectiveness in formal written communications?
4. Identify and give a one-sentence description of each of the reasons why communications fail.
5. Good communications require continual planning and analysis. Explain.
6. What are the basic elements of any control process?
7. How can the performance of people or departments be measured when their outputs are nonquantifiable?
8. How does a manager determine whether or not he has realized or achieved his objectives?
9. Discuss why and how the four functions performed by every manager are interrelated and interdependent.

## Incident 18–1

Doug Clemens, foreman of the warehouse for Grey Line Trucking Company, has a new inventory system he wants to initiate. He called a meeting of his employees to inform them of the new system. During the meeting Jeff Ripko, one of Grey Line's best employees, stated, "The system won't work without some very important changes." "Ripko," replied Doug Clemens, "I'm not going to argue about a system that has worked for other companies. I think you're just too set in your ways to accept a change."

"You know very well, Mr. Clemens, that I'd be the first to accept a change that was good for Grey Lines," replied Ripko. "But, we have to make some important changes in the system you're proposing before we install it here."

Doug Clemens answered, "Ripko, talk to me after the meeting. Your comments indicate that you obviously don't understand the system." Addressing the entire group, Doug Clemens asked, "Are there any questions?" There were no questions and the meeting was adjourned.

(1) What communication problems do you see in this incident?
(2) How can these problems be overcome?
(3) How has Clemens affected the employees' cooperation during this meeting?
(4) Has he really communicated his message? What message did the employees really hear?
(5) What do you think Doug's communication philosophy is?
(6) Why were there no questions at the end of the meeting?
(7) What suggestions would you have for Doug to improve his communication skills?

## Incident 18–2

When the Excell Tool and Die Co. was small, it had no trouble in controlling the flow of orders through the shop so that production was efficient and customer orders went out on time. Now that it has grown in size to over 100 employees, orders are not always processed efficiently, deliveries are delayed, and costly returns by customers are increasing. Alice Sutton, the company's treasurer, has asked for a complete review of the control system to determine what is wrong and what improvements need to be made. Alice actually traced an order through the factory and found the following:

(a) Most jobs in the tool and die industry are bid for by numerous companies from blue prints provided by the customer. Excell's bid is based upon a conference between the shop foreman and owner of the company.
(b) Those jobs that are obtained are forwarded to the shop foreman. The foreman figures out what parts and processes are needed to complete the job and also schedules the completion date for each part of the job.
(c) The shop foreman then assigns the appropriate number of men to the job. They are under the direction of at least one master tool and die maker.
(d) Each worker gets the tools, materials, and supplies needed to do the job.
(e) The master tool and die maker reports to the shop foreman when each part of the job is finished.
(f) The shop foreman checks these reports against his schedule for the completed job and pushes if he feels the job is falling behind schedule.
(g) One week before the job is completed the foreman notifies the treasurer, who prepares the necessary billing for the completed job.
(h) The finished job and billing are shipped or delivered to the consumer.

(1) What parts of the control process are not being performed or are being poorly performed?
(2) What suggestions do you think Alice Sutton should make for improving this control process?
(3) How would you go about introducing these changes so that these people who are involved will accept them?

# THE INFORMATION PROCESS

Information should be gathered concerning the internal operations of the business system in order for management to plan and control the activities of each process as well as the total business system as a whole. Likewise, information on the internal operations of the firm is needed by outsiders such as creditors, stockholders, and potential investors in order to evaluate management's effectiveness in operating the firm. Information that is useful to management for internal planning and control and evaluated by outsiders as a reading on the firm's efficiency can be found in accounting, financial, and other statistical data.

Information is also desirable in order to evaluate changes in the external environment. This information can then serve as the basis for changes in strategy which will have to be made in order for the business to adapt to the changing environment. Such information as market research and economic forecasting data is critical in laying the path the firm plans to follow.

Information, in the form of reports or otherwise, becomes the basis upon which a department head or a group such as a committee makes a decision or forms a judgment relating to a particular problem. The steps which comprise the information process may be diagrammed as follows:

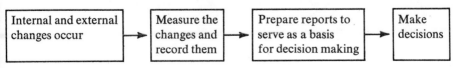

The information process will be discussed in the following four chapters: Chapter 19, Internal Information Process—Financial Accounting; Chapter 20, Internal Information Process—Managerial Accounting; Chapter 21, Research: Generating Additional Generation; and Chapter 22, Tools to Aid in the Utilization of Information.

# 19

# Internal Information Process— Financial Accounting

The manager is continually confronted with the necessity of making decisions concerning the internal operations of the business. Some of these decisions are rather routine, whereas others may affect the very survival of the firm. Although decision making is difficult, this chore is made easier when the manager has access to the necessary financial information. Just as the pilot of an airliner relies upon the air traffic control tower for guidance in making a landing, so too, the manager of a firm relies upon accounting information for guidance in making decisions. In addition to the manager, outsiders such as creditors, stockholders, and potential investors (just to name a few) require financial information which can be used as a basis for making decisions.

This chapter covers the nature of financial accounting and the users of the information it provides; the basic approach the accountant follows in preparing financial statements; and some important analytical tools used in analyzing financial statements. However, before these areas are discussed, it is necessary to first examine the relationship between the information process and the total business system.

## The Information Process and the Business System

Information flows throughout the business system in the same way as the other resources used by the business. Each of the processes (financial, production, distribution, manpower) has an information flow which monitors how that process is being performed and indicates where further changes will have to be made. In the case of a small sole proprietorship, the owner and operator may evaluate all available information and make decisions based upon it. In the case of a large corporation, a number of managers will have access to information affecting their departments as well as the total business system. Each manager will in turn evaluate this information and make decisions based upon it. Thus, information is like the backbone and nervous system of the body. Like the nervous system it monitors the various separate processes of the business system. And like the backbone it ties together the separate processes into an operating whole. The flow of information needed for each process will be briefly discussed.

Through the financial process, funds flow into the business, are used, and eventually flow out of the business. Information is needed to monitor and make decisions about this flow of funds. The financial manager, for example, utilizes information when the firm is first being organized. The manager of the information process accumulates data relating to the estimated funds required to operate the business and the profits which should be realized. This type of information is of utmost importance to those outsiders such as stockholders and creditors who are contemplating advancing funds to the firm. However, it is important to note that the manager of the information process simply accumulates and reports this information. It is the responsibility of the production manager, the distribution manager, and the financial manager (among others) to work closely with the information manager in compiling the necessary estimates concerning potential revenues and expenses.

Once the firm begins full operation, the financial manager continues to rely upon information to plan and control the firm's funds. Information contained in the earnings statement, the statement of financial position, and other summary or detailed reports will be helpful to the financial manager in planning and controlling the acquisition of long-term and short-term funds, in selecting the proper form of business organization to utilize, and in electing the necessary tax provisions to minimize the outflow of funds as taxes.

Through the production process materials and equipment flow into the business, are used, and eventually flow out of the business. The production manager requires information relating to the transformation of inputs into outputs. Through the accumulation of material, labor, and overhead costs, the information process provides production with the actual costs incurred in manufacturing a product or providing a service. However, the production manager is not only interested in terms of actual costs but also in terms of what costs should have been. This requires standards. It is the responsibility of the production manager to develop a set of cost standards for producing a product or providing a service. Through the information process, data in the form of performance reports is accumulated relating to the actual costs incurred. These performance reports are then compared to the predetermined standards in order that the production manager may determine which activities adhered to standards and which did not. Internal information is also provided in order to control such elements as the amount of inventory on hand, the amount of scrap or waste, and product or service quality levels.

In addition to internal information, the production manager also utilizes external information in the form of published periodicals, books, and other reports. External information provides suggestions of what others have done to improve their production processes.

Through the distribution process, ideas flow into the business, are used, and products or services flow out to consumers. The distribution manager uses internal information to determine which products account for most of the firm's sales, which products are unprofitable and therefore should be eliminated, which territories or customers account for most of the firm's sales, and so on. Information on the costs of producing a product or providing a service can be used for pricing purposes. Information relating to transportation costs provides a basis for selecting the proper mode of transportation in order to minimize cost and yet provide good service.

The distribution process, probably more than any other process, makes extensive use of external information. The use of such published information as census data helps the distribution manager to analyze the number and types of people within a market area. External information is also generated through the use of questionnaires, interviews, or observations. This type of information assists the distribution manager in answering such questions as "What motivates customers to buy the firm's products?" or "What characteristics are representative of most of the firm's customers?"

Through the manpower process, human resources flow into, are used, and eventually flow out of the business. The manpower manager requires internal information relating to absenteeism and turnover of employees in order to plan properly and control personnel requirements. The manpower manager also makes use of external data. Such information as the skills available within a particular community or the going wage in a community are important in determining both the number and kind of employees the firm will hire and the wage to be paid. Data are also generated concerning the attitudes and feelings of employees.

Although this discussion emphasizes the information utilized by managers of the various processes, it is important to realize that the manager of a small business also requires information. In fact, the manager of a small business will most likely be responsible for both accumulating and interpreting information affecting all aspects of his business. At the other extreme, top-level management of large business organizations require information to make total business decisions. As an example, information is needed to make certain that the goals of each process are consistent or compatible with the goals of the firm as a whole.

## The Nature of Financial Accounting

In broad terms, accounting can be defined as that art concerned with the recording, classifying, summarizing in good form, and interpreting of financial data. Because accounting provides financial information needed by managers, investors, creditors, and other interested groups, it is often referred to as the "language of business." Financial accounting is designed to periodically provide information concerning the overall operating activities of the firm, rather than reporting the activities, for example, of one process within the firm or of day-to-day operations. In addition to business firms which are profit oriented, many nonprofit organizations need accounting information. These include churches, schools, governmental agencies, hospitals, charities, and clubs.

In order to provide the information needed by various interested parties, it is necessary to design an accounting system to record transactions and events which affect the firm's financial position and results of operations. The discussion which follows examines the fundamental accounting equation used by the accountant to record financial information.

### THE ACCOUNTING EQUATION

**Assets** are defined as economic resources (properties) owned or controlled by the business. The rights or claims to these assets are equities. In other words, if a business has $20,000 in assets, there must in turn be equities in these assets amounting to $20,000. This relationship may be expressed in the following manner:

$$\text{Assets} = \text{Equities}$$

Rights or claims to assets are generally held by two parties: the owner or owners of the business and creditors. The equity of the owner or owners in the assets of the business is called owners' equity. For example, if John Roberts invests $5,000 of his personal savings to start up a bicycle repair shop, it would be expressed as follows:

$$\text{Assets} = \text{Owner's Equity}$$
$$5,000 \qquad \$5,000$$

The equity of creditors in the assets of the business is **liabilities.** Therefore, if John Roberts also borrows $3,000 from a local bank in order to start his new business, the relationship will be expanded:

$$\text{Assets} = \text{Liabilities} + \text{Owner's Equity}$$
$$8,000 = \quad \$3,000 \quad + \qquad \$5,000$$

This relationship may be described as the fundamental formula in accounting. If the records of a business are to be properly maintained, every transaction from the very simplest to the most complex must be recorded so as to adhere to this relationship. Liabilities are listed in the accounting equation before owner's equity because creditors of a business have first claim or right to the assets. That is, if John Roberts elected at a latter date to sell his bicycle repair shop for cash, any creditors who have a claim in these assets must be paid first. Once the creditors are paid in full, the remaining money would belong to the owner. To illustrate that the claims of the owner or owners in the assets of a business are secondary to the claims of creditors, the accounting equation may be written as follows:

$$\text{Assets} - \text{Liabilities} = \text{Owner's Equity}$$

Mr. Roberts, as a businessman, is interested in operating his bicycle repair shop at a profit. This requires an inflow of **revenue** which exceeds operating expenses. Revenue may be defined as the inflow of assets such as cash or accounts receivable resulting from the sale of a good or service. An **expense** is defined as the cost of goods or services used up in the process of earning revenue. Both revenue and expenses have an effect upon the accounting equation. Revenue increases assets on the left side of the equation and owner's equity on the right side. Conversely, expenses decrease assets on the left side of the equation and decrease owners' equity on the right side. The fundamental accounting equation can be expressed in the following matter to show the recognition of revenue and expenses:

$$\text{Assets} = \text{Liabilities} + \text{Owner's Equity} + (\text{Revenues} - \text{Expenses})$$

This fundamental equation must always balance. If at any time the equation is out of balance, an error has been made in recording a transction.

## TRANSACTIONS AND THEIR EFFECT ON THE ACCOUNTING EQUATION

Accounting is concerned, among other matters, with recording financial transactions. A transaction may be defined as an economic event relating to the exchange of money, goods, or services with another person or firm which must be recorded. Before the recording of transactions is discussed, it is first necessary to examine briefly two concepts which the accountant adheres to in recording financial transactions and events. These two concepts are the entity concept and the cost concept.

### THE ENTITY CONCEPT

Under this concept, a business is looked upon as separate and distinct from its owners. The business is considered an economic unit which has its own assets, liabilities, and owners' equity. If an individual owns two businesses, such as a clothing store and an automobile dealership, separate records will be maintained for each. Furthermore, the personal assets of the owner such as his home, life insurance, furniture, car, and savings will not be intermingled with the assets of the business.

### THE COST CONCEPT

In transactions involving the acquisition of an asset, the accountant adheres to the cost principle. This means that all assets acquired are recorded at cost. Cost is a good measure of the fair value of an asset, because it is the amount which results from a transaction between a buyer and a seller who are independent of each other.

The discussion below describes a few transactions to show the effect of these events upon the accounting equation. For purposes of illustration, assume that

Mr. John R. Witzel decides to open a new sporting goods store on January 1, 19X1. The store is to be operated by Mr. Witzel as a sole proprietorship and is given the name "Witzel's Sporting Goods." The events described below represent the transactions which Mr. Witzel consummated during the first year (19X1) of the store's operation. The changes which take place in the assets and/or equities are explained for each transaction.

## 19X1 Transactions

(a) Mr. Witzel deposits $40,000 of his personal savings in a checking account opened at the local bank in the name of Witzel's Sporting Goods. As a result of this transaction, assets are increased by $40,000 in the form of cash, and owner's equity is likewise increased by $40,000. The accounting equation for Witzel's Sporting Goods appears as follows:

|  | Assets = | Owner's equity |
|---|---|---|
|  | Cash = | J. R. Witzel, equity |
| Bal. before (a) | 0 | 0 |
| (a) | $40,000 | 40,000 |
| Bal. after (a) | $40,000 = | 40,000 |

(b) Mr. Witzel acquires land for $20,000, paying cash. The effect of this transaction is to increase the asset Land $20,000 and to reduce the asset Cash by $20,000 as indicated below:

|  | Assets | | Owner's equity |
|---|---|---|---|
|  | Cash | Land | J. R. Witzel, equity |
| Bal. before (b) | 40,000 | | 40,000 |
| (b) | −20,000 + | 20,000 | |
| Bal. after (b) | 20,000 + | $20,000 = | 40,000 |

Notice that transaction (b) does not result in an increase in total assets but merely a change in the composition of total assets.

(c) A building costing $45,000 is purchased by Mr. Witzel, who pays $12,000 in cash and borrows $33,000 from the bank after signing a mortgage note which matures in nine years, or in 19X9. This transaction increases the asset Building and decreases the asset Cash on the left side of the equation and increases the liability Mortgage Payable on the right side.

|  | Assets | | | | Liabilities+Owner's equity | |
|---|---|---|---|---|---|---|
|  | Cash | + Land | + | Bldg. | Mortgage payable | J. R. Witzel, equity |
| Bal. before (c) | 20,000 + | 20,000 | | | | 40,000 |
| (c) | −12,000 | | + | 45,000 | +33,000 | |
| Bal. after (c) | 8,000 + | 20,000 | + | 45,000 = | 33,000 + | 40,000 |

(d) As previously noted, the primary objective of a business is to earn a profit. In the case of a retail store, such as Witzel's Sporting Goods, a profit is made by selling merchandise at a price which exceeds the cost of the goods sold added to operating expenses. Therefore, during the year Mr. Witzel acquires on account merchandise consisting of all kinds of sporting goods at a cost of $55,000. The effects of this transaction are shown below.

|  | Assets | | | | Liabilities + Owner's equity | | |
|---|---|---|---|---|---|---|---|
|  | Cash | + Merch. inven. | + Land | + Bldg. | Acct. payable | + Morg. payable | + J.R.W. equity |
| Bal. before (d) | 8,000 |  | 20,000 | 45,000 |  | 33,000 | 40,000 |
| (d) |  | 55,000 |  |  | +55,000 |  |  |
| Bal. after (d) | 8,000 | + 55,000 | + 20,000 | + 45,000 = | 55,000 | + 33,000 | + 40,000 |

(e1) During the year Mr. Witzel sells $80,000 of merchandise. Of this total, $50,000 is for cash and the remainder, $30,000, is on account. The effect of selling merchandise on the accounting equation is to increase both assets and owner's equity in the following manner:

|  | Assets | | | | |
|---|---|---|---|---|---|
|  | Cash | + Acct. rec. | + Merch. inven. | + Land | + Bldg. |
| Bal. before (e1) | 8,000 |  | 55,000 | 20,000 | 45,000 |
| (e1) | 50,000 | + 30,000 |  |  |  |
| Bal. after (e1) | 58,000 | + 30,000 | + 55,000 | + 20,000 | + 45,000 |

|  | Liabilities + Owner's equity | | |
|---|---|---|---|
| = | Accts. payable | + Morg. payable | + J. R. W. equity |
|  | 55,000 | + 33,000 | + 40,000 |
|  |  |  | + 80,000 |
| = | 55,000 | + 33,000 | + 120,000 |

(e2) The cost of the merchandise sold during the year amounts to $40,000. This expense, called Cost of Goods Sold, results in a decrease of both assets and owners' equity. The accounting equation now appears as follows:

|  | Assets | | | | |
|---|---|---|---|---|---|
|  | Cash | + Acct. rec. | + Merch. inven. | + Land | + Bldg. |
| Bal. before (e2) | 58,000 | + 30,000 | + 55,000 | + 20,000 | + 45,000 |
| (e2) |  |  | − 40,000 |  |  |
| Bal. after (e2) | 58,000 | + 30,000 | + 15,000 | + 20,000 | + 45,000 |

|  | Liabilities + Owner's equity | | |
|---|---|---|---|
|  | Accts. payable | + Morg. payable | + J. R. W. equity |
|  | 55,000 | + 33,000 | + 120,000 |
|  |  |  | − 40,000 |
| = | 55,000 | + 33,000 | + 80,000 |

In order to determine the Cost of Goods Sold figure of $40,000, it was necessary for Mr. Witzel to take a physical count of the merchandise inventory on hand at the end of the year or December 31, 19X1. This is accomplished by

making a detailed listing of the merchandise on hand and multiplying each type
of merchandise by its purchase price. Once the ending inventory is determined,
the cost of goods sold is computed as follows for the Witzel's Sporting Goods
Store:

| | |
|---|---:|
| Merchandise inventory January 1, 19X1 | $ —0— |
| Plus purchase during the year | 55,000 |
| Goods available for sale | 55,000 |
| Less merchandise inventory, December 31, 19X1 | 15,000 |
| Cost of goods sold during the year | $40,000 |

(f) Mr. Witzel receives $13,000 from customers who purchased merchan-
dise on account. On the other hand, Mr. Witzel pays out $28,000 in cash to
suppliers from whom merchandise was purchased on account. The effect of
these transactions is illustrated below.

|  | Assets | | | | |
|---|---|---|---|---|---|
|  | Cash + | Acct. rec. | + Merch. inven. | + Land + | Bldg. |
| Bal. before (f) | 58,000 + | 30,000 | + 15,000 + | 20,000 + | 45,000 |
| (f) | +13,000 − | 13,000 | | | |
| | −28,000 | | | | |
| Bal. after (f) | 43,000 + | 17,000 | + 15,000 + | 20,000 + | 45,000 |

|  | Liabilities + Owner's Equity | | |
|---|---|---|---|
| = | Accts. payable | + Morg. payable | + J. R. W. equity |
| = | 55,000 | + 33,000 + | 80,000 |
| | −28,000 | | |
| = | 27,000 | + 33,000 + | 80,000 |

(g) The following general and administrative expenses are incurred during
the year, for which Mr. Witzel pays cash:

| | | |
|---|---:|---:|
| Salaries and wages | $15,000 | |
| Advertising | 1,000 | |
| Insurance expense | 1,000 | |
| Supplies | 200 | |
| Heat, light, and power | 700 | |
| Property taxes | 2,000 | |
| Interest expense | 2,100 | |
| Total | | $22,000 |

Again, since expenses reduce both assets and owners' equity, the effect on the
accounting equation is as follows on the next page.

Notice that after each transaction described is recorded, the accounting
equation is always in balance. That is, assets equals liabilities plus owner's
equity. This is because an increase, for instance, on one side of the accounting
equation is matched either by a decrease on the same side of the equation and/
or by an increase on the opposite side of the equation.

|  | Assets | | | | |
|---|---|---|---|---|---|
|  | Cash + | Acct. rec. + | Merch. inven. + | Land + | Bldg. |
| Bal. before (g) | 43,000 + | 17,000 + | 15,000 + | 20,000 + | 45,000 |
| (g) | −22,000 | | | | |
| Bal. after (g) | 21,000 + | 17,000 + | 15,000 + | 20,000 + | 45,000 |

|  |  | Liabilities + Owner's Equity | | |
|---|---|---|---|---|
| = |  | Accts. payable + | Mortg. payable + | J. R. W. equity |
|  |  | 27,000 + | 33,000 + | 80,000 |
|  |  |  | − | 22,000 |
| = |  | 27,000 + | 33,000 + | 58,000 |

The transactions described above for Witzel's Sporting Goods during the year 19X1 are summarized in Exhibit 19–1. Each transaction is identified by letter and the final balance for each account at year end is shown at the bottom of the table. The information in this table will be used next to construct the financial statements for Witzel's Sporting Goods. The two primary financial statements which represent the end product of financial accounting are the balance sheet and the income statement.

## BALANCE SHEET

The balance sheet is called the statement of financial position because it provides a summary of the firm's assets, liabilities, and owners' equity as of a particular date. Observe the balance sheet in Exhibit 19-2 for Witzel's Sporting Goods store. The heading on the balance sheet indicates the name of the firm, the title of the statement, and the date. Note also that total assets of $118,000 equals total equities of $118,000. The equities of a business are divided into two parts, liabilities and owners' equity.

### ASSETS

Assets are economic resources owned or controlled by the business. There are three primary classifications of assets which appear on a firm's balance sheet: current assets, fixed assets, and other assets.

*Current Assets.* A current asset is one which will be converted to cash within one year or within the operating cycle and be available for operating the business. Common examples of current assets include cash, accounts receivable, merchandise inventory, and prepaid items such as rent and insurance. Current assets are listed in the balance sheet in the order of their **liquidity,** that is, the amount of time it takes to convert them into cash. Total current assets for the Witzel's Sporting Goods store amount to $53,000.

*Fixed Assets.* A fixed assets is one which will be used in the business over a long period of time for the purpose of carrying out the regular activities of the

## EXHIBIT 19-1
### Witzel's Sporting Goods
### Summary of Transactions
### Year 19X1

| Transaction | Assets | | | | | = | Liabilities and Owner's Equity | | |
| --- | --- | --- | --- | --- | --- | --- | --- | --- | --- |
| | Cash + | Accounts Receivable + | Merchandise Inventory + | Land + | Building | = | Accounts Payable + | Mortgage Payable + | J. R. Witzel's Owner's Equity |
| | −0− | −0− | −0− | −0− | −0− | = | −0− | −0− | −0− |
| (a) | + 40,000 | | | | | | | | + 40,000 |
| (b) | − 20,000 | | | + 20,000 | | | | | |
| (c) | − 12,000 | | | | + 45,000 | | | + 33,000 | |
| (d) | | | + 55,000 | | | | + 55,000 | | |
| (e1) | + 50,000 | + 30,000 | | | | | | | + 80,000 |
| (e2) | | | − 40,000 | | | | | | − 40,000 |
| (f) | + 13,000 | − 13,000 | | | | | | | |
| (g) | − 28,000 | | | | | | − 28,000 | | |
| | − 22,000 | | | | | | | | − 15,000 |
| | | | | | | | | | − 1,000 |
| | | | | | | | | | − 1,000 |
| | | | | | | | | | − 200 |
| | | | | | | | | | − 700 |
| | | | | | | | | | − 2,000 |
| | | | | | | | | | − 2,100 |
| Totals | 21,000 + | 17,000 + | 15,000 + | 20,000 + | 45,000 | = | 27,000 + | 33,000 + | 58,000 |

## EXHIBIT 19-2

*Witzel's Sporting Goods*
*Balance Sheet*
*December 31, 19X1*

### Assets

| | | |
|---|---|---|
| Current assets | | |
|   Cash | $21,000 | |
|   Accounts receivable | 17,000 | |
|   Merchandise inventory | 15,000 | |
|     Total current assets | | $ 53,000 |
| Fixed assets | | |
|   Building | $45,000 | |
|   Land | 20,000 | |
|     Total fixed assets | | $ 65,000 |
| Total Assets | | $118,000 |

### Liabilities

| | | |
|---|---|---|
| Current liabilities | | |
|   Accounts payable | $27,000 | |
|     Total current liabilities | | $ 27,000 |
| Long-term liabilities | | |
|   Mortgage payable, 8% | | |
|     (due January 1, 19X9) | | 33,000 |
|     Total Liabilities | | $ 60,000 |
| Owner's equity | | |
|   J. R. Witzel, equity | | $ 58,000 |
| Total Equities | | $118,000 |

firm. Examples include machinery and equipment, buildings, and land. Witzel's Sporting Goods has $65,000 invested in its fixed assets.

*Other Assets.* Most assets of a small business will be included under the two categories mentioned above. Those assets which are not current or fixed are called Other Assets. Investments to be held over a long period of time, such as ownership of a subsidiary or investments in land held for the purpose of future expansion, are two examples of other assets.

## LIABILITIES

Liabilities are economic obligations of an enterprise. That is, they represent the debts of the firm. Two common ways in which liabilities are created are the purchase of merchandise on credit and the borrowing of money from a bank. In the event a firm becomes insolvent due to its inability to pay its debts, the creditors have first claim upon the assets of the firm. After these claims have been satisfied, any remaining assets are distributed to the owners. Two primary classifications of liabilities which appear on the balance sheet are current liabilities and long-term liabilities.

*Current Liabilities.* Those liabilities due within twelve months are classified as current. The most common example is accounts payable which result from purchase of goods and services on credit. Other current liabilities include notes payable, taxes payable, wages payable, and interest payable. Current liabilities are listed in the order of their settlement or liquidation. That is, those which are due first are listed first. Total current liabilities of the Witzel's Sporting Goods store amount to $27,000.

*Long-Term Liabilities.* Liabilities which will not be settled or paid within the next year are classified as long-term. A note due in two years and a mortgage due in the next thirty years are both examples of long-term debt. However, that portion of the mortgage due within the next twelve months should be classified as a current liability. No particular order is used to list long-term debts in the balance sheet. The single long-term debt for which Witzel's Sporting Goods is responsible is a mortgage of $33,000.

OWNERS' EQUITY

Owners' equity represents the claims of the owner or owners against the assets of the firm. It is computed by subtracting total liabilities from total assets. The owners' equity of the Witzel's Sporting Goods store on December 31, 19X1 is computed as follows:

|  |  |
|---|---|
| Total assets | $118,000 |
| Total liabilities | 60,000 |
| Owners' equity | $ 58,000 |

The composition of Mr. Witzel's equity of $58,000 is as follows:

|  |  |
|---|---|
| Original investment in the store | $40,000 |
| Earnings for the year 19X1 | 18,000 |
| Total equity | $58,000 |

The owners' equity section of the balance sheet is slightly different if the enterprise is formed as a partnership or as a corporation. For example, if Mr. Witzel elected to form a partnership with Miss Edison and each invested $20,-000 in the sporting goods store, the equity section of the balance sheet would appear as follows on December 31, 19X1:

| Partners' equities: |  |
|---|---|
| J. R. Witzel, capital | $29,000 |
| M. M. Edison, capital | 29,000 |
| Total partners' equity | $58,000 |

The composition of each partner's capital of $29,000 is as follows:

|  |  |
|---|---|
| Original investment | $20,000 |
| Earnings for the year 19X1 assumed to be shared equally ($18,000 × ½) | 9,000 |
| Amount of each partner's capital | $29,000 |

On the other hand, if Mr. Witzel elected to form a corporation, the equity section of the balance sheet would appear as follows:

| Stockholders' equity: | |
|---|---|
| Capital stock | $40,000 |
| Retained earnings | 18,000 |
| Total stockholders' equity | $58,000 |

Notice that in the case of a corporation, earnings are classified separately from initial investment of the stockholders. This is accomplished by using an account called Retained Earnings which represents total earnings accumulated in the corporation since its inception.

## THE INCOME STATEMENT

The income statement, often referred to as the statement of earnings, reports the results of operations or profits of an enterprise for a specified period of time. In preparing the income statement, the accountant uses the matching concept. Under this concept, the income of a particular period is matched against the expenses of the same period.

The income statement for Witzel's Sporting Goods is shown in Exhibit 19-3. The revenues of $80,000 represent total earnings for the firm over the past twelve months. Likewise, the expenses of $62,000 represent the total costs incurred over the past year. A net income of $18,000 was realized because revenues exceeded expenses. When expenses exceed revenues, the result is a net loss. In order to facilitate the business manager in making decisions, income statements as well as balance sheets are often prepared quarterly or monthly.

### REVENUES

Revenue is defined as the inflow of assets resulting from the sale of merchandise or services. For example, if a firm sells merchandise to a customer for cash, the sale increases the asset Cash. If the sale is made on credit, the asset increased is Accounts Receivable. The primary source of revenue for a retailer, wholesaler, or manufacturer is sales of the firm's products. The primary source of revenue for a professional person such as a doctor, lawyer, C.P.A., or architect is providing services to clients. Other sources of revenue include gains on the sale of assets other than merchandise inventory, interest or dividends on investments, and sale of by-products. Investments of additional money in the firm by the owner or money borrowed from a bank does not qualify as revenue.

### EXPENSES

Expenses represent the cost of goods or services used in the process of earning revenue during the period. For example, Witzel's Sporting Goods sold merchandise costing $40,000 to generate total sales for the year of $80,000, resulting in a gross profit on sales of $40,000. The difference between sales and cost of goods sold is referred to as *gross profit* because operating expenses need to be subtracted from it.

## EXHIBIT 19-3

*Witzel's Sporting Goods*
*Income Statement*
*For the Year Ended December 31, 19X1*

| | | | |
|---|---|---:|---:|
| Revenue from sales | | | |
| Sales | | | $80,000 |
| Cost of merchandise sold | | | |
| Merchandise inventory, January 1, 19X1 | | $      0 | |
| Purchase | | 55,000 | |
| Merchandise available for sale | | 55,000 | |
| Less merchandise inventory, Dec. 31, 19X1 | | 15,000 | |
| Cost of merchandise sold | | | 40,000 |
| Gross profit on sales | | | $40,000 |
| Operating expenses | | | |
| Selling expenses | | | |
| Sales salaries and wages | $9,000 | | |
| Advertising | 1,000 | | |
| Store supplies | 100 | | |
| Total selling expenses | | 10,100 | |
| Administrative expenses | | | |
| Office salaries | 6,000 | | |
| Insurance expense | 1,000 | | |
| Office supplies | 100 | | |
| Heat, light, and power | 700 | | |
| Property taxes | 2,000 | | |
| Interest | 2,100 | | |
| Total administrative expenses | | 11,900 | |
| Total operating expenses | | | 22,000 |
| Net income | | | $18,000 |

Operating expenses are often classified into two subheadings: selling expenses and administrative expenses. Selling expenses include those associated with the selling function of the store, such as sales salaries, store supplies, and advertising. Total selling expenses for Witzel's amounted to $10,100. Administrative expenses include those associated with the administrative function of the store, such as office salaries, office supplies, and insurance. Total administrative expenses (also commonly called *general expenses*) for Witzel's amounted to $11,900. Total operating expenses therefore amounted to $22,000 ($10,100 + $11,900).

The value in preparing financial statements lies in the information which may be obtained from them which will serve as a basis for decision making either by management or outsiders. Therefore, we will next turn our attention to two areas: those individuals or groups of individuals who use information contained in the financial statements of a business organization and some basic tools of statement analysis.

## Users of Accounting Information

Managers of a business enterprise rely upon timely reports provided by the accountant in making decisions which affect the very survival of the firm. Quarterly and monthly income statements and balance sheets are prepared to provide the business manager with a current summary of the firm's earnings and its ability to meet current obligations.

Bankers and other lenders require financial reports in order to determine the ability of the firm to meet its financial obligations as they mature. Credit-granting institutions are interested in the earning record of the firm, the value of its total assets, and the total amount of liabilities currently outstanding (unpaid). Because securing adequate credit is most important in the operation of a business, it is vital that adequate financial reports be prepared to serve the needs of current and potential lenders.

For those business establishments organized as corporations, financial reports are needed to provide information both for present and potential stockholders. Current and past dividends paid by the firm, its earnings trend, the comparison of its earnings with other firms in the same industry, the amount spent for new product development, and plant acquisitions or mergers are types of information required by investors. By carefully examining financial reports of different firms, the investor is better able to select that firm which will satisfy his particular needs. Furthermore, once he makes his investment, the investor continues to utilize accounting data to determine the desirability of investing additional money or perhaps of withdrawing all or a portion of the investment.

The computation and reporting of taxable income is required by federal, state, and local governments. In accordance with the Internal Revenue Code, taxable income from sole proprietorships and partnerships must be reported on Form 1040. Income of a corporation must be reported on Form 1120. In addition to the federal tax, state and local governmental units may require the filing of special reports relating to property taxes, sales taxes, or payroll taxes, just to mention a few. Many federal regulatory agencies, such as the Federal Power Commission and the Interstate Commerce Commission, require reports based upon accounting data.

Other users of accounting information include employees, customers, unions, financial advisors, lawyers, financial press and reporting agencies, trade associations, and the stock exchange.

## Tools of Statement Analysis

These users of accounting data need to understand some of the more important analytical tools used to get the necessary information from the financial statements.

## INTRASTATEMENT RATIOS

### BALANCE SHEET RATIOS

The two balance sheet ratios examined are the current ratio and the ratio of owners' equity to total equity. Each of these ratios is computed by using information included in the Witzel's Sporting Goods balance sheet.

*Current Ratio* (Current assets/Current liabilities).    The current ratio is one of the primary ratios which is carefully examined by bankers, management, and others interested in analyzing the firm's financial position. This ratio is also referred to as the *working capital ratio* because working capital represents the excess of current assets over current liabilities. The working capital of the Witzel's Sporting Goods store amounts to $26,000:

| | |
|---|---|
| Current assets | $53,000 |
| Current liabilities | 27,000 |
| Working capital | $26,000 |

The current ratio is computed by dividing current assets of $53,000 by current liabilities of $27,000, which gives 2.30 to 1. This means that Witzel's Sporting Goods has $2.30 of current assets for each $1.00 of current liabilities.

The higher the firm's current ratio, the greater is the firm's ability to pay its debts as they mature, to take advantage of purchase discounts offered by suppliers, and to stimulate sales by allowing sales discounts to customers. Although some firms require greater amounts of working capital than others, the general feeling among bankers and other lenders is that a current ratio of 2.0 to 1.0 is adequate.

Maintaining a good current ratio is important to the financial well-being of a firm. Nevertheless, the business manager must be careful to avoid overdoing it. A firm with more working capital than it needs to operate with should consider investing the excess in marketable securities or other assets which will earn a return for the business.

*Ratio of Owners' Equity to Total Equity* (Owners' equity/Total capital).    The ratio of owners' equity to total equity for Witzel's Sporting Goods is determined by dividing owners' equity of $58,000 by total equity of $118,000, which amounts to 49.2 percent. This ratio shows the proportion of the total equity of the firm supplied by the owner. This means then that 50.8 percent (100 percent minus 49.2 percent) of the total equity was provided by the store's creditors. In other words, of every $1.00 invested in the sporting goods store, $0.49 is provided by the owner and $0.51 is provided by creditors.

From the viewpoint of the creditor, the ratio of owners' equity to total capital reflects the amount of protection available to the firm's creditors. Consequently, the higher the ratio the greater the security afforded the creditors. On the other hand, from the viewpoint of an owner, it is possible that the ratio may be too high. Whenever a firm can earn a return on investment greater than the interest charged by the lender, it is advantageous to borrow. For example, if the business manager borrows money at 6 percent and then invests the money in his business and earns a return of 8 percent, he is increasing his profits. This techique is referred to as *trading on equity* and is discussed in more detail in chapter 4.

## INCOME STATEMENT RATIOS

The analytic tools based solely on information contained in the income statement are examined below. These include the operating ratio and the number of times interest expense earned.

*Operating Ratio* (Operating expenses/Sales). The operating ratio relates revenues to expenses. The operating ratio for Witzel's Sporting Goods is determined as follows: $62,000/$80,000 = 77.5 percent. This means that for every $1.00 of sales realized by the Witzel's Sporting Goods store, $0.775 is spent on operating expenses. Therefore, if a firm had an operating ratio of 100 percent, it would not be making a profit. For those firms which operate with a high operating ratio, it is of utmost importance that the business manager continuously be alert for possible savings in operating costs. Because of competition from other firms in the same business, it is usually difficult to raise selling prices without suffering a loss in sales.

*Times Interest Expense Earned* ((Net income + Interest expense)/Interest expense). Creditors who provide a business with long-term funds are interested in the ability of the firm to make interest payments over the term of the loan plus the principal when the loan matures. One means of measuring this ability is to compute the number of times interest expense was earned during a fiscal year. This computation is illustrated below by using information included in the income statement of Witzel's Sporting Goods:

$$\frac{\$18,000 + \$2,100}{\$2,100} = \frac{\$20,100}{\$2,100} = 9.57$$

Since interest expense is deducted in arriving at net income on the income statement, it is necessary to add back interest expense in order to obtain a true measure. If a firm continuously earns sufficient profit to cover its interest expense a minimum of two times each year, long-term creditors are considered to have a secure investment. Using a ratio of 2.0 as a benchmark, the creditors of Witzel's appear to have little to worry about with a ratio of 9.57.

## INTERSTATEMENT RATIOS

There are a number of ratios which can be computed based upon information obtained from the balance sheet and the income statement. Three interstatement ratios which are commonly used by analysts are rate of return on total assets, rate of return on owners' equity, and turnover of merchandise inventory.

*Rate of Return on Total Assets* ((Net income + Interest expense)/Total assets). The rate of return on total assets for Witzel's Sporting Goods store is 17.0 percent. This is determined by dividing the net income of $18,000 plus interest expense of $2,100 by the total assets of $118,000. In order to get a more accurate measure of the return on total assets, it is necessary to add back interest paid creditors because it represents a return for the assets they have provided the firm. The figure of 17.0 percent reflects how well assets were employed in generating a return for Mr. Witzel. In large corporations, stockholders consider this ratio as one tool of measuring how well management is performing its job. Other things being equal, the higher the ratio, the better the job.

Observe that Mr. Witzel is successfully trading on equity. The rate of return of 17.0 percent exceeds the interest rate of 8 percent on the mortgage payable of $33,000. Therefore, by borrowing money, Mr. Witzel is able to increase the profits of the sporting goods store.

*Rate of Return on Owners' Equity* (Net income/Owners' equity). One of the primary reasons for investing money in a business venture is the expectation of earning a return on the investment. To determine the return on Mr. Witzel's investment he simply divides the net income of $18,000 by owners' equity of $58,000. The result is a return on owners' equity of 31 percent. If Mr. Witzel is satisfied with his return, he will most likely continue his present operation. On the other hand, if he is aware of alternative investments which will generate greater rewards, he may elect to sell the sporting goods store and invest elsewhere.

*Turnover of Merchandise Inventory* (Cost of goods sold/Merchandise inventory). A turnover may be defined as the number of times one asset is converted into another asset during the year. When an asset such as merchandise inventory is sold, it is converted sooner or later into cash. By converting inventory into cash frequently, the businessman is able to reduce the amount of capital needed to operate his business. Therefore, the business manager is interested in maintaining a high turnover of inventory, while at the same time providing good service to the firm's customers. The Witzel's Sporting Goods store turns its inventory over 2.67 times per year. This is arrived at by dividing cost of goods sold of $40,000 by merchandise inventory of $15,000. Because the turnover appears to be rather low for a sporting goods store, it may be that Mr. Witzel could reduce his inventory by eliminating slow-moving items. For example, if the inventory could be reduced to $10,000 without affecting sales, the turnover rate would increase from 2.67 to 4.0 times per year.

If the ending inventory (inventory at the date of the financial statements) is not representative of the normal inventory maintained during the year, an average of the beginning and ending inventory should be used in the turnover computation.

## INTERPRETATION OF OPERATING DATA

The ratios computed above are used to help understand the operations of the Witzel's Sporting Goods store. These same ratios are equally applicable to partnerships and corporations, whether large or small. In order to interpret these ratios, it is necessay to have some standards or guidelines which may be used as a basis for comparison. Without such a basis, a statement reader is unable to determine whether a particular ratio is average, above average, or below average.

One of the most useful means of interpreting the ratios of a company is to compare them with the same ratios of similar companies in the same industry. Information of this type can be computed from the financial statements which are included in the annual reports of large corporations whose stock is traded on the New York or American stock exchanges.

For smaller businesses, such as Witzel's Sporting Goods store, financial ratios and other statistics on sporting goods stores of similar size would probably be available through a trade association. Many industries have developed trade associations which compile a myriad of data on the financial operations of member firms. Using standards or average ratios as a guide, Mr. Witzel can more effectively interpret his financial situation. For example, if the statistics indicate that the average yearly inventory turnover is 6.2 for similar sporting goods stores, Mr. Witzel would conclude that some adjustments must be made to increase the present turnover of 2.67. Likewise, if the average rate of return on total assets for similar sporting goods stores is greater than 17.0 percent, Mr. Witzel would want to search for various ways of improving his return.

For those firms which do not belong to a national or local trade association, information is often available through such sources as Dun and Bradstreet.

TREND ANALYSIS

Anther technique available to the business manager is to compare ratios of one period with ratios of prior periods. Simply looking at a particular ratio does not tell much. However, by making comparisons, it is possible to determine which ratios represent a favorable trend and which ratios represent unfavorable trends. As an example, Witzel's Sporting Goods store earned 17.0 percent on total assets invested in the business during the year 19X1. In subsequent years, this ratio should again be computed in order to develop a trend over time. This trend would reflect one measure of Mr. Witzel's performance in managing the store. The following examples taken from the Wall Street Journal illustrate two types of trend analysis:

> U. S. new-car sales hit 188,818 units in the Jan. 1–10 period, up 16.4 percent from a year earlier on a daily-rate basis but trailing the 1966 record.
> Xerox's net income climbed 17 percent last year to a record $249.5 million, while revenue rose 23 percent to $2.42 billion, also a high. Its chairman forecast "satisfactory performance" in 1973.[1]

These results for the Xerox Corporation indicate that both revenue and net income increased to a record high. Nevertheless, you cannot conclude that whenever there is an increase in sales or revenue, there will likewise be an increase in net income. In fact, there have been instances in which income has

---

1. *Wall Street Journal,* January 11, 1973, p. 1.

declined while sales increased. At Monsanto Co. of St. Louis, the nation's third largest chemical company, sales have been increasing but profits have been declining. Since the beginning of 1966, Monsanto's sales have continued to increase but its net income has started to decline. In fact, in 1970, while sales inched up to $1.97 billion, profits fell drastically to $77.9 million.[2] How is it possible for income to decline when sales are increasing? The answer is that the cost of operating the business, such as selling and administrative expenses and reasearch and development costs, jumped more than sales.

Although Monsanto is one of America's largest corporations, the same types of trends can take place in a small business such as Mr. Witzel's Sporting Goods store. In analyzing the operations of a company, it is not adequate to simply look at one trend such as sales and ignore other information which may be very important.

## Summary

Both the business manager and those outside the firm need information in order to make decisions regarding a variety of business matters. Much of this information is communicated to interested people through the balance sheet and the income statement. In order to understand the information contained in these two financial reports, it is helpful if statement readers have some knowledge concerning the fundamental accounting equation and the effects transactions and events have upon the equation.

The balance sheet, which is also called the statement of financial position, contains a summary of the firm's assets, liabilities, and owners' equity as of a particular date. Two balance sheet ratios, among others, which are used in analyzing a firm's financial position are the current ratio and the ratio of owners' equity to total equity. The income statement, also called the statement of earnings, reports the results of operations of a firm for a specified period of time. Two ratios which are based solely on information contained in the income statement are the operating ratio and the number of times interest expense earned. In addition, a number of ratios are computed by utilizing information from both the balance sheet and the income statement.

In order to interpret the answers provided by calculating a ratio properly, it is important that the statement reader have certain guidelines which may be used as a basis for comparison. Trend analysis provides additional insight into determining whether a given ratio is favorable or unfavorable.

## QUESTIONS

1. Discuss the information process in relation to the:
   (a) Production process
   (b) Distribution process

---

2. *Business Week,* November 4, 1972, p. 71.

(c)  Manpower process
(d)  Financial process
(e)  Management process

2. (a)  What is the fundamental accounting equation?
   (b)  What is the purpose for listing liabilities in the accounting equation before owners' equity?

3. Define the following terms and give two examples of each.
   (a)  Asset
   (b)  Liability
   (c)  Owners' equity
   (d)  Revenue
   (e)  Expense

4. Discuss the following concepts briefly.
   (a)  Entity concept
   (b)  Cost concept
   (c)  Matching concept

5. (a)  What does the balance sheet and the income statement show?
   (b)  What is the difference between the following:
       (1)  Current assets and fixed assets
       (2)  Current liability and long-term liability
       (3)  Owners' equity section of the balance sheet for a sole proprietorship and for a corporation

6. (a)  List five individuals or groups who utilize accounting information.
   (b)  What specific types of information are they interested in and why?

7. (a)  List six kinds of tools used for statement analysis purposes.
   (b)  Explain how each tool listed in part (a) is computed.

8. In order to properly interpret information calculated in various ratios, what types of guidelines should the businessman utilize?

9. (a)  Explain the meaning of the term *physical count*.
   (b)  Using the following information, compute the cost of goods sold for a retail store:

   | | |
   |---|---|
   | Ending merchandise inventory | $26,000 |
   | Cost of purchases during the year | 62,000 |
   | Beginning merchandise inventory | 20,000 |

10. What is the difference between intrastatement ratios and interstatement ratios?

## Incident 19–1

Bev Jones decided to start a new jewelry store on January 1, 19X1. The store is to be operated as a sole proprietorship and is called Jones Jewelry. The transactions listed below represent those which Ms. Jones entered into during the course of the year.
(a) Ms. Jones deposited $30,000 in a checking account in the name of Jones Jewelry.

**EXHIBIT 19–4**
*Jones Jewelry*
*Summary of Transactions*
*Year 19X1*

| | Assets | | | | | = | Liabilities + Owners' Equity | | |
| --- | --- | --- | --- | --- | --- | --- | --- | --- | --- |
| | | *Accounts* | *Merchandise* | | | | *Accounts* | *Mortgage* | *Bev Jones* |
| *Transactions* | *Cash* | + *Receivable* | + *Inventory* | + *Land* | + *Building* | = | *Payable* | + *Payable* | + *Owners' Equity* |

(b) Land was acquired for $4,000 cash.
(c) A building was purchased for $27,000. Mrs. Jones paid 10 percent down and assumed a 20-year mortgage note for the remainder.
(d) During the year $60,000 of merchandise was purchased on account.
(e) Sales for the year amounted to $90,000. One-third of the sales were on account and the remainder were cash sales.
(f) At the end of the year, she took a physical count of the merchandise inventory on hand and determined the total cost of goods sold to be $15,000.
(g) $20,000 was received from customers who previously purchased merchandise on account.
(h) Ms. Jones paid cash for the following selling and administrative expenses:

| | |
|---|---:|
| Salaries and wages | $12,000 |
| Advertising | 750 |
| Insurance | 600 |
| Supplies | 400 |
| Heat, light and power | 500 |
| Property taxes | 1,500 |
| Interest Expense | 2,000 |
| Total | $17,750 |

(1) In order to show the effect of each transaction upon the accounting equation, complete Exhibit 19–4 in a manner similar to Exhibit 19–1 (page 324).
(2) Based upon the information summarized in your table for question (1), construct a balance sheet and an income statement for Jones Jewelry.
(3) Based upon information included in the financial statements for Jones Jewelry, compute the following ratios:
  (a) The current ratio
  (b) The ratio of owners' equity to total equity
  (c) The operating ratio
  (d) Times interest expense earned
  (e) Rate of return on total assets
  (f) Rate of return on owners' equity
  (g) Turnover of merchandise inventory

# 20

# Internal Information Process—
# Managerial Accounting

In Chapter 19 emphasis was placed upon financial accounting. In this chapter the emphasis is on managerial accounting. Managerial accounting is a method for the accumulation of information for two major purposes: determining the cost of producing a product and planning and controlling operations. Before these two purposes are discussed in some detail the nature of managerial accounting will be explored by being contrasted with financial accounting.

### Managerial Accounting Versus Financial Accounting

These two terms (financial and managerial) simply indicate the different manners in which accounting information is utilized. Financial accounting is concerned with providing information primarily to outsiders who have a special interest in the firm. As indicated in Chapter 19, these outsiders include stockholders, lenders, suppliers, customers, unions, potential investors, and government. These outsiders are not concerned with information relating to the day-to-day operating aspects of a firm, but rather with information which reflects overall operating activities. This type of information is provided by financial reports such as the income statement and the balance sheet.

Managers of a business likewise require information which is provided in the financial statements. In addition, however, they need information which will assist them in planning and controlling the operating activities of the business. The manager plans for the future by establishing objectives and the methods by which they can be realized. The manager then controls operations by making certain that actual results are consistent with plans. The managerial accountant facilitates the planning function by participating with others in the preparation of standards and budgets. For example, a company foreman establishes the standard amount of time an employee should spend on producing a product or providing a service. The accountant then converts this quantity into dollars and cents by multiplying the standard time (established by the foreman) by the wage the employee receives, to determine the standard cost of labor going into each product or service produced. In similar fashion, the sales manager prepares a budget for the next fiscal year relating to the activities of the distribution process. The budget expresses the sales manager's objectives in financial or quantitative terms. Much of the information needed in preparing such a budget such as prior year's sales and expenses is provided by the accountants.

Once plans have been determined, the managerial accountant facilitates the control function through the preparation of performance reports. The performance report contains information on actual operating results. For example, a performance report could be developed to compare the actual amount of labor cost incurred for an employee to produce a product or provide a service with predetermined standard labor costs. Likewise, a performance report would show how well the actual results conformed to the budget established by the sales manager. Where there are differences between plans and actual results, the manager must take appropriate action to eliminate inconsistencies.

## Cost Determination

In order to determine the total cost of merchandise inventory the firm has on hand at any time during the year, it is necessary to know the cost of producing each unit. The balance sheet and the income statement cannot be prepared until the firm's ending merchandise inventory has been determined, because the ending merchandise inventory is an asset on the firm's balance sheet and is used in determining a firm's cost of goods sold on the income statement.

Determining the cost of a product being held for resale to others is a more difficult task for a manufacturer than it is for a retailer or a wholesaler. For example, if a retailer or a wholesaler wants to know the cost of acquiring a particular product, he simply refers to the purchase invoice which states the quantity purchased and the cost per unit.

However, a manufacturer does not acquire finished goods from others. Instead he purchases raw materials, labor, and overhead in order to produce a finished product. As a result, the manufacturer must utilize a more sophisticated cost accounting system in order to determine the cost of producing a particular product. For this reason, this discussion emphasizes the method by which the accountant accumulates the cost of materials, labor, and overhead in order to determine the cost of producing a particular product.

In the previous chapter financial information was accumulated on Witzel's Sporting Goods store which is owned and operated by John R. Witzel. Now assume that Witzel decides to expand his business venture by manufacturing baseball and softball bats on a small scale. Some of these bats will be sold to customers through his own retail store but the majority will be sold to wholesalers in the southern part of Michigan. In order to operate the factory effectively, Mr. Witzel has hired a production manager, a distribution manager, and an accountant to handle financial and information matters.

## JOB ORDER COST SYSTEM

Because of the various types of bats which Witzel Manufacturing Co. produces, the firm's accountant has elected to use a job order cost system as a means of determining the cost of manufacturing each job lot of ball bats. A job lot is a quantity of identical items. For example, a job lot would be 500 28-inch baseball bats or 500 32-inch soft ball bats. Each of these job lots is sufficiently different to be identified as a separate product. Under a job order cost system, the costs of raw material, direct labor, and factory overhead are accumulated on a job cost sheet for each particular job lot worked on.

To illustrate the manner in which a job order cost system is used, assume that a production worker is starting a new job lot consisting of 480 32-inch baseball bats. Three types of manufacturing costs will be incurred in the production of these bats:

(1) Direct materials
(2) Direct labor
(3) Manufacturing overhead

Each of these three costs will be discussed.

### DIRECT MATERIALS

Direct materials cost represents the cost of those materials which are incorporated into the product being manufactured. In the manufacturing of ball bats, the direct materials consist of wood, varnish or paint to protect the wood, and perhaps tape for the handle. When a company purchases raw materials to be used in the manufacturing of a product, these materials are first placed in a storeroom under the custody of a storekeeper. It is the storekeeper's responsibility to keep proper count of the materials on hand and to issue materials only upon receipt of a signed materials requisition form. A copy of such a form is presented in Exhibit 20–1.

EXHIBIT 20–1

| Materials Requisition | | | |
|---|---|---|---|
| Job. No._____17_____     Requisition No._____35_____<br>Department___Production___     Date___March 15, 19X1___<br>Authorized by_____ | | | |
| Description | Quantity | Unit cost | Amount |
| Wood | 80 cubic feet | $3.80 per cu. ft. | $304.00<br>Total $304.00 |
| Person Issuing___Sam Jones___     Person Receiving_Ed Sutton_ | | | |

Before issuing the necessary materials, the storekeeper checks to make certain that the materials requisition form is signed by an individual with proper authority, such as a plant foreman or the plant superintendent. Upon issuance of the material, one copy of the material requisition form is sent to the accounting department where it is recorded on a job cost sheet.

## DIRECT LABOR

Direct labor costs represent the wages of those workers who work directly on the product being manufactured. For example, in the Witzel Manufacturing Co., the wages of those employees who work with machines and tools needed to shape lumber into ball bats are referred to as direct labor costs. In order to determine how much time each employee spends on a particular job lot, it is necessary that a labor time ticket be filled out. For example, if an employee of the Witzel Manufacturing Co. worked on two separate job lots (lots number 16 and 17) during the day, the labor time ticket would appear as in Exhibit 20–2.

A copy of each job ticket, like the material requisition form, is sent to the accounting department at the end of each work day. This information is recorded by someone in the accounting department on a job cost sheet.

## MANUFACTURING OVERHEAD

The third type of manufacturing cost is manufacturing overhead. Overhead includes all production costs other than direct material and direct labor. For the Witzel Manufacturing Co. some of the overhead costs would be salaries of the plant foreman, raw materials storekeeper, and plant janitor; depreciation on the plant and equipment; utilities such as water, gas, and electricity; and property taxes on the factory building. Manufacturing overhead differs from direct labor and direct materials in that these costs cannot be directly associated with the products being produced. For example, when a company

EXHIBIT 20–2

| | | | | | |
|---|---|---|---|---|---|
| | | Work Ticket | | | |
| Employee No. 3 | | | Work Ticket No. 6 | | |
| Employee Name Joe Brown | | | Date March 15, 19X1 | | |
| Description of Work cutting & sanding | | | | | |
| Department No. | | | | | |
| | | | Time | | |
| Start | Stop | Job number | Hours worked | Rate per hour | Labor cost |
| 8:00 AM | 12:00 PM | 16 | 4 | 3.00 | $12.00 |
| 1:00 PM | 5:00 PM | 17 | 4 | 3.00 | $12.00 |
| Employee | | | Foreman | | |

incurs $1,000 in depreciation expenses on its factory equipment for a year, how much of this depreciation should be allocated to each product or job lot produced during the year? How much of the foreman's yearly salary of $14,000 should be charged to each product or job lot produced during the year? For direct material and direct labor this is not a difficult determination to make. That is, the material and the labor can be directly traced to the job lot being produced by simply examining the material requisition forms and the time tickets. However, overhead costs are indirect. There is no direct relationship between the products being produced and the overhead costs incurred. A firm's total overhead costs apply to all job lots or products that are produced during the year.

In order to resolve this dilemma, accountants use a predetermined overhead rate to allocate overhead to the products produced during the year. A predetermined overhead rate relates total manufacturing overhead costs to another cost factor which can be directly associated to the product being produced. Such cost factors as direct labor cost, direct labor hours, and machine hours are common examples.

In order to determine an overhead rate, three steps must be followed at the beginning of the firm's fiscal year:

(1) Estimate the amount of overhead costs expected to be incurred. This is often referred to as budgeted overhead.

(2) Establish the basis used to allocate the overhead costs to each product produced during the year (such as direct labor costs). This is referred to as the overhead application base.

(3) Calculate the overhead rate by dividing the budgeted overhead by the overhead application base (2).

To illustrate the computation of a predetermined overhead rate for the Witzel Manufacturing Co., assume the following information was compiled on January 1, the beginning of the firm's fiscal year:

Step No. 1
Budgeted overhead:

| | |
|---|---:|
| Foreman's salary | $14,000 |
| Janitorial service | 6,000 |
| Depreciation of building and equipment | 11,000 |
| Property taxes on building and equipment | 5,000 |
| Insurance on building and equipment | 2,000 |
| Utilities | 4,000 |
| Repairs and maintenance | 8,000 |
| Total | $50,000 |

The Witzel Manufacturing Co. uses as its overhead application base total direct labor cost for the fiscal year. These costs were estimated by the firm's accountant and the plant foreman to amount to approximately $40,000 during the new fiscal year.

Step No. 2
Overhead application base:            $40,000

The firm's overhead rate, expressed as a percentage, is computed in the following manner:

Step No. 3
Overhead application rate:

$$\frac{\text{Budgeted overhead}}{\text{Overhead application base}} = \frac{\$50,000}{\$40,000} \text{ or } 125\%$$

This percentage may be interpreted to mean that for every $1.00 of direct labor cost spent in producing a job lot of ball bats, overhead in the amount of $1.25 ($1.00 $\times$ 125%) will be allocated to that particular job lot of ball bats.

When a particular product or job lot is completed, the accounting department uses the information provided on the material requisition form, the labor time ticket, and the predetermined overhead rate to determine the total cost of producing a specific product or job lot. This information is summarized on a job cost sheet such as the one illustrated in Exhibit 20–3 for the Witzel Manufacturing Co.

If the accountant for the Witzel Manufacturing Co. prepares quarterly (every three month) financial statements, then the cost of the 480 baseball bats completed on job number 17 (see Exhibit 20–3) would be included as a part of the firm's ending inventory on March 31, 19X1 (assuming the bats were not sold). The important point is that accumulation of actual costs for raw materials, labor, and overhead is vital if the accountant is to determine the cost of the firm's inventory. Although the accountant accumulates these costs, it is necessary that factory workers fill out time tickets, storekeepers issue raw material requisition forms, and overhead application rates be determined with the help of foremen and others. As previously indicated, the

EXHIBIT 20–3

*Job Cost Sheet*

Job description_____ 480 32″ baseball bats _____ Job No.____17____

Date Started_____ March 15 _____ Date Completed_____ March 20 _____

| Date | Materials | | Labor | | Overhead costs applied | | |
|---|---|---|---|---|---|---|---|
| | Requi-sition no. | Amount | Time ticket no. | Amount | Date | Rate | Amount |
| March 15 | 35 | $304.00 | T-5 | $ 12.00 | | | |
| 16 | | | T-6 | 24.00 | | | |
| 17 | | | T-7 | 24.00 | 3/20 | 125% of | $165.00 |
| 18 | 36 | 359.00 | T-8 | 24.00 | | direct | |
| 19 | | | T-9 | 24.00 | | labor | |
| 20 | | | T-10 | 24.00 | | costs | |
| | | | | | Summary of costs | | |
| | | | | | Materials | | $663.00 |
| | | | | | Labor | | $132.00 |
| | | | | | Overhead | | $165.00 |
| | | | | | Total cost of the | | |
| | | | | | job lot | | $960.00 |
| | Total | $663.00 | Total | $132.00 | Cost per bat | | $ 2.00 |

statement of financial position (balance sheet) and the statement of earning power (income statement) cannot be prepared without first determining the cost of a firm's inventory. Since the income statement and the balance sheet are used frequently by management as well as outsiders for decision making, it is important that the managerial accountant develop a system for accumulating raw material, labor, and overhead costs to determine a firm's cost of goods sold and its ending inventory.

Actual costs are also accumulated for purposes of controlling operations. In fact, actual costs incurred by a firm represent a basic part of the control mechanism used by accountants in helping management control operations. Control and planning are the second area of the discussion on managerial accounting.

## Planning and Control

There are two basic tools which accountants use to provide a means of planning and controlling operations: standard costs and budgets. Each of these will be discussed.

## STANDARD COSTS

The discussion above explains how costs are accumulated as production of a particular product takes place. Although the information accumulated on raw material, direct labor, and manufacturing overhead provide management with a measure of the cost incurred in producing a product, management requires additional information in order to properly control operations. That is, managers are as much concerned with what costs should have been as they are with what costs actually were. In order to ascertain what costs should have been, it is necessary for the accounting department (in conjunction with the other departments) to develop standard costs for raw materials, labor, and overhead.

Standard costs are predetermined costs which should be attained under normal operating conditions. As such they represent a par which the firm shoots for in much the same fashion as a golfer shoots for par on a golf course. When comparing actual costs incurred against standard costs, any differences are referred to as *variances*. If the actual cost is smaller than the applicable standard cost, the difference is called a favorable variance. Conversely, if the actual cost is greater than the standard cost, the difference is called an unfavorable variance. Unfavorable variances are examined carefully by appropriate personnel in order to determine why the variance occurred and the necessary steps to take in order to accomplish the firm's objectives.

Standards can be determined for materials, labor, and overhead which can then be utilized to enable management to control operations more effectively.

## MATERIALS

Material standards are divided into two types: material quantity standards and material price standards. Engineering studies or simply prior experience are often the means for determining the standard amount of raw materials which should be required to manufacture a product. The standard price to be paid for the raw materials which enter into the manufacturing of a product could be established by the purchasing agent with approval from top management.

If the actual quantity of materials used in manufacturing a product or providing a service exceeds the standard quantity, the difference is referred to as a *quantity variance*. If the actual price paid to acquire the direct materials differs from the standard price, the difference is called a *price variance*. To illustrate the computation of these two variances, assume that the Witzel Manufacturing Co. receives an order from a wholesaler in Michigan for 360 32-inch softball bats. The Witzel Manufacturing Co. has established the following standards: the equivalent of one cubic foot of wood will produce three ball bats; the price per cubic foot is $3.75. According to the job cost sheet, the actual direct material cost incurred in producing the bats amounted to $532.00. The total direct materials variance therefore amounted to $82.00, computed as follows:

| | | |
|---|---|---|
| Actual: | 140 cubic feet × 3.80 | $532.00 |
| Standard: | 120 cubic feet × 3.75 | 450.00 |
| | Total direct materials variance | $ 82.00 |

The question which management must ask themselves at this point is why actual material costs exceeded standard material costs by $82.00? The answer to this question is provided by breaking up the total materials variance into two separate figures: material quantity variance and the material price variance. The method of computing each variance is shown below:

| | | |
|---|---|---|
| Material quantity variance | | |
| Actual quantity | 140 cubic feet | |
| Standard quantity | 120 cubic feet | |
| Difference—unfavorable | 20 cubic feet | |
| Times standard price per cu. ft. | $3.75 | |
| Unfavorable quantity variance | | $75.00 |
| Material price variance | | |
| Actual price | $3.80 per cu. ft. | |
| Standard price | 3.75 per cu. ft. | |
| Difference—unfavorable | $ .05 | |
| Times actual quantity of cu. feet | 140 | |
| Unfavorable price variance | | 7.00 |
| Total direct material cost variance—unfavorable | | $82.00 |

The next step for the accountant is to report the variance to the appropriate officials within the organization. For example, the unfavorable price variance of $7.00 should be reported to the purchasing agent, who should in turn take whatever action is deemed necessary to make sure it does not happen again. Because the purchasing agent paid a price greater than the standard established, consideration should be given to buying from another supplier or perhaps buying a substitute product which costs less.

The unfavorable quantity variance of $75.00 should be reported to the production foreman. This variance may have resulted from certain production workers who were careless in handling the material. On the other hand, the quality of the material used might not have been up to par, and therefore the purchasing agent would again be responsible.

## LABOR

Labor standards are also divided into two types: labor efficiency standards and labor rate standards. Labor efficiency standards relate to the amount of time required to manufacture a product or provide a service. This standard is often established by means of time and motion studies. Through these studies it is possible to determine the most efficient method of accomplishing a particular labor operation. For example, a time and motion study for the Witzel Manufacturing Co. would indicate the amount of time which should be spent on cutting, sanding, and painting each ball bat.

The standard labor rate the firm feels each employee should receive is not subject to as much control as the labor efficiency standard, because the wage rate, in most large companies, is determined by the union contract. In the case of smaller companies where employees do not have union representation, the wage rate is determined to a large extent by the law of supply and demand for workers in each community.

Should the actual amount of labor used in producing a good or providing a service differ from the standards, the firm will have a labor efficiency variance. Similarly, if the actual wage rate paid production workers differs from the standard wage rate, the firm will experience a labor price variance. Again, using the same illustration, assume that the standard time established to produce one ball bat is five minutes, or twleve bats per hour. The standard labor rate is $3.00 per hour. Furthermore, assume that the actual costs incurred (as reported in the job cost sheet) for direct labor in producing the 360 soft ball bats amounted to $110.25. The total direct labor variance therefore amounted to $20.25, computed as follows:

| | | |
|---|---|---|
| Actual: | 35 hours × 3.15 | $110.25 |
| Standard: | 30 hours × 3.00 | 90.00 |
| | Total direct labor variance | $ 20.25 |

The labor variance, like the material variance, may be broken up into two distinct variances: the labor efficiency variance and the labor rate variance. The method of computing each variance is illustrated below.

| | | |
|---|---|---|
| Labor efficiency variance | | |
| Actual time | 35 hours | |
| Standard time | 30 hours | |
| Variance—unfavorable | 5 hours | |
| Times standard wage rate | $3.00 | |
| Unfavorable efficiency variance | | $15.00 |
| Labor rate variance | | |
| Actual rate | $3.15 | |
| Standard rate | 3.00 | |
| Variance—unfavorable | .15 | |
| Times actual hours worked | 35 | |
| Unfavorable rate variance | | $ 5.25 |
| Total direct labor cost variance—unfavorable | | $20.25 |

In this case, the unfavorable efficiency variance may have occurred because of a number of factors. The machines used in the production process may have broken down and needed repair, the raw material may have been defective, or the production workers involved may have been inexperienced. Regardless of the reason, management should search for ways to implement improved operations and eliminate the unfavorable variance.

The unfavorable labor rate variance may also be the result of a number of factors. Perhaps one of the most common reasons for this variance is that the foreman may have used a more experienced worker (earning a higher hourly wage) than the job demanded.

## OVERHEAD

The third element which makes up the cost of manufacturing a product or providing a service is called manufacturing overhead. This cost, however, differs significantly from the direct labor costs and direct material costs in at least three respects. First, manufacturing overhead consists of a number of costs such as rent, insurance, depreciation, utilities, supervision, and so on. Second, although overhead is a significant cost in total, many of the individual costs which comprise overhead are rather small in dollar value compared to direct labor costs or direct material costs. Third, unlike direct material costs and direct labor costs, which can be directly associated with a particular product or job lot, overhead is an indirect cost. These costs cannot be traced directly to a particular product or job lot. Because of the differences in overhead costs, as compared to direct costs, it is necessary for accountants to develop some rather sophisticated techniques to control these costs. Rather than discussing these control measures in this text, we would encourage interested readers to refer to a principles of accounting textbook.

## TIMING OF PERFORMANCE REPORTS

The extent to which standards assist personnel within the firm in controlling operating activities depends largely upon the timing of performance reports. In order to be of maximum usefulness in controlling labor and material costs in particular, these reports should be issued daily to individuals responsible for these costs. In those firms which have access to computers, such reports are often issued hourly. To illustrate, if the actual amount of material used in producing a product exceeds the standards established by the firm, such a difference should be reported immediately or daily at the latest in order that the appropriate supervisor may take corrective action. Reporting such a variance weekly or monthly may result in extra costs which might otherwise have been avoided.

This discussion relates to the planning and controlling of only one segment of the business firm—production. However, the use of cost standards and interpretation of variances can be used for planning and control in all segments of business operations. It is not realistic to plan and control one process of business operations such as production and, at the same time, ignore other processes such as distribution.

For example, standards may be developed for order filling costs, such as warehousing, packing, and shipping. To illustrate, assume that the following standards have been developed for packing one carton of ball bats:

| | |
|---|---|
| Direct labor | $ .75 |
| Tape and string | .05 |
| Carton | .25 |
| Labels | .10 |
| Total per carton | $1.15 |

During the first week of March, 100 cartons of ball bats were packed for shipment to various buyers. Exhibit 20–4 represents a performance report for the first week in March. As is the case with production standards, the variances will be analyzed by appropriate personnel (such as the foreman in charge of packing) in order to determine the appropriate steps which should be taken.

EXHIBIT 20–4

*Packing Operation Performance Report*
*Week 1, March, 19X1*
*Cartons Packed—100*

| Item | Total standard cost | Actual cost | Variance |
|------|---------------------|-------------|----------|
| Direct labor | $ 75.00 | $ 90.00 | $15.00 unfavorable |
| Tape and string | 5.00 | 5.00 | -0- |
| Cartons | 25.00 | 30.00 | 5.00 unfavorable |
| Lables | 10.00 | 9.00 | 1.00 favorable |
| Totals | $115.00 | $134.00 | $19.00 unfavorable |

In the area of distribution costs, planning and control can be very effective when these costs are routine (such as those used in the illustration.) Other distribution costs which are not subject to standardization, such as product research and development costs or advertising costs, are more difficult to plan and control. Nevertheless, by working closely with distribution managers, accountants have developed more advanced techniques in order to help in controlling these costs. Those readers who have an interest in these techniques should consult textbooks in managerial accounting.

Another tool available to management in planning and controlling operations is the budget. The budget is one means whereby management can coordinate the activities of all processes of the business system. In the discussion which follows these aspects of budgets plus administering and preparing budgets will be covered.

## BUDGETING

Budgets are a part of our everyday lives. For example, most people try to live within their budgets. That is, they try not to spend more than they earn. This is not always easy for the simple reason that wants and desires are unlimited, whereas income is limited. Nevertheless, by following a budget, expenses can be better controlled. However, a budget is much more than simply a tool used to help minimize expenses. A budget, if properly utilized, forces you to think ahead and to plan goals or objectives. It also is a means of controlling activities. If actual results do not conform to plans, you are motivated to take corrective action in order to get back on course. For example, assume a salesman establishes the following plan of action for the month of June: fifteen calls per week on new customers or a total of sixty for the month; sell $700 of merchandise each week or $2,800 for the month; and keep traveling and entertainment expenses to $200 per week or $800 for the month. On June 15, the hypothetical salesman compares his actual results with the plans he established on June 1.

As a result of his performance, the salesman concludes that it will be necessary for him to work a ten-hour schedule each day, (rather than the usual

|                              | *Two weeks* | | |
|                              | *Original Plan* | *Actual Results* | *Variation* |
|------------------------------|-----------|------------|-----------------|
| Sales calls                  | 30        | 20         | 10 unfavorable  |
| Sales made                   | $1,400    | $1,100     | 300 unfavorable |
| Traveling and entertainment  | 400       | 325        | 75 favorable    |

eight) for the remainder of the month and improve his personal selling techniques. He also concludes that he can spend more on entertainment for his clients. This simple illustration emphasizes two objectives of budgeting: first, the budget forces the businessman to plan or establish the goals he wishes to achieve; second, by comparing actual results with predetermined goals, he can determine how well he is adhering to his goals. If actual results are not up to plan, he must take corrective action. By so doing, the businessman is better able to control his operations.

The benefits of budgeting for the small businessman are also available to the larger business firm. Furthermore, because larger business firms generally consist of a number of employees and departments, the use of a comprehensive or master budget helps management to coordinate its separate activities. A comprehensive budget is a financial plan for all of the operations of a business which is prepared in the form of forecasted financial statements. This master budget can be an important tool in helping management to operate the business as a system rather than as separate departments.

## COORDINATION AMONG DEPARTMENTS

In a business firm with separate departments it is important that the goals or objectives of each department are consistent with the goals of the firm. If the goal of the firm is to maximize profits, then each department should do its part in helping the firm to maximize profits. A common problem in business firms today is the tendency of each department head to think only of the problems his particular operation faces without consideration of the problems of other departments. For example, in establishing a budget for the production department, the production manager may plan to produce one million units of a particular product during the next fiscal year. However, the sales manager is convinced that his staff can only sell one-half million units during the next fiscal year. If the production manager does in fact go ahead and produce a million units, the result may be that the financial manager will find it necessary to borrow sufficient funds to build the necessary warehouses to store the excess production, or perhaps the excess production will have to be sold at reduced prices. This example points out a lack of coordination between departments which is so vital to the success of the firm as a whole. The production manager's department has done a masterful job by attaining the goals originally set. However, the firm has incurred additional costs because of the need to invest in an additional warehouse or sell products at reduced prices. As a result, the firm did not attain its goal of maximizing profits. Situations such as the one above are common in the business world, and even happen in industry-leading companies.

> Mrs. Handler (one of the original founders of the Mattel Corporation) concedes she was too bullish. "We geared up production that was too high for our sales," she says . . . Suddenly, toy departments were overstocked. The pipeline jammed, and Mattel found itself with a mounting inventory. The Company estimates that it and Topper were stuck with $25 million to $30 million of unsold racers; some sources say the amount was two or three times that. In any case, Mattel had to unload its inventory at distress prices over the next couple of years.[1]

In order to achieve coordination between departments, a budget committee is often formed, consisting of the managers of each department along with top-level management such as the president and vice-presidents. The budget committee in turn selects a budget officer who is responsible for implementing the budget. Because of the nature of the data which enter into the compilation of a budget, the budget officer is generally an accountant. However, it is important to realize that the accountant does not prepare the budget. As indicated above, each budget is prepared by the department to which it applies. When a department head prepares a budget which is later approved by the budget committee, he will be motivated to adhere to the budget because of his participation in its preparation. On the other hand, if the accountant prepared the budget for a particular department such as production, the production head might well conclude that the accountant does not understand what he's talking about, and consequently he might ignore the budget.

The primary role of the accountant is to convert, where necessary, the goals of the various departments into dollars and cents. For example, the production manager may establish a goal of producing 10,000 units of a product during the month of June. The accountant's job is to convert this physical quantity into money terms so that a production budget may be prepared. In addition, the accountant is responsible for preparing performance reports which are compared to the original budgets to measure compliance of actual results with plans.

## THE BUDGET COMMITTEE

Initially in the preparation of a comprehensive budget in the form of forecasted financial statements, each department manager must determine the goals for his particular department. Operating data relating to the ensuing fiscal year such as expected sales, units of production, raw material purchases, number of employees required, inflow of cash, and so on must be prepared by individual departments responsible for such data. In other words, the distribution manager prepares the sales budget, the production manager prepares the production budget, the financial manager prepares the cash budget, and so on.

---

1. *The Wall Street Journal,* June 20, 1973, p. 21.

The next step is to coordinate the goals of each department so that the goals of the firm as a whole will be realized. It is important during this step for the members of the budget committee to work together in ironing out the problems which the goals of one department may cause another department. For example, if the sales manager estimates that his department can sell twice as many products as the production department is presently capable of producing, consideration must be given to expanding production facilities. A decision of this nature must be carefully worked out by such individuals as the production manager, the financial manager, and the personnel manager. Expanding production will require additional employees as well as additional funds. By working out problems of this nature the budget committee plays an important part in developing individual budgets for each department which will serve the best interests of the firm.

By working together, each member on the budget committee is motivated to broaden his thinking. Each member is forced to recognize the goals of the firm as a whole and the role his department can play in achieving these goals. This requires that each department head think in terms of the way in which his department may utilize the strengths of other departments or assist in alleviating weaknesses of the other departments.

Once the individual budgets are constructed for each department, they are then brought together to form a master budget which represents the budget for the entire firm. Some of the individual budgets which comprise the master budget are the sales budget, production budget, cost of goods sold budget, and selling and administrative expense budget.

### SALES BUDGET

The sales budget is usually the first budget prepared, because information in other budgets such as the production budget will vary depending upon the number of units expected to be sold. The sales budget for the Witzel Manufacturing Co. is presented in Exhibit 20–5.

### EXHIBIT 20–5

*Witzel Manufacturing Co.*
*Sales Budget*
*For the month ending January 31, 19X1*

| Product | Unit sales volume | Unit selling price | Total sales |
|---|---|---|---|
| Softball bats | 2,000 | $6 | $12,000 |
| Baseball bats | 3,000 | $7 | 21,000 |
| Total sales | | | $33,000 |

The different sources of information used to estimate sales are explained in chapter 3. These include, among others, survey of potential buyers, market tests, expert opinions, data accumulated by private research firms, and data published by the government.

## PRODUCTION BUDGET

Once the sales budget is finalized, the production budget can be prepared. The number of units to be manufactured during the year depends upon two factors: the expected number of units to be sold and the levels of inventory at both the beginning and the end of the year. The formula for the required units of production is: units expected to be sold plus units in desired ending inventory minus units in beginning inventory. The production budget for the Witzel Manufacturing Co. appears in Exhibit 20–6. below.

### EXHIBIT 20–6

*Witzel Manufacturing Co.*
*Production Budget*
*For the month ending January 31, 19X1*

|  | Softball | Baseball |
|---|---|---|
| Ball bats required to meet expected sales | 2,000 | 3,000 |
| Desired ending inventory of ball bats, January 31, 19X1 | 300 | 450 |
| Total ball bats required | 2,300 | 3,450 |
| Ball bats beginning inventory January 1, 19X1 | 250 | 350 |
| Quantity of bats to be manufactured | 2,050 | 3,100 |

Once the quantity of units to be manufactured has been determined, the next step is the preparation of the direct materials budget, the direct labor budget, and the manufacturing overhead budgets. These budgets provide information on the expected cost of the units to be manufactured.

## COST OF GOODS SOLD BUDGET

By combining the total cost of units to be manufactured along with figures on beginning and ending inventories, a cost of goods sold budget can be prepared. An example of such a budget for the Witzel Manufacturing Co. is presented in Exhibit 20–7.

### EXHIBIT 20–7

*Witzel Manufacturing Co.*
*Cost of Goods Sold Budget*
*For the month ending January 31, 19X1*

| | |
|---|---|
| Beginning inventory of ball bats, January 1, 19X1 | $ 3,000 |
| Total manufacturing costs | 25,000 |
| Cost of ball bats available for sale | 28,000 |
| Less ending inventory of ball bats, January 31, 19X1 | 3,750 |
| Cost of goods sold | $24,250 |

## SELLING AND ADMINISTRATIVE EXPENSE BUDGET

The sales manager and the office manager are responsible for preparing budgets of the estimated expenses which will be incurred in their departments.

These expected costs are not only based upon expected sales but also upon expected wage increases for employees, increases in the cost of office supplies, and past experience. The selling and general expense budget for the Witzel Manufacturing Co. appears in Exhibit 20–8.

EXHIBIT 20–8

*Witzel Manufacturing Co.*
*Selling and Administrative Expense Budget*
*For the month ending January 31, 19X1*

| | | |
|---|---:|---:|
| Selling expenses | | |
|     Sales salary and commissions | $2,000 | |
|     Traveling and entertainment | 1,000 | |
|     Advertising | 1,000 | |
|     Depreciation of delivery equipment | 500 | |
|     Total selling expenses | | $4,500 |
| Administrative expenses | | |
|     Office salaries | $1,200 | |
|     Office supplies | 200 | |
|     Depreciation of office equipment | 250 | |
|     Insurance | 50 | |
|     Property taxes | 100 | |
|     Total administrative expenses | | $1,800 |
| Total operating expenses | | $6,300 |

Budgets are often called forecasted financial statements. Upon completion of the sales budget, the cost of goods sold budget, and the selling and administrative expense budget, the budget committee is in a position to prepare a budgeted income statement for the firm as a whole. The budgeted or forecasted income statement for the Witzel Manufacturing Co. is presented as the first column of figures in Exhibit 20–9.

In addition, preparation of a cash budget along with a plant and equipment budget will enable the budget committee to prepare a budgeted balance sheet for the firm. These two budgets—the budgeted income statement and the budgeted balance sheet—comprise what is commonly called the firm's master budget. Once it is finalized by the budget committee, the master budget is presented to the board of directors (in the case of a corporation) or other top-level executives for final approval.

## TIME PERIOD OF BUDGET REPORTS

Management must decide how far ahead to look in preparing a budget. Generally, budgets are prepared to conform to the firm's fiscal year. For example, if a business uses the calendar year as its twelve-month period, the budget will likewise cover the calendar year. However, in order to provide management with a means of comparing actual results with plans, the yearly budget is often broken up into monthly periods. Comparisons at the end of each month provide management with information that is valuable in determining whether or not the firm is on course in attaining its goals. In Exhibit 20–9 the actual

EXHIBIT 20–9

*Witzel Manufacturing Co.*
*Income Statement and Variations from the Budget*
*For the month ending January 31, 19X1*

| | Budget | Annual results | Variations |
|---|---|---|---|
| Sales (Exh. 20–5) | $33,000 | $34,000 | $+1,000 |
| Cost of goods sold (Exh. 20–7) | | | |
|   Beginning inventory, Jan. 1, 19X1 | 3,000 | 3,000 | None |
|   Total manufacturing costs | 25,000 | 26,000 | +1,000 |
|   Cost of goods available for sale | $28,000 | $29,000 | $+1,000 |
|   Ending inventory, Jan. 31, 19X1 | 3,750 | 3,800 | + 50 |
|     Cost of goods sold | $24,250 | $25,200 | $+ 950 |
| Gross profit | $ 8,750 | $ 8,800 | $+ 50 |
| Operating expenses (Exh. 20–8) | | | |
| Selling expenses | | | |
|   Sales salary and commissions | $ 2,000 | $ 2,200 | $+ 200 |
|   Traveling and entertainment | 1,000 | 750 | − 250 |
|   Advertising | 1,000 | 900 | − 100 |
|   Depreciation of delivery equipment | 500 | 500 | None |
|     Total selling expenses | $ 4,500 | $ 4,350 | $− 150 |
| Administrative expenses | | | |
|   Office salaries | $ 1,200 | $ 1,200 | $ None |
|   Office supplies | 200 | 225 | + 25 |
|   Depreciation of office equipment | 250 | 250 | None |
|   Insurance | 50 | 50 | None |
|   Property taxes | 100 | 100 | None |
|     Total administrative expenses | $ 1,800 | $ 1,825 | $+ 25 |
| Total operating expenses | $ 6,300 | $ 6,175 | $− 125 |
| Income from operations | $ 2,450 | $ 2,625 | $+ 175 |

results for January, when compared to the budgeted figures for January, reflect variations which are mostly favorable. Income from operations exceeded the firm's goal by $175. Through proper interpretation of those variations which are significant, management is in a position to take corrective action where necessary.

In addition to yearly, quarterly, or monthly budgets which are classified as short range, companies also prepare budgets covering three, five, or ten years into the future. These budgets, classified as long range, are used to plan and control plant equipment acquisitions and product changes.

## Summary

In addition to information contained in the financial statements, the manager needs information which will help him in making decisions which affect the day-to-day operating of a firm. Managerial accounting provides information for two basic purposes: (1) cost determination for valuing inventories and computing net income and (2) planning and controlling the various activities of the firm.

To determine the cost of manufacturing a product, a firm must develop a cost accounting system to record and accumulate the costs incurred for material, labor, and overhead. These costs are used to value a firm's ending inventory, which will appear as a current asset on the balance sheet and will also be used to compute the cost of goods sold on the income statement. In addition, the accumulation of actual costs is instrumental in order for management to control operations effectively.

Through the utilization of standard costs for labor, material, and overhead, the production process determines what costs should be incurred in manufacturing a product or providing a service. By comparing actual costs incurred with predetermined cost standards, management is able to determine which activities need correcting. Standard costs can also be utilized to plan and control distribution costs, manpower costs, and other areas which comprise the business system. In similar fashion, the use of budgets forces department managers to plan ahead by establishing certain goals they wish to achieve. The managerial accountant then accumulates actual costs incurred on performance reports which are compared to the budgeted figures. Any significant differences which are unfavorable are then brought to the attention of management. Through use of a comprehensive budget, the managerial accountant plays a role in helping management to not only plan and control operations for the firm as a whole, but also to coordinate the various processes which make up the business system.

## QUESTIONS

1. Distinguish financial accounting from managerial accounting.
2. Why is it necessary that the managerial accountant determine the cost of a firm's ending merchandise inventory?
3. (a) List the three types of costs which are incurred by a firm in producing a product. Define each type.
   (b) What is a job order cost system?
4. What three steps must be followed in determining a firm's predetermined overhead rate?
5. Is management only concerned with those costs which were actually incurred in producing a product or providing a service?
6. (a) Define *standard cost*.
   (b) Explain how standard costs are developed for direct materials and direct labor.
7. Explain the meaning of the terms *favorable variance* and *unfavorable variance*.
8. "The extent to which standards assist personnel within the firm in controlling operating activities depends to a large extent upon the timing of performance reports." Explain.

9. (a) How does a budget help top management to coordinate the activities of separate departments within a business system?
   (b) Should the managerial accountant prepare the budget for each process such as production or distribution? Explain.

10. (a) Define the meaning of the term *master budget.*
    (b) List four individual budgets which comprise the master budget.
    (c) Which of the individual budgets is prepared first? Explain.

11. How far ahead should management look in preparing a budget?

## Incident 20–1

A company has established the following standard costs for material and labor to produce one unit of its finished product:

| | |
|---|---|
| Materials (4 units at $1.50 per unit) | $6.00 |
| Direct labor (2 hours at $3.00 per hour) | $6.00 |

During the month of January, the company produced 1000 units of finished product and incurred the following costs:

Materials (4200 units at $1.60 per units)
Direct labor (1900 hours at $3.10 per hour)

(1) Isolate the material and labor variances into price and quantity variances.
(2) For each variance computed in (1), explain to whom the variance should be reported in the firm and why.

## Incident 20–2

(1) The ABC Manufacturing Co. produces briefcases. Using the information given below, prepare a sales budget, a production budget, and a cost of goods sold budget for the month of January.

| | |
|---|---|
| Expected units to be sold in January | $ 2,500 |
| Unit's selling price | $ 8 |
| Desired ending inventory at Jan. 31 | 250 units |
| Beginning inventory at Jan. 1 | 200 units |
| Cost of units in beginning inventory | $ 1,000 |
| Cost of units in ending inventory | $ 1,250 |
| Total manufacturing costs incurred during January | $12,750 |

(2) Using the information prepared in (1), prepare a budgeted income statement for the month of January. Assume that total selling expenses amounted to $2,000 and total administrative expenses amounted to $1,500.

# 21

# Research:
# Generating Additional
# Information

The manager makes decisions or solves problems in many areas where financial and accounting information is necessary. However, decisions must be made in other areas, where financial and accounting information is of little value. Examples of such problems or decision areas would include: How can employee absenteeism be reduced? What is my product's image? How can I improve production efficiency? Is my advertising really effective? How are conditions changing in my market? How can my business stay ahead of competition with new products?

In fact, three of the processes which are included in every business system pose many problems for which accounting and financial information cannot be used. The three are the production, distribution, and manpower processes. In addition to these three processes, if the business system is to be adaptive in a changing environment, information concerning business conditions on both a local and national basis must be obtained and analyzed. The problem of being competitive in a changing environment can only be solved with information on the nature of conditions the businessman will face in the future.

In this chapter, the concept of research will be explored. Research is the way the manager generates the information to help solve many of his competitive adaptation, production, distribution, and manpower problems. After discussing the concept of research, its application to these four problem areas will be discussed. Accounting and financial information is good for solving accounting and financial problems. Research, on the other hand, is the way information is gathered to help the manager solve a multitude of other problems he faces. In other words, relying on accounting and financial information will only help solve some of the problems facing the manager of a business system.

## Research and Business

At first glance the term *research* might cause images of the scientist in the laboratory. Probably very few people associate the term *research* with business or managers. In fact very few people think of managers or businessmen as researchers. Yet what does a researcher do? In general, researchers obtain facts and information and interpret these data. Those involved in cancer research, for example, gather facts and information under various conditions and experiments until a conclusion is reached. When you "research" a topic for a term paper or class project, you gather and interpret facts and information. And the manager also gathers and interprets facts and information when he, for example, forecasts future business conditions.

There are many types or variations of research. The scientist is involved in pure exploratory research. He is looking for new ideas or relationships. Unlike the scientist, the manager does very little pure research. Most business research carried on by managers could be classified as *descriptive research*. Descriptive research attempts to obtain a complete and accurate description of an event or situation. For example, answers to the following types of questions require descriptive research: how many of the business' consumers are over forty years old? What is the average life of our product? What volume of sales did each of our competitors do last year? How do our employees feel about joining a union? Are employees in general dissatisfied with their jobs? Does the number of faulty products produced increase or decrease on certain days of the week? How many people see our advertisement? To answer these questions and others requires research or information. Based upon this descriptive information, or descriptive research, the manager makes decisions on how things should be done; he solves problems. For example, describing or obtaining information on where most of a business' consumers live will have a definite impact on certain problems that must be solved in designing the business' distribution process. Or a description of employee attitudes will have an effect on such elements of employment as wages, hours, and working conditions.

How a manager goes about gathering and interpreting information will definitely have an effect on the course of action he takes. If the information is incomplete, solutions or suggestions based upon this information will be weak. In other words, how well a business or manager does descriptive research will determine its value in helping the manager make complete decisions. Basically, any kind of research can either be unsystematic or systematic in nature.

Unsystematic research is sporadic, incomplete, or biased. For example, if you were asked to research the topic of "unions" and you only read one article written by the head of the Teamsters, it would have to qualify as unsystematic research. If the manager notices sales dropping and concludes, based upon a conversation with one customer, that the product's package is the cause, he also has conducted unsystematic research. In both cases, information has been gathered and interpreted, yet the information is incomplete and biased.

Systematic research, on the other hand, is thorough, rational, and objective. All information pertaining to a point or problem is sought and objectively interpreted. In the physical sciences (chemistry, biology, physics) research is more often than not systematic. The sciences have a special name for systematic research: the scientific approach. Business research, however, usually is nonscientific in nature. Most business research, which has been classified as descriptive research, cannot in fact, be scientific due to the nature of the information managers need. Business information is not as exact as that with which the physical sciences deal. The reasons sales decrease or employees quit can be varied, with none clear or orderly. For example, ten employees may quit because of pay, family troubles, better job offers, troubles with fellow workers, just for a change, and so on. Exactly which reasons or their relative importance to one particular employee in his decision to quit may be very hard to determine. Yet because business descriptive research cannot be scientific is no excuse for it being unsystematic. Decisions based upon poor quality, biased, or incomplete information result in either an inaccurate reading of the situation as it exists, more problems, or a failure to solve the original problem. This discussion, then, will emphasize systematic rather than unsystematic business research.

### Systematic-Descriptive Business Research

Three factors affect how systematic the business research will be:
(1) Objectivity of the investigator
(2) Accuracy of the information-gathering device
(3) Degree to which the research is exhaustive

## OBJECTIVITY OF THE INVESTIGATOR

The manager, to achieve objectivity, should always strive to eliminate his own personal bias. The ideal would be to become an impartial observer gathering and interpreting facts and information. The impartial observer bases his judgments on facts, not on notions or intuitions. This is difficult because the manager is not an impartial outsider, but lives within the business system. He has a stake in what happens, which can easily cause him to become subjective in his research efforts. Subjectivity may cause certain information to go unexamined because "I know what the answer will be," or other information to be misinterpreted because "My experience tells me that just can't be true."

Business research constantly presents the opportunity for subjectivity. The manager must always be aware of this and force himself to look at things objectively. One very simple way to do so is to ask the following question: "If a stranger were to research this area, would he have gathered different information or interpreted the present information in a different way?"

## ACCURACY OF THE INFORMATION-GATHERING DEVICE

Probably the main reasons for worrying about objectivity in business research is the lack of accurate information-gathering devices. In fact, one thing that distinguishes research in the physical sciences from research in business is the lack of accurate information-gathering devices. For example, contrast the accuracy of the information obtained from measuring electronically the number of heart beats per minute with that obtained in determining how employees feel about their jobs. Most of the information obtained through business research relates to opinions, attitudes, or performance figures. Information-gathering devices are not refined enough to measure a person's opinions or attitudes accurately. This appears to be a limitation business researchers have to live with. Realizing this limitation, care should be taken to choose the most accurate information-gathering device available. The business researcher has two choices in gathering descriptive information, using already published information, or collecting information via questionnaires, interviews, or observations. Depending on the circumstances, one method will be more accurate than the other.

## GATHERING ALREADY PUBLISHED INFORMATION

There is a wealth of published information available to the manager which is usually free. In this context the amount of information gathered by the manager is only limited by his awareness of sources.

*Census of the United States.* There are six different censuses made by the Bureau of the Census. Each should be of some interest to the manager doing descriptive research. The *Census of Population* is made every ten years; the last one was in 1970. This census provides a count of all individuals in the U.S. by state, county, city, and metropolitan area. In addition, sociological and economic characteristics such as age, sex, race, citizenship, education, family status, occupation, employment status, and income are presented. The *Census of Housing* is made with the census of population but is based upon a count of dwelling units. Information includes number of occupied and unoccupied dwellings, race of occupant, year built, rent paid, number of rooms, value, and type of structure. The *Census of Business* consists of censuses of wholesaling, retailing, and service trades. For each type of business, information on kinds of businesses, the functions they perform, sales volume, number of stores, sales by commodity, number of establishments, employment, and legal form of organization is provided. This information is broken down for each county and for larger cities. The *Census of Manufacturers* furnishes information on manufacturers: number of establishments, quantity of specific products produced, value of products produced, cost of materials and equipment, and wages paid. This census provides information on all the major industries in the U.S. The *Census of Agriculture* gathers various information about farms and farm operations in the U.S. The *Census of Minerals* provides information on the mineral industry, including fuels, metallic ores, stone, sand and gravel, and clay.

*Registration Information* is available on a wide range of subjects, such as births, deaths, marriages, unemployment, automobile registrations, and school enrollments.

*Summary Volumes of Information.*   There are a number of publications which summarize information from many sources. Examples would include:

1. *Statistical Abstracts of the United States.* These include information on most industrial, social, political, and economic organizations of the United States.

2. *Survey of Current Business.* This is a monthly, comprehensive source of much data covering economic and industrial activity in the United States.

3. *Monthly Labor Review* and *Handbook of Labor Statistics.* Information on employment, wages, and labor turnover is presented in these two publications.

4. *Federal Reserve Bulletin.* Information on banking, retailing, consumer prices, consumer credit, and national income is presented in this publication.

Published information of this sort has many applications to the business situation, some of which will be discussed later in this chapter. The basic concern now, however, is with the accuracy of published information. All published information has been collected by someone. Before using this information, the manager should evaluate the circumstances under which it was collected. Just because it is printed does not mean that it is accurate. The organization publishing the information is a good indication of its accuracy. The Bureau of the Census, for example, has a large amount of money and people available to assure accurate information collection. Other smaller sources may be less accurate in their reporting procedures.

In addition to information which others publish, the manager has various information on record which might be useful in solving a problem or evaluating a situation. This would include such information as salesmen's reports, operating statistics, and information about employees such as absences and wages. Many times this information cannot be used because it has not been collected. The utilization of this information is largely a matter of establishing a systematic method of recording.

In many cases published information does not fit the manager's needs. In these situations he must then turn to collecting his own information.

## GATHERING UNPUBLISHED INFORMATION

In gathering new information the manager has a choice of at least three devices: questionnaire, interview, and observation.

*The questionnaire.*    A list of questions to be answered by someone is called a *questionnaire*. Most people have participated in surveys conducted by various businesses. In fact, the biggest advantage of questionnaires is their widespread use. If the manager wants the opinion or attitude of people—be they employees or consumers—giving them a questionnaire to fill out is probably the approach he would take. He can think through the questions beforehand and design the questionnaire to get exactly that information needed.

However, certain disadvantages to the questionnaire method may lead the manager to suspect its accuracy. First is the general unwillingness of people to fill in questionnaires. If response is placed on a voluntary basis, it is not uncommon for only 10 percent of the people given questionnaires to return them. On the other hand, if response is mandatory, people may not answer the questions truthfully. This method should always raise doubts about how those people who did not respond would have answered the questions and whether those who did respond answered them truthfully. A second disadvantage with questionnaires is the possible inability of people to answer the questions. Some people may not be able to tell why they bought a particular product or dislike a particular manager. Most opinions or attitudes have many causes, some of which are unknown to the person who has them. Furthermore, some people may misinterpret the question being asked on the questionnaire, resulting in an incorrect response. A final disadvantage is the tendency of the questioner to build his bias into the questions; this, however, can be controlled by careful objective review of the questionnaire before it is given.

*The Interview.*    In a personal interview with customers or employees, the manager can increase the accuracy of the information he obtains. He can get people to answer questions and can explain questions that are not clear. In addition, he can encourage the person to answer questions more fully and observe how the person is answering the question. These will help improve the accuracy of the information obtained.

There are again, however, certain disadvantages with an interview which might decrease its accuracy as a information-gathering device. An interviewer is likely to bias a response. For example, an employee may tell the manager what he thinks the manager would like to hear rather than his real feelings. In filling in a questionnaire, the person can be anonymous and thus is more likely to relate his true feelings. A face-to-face interview gives the person nothing to hide behind, which may affect his response.

These disadvantages point to a combination of both questionnaire and interview as a way of increasing the accuracy of the information. The manager might want the same people to fill in a questionnaire and then be interviewed, or divide people into two groups—one filling in the questionnaire and the other being interviewed. In either situation discrepancies in the information would lead the manager to suspect its accuracy.

*Observation.*    Rather than asking people questions, it is sometimes better just to observe their actions. For example, instead of asking employees how they spend their time on the job, the manager might observe them for a number of days. Or instead of asking salesmen how they sell the product, the manager may simply watch a number of sales calls.

Gathering information by observation is more objective and accurate than other methods. Events are recorded as they occur, and the manager does not have to rely on the willingness or ability of a person to report what happened.

However, observation does have its disadvantages also. First, observation cannot be used to indicate a person's attitudes or beliefs. Thus, some information simply cannot be obtained by observation. Second, observation is a costly method of obtaining information. It takes a lot of time to observe the actions of very few people. And, finally, the presence of an observer may change the way people normally act. When someone knows he is being watched his actions may and often do change. Thus, the observer may get an inaccurate impression of what is happening. He may think that something is normal when in fact it is abnormal.

In summary, it is difficult to get accurate information, regardless of which information-gathering device is employed. The business researcher should be aware of this difficulty and with this in mind should temper his conclusions which are based upon information.

## THE DEGREE TO WHICH THE RESEARCH IS EXHAUSTIVE

If the manager gathers incomplete information with devices that by their very nature are not completely accurate, he will have unreliable data. To guard against this, information should be obtained from many sources and through many devices. The manager should never be too sure that he has all the information. Systematic research is exhaustive. Even though some results may be inaccurate, if enough data have been gathered, the manager will uncover these inaccuracies. In the final analysis, the manager who performs systematic research will have greater assurance in the decision he makes. He can feel confident that he has all the information that could be obtained and interpreted. He has been systematic in the methods used and information gathered. Now he can make an objective decision or evaluation. Systematic research and exhaustive research does not provide the manager with answers; it just makes it more likely that he will come up with the right answers or conclusions, and decreases the chance of a wrong decision.

With this definition of descriptive business research and the methods and problems involved, the discussion can turn towards applications to some of the problems research can help the manager solve. These problems will be discussed in four major topics: problems in competitive adaptation, production, distribution, and manpower.

### Competitive Adaptation and Business Research

How competitive a business will be depends upon how adaptive it is to changing conditions. The business system is constantly adjusting to a changing environment. Descriptive business research which indicates these changes is therefore central to the business system's success and survival. Business research which deals with future changes is called **forecasting.** Forecasting is the process of defining future conditions in that environment in which a given business competes before they happen.

Without some foreknowledge of how events are likely to change, the businessman is assuming that what he is doing now will continue to be the right thing to do in the future. This is obviously a dangerous assumption. However, with the proper information the businessman can consider the impact of future conditions on his business and adjust his activities to meet changing conditions. Forecasting is thus vital to the modern business system.

The manager who does a good job of forecasting has information available to answer the following questions: What is the industry outlook for future sales volume and profit level? What is future demand for my good or service likely to be? What will my competition be like in the future? How will the general economy look in the future? Forecasting, as other forms of business research, relies on information which is obtained from two sources: published information and information generated by the businessman himself.

## PUBLISHED INFORMATION AND FORECASTING

Two prominent sources of information about general economic conditions are available to the businessman. The Department of Commerce and Securities and Exchange Commission annually publishes a *Survey of Current Business,* and McGraw-Hill publishes an annual study appearing in the magazine *Business Week*. These economy-wide surveys seek a base for forecasting broad economic trends such as business investment, expenditure, and even general economic conditions. These broad surveys, among others, are only useful as a first approximation of what economic conditions might be in the future. For more specific information the businessman must rely on the information he generates himself.

## GENERATING INFORMATION AND FORECASTING

Specific information for forecasting purposes is usually generated through an opinion survey. Opinion surveys assume that future changes in part depend upon what people presently believe or presently plan for the future.

An individual business can conduct a survey of its actual customers to determine how their product or service demands might change in the future. Or the business might survey its sales force to get their opinion on how future product demand will change. This approach takes into account that salesmen continually talk to consumers, hearing their complaints and desires. They also see how consumers are reacting to competitor's products. Salesmen are thus in an excellent position to offer an opinion on future changes in the immediate market.

The businessman also has to be sensitive to events happening in his market. Unfortunately much of this sensitivity must be an intuitive feel for the market place. For example, are possible substitutes for the firm's product being developed and accepted by consumers—steam for gas, bicycles for cars, poultry for beef? What *technological* changes will affect the future of the firm's product? Technology may change the availability and price of raw materials—for example, industrial man-made diamonds. It can also affect established methods of production—for example, computerized machinery is displacing some man-operated machinery. In addition changes in future costs must be predicted. At a minimum, changes in labor and material costs must be estimated. Changing costs in these two areas alone can have dramatic impact on the future profitability of the firm.

Research, or the gathering of information for forecasting purposes, although descriptive, is characterized by uncertainty. Nevertheless, based upon the information gathered from various sources, the businessman will improve his ability to forecast future conditions. He can never be certain of such predictions or forecasts, because conditions and events in the economy are changing too rapidly. Failing to make a forecast or prediction in essence means the businessman trusts his future success to chance or luck. Forecasting, on the other hand, provides a base for adapting to changing conditions as the businessman sees them. No one knows what the future will be. The successful, adaptive businessman tries to minimize this uncertainty by trying to predict future changes.

### The Production Process and Business Research

Business research into production can be aimed at providing information to either improve or adjust any element of the production process.

## PUBLISHED INFORMATION AND PRODUCTION

Published information provides the businessman with suggestions of what others have done to improve their production processes. Searching for this information is research. Many books have been written on the subject of production. Of equal importance are the numerous periodicals in the area of production, including *Factory Management, Modern Plan Operation and Maintenance,* and *Production.* A wealth of information and ideas on improving any element of the production process can be found in these periodicals. For those businesses involved in producing a service, numerous special-interest periodicals such as *Food and Equipment Product News, Carpet Review, Furniture News,* and *Purchasing,* are available. Published information indicates what others have done and helps the businessman formulate decisions concerning changes in his production process.

## GENERATING INFORMATION AND PRODUCTION

Internal, descriptive production information is generated for two reasons: first to control the elements of the production process and second to serve as a basis for suggesting production changes. Much of this information is a matter of keeping up-to-date records, but it still qualifies as business research because it must be gathered and interpreted by the businessman.

The area of inventory control is an example of the types of information that need to be generated to control part of the production process. A very single, objective means for controlling inventory uses the maximum, minimum, and reorder points. The maximum is the largest amount of a given item that should be on hand. The minimum is the smallest amount that should be in storage. The reorder point is the quantity on hand which signals that a new supply must be ordered. To establish these maximum, minimum, and reorder points the following information is needed:

(1) Average usage of the part or materials (per day, week, etc.)

(2) The time needed to procure needed parts or materials.

(3) Maximum usage during this procurement time.

(4) Minimum usage during this procurement time.

(5) The economic order quantity.

Generating this information for the most part involves keeping accurate records of past events. Assume that the Jiffy Trailer Co. has recorded the following past experiences with the use of camping trailer taillight fixtures.

(1) Average daily usage, 10 light fixtures

(2) Procurement time, 30 days

(3) Maximum usage during this procurement time, 600 light fixtures

(4) Minimum usage during this procurement time, 60 light fixtures

(5) Economic order quantity, 800 light fixtures

The point at which these light fixtures should be reordered would be set at that quantity which will keep the optimum number on hand and supply the proper amounts to production at the time and place needed. This reorder point is determined by evaluating procurement time (2) and the maximum usage during this procurement time (3). The reorder point is that quantity at which, with maximum usage, the quantity will be reduced to zero during the thirty-day procurement time. Thus, the reorder point for the camping trailer fixtures is 600 units. When the number of fixtures on hand has been reduced to 600, a purchase order for 800 units needs to be sent to the supplier.

If there were maximum usage during this thirty-day procurement time, the stock of light fixtures would be reduced to zero. Under average conditions, only ten units are used per day, or 300 for the thirty-day procurement time. Thus, under average conditions the quantity left on hand after thirty days would be 300 (600 — 300). Thus, 300 units represents the minimum quantity needed to insure against maximum usage.

When the order quantity arrive, it is added to the quantity on hand. If there has been minimum usage (60), the amount on hand would be 540 (600 — 60). When the order quantity is added to this amount, Jiffy Trailer Co. would have the maximum quantity it should have on hand, 1,340 (800 + 540). Since minimum usage would occur only during the lightest months of production there should never be more than 1,340 units on hand. For Jiffy, the standard quantities of light fixtures are as follows:

(1) Maximum number of units to be held in inventory, 1,340
(2) Minimum number of units to be held in inventory, 300
(3) Reorder point, 600
(4) Economic order quantity 800

The economic order quantity (4) is an important part of these standards. Its determination shall be discussed in a later chapter.

This example shows the way information can be generated and utilized to aid the businessman in improving the production process. Additional information or research into such diverse areas as waste or scrap level, machinery evaluation, work station design, alternative plant layout evaluation, evaluation of order-handling system, quality inspection, determining performance standards, machinery maintenance, or shipping systems, are all important to an efficient production process. All of the information needed in these areas can be generated internally by the businessman.

## The Distribution Process and Business Research

Business research in the distribution area is commonly called *market research*. Probably more descriptive research is done in distribution than in any other area of the business. Market research is how a business system keeps in touch with its consumers. The central role consumers play in determining a business' success or failure is an indication of why so much time and money is put into marketing research. Changing consumer demands, attitudes, and opinions affect every element of the distribution process, from product design to promotional efforts and physical distribution. Being aware of what the particular consumer demands, attitudes, and opinions are is therefore central to the success of the business system.

### PUBLISHED INFORMATION AND MARKETING RESEARCH

The census information is widely used in marketing research. It can be used:

(1) To analyze the number and type of people within a market area
(2) To analyze various methods of physical distribution
(3) To lay out sales territories
(4) To locate retail stores and warehouses
(5) To determine representative samples of the population for marketing research studies.

In addition to census data, the various registration information such as births, deaths, and marriages is invaluable for some businesses such as photographers, diaper services, life insurance companies, etc.

When published information can help solve a problem, it only makes economic sense to use it. Market research is not necessarily the generation of new information. Only after all the published information has been evaluated, should the businessman consider generating new market information. In some cases the published information may not be available or may be incomplete in an area the businessman is concerned with. For these cases new, specific information must be generated.

## GENERATING INFORMATION AND MARKET RESEARCH

This is the most familiar kind of business research. Most people have answered a questionnaire, responded to an interviewer, or redeemed product coupons. Many distribution questions cannot be answered with published information. For instance, how are the firm's product, price, name, and package seen by consumers? What influences the firm's consumers' buying decisions? Why do people buy or not buy the product? What advertising message and medium is most effective? What channel of distribution will be best received by consumers? The information to answer these questions must come from the specific consumers of a particular product.

The methods of generating information to answer these questions are the same for any type of business research. Marketing researchers can either use a questionnaire, interview, or observation. The researcher may use a combination of any of these three approaches. For example, the executives of one bank were concerned with the image customers were forming about the bank and its employees. In a questionnaire the following question was asked:

Check any number of the following words which best describe First National Bank:

_____ Warm
_____ Institutional
_____ Business-like
_____ Relaxing
_____ Cold
_____ Pleasant

In addition to the questionnaire, people were hired to make transactions such as opening a checking account, buying travelers checks, and depositing money. After each transaction the person recorded his general impressions of how bank employees treated them. These two methods allowed bank managers to see the image being projected by the bank and its employees, as well as where improvement could be made. The different types of questionnaires, interviews, or observation which can be used are only limited by the businessman's imagination. However, since much of this information is consumer opinion or attitude, the businessman must be very careful that the information is gathered systematically. Questionnaires, interviews, and even observation can be biased, resulting in weak decisions based upon faulty information.

When generating market information, more so than in any other type of business research, the entire study must be evaluated to insure that it is systematic. The method of gathering information which is chosen must be most likely to be accurate in the situation. For example, counting the number of cars which pass by a given intersection is likely to be more accurate than asking people how many times they drive on a particular road in any given week. The investigator must also force himself to be objective both in gathering and interpreting the information. An interviewer can, if he is not careful, influence the way people respond to his questions. For example: "More sophisticated people like to watch X television show. Do you like to watch X television show?" To answer in the negative would imply that the person is not sophisticated. Therefore, most people would answer yes even if they did not watch X television show.

Since market surveys do not cover all the consumers of a product, care must be taken that those included in the sample are representative of the total consumers. For example, asking only high school seniors what they want in a car's styling and performance would not give results which represent the total car-buying population.

The whole area of market research is too extensive to cover here. However, it is important to understand that when describing consumer attitudes, beliefs, or opinions, systematic research is a necessity. Incomplete, biased market information is probably more dangerous than any other kind, since so many business decisions are based on what the consumer wants and needs.

## The Manpower Process and Business Research

Information about people is necessary to control and improve the use of this resource. Unlike the other resources used by the business system, the human being has feelings and opinions that must be taken into consideration in utilizing him as a resource. In addition to employee opinions, published information can be used to control and improve the use of manpower.

### PUBLISHED INFORMATION AND MANPOWER RESEARCH

Published manpower information is gathered from two sources, the community where employees live and internal employment records.

Each business competes for employees in a given labor market. Employees are only willing to travel so far to work. Thus the location of the business defines the labor market which will be available to the business. There is usually competition with other businesses for a limited number of skilled employees within this labor market. This is true regardless of the skill: secretarial, machinist, tool and die maker, accountant. To be competitive in a labor market an individual businessman needs to find out two pieces of information: first, how many people in this labor market have certain skills and second, what is the going wage for these various types of employees. The local chamber of commerce or various local trade associations often have this information.

The businessman should be concerned with the available skills and the going wage for the following obvious reasons. First, if a skill necessary for the business operation (tool and die makers, for example) is in short supply, the businessman must assume the responsibility for increasing the supply. The supply can be increased by setting up training programs or recruiting and moving people from other parts of the country into the immediate community within which the business operates. Although this alternative seems drastic, if the skills needed are not available, the only other way is for the business to operate without them or select a new location. Second, to compete for employees the businessman must be sure his wages are competitive. All other things equal, you can guess the result of two businesses offering tool and die makers $6.00 and $8.00 an hour, respectively. Wages are the initial means of competing for employees in a given labor market.

This general labor market information helps the businessman plan his strategy for attracting the right type and number of employees. There are also certain journals to aid the businessman in performing the various phases of the manpower process. Among these are *Personnel, Personnel Administration,* and *Personnel Psychology.*

To control and improve the utilization of the human resource various information already on record should be evaluated. Two general types of information should be evaluated. They are labor turnover and absenteeism.

Labor turnover is simply the number of people leaving, or being separated from the business. A turnover rate can be calculated by using the following formula:

$$\text{Turnover rate} = \frac{\text{Number of employees separated during a given time period}}{\text{Number of employees working during that same time period}} \times 100$$

For example, if a business employed 500 people during the month of December and ten were separated, the turnover rate would be:

$$10/500 \times 100 = 2\%$$

In addition to turnover, the absence of some employees from their jobs can be disruptive to production. To combat absenteeism it is first necessary to determine its extent. Absenteeism is defined as a failure of workers to report on the job when they are scheduled to work. In order to standardize the measurement of absenteeism, the Bureau of Labor Statistics suggests the following formula:

$$\frac{\text{Absenteeism}}{\text{rate}} = \frac{\text{Man days lost during a period} \times 100}{\text{Number of workers} \times \text{Number of days worked}}$$

Thus, if the same business employed 500 people who worked twenty days in December lost five man-days due to absence, absenteeism rate would be:

$$\frac{\text{Absenteeism}}{\text{rate}} = \frac{5 \text{ days lost} \times 100}{500 \text{ workers} \times 20 \text{ days worked}} = 5\%$$

Turnover and absenteeism rates are important to analyze for two reasons. First, they help the businessman in planning for future manpower needs. If the absenteeism rate of 5 percent is constant the businessman can plan for adding part-time labor or shifting the work schedule to accommodate a less than full labor force. And if the turnover rate of 2 percent is stable, the businessman knows ahead of time that he will have to find and hire ten new employees every month. He can thus plan for this. Secondly, any increase or abnormally high turnover or absenteeism rates indicate that something needs correcting. Absenteeism may simply be a result of illness such as a flu epidemic. Where illness can be ruled out, high absenteeism or turnover usually indicates employee discontent. They may be bored, unhappy with working conditions, unhappy with particular supervisors, or have any number of reasons. These reasons need to be investigated and corrected, if possible.

To correct the causes of absenteeism and turnover it is necessary to determine first who are the firm's highest absenteeism and turnover people. Usually the businessman finds that 80 percent of the absences and turnover problems are caused by 20 percent of the employees. Identifying these 20 percent is a first step in curing the problem. Second, the businessman can analyze any pattern when absenteeism and turnover are highest. Examples might include opening days of deer season, Fridays, and Christmas. Third, the businessman would want to determine if the 20 percent of the labor force works in a particular part of the business or under a particular supervisor. The control of turnover and absenteeism depends upon their causes. When the causes are uncovered, steps can be taken to eliminate them.

Turnover, absenteeism, and in general gaining employee cooperation can be linked to employee attitudes and feelings. Information about feelings and attitudes must be generated by the businessman.

## GENERATING INFORMATION AND THE MANPOWER PROCESS

The primary type of manpower information generated by the businessman concerns employees' attitudes and feelings. Employee attitudes can and do affect their work. Certain management practices, such as decisions made and how management acts in carrying out various duties, influence employee attitudes. Thus, employee attitudes are affected by what the management of a business does and how it does what it does.

There are a number of methods available to generate employee attitude information. They all, however, boil down to asking the employees to express their opinions. Their opinions can either be gained through interviews or questionnaires. For example, the employee might be asked to respond to the following types of questions:

When your supervisor gives orders, does he:

_____ Tell you to do a thing in a way that makes you feel like doing it?
_____ Make you mad because of the way he tells you?

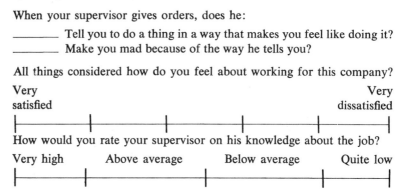

An employee's attitude about the business or his immediate supervisor can affect his work. For every decision the businessman makes or action he takes in getting the work done, employees have an opinion or attitude. The businessman should be concerned about his employees' attitudes. In some cases they are based on false information and can be corrected. In other cases, they are based on true situations, which, if possible, must be remedied. If they are not corrected the businessman will have problems on his hands in the future.

Whatever employees' attitudes are, the businessman should know them and then correct those that are detrimental to performing the work of the business system.

## Summary

Information other than accounting and financial is needed to direct and control various processes within the business system. In fact, decisions in three processes—production, distribution, and manpower—are based on information of a nonfinancial nature. In obtaining and interpreting this information the businessman involves himself in business research. Throughout this chapter the necessity of performing business research in the production, distribution, and manpower processes systematically has been stressed. Unsystematic business research leads to biased information and weak decisions. The next chapter discusses putting this information into meaningful terms for business decision making.

## QUESTIONS

1. What is the difference between the information generated through accounting and financial documents and that generated by descriptive business research?
2. Differentiate between systematic research, unsystematic research, and business research.
3. What specific factors effect how systematic the research will be?
4. What are the advantages and disadvantages of each of the following information-gathering devices?
   (a) The questionnaire
   (b) Published data
   (c) The interview
   (d) Observation
5. Describe the concept of forecasting and indicate what information the businessman would need to make an accurate forecast.
6. Describe how the businessman would go about performing a market research study to evaluate the buying habits of his consumers.
7. What types of manpower information are necessary to better control and utilize this resource?

## Incident 21–1

Bill Bard, president of the Hardy Meat Company, has watched his company grow from an idea into a profitable business. The Hardy Meat Company concentrates on processing meat and meat by-products into convenient lunch meats: bologna, summer sausage, liverwurst, pickle loaf, etc. Hardy Meats are displayed and sold in most of the chain grocery stores throughout the nation.

Bill recently decided to introduce a new concept in selling lunch meats. The new concept is a prepared tray of hors d'oeuvres. The hors d'oeuvres would be made of cheese, lunchmeat, shrimp, and oysters in varying combinations and offered in an attractive ready-to-serve package. Bill felt that the novel idea and convenience it offered consumers, with the attractive ready-to-serve package, would gain good buyer acceptance. He was particularly anxious to evaluate his new idea's potential.

Bill asked Dennis Hutter, director of new products, to prepare a sales forecast for the new idea. He also asked Francine Kuk, Hardy Meats' sales manager, to prepare the same type of forecast. Once these two reports were in Bill planned on making his decision. He realized that the two managers would probably turn in two different reports. Dennis Hutter tended to be excessively cautious in his forecasts of products sales. Francine Kuk, based on her belief in her salesmen's capabilities, usually developed optimistic forecasts. But Bill felt that since he knew these facts he could put each report in its proper perspective and make a good decision.

(1) Evaluate how systematic Bill Bard's research process is.

(2) What additional information do you think Bill needs before making his decision?

(3) Given the time and money, how would you prepare the forecast for Hardy Meat Company?

## Incident 21–2

Richard Thornton, chairman of the board of Diodeconductors International, feels the company has long ignored employee attitudes and feelings. To remedy this he proposed and got approval at the last board meeting for funds to conduct an employee attitude survey. Richard has issued the following directive to Lewis Selzer, head of industrial relations for Diodeconductors International:

> Lewis, I want your department to set in motion a systematic interview procedure which would result in an individual interview with each employee. The board wants to know how the employees feel about this company, what their complaints are, what changes they would like to see made, what things would keep them with Diodeconductors International. Since there will probably be different ideas expressed by different people I feel it is necessary to do two things. First, each interview should be taped. I don't see any reason why the employee needs to know that such recordings are being made. Second, each employee's department and salary classification needs to be identified during this interview. This will allow us to group the interview into similar categories. Finally Lewis, I think we need to emphasize at the start of the interview that the information provided will be strictly confidential and that no report or names will be disclosed to fellow employees or their superiors.

Lewis Selzer was taken back by the magnitude of interviewing 15,000 employees and questioned the value of the information that will be received during these interviews.

(1) What are the strengths and weaknesses of the research process Richard Thornton is proposing to Lewis Selzer?

(2) How would you suggest Lewis go about implementing this directive?

(3) Develop a list of questions that should be included in the interview to gain the types of information Richard Thornton wants.

(4) What alternative methods would you suggest to Lewis instead of the interview?

(5) Prepare a presentation for each alternative suggested that would convince Richard Thornton to change his mind. Each presentation should include examples of the way the information Richard Thornton wants will be obtained.

# 22

# Tools to Aid in the Utilization of Information

The great bulk of information generated and needed to make business decisions, as presented in Chapters 19, 20, and 21, can be overwhelming. There is always a risk that the manager will be buried in unnecessary information, ignore important information, or "fail to see the forest for the trees." The business manager many times needs to summarize a lot of information into a few meaningful summary statements or graphs so that he can concentrate on the problems at hand. This chapter first discusses how vast amounts of information can be stored, presented, and utilized through the computer. Second, we will cover the presentation of data by means of graphs as well as through the computation of those averages often referred to as **measures of central tendency.**

Included at the end of this chapter is an appendix. In appendix A, consideration is given to the volume–profit dilemma which every businessman must face. In appendix B attention is directed to another universal problem in business, the level of inventory to have on hand during any one period of time.

## The Computer

The term **data processing** refers to the collecting, processing, and reporting of information. The tools used to accomplish these tasks vary. For example, the processing of information may be manual, automatic, or electronic. Under a normal system, the processing of data is performed primarily by hand. An automatic system uses a machine to facilitate the processing of information. Such a system is commonly referred to as ADP (automatic data processing). However, when the machine being utilized is an electronic computer, the system of data processing is then referred to as EDP (electronic data processing).

Because of its widespread use in business as well as its seemingly unlimited capacity for processing of business data, the concern in this chapter is directed at the computer. Computers will not be examined in depth, but rather you will be introduced to a few basic computer components as well as to how the computer can be used to process and report information needed for decision making.

## COMPUTER COMPONENTS

The basic units which comprise an electronic data processing system are diagrammed in Exhibit 22–1. The three components in the center of the dia-

### EXHIBIT 22–1

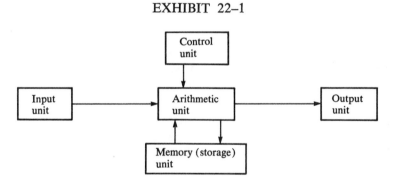

gram (the control unit, arithmetic unit, and memory unit) comprise the heart of the EDP system. In addition, however, extra components such as the input unit and the output unit are necessary. These extra components are usually referred to as **hardware.** Each of these components will be discussed separately.

### THE INPUT OF INFORMATION

In order for the EDP system to process information, it is first necessary that source data be introduced into the computer along with instructions on how to process the data. Two of the most popular input media used today are punched cards and magnetic tape.

*Punched Cards.* A typical punched card contains twelve horizontal rows and eighty vertical columns. Information is recorded on a card by means of a keypunch machine which is operated by a person. The keypunch operator transfers information from a source document (such as a sales invoice) to the cards by punching holes in certain locations of the columns. An example of data represented on a punched card is shown in Exhibit 22–2. Once information is

EXHIBIT 22–2

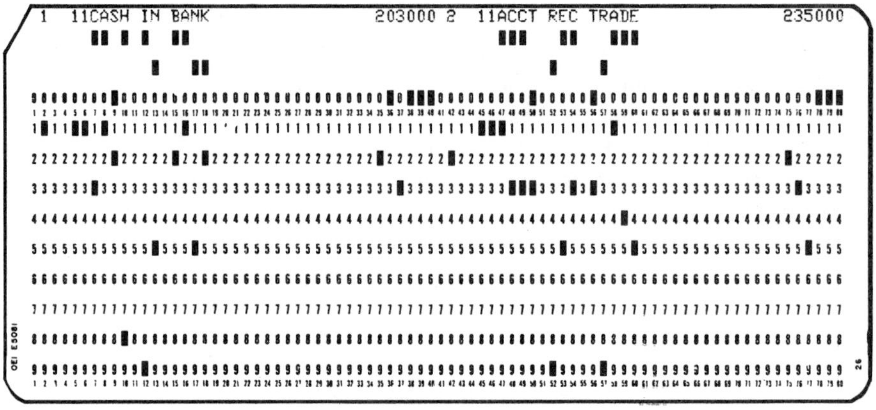

punched into the card, it is introduced into the computer by means of a card reader, which converts the data on cards into electronic impulses.

*Magnetic Tape.* Instead of information punched on cards, it is also possible to record information on tapes in the form of magnetized spots which are referred to as *bits.* Once the information is recorded on the tape, it may either be retained for future use or erased. Because the computer can process information much faster when it is recorded on tape than on punched cards, magnetic tape is becoming increasingly popular as an input medium for EDP systems.

## THE PROCESSING OF INFORMATION

The processing of information is performed by the central processing unit (CPU) of the computer. The CPU consists of the control unit, the arithmetic unit, and the memory (storage) unit.

*The Arithmetic Unit.* This unit performs the functions of addition, subtraction, multiplication, and division. Furthermore, it makes basic comparison operations needed for decision purposes. For example, in the processing of a payroll, it is necessary that the computer calculate each employee's F.I.C.A. (social security) tax. However, before making such a calculation, the computer must first determine if each employee's year-to-date earnings exceed the maximum earnings which are subject to such a tax. For example, 1974 earnings in excess of $13,200 are not subject to F.I.C.A. tax. By comparing an employee's total earnings for the year with the total earnings subject to such a tax, the computer is able then to make a decision. That is, it either calculates the additional F.I.C.A. tax or does not make such a computation.

*The Memory Unit.* This unit represents the filing cabinet of the computer because information stored in memory is held in a specific location. Each location is assigned a particular address so that the computer knows at all times where information is stored. Three types of data are held in storage: data awaiting processing, data currently being processed, and data already processed but awaiting output. In addition, the computer program is stored in the memory unit. The computer program is a sequence of instructions which the computer follows in carrying out a specific operation. At one time it was necessary for computer programmers to write instructions in a language which computers understood. These machine languages required the use only of ones and zeros as letters. Today, however, computer languages such as COBOL (Common Business Oriented Language) are very popular in business firms. Rather than being a pure machine language, COBOL uses English. The computer has a compiler unit which translates the English into pure machine language.

*The Control Unit.*   This unit interprets the instructions outlined in the computer program and directs the activities of all the computer units. This makes the control unit a very powerful tool and, in fact, it is often described as the "central nervous system" of the computer. The control unit, by interpreting the stored computer program, instructs the input unit as to what data is needed and where in storage it is to be located. Similarly, it instructs the arithmetic unit as to the type of calculation to be performed on certain data, where these data can be located in the memory unit, and where to place the resulting data upon completion of processing. Finally, the control unit instructs the output unit as to which data are to be released and where such data are located in the computer's memory unit.

## THE OUTPUT OF INFORMATION

The output unit is a device which accepts processed data from the computer's memory unit. The output may be in a form which the user can immediately read, such as print-out copy. For example, the balance sheet in Exhibit 22–3 is a computer print-out. Financial transactions were fed into the computer by means of punched cards. The computer was instructed by means of a program to process these transactions and to print out a balance sheet.

## CAN A COMPUTER THINK?

Although the computer is a very sophisticated machine, there is one thing it cannot do—think. The computer can only do what a human being tells it to do. Therefore, if incorrect instructions or incorrect information are fed into the computer, the output from the computer will likewise be incorrect. A phrase often used to describe this is *GIGO,* which simply means: "Garbage In, Garbage Out." Despite the computer's inability to think, its usefulness lies in the fact that it can do three rather simple things superlatively well:[1]

(1)  It can retrieve almost instantly any stored piece of information;

(2)  It can compare two numbers and perform any mathematical operation with them;

(3)  It can perform any combination of these functions in specified sequence —a program—without additional human intervention.

1. Robert Compbell, "How the Computer Gets the Answer," *Life Educational Reprint, 33*. Chicago: Time Incorporated, 1967, p. 3.

## EXHIBIT 22–3

```
         BALANCE SHEET
         *************

     ASSETS
     ------

 CURRENT ASSETS
 --------------

  1     CASH IN BANK                          2030.00

  2     ACCT REC TRADE                        2350.00

  5     STORE SUPP                             210.00

 20     MDSE INV WASHERS                      2070.00

 22     MDSE INV DRIERS                       2160.00
                                           ----------

                                                      8820.00
                                                   ----------

        TOTAL ASSETS                                 8820.00
        ------------                              **********



     LIABILITIES AND EQUITIES
     ------------------------

     LIABILITIES
     -----------

 CURRENT LIABILITIES
 -------------------

  6     ACCRUED SAL PAY                        700.00

  7     ACCT PAY T/AJAX                       6360.00
                                           ----------

                                                      7060.00
        EQUITIES
        --------

  8     CAPITAL STK                          1000.00

 40     RETAINED EARNINGS                     760.00
                                           ----------

                                                      1760.00
                                                   ----------

        TOTAL LIABILITIES AND EQUITIES               8820.00
        ------------------------------            **********
```

## APPLICATIONS OF THE COMPUTER

The computer is designed to handle large amounts of information rapidly. For this reason, use of the computer is common today in such operations as the processing of payroll or the maintaining of perpetual records on the level of each inventory item in stock. In addition, however, the computer is an excellent tool in helping the business manager solve complex problems. Some basic illustrations of how the computer is applied in business firms today are given below.

### PAYROLL

Due to the routine and repetitive nature of payroll processing, the business manager is often able to reduce payroll preparation costs through computers. The accuracy and speed with which the computer works enable the firm to reduce both the number of errors which frequently occur under a manual system as well as the time needed to process the payroll.

In calculating each employee's take-home pay, the computer first determines each employee's gross pay for the payroll period. Deductions from gross pay include certain taxes which are withheld by the employer and later paid to the government at periodic intervals. These include amounts for state and federal income taxes, as well as F.I.C.A. taxes. Other deductions may include money withheld for retirement, credit union, savings bonds, charitable contributions, union dues, and so on. Once each employee's net pay is determined, the computer then prints for each employee his payroll check which includes a statement (attached to the check) summarizing the employee's gross income and deductions.

The computer also has the capacity to print reports summarizing each employee's gross pay and deductions for the entire year. For example, the form W-2 which each employee is required to include when filing his federal, state, and local income tax return can be furnished by the computer at the end of the calendar year. Other reports provided by the computer include those which must be submitted periodically by the employer to the state and federal governments showing the amount of state and federal unemployment taxes payable by the employer. In addition to government units, other organizations such as insurance companies, credit unions, regulatory agencies, and labor unions utilize data relating to a firm's payroll which can be compiled and printed accurately and quickly by the computer.

### INVENTORY CONTROL

The computer's ability to make comparisons of certain information and then to act, based upon the results of such comparisons, makes it very valuable in controlling inventory costs. Assume that the manager of a department store places an order with a salesman of the Snap Shot Wholesale Co. for 100 units each of five different types of camera models to be shipped via airplane. The salesman would feed all of this information into his company's computer. The computer would in turn print the name and address of the purchaser on a sales invoice. Then, according to instructions stored in the computer's memory, the computer would compare the existing balance of each camera model in stock (also stored in the computer's memory) with the number ordered. If sufficient quantities are in stock, the computer automatically completes the sales invoice by printing the description of each model purchased, the quantity, unit selling price, and total sales price for the order. Furthermore, delivery instructions are printed by the computer.

In order to maintain a current balance for each model of camera in stock, the computer subtracts the number of cameras purchased from each category affected. If the resulting balance is less than the firm's minimum acceptable stock level, the computer automatically issues a purchase order for additional cameras.

## BLENDING OF RAW MATERIALS

Complex problems which would require considerable time to solve if done by hand are often solved quickly by the computer. For example, assume that a firm manufactures dog food by blending five types of raw materials: meat by-products, beef, soy flour, soybean oil, and salt. Because the firm is interested in meeting the minimum requirements of animal nutrition, one unit of dog food must contain thirty-two units of vitamins, sixteen units of a given mineral complex, and forty-eight calories. Management wants to ascertain the amounts of each raw material which must be blended into the dog food in order to attain the minimum standards at the least cost to the firm.

A problem such as this can be solved through linear programming. Linear programming is a powerful mathematical tool which the business manager can use to compute that combination of variables (in the example above the variables are the five raw materials) which will minimize the firm's total cost yet allow the firm to maintain certain minimum standards. Although linear programming problems can be solved by hand, the number of calculations involved can be immense when there are more than three variables. However, through utilization of a computer, such problems can be solved in a matter of minutes.

## OTHER APPLICATIONS

A number of firms use computers to print out their budgets, performance reports, and financial statements. The use of the computer reduces the amount of time management must wait before receiving these reports. Computers are also used to simulate the business operations of a company in order to train management personnel in much the same fashion that airlines use flight simulators in training their pilots. The research and development area of a firm can utilize the computer to solve some scientific problems that arise in developing new products. Customer services can be improved through use of the computer. For example, insurance companies feed relevant facts obtained from customers into a computer. The computer, in turn, after considering each individual's specific needs, prints out a recommended insurance program.

The use of the computer as a tool in helping to solve management's problems is limited only by the imagination and ingenuity of man. Although computers are expensive, they are by no means limited only to big businesses. Through time sharing, smaller businesses are able to capitalize on computer benefits.

## TIME SHARING

Many small businessmen cannot economically justify the purchase of a computer because of the fact that it would sit idle much of the time. Nevertheless, these same businessmen have a real need for computer services at certain periods of time throughout the working cycle. To solve this dilemma, a method referred to as **time sharing** has been developed. Time sharing is a term used to describe a system whereby a number of users situated at various locations use the same computer via separate input/output terminals. The only investment which each businessman must make is in the input/output devices (alternatively these terminals can be rented). The computer itself is located at a service center. The service center charges each user an installation fee plus a fee for the amount of computer time used in the processing of information. This is similar to the way in which you are charged for telephone service. This is a very attractive service for smaller businessmen, in that each pays only for the actual computer time he uses. Furthermore, the businessman has access to a computer which can be used in processing information and solving problems.

### Data Presentation

Every business manager often has too little time during the course of a working day. It is therefore of vital importance that information be presented in proper format so that the business manager can comprehend it quickly and correctly. To understand the importance of presenting data in good form, look at the following example. John Brown, sales manager for Downtown Chevrolet, is interested in determining the number of new cars each of his twenty salesmen sold during the past year. He has accumulated the data in Exihibit 22–4. These figures are *ungrouped,* in that each salesman's output is listed separately. That

EXHIBIT 22–4

*Number of Cars Sold by Twenty Salesmen during 1973*

| Salesman | Cars sold | Salesman | Cars sold |
|----------|-----------|----------|-----------|
| A | 33 | K | 30 |
| B | 42 | L | 24 |
| C | 48 | M | 32 |
| D | 33 | N | 40 |
| E | 33 | O | 27 |
| F | 39 | P | 46 |
| G | 30 | Q | 21 |
| H | 35 | R | 37 |
| I | 31 | S | 16 |
| J | 28 | T | 45 |

is, the sales manager simply listed the names of the twenty salesmen in alpha-
betical order and then determined for each salesman his total sales during the
year. Presenting information in this manner makes it very difficult for John
to interpret without spending a lot of time examining the table.

An improvement in the presentation of the information would be to list the
number of cars sold by each salesman in an **array.** An array is a listing of numbers in a table such that the lowest number is recorded first and the highest
number is recorded last. The information in Exhibit 22–5 is converted into an
array.

EXHIBIT 22–5

*Number of Cars Sold by Twenty Salesman during 1973*

| Salesman | Cars sold | Salesman | Cars sold |
|----------|-----------|----------|-----------|
| S | 16 | D | 33 |
| Q | 21 | E | 33 |
| L | 24 | H | 35 |
| O | 27 | R | 37 |
| J | 28 | F | 39 |
| G | 30 | N | 40 |
| K | 30 | B | 42 |
| I | 31 | T | 45 |
| M | 32 | P | 46 |
| A | 33 | C | 48 |

By listing the information systematically the sales manager can anlyze the
data more easily. For example, by simply glancing at Exhibit 22–5 the sales
manager can see that the number of cars sold during the year by each salesman varied from a low of sixteen to high of forty-eight, or a range of thirty-two
cars (48 —16). The sales manager can quickly see that most of the salesmen
achieved sales of around thirty to thirty-nine cars. Furthermore, it is evident
to the sales manager that the highest-producing salesman sold three times as
many cars as the lowest-producing salesman (16 $\times$ 3 = 48).

## A FREQUENCY DISTRIBUTION

Although information in an array enhances the understanding and interpreting of the data, another technique is available which is a further improvement. This technique is a **frequency distribution.** A frequency distribution is an
arrangement of data into categories or classes along with an indication as to
the frequency or number of observations in each of the classes. Exhibit 22–6
contains a frequency distribution of the twenty salesmen in the example.

Notice that each of the seven classes of data in Exhibit 22–6 has a lower
and upper limit. For example, the first class listed, which has a class frequency
of one, has a lower class-limit of 16 and an upper class-limit of 20. The last
class listed, which has a class frequency of two, has a lower class-limit of 46 and
an upper class-limit of 50. Furthermore, the range of each of the seven
classes is five (i.e., the first class shown includes the numbers 16, 17, 18, 19

EXHIBIT 22–6

*Number of Cars Sold by Twenty Salesmen during 1973*

| Number of cars sold | Number of salesmen (frequency) |
|---|---|
| 16–20 | 1 |
| 21–25 | 2 |
| 26–30 | 4 |
| 31–35 | 6 |
| 36–40 | 3 |
| 41–45 | 2 |
| 46–50 | 2 |
| | 20 |

and 20). Although the frequency distribution in the table here has seven classes, there is no set number which must be used.

By arranging the number of cars sold into classes or categories, the sales manager is better able to evaluate the performance of his men. For example, examination of Exhibit 22–6 indicates that most of the salesmen are in the category of 31 to 35 cars. In addition, the sales manager can quickly calculate that 10 percent of the salesmen fall into the highest class of 46 to 50 cars, and only 5 percent fall into the lowest class of 16 to 20 cars.

## GRAPHIC ILLUSTRATIONS

Another medium for presenting information is a graph. Two of the more popular graphic illustrations are the **histogram** and the **frequency polygon.** Exhibit 22–7 is an illustration of an histogram which depicts the frequency distri-

EXHIBIT 22–7

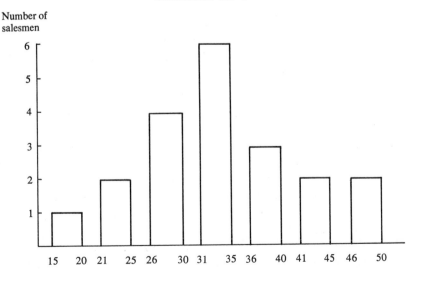

bution presented in Exhibit 22–6. Notice that the height of each bar in Exhibit 22–7 represents the number of salesman in each category, whereas the horizontal axis represents the number of cars sold, which make up the lower and upper limits of each class. For example, by referring to Exhibit 22–7, the sales manager can see that the number of salesmen whose sales record for the year falls into the class of 31 to 35 is six.

In addition to illustrating the frequency distribution in the form of a histogram, it is possible to construct a frequency polygon. In order to construct the polygon it is first necessary to determine the midpoint at the top of each histogram bar. For example, the midpoint on the first bar (the class of 16 to 20) is 18 (16 + 20/2 = 18). A straight line is then drawn, connecting each of the midpoints associated with each histogram bar. This is illustrated in Exhibit 22–8. The line so drawn is a frequency polygon. In Exhibit 22–9, the frequency polygon is drawn without the histogram.

EXHIBIT 22–8

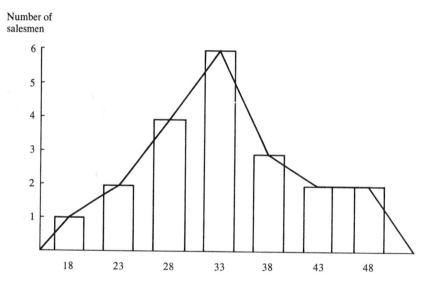

## MEASURES OF CENTRAL TENDENCY

Another means of presenting large quantities of numbers in concise form is to compute a measure of central tendency or average. That is, it is one figure which is representative of a group of figures. However, the business manager must be careful when looking at average figures because the word *average* can be understood in different ways. The discussion which follows includes three measures of central tendency: the arithmetic mean, the median, and the mode.

### ARITHMETIC MEAN

The arithmetic mean is the most popular of the three measures mentioned above. When most people speak of an average, they usually are referring to the

EXHIBIT 22–9

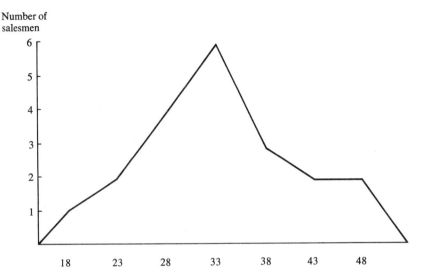

Number of
salesmen

arithmetic mean. The mean is computed for a particular list of figures by adding the figures and dividing by the number of figures in the list. The equation used to compute the mean may be expressed as follows:

$$\bar{x} = \frac{\Sigma x}{n}$$

The term $(\bar{x})$ represents the mean, $(\Sigma x)$ is the sum of the figures in a particular list, and $(n)$ represents the number of figures in the list. As an example, the mean number of cars sold by the twenty salesmen discussed earlier is 33.5. It is computed as follows:

$$\bar{x} = \frac{\Sigma x}{n}$$

$$\text{or } \bar{x} = \frac{670}{20} = 33.5$$

One of the disadvantages of the mean is that if there are unusually large or small numbers included in the list, the mean may not reflect a true average. For example, assume that five salesmen sold the following number of units of their product during the month of September:

| Salesman | Number of units sold |
|---|---|
| A | 10 |
| B | 15 |
| C | 18 |
| D | 19 |
| E | 78 |

The arithmetic mean of this list of numbers is 28 ($140 \div 5 = 28$). Although twenty-eight is the true mean of the units sold by the five salesmen, it hardly reflects the average number of units sold during September by salesmen A, B, C, or D.

## THE MEDIAN

The second measure of central tendency is called the *median*. The median may be defined as the value of that figure which divides a list of figures into two equal parts. To calculate the median it is first necessary to list the figures in an array (an arrangement of figures from lowest to highest). The next step is to locate that number which separates the list into two equal groups such that the number of figures in one group is equal to the number of figures in the other group. In other words, if the seven figures 3, 5, 7, 9, 11, 13 and 15 were in a group, the median figure would be the fourth figure in the list, or the number 9.

The following formula is often used in the computation of the median $M$ for $n$ numbers:

$$\text{Location of } M = \frac{n+1}{2}$$

The letter $M$ represents the median and the letter $n$ reflects the number of figures in the list. Using the previous example, the fourth largest number in the array is the median. That is, $(7 + 1) / 2 = 4$. Notice that the figure 4 is not the median figure, but rather it indicates the number of figures which must be counted off in the array until the median value, the figure 9, is found.

Whenever the number of figures in a list is uneven there will be a median figure. However, when the list contains an even number of figures, such as the sales records of the twenty salesmen, a median figure must be computed. For example, an array of the list of the cars sold by twenty salesmen during 1973 as shown in Exhibit 22–5 would be: 16, 21, 24, 27, 28, 30, 30, 31, 32, 33, 33, 33, 35, 37, 39, 40, 42, 45, 46, and 48. The median number of cars sold by the twenty salesmen would be between the tenth and eleventh figures, computed as follows:

$$\text{Location of } M = \frac{20+1}{2}, \text{ or } 10.5$$

In practice the assumption is made that the median is located halfway between the two middle figures. Therefore, the median figure would be determined by adding the tenth (33) and the eleventh (33) figures and dividing the total of 66 (33 + 33 = 66) by 2, to get 33.0.

Thus before a median value can be computed, it is necessary to list the figures in an array. This, of course, can be quite time-consuming when the list of figures is large. On the other hand, the median figure of a group of figures is not affected by extreme numbers, as the mean is. For example, the median value of the numbers 2, 4, 6, 8, and 12 is 6. Similarly, the median value of the numbers 2, 4, 6, 8, and 40 is also 6.

## THE MODE

The third measure of central tendency is the *mode*. The mode is that value in a series of figures which occurs with the highest frequency. For example, the modal number of cars sold by the twenty salesmen in the example is 33.

An interesting quality of the mode is that the modal value need not be numerical. For instance, it may relate to categories of products. If, for example, more people in America bought Chevrolet Impalas last year than any other kind of automobile, then the Chevrolet Impala is the modal car. Again, if a poll taken of women in the state of Indiana disclosed the fact that most women favor the color red above all others, then red is the modal color among women in Indiana. If more Americans mail their federal income tax returns in to the Internal Revenue Service on April 15th than on any other date, then April 15th is the modal date for mailing federal tax returns.

Perhaps the biggest disadvantage of the mode is that there is often no mode. As an illustration, assume that a college offers six sections of Introduction to Business and that the following numbers of students are enrolled in each section: 32, 34, 39, 42, 48, and 51. Because no one value occurs more frequently than any other value, there is no modal class size in this example.

## WHICH MEASURE SHOULD THE BUSINESS SELECT?

Now that the three measures of central tendency have been presented, the next question might be which measure a businessman should use. The measure selected will often depend upon the nature of the problem. As an illustration, assume that a manager is interested in determining the number of daily rejects of Product X which can be expected during each working day in the month of February. In order to estimate this, the manager first reviews the number of rejects of Product X which occurred during each of the twenty-three working days in January. These were as follows (listed in array form):

| 8 | 10 | 10 | 12 | 14 |
|---|----|----|----|-----|
| 9 | 10 | 10 | 12 | 14 |
| 9 | 10 | 10 | 13 | 200 |
| 9 | 10 | 11 | 13 | |
| 9 | 10 | 11 | 14 | |

The mean number of rejects of Product X is computed as follows:

$$\bar{x} = \frac{\Sigma x}{n} = \frac{488}{23} = 21.2$$

The median number of rejects of Product X is arrived at as follows:

$$\text{Location of } M = \frac{n+1}{2} = \frac{23+1}{2} = 12$$

Therefore, the median number is equal to the twelfth number in the array, or 10.

The modal number of rejects is also 10 because 10 is that number of rejects which occurs with the highest frequency.

In this illustration the median and the modal values both reflect the number of daily rejects which the manager can expect in February. On the other hand, the mean value of 21.2 hardly reflects the number of daily rejects which occurred in January, and therefore it is a poor indicator of what the manager should expect in February.The mean, in this case, was distorted by one day with an extreme number (200) of rejects.

## Summary

Once information, both internal and external, is accumulated, the business manager has available certain basic tools to aid in the utilization of information. Although there are a wide variety of such tools, the discussion in this chapter was limited to some of the more common ones. The availability of the computer has significantly reduced the amount of time needed for the processing and analyzing of information. Although the computer is an expensive machine, small businessmen can take advantage of its capacity through time-sharing services.

Perhaps the one method which many managers overlook is presenting information in proper format. Use of such basic techniques as presenting data in an array or utilizing a graph often can increase the reader's comprehension of the information. In addition, proper data presentation reduces the amount of time needed to review the information.

## The Information Process in Retrospect

The information process provides both internal and external data to each of the processes which comprise the business system. The information is used by the business manager as a basis upon which decisions are made. Without information, the business manager would be forced to rely upon his personal intuition in making a decision. Although relying upon a hunch sometimes works, it is a poor substitute for real facts.

In this section internal information, external information, and methods to aid in the utilization of this information have been looked at. The accountant provides two types of internal information: financial and managerial. Financial accounting is concerned with providing information which reflects the overall operating activities of the business firm rather than the reporting of day-to-day activities. Such reports as the income statement and the balance sheet are examples of the output of financial accounting. However, in order to have a good comprehension of the information included in these financial statements, it is helpful if the business manager, as well as those outside the firm, have some knowledge of the fundamental accounting equation and the effects transactions and events have upon this equation. Once they have this basic understanding, they are then in a position to use the balance sheet and the income statement as a basis upon which to evaluate the firm's financial position and its operating results.

On the other hand, managerial accounting is chiefly concerned with reporting the day-to-day activities of the firm. Information accumulated by the managerial accountant is used for two purposes: first, to determine the cost of producing a product or a service, and second, for planning and controlling operations. The managerial accountant works closely with others in the organizational framework in helping to develop standards for material, labor, and overhead costs. These standards are then used as criteria for evaluating actual results. In this manner, management is able to determine the activities which need correcting. Similarly, the managerial accountant compares actual results realized over a period of time with predetermined goals or plans as expressed in the firm's budget. If actual results are not consistent with plans, the business manager is stimulated to adjust these activities in order to realize his goals.

Information other than accounting or financial data is likewise required by the business manager in order to direct and control various activities of the firm. Many decisions which are made in the areas of marketing, production, and manpower are based upon external data. Such information may be accumulated through the gathering of published information such as that reported in the *Census of Business*. Information which has not been published may be obtained by the firm through the use of questionnaires, interviews, or observations. In order to avoid the collection of biased information, the business manager should attempt to make his research efforts systematic.

Once information, either internal or external, is collected, it is important that the business manager has an understanding of certain tools which he may utilize to assist him in his role as a decision maker. For example, simply having a basic understanding concerning the proper presentation of information will both reduce the time spent in examining the data and improve the businessman's comprehension of the data. Furthermore, use of a tool such as computers may enable the manager to accumulate information which would affect the very survival of the firm.

We will now turn our attention to two additional tools: volume profit analysis and economic order quantity (EOQ) analysis. Both of these, which are covered in appendix A and B respectively, provide additional quantitative information needed by the businessman in planning and controlling business activities.

## QUESTIONS

1. (a) Name the basic components of a computer.
   (b) Describe briefly the functions performed by each component.
   (c) List two input media used for introducing data into the computer.

2. (a) What is a computer program?
   (b) Is it necessary to write a computer program in machine language? Explain.

3. Can a computer think? Explain.

4. The computer is an excellent tool for helping the business manager solve a wide variety of problems. List ten such applications.

5. Explain the term *time-sharing*. Why is it helpful to the small businessman?

6. (a) Explain what is meant by listing information in an array.
   (b) Explain what is meant by listing information in a frequency distribution.

7. The following list of numbers represents the grades received by 37 students on an accounting examination:

| 90  | 83 | 74 | 79 | 96  | 72 | 77 |
|-----|----|----|----|-----|----|----|
| 63  | 87 | 73 | 64 | 95  | 78 | 49 |
| 100 | 82 | 63 | 62 | 100 | 78 | 93 |
| 85  | 88 | 87 | 78 | 98  | 79 | 67 |
| 65  | 75 | 67 | 90 | 62  | 81 | 78 |
| 63  | 94 |    |    |     |    |    |

From this listing of grades, compute the mean, median, and modal grades.

8. (a) Explain one of the disadvantages of using the mean as a measure of central tendency.
   (b) Is the disadvantage you cited in part (a) also a disadvantage in using the median as a measure of central tendency?

9. (a) Prepare a list of ten figures in which there is a modal number.
   (b) Prepare a list of ten figures in which there is no modal number.

10. Give two examples of modal values which are not numerical values.

## Incident 22–1

Julia Brown is the sales manager in charge of color television sets at a large department store in South Bend, Indiana. She is responsible for twenty salespeople, each of whom is paid a salary plus commission on each set sold. In order to reward those salespeople who have achieved above average sales for the year, the board of directors is considering paying a year-end bonus, for the first time since the store's inception. The board is scheduled to meet in two weeks, and the secretary of the board has requested Ms. Brown to present information she feels will be helpful in determining who should receive the year-end bonus.

Julia is very much in favor of rewarding those members of the sales force whose sales were above average during the year. However, she realizes that the word *average* can be defined in different ways. Therefore, she has decided to ask you, as her assistant, to do the following:

(1) Compute the mean, median, and modal number of color television sets sold during the year. The information on page 393 has been made available to you.

(2) Which measure do you feel the board of directors should select? Explain your decision.

(3) In order to provide the board with a visual graph of the sales achieved by the salesmen, Ms. Brown has asked you to prepare a bar chart. She has suggested

## Number of Color Sets Sold by Twenty
## Salespeople During 1973

| Salesperson | Sets sold | Salesperson | Sets sold |
|-------------|-----------|-------------|-----------|
| A | 67 | K | 61 |
| B | 97 | L | 65 |
| C | 85 | M | 49 |
| D | 67 | N | 81 |
| E | 67 | O | 55 |
| F | 79 | P | 43 |
| G | 71 | Q | 93 |
| H | 61 | R | 75 |
| I | 57 | S | 33 |
| J | 63 | T | 91 |

that seven classes of sets sold be used, each with an interval of ten. Draw the graph.

(4) What other factors would you suggest that the board of directors take into consideration in determining which of the 20 salespeople are to receive a year-end bonus?

# Volume–Profit Analysis

Management is continually faced with such questions as: What level of sales is required to break even? What volume of sales is required in order to earn a desired profit? What effect will changes in the selling price of a firm's product or changes in the cost of doing business have upon the firm's profits? These questions are often asked when management is thinking in terms of introducing a new product to the market or evaluating current operating activities.

Answers to these questions can be made available through volume–profit analysis. This analysis reflects the effects which changes in the volume of sales will have upon a firm's profits. Another name for this type of information is **break-even point** *analysis*. The break-even point for a firm is that point where total sales for a given period are equal to total expenses for the same period. This is the point where a firm earns zero profits.

The discussion which follows considers two types of analysis which a businessman may use to compute the firm's break-even point, as well as the amount of profits or losses associated with various levels of sales volume. These include graphic analysis and formula analysis.

### GRAPHIC ANALYSIS

In order to construct a volume–profit graph, it is necessary to understand the nature of different expenses and how they respond to changes in volume. Therefore, a brief review of certain terminology is appropriate at this point: *A variable expense* is one which varies in direct proportion to a change in sales volume. *A fixed expense* is one which remains constant as sales volume changes. *Total expenses* equal variable expenses plus fixed expenses. To understand the computation of the break-even point for a retail store, assume the following situation.

Sam Stark is the owner and operator of a bicycle shop across the street from a small state college in Big Springs, California. Mr. Stark has limited his inventory to girls' and boys' ten-speed bicycles due to the current demand for them. He is interested in determining the number of bicycles he would have to sell each month in order to break even. He has accumulated the following information:

| | | |
|---|---|---|
| Selling price per bicycle (either girls' or boys') | | $ 100 |
| Cost per bicycle (variable expenses) | | 50 |
| Cost of operating the shop (fixed expenses) | | |
| Rent | $300 | |
| Utilities | 75 | |
| Insurance | 50 | |
| Bookkeeping and accounting | 100 | |
| Sales clerk's salary | 400 | |
| Office and store supplies | 50 | |
| Miscellaneous | 25 | |
| Total fixed expenses | | $1,000 |

One means of ascertaining the level of sales necessary for Mr. Stark to break even each month is to construct a break-even graph. One such graph is presented in Exhibit 22–10. The vertical axis represents dollars of revenue or expense. Since both sales and expenses are in dollars they can both be represented on the same axis. The horizontal axis represents units sold. In the example, the units are bicycles. The size of Mr. Stark's store is such that the maximum number of bicycles which can be sold in any one month is 60, giving a monthly sales volume of $6,000 ($100 × 60). Since this amount represents store capacity for any one month, the vertical axis stops at $6,000 and the horizontal axis ends at 60 bicycles. The revenue line is plotted on the break-even chart by connecting two points. One point is the intersection of $0 and a sales volume of zero; the second point is $6,000 and a sales volume of 60 bicycles. The fixed expense line parallels the horizontal axis, connecting the vertical axis at the $1,000 expense level. Fixed expenses remain constant regardless of the volume of bicycles sold. The variable expense line slopes upward because these costs vary in proportion to the units sold. Notice that the variable expense line starts on the vertical axis at the fixed expense level of $1,000 rather than $0. In other words, if Mr. Stark experienced a month in which he sold no bicycles, he

EXHIBIT 22–10

*The Stark Bicycle Shop Monthly Volume Profit Graph*

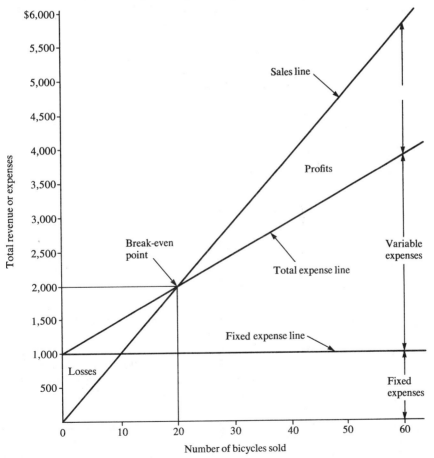

would incur $1,000 of fixed expenses even though his variable expenses would be zero. And when he sells 30 bikes, his fixed expenses, as shown, are still $1,000, even though his total expense increases to $2,500. The additional $1,500 in expense is variable expenses (30 bicycles × $50 = $1,500).

Since variable expenses are added on top of fixed expenses on the graph, the variable expense line becomes the total expense line. As previously defined, total expenses are equal to variable expenses plus fixed expenses. The total expense line is also plotted on the chart by connecting two points. The first point is the level of $1,000 total expenses at zero volume; the second point is $4,000, which represents total expenses at a sales volume of 60 bicycles ($1,000 fixed expense + $3,000 variable expense).

The point on the graph where the total expense line intersects the revenue line is called the break-even point. On the chart in Exhibit 22–10, this intersection takes place at a point which is equal to sales of 20 bicycles or $2,000 revenue per month (20 × $100). Total monthly sales of $2,000 will be exactly equal to $2,000 of total monthly expenses, and therefore profit will be zero. In equation form, break-even is the point at which:

$$\text{Sales} = \text{Fixed expenses} + \text{variable expenses}$$

A monthly income statement assuming sales at the break-even point would appear as follows:

### THE STARK BICYCLE SHOP
*Income Statement*
*For the Month Ended January 31, 19X1*

| | | |
|---|---:|---:|
| Sales | | $2,000 |
| Cost of goods sold ($50 × 20) | | 1,000 |
| Gross profit | | $1,000 |
| Cost of operating the shop: | | |
|   Rent | $300 | |
|   Utilities | 75 | |
|   Insurance | 50 | |
|   Bookkeeping and accounting | 100 | |
|   Sales clerk's salary | 400 | |
|   Office and store supplies | 50 | |
|   Miscellaneous | 25 | 1,000 |
| Net profit | | $ 0 |

One of the advantages of using a break-even graph is that the businessman can determine simply by looking at the graph the amount of profit or losses which will be realized at different levels of sales volume. For example, at a sales volume of forty bicycles per month, total sales will amount to $4,000 and total expenses will amount to $3,000, resulting in a monthly profit of $1,000. On the other hand, at a sales volume of ten bicycles each month, total sales will amount to $1,000 and total expenses will amount to $1,500, leaving a loss for the month of $500.

Nevertheless, the break-even graph has a limitation in that it is static. This means that the underlying information used to construct the graph, such as selling price per unit, variable expense per unit, and fixed expenses, does not change. For example, if a businessman is thinking in terms of reducing his selling price, it would be necessary to construct a new graph in order to determine what effect this decision would have upon the firm's break-even point. This can be a time-consuming process. This limitation can be overcome, however, by utilizing the formula approach to finding the break-even point.

## THE FORMULA ANALYSIS

The formula used to compute the break-even point in units is as follows:

$$\text{B-E.P. in units} = \frac{\text{Total fixed expenses}}{\text{Contribution margin per unit}}$$

Again, using Sam Stark's bicycle shop, the numerator in the formula is the monthly fixed expenses, or $1,000. The denominator, or contribution margin per unit of sales, is equal to the difference between unit selling price and unit variable cost. For Mr. Stark's bicycle shop, contribution margin is computed as follows:

| | |
|---|---|
| Selling price of each bicycle | $100.00 |
| Cost of each bicycle (variable cost) | 50.00 |
| Contribution margin per unit | $ 50.00 |

Therefore, the monthly break-even point in terms of bicycles is determined in the following manner:

$$\text{B-E.P. in units} = \frac{\$1,000}{\$50} = 20 \text{ bicycles}$$

Notice that when a bicycle is sold, Mr. Stark will have $50 ($100 − $50) which can be applied towards covering his fixed expenses. In the example, twenty bicycles must be sold each month before Mr. Stark will cover his monthly fixed expenses of $1,000. Once the fixed expenses are covered, the $50 of contribution margin provided on each bicycle sold represents a contribution to total profits.

Since a business organization is not interested in simply breaking even but rather in earning a reasonable profit, the formula approach can also be used to determine the number of units which must be sold in order to earn a desired profit. This is accomplished by expanding the numerator in the formula to include desired net profit:

$$\frac{\text{Sales in units at}}{\text{desired profit level}} = \frac{\text{Total fixed expenses} + \text{Net profit}}{\text{Contribution margin per unit}}$$

Now that the effects differences in sales volume have upon profits and expenses have been explained, the ways volume–profit analysis can be used by the businessman can be discussed. There are two major problem areas where volume–profit analysis is helpful:

(1) Decisions on changing present sale price.
(2) Decisions on changing present expenses.

## DECISIONS ON CHANGING PRESENT SELLING PRICE

During the month of June, Sam Stark is giving serious consideration to having a sale by reducing the selling price of each bicycle from $100 to $90. He is concerned with the impact this would have upon his break-even point and how many units he would have to sell in order to maintain a profit of $1,000 for the month.

*Solution.* By reducing the selling price of each bicycle $10, the contribution margin per unit sold will decrease from $50 ($100 − $50) to $40 ($90 − $50). As a result, the break-even point in terms of units will increase from 20 to 25. This is computed as follows:

$$\text{B-E.P. in units} = \frac{\$1,000}{\$40} = 25 \text{ bicycles}$$

Although selling price per unit would decrease as a result of the sale, fixed expenses of $1,000 per month would remain constant. Since a smaller contribution margin would be earned on each bicycle sold, it would take five extra sales to cover these fixed expenses.

The number of bicycles Sam would have to sell to maintain his profit level of $1,000 a month at the lower price would be calculated as follows:

$$\frac{\text{Units required to earn a}}{\text{profit of \$1,000}} = \frac{\$1,000 + \$1,000}{\$40} = 50 \text{ bicycles}$$

At a selling price of $100 for each bicycle, Sam is able to earn a profit of $1,000 per month by selling forty bicycles. Consequently, if Sam is of the opinion that reducing the selling price of each bicycle by $10 will increase sales for the month of June by at least ten units, then he will maintain his monthly profit of $1,000. Of course, reducing the selling price may result in an increase in sales of more than ten units, thereby increasing Sam's monthly income.

## DECISIONS ON CHANGING PRESENT EXPENSES

Sam Stark has accumulated $25,000 in personal savings and is thinking about buying the store he now rents. The fixed expense of $300 per month would be eliminated. However, Sam would then be required to assume ownership expenses such as property taxes, insurance, and depreciation on the building. These expenses would amount to an average of $150 per month. Sam is interested in knowing if this reduction will affect his break-even point as well as his profit.

*Solution.* Total fixed expenses would be reduced from $1,000 per month to $850 ($1,000 − $300 + $150). Since the contribution margin per bicycle sold will not be reduced, it will take fewer sales to cover the reduced fixed expenses. The new break-even point in units would be seventeen bicycles per month rather than twenty. This is calculated as follows:

$$\text{B-E.P. in units} = \frac{\$850}{\$50} = 17 \text{ bicycles}$$

If Sam sells forty bicycles a month, the decision to buy the store rather than rent will increase his monthly income from $1,000 to $1,150. This is shown below:

|                    | *Rent store* | *Purchase store* |
|--------------------|--------------|------------------|
| Sales              | $4,000       | $4,000           |
| Cost of goods sold | 2,000        | 2,000            |
| Gross profit       | 2,000        | 2,000            |
| Operating expenses | 1,000        | 850              |
| Net profit         | $1,000       | $1,150           |

The impact of any decision which will affect the various elements of the break-even formula can be calculated. For example, the effects of increasing advertising, changing to a lower cost supplier, expanding of facilities, or adding salesmen could be determined. The businessman could evaluate how these changes will affect profits and thus be in a better position to evaluate the decision.

In addition, many firms use the break-even point as a goal they hope to reach as soon as possible during the course of the fiscal year. For example, a large corporation such as General Motors may set as one of its goals to sell sufficient cars by the midpoint of each year to reach the firm's break-even point for the year. Those cars sold during the second half of the year contribute to the firm's profit. Sam Stark may set a goal to sell twenty bicycles during the first two weeks of each month in order to break even for the month. Any sales during the second half of the month would then contribute to profits. He can thus tell how he and his salesmen are performing during the month and indicate where or when he is going to have a bad month, which then becomes an aid to controlling his operations.

A second universal problem faced by all businessmen is determining how much inventory to order at any one time as well as when to order the inventory. This is the subject of appendix B.

## Incident 22–2

The Wood Company makes and sells baseball bats. The following facts are taken from the firm's records:

    Present sales volume: 600,000 bats per year
    Present selling price of each bat: $0.60 per bat
    Fixed costs per year: $120,000
    Variable costs per year: $0.30 per bat
    Total assets of the Wood Company: $100,000

Find the appropriate answer for each blank space.

(1) The present sales break-even point is equal to $_____.
(2) The present earnings for a year amounts to $_____.
(3) _____ units must be sold in order for the company to earn a 10 percent rate of return on total investments.
(4) Market research indicates that if the selling price were reduced $0.10 per unit, 200,000 additional units could be sold. If the Wood Company then reduces its prices, earnings for a year will amount to $_____.
(5) If fixed costs were increased by 20 percent, the new sales break-even point would be $_____.

# Inventory Planning and Cost Control

Determining the amount of merchandise inventory a firm should have on hand is not easy. Business managers differ on the methods they use, depending, for the most part, on their individual interests. For example, the production manager wants large quantities of raw materials in order that production lines will continuously operate at optimum output with no interruptions. Likewise, the distribution manager is interested in having abundant supplies of all items so that every customer will be satisfied. On the other hand, the financial manager realizes that money invested in excess inventories could be earning interest if invested elsewhere. Furthermore, excessive inventories may become obsolete or deteriorate, resulting in additional losses to the firm.

Rather than looking at each process such as distribution or production separately, the systems approach to operating a business would suggest that the inventory level to be maintained would be that level which most benefits the firm as a whole. This level would be somewhere in between the two extremes. In order to determine the proper amount of inventory to have on hand, it is necessary to understand carrying costs and ordering costs associated with inventories and the manner in which these costs can be minimized. These topics are discussed in some detail below.

## CARRYING COSTS AND OPERATING COSTS

As described above, management is interested in maintaining sufficient levels of inventory to meet the demands of its customers. On the other hand, management is also concerned about minimizing the costs associated with carrying merchandise in inventory. For example, the items listed below are all costs a firm incurs in carrying goods in inventory:

Insurance
Personal property taxes
Cost of storage space
Risk of obsolescence and deterioration
Handling and clerical costs
Interest on money tied up in inventory

Ordering costs include, for the most part, those costs associated with initiating the order and the subsequent receipt of the goods. Initiating the order requires the costs of both clerical labor and office supplies. When the order is received, costs are incurred for the inspection and handling of the merchandise.

One means of reducing the carrying costs would be for the firm to order more frequently in smaller quantities. This would reduce the level or amount of goods on hand at any one point in time, thereby reducing carrying costs. However, this technique results in increasing ordering costs. Conversely, a firm can reduce its ordering costs by ordering less frequently and in larger volumes. However, this then results in larger carrying costs.

One means of resolving this dilemma is for the firm to order that quantity which minimizes total annual costs associated with inventory. That quantity is referred to as the *economic order quantity* (EOQ).

## HOW MUCH SHOULD A FIRM ORDER?

The Kool Company, a manufacturer of air conditioners, purchases electric motors from outside suppliers. The cost of carrying one motor in inventory for a year has been estimated to be $5.00, which consists of the following:

| | |
|---|---|
| Interest costs for money borrowed to purchase motors in inventory, 8% × $30.00 | $2.40 |
| Insurance, taxes etc. | 2.60 |
| Annual carrying cost per motor | $5.00 |

Each time an order is placed with a supplier, the firm incurs a cost of approximately $75.00. This is estimated in the following manner:

| | |
|---|---|
| Clerical costs | $10.00 |
| Paper work and postage | 5.00 |
| Inspection | 40.00 |
| Handling | 20.00 |
| Cost of each purchase order | $75.00 |

The firm expects to produce 24,000 air conditioners during the current year. It will place orders for motors twelve times a year, ordering 2,000 motors each month. The firm assumes that they will have 2,000 units on hand at the beginning of each month and zero units at the end of each month, thus resulting in an average inventory of 1,000 units (2,000 ÷ 2 = 1,000) during the month.

Using the information in this illustration, total annual costs (carrying costs plus ordering costs) for the electric motors can be computed as follows:

| | | |
|---|---|---|
| Carrying costs of electric motors | | |
| Average inventory in units (2,000/2) | 1,000 | |
| Multiplied by annual carrying cost | $ 5 | |
| Total annual carrying cost | | $5,000 |
| Ordering cost of electric motors | | |
| Number of purchase orders | 12 | |
| Multiplied by cost of each purchase order | 75 | |
| Total annual ordering costs | | $ 900 |
| Total annual carrying and ordering costs | | $5,900 |

One question which might be asked at this point is what total inventory costs would amount to if the Kool Company placed purchase orders twice a month rather than once, with each purchase for 1,000 motors rather than 2,000? The solution to this question is:

| | | |
|---|---|---|
| Carrying cost of electric motors | | |
| Average inventory in units (1,000/2) | 500 | |
| Multiplied by annual carrying costs | $ 5 | |
| Total annual carrying costs | | $2,500 |
| Ordering cost of electric motors | | |
| Number of purchase orders | 24 | |
| Multiplied by cost of each purchase order | $75 | |
| Total annual ordering cost | | 1,800 |
| Total annual carrying and ordering costs | | $4,300 |

Notice that by doubling the number of purchase orders the firm places each year, it doubles the ordering cost from $900 to $1,800 per year for an increase of $900. However, total annual carrying costs were reduced from $5,000 to $2,500, which represents a decrease of $2,500. By trading off $2,500 of carrying cost for an additional $900 in ordering cost, the firm has reduced total costs by $1,600.

The next step in the analysis would be to determine if total costs could be reduced further. That is, by increasing the number of purchase orders to more than twenty-four per year, could the Kool Company reduce total annual costs below $4,300? The approach used above could be followed to determine the result. However, this approach is a trial-and-error method, in that a business manager must make a number of calculations before he finally arrives at the economic order quantity (EOQ) for which he is searching. In order to save time, a formula has been developed which will provide management with the answer it is looking for immediately. This widely used formula may be expressed as follows:

$$Q = \sqrt{\frac{2PC}{S}}$$

$Q$ = size of each order; $P$ = annual quantity of units to be used; $C$ = cost of placing one order; and $S$ = annual cost of storing one unit in inventory for one year. Substituting the information given earlier into this formula, the size of each order should be:

$$Q = \sqrt{\frac{2\,(24{,}000)\,(75)}{5}}$$

$$Q = \sqrt{\frac{3{,}600{,}000}{5}}$$

$$Q = \sqrt{720{,}000}$$

$$Q = 848$$

With an EOQ of 848 motors, it would be necessary for the firm to place approximately twenty-eight orders each year. The annual carrying cost and the ordering cost for this size order can be determined by following the procedures described earlier:

| | | |
|---|---|---|
| Carrying cost of electric motors | | |
| Average inventory in units (848/2) | 424 | |
| Multiplied by annual carrying costs | $ 5 | |
| Total annual carrying cost | | $2,120 |
| Ordering cost of electric motors | | |
| Number of purchase orders (24,000/848) | 28 | |
| Multiplied by cost of each purchase order | $75 | |
| Total annual ordering cost | | 2,100 |
| Total annual carrying and ordering cost | | $4,220 |

In this example, the question of how much to order has been answered, but the question of when to order has been ignored.

## WHEN TO ORDER?

To solve this problem for the Kool Company, it is necessary to consider the following information:

Air conditioners to be produced during current year, 24,000 units

Economic order quantity, 848 motors

Lead time, 5 working days

Average daily usage of motors, 75 motors

Lead time represents the number of working days it takes to receive the motors after the purchase order is sent. Since the Kool Company uses seventy-five motors each working day and the lead time is five working days, it will be necessary for the firm to place a purchase order whenever the number of motors in inventory declines to a level of 375 units ($75 \times 5 = 375$). This is the reorder point.

Therefore, in theory, the firm would purchase 848 motors when the inventory reached the reorder point of 375 motors. Since it would take five working days for the merchandise to arrive, the inventory level would be zero on the day of receipt. When the motors are placed in inventory, the level would again increase to 848 units and the Kool Company would not reorder until the inventory again declined to a level of 375 motors. All of this, of course, assumes that the firm uses an average of seventy-five motors each working day.

However, in practice a firm can never be certain of what the demand for its products will be. If demand for air conditioners increased, the Kool Company might increase output beyond seventy-five units a day to meet the sudden spurt in demand. If, for example, production was increased to 100 units a day or the lead time needed for delivery suddenly increased to six or seven working days, the Kool Company would experience a stockout of electric motors for a few days. In order to prevent this from happening, a firm should use a safety stock as a buffer. The amount of safety stock the firm wishes to have on hand depends to a large extent upon past experience and expected future conditions. For example, if the Kool Company can produce at a maximum capacity of ninety air conditioners a day, then perhaps the firm should consider reordering when the inventory level declines to 450 units ($90 \times 5 = 450$). In this situation, the safety stock would be equal to $450 - 375$, or 75 motors. This would mean the firm could operate at maximum capacity during the lead time and still not experience stockout.

## SUMMARY

Although management is most interested in having adequate amounts of inventory on hand to satisfy the needs of customers, it is also concerned with minimizing the total costs associated with ordering and carrying inventories. In order to solve this dilemma, it is necessary to give consideration to three factors: (1) how much to order, (2) when to order, and (3) safety stock.

In measuring how much to order, the firm is concerned with minimizing total ordering costs and carrying costs incurred during the year. The amount arrived at is the firm's economic order quantity (EOQ). Next the firm must determine when to order the merchandise. To solve this problem, consideration must be given to the number of days required for delivery of the merchandise. However, in order to avoid stockout conditions, the firm should have a safety stock as a buffer.

**Incident 22–3**

The Wood Company uses 400,000 units of lumber in manufacturing baseball bats. Production is carried out evenly throughout the year. The cost of one unit of lumber is $2.40. The cost of placing an order for lumber amounts to $100. Carrying costs amount to $1.00 per unit for a year. The Wood Company receives a shipment of lumber five days after it is ordered.

(1) What is the Wood Company's economic order quantity?
(2) Based upon the following information, what is the Wood Company's reorder point?
    (a) Units of lumber to be used during year—400,000
    (b) EOQ—8,944
    (c) Average daily usage of lumber—1,600
    (d) Lead time in days—3
(3) Assume the Wood Company has the capacity to use 2,000 units of lumber per day and operates at full capacity whenever there are sudden spurts in the demand for baseball bats. How much safety stock should the company maintain?

# VIII

# THE BUSINESS SYSTEM
# IN THE FUTURE AND
# IN RETROSPECT

The business environment in which the firm operates does not remain constant, but rather is continuously changing. In order for the firm to survive and remain a viable entity in the community, it is vital that the business manager remain abreast of what is happening around him. The demands placed upon business firms today by society are greater than ever before. It is no longer enough for the firm to produce a good or service and provide jobs for workers. As we shall discover in Chapter 23, today's firm must concern itself with the health of our environment, the injustices which exist in our society, and employee attitudes about job satisfaction.

In addition to social responsibilities, today's business manager must give consideration to current trends which reflect the direction in which many firms are headed. One of these trends, which will be discussed in Chapter 24, is the growing commitment on the part of many firms to sell in one or more foreign markets rather than being restricted simply to markets in the United States. A second trend is business combinations. Because of certain advantages inherent in being large, a number of business managers are anxious to combine two or more firms. This subject will be handled in Chapter 25.

In Chapter 26 we will review and reemphasize the interrelationships among the six processes discussed in this text: the financial, production, distribution, manpower, management, and information processes. Also included will be a discussion of the alternatives open to the student who wants to major in a particular field or business in total.

# 23

# Changes Affecting Business

Business today is still responsible for its traditional role of providing for economic growth, creating jobs for workers, and producing goods and services demanded by the public. However, changes are taking place in the business world which are not only changing the way in which many people live, but also the manner in which business managers conduct their operations. This chapter begins by looking briefly at **automation,** and then at two changes affecting business which are largely the result of automation: (1) shortening the laborer's work week, and (2) changing attitudes of workers towards their jobs.

We then will examine in some detail a change which is of primary concern to the business manager today—social responsibility. The following social responsibilities of the business manager will be considered: (1) the need to make work more meaningful for employees, (2) the need to eliminate discrimination against minority workers, and (3) the need to improve the environment.

## Automation

One factor which is having a significant impact upon the manner in which the business manager conducts his operations today is automation. Automation may be defined as that process whereby goods or services are produced with the use of automatic machines with little or no assistance from human beings. Because machines operate at such high speed and with pinpoint accuracy, workers in the United States today are able to produce more goods and services than ever before. For example, in one automated plant, 130 employees can manufacture 750 railroad wheels in one day. Without the automated equipment, it would require more than two days for the same 130 employees to produce the 750 wheels.

People differ in their opinions on the long-run effects of automation on the well being of society. For example, some hold the view that automation will eliminate many jobs. That is, work which was previously performed by people will be performed by a machine. The result, many feel, will be increased unemployment. In order for the unemployed to survive, the argument is given, the government will need to provide a minimum guaranteed income for everyone.

On the other hand, there are those who hold the view that automation will not eliminate jobs but rather create a demand for additional jobs. Although some of these jobs may be filled by individuals who do not possess a particular trade or skill, the majority of such jobs will be such that only skilled individuals will be able to man them. Consequently, many contend that automation does not represent a threat to unemployment but rather it provides a challenging opportunity for businessmen and the government to retrain those workers who are unskilled.

Regardless of the view you hold, it does appear that automation is having an effect upon two aspects of the American worker's life: (1) it will further the trend towards a leisure-oriented society, and (2) it will decrease the importance of work to many people.

## TREND TOWARD MORE LEISURE

In the past, as the productivity of workers has increased, the number of hours worked per week have decreased. For example, between 1850 and 1900, the work week was reduced by approximately two hours each decade; between 1900 and 1940 the work week was reduced by some four hours. However, since 1940, cut-backs in the work week have taken place at a slower rate. According to figures compiled by the Bureau of Labor Statistics, the average work week of production workers on private nonagricultural payrolls as of September, 1973, was 37.3 hours.[1] Taking up the slack is greater numbers of holidays and longer vacations. The following excerpt from *Business in Brief* illustrates this trend:

> Declines in the work week, which fell from seventy hours in 1850 to around forty hours by 1964, have slowed down a bit. But coming along to take up the slack are more holidays and longer vacations, which since 1946

---

1. U. S. Department of Labor, Bureau of Labor Statistics, *Monthly Labor Review,* November, 1973, p. 99.

alone have provided the nation's workers with an additional ten days annually of respite and recreation.[2]

## THE FOUR-DAY WORK WEEK

Perhaps the newest change to come along in the scheduling of work is the four-day work week. Basically, in those firms which have adopted this work schedule, workers put in ten hours a day for four days rather than the traditional eight hours per day for five days. Although the total number of hours worked each week remains forty, the effect of a four-day work week is to lead to greater leisure orientation for workers, because they have the opportunity to enjoy three-day weekends. Another current advantage is that, with the energy crisis, the four-day plan reduces traveling costs for many workers. It is uncertain at this time whether the four-day work week will become common. One recent study reports conversions from the five-day to the four-day plan at around seventy firms each month. A number of firms which have adopted this new schedule report that overall employee morale has increased. Furthermore, some firms have experienced a reduction in employee absenteeism and employee turnover.

## THE IMPORTANCE OF WORK

Given the fact that the worker has been able to produce more and more goods and services in less and less time, the next question is the attitude of workers towards their jobs. The first impression would probably be that today's group of working men and women in America are the happiest and most contented of any group in the history of this country. They experience working conditions which are far superior to those of only a few decades ago. No longer are workers required to work seventy or eighty hours per week. Sweat shops are a thing of the past. Women and children are not subject to the hazardous and painful labor which was common during the nineteenth century. Furthermore, the economic well-being of American workers has never been higher. This is for the most part due to the development of unions, to legislation passed by Congress which has been favorable to the worker, and to dramatic changes in the personnel policies of American firms. It is not uncommon for today's worker to own two cars, vacation for two or three weeks each year, and send his children to college. Many workers who are laid off for a portion of the year are entitled to unemployment benefits, which frequently amount to as much as 90 or 95 percent of their regular wages. For those who are unable to work, the government and business have established supplemental benefits in the form of workmen's compensation, social security, and others.

Nevertheless, despite the progress and the many benefits which today's workers have realized, many workers today are expressing a very real discontent with their work. Many do not view their jobs as being important or interesting. Much of the blame for this attitude has been placed upon the widespread utilization of automated machines and techniques.

---

2. New York: The Chase Manhattan Bank, July–August, 1964, p. 2.

In an automated plant, machines control their own operations with little assistance from people. Consequently many workers no longer participate directly in the final product or service produced. This is particularly true of blue collar and clerical workers who generally have low-level responsibility. The following quotation from an interview with workers in an automated plant seems to illustrate the lack of pride and the absence of a sense of accomplishment in the work performed by an individual:

> I don't like the lack of feeling responsible for your work. The feeling that you're turning out more work but knowing its not yours really and not as good as you could make if you had control of the machine.[3]

Furthermore, the Report of a Special Task Force concerning Work in America summarizes the results of a 1970–1971 survey of white male blue-collar workers. The survey shows that fewer than 50 percent claimed that they were satisfied with their jobs most of the time.

There is in America today a situation in which blue-collar and clerical workers are earning real income and receiving other benefits which are the best in the history of the American worker. Yet work satisfaction appears to be decreasing. In addition, this very situation also appears to be common for many white-collar workers.

Again, according to a Report of a Special Task Force on Work in America, one of the most reliable single indicators of job dissatisfaction has been the response to the question: "What type of work would you try to get into if you could start all over again?" Exhibit 23–1 reflects the percentages in oc-

## EXHIBIT 23–1

*Percentages in Occupational Groups who would Choose Similar Work Again*

| Professional and lower white-collar occupations | % | Working-class occupations | % |
|---|---|---|---|
| Urban university professors | 93 | Skilled printers | 52 |
| Mathematicians | 91 | Paper workers | 42 |
| Physicists | 89 | Skilled autoworkers | 41 |
| Biologists | 89 | Skilled steelworkers | 41 |
| Chemists | 86 | Textile workers | 31 |
| Firm lawyers | 85 | Blue-collar workers, cross-section | 24 |
| Lawyers | 83 | Unskilled steelworkers | 21 |
| Journalists (Washington correspondents) | 82 | Unskilled autoworkers | 16 |
| Church university professors | 77 | | |
| Solo lawyers | 75 | | |
| White-collar workers, cross-section | 43 | | |

Source: *Work in America*, A Report of a Special Task Force to the Secretary of Health, Education and Welfare, Washington, D. C.: 1973, p. 16.

---

3. W. Faunce, E. Hardin, and E. Jacobson, "Automation and the Employee," *Annals of the American Academy of Political and Social Science,* March, 1962, pp. 60–68.

cupational groups who would choose similar work again. Of interest is the fact that in a cross-section of blue-collar workers, only 24 percent would choose similar work again. On the other hand, a cross-section of white-collar workers which includes professionals shows that 43 percent would choose similar work again. The data in the exhibit also reflect the fact that a much larger percentage of professional people would choose similar work than would unskilled workers. Certainly the information in the exhibit suggests that the level of responsibility and the skill required in his work has a significant impact upon the degree of satisfaction an individual realizes from his job.

Changing the attitudes of workers towards their jobs is obviously very difficult. Nonetheless, a number of firms today are realizing the importance of a satisfied and highly motivated work force to the long-run survival of the firm. As a result, many firms are implementing new techniques which are having a positive effect upon the way in which workers view their jobs. Improving job satisfaction is part of the social responsibility which more and more business manager are assuming today.

## Social Responsibility

*Social responsibility* is a new term which has become increasingly popular within the the past decade because of the increased emphasis being placed upon the need to clean up the environment and improve the quality of life for all Americans. Business managers are said to act in a socially responsible manner whenever their decisions and actions reflect a willingness to use society's resources for broad social ends and not solely for purposes of increasing the firm's profits.

However, there are opposing views as to whether a business manager should in fact assume the function of social responsibility. On the one side are those who contend that the only responsibility of business in a free enterprise system is to make a profit. As long as the firm operates within the laws established by society, its only goal should be to maximize its profits; and this goal should not be blurred by social responsibilities. People who hold this view emphasize that managers of a corporation, for example, act as agents for the firm's stockholders. Therefore their primary responsibility is to increase the wealth of each stockholder. In other words, when the business manager of a corporation acts in a socially responsible manner he is spending money which rightfully belongs to the firm's stockholders. These people also point out that it is the function of the government to concern itself with the general welfare of society and that only under a socialist system would business be expected to assume any form of social responsibility.

At the other end of the spectrum, there are those who contend that the business manager does have a responsibility to meet today's crucial social and environmental problems. Such individuals point out that it is not inconsistent for a firm to assume its social responsibilities while at the same time striving to maximize its profits. In fact, to ignore such social responsibilities as pollution control and discrimination against minority groups is to reduce profits in the long run. Furthermore, attention is directed to the fact that public interest groups and the government are becoming increasingly impatient with the business world. Unless positive action to implement policies which are socially oriented is taken soon, laws will be passed which will reduce the freedom, flexibility, and independence which business managers now enjoy.

Of the two views described, it is rather evident that the one toward which we are moving is for business managers to assume certain social responsibilities rather than avoiding them. In a 1969 survey of the 500 largest corporations in America, *Fortune* magazine reported that only 10 percent of the companies felt that the sole concern of business should be making profits.[4] On the other hand, 42 percent believed that while the first priority of business is to make a satisfactory profit, the firm should then undertake social responsibilities which might not themselves be profitable. Some of the more fruitful areas of social responsibility presently being explored by a number of firms include work satisfaction, fairness in hiring practices, and pollution control.

## WORK SATISFACTION

As mentioned earlier, workers in America have recently been able to produce more goods and services in less time. Despite the remarkable progress in productivity, many of today's workers appear to be experiencing growing dissatisfaction with their work. They do not find their work meaningful, and therefore their jobs do not provide the necessary fulfillment to make life interesting and eventful. As one observer put it, "without work all life goes rotten; but when work is soulless, life stifles and dies."[5] In the book *Wheels,* the author Arthur Hailey, gives several examples of production workers intentionally damaging automobiles on the production line. The explanation for such behavior is not difficult to understand when the repetition and lack of control which most of these assembly line workers experience are considered. Certainly, automobile plants are not exceptional. The production line concept of work has left many workers in all kinds of industries with monotonous jobs which lack meaning.

Because many production and assembly line workers find their jobs meaningless, some turn to alcoholism and drug addiction. Others develop various symptoms of poor mental health. As a result, sabotage, absenteeism, and turnover of employees are on the increase. All of this means additional costs to the business manager in producing a product or providing a service.

A growing number of business managers are beginning to realize the importance in having workers view their jobs as meaningful. Because work is so vital to the lives of most workers, a number of plants are experimenting with ways in which work can be redesigned to make it more satisfying. Following are examples of how three firms have successfully redesigned both blue- and white-collar jobs:

---

4. September, 1969, p. 94.
5. Arthur Hailey, *Wheels.* Garden City, N. Y.: Doubleday and Co., Inc., 1971, pp. 167–69.

At the Bankers Trust Company, many typists had repetitious jobs that entailed recording stock transfer data. Production was low, quality was poor, attitudes slack; absenteeism and turnover were high. The workers decided to try to redesign their own work tasks. Among other changes, they eliminated the work of a checker, and of a special group that made corrections by assuming these responsibilities themselves. This change permits a $360,000 annual savings, and the social problems have been largely eliminated. Similar results have been reported at Traveler's Insurance with keypunch operators.

On a Corning Glass assembly line, women workers formerly assembled hot plates for laboratory use. Now, each worker assembles a whole plate. Employees put their initials on each final product to allow identification with the work and to reference customer complaints. They also are given the opportunity to schedule their work as a group, and to design work flow improvements. Quality checks previously made by a separate group are conducted by the workers themselves. In six months following the change, rejects dropped from 23 percent to 1 percent, and absenteeism from 8 percent to 1 percent. During this same time, productivity increased. Also, the reputation of this division as an undesirable place to work was reversed. Other job change projects have been conducted at Corning with more complex instruments.

Motorola Inc. has restructured an assembly operation so that each employee involved in the experiment, instead of working on one or two components of the total product, now puts together the entire combination of eighty different components. Each employee is personally responsible for the quality of his receivers. His name appears on each of his units, and he must personally repair any unit that does not meet testing requirements. Early results from the experiment indicate that the technique of individual assembly requires 25 percent more workers, as well as a more detailed training program. However, these greater costs are just about offset by higher productivity, by the need for less inspection, by lower repair costs, by improved quality, and by reduced employee turnover and absentee rates.[6]

The benefits which are realized as a result of work redesign have been very encouraging to the workers involved. As these examples illustrate, the variety of work can be increased and consequently the monotony and boredom which is characteristic of assembly line jobs minimized and in some cases eliminated. Since these workers have more control over more aspects of their jobs, they are motivated to utilize all of their potential in order to improve their own production techniques. This leads to greater job satisfaction because workers begin to recognize that they are not only needed by the firm but that they play an integral part in the making of certain decisions necessary to the long-run survival of the firm.

In addition, the firms benefit from these programs. Although there are usually added costs for training purposes, total costs to the firm are often reduced

---

6. *Work in America,* A Report of a Special Task Force to the Secretary of Health, Education, and Welfare, Washington, D. C.: 1973, pp. 99–101.

because workers produce more goods at a higher level of quality. Absenteeism and turnover rates are reduced. Employee morale and motivation are increased. Furthermore, because workers realize a greater sense of personal worth, many work redesign programs have resulted in more workers participating in community projects such as the United Fund.

## MINORITY GROUPS AND HIRING PRACTICES

*Minority workers* include primarily blacks, Indians, and Spanish-speaking Americans. For the most part, they represent those members of the society who have not had job opportunities opened to others who are more fortunate. One means of measuring the extent to which minority workers have been unable to keep pace in society is to compare the earnings of both groups. For example, whereas all adult males in the United States in 1969 earned a median income of $6,429, minority males earned a median income of $3,991. The difference of $2,438 reflects the discrimination which exists in the hiring and promotion policies of numerous firms throughout the country.

Despite the fact that minority workers have not kept pace, this does not mean that progress is not being made. In fact, during the decade of the sixties, impressive progress was realized. A joint study by the Bureau of Labor Statistics and the Bureau of the Census reports that "Negroes now are more likely to have higher incomes, hold better jobs, and live in better homes than they did a decade ago."[7] Nevertheless, this same study reports that wide discrepancies still remain.

Eliminating the discrepancy in job opportunities is largely a role of the business manager in America. Of course, many business managers contend that their real concern is with maximizing profits rather than with helping people. However, a growing number of business managers are beginning to realize that to help the minority worker help himself is very consistent with the self-interest motive of maximizing profits. This is reflected in a speech delivered by Henry Ford II on April 7, 1969, at Yale University:

> It is clearly in the self-interest of business both to enlarge its markets and to improve its work force by helping disadvantaged people to develop and employ their economic potential. Good employees are any company's most valuable resource. Good employees are also hard to find. Any company that limits its access to good employees by imposing such irrelevant criteria as race or color is also limiting its profit potential.[8]

The fact that business managers are exercising their social responsibility in regard to the hiring of minority workers is reflected in the formation in 1968 of the National Alliance of Businessmen. Working in conjunction with the federal government, the alliance encourages business managers to employ the hard-core unemployed.

---

7. U. S. Department of Labor, Bureau of Labor Statistics, "Progress of U. S. Negroes During the 1960s," *Monthly Labor Review*, April, 1970, p. 64.
8. "Business and Society's Problems," reprinted in *Issues in Business and Society*, George A. Steiner (ed.). New York: Random House, Inc., 1972, p. 167.

In addition to employment in assembly line and blue-collar jobs, progress is also being made in professional jobs. According to figures released by the Bureau of Labor Statistics, minority workers are also beginning to hold higher level positions in society. In 1957, 3.7 percent of all minority workers held professional and technical positions. By 1972, this percentage had increased to 9.5 percent.[9]

## WOMEN

Another group of individuals who are also recognized as being discriminated against is women. In general, women earn less, hold lower status jobs, and experience greater unemployment than men. The discrepancy in the earnings of women versus men is rather large. For example, the average female employee in 1970 earned approximately 59 percent of the wages paid to a similarly employed man. Although women today can be found in virtually every job listed by the Bureau of the Census, the great majority of women work in occupations which have been traditionally characterized as a "woman's job." This is reflected in the data in Exhibit 23–2.

### EXHIBIT 23–2

*Employed Married Women by Occupation, 1972*

Percent distribution:

| | | | |
|---|---|---|---|
| Professional | 16.2 | Operatives | 14.4 |
| Farmers and farm managers | .3 | Private household workers | 3.0 |
| Managers and administrators | 4.9 | Service workers | 16.7 |
| Clerical | 33.9 | Farm laborers and foremen | 1.5 |
| Salesworkers | 7.0 | Laborers | .8 |
| Craftsmen, foremen | 1.3 | | |

Source: U.S. Bureau of the Census, *Statistical Abstract of the United States: 1973*, 94th ed. Washington, D.C.: 1973, p. 223.

Notice that while only 4.9 percent of employed married women are working as managers and administrators, 33.9 percent are employed in clerical jobs, which include stenographers, typists, and secretaries, Although 16.2 percent are employed in professional jobs, approximately two-thirds of these jobs account for those women employed as either nurses or teachers. Furthermore, most women teach in the primary grades, whereas most men teach in the high schools. It is relatively rare for a woman to hold a teaching position in a university.

Although there is discrimination in the hiring and promotion policies of many firms in regard to women, progress is being made to eliminate this injustice. The number of women partcipating in the labor force is higher than ever as shown in Exhibit 23–3.

---

9. U. S. Bureau of the Census, *Statistical Abstract of the United States: 1973*, 94th ed. Washington, D. C.: 1973, p. 234.

EXHIBIT 23–3

*Participation Rates of Females in the Labor Force
1960 to 1972 and Projections to 1985*

| Year | Participation rates |
|------|---------------------|
| 1960 | 37.1 |
| 1970 | 42.8 |
| 1971 | 42.8 |
| 1972 | 43.3 |
| 1980 | 45.0 |
| 1985 | 45.6 |

Source: U.S. Bureau of the Census, *Statistical Abstract of the United States: 1973*, 94th ed. Washington, D.C.: 1973, p. 220.

Whereas 37.1 percent of all females over the age of sixteen participated in the labor force in 1969, 43.3 percent participated in 1972. Furthermore, the projected trend is that labor force participation on the part of women will increase.

The fact that business managers in the United States are becoming increasingly sensitive to the needs of women is apparent in a recent survey of more than 100 businesses and industrial firms. The results show the following:

> The firms plan to hire one-fifth more women college graduates from the class of 1970 than from the previous classes. Two-fifths or more of the firms indicated that more women would be hired in engineering, data processing, or accounting positions if qualified women could be found.[10]

In addition, *Business Week* and other sources have indicated that women graduates are currently being employed in entry-level executive jobs that were at one time considered closed to females. Not only are opportunities more plentiful today for members of all minority groups, the competition among firms to hire good people is very keen. This fact is reflected in the following statement:

> Ex-Cell-O Corp. launches a summer intern program aimed at black engineering students. At a division of Johnson & Johnson, "well over half" of this summer's student interns are women or minorities, up from 20 percent in 1970. With competition to hire blacks and women stiffening, a large petroleum company admits its intern program seeks to "get a foot in the door for getting the top-notch people when they graduate."
>
> The intern programs pay off at many firms. Public Service Co. of Colorado will hire its first female engineer next month; she had worked as an intern last summer. In Chicago, Commonwealth Edison estimates it hires one-third or more of its interns upon graduation. "What I saw during the summer really sold me on the company," says a Negro engineer and former intern whom the utility landed in 1970.[11]

---

10. *Monthly Labor Review*, June, 1970, pp. 19–29.
11. *Wall Street Journal*, June 26, 1973, p. 1.

## POLLUTION CONTROL

Even though man has always polluted his surroundings, the dangers to the environment were not significant before the industrial revolution, because most people lived in uncrowded rural areas and most goods were produced by hand rather than by machines. However, ever since the industrial revolution, large urban areas have been developing. The large factories and people crowded into smaller areas resulted in the pollution of air and water surrounding our larger cities. During the 1900s pollution problems grew worse with the invention of automobiles and airplanes, along with new production techniques requiring more and more machines. Gases and smoke dirty the air; chemicals poison the water, and fertilizers and pesticides damage the soil.

However, it was not until the latter part of the 1960s that people became truly concerned about the environment. The following statement illustrates the extent to which various industries had contributed to the pollution of the Ohio River:

> At Midland, Pa., pipes from a Crucible Steel Corp. titanium plant spew a bright green, poisonous waste fluid into the river. At Steubenville, Ohio, iron oxide from steel company blast furnaces stains the river a reddish brown. Just below Wheeling, West Va., an Ashland Oil Co. plant pours a bluish-black goo down a bank into the water. Upstream at Aliquippa, Pa., oil discharged from a Jones and Laughlin Steel Corp. plant leaves irridescent splotches that flash green and blue as they float lazily away with the current.[12]

Of course, it would be incorrect to blame industry for all these problems. In the case of the Ohio River, raw sewage is contributed by 300 communities which are located either on the river or along its tributaries. None of these communities have sewage plants.

This picture of one river reflects in many ways what is happening to much of the water supply as well as the air. Business managers are just beginning to answer to their social responsibility in this area. As indicated previously, the primary goal of business is to make a profit which represents a reasonable return for the risks assumed. However, many business managers now realize that neglecting the environment in which business works will, in the long run, have a negative or eroding effect upon the firm's profits. In other words, maintaining clean air, clean water, and so on is good business. Many firms which are located in our urban areas are already realizing this point. The decay of many large cities is destroying the very marketplace in which business transactions are made.

There are many examples today of changes which business firms have implemented in order to protect the environment. A number of manufacturing firms are installing filters and other devices in their smoke stacks which prevent pollution from escaping into the air. A case in point, the Mead Corporation (a pulp

---

12. *Wall Street Journal,* March 17, 1969, p. 1.

and paper mill which has its headquarters in Dayton, Ohio) has invested millions in pollution control facilities at its paper mill in Escanaba, Michigan:

> Among other things, the company has repeatedly increased its outlays for pollution abatement equipment, to a current total of about $16 million for air and water controls. Moreover, officials at the mill say they're under directions from James W. McSwiney, Mead's Chairman, to put concern about pollution ahead of concern about production.[13]

To reduce the pollution that is emitted by automobile engines, gasoline refineries are producing no-lead gasoline. Most 1975 cars will require unleaded gasoline because of catalytic muffler emission control systems which are being installed by the automobile manufacturers.

Many of these innovations came about because laws were passed which require business firms to raise their environmental protection standards. Most notable of these laws has been the Clean Air Act of 1970. Nonetheless, voluntary efforts on the part of business managers are becoming more widespread. The following example illustrates this:

> One company that has won praise from pollution fighters for its voluntary efforts is National Steel Corporation. When it added a giant new steel-making shop to its plant at Weirton, West Virginia, in 1967, National installed extensive water pollution control equipment that is said to make its waste water cleaner than that of most cities. After the equipment was installed, a high sludge mass—two inches thick and 2,500 feet long—slowly disappeared from alongside the plant. The sludge had built up from oil discharged by the plant before the new equipment was installed.[4]

In the future, it is expected that more and more companies will voluntarily implement changes which will have a positive effect upon the environment.

## SOCIAL RESPONSIBILITY IN REVIEW

In this discussion of the business manager's social responsibilities, emphasis has been placed on the importance of improving workers' attitudes towards their jobs, eliminating discrimination in hiring policies, and cleaning up the environment. Other steps must also be taken to improve truth in advertising, product safety, product quality, and so on. To help make certain that business managers carry out their social responsibilities, a number of experts are calling for a "social audit" of business firms in the United States by outside consultants. This social audit would be similar to the fianancial audit which is conducted by the certified public accountant. The purpose of the social audit would be to review the record of the firm's social accomplishments.

Although progress is being made in the various areas of social responsibility, it is important to realize that business managers are not sacrificing their traditional responsibilities of providing for economic growth, employing people, and producing goods and services. They are, on the contrary, recognizing the

---

13. *Wall Street Journal,* June 29, 1973, p. 1.
14. *Wall Street Journal,* March 17, 1969, p. 1.

social responsibilities as being an additional role which business must assume along with individual citizens and the government.

## Summary

Automation is a process whereby goods or services are produced with the use of automatic machines with little or no assistance from human beings. It has increased the productivity of American workers, thereby increasing the amount of leisure time they can enjoy. The average work week today for production workers is around 40.6 hours, whereas in 1850 production workers put in 70 hours per week. Furthermore, a growing number of firms are adopting the four-day work week, resulting in a three-day weekend for many workers. On the other hand, automation has tended to decrease job satisfaction by narrowing the amount of responsibility which workers must assume.

Social responsibility is a term which reflects a willingness on the part of business managers to act for the good of society and not solely for purposes of maximizing the firm's profit picture. When a business manager acts in a socially responsible manner he may also be improving the firm's profits, because employees, customers, minority groups, and the public in general approve of those firms which act in a socially responsible manner. Their approval is exercised by purchasing the firm's goods or services and, in the case of employees, working harder for the long-run survival of the firm.

Three primary areas of social responsibility which are of concern to the business manager were discussed in this chapter. The first is improving job satisfaction. Through redesign of work tasks, it is possible to make work more meaningful, thereby reducing absentee rates and employee turnover, as well as improving the quality of goods or services produced. The second is eliminating discrimination in hiring practices. Although this was a major problem prior to the seventies, recent practices indicate that business firms are opening their doors to all minority groups, including women. Nevertheless, much remains to be done before discrimination is eliminated. The third is protecting the environment against pollution. Even though much remains to be done in this area, many firms are voluntarily taking action to clean up water, air, and soil which have become dirtied because of the past carelessness of firms and individual people.

## QUESTIONS

1. (a) Define *automation*.
   (b) In your opinion, will automation eliminate jobs?
2. Describe the two aspects of an American worker's life which automation appears to be affecting.
3. (a) Explain the four-day work week.
   (b) Would you prefer a four-day or five-day work week? Explain.

4. According to data presented in a table in Chapter 23, only 24 percent of blue-collar workers would choose similar work again. In your opinion, why is this percentage so low?

5. (a) Explain the meaning of the term *social responsibility* as it relates to the business manager.

   (b) Discuss the opposing views as to whether a business manager should in fact assume the role of social responsibility. Which view do you hold?

6. (a) Explain the technique which the Corning Glass Co. implemented to improve job satisfaction for its employees.

   (b) What were the results?

7. Cite some data or other information which would indicate that business firms are beginning to make real progress in the hiring of minority workers.

8. Discuss the following statements: "A business manager who is interested in maximizing his profits will not concern himself with protecting the environment."

9. Give two examples which illustrate the fact that business managers are concerned with protecting the environment.

10. (a) What is meant by a *social audit?*

   (b) Should the person or persons who conduct a social audit be employees of the firm being audited? Explain.

# 24

# International Business

Business manager today are not restricted to their home markets in seeking customers for their goods and services. A new frontier—the world market—is just beginning to be explored. There are two common means by which the business manager may participate in this world market. The first is to exchange goods or services with another country, thereby becoming an active participant in international trade. Although business managers in the past have traded with foreign nations, the volume of such trading was generally small. However, since World War II the magnitude of trade between nations has reached unprecedented levels. Today, it amounts to over $300 billion.

The second means by which the business manager may participate in the world market place is to construct a subsidiary plant in a foreign market. Since 1950, the construction of plants in foreign markets has become so widespread that experts are comparing its impact upon the business environment with that of the industrial revolution.

## International Trade

The first question to ask is why nations engage in trade with each other. The answer can perhaps be best explained by looking first at individuals. In the free world those people who specialize in a particular trade or profession are able to raise their standards of living by producing a good or service and in turn exchanging with others for other goods and services rather than trying to do everything for one's self. For example, assume that a farmer specializes in the production of wheat. The money which he receives from selling his wheat is then used to purchase those items which he needs, such as a car, farm equipment, life insurance, clothing, radio and television, dental services, and an education for his children. If a wheat farmer were to try to produce not only wheat but also attempt to educate his own children, build his own farm equipment or television, fix his children's teeth, and so on, the results would be less than satisfactory. In fact, his family would have a very low standard of living.

This same reasoning also applies to nations throughout the world. A nation can increase its wealth and the standard of living for its people by specializing. That is, it produces and exports those goods which it can produce more efficiently than other nations and exchanges for imports those goods which it is least efficient in producing. This reasoning is often referred to as the "principle of **absolute advantage.**"

## THE PRINCIPLE OF ABSOLUTE ADVANTAGE

*Absolute advantage* is a term used to describe a condition in which one country can produce a product more efficiently than another country. For example, because of soil and climate, farmers in Brazil can produce coffee more efficiently than farmers in the United States. Consequently, Brazil is said to have an absolute advantage over the United States in the production of coffee. Similarly, Cuba has an absolute advantage over the United States in the production of sugar. Conversely, the United States would have an absolute advantage over Brazil and Cuba in the production of wheat and corn. The principle of absolute advantage is very important because it helps to explain why countries (or businessmen) specialize in the production of certain goods and then trade with other countries for those goods which are scarce. Exchanging of goods between nations is referred to as *international trade*.

In order to explain the advantages of international trade, an example will be used. Assume that Country A and Country B are both capable of producing onions and soybeans. Also assume, for purposes of simplifying the illustration, that each country has 1,000 acres of land, 40 percent allocated to the production of onions and the remainder (60 percent) to the production of soybeans. Country A produces 60 tons of onions and 120 tons of soybeans. Country B produces 100 tons of onions and 80 tons of soybeans. This information is shown in Exhibit 24–1.

Notice that both countries produce a total of 180 tons of onions and soybeans in a year. Nevertheless, the data reflect the fact that Country A has an absolute advantage over Country B in the production of soybeans, because Country A can produce 120 tons of soybeans on 60 percent of its land whereas Country B produces only 80 tons of soybeans on 60 percent of its land. Conversely, Country B has an absolute advantage over Country A in the produc-

## EXHIBIT 24–1

*For the Year 19X1*
*Production of Onions and Soybeans*
*(in tons)*
*Without Specialization*

| Country | Onions | Soybeans | Total |
|---------|--------|----------|-------|
| A | 60 | 120 | 180 |
| B | 100 | 80 | 180 |
| | 160 | 200 | 360 |

tion of onions. That is, Country B produces 100 tons of onions on 40 percent of its land whereas Country A produces 60 tons on the same amount of land.

Now consider the advantages which both countries would realize through specialization and exchange. Should Country A devote 100 percent of its land to the production of soybeans rather than 60 percent, it would produce 200 tons of soybeans ($120/60\% = 200$). By planting 100 percent of its land in onions, Country B would produce 250 tons of onions. These results are reflected in Exhibit 24–2.

## EXHIBIT 24–2

*For the Year 19X2*
*Production of Onions and Soybeans*
*(in tons)*
*With Specialization*

| Country | Onions | Soybeans | Total |
|---------|--------|----------|-------|
| A | 0 | 200 | 200 |
| B | 250 | 0 | 250 |
| | 250 | 200 | 450 |

Notice that if each country produces that product in which it has an absolute advantage, total production of onions and soybeans is increased from 360 tons (see Exhibit 24–1) to 450 tons (see Exhibit 24–2). Before specialization, Countries A and B were capable of producing 160 tons of onions and 200 tons of soybeans (see Exhibit 24–1). With specialization, Country A is capable of producing 200 tons of soybeans and Country B is capable of producing 250 tons of onions.

As a result of specialization, the two countries will trade with each other in order for Country A to obtain onions and Country B to obtain soybeans. If Country B trades 100 tons of onions to Country A in exchange for 80 tons of soybeans the result would be as shown in Exhibit 24–3. The advantages of specialization and trade are evident when Exhibit 24–3 is compared with Exhibit 24–1. Before specialization, Country A had 60 tons of onions and 120

EXHIBIT 24–3

*Distribution of Onions and Soybeans*
*(in tons)*
*After Trade Between Countries A and B*

| Country | Onions | Soybeans | Total |
|---------|--------|----------|-------|
| A | 100 | 120 | 220 |
| B | 150 | 80 | 230 |
|  | 250 | 200 | 450 |

tons of soybeans, for a total of 180 tons. After specialization and trading, Country A has 100 tons of onions and 120 tons of soybeans, or a total of 220 tons. In other words, Country A increased its onions by 40 tons while maintaining its soybeans at 120 tons. Country B ends up with 150 tons of onions and 80 tons of soybeans. Although Country B's amount of soybeans remains constant, it was able to increase its holdings in onions by 50 tons.

Because nations around the world (even those behind the iron curtain) realize the advantages to be derived from international trading, there have been a number of developments since World War II which have facilitated the exchange of goods and services between countries. These include the General Agreements on Tariffs and Trade (GATT); the International Monetary Fund; the World Bank; and the Export-Import Bank.

## THE GENERAL AGREEMENT ON TARIFFS AND TRADE

Before World War II, the amount of international trade between nations was limited because of the restricted trade barriers at that time. The two most common devices which a country can utilize to restrict the importation of goods and services are **tariffs** and **trade quotas.** A *tariff* is a tax assessed on each good being imported from another nation. For example, assume that the United States assesses a 10 percent tariff on the value of all Volkswagons imported from Germany. The effect would be to increase the cost of Volkswagons to retail car buyers in America, thereby restricting the number of Volkswagons sold. Such a tariff would supposedly afford some protection to American automobile manufacturers. A *quota,* on the other hand, does not represent an additional tax but rather it restricts the number of units of a particular good which may be imported. The quota on Volkswagons entering the United States might be set at 500,000 per year.

It was not until after World War II that the major trading nations of the world began to liberalize trade by reducing or eliminating trade barriers. One of the most notable accomplishments of the free trade movement was the creation in 1947 at Geneva of the General Agreement on Tariffs and Trade (commonly referred to as GATT). Twenty-two countries participated in the original signing of the tariff agreement. Today, some ninety countries accounting for over four-fifths of the world's trade are members of GATT. The primary purpose of this agreement has been to foster the exchange of goods and services between participating countries through the lowering of tariffs and other barriers. For example, one of the results has been the conception of the most favored nation clause, which prevents discrimination among nations. For example, if Country A were to offer Country B a tariff concession, the most favored nation clause would require that Country A offer a similar concession to the other countries which are members of GATT. Because of the liberalization in trade policies which GATT has brought about, business managers in the United States and throughout the free world have been able to develop markets for their products which at one time were considered closed.

## THE INTERNATIONAL MONETARY FUND

When exchange rates are unstable, businessmen assume a great deal of uncertainty when they engage in international trade. Such was the case prior to World War II. In order to overcome this barrier to international trade, the International Monetary Fund (IMF) was established in 1944 at the forty-four nation Bretton Woods Conference. Today, over 100 nations are members of the fund. Because of its large financial resources (over $28 billion), the IMF is able to allow those nations with balance of payments problems the opportunity to continue trading. Business firms in the United States and other countries do not deal directly with the IMF. Nevertheless, establishment of the IMF has benefitted the businessman through the development of world markets.

## THE WORLD BANK

The International Bank for Reconstruction and Development, often referred to as the World Bank, is an agency of the United Nations. The World Bank makes over $1 billion of long-term loans a year to member governments to help in the financing of investments in such areas as education, agricultural and industrial projects, and health care. Like the IMF, more than 100 countries are members of the World Bank. The bank obtains its funds from member countries and in turn loans funds to member countries which are unable to obtain financial backing at reasonable terms from other sources.

The World Bank has helped to foster international trade and has benefitted the American economy. A good portion of the $1 billion in annual long-term loans is used to purchase equipment and other goods produced in the United States. Furthermore, when underdeveloped nations help themselves, they raise their standards of living and eventually become potential markets for goods produced in the United States and other countries.

## THE EXPORT-IMPORT BANK OF THE U. S.

Although the United States Export-Import Bank was established before World War II in 1934, it has in recent years provided significant assistance to businessmen who are interested in exporting their goods and services abroad.

Its impact upon international trade is reflected in the following statement extracted from EXIM/BANKER:

> Its assistance has now reached the point where, during the past three fiscal years alone, Eximbank authorizations have supported U. S. transactions with an export value of some $15 billion. The *immediate* result of this support has been to provide additional orders for U. S. industry and increased employment for U. S. labor. An equally important *longer-range* result is that the foreign projects financed by Eximbank have resulted in economic growth which has expanded world markets for U. S. goods and services.[1]

## INTERNATIONAL TRADE TODAY

Because of the favorable developments in free trade, including those discussed above, the exchange of goods and services between nations is growing significantly each year. Figures compiled by the *Survey of Current Business* show that exports of goods and services from the United States in 1972 amounted to $73.75 billion. This represents an increase of 11½ percent over 1971. On the other hand, imports of goods and services into the United States amounted to $77.75 billion, or an increase of 19 percent over 1971.

The trend towards specialization and exchange between nations means that the business manager has a larger market in which to sell his products. Rather than being restricted to a local, regional, or even national market, the business manager has an opportunity to sell in a global or world marketplace. Although international trade is becoming increasingly popular, not every firm must sell abroad in order to earn a good profit. Nevertheless, it is important in today's world economy for many business managers to give serious consideration to the potential markets which may exist for their products or services in other countries. Serving such markets could present a real opportunity for maximizing profits.

In order to determine whether or not there is a potential market for his product in foreign nations, the business manager should be aware of the types of goods which are exported from the United States and the areas to which these goods are sent. In the remainder of the discussion on international trade, consideration will be given to four factors: (1) the primary types of commodity groups exported from the United States, (2) the areas to which these goods are sent, (3) comparison of exports to imports, and (4) the services available to a small firm which wishes to sell abroad.

## COMMODITY GROUPS EXPORTED

Data in Exhibit 24–4 show the type of goods which businessmen in the United States exported to other countries during the years 1960 and 1972. Of interest is the fact that each of the first five commodity groups listed accounts for a small percentage of total domestic exports in 1972 as compared to 1960.

---

1. July, 1972, p. 4.

EXHIBIT 24–4

*Domestic Exports, by Selected Commodity Groups*
*1960 and 1972*

| Commodity | 1960 | 1972 |
|---|---|---|
| | \<\<Percent of total\>\> | |
| Food and live animals | 13.2 | 11.6 |
| Beverages and tobacco | 2.4 | 1.9 |
| Crude materials, unediable except fuels | 13.7 | 10.3 |
| Mineral fuels and related materials | 4.1 | 3.2 |
| Chemicals | 8.7 | 8.4 |
| Machinery and transport equipment | 34.3 | 43.7 |
| Other manufactured goods | 18.7 | 16.5 |
| Unallocated | 4.9 | 4.4 |

Source: U.S. Bureau of the Census, *Statistical Abstract of the United States: 1973*, 94th ed. Washington, D. C.: 1973, p. 784.

For example, in 1960, food and live animals accounted for 13.2 percent of the total United States exports. However, in 1972 it accounted for only 11.6 percent. On the other hand, the other two commodity groups listed in the table (Machinery and transport equipment and Other manufactured goods) accounted for a larger percentage of total exports. In 1960, these two groups accounted for 53 percent (34.3 + 18.7) of total exports and in 1972 they accounted for 60.2 (43.7 + 16.5) percent. These figures reflect the fact that manufactured goods rather than primary goods (foods and raw materials) predominate international trade today. Prior to 1960 this was not the case. That is, raw materials accounted for a larger percentage of United States exports than did manufactured goods.

## WHERE GOODS ARE SENT

In Exhibit 24–5 information is provided on the different continents to which American businessmen exported merchandise. The continents of Europe and North America accounted for 64.6 percent of United States exports in 1972. In terms of specific countries, the following ten are the most important customers of goods exported from the United States: Canada, Japan, West Germany, United Kingdom, Mexico, France, Italy, Netherlands, Australia, and Brazil. Perhaps the most interesting development in international trade during the sixties and early seventies has been the increase in trade with the Soviet Union and China.

Relations between the United States and the Soviet Union improved dramatically during the decade of the 60s. As a result, United States businessmen have become increasingly aware of the potential markets in the Soviet Union for goods produced in the United States. The fact that firms in the United States

EXHIBIT 24–5

*Exports of Merchandise by Continent*
*1960 and 1972*
*(In Billions of Dollars)*

| Continent | 1960 | 1972 |
|---|---|---|
| Africa | .8 | 1.6 |
| Asia | 4.1 | 11.3 |
| Australia and Oceania | .5 | 1.0 |
| Europe | 7.4 | 16.2 |
| North America | 5.5 | 16.0 |
| South America | 2.2 | 3.7 |
| Total | 20.5 | 49.8 |

Source: U.S. Bureau of the Census, *Statistical Abstract of the United States: 1973,* 94th ed. Washington, D. C.: 1973, page 780.

are giving serious consideration to the Soviet market is reflected in the industrial exhibit which American businessmen stage in the U.S.S.R. annually. The following excerpt represents an example of the purchases which were made by the Soviet Communists at the 1973 exhibition:

> The U.S. businessmen knew that when the Communists bought they would buy big. So far this year, Soviet purchases from U.S. exhibitors have included $68 million worth of Caterpillar earthmovers and $25 million worth of International Harvester compressors and generators.[2]

In comparison with the U.S.S.R., trade with China is very small. Nevertheless, great strides have been made in the past few years. For example, during 1973 trade between China and the United States expanded by $800 million. In 1972 the total was only $92 million. The kinds of products which China purchased from U.S. businessmen are depicted in the following statement:

> So far, the new link is proving to be a bonanza for U.S. firms; the Chinese import nearly fifteen times as much from the U.S. as they export. Among the biggest ticket items to date are some 4,000,000 tons of grain, ten Boeing 707 jetliners valued at $150 million, and eight ammonia plants to be built by M. W. Kellogg Co. for $200 million. The Chinese are also anxious to do business with giant American oil companies such as Exxon, Mobil, and Caltex, and makers of petroleum exploration and drilling equipment, including U.S. Steel International, Phillips Petroleum, and Baker Oil Tools.[3]

## EXPORTS COMPARED TO INPORTS

The graph in Exhibit 24–6 shows that the United States exports exceeded United States imports until 1971. Since then, imports have exceeded exports, with the gap widening. For the year 1972 the United States exports of mer-

---

2. *Time,* December 3, 1973, p. 104.
3. *Time,* December 31, 1973, p. 53.

## EXHIBIT 24–6

*Merchandise Exports and Imports: 1960 to 1972*

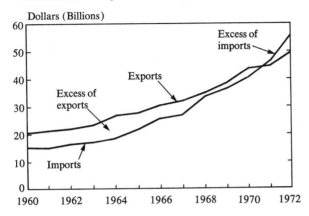

Source: U.S. Bureau of the Census, *Statistical Abstract of the United States: 1973*, 94th ed. Washington, D. C.: 1973, p. 762.

chandise amounted to $49.8 billion. Imports of merchandise amounts to $55.6 billion for the same period. As a result, the United States experienced a trade deficit during 1972 of $5.8 billion. However, in 1973 there was a complete turnaround. United States firms exported $70.8 billion of goods abroad and imported $69.1 billion. As a result, the United States realized a trade surplus of $1.7 billion. In comparison to 1972, exports increased 44 percent during 1973. The February 18, 1974, issue of *Commerce Today* outlines four reasons for this export expansion:

> First, the strong acceleration in foreign economic activity stimulated demand for a wide variety of U. S. products, especially machinery and industrial materials; secondly, the exchange rate shifts over the past two years have improved the price competitiveness of U. S. products in foreign markets; thirdly, extremely tight supplies of farm products overseas, due to smaller crops in many countries, stimulated a huge expansion in U. S. agricultural exports; fourth, domestic price controls made exporting especially profitable and provided incentive for American firms to step up their sales efforts abroad.[4]

## HOW DOES A SMALL FIRM MARKET ITS PRODUCTS ABROAD?

Large companies often have their own export departments, which are responsible for making connections with foreign markets. Unfortunately, the small firm does not generally have sufficient capital to established its own export department. Consequently, it must look to other methods if it is interested in selling abroad. One method, which is growing in popularity in the United States, is to utilize an *export management company* (EMC). It is estimated that

4. P. 8.

between 600 to 1,000 EMC's are in business today, helping small businessmen market their products abroad. The following example illustrates the way in which an EMC can help a small firm develop markets in foreign countries for its product:

> Fifteen years ago, Chet Conk had built up a nice little product: blanks.
> Mr. Conk's blanks are film-coated aluminum discs that are used to make master recordings. Since each master can be used to press thousands of phonograph records, there is a limit to the domestic demand for blanks.
> What to do? Mr. Conk decided to push exports. He got together with Singer Products Co. of New York, an exports-management firm whose business is finding and exploiting foreign markets for small and medium-sized U. S. manufacturers.
> And here's the happy ending. The export sales of Mr. Conk's company, Transco Products of Linden, N. J., have since grown from about $10,000 a year to just about $1 million annually. Transco now ships about 50 percent of its blanks abroad; it has around 60 percent of the world market and sells to buyers in more than 100 countries.[5]

Most small businesimen do not understand the needs of foreign markets, let alone the complexities of trade laws. Consequently, working with an EMC can reduce many of the problems and worries which a small firm might realize if it tried to export on its own.

A second method available to a small firm is to sell its products outright to an *export merchant*. The export merchant in turn resells the merchandise in a foreign country for his own account. This method would appear to work best for those firms which are interested in selling abroad periodically rather than developing a solid market abroad.

A third means of exporting merchandise for the small firm is the *export broker*. Rather than purchasing the merchandise to be exported, the export broker brings the seller and the buyer together. His fee is based on a percentage of the sales he has arranged. For instance, "Tatum Farms of Georgia began exporting hatching eggs and baby chicks at the end of 1963 through an export broker. Subsequently, the firm sold some 70 percent of its production abroad."[6]

*Literature Available to the Small Company.*   The business manager of a small firm wishing to export should take advantage of the many materials which are now available. For example, the Small Business Administration publishes a 134-page book entitled "Export Marketing for Smaller Firms." This book outlines for the manager of a small company the problems he will probably encounter and the sources of assistance available to him. Furthermore, publications of the United States Department of Commerce and its Bureau of International Commerce provide information necessary for the proper evaluation of foreign markets.

---

5. *Wall Street Journal,* July 13, 1973, p. 1.
6. Vern Terpstra, *International Marketing.* New York: Holt, Rinehart and Winston, Inc., 1972, p. 10.

## The Multinational Firm

The discussion thus far has centered on international trade. Up until 1950 the primary means of conducting international business was through international trade. Some companies had made direct investments abroad before World War II in the agricultural and extractive industries. However, their primary reason for doing so was to extract materials for use back in the United States. At the start of the fifties, there was a major shift in the conduct of world business. Business firms in the United States started to invest heavily in subsidiary plants abroad with the intent of producing products to sell largely in these and other foreign countries. Through their experiences with exporting, a number of firms became familiar with the market conditions abroad. They were not hesitant to invest in manufacturing and distribution facilities. The country in which the goods were produced was also the same country in which the goods were marketed. Business firms which followed this pattern became known as *multinational companies.* According to *Business Week,* a company must meet two tests before it can be classified as multinational:

(1) It has a manufacturing or some other form of direct investment in at least one foreign country.

(2) It has a global perspective. All basic decisions concerning marketing, production, and research are made in terms of the alternatives available to it throughout the world.[7]

In addition to the above, the multinational firm is one which realizes at least 20 percent of its sales and profits from international operations. Exhibit 24–7

### EXHIBIT 24–7

*Examples of U. S. Multinational Firms*

| Company name | % of earnings from foreign operations as of 1972 |
|---|---|
| Coca-Cola | 55 |
| Gillette | 51 |
| Hoover | 60 |
| IBM | 54 |
| Revlon | 38 |
| Sunbeam | 38 |
| Xerox | 46 |

Source: *Business Week,* January 12, 1974, p. 53.

gives a few examples of United States corporations which would be properly classified as multinational companies. A firm which realizes less than 20 percent of its sales and profits from international operations is properly classified as simply a firm with international investments.

---

7. "Multinational Companies: How U. S. Business Goes World Wide," *Business Week,* April 20, 1963, p. 63.

In contrast to the multinational firm, a firm which both produces and sells its goods or services in only one country is called a *uninational firm.* A company which produces its products in one country and exports some or all of its goods to a foreign market is not a uninational firm. Rather, such a firm is said to be involved in international trade, but it is not properly called a multinational firm.

The distinction between these three types of firms is illustrated in Exhibit 24–8. In case A the production process and the distribution process are both

EXHIBIT 24–8

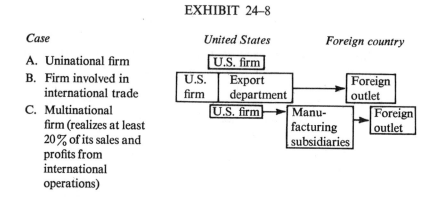

| *Case* | *United States* | *Foreign country* |
| --- | --- | --- |
| A. Uninational firm | | |
| B. Firm involved in international trade | | |
| C. Multinational firm (realizes at least 20% of its sales and profits from international operations) | | |

conducted in the United States. Therefore the firm is classified as uninational. Notice that the firm does not export its goods abroad nor does it own a subsidiary plant in a foreign country. In case B, the production process is carried on in the United States. However, in this case the company sells its products in both the United States market and also in a foreign market, by exporting its manufactured goods abroad. In case B the firm is shown as having its own export department which is responsible for carrying out export activities. As previously mentioned, a firm can also export through export management companies (EMC) and other brokers. In case C, the parent firm produces and sells its products in the United States. In addition, goods are produced in and sold through a foreign affiliate. Consequently, because of the direct investment which has been made in a foreign country and, assuming management has a global perspective as regards decision making, case C is appropriately called a multinational firm.

## COUNTRIES IN WHICH DIRECT INVESTMENTS ARE MADE

In 1972, the value of United States direct investments abroad amounted to $94 billion. This represents an increase of approximately $7.8 billion over 1971. For several years, firms in the United States have been increasing their direct investments abroad by around 9 percent each year. Data in Exhibit 24–9 reflect the primary areas in which United States firms have invested.

When compared to 1971, direct investments in Europe and Canada increased by $3.1 and $1.8 billion respectively during the year 1972. In fact, as of the end of 1972, the $25.8 billion invested in Canada and the $30.7 billion

EXHIBIT 24–9

*U.S. Foreign Direct Investments by Area, 1971 & 1972 (Preliminary)*

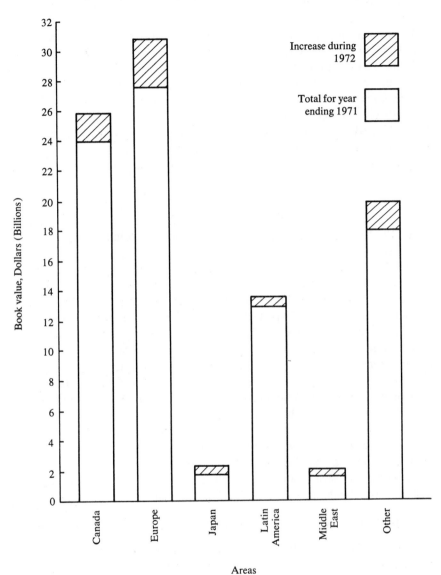

invested in Europe together accounted for over 60 percent of the total $94.0 billion invested in foreign countries. There appear to be three primary reasons for this high percentage. First, the standards of living in Canada and the European countries such as Belgium, France, Germany, Switzerland, Italy, and the Netherlands are relatively high. As a result, firms in the United States have been able to develop a number of markets for their products in those areas. Secondly, the political ties which the United States government has with these countries are such that American firms consider their investments safe. That is, the chances of their property being confiscated by the foreign governments are extremely low. Third, in the case of Canada, its close geographical proximity to the United States is very attractive to many firms.

Direct investment in Latin America increased from $13.0 billion at the end of 1971 to $13.5 billion at the end of 1972 (see Exhibit 24–9). This makes the Latin American countries, such as Mexico, Panama, Argentina, Brazil and Venezuela, third behind Europe and Canada in terms of direct investments by American firms. Surprising as it may seem today, in 1929 Latin America was first, with $3.5 billion invested by American firms. This represented 41 percent of total United States direct investments in that year. However, because of the more rapid pace at which Europe and Canada have developed economically and politically, Latin America lost its number one ranking.

### INDUSTRIES IN WHICH DIRECT INVESTMENTS ARE MADE

Earnings on the $94.0 billion of United States direct investments abroad during 1972 amounted to $12.4 billion. Exhibit 24–10 indicates the types of industries in which United States firms have invested for the years ending 1971 and 1972. The largest increase was in the manufacturing industry. Whereas investment in manufacturing amounted to $35.5 billion at the end of 1971, it increased around $4.0 billion during the year 1972 for a total of $39.5 billion. This represents over 50 percent of the total increase in United States direct investments during the years 1972. Most of this increase of $4.0 billion was in the developed areas such as Canada and Europe rather than the underdeveloped areas such as Latin America or the Middle East.

At the end of 1971, $24.3 billion was invested in the petroleum industry. This compares with $26.4 billion invested at the end of 1972. The increase of $2.1 billion was brought about by the increasing demand around the world for additional energy. This demand has become critical during 1973 and 1974, and therefore we can expect direct investments in this industry to increase significantly during the decade of the seventies.

The Other industries category, which increased $1.5 billion during 1972, includes trade, banking, public utilities, and agriculture.

### OTHER COUNTRIES INVESTING IN THE UNITED STATES

American investment abroad is not a one-way street. In fact, according to the *Survey of Current Business,* direct investments in the United States increased significantly in the 1960–1972 period. Whereas in 1960 these investments amounted to $6.9 billion, in 1972 total investments amounted to $14.4 billion. The distribution of foreign direct investments by industry and country of ownership for years 1962 and 1971 is presented in Exhibit 24–11. The graphs provide ample evidence that, as time passes, we are increasingly living in a world economy. Business managers in foreign countries see the same opportunities in America that business managers in America see in foreign countries. They invest in a broad variety of American businesses.

EXHIBIT 24–10

*U.S. Foreign Direct Investments by Industry*
*1971 & 1972 (Preliminary)*

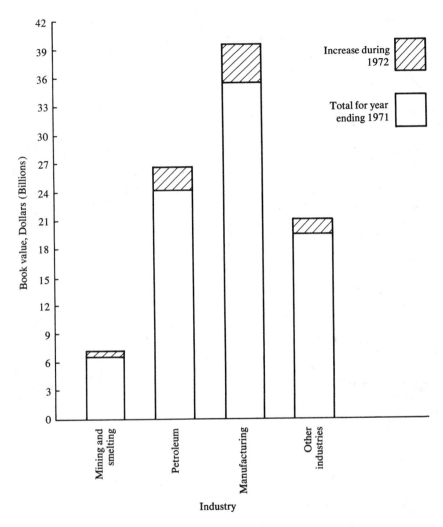

Industry

Heavily armed with dollars, investors from abroad are buying into the American economy at a record clip. They are purchasing everything from farmland to fishing fleets, taking over well-known American corporations through stock purchases and setting up new plants to produce such varied goods as Swedish Volvos in Virginia and Japanese teriyaki and soy sauce in Wisconsin.

The foreign investments are cropping up in many forms around the nation. They range from Japanese purchases of hotels in Hawaii and farmland in the Midwest to planned plants by a French tire maker and a German diesel-engine parts company in South Carolina. Wall Street has also witnessed a rash of takeover bids in the past year, including successful

EXHIBIT 24–11

*Distribution of Foreign Direct Investments in the United States,*
*1962 and 1971*

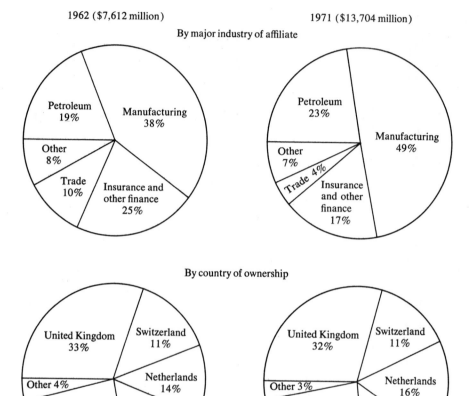

Source: U.S. Department of Commerce, *Survey of Current Business*, February 15, 1973, p. 32.

tender offers by British-based concerns for such well-known companies as Gimbel Brothers, Inc. (department stores), Grand Union Co. (supermarkets), and TraveLodge International Inc. (motels).[8]

Although such investment by foreign firms in the United States is resented by many Americans, it is important to realize that the United States has six times as much invested abroad ($94.0 billion) as foreigners have invested

---

8. *Wall Street Journal*, January 22, 1974, p. 1.

($14.4 billion) in America. Certainly, the United States cannot expect to close the door on foreign investments and still expect American firms to be welcomed with open arms around the world.

## To What Extent Should American Firms Engage in Business Abroad?

Earlier in this chapter three types of companies—the uninational firm, the firm involved in international trade, and the multinational firm—were described. The question which might be asked at this finishing point is to what extent the firm should become involved in world business.

This is a question which each business manager should ask himself. The answer will, of course, vary, depending upon the resources of the firm and the type of market the firm is presently serving. In many, if not most, instances, the businessman may have no desire whatsoever to serve a foreign market. Wishing to remain a uninational firm does not in any way imply that the business manager is uninterested in maximizing his profits. Since the marketplace in the United States is so vast, many firms have not yet begun to tap all of their potential customers at home, let alone abroad. Certainly the businessman of an American firm has more familiarity with the markets to be served, the nature of his competition, and the kinds of problems to be solved in this country than he does in a foreign market.

For those business managers who have a real interest in entering foreign markets, consideration must be given to the means by which this goal will be accomplished. For those businessmen who have not previously served foreign markets, the most logical approach may will be to export through a trade specialist such as an export management company. Since the business manager may not understand the needs of customers in foreign markets nor the various trade laws, he can learn over time through services provided by an EMC or an exporter. Once he has gained experience and developed a market abroad for his product, he may then give consideration to developing an export department as an integral part of the firm. He may simply assign export related duties and responsibilities to present executives of the firm, or he may establish a completely new department.

In certain instances it may not be possible to export goods to another country because of high import quotas and/or tariffs. In these situations it may be possible for the business manager to construct production and distribution facilities abroad. In other instances he may decide to produce and distribute the firm's products abroad in order to avoid the transportation costs and other expenses associated with exporting. A number of foreign nations encourage the development of subsidiary plants in their countries by providing certain incentives such as reduced taxes. Although the development of a multinational firm usually requires a large amount of capital, hundreds of small and medium-sized companies have invested in subsidiary plants in foreign countries.

## Summary

According to the principle of absolute advantage, a nation should export those goods which it can produce more efficiently than other nations can and import those goods which it is least efficient in producing. The result should be that the standard of living for all people and each country throughout the world will be increased. The fact that many nations today adhere to this principle is reflected in the liberal trade agreements and other innovations which have been implemented since World War II. These include GATT; the International Monetary Fund; the World Bank; and the Export-Import Bank.

Business managers are participating in the world marketplace today at unprecedented levels. This participation is achieved primarily through international trade and international investments. A firm is involved in international trade when it exchanges goods or services with residents of another country. During 1972, manufactured goods accounted for over 60 percent of all goods exported from the United States. The primary recipients of exports from the United States were Europe and Canada. Because American imports exceeded exports during 1971 and 1972, the United States government is encouraging business firms to increase their exports. As a result, the United States experienced a trade surplus during 1973. Three methods available to the small firm which is interested in selling abroad include the export management company, the export merchant, and the export broker.

A major shift in the manner in which the business manager served the world came about after 1950. Rather than simply exporting goods across national borders, business managers began to establish subsidiary plants in foreign nations. As a result, goods are sold in the same foreign market in which they are produced. In 1972, the United States' direct investments abroad amounted to $94.0 billion. On the other hand, direct investments in the United States by foreign firms amounted to $14.4 billion.

Because of international trade and international investment, today there truly is a world market. Although the majority of United States firms today are uninational, with each passing year more and more become involved in international business.

## QUESTIONS

1. Explain the principle of absolute advantage.
2. What do each of the following represent?
   (a) Tariff
   (b) Quota
   (c) GATT
   (d) World Bank
   (e) IMF
   (f) Export-Import bank

3. Explain the meaning of the term *International Trade*.

4. In your opinion, why has international trade become increasingly popular today among so many nations, including communist countries?

5. (a) The United States Bureau of the Census divides U. S. exports into seven select commodity groups. What are these and which two groups account for over 50 percent of American exports?
   (b) To which continents does the United States export merchandise? Of these, which two account for over 64 percent of the total?

6. Do you feel that the present trend whereby the United States trades with the communist countries of Russia and China will continue and increase in volume? Explain.

7. List and explain the three methods available to the small business manager who is interested in selling his product abroad.

8. (a) What is a uninational firm?
   (b) What is a multinational firm?
   (c) How do uninational and multinational firms differ from a firm which is involved in international trade?
   (d) Could a multinational firm also be involved in international trade? Explain.

9. (a) In which areas of the world are United States direct investments held?
   (b) In what specific area was the largest increase (in terms of dollars) recorded during the year 1972? How much was this increase?

10. (a) Do other countries around the world invest in the United States? How much did they have invested at the end of 1972? Is this amount greater or smaller than American investments abroad?
    (b) Which country accounts for the largest percentage of foreign direct investments in the United States?

11. Express your opinion on the following statement: "As American citizens, we should become upset with foreigners investing in our country, and write our congressmen, insisting that they pass legislation preventing future investments."

# 25

# External Growth Through Business Acquisitions

Every business manager is concerned about the growth of his firm. If a firm is not growing, it is most likely loosing ground to competitors and therefore dying. Growth can be measured in different ways. For example, the business manager may compare the firm's total assets at the end of 19X5 with those it owned at the end of 19X4. Comparisons are also made between two periods in terms of yearly profits, sales revenue, number of people employed, number of products or services produced, percentage share of the market, and so on.

One way in which a firm can achieve growth is through acquiring other firms. The purpose of this chapter is to examine the following aspects of business acquisitions: the formal plans for combining firms such as mergers and consolidations, the different growth patterns by which a firm expands externally, motives for buying or selling, and the federal laws which control business acquisitions. However, before examining these different areas internal growth will be differentiated from external growth.

## Internal Versus External Growth

Growth may be achieved either internally or externally. The primary source of funds used by a firm for internal growth is retention of the firm's earnings rather than paying such earnings to the firm's owners in the form of withdrawals or dividends. In addition, funds for internal growth are acquired through the issuance of securities such as stocks and bonds. These funds are then used by the firm to expand production, hire additional personnel, and acquire other resources necessary for the expansion of the firm. Many of the largest business firms in the United States today achieved their present position through internal growth. Perhaps the best example is the Ford Motor Company.

External growth is realized through business acquisitions. The term *acquisition* is used here to describe the combining of two or more independent entities into a single entity. Because of certain advantages which are inherent in external growth, this has become a popular means of expanding operations. Exhibit 25–1 discloses the number of acquisitions recorded between 1960 and

EXHIBIT 25–1

*Acquisitions—Manufacturing and Mining Concerns
Acquired: 1960 to 1971*

| Year | Total | Year | Total |
|------|-------|------|-------|
| 1960 | 844   | 1967 | 1,496 |
| 1963 | 861   | 1968 | 2,407 |
| 1964 | 854   | 1969 | 2,307 |
| 1965 | 1,008 | 1970 | 1,351 |
| 1966 | 995   | 1971 | 1,011 |

Source: U. S. Bureau of the Census, *Statistical Abstract of the United States: 1973*, 94th ed. Washington, D. C.: 1973, p. 486.

1971. By far and away the two most popular years for business combinations were 1968 and 1969. The figure for 1971 of 1,011 acquisitions is the lowest since 1967. Nonetheless, figures released by Grimm & Co. (a Chicago-based consulting firm) indicate slightly more than 1,200 acquisitions for 1972. The firm predicts a 5 percent increase in acquisitions for 1973.

## Formal Plans for Combining Firms

Three of the more popular plans available to the business manager who is interested in acquiring other firms are **mergers, consolidations** and **holding companies.** A merger occurs when one firm acquires the assets of another firm, with the acquiring firm surviving and the acquired firm being dissolved. A merger may be described by the following formula: $X + Y = X$. The $Y$ firm is absorbed by the $X$ firm and therefore is dissolved.

A consolidation takes place when two firms dissolve their separate operations by combining their assets and liabilities to form a new entity. A consolidation may be expressed by the following formula: $X + Y = Z$. In this case, the Z firm is a new entity organized for the purpose of taking over both X and Y, which are dissolved.

A holding company is established when the acquiring firm purchases a sufficient number of shares of stock necessary to control another corporation. The acquiring firm or holding company is usually formed simply to own and vote the shares of the firm or firms which it acquires. In other words, the holding company itself is usually not involved in the manufacturing of a product. The interesting aspect of a holding company is its ability to control large amounts of assets with relatively little investment. To illustrate, assume that the XYZ Corporation has the following capital structure:

*The XYZ Corporation*
*Balance Sheet*
*December 31, 19X1*

| Assets | | Equities | | |
|---|---|---|---|---|
| Current assets | $1,000,000 | Current liabilities | $ 250,000 | |
| Fixed assets | 3,500,000 | Long-term liabilities | 1,250,000 | |
| Other assets | 500,000 | Total liabilities | | $1,500,000 |
| | | Preferred stock | 2,000,000 | |
| | | Common stock | 1,000,000 | |
| | | Retained earnings | 500,000 | |
| | | Total Stockholders' Equity | | 3,500,000 |
| Total Assets | $5,000,000 | Total Equities | | $5,000,000 |

Assume further that the ABC Holding Co. is interested in acquiring control of the XYZ Corporation. In order to do so it would be necessary to purchase 50 percent of the common stock of the XYZ Corporation, or $500,000. This is because common stockholders are usually the only stockholders entitled to vote for directors and on major decisions affecting the firm. Now assume that there are four other firms with the same capital structure as the XYZ Corporation which the ABC Holding Co. is interested in controlling. The ABC Holding Co. would have to pay out $2,500,000 ($500,000 × 5 = $2,500,000) in order to gain control of these five corporations. This investment, however, would control five corporations with total assets of $25,000,000 ($5,000,000 × 5). Thus by acquiring 10 percent of each firm's assets ($500,000/$5,000,000 = 10%), the ABC Holding Co. is able to control 100 percent of the $25,000,000 in assets.

## The Growth Pattern of a Firm

When one firm acquires another firm, it will most likely grow in one of three ways: vertical expansion, horizontal expansion, or conglomerate expansion.

## VERTICAL EXPANSION

Vertical expansion takes place when a company expands its operations into areas previously performed by others for the firm. Vertical expansion may occur in two directions: forward towards the firm's customers or backwards towards the source of the firm's raw materials. For example, a manufacturer of ice cream would achieve vertical expansion backwards through the acquisition of a dairy farm. This would provide the firm with its source of raw material—milk. Vertical expansion forward would be realized by acquiring ice cream stores. This would provide an outlet for the firm's finished produce—ice cream.

One of the primary motives for vertical expansion is that the firm's profit margin is widened. That is, profits which originally accrued to the firm's supplier or its distributor now accrue to the manufacturer. Because of the severity of competition which most firms experience in the business world today, many find vertical expansion one approach to staying in business.

## HORIZONTAL EXPANSION

Horizontal expansion takes place when a firm acquires a competitor. For example, in the illustration above, the ice cream manufacturer would expand horizontally by acquiring another firm which produces ice cream. Such an acquisition would give the firm a larger share of the market. However, because of the antitrust laws, the business manager must move cautiously whenever a competing firm is going to be acquired. These laws will be examined later in this chapter.

## CONGLOMERATE EXPANSION

A firm becomes a conglomerate when it acquires other companies which produce products that are unrelated to the product produced by the acquiring firm. For example, if the ice cream manufacturer acquires a firm which manufactures baby furniture, a conglomerate would be formed. There are many extremely large, extremely familiar organizations today which, through a number of acquisitions, have become conglomerates. These include such firms as Gulf & Western, Litton Industries, LTV, Textron, Inc., and ITT.

The primary advantage of the conglomerate form of organization is that it can achieve a more stable earnings record, because cyclical declines in one industry are offset by cyclical expansion in another industry. Furthermore, a firm which acquires companies in industries different from its own is usually not subject to antitrust laws.

The popularity of the conglomerate expansion route for large firms is reflected by the data in Exhibit 25–2. For example, in 1968, which was the bumper year for business combinations, 207 firms with assets each of $10 million or more were acquired. Of these, 175, or 85 percent, represented conglomerate acquisitions on the part of the acquiring firms. For 1971, 88 percent of the 66 acquisitions were conglomerate acquisitions.

EXHIBIT 25–2

*Large Manufacturing and Mining Concerns Acquired[1]*
*1960 to 1971*

| | | Number | |
| | | Horizontal and vertical acquisitions | Conglomerate acquisitions |
| Year | Total | | |
|---|---|---|---|
| 1960 | 64 | 20 | 44 |
| 1965 | 91 | 27 | 64 |
| 1968 | 207 | 32 | 175 |
| 1971 | 66 | 8 | 58 |

Source: U. S. Bureau of the Census, *Statistical Abstract of the United States: 1973*, 94th ed. Washington, D. C.: 1973, p. 486.

## DO SMALL FIRMS ENGAGE IN BUSINESS COMBINATIONS?

Most people think only of large corporate firms as being involved in business combinations. It is true that big business does play a large role in the business acquisitions consummated each year. Nonetheless, as Exhibit 25–3 indicates,

EXHIBIT 25–3

*Acquisitions—Manufacturing and Mining Concerns Acquired*
*By Size of Assets of Acquiring Concern*
*1968 and 1971*

| Assets of acquiring concern (million $) | 1968 | | 1971 | |
| | Firms acquired | Percent | Firms acquired | Percent |
|---|---|---|---|---|
| Under 1.0 | 144 | 6.0 | 141 | 13.9 |
| 1.0–4.9 | 364 | 15.1 | 102 | 10.1 |
| 5.0–9.9 | 250 | 10.4 | 84 | 8.3 |
| 10.0–49.9 | 816 | 33.9 | 277 | 27.4 |
| 50.0–over | 833 | 34.6 | 407 | 40.3 |
| Total | 2,407 | 100.0 | 1,011 | 100.0 |

Source: U. S. Bureau of the Census, *Statistical Abstract of the United States: 1973*, 94th ed. Washington, D. C.: 1973, p. 486.

small firms are very much involved in the acquisition of other concerns. For example, in 1968, 6 percent of the acquiring firms had assets of under $1 million. In 1971 this percentage had more than doubled to 13.9 percent. The majority of these business combinations would be of the vertical or horizontal pattern.

### Motives for Acquiring Another Firm

Certain advantages resulting from business acquisitions have already been discussed. For example, vertical expansion widens the firm's profit margin.

---

1. Includes all concerns with assets of $10 million and over.

Horizontal expansion increases the acquiring firm's share of the market. In addition to these, there are other reasons why a business manager might decide to acquire another firm. It is not the intention of this chapter to cite all of the possible motives. Rather, four dominant motives will be examined.

## TO SAVE VALUABLE TIME

When a firm invests funds in the research and development of a new marketable product, there is no assurance that the product will ever be developed. Furthermore, if the product is developed, problems relating to production and distribution of a new product must be solved. All of this obviously takes months and, in many instances, years. As a result, a business manager who is interested in expanding his operations may find that valuable time can be saved by acquiring another company which is already selling a product or service that has gained wide acceptance in the market place.

## TO STABILIZE SALES

Two firms which sell their products in different seasons of the year can stabilize sales by combining their operations. For example, a firm which produces ball bats could stabilize its annual sales by combining with a firm which produces snow skis.

In addition to seasonal products, firms which produce capital goods such as machinery, equipment, and other durable goods experience cyclical variations in sales. That is, periods of sales growth are followed by periods of sales decline. Again, in order to stabilize sales, firms in the capital goods industry frequently acquire firms in nondurable industries which are less subject to cyclical fluctuations.

## TO OBTAIN KEY PERSONNEL

One firm may acquire another in order to obtain key personnel who possess talents which are needed by the acquiring firm. For example, when a public accounting firm acquires another firm of public accountants, the most important resource obtained in the acquisition is the CPAs on the staff of the acquired firm. Similarly, a manufacturing firm may be interested in doing research and development on new products. Rather than developing its own department by hiring engineers and other technical personnel, the firm could acquire a small independent company currently involved in research and development of new products. Again, the primary purpose of such an acquisition would be the securing of competent personnel whose skills may have a definite impact upon the success of the firm. Of course, it is of primary importance that the acquiring firm is certain that the key personnel of the acquired firm will remain with their new employer.

## TO REALIZE TAX BENEFITS

If a firm has accumulated operating losses on its books, it may be able to save considerable tax dollars by acquiring another firm which is operating at a profit. For example, assume that Firm A has operated at a loss of $25,000 each year during the last two years. As a result, it has accumulated operating losses of $50,000 (2 × $25,000 = $50,000). Furthermore, assume that Firm B is a profitable entity which earns $100,000 per year. According to the Internal Revenue Code, Firm A can offset its $50,000 of operating losses against other operating income. One means of generating this other income would be for Firm A to acquire B.

Since Firm B has earnings before taxes each year of $100,000, it is required to pay $41,500 in federal taxes. This is computed as follows:

| | | |
|---|---|---|
| Firm B's earnings before taxes | | $100,000 |
| Taxes due: | | |
| 22% × $25,000 | $ 5,500 | |
| 48% × excess or $75,000 | 36,000 | |
| Total federal taxes | | $ 41,500 |

However, if Firm A were to merge with Firm B, federal income taxes would be reduced to $17,500. This is arrived at in the following manner:

| | | |
|---|---|---|
| Firm B's earnings before taxes | | $100,000 |
| Firm A's accumulated operating losses | | (50,000) |
| Net earnings before taxes | | $ 50,000 |
| Taxes due: | | |
| 22% × $25,000 | $ 5,500 | |
| 48% × excess or $25,000 | 12,000 | |
| Total federal taxes | | $ 17,500 |

In other words, Firm A can realize a savings of $24,000 in taxes ($41,500 — $17,500 = $24,000) by acquiring Firm B. Such savings could be used by Firm A to help finance the acquisition.

## Motives for Selling

As with buying, there are many reasons why an owner-manager elects to sell his business to an acquiring firm. Four of the more compelling reasons appear to be the following: (1) to acquire for growth; (2) to retire; (3) to solve internal disputes; and (4) to divest.

### TO ACQUIRE FUNDS FOR GROWTH AND DEVELOPMENT

Many smaller firms are successful in that they are producing a quality product and earning a good return on the capital invested. However, because of increasing demand for the firm's product such a company may need to expand, yet lack the necessary funds to do so. Furthermore, such a firm may be interested in starting a research and development department in order to develop new products for the growth and well-being of the organization. Banks and other lending sources may be unwilling to provide the amount of capital necessary for the type of expansion the owner-manager is interested in pursuing.

One alternative open to the owner-manager is to sell his firm to a larger firm. For example, Firm Small could be absorbed into Firm Large. In exchange for the assets acquired by Firm Large, the owner of Firm Small receives stock representing ownership in Firm Large. The result of this combination is that the necessary funds are now available to expand the acquired firm into a bigger-profit making operation. Furthermore, the combination agreement may provide that the owner of Firm Small will be employed in an administrative position with Firm Large.

## TO RETIRE

The owner of a family business may be ready to retire with no one in the organization capable of assuming the responsibilities needed for the long-run survival of the firm. One avenue available to the owner would be to sell his firm, receiving in exchange stock in the acquiring corporation. Dividends on the shares so received would provide a source of income for the retired owner. This method is particularly beneficial when the acquiring corporation is a large firm whose shares are actively traded on a stock exchange. These shares have a ready market value and can be sold at any time without difficulty. This feature is particularly important in the event the retired owner dies. Since his estate might well be large, the estate taxes in turn would be significant. Should the surviving family require additional cash to pay the taxes, they could simply sell some of the stock. If the retired owner sells his business to a firm whose stock is not actively traded on an exchange, he would most likely be interested in receiving cash in exchange rather than stock.

## INTERNAL DISPUTES

The selling firm may have significant problems internally as a result of disagreements between owners. For example, in the case of a partnership, one owner may wish to expand by diversifying the existing product line, whereas the other owner may be vehemently opposed to such a move. If neither owner is willing to give in to the other's wishes, their only recourse may be to sell the firm.

## TO DIVEST

Not infrequently a firm wishes to sell a company which it previously acquired through a business combination. This is referred to as *divesting of an acquisition*. A firm may divest for the following reasons: the acquisition does not prove to be as profitable as management had expected, the potential growth of the firm is less than management had planned, or perhaps the antitrust laws were violated and the acquiring firm was told to divest in order to preserve competition. An example of that reason is reflected in the ITT situation discussed below:

> For the past two and one-half years, International Telephone & Telegraph Corp. has been trying without success to find a buyer for its Levitt home-

building business, which the giant conglomerate is under a Justice Department order to sell. Last week a buyer finally surfaced. He was none other than William J. Levitt, the 67-year-old creator of the celebrated Levittown instant suburbs, who sold the business to ITT in 1968. Levitt signed a letter of intent to take the company back and said that he will operate it as a privately owned concern under its original name of Levitt & Sons. The deal, if approved by the Justice Department, will make the company one of the few ever to enter the maw of a giant conglomerate and come out again years later in recognizable shape under its original owner.[2]

## Antitrust Laws

As mentioned in the first chapter of this text, competition is the cornerstone of the economic system in the United States. Nevertheless, in order to seek security, some businessmen have sought to decrease the amount of competition that their firms have to undergo. One of these methods has been the acquisition of other companies.

This became particularly evident during the latter part of the nineteenth century when numerous concerns, both large and small, entered into various forms of business combinations in order to restrict competition. For example, in a period between 1870 and 1882, Standard Oil of Ohio was able to acquire a sufficient number of companies to enable it to control some 90 percent of trade in refined petroleum products. In 1890, because of a series of horizontal acquisitions, the American Sugar Refining Co. controlled 98 percent of the sugar refining business.

In order to preserve competition, in 1890, the federal government enacted the Sherman Act. This Act contained two main prohibitions:

Section 1: Every contract, combination in the form of trust or otherwise, conspiracy, in restraint of trade or commerce is hereby declared to be illegal.

Section 2: Every person who shall monopolize, or attempt to monopolize, or combine or conspire with any other person or persons to monopolize any part of the trade or commerce, . . . shall be deemed guilty of a misdemeanor.

Although the wording to these two sections appears clear, the courts have varied over the years in their interpretation of the act. The following brief court decisions spanning the years 1911 through 1953 provide some insight into the inconsistency of the courts:[3]

Out of the Standard Oil and American Tobacco cases of 1911 the courts developed the "rule of reason," which stated in effect that not every contract or combination in the restraint of trade is to be deemed illegal. . . .

2. *Time,* February 25, 1974, pp. 85–86.
3. Campbell R. McConnell, *Economics: Principles, Problems and Policies.* New York: McGraw-Hill Book Co., 1963, p. 595.

> Then in 1920 . . . It was ruled [in the U. S. Steel case] that the mere fact
> that a firm is large and that it posesses monopoly power is not in violation
> of the antitrust laws. Violation hinges upon the *use* of monopoly power.
> But a quarter of a century later in the Alcoa case of 1945, the courts did
> a turnabout from the U. S. Steel case. . . . The acquisition or possession of
> monopoly power as such is a violation of the antitrust laws. Then in 1953
> in the Du Pont Cellophane case, the courts mellowed once again . . . con-
> cluding . . . that although Du Pont clearly monopolized the production of
> cellophane, it faced significant competition from . . . other wrapping ma-
> terials.

This brief mention of a few of the more important decisions shows that
what is legal or illegal is often a matter of subjective opinion of federal judges.
In the 1911 and 1920 cases cited above, the courts interpreted the Sherman
Act rather loosely. However, in the 1945 case, the courts applied a vary strict
interpretation of sections one and two. Then, in the 1953 case, the judges ap-
peared to relax their interpretation once again. The courts today appear to
have returned to the strict interpretation which characterized the 1945 case
involving U.S. Steel.

## THE IBM-TELEX CASE

In order to provide additional guidelines so as to make interpretation of the
Sherman Act less subjective, Congress passed the Clayton Act, in 1914. The
Clayton Act strengthened the Sherman Act by defining several practices as
being unlawful. For example, Section 1 of the Clayton Act forbids sellers "to
discriminate in price between different purchasers of commodities." It was
this section which Judge Christensen cited in his recent landmark decision in
the IBM-Telex case. As reported in the September 22, 1973 issue of *Business
Week*,[4] Judge Christensen found the following:

> IBM clearly violated Section 2 of the Clayton Act . . . the court found
> that IBM's pricing changes were not merely competitive reactions to the
> market place, but were directed "not at competition in an appropriate
> competitive sense, but at competitors and their viability as such." In other
> words, the judge is convinced that IBM tried to put its competitors out of
> business, rather than merely competing for a share of market with them.

Telex Chairman Roger M. Wheeler phrased the judge's decision as follows:

> It's fantastic . . . a monopoly in action . . . a court that restored competition
> to an industry : . . . a judge who had the guts to call it the way he saw it.

It is expected by many that this decision (which has been appealed by IBM)
may well pave the way for additional breaking up of giant IBM.

In conclusion, there exist today many valid reasons for business combinations. However, before a business manager decides to expand his firm by acquiring another firm, he must recognize that such an acquisition may lessen

---

4. Pp. 18–19.

competition. If this lessening of competition is significant or unreasonable, the business manager may be violating the antitrust laws.

## Summary

A business firm can achieve growth either internally or externally. A firm grows internally through the reinvestment of its earnings or the sale of additional stocks and bonds. External growth is achieved through business acquisitions. In this chapter the term *acquisition* is used to describe the combining of two or more independent entities into a single firm. Three formal plans of bringing about a business combination are mergers, consolidations, and holding companies. In a merger, the acquiring firm survives and the firm acquired is dissolved. In a consolidation, a new entity is formed, with both the acquired firm and the acquiring firm being dissolved. A holding company is formed for the sole purpose of controlling another firm. This is achieved by the purchase of a controlling interest in the voting stock of the acquired firm. The interesting aspect of a holding company is its ability to control large amounts of assets with relatively little investment.

External growth follows one of three patterns: horizontal, vertical, or conglomerate. Horizontal growth occurs when a firm acquires a competitor. Vertical growth takes place when the acquiring firm acquires either a supplier firm or a customer firm. Conglomerate growth is realized when a firm acquires a company in another industry. That is, the products produced by the acquired firm are unrelated to those produced by the acquiring firm.

Four motives for acquiring another firm are, (1) to save valuable time, (2) to stabilize sales, (3) to obtain key personnel, and (4) to realize tax benefits. Motives for an owner to elect to sell include (1) to acquire funds for growth and development, (2) to retire, (3) to solve internal disputes, and (4) to divest.

Because business combinations have an impact upon competition, the federal government has enacted a number of antitrust regulations. The two most used are the Sherman Act and the Clayton Act. The purpose of these laws is to preserve competition.

## QUESTIONS

1. List five ways in which a business manager can measure a firm's growth between two points in time.
2. List and explain three formal plans for combining two or more firms.
3. A holding company controls assets of over $10,000,000 with an investment of only $1,000,000. Develop your own example which would illustrate how this situation could come about.

4. Explain the following terms:
   (a) Vertical expansion
   (b) Horizontal expansion
   (c) Conglomerate expansion

5. What advantage might a firm realize by expanding vertically? Horizontally? As a conglomerate?

6. To what extent did small firms (assets of less than $1 million) engage in business acquisitions of manufacturing and mining concerns during 1971?

7. (a) List the four motives discussed in this text for acquiring another firm.
   (b) List four other motives which you personally feel explain why a business manager would acquire another firm.

8. (a) List the four motives discussed in this text which explain why an owner would sell his firm.
   (b) List four other motives which you personally feel account for an owner's selling his firm.

9. Have the courts been consistent over the years in their interpretation of the antitrust laws? Explain.

# 26

# The Business System: A Restatement

In this final chapter, two areas will be discussed. First, we will try to review and reemphasize the nature of the business system. With a very broad brush, the previous chapters will be brought together to cover the business system in total as well as the six processes which are performed within *every* business system. The purpose is to emphasize once again the interrelationships of each of these processes as well as the interdependence of the business system with the environment in the United States.

It is appropriate to conclude the text with a section which discusses career opportunities and possible courses of study to achieve these opportunities. After reading this second part of the chapter, you should have a better indication of what you want to pursue as well as how your pursuit is related to the total operation of a business system.

## Environmental Realities in the United States

No business is run in a vacuum or immune to the environmental realities of the country. Regardless of the size of the firm, all business activity occurs in an environment which has been molded over the years by society. This environment represents the sum of three interrelated systems: the social system, the economic system, and the governmental system. Since these three systems intertwine, they are inseparable elements of the total environment.

The social system is the cultural beliefs and values of the people. In the United States, for example, people believe deeply in the equality and freedom of individuals. These cultural values are in turn reflected in the economic system. Every economic system exists to produce the goods and services of a society, but in the United States the economic system rests on guaranteeing the equality and freedom of individuals, be they producers or consumers. Consumers are free to choose those goods or services which they wish to purchase. Firms are free to produce those goods and services which they feel will satisfy the wants and needs of individuals. If a business predicts accurately what the consumer wants and provides the goods or services at a price consumers are willing to pay, it will be successful. On the other hand, if it is unable to determine the wants and needs of consumers, it will be a failure.

However, if freedom is allowed to run without restraint or interference, the result could be complete loss of freedom. The powerful and influential would gain at the expense of others. Therefore, in order to preserve the individual's freedom of choice, a political system has been devised. The government consists of three branches, each of which plays an active role in protecting business from business, consumers from business, and employees from employers. In addition, through governmental intervention, efforts are continuously being made to promote the economy by maintaining high employment and stable prices.

Within this environment the business manager must make decisions which will have a direct bearing upon the future success or failure of the firm. The goals or objectives of the firm will guide the business manager in making these decisions. Although the primary goal of every business is to survive, that goal is too broad to provide much guidance for the business manager in his role as a decision maker. However, this primary goal can be made more specific by thinking of four secondary goals which every business must achieve to be successful. These four secondary goals are to produce a competitive good or service, to make a profit, to gain society's acceptance, and to live up to the responsibility of the various publics business deals with from day to day. All business decisions should be made to help achieve these four goals. However, when the business manager makes a particular decision it may appear that he is emphasizing one particular secondary goal and ignoring the other three. This might be true, but the smart business manager realizes that, in the long run, the business can survive only if each of the secondary goals is realized to a certain degree.

This obviously makes the businessman's job a very formidable one. Decisions cannot be made in a vacuum, but rather a number of separate factors must be considered if the primary goal of survival is to be attained. The systems approach helps put into perspective all the factors and relationships which must be considered by the business manager in making decisions.

## The Systems Approach

Under the systems approach the component parts of a system are defined and their interrelationships studied to help increase the efficiency of accomplishing some purpose or goal. A business can be viewed as an on-going system with distinct, definable components. These components have been called *processes*. The six processes within every business system which help the business achieve the goal of survival are:

(1) The business must finance its efforts.
(2) Something of value must be produced.
(3) The good or service must be distributed to the consumer.
(4) Someone must manage the business system.
(5) Manpower, in the form of workers and managers, must be employed.
(6) Information must be obtained.

The systems approach forces the business manager to examine first how to improve the performance of each separate process and second how to coordinate each of these processes to achieve the goal or objective of the business. The decisions he makes in these two areas will ultimately determine the success of the organization. If one process is allowed to dominate, the total business system will suffer. In order to reinforce the concept of the systems approach to operating a business, we will once again examine briefly each of the six processes and the interdependence of each in the total business system.

## THE FINANCIAL PROCESS AND THE BUSINESS SYSTEM

Once the business manager has conceived of a particular good or service which he feels will satisfy the unfilled wants and needs of the consumer, he is ready to begin the financing of his business venture. The financial process of a firm is concerned primarily with that series of events leading to the acquisition of funds. In order to maximize the funds flowing into the firm, the business manager must be aware of the advantages and disadvantages of the various forms of business organization, the various sources of long-term and short-term financing, and the federal income tax regulations.

Through the financial process funds are raised which in turn are used to finance the activities of the other processes included in the business system. The production, manpower, and distribution processes each utilize funds to acquire the necessary resources needed to produce the goods or services and make them available to the consumer. This makes the financial process an interdependent part of the total business system. Once the business is operating, the other processes generate funds which are utilized by the financial process. For example, the production process creates a good or service which in turn is sold and shipped via the distribution process. These activities bring into the firm additional funds which the financial process has in custody. Furthermore, the information process generates data which is made available to the financial process for planning and control purposes.

## THE PRODUCTION PROCESS AND THE BUSINESS SYSTEM

Once the necessary funds are obtained, the production process can be initiated. The production process is concerned with that series of events which combine men and machines for the purpose of attaining and transforming raw materials into finished goods or services. Funds provided by the financial process are used to acquire men, machinery and equipment, raw materials, and so on. With these resources the business manager is able to convert his ideas into a tangible good or service. The production process, like the financial process, is also related to the other processes of the business system. Once the good or service is produced, the distribution process must price, promote, sell, and transport the product to the firm's customers. The attitudes of customers concerning the product are in turn obtained by the distribution process and communicated back to the production process. With this information adjustments are made in the quality or style of the product in order to better satisfy the wants and needs of the consumer. Changes in the style of the product would likewise require changes, perhaps in the pricing and transporting of the product. It is obvious that the activities of the production and distribution processes are closely intertwined. Adjustments in one process often directly affect the other process.

The production process also affects and is affected by the other processes within the firm. The manpower process provides labor needed to convert ideas into a good or service. The type of labor required will vary depending upon the type of product produced. Through the information process, data are made available to the production process to be used for planning and control. For example, information on product quality level assists the manager in improving the performance of the production process.

## THE DISTRIBUTION PROCESS AND THE BUSINESS SYSTEM

The production of goods and services is only the beginning. Unless these goods and services are purchased by someone, they have no value. However, in order for goods and services to be purchased, they must be distributed. The distribution process represents that series of events or activities necessary to move goods or services from the point of production to the consumer. Some of the specific activities included in the distribution process are retailing, wholesaling, pricing, advertising, selling, and transportation.

The distribution process is closely related to the financial process and the production process. After an idea has been conceived, financial backing arranged, and the good or service produced, it is the distribution process which makes the goods or services available to the consumer. In order for the firm to realize its objectives, it is vital that the financial process, the production process, and the distribution process perform in a coordinated and efficient manner. A less than satisfactory performance within one of these processes has an adverse impact upon the other processes. As a result, the firm will fail to achieve its overall goals.

After generating funds through the financial process, creating goods and services through the production process, and hiring employees via the manpower process, the activities within the distribution process can be performed. Upon sale, funds in the form of sales revenue are returned to the firm. These funds in part allow the production process to continue. Data generated via the information process can be used to judge the success or failure of the distribution process. If the firm's customers are satisfied, this fact will be reflected in such reports as the financial statements.

## THE MANPOWER PROCESS AND THE BUSINESS SYSTEM

The manpower process is that series of events which focuses on the attainment and maintenance of a productive labor force. Certainly, no business firm will realize its goals without people. Since each of the other processes of the business firm requires people to carry out their various activities, a strong relationship exists between these processes and the manpower process. This is especially true with producton and distribiution. It takes people to operate the necessary equipment needed to convert raw materials into a finished product. Likewise, people are needed in order to price, promote, and sell the finished product or service. The manpower process must provide competent personnel if these activities are to be performed efficiently. The goods and services produced and sold by people result in a flow of funds into the firm. These funds are in turn used by the financial process to pay workers for their various talents, to purchase raw materials, and to finance the acquisition of additional plant and equipment.

The manpower process also provides personnel needed to fill both the professional and clerical jobs created by the activities required within both the information and management processes. The information process generates employee data and information. This information helps management evaluate how human resources are being used or misused in performing the activities which comprise the other processes. Data are gathered on such categories as absenteeism, accident rates, productivity, sales commissions, customer complaints, and payroll. Furthermore, the management process carefully evaluates each employee or group of employees in order to determine what adjustments are needed in order to help improve or maintain employee performance. For example, improving the physical environment in which the employee works may improve his performance. Or allowing a worker more control and responsibility over his area of work may improve morale and job satisfaction, resulting in better job performance.

## THE MANAGEMENT PROCESS AND THE BUSINESS SYSTEM

The financial, production, distribution, manpower, and financial processes each require a manager who is concerned with planning, organizing, directing, and controlling the activities of each particular process. Of course, if the business is small, one individual may well perform this function. As the business grows, each process may have its own manager.

Through the management process the separate processes of the firm are merged into one system. In very real terms, the management process is involved in running the entire business system and each of the separate processes. The manager accomplishes this by first considering the objective of the business and secondly combining the various processes so as to accomplish this purpose. Viewing the business as a system enables the manager to place each of the processes of the firm in proper perspective. In addition to fitting the various processes of the firm into a meaningful system, the management process maintains this delicate balance by carefully considering the effect of each decision upon the firm's welfare. In short, managers not only give life to the business system, but also serve as a catalyst whose influence is felt throughout the business system.

## THE INFORMATION PROCESS AND THE BUSINESS SYSTEM

The information process is that series of events which measures changes taking place in both the internal operations of the firm and the external environment. Each of the other processes has an information flow which monitors how that process is being performed and indicates where further changes need to be made.

The financial process utilizes data provided by the information process to plan and control the firm's inflow and outflow of funds. Much of this information is contained in the firm's financial statements and forecasts of future sales. In an effort to control both costs of production and levels of quality, the production process uses internal data gathered by the information process and presented in the form of performance reports. The production process works closely with the information process in developing information needed for this report. The performance report compares actual costs incurred against predetermined standards. Unfavorable variances are examined carefully to determine their cause. In addition, the production process utilizes external information in the form of published reports which provide insight into methods of improving production techniques.

Data accumulated by the information process allow the distribution process an opportunity to learn which of the firm's customers, territories, or products account for the largest share of the firm's profits or sales. Although the information process gathers and analyzes this kind of data, it depends upon salesmen to report their individual sales accurately and consistently. External data in the form of census information, questionnaires, interviews, and observations provide additional information. The distribution process and the information process analyze the information received in order to better understand who the customers are and what motivates them to buy.

The manpower process is able to plan and control personnel requirements more effectively through data obtained by the information process concerning absenteeism and turnover of employees. Surveys, interviews, and other techniques are used to determine employee attitudes and feelings towards their jobs.

In a small firm the owner will most likely be responsible for both the accumulating and the analyzing of information needed to monitor the various processes of the business. In a large firm, many individuals will be involved in generating and anlyzing information. In a firm which accepts the systems approach to decision making, information is required which will assist managers in determining if the goals of each process are in line with the goals of the firm as a whole.

## THE SYSTEMS APPROACH IN RETROSPECT

Throughout this text is the central theme that no one decision made within a business can be made in a vacuum. Six functions or processes are identified as being present in every business system, regardless of size or purpose. Decisions made in any one process affect the decisions and operations of the other five processes. The systems concept provides the vehicle for integrating what on the surface appear to be independent functions performed within a business. It is our hope that you have gained an understanding of how to perform each process, the interrelationships and interdependence of the six processes with the business system, and the various "realities" in the environment which limit the modern businessman's freedom.

## Career Opportunities Open to Business Students

For some, choosing a career is relatively easy. They somehow know exactly what they want to be and pursue their chosen profession through high school and beyond with little or no interruption. However, for many others, deciding on future work is very difficult. Some are fortunate and in time find a profession which is stimulating and rewarding. Others, after years of searching, find themselves locked into a particular job which they neither enjoy nor perform effectively.

In the discussion below we will look briefly at a few of the many job opportunities which exist today in the business world. You should have some insight into one or more careers which appeal to your liking.

## THE STUDY OF BUSINESS IN COLLEGE

Students presently attending two-year or four-year colleges will have the opportunity to study the basic courses in business which include (among others) principles of accounting, marketing, finance, management, computer programming, along with business law, economics, and so on. There are many job openings in business firms today for those students who have a junior college education. For those who wish to pursue a bachelor's degree in business administration, it will be necessary to enroll in a four-year college or university. Students majoring in a particular area of business will usually enroll in the college of business administration, which most often has four departments: accounting, marketing, management, and finance.

This text examines the six processes which comprise the business system. The four departments which make up colleges of business administration offer courses which provide an in-depth coverage of each process. The process or processes which each department is responsible for are as follows:

| | |
|---|---|
| Information process | Department of Accounting |
| Distribution process | Department of Marketing |
| Financial process | Department of Finance |
| Production process | Department of Management |
| Manpower process | Department of Management |
| Management process | Department of Management |

## ACCOUNTING AS A CAREER

Accounting is concerned with the art of recording, classifying, summarizing, and interpreting financial information. In addition to accounting courses, the student majoring in accounting will probably take courses in marketing, management, finance, economics, law, statistics, and so on in order to acquire an appreciation for the total business system.

The profession of accountancy has reached a stature today which is comparable to such professions as law and engineering. Such recognition is due primarily to the rigorous requirements which must be met before an individual can be granted the right to practice as a certified public accountant (C.P.A.). These requirements include: (1) successful completion of the uniform C.P.A. examination, which is a national examination given in May and November of each year; (2) fulfillment of the experience requirement as stipulated by each state (experience required varies from one to five years); (3) receipt of a license by the certifying state, designating the recipient a C.P.A.

Although the C.P.A. designation is a valuable credential for the accountant, many jobs in the accounting area do not require that the accountant be certified. There are three primary avenues which the accountant may travel: public, private, and governmental. Generally speaking, an accountant engaging in public practice will be expected to become certified. On the other hand, certification is not mandatory for those accountants pursuing a career in industrial or governmental organizations.

### PUBLIC ACCOUNTING

An accountant who is engaged in the practice of public accounting provides services to clients on a fee basis in much the same way a dentist charges his patient a fee for services rendered. Services provided by a public accountant are usually divided into three areas: auditing, taxes, and management services.

*Auditing.* An audit is an independent review of the firm's financial records. Upon completion of an audit, the C.P.A. expresses an opinion concerning the fairness of the firm's financial statements. This opinion is often referred to as the *auditor's report.* A C.P.A. is requested by various groups or individuals to perform an audit. For example, a bank would frequently request a C.P.A. to audit the records of a firm before making a decision concerning a large loan.

*Taxes.*   Due to the increasing complexity of federal and state tax laws, the C.P.A. is frequently called upon by both individuals and firms to prepare their tax returns. Because of the C.P.A.'s expertise in financial matters and his understanding of tax regulations, he is often able to minimize his client's tax liability.

*Management Advisory Services.*   When a C.P.A. audits a firm's records he becomes very much aware of the firm's weaknesses in regard to its system of accounting. As a result, the accountant is in an excellent position to advise management on certain changes which the firm should implement in order, for example, to safeguard assets or lower operating expenses.

## PRIVATE ACCOUNTING

When an accountant engages in private accounting he is hired by a firm as one of its employees. In many instances, an accountant who has four or five years of experience in public accounting will be hired by a firm to be its controller or chief accountant. The accountant engaged in private practice is primarily concerned with three goals: (1) accumulating information in order to help management plan and control the day-to-day operations of the firm; (2) accumulating data needed to determine the cost of producing a product or providing a service; (3) reporting information to management which will provide a basis for making special decisions such as, for example, the acceptance or rejection of a new product line. Each of these three goals reflects the fact that the private accountant plays a key role in helping the business manager operate his firm.

## GOVERNMENTAL ACCOUNTING

In addition to private and public accounting, an accountant can also elect to serve the government in a local, state, or federal capacity. Such agencies of the federal government as the Internal Revenue Service, the General Accounting Office, and the Federal Bureau of Investigation are always looking for individuals with expertise in accounting.

## DATA PROCESSING AS A CAREER

Careers associated with computers are closely related to accounting, because computers are very much a part of the overall function of recording, classifying, and summarizing of information. Three basic jobs associated with computers are computer operator, computer programmer, and systems analyst.

## COMPUTER OPERATOR

The computer operator, by working at a console, controls the CPU (Central Processing Unit) along with the input and output units. He operates the computer in accordance with the instructions prepared by the programmer.

## COMPUTER PROGRAMMER

The programmer is responsible for writing instructions in a language and format which can be understood by the computer. The programmer begins with a particular problem which requires solving. With the use of flow charts, the programmer organizes and analyzes the problem into its component parts, puts these parts together in a logical framework, and writes a program which tells the computer what to do. The computer programming profession offers the greatest job opportunities of any in the computer industry.

## SYSTEMS ANALYST

The systems analyst is responsible for designing the entire electronic data processing system so that the information goals of the firm will be realized. He is responsible not only for assembling the necessary equipment, but also for training others, such as the programmer and operator, to do their respective jobs.

Other occupations associated with an electronic data processing system are the key punch operator, the librarian, and the data processing manager.

## EMPLOYMENT PROSPECTS

The information in Exhibit 26–1 shows the job outlook for accountants and related occupations through the decade of the seventies.

### EXHIBIT 26–1

*Outlook for Jobs through the Seventies
in Accounting and Related Occupations*

| Occupation | Estimated employment 1970 | Average annual openings to 1980 |
|---|---|---|
| Accountants | 491,000 | 31,200 |
| Excellent opportunities. Strong demand for college-trained applicants. Graduates of business and other schools offering accounting should have good prospects. | | |
| Systems analysts | 100,000 | 22,700 |
| Excellent opportunities due to rapid expansion of electronic data processing systems in business and government. | | |
| Statisticians | 24,000 | 1,500 |
| Very good opportunities for new graduates and experienced statisticians in industry and government. | | |

Source: U. S. Department of Labor, as used in University of Notre Dame, *Placement Manual*. Placement Publications, Inc. Rahway, N. J.: Spring, 1974, pp. F-4–F-7.

## MARKETING AS A CAREER

The study of marketing is concerned with those activities which direct the flow of goods and services from the producer to the consumer. A student majoring in marketing not only learns the principles of marketing but also the relationships of marketing with other processes of the firm. The marketing curriculum of a university provides training for men and women who are interested in pursuing careers such as personal selling, advertising, product design, purchasing, transportation, and retailing. Once a student receives a degree in marketing, he will most likely start out in the field of selling.

## SALES JOBS VARY

The type of sales job an individual has will vary according to the kind of business which employs him. For example, a salesman may sell for a manufacturer, for a wholesaler, or for a retailer. Furthermore, the sales job will vary according to the customer to whom the salesman is selling. For example, when selling for a manufacturer, a salesman may sell directly to the final consumer or to another business firm such as a wholesaler or retailer.

After an individual has gained experience in selling and has proven himself to be a creative and productive salesman, he may then be promoted to a sales management position. For example, a firm selling a number of different products may appoint a product sales manager to be in charge of those salesmen selling a particular product or group of products. Or a firm selling in different territories may employ territorial sales managers. A company which divides its total market into regions would employ a regional sales manager for each region. Such a sales manager would be responsible for hiring, training, and supervising the salesmen in his particular region.

From product sales manager or territorial sales manager, an individual may climb to the top sales position within the firm—the chief sales executive. In this position, he is responsible for all activities relating to sales.

On the other hand, rather than being employed by a firm as a salesman, a businessman may elect to be an independent salesman by going into business for himself. Such salesmen are referred to as manufacturers' agents or manufacturers' representatives.

Of course, once someone has gained experience in selling, he may decide to move into other areas of marketing in which he can utilize the experience he has gained through sales. For that matter, he may elect to begin his career in one of the other areas of marketing mentioned earlier. Excellent opportunities exist today in the fields of advertising, packaging, physical distribution, promotion, marketing research, product development and design, consumer behavior, and so on.

## EMPLOYMENT PROSPECTS

The outlook for jobs in the marketing area through the seventies, as reported by the U.S. Department of Labor, are shown in Exhibit 26–2. Of course, there are many job opportunities in the marketing area. The employment prospects cited in the exhibit should, however, give you a feel for the future opportunities in marketing.

## FINANCE AS A CAREER

In the curriculum of finance, the student learns both the instruments and the institutions of finance. In order to familiarize the students with other areas which impinge upon financial decisions, most curriculums integrate into the

EXHIBIT 26–2

*Outlook for Jobs Through the Seventies
in Marketing and Related Occupations*

| Occupation | Estimated employment 1970 | Average annual openings to 1980 |
|---|---|---|
| Manufacturer's salesmen | 510,000 | 25,000 |

Favorable opportunities for well-trained workers, but competition will be keen. Best prospects for those trained to handle technical products.

| | | |
|---|---|---|
| Advertising workers | 141,000 | 8,400 |

Slow growth. Opportunities will be good, however, for highly qualified applicants, especially in advertising agencies.

| | | |
|---|---|---|
| Marketing research workers | 23,000 | 2,600 |

Excellent opportunities, especially for those who have graduate degrees. Existing marketing research organizations are expected to expand and new research departments and independent firms set up.

| | | |
|---|---|---|
| Public relations workers | 76,000 | 4,400 |

Rapid increase due to population growth and rise in level of business activity. An increasing amount of funds will be allocated to public relations work.

Source: U. S. Department of Labor, as used in University of Notre Dame, *Placement Manual.* Placement Publications, Inc. Rahway, N. J.: Spring, 1974, pp. F-4–F-7.

finance program courses in taxes, economics, governmental regulations, business law, accounting, and management. These additional courses provide the future financial manager with an appreciation of the total business system. Three of the more popular areas of finance, discussed below, are: institutional finance, brokerage and investments, and business finance.

## INSTITUTIONAL FINANCE

An individual specializing in this area of finance would work for a financial institution such as a bank, savings and loan association, or credit union. These institutions perform two services: (1) they safeguard the deposits of households and business firms, and (2) they make loans to households, firms, and others who need additional money for a variety of reasons. An individual pursuing a career in institutional finance will be acting as an intermediary between depositors (savers) and borrowers (investors).

## BROKERAGE AND INVESTMENTS

Although there are many types of brokers in the United States perhaps the most familiar is the securities broker. The securities broker answers questions, gets quotations, obtains information, and executes orders in various securities for his customers. These securities, such as stocks and bonds, are bought and sold for investors by the broker through a stock exchange such as the New York and American exchanges.

## BUSINESS FINANCE

This is the area of the finance field to which we have given our attention in the text. The individual pursuing a career in business finance will be responsible for both the acquisition of funds for the firm and the allocation of funds to various departments within the firm. The managers of finance must have a keen awareness of the various forms of business organization, the means of obtaining sufficient funds for the firm under the most favorable terms, and the federal income tax regulations.

## EMPLOYMENT PROSPECTS

There are a number of fields open to an individual who majors in finance. The job outlook for two of these is presented in Exhibit 26–3.

### EXHIBIT 26–3
*Outlook for Jobs Through the Seventies in Finance Related Occupations*

| Occupation | Estimated employment 1970 | Average annual openings to 1980 |
|---|---|---|
| Bank officers | 174,000 | 11,000 |
| Employment is expected to grow rapidly as the increased use of computers enables banks to expand their services. | | |
| Securities salesmen | 200,000 | 11,800 |
| Good opportunities. | | |

Source: U. S. Department of Labor, as used in University of Notre Dame, *Placement Manual.* Placement Publications, Inc. Rahway, N. J.: Spring, 1974, pp. F-4–F-7.

## MANAGEMENT AS A CAREER

The management of business firms has in the past been taken for granted. The successful salesman, the best worker, or the best engineer was promoted to a managerial position. In some cases these promotions were wise, but in many cases the successful salesman turned out to be a failure as a manager. The successful "doer" of a task is not always the successful manager of a group of people performing the same task. This conclusion does not help solve the wide demand for managerial talent in the economy. In fact, with the rising costs and competition and rapidly changing technology and consumer's demands, the cry for managerial excellence is increasingly being heard from both private and public institutions.

In any institution, two broad types of managers exist: functional managers and general managers. Functional managers manage employees within *one* functional area in business. Examples would include managers of engineers, lawyers, accountants, scientists, etc. In addition to managerial training they usually must possess some degree of expertise in the functional area they are managing. General managers manage broader areas than functional managers and usually manage managers rather than workers. Examples would include presidents, vice-presidents, product-line managers, heads of departments or divisions, plant managers, etc. There is a great demand in public and private institutions for *both* types of managers. This can be illustrated by reviewing the growing job opportunities within the distribution, financial, information, production, and manpower processes. Not only are the job opportunities increasing in these areas but so too are the demands for managers to manage these employees.

In response to this demand colleges, both on the graduate and undergraduate levels, have created a course of study designed to train students in managerial techniques, principles, and functions. This course of study is centered around the fact that managers get work done through other people rather than doing the work themselves. What a manager does is plan, organize, direct, motivate, and control the efforts of those who are subordinates and make decisions that affect the operations for which he is responsible. Most curriculums in management are designed to help the student be a better planner, organizer, director, motivator, controller, and decision maker. Because of the vast variety of

EXHIBIT 26–4

*Outlook for Jobs Through the Seventies*
*In Management Related Occupations*

| Occupation | Estimated employment 1970 | Average annual openings to 1980 |
|---|---|---|
| Personnel workers | 160,000 | 9,100 |
| Favorable outlook especially for college graduates with training in personnel administration. More workers will be needed for recruiting, interviewing, and psychological testing. | | |
| Purchasing agents | 167,000 | 5,400 |
| Good prospects. Demand strong for business administration graduates who have courses in purchasing. Demand also will be strong for graduates with backgrounds in engineering or science to work in firms manufacturing chemicals, complex machines, and other technical products. | | |
| Managers and assistants (hotel) | 195,000 | 14,400 |
| Favorable outlook, especially for those who have college degrees in hotel administration. | | |
| Hospital administrators | 17,000 | 1,000 |
| Very good opportunities for those who have masters degrees in hospital administration. Applicants without graduate training will find it increasingly difficult to enter this field. | | |

Source: U. S. Department of Labor, as used in University of Notre Dame, *Placement Manual.* Placement Publications, Inc. Rahway, N. J.: Spring, 1974, pp. F-4–F-7.

knowledge needed, management majors are required to take courses from many departments and areas. Typical of the types of course areas needed would be psychology, statistics, operations research, business law, accounting, finance, marketing, organization theory, and labor relations.

The job of a manager is probably one of the most demanding and personally rewarding jobs within modern institutions. Exhibit 26–4 gives just a brief illustration of some of the opportunities facing the modern manager.

What most students forget is that managerial talent is not only demanded by business institutions. Governments, hospitals, prisons, schools, and many other public institutions sorely need professional managerial talent. The management of public institutions has been ignored in the past. In the future this will not be so. Public management will become the growth area of the future. The insightful student who intends to pursue a managerial career will define his opportunities to include both private and public institutions.

## SUMMARY

The environment in which the business firm operates today is composed of three systems: the social system, the economic system, and the governmental system. The social system consists of the cultural beliefs and values of the people. Through the economic system, business firms are free to produce those goods and services which consumers desire. In order to maintain the freedom of choice for both producers and consumers, a governmental system consisting of three branches has been devised.

Within this environment, the business manager must make decisions which will affect the success or failure of the firm. To be successful, every business must realize the following four goals: (1) produce a competitive good or service, (2) make a profit, (3) gain society's acceptance, and (4) live up to the responsibility of its various publics.

If he is to realize these four goals, the business manager cannot make decisions in a vacuum. On the contrary, he must view the business firm as an ongoing system of six identifiable processes; finance, production, distribution, manpower, management, and information. He must coordinate each of these six processes in order to achieve the overall goals of the firm. If one process is allowed to dominate, the total business system will suffer.

It is our hope that those of you who find the study of business an exciting and stimulating experience will pursue one of the many career opportunities open today for business students.

## QUESTIONS

1. Now that you have had an opportunity to study the various activities of the business manager and the environment in which the business firm operates,

discuss in your own words the meaning of the "systems approach" to operating a firm.

2. (a) What do the initials C.P.A. represent?
   (b) List the three requirements which an accountant must satisfy in order to be called a C.P.A.

3. Distinguish public accounting from private accounting.

4. (a) Services provided by a public accountant can be divided into three areas. List these three areas.
   (b) The accountant engaged in private practice is primarily concerned with accumulating information which will help the business manager operate his firm. List three areas in which the private accountant accumulates information.

5. What are three jobs open to individuals interested in pursuing a career in data processing?

6. In what way do sales jobs vary?

7. List eight occupations which a student of marketing might pursue.

8. List three areas a student of finance might wish to pursue.

9. The manager of finance for a business firm must have, among others, a keen awareness of three subjects. List these three subjects.

10. Distinguish the functional manager from the general manager.

11. Is managerial talent only demanded by business firms?

12. Evaluate the job outlook through the seventies for the following occupations:
    (a) Accountants
    (b) Advertising workers
    (c) Securities salesmen
    (d) Personnel workers

# Glossary

**Absolute advantage**—The principle by which a nation produces and exports those goods and services which it can produce more efficiently than other nations and exchanges its products for those goods which it is less efficient in producing, thereby increasing its wealth and the standard of living of its inhabitants.

**Administrative expenses**—An operating outlay resulting from the administrative function.

**Advertising**—A type of indirect comunication used by a seller to reach many potential customers at one time.

**Arbitration**—A process of settling a dispute between two parties in which a third party hands down a decision binding upon both parties.

**Array**—A listing of numbers in a table such that the lowest number is recorded first and the highest number is recorded last.

**Assets**—Economic resources (properties) owned or controlled by a business.

**Authorized shares**—The number of shares of stock which a corporation is permitted to issue.

**Automation**—That process whereby goods or services are produced by an automatic machine with little or no assistance from human beings.

**Break-even point**—The point where total sales for a given period equal total expenses for the same period; the point where the firm operates at zero profits.

**Business system**—A man-directed, multigoal, adaptive network of processes which interact to achieve a goal or plan.

**Capitalism**—An economic system where the production and distribution of goods and services is not organized and planned by some central authority, but is regulated by the market.

**Cash forecast**—A schedule which summarizes the expected cash receipts to be realized in the future, the estimated expenditures to be incurred, and the resulting cash balance.

**Collateral**—Security, such as property, given as a pledge.

**Collective bargaining**—The process in which the businessman or woman negotiates with representatives of the employees over matters pertaining to wages, hours, and working conditions.

**Common stock**—That stock issued by a corporation when only one class of stock is issued; equity which confers voting rights to the owner.

**Communications**—The passing of information from one person to another or from one person to a group of people.

**Consolidation**—The process in which a new firm is created by two firms which dissolve their separate operations and combine their assets and liabilities.

**Consumer**—An individual with a specific, definable desire, with the economic ability and the motivation to satisfy the desire.

**Continuous manufacturing**—A continuous, uninterrupted flow of inputs, goods in process, and outputs.

**Contract**—A document of binding arrangements for the future agreed upon by two separate parties which enables a business to expand beyond personal relationships.

**Corporation**—A form of business organization in which ownership and management can be separated; a business which is "an artificial being, invisible, intangible and existing only in the contemplation of the law" (John Marshall).

**Cost plus**—A single approach to pricing products where a predetermined mark-up is added to the cost of the product to arrive at the product's price.

**Cumulative stock**—Stock which pays dividends from year to year.

**Data processing**—The collecting, processing, and reporting of information.

**Debentures**—Unsecured bonds in which no property is pledged as security.

**Debt**—Funds which a business obtains from creditors.

**Direct labor**—Costs incurred for employees working specifically on goods being manufactured.

**Direct materials**—Materials incorporated into a product being manufactured which become a part of the final product.

**Distribution costs**—Selling expenses and those costs incurred in directing the flow of finished goods from the production department to the consumer or user.

**Equity**—The rights or claims to assets.

**Expenses**—The costs of goods or services used up in the process of earning revenue.

**Fixed asset**—A property item such as land, building, or machinery, expected to be used in a business over a long period of time.

**Fixed cost**—A cost which remains constant over varying levels of production.

**Flow control**—The process by which a continuous manufacturer controls the entire flow of raw materials through the various manufacturing operations rather than controlling each order.

**Forecasting**—Business research which deals with future changes.

**Franchise**—A business which has been granted the right to sell or distribute a manufacturer's means of combining the advantages of both big and small businesses.

**Free enterprise**—A system where the production and distribution of goods and services is not organized and planned by some central authority.

**Frequency distribution**—Arrangement of data into categories or classes along with an indication of the number of observations in each category.

**Frequency polygon**—A graph consisting of a line connecting the midpoints of each of a series of histogram bars, where each bar represents a category or group of data.

**Group**—Any number of people who interact with one another, identify themselves as a group, and have a purpose.

**Hardware**—The physical components of a computer system—electronic, mechanical, or magnetic.

**Histogram**—A graphic presentation of a frequency distribution with bars which show the number of observations in each category of data.

**Holding company**—A business which owns stock in other companies sufficient to control them.

**Indenture**—An agreement which outlines various restrictions and terms to which a corporation must adhere.

**Interest**—A charge for the use of money.

**Intermittent manufacturing**—A manufacturing process with uneven flow of inputs, goods in process, and outputs.

**Inventory**—The value of the goods or stock of a business.

**Job summary**—A statement of the basic tasks performed on a job.

**Liabilities**—In accounting, the equity of creditors in the assets of a business.

**Limited liability**—Characteristic of owners of stock in a corporation in which personal assets of the stockholders are not available to creditors of the corporation.

**Line of credit**—Amount of money available to a firm from a bank, whereby the firm can borrow up to a set limit simply by requesting the amount desired.

**Liquidity**—The time required to convert assets into cash.

**Long-term debt**—Those liabilities of the firm which will not mature within a period of twelve months.

**Management:**   **Top**—President of a company and department heads;
**Middle**—Subordinate managers within the departments;
**First-level**—Supervisors of operating employees.

**Management process**—The process of planning the direction a business will take in the future, organizing its resources, directing its efforts, and setting in motion a system for control.

**Manpower process**—Attaining and maintenance of a productive labor force.

**Manufacturing**—Operations to transform raw materials into finished goods.

**Manufacturing overhead**—All factory costs not classified as direct materials and direct labor.

**Market**—A group of businesses and consumers interested in the same product.

**Measure of central tendency**—Presentation of data by means of a graph as well as through computation of averages.

**Mediation**—The process of settling a dispute between two parties through a third person who intervenes with suggested, but not binding, solutions.

**Medium (media)**—Any form or method of communication.

**Merger**—Acquisition of one firm by another, with the acquiring firm being dissolved.

**Mortgage**—A transfer of title of property from a borrower to a lender, upon condition that title will be returned upon payment of debt.

**Mutual agency**—Property of partnerships under which partnership is bound by any agreements or contracts entered into by any partner.

**Net income**—Total sales less total expenses.

**No par stock**—Stock issued with no assigned value.

**Order control**—The process by which an intermittent manufacturer controls operations through each order separately.

**Outstanding shares**—Portion of authorized shares of stock which have been issued to stockholders.

**Par value**—Stock to which a face value—such as $100, $10, or $5—has been arbitrarily assigned.

**Participating stock**—Preferred stock in which the stockholder has a right to dividends in excess of a predetermined percentage.

**Partnership**—An association of two or more persons as coowners of a profit-making business.

**Policy**—A formal statement of a manager's beliefs about a given area.

**Preferred stock**—Stock which receives certain preferential treatment.

**Principal**—Money loaned by the lender (contrast with **Interest).**

**Procedure**—A statement of sequence of steps to be taken to achieve a specific purpose.

**Process**—A series of actions or operations definitely conducive to some end.

**Procurement**—Process of obtaining the proper materials, equipment, supplies, and other inputs to be used within a business.

**Product**—Whatever satisfies consumer demands.

**Product cost**—Direct materials, direct labor, and manufacturing overhead.

**Production process**—Series of events which creates value in the form of finished goods and services.

**Promotion**—Part of the distribution process which furthers sales.

**Proprietorship**—A business totally owned and controlled by one person.

**Purchase order**—Legally binding contract which contains conditions of sale plus any other records the business man or woman feels should be included.

**Quality control**—Process of assuring that finished goods will meet a desired specification or quality level.

**Rate of return on investment**—A measure of performance computed by dividing earnings per period by average investment in assets over the period.

**Retailers**—Institutions which sell products to the ultimate consumer.

**Retained earnings**—Amount remaining after distribution of dividends to stockholders.

**Revenue**—Inflow of assets resulting from the sale of goods or services.

**Rules**—Statements of required or mandatory behavior.

**Short-term debt**—Those liabilities of the firm which must be paid within a period of twelve months.

**Staff unit**—Group of employees who take from other managers those administrative jobs outside their area of specialization.

**Stockholders**—Owners of a corporation.

**System**—A set of component parts related in the accomplishment of some purpose.

**Tariff**—A tax assessed on goods imported from another nation.

**Time-sharing**—System in which a number of users at different locations utilize the same computer through separate input/output channels.

**Trade quota**—A restriction on the number of units of a particular goods which may be imported.

**Trading on equity**—A means of obtaining money through issuing bonds or stock rather than through debt.

**Union**—A formal organization of workers.

**Unissued shares**—Shares of a corporation which are authorized but unissued.

**Unlimited liability**—The right of a firm's creditors to the assets of the firm and the personal assets of the owners; characteristic of proprietorship and partnership.

**Variable overhead**—Costs which vary in relation to changes in production.

**Wholesaler**—A firm which supplies other firms with the input used in their businesses.

**Working capital**—Current assets minus current liabilities; includes cash, accounts receivable, and merchandise inventory.

# Index

Absenteeism, 371, 412
Absolute advantage, defined, 422
Accounting, defined, 459
Accounting equation, 318–23
Accounts receivable
    factoring, 74–75
    and revenue, 327
Acquisition
    advantages to buyer, 444–46
    advantages to seller, 446–48
    defined, 441
    to restrict competition, 448
Administrative expenses
    and distribution costs, 35
    types of, 36
Advertising
    brand names, 174
    dog food, 175
    expectations of, 173–74
    for job applicants, 216–17
    media evaluation, 176–78
    and product life cycle, 179–81
    when to use, 172–73
    writing an ad, 174–75
*Advertising Age,* 176
Age Discrimination in Employment Act
    (1967), 224
Agriculture, Department of, 11
American Cancer Society, 82
American Stock Exchange, 42, 333, 464
American Sugar Refining Company, 448
Antitrust laws, 9–10
Arbitration, defined, 253
Arithmetic mean, defined, 387
Array, defined, 384
Assets
    current, defined, 323
    defined, 318
    other, defined, 325
    withdrawal of, and corporation, 43
    withdrawal of, and partnership, 41
Audit, defined, 459
Authorized shares of stock, defined, 47–48
Automobile Information Disclosure Act
    (1958), 11
Avon, 158

Balance of payments, and IMF, 425
Balance sheet
    explained, 323
    ratios explained, 330–32
Bayer aspirin, 174
*Better Homes & Gardens,* 172, 176, 177
Bids, *see* Quotations
Blacks, in labor force, 233
Bonds
    collateral trust, 55
    convertible, 56–57
    debentures, 56
    income bonds, 56
    mortgage, 55
    taxing of, 90–91
    values discussed, 58
    with special features, 56
Boy Scouts of America, 82
Break-even point, defined, 394
Bretton Woods Conference (1944), 425
Budget
    types of, 352–54
    use of, 349–50
Budget committee, 351–52
Budget reports, timing of, 354–55
Bureau of the Census, 361, 362, 414, 415
Bureau of Labor Statistics, 371, 408, 414,
    415
Business
    failures of, 5–6, 31, 199
    functions of, 21–22
    goals of, 16–20
    promotion of, 31–32
    small, defined, 272
    small, strengths of, 275–77
    small, weaknesses of, 277–81
Business manager
    and pollution, 417–18
    and social responsibility, 411–12
Business objectives
    achieving, 265–67
    general, 453
    selecting, 263–65
    small business, 272–75
    value of, 267–68
Business processes
    related to college departments, 459

Business system
  described, 22
  establishing standards of, 307
  and the information process, 316–18
  management control of, 306–7
*Business Week,* 54, 365, 416
Businessman
  defined as manager, 259
  and employee informal group, 247–48

Capitalism, 4
*Carpet Review,* 366
Carriers of freight traffic, 189–90
Cash forecast
  and bank loans, 69
  defined, 65
*Census of Agriculture,* 362
*Census of Business,* 361
*Census of Housing,* 361
*Census of Manufacturers,* 361
*Census of Minerals,* 362
*Census of Population,* 361
Central Processing Unit (CPU), components of, 378–79
Chase Manhattan Bank of New York, 271
Chattel mortgage, defined, 76, 77
Chicago *Tribune,* 172
Chicanos, in labor force, 232–33
Civil Rights Act (1964), 222–24
CL (car-load rate), 192
Clayton Act (1914), 9, 10, 449
Clean Air Act of 1970, 418
COBOL, defined, 379
Coca-Cola Company, 174
Collateral
  defined, 67
  loan requirements of, 70
  trust bonds, 55
Collective bargaining, 252–53
Commerce, Department of, 365
Commercial paper, defined, 73
Committee for Economic Development, 272
Commodity groups, as exports, 426
Common carriers, defined, 189
Common stock
  and convertible bonds, 56–57
  investment in, 49
  taxing of, 90–91
  values discussed, 58
Communication
  factors of, 301–2
  failures of, 304–6
  oral, 303–4
  written, 302–3
Communication Act (1934), 11
Competitive edge in distribution, 137
Computer
  abilities of, 379
  applications of, 381–83
Conglomerate, defined, 443

Consolidation, defined, 441–42
Consumer
  defined, 137–38
  industrial, 139–41
  ultimate, 141–47
Consumer protection laws, 10–12
Contract
  application of, 12–13
  labor, 253
  partnership, 41
  as purchase order, 110–11
Contract carriers, defined, 189
Convertible bonds, and common stock, 56–57
Corporation
  and bond advantage, 54
  and equity funds, 47–53
  explained, 42–44
  funding, 39, 44
  limited liability, 48
  number of, 39
  taxation of, 80, 84–86
Cost estimation, 34–36, 38
Cost of goods sold budget, 353
Cost-plus approach, defined, 154
CPU, *see* Central processing unit
Current ratio, computation of, 330

Data processing
  as a career, 460–61
  defined, 376–77
Debentures, defined, 56
Debt funds, 46
Departmentalization, types of, 291–94
Direct cost, 348
Direct labor
  cost of, 341, 348
  and product cost, 34, 36
Direct materials
  cost of, 340, 348
  and product cost, 34, 36
Discounts, 68, 69
Distribution costs, defined, 35
Distribution process
  defined, 455
  and industrial consumer, 141
Divesting of an acquisition, defined, 447
Dividend
  declaration of, 49
  stockholders' right to, 49
  calculation of rate, 50
  rate, stock, 49
Dunn and Bradstreet, 5

Economic system, defined, 453
Employee
  attitudes of, 372–73
  cooperation of, 237–38
  discipline of, 238–39
  ESP model of, 235–36

Employee (continued)
  group effect on, 245–48
  hiring of, 219–21
  legislation protecting, 250–52
  qualifications of, 213
  rational-economic model of, 234–35
  turnover of, 412
Employment agencies, 217–18
Endorsements, defined, 72–73
Equal Employment Opportunity Commission, powers of, 224
Equal Pay Act (1963), 224
Equity funds
  as common stock, 47
  defined, 46
  as preferred stock, 47
  and retained earnings, 47, 52–53
  types of, 46
Expansion
  and key personnel, 445
  and research and development, 445
  and small firms, 444
  and stabilization of sales, 445
  and tax savings, 445–46
  types of, 443
Expense
  defined, 319
  types of, 327–28
Export broker, function of, 430
Export management company (EMC), 429–30, 437
Export merchant, function of, 430
Exports
  commodity groups, 426
  compared to imports, 428.
  reflect political relations, 427
  small business and, 429–30

*Factory Management,* 366
Fair Labor Standards Act (1938), 224
Federal Alcohol Administration Act (1935), 11
Federal Bureau of Investigation, 460
Federal Communications Commission, and advertising, 11
Federal government, financial assistance to small business, 271–72
Federal government economic activity
  executive branch, 13–14
  judicial branch, 12–13
  legislative branch, 8–13
Federal Hazardous Substances Labeling Act (1960), 11
Federal Mediation and Conciliation Service, 253
Federal Power Commission, 329
*Federal Reserve Bulletin,* 362
Federal Trade Commission, 9–12
Federal Trade Commission Act (1914), 9–11

Federal Unemployment Tax Act, 225
Field warehousing, defined, 75
Finance, as a career, 462–64
Financial accounting, defined, 338–39
Financial process, defined, 454
Financial reports, use of, 329
Firestone, 158
Fixed assets
  defined, 37, 323–25
  and sales and leaseback, 60
Fixed cost
  defined, 34
  and manufacturing overhead, 34
Flow control, defined, 122–23
Food and Drug Administration, 10–11
*Food and Equipment Product News,* 366
Ford Motor Company, 5, 31, 53, 57
Forecasting
  defined, 365–66
  and published information, 365
Foreign investments
  extent of, 432–34
  industries involved in, 434
  in U.S. firms, 434–37
*Fortune,* 412
Franchise, 39
Free enterprise, 4
Freight traffic, statistics of, 186–89
Frequency distribution, defined, 384
Frequency polygon, defined, 385–86
*Furniture News,* 366

General Accounting Office, 460
General agreements on tariffs and trade (GATT), 424–25
General Motors, 19, 40, 271, 292
GIGO (Garbage In/Garbage Out), defined, 379
Goods in process, defined, 116
Grain market, New York City, 166
Grievance procedure, defined, 253–54
Gross profit, defined, 327
Group behavior, effect of on employee, 246–47
Group, defined, 245
Gulf & Western, 443
Gulf Oil Company, 54

*Handbook of Labor Statistics,* 362
Hardware, defined, 377
Hiring practices
  minority groups, 414
  women, 415–16
Histogram, defined, 385–86
Holding company, defined, 442
Holiday Inn, 32

Income
  adjusted gross, 82–83
  gross, 80–81

Income (continued)
    net, calculation of, 32–33, 327
    participation of in partnership, 41
    predicted household annual, 142
    recreation expenditure, 143
    salary plus commission, 171
    saving of, 142
    straight commission, 171
    straight salary, 171
Income bonds, 56
Income estimation, 33–34, 38
Income statement, 327, 331, 344
Income tax, as cost, 35
Indenture, defined, 54
Indians in labor force, 232–33
Industrial compensation laws, 225
Information
    computer processing of, 377–79
    forecasting, 365
    and manpower process, 372–73
    manpower research and, 370–72
    marketing research and, 368–70
    and production process, 366
    use of published, 362
    use of unpublished, 362–64
Information process, defined, 457
Inspection, 123–25
Interest
    average rate of, 71
    bank loan repayment, 70
    computation of, 64–65
    defined, 53
Internal growth, funding, 440–41
Internal Revenue Code, 79, 329
    and corporate taxation, 80
    and incorporation laws, 89
    tax on accumulated earnings, 89–90
    tax deductions, 83
Internal Revenue Service, 79, 225, 460
International Association of Machinists, 250
International Bank for Reconstruction and
    development, *see* World Bank
International Brotherhood of Electrical
    Workers, 250
International Brotherhood of Teamsters,
    Chauffers, Warehousemen, and Helpers
    of America, 249
International Business Machines, 6
International Monetary Fund (IMF), 425
International Telephone and Telegraph,
    443
International trade
    defined, 422
    electing to participate in, 437
    and exports, 426–27
Interstate commerce, federal legislation,
    10
Interstate Commerce Commission, 189,
    329
Interview, use of, 363

Intrastate commerce, 10
Inventory
    cost determination, 339–40
    defined, 37
Inventory control, defined, 367–68
Investment, estimate of initial, 36–39
Invoice, defined, 111

Jet Way, Inc., 189
Job applicants
    advertising for, 216–17
    and employment agencies, 217–18
    recommended, 216
    recruiting of, 218–19
    unsolicited, 216
Job cost sheet, use of, 343
Job lot, defined, 340
Job order cost system, defined, 340
Job satisfaction, 410–11
Job specialization and organizational struc-
    ture, 290–91
Job summary, defined, 213
Job ticket and direct labor costs, 341–42
Jobs
    analysis of, 213
    creation of, 212
    measurement of output, 307–9
    organization of, 289–90
Justice, Department of, 10

K-Mart, 159
Korvetts, 159

Labor
    calculation of turnover, 371
    as cost and resource, 212
    division of, 286
Labor efficiency standards, defined, 346–47
Labor efficiency variance, defined, 347
Labor force
    changes in, 215
    described, 229–33
    predictions on size of, 230
    sexual division of, 230
    white- vs. blue-collar, 250
    women, 415–16
Labor rate standards, defined, 346–47
Labor rate variance, defined, 347
Lawrence, Mass., 8, 222
LCL (less than carload) rate, 192
Leases, defined, 60
Lee Way Motor Freight, 189
Legislation
    antidiscrimination, 222–24
    employee protection through, 224–25,
        250–52
Leisure, increase of, 408–9
"Let the buyer beware," 10
Liabilities
    creation and redemption of, 325
    current, defined, 326

Liabilities (continued)
  defined, 318
  limited, defined, 42
  long-term, defined, 326
Line of credit, defined, 72
Liquidity, defined, 323
Litton Industries, 443
Lockout, 253
Long-term debt
  bonds, 54–57
  defined, 47
  funds, 53–61
Long-term funds
  expense of, 331
  leases, 60
  sales and leaseback, 60–61
  trading on equity, 59–60
Long-term motgage notes, defined, 47
Los Angeles *Times,* 172
LTL (less than truckload) rate, 192

*McCall's,* 172
McDonald's, 32, 174
McGraw-Hill Book Company, 365
Machinery
  general-purpose, 119, 120, 121
  special-purpose, 120, 121
Magazine advertising, 176–77
Magnetic tapes, defined, 378
Management
  as a career, 464–66
  control of business system, 306–7
  levels of, 294–96
Management process
  defined, 457
  and planning, 263
Manpower process, defined, 456
Manufacturing
  continuous, defined, 117
  intermittent, defined, 117
  operation of continuous, 120–21
  operation of intermittent, 119, 121
Manufacturing cost
  direct labor, 341
  direct materials, defined, 340
  manufacturing overhead, 341–43
Manufacturing design and manufacturing
    operations, 119–21
Manufacturing operation, consumer demand, 117
Manufacturing overhead
  defined, 347–48
  and product cost, 34, 36
Manpower process, and generating information, 372–73
Manpower research and published information, 370–72
Marketing, as a career, 461–62
Marketing research, 368–70
Marshall, Chief Justice John, 42

Materials
  price standards of, 345
  quantity standards of, 345
  requisition form, 340, 341
Maytag, 160
Mead Corporation, 417
Measures of central tendency
  explained, 386–89
  selection of, 389–90
Median, defined, 388
Mediation, defined, 253
Medicare, 225
Merchandise Mart (Chicago), 166
Merger, defined, 441
The Miami Beach *Sun Reporter,* 172
Miles Laboratory, 271
Minority groups and hiring practices, 414
Mode, defined, 389
*Modern Photography,* 176
*Modern Plant Operation and Maintenance,*
    366
Monsanto Compay, 334
*Monthly Labor Review,* 362
Mortgage bonds, defined, 55
Multinational firm, defined, 431
Mutual agency
  and corporation, 43
  of partnership, 41

Nader, Ralph, *Unsafe at Any Speed,* 19
National Aeronautics and Space Administration, 104
National Alliance of Businessmen, 414
National Labor Relations Board, powers
    of, 251–52
Net loss, 327
New Deal, 8
New York, city of, 166
New York Stock Exchange, 42, 333, 464
Newspapers, advertising in, 176
*Newsweek,* 166
Nixon, Richard M., 13
No-par stock, 48

Observation, use of, 363–64
Oklahoma City *Journal,* 172
Operating ratio, 331
Opinion survey, use of, 365–66
Order control, defined, 121–22
Organization, pyramid of, 294
Orientals in labor force, 233
Outstanding shares of stock, defined, 48
Overhead rate, calculation of, 342–43
Owners' equity
  accounting of, 326–27
  computation of ratio to total equity, 330–
    31
  defined, 318
  rate of return on, 332

Par value, 48
Participating stock, 50–51
Partnership
  and equity funds, 47
  explained, 40–42
  funding of, 39, 44
  incorporation of, 89
  limited life, 41
  and mortgage note, 55
  as a tax unit, 80, 84
Pay Board, 13
Penn Central Railroad, 5, 18
Penney, James Cash, 6
Performance reports
  defined, 339
  timing of, 348
*Personnel,* 371
*Personnel Administration,* 371
*Personnel Psychology,* 371
Philadelphia Authority for Industrial Development, 54
Plan, defined, 263
  *See also* Planning
Planning
  and business problems, 269–71
  value of, 269–70
Playboy Corporation, 6
Policy, defined, 268–69
Pollution, control of, 417–18
*Popular Mechanics,* 176
Post Office Department, fraud, 11
Preferred stock
  cumulative, 49–50
  investment in, 49
  noncumulative, 50
  nonparticipating, 50–51
  participating, 50
  taxation of, 90–91
  values discussed, 58
Price Commission, 13
Price variance, defined, 345
Principal
  and calculation of interest, 64
  defined, 53
Private carriers, defined, 189
Procedure, defined, 269
Process, defined, 21
Procurement, defined, 103
Product departmentalization, defined, 292–93
Product
  cost, estimation of, 34–36
  introduction of new, 151–53
  life cycle of and advertising, 179–81
  life cycle of, 150–51
  life cycle of and pricing, 155–56
  penetration pricing, defined, 155
  skim pricing, defined, 155
*Production,* 366
Production budget, 353

Production process
  defined, 97, 455
  and published information, 366
Promissory note
  characteristics of, 70
  as commercial paper, 73
  and guarantor, 72
Public accountant (CPA), defined, 459
Public warehousing, defined, 75
Punched cards, defined, 377–78
Purchase contracts, defined, 47
Purchase invoice, 339
*Purchasing,* 366
Purchasing requisitions, value of, 107–8
Purina Company, 175

Quantity variance, defined, 345
Questionnaire, use of, 363
Quotations, requesting, 109

Radio advertising, 177–78
Rate of return on investment
  defined, 37
  and trade area, 200
Rate of return on total assets ratio, defined, 331–32
Rate of return on owners' equity, ratio of, 332
Rating, defined, 190
Ratios, types of, 330–32
*Reader's Digest,* 172
Receiving report, 111–12
Red Cross, 82
Reference group, defined, 145
Research
  discussion of, 359–60
  systematic-descriptive, 360–64
Resources, assembly of and promotion, 37–39
Retail store
  defined, 198–99
  failures of, 199
  location of, 201–2
  trading area of, 199–201
Retained earnings, defined, 50
Revenue, defined, 319, 327
Robinson-Patman Act (1936), 9, 10
Roosevelt, Franklin D., 8
Rules, defined, 269
Ryder Truck, 189

Sabotage, 412
Sales budget, 352
Sales force, development of, 169–71
*Saturday Evening Post,* 5
Sears-Roebuck, 6, 133
Schedule, developing for manufacturing, 122
Secondary products, defined, 105
Secured bonds, types of, 55

Securities Act, 11
Securities and Exchange Commission, 11, 12, 365
Selling, personal
  disadvantages of, 168–69
  expectations of, 167–68
  when to use, 166–67
Selling and administrative expense budget, 353–54
Selling expenses
  and distribution costs, 35
  types of, 36
Semantics, defined, 304–5
Service industry, types of, 276–77
Sherman Act (1890), 9, 10, 448–49
Shops, types of, 119
Short-term debt, defined, 47
Short-term funds
  assignment, 74
  cash discount, 69
  chattel mortgages, 76
  and commercial banks, 69–70
  commercial paper, 73
  factoring of accounts receivable, 74–75
  field warehousing, 75
  general discussion of, 63–64
  public warehousing, 75
  trade credit, 67–68
  trade discounts, 68–69
  trust receipt loans, 76
Singer, 158, 202
Small Business Administration
  establishment of, 38
  and exports, 430
Small Business Administration Act, 272
Social Security Act, 218, 225
Social system, defined, 453
Sole proprietorship
  compared with partnership, 41
  and equity funds, 47
  explained, 39–40
  incorporation of, 89
  and mortgage note, 57
  as a tax unit, 80, 84
  funding of, 39, 44
Specialization, in production, 423–24
Standard costs, defined, 345
Standard Oil of Ohio, 7, 448
*Statistical Abstracts of the United States*, 362
Stock
  authorized shares, 47–48
  common, and convertible bonds, 56–57
  earnings per share, 91
  investment in, 49
  no-par, 48
  outstanding shares, 48
  par value of, 48
  split of, 51
  stated value of, defined, 48

taxing of, 90–91
  unissued shares, 48
Stock purchase warrants, defined, 57
Stockholders
  basic rights of, 48–49
  corporate ownership, 47
  defined, 42
  and liquidation, 51
Strike, use of, 253
Supreme Court, U.S., 251
Subchapter S Corporation
  defined, 88–89
  tax on accumulated earnings, 90
*Survey of Current Business,* 362, 365
Systems approach
  components of, 454
  and decision making, 453


Taft-Hartley Act (1947), 250–52
Tariff, defined, 424
Tax
  on accumulated earnings, 89–90
  on bonds, 90–91
  constitutional amendment, 79
  as a cost, 36
  individual income, 80–84
  rate of, and corporation, 44
  rate of, and partnership, 44
  rate of, and sole proprietorship, 44
Television advertising, 177
Texaco, 156, 174
Textron, Inc., 443
Thom McAn, 158
Time sharing, defined, 383
Times interest expense earned ratio, 331
TL (truckload) rate, 192–93
Trade quota, defined, 424
Trading on equity, defined, 59–60
Transportation costs and plant location, 197–98
Transportation rates
  class rates, 190
  commodity rates, 191
  and distribution costs, 193
  diversion in transit, 192
  incentive rates, 192–93
  transit privilege, 192
Treasury Department, 79
Trend analysis, explained, 333–34
Trust receipt loans, defined, 76
Turnover of merchandise inventory, ratio, 332


Unemployment, estimates of, 217
Unfair labor practices, defined, 251
Uniform Commercial Code (1962), 12
Uniform Partnership Act, 40
Uniform Warehouse Receipt Act (1907), 75

Uninational firm, defined, 432
Unions
  as formal groups, 244
  growth of, 248–50
  membership of, 249
Uniroyal, 160
Unissued shares of stock, defined, 48
United Airlines, 271
United Auto Workers, 249
United Brotherhood of Carpenters and Join-
    ers of America, 250
U.S. Census of Business, 200
U.S. Constitution, 79
United States Export-Import Bank, 425–26
United Steelworkers of America, 250
Unlimited liability
  defined, 40
  of partnership, 41

Variable overhead and manufacturing over-
    head, 34
Variances, defined, 345

Wages
  general, 346–47
  of textile workers, 222
*Wall Street Journal,* 217, 333

Warehouse
  private, 194–95
  public, 195–96
  receipt as credit, 196
  use of, 193–94
Western Electric, 271
Wheeler-Lea Act (1938), 9, 11
*The Wide World of Sports,* 177
Winston cigarettes, 156, 174
Work
  measurement of, 307, 308
  organization of, 285–89
Work orders, defined, 122
Work ticket, use of, 341
Work week, decrease of, 408–9
Working capital
  defined, 37
  and sales and leaseback, 60
  ratio, 330
Workmen's compensation, *see* Industrial
    compensation laws
World Bank, 425
Wyoming, 6

Xerox Corporation, 333

Yale University, 414